The
Politics of
International
Economic
Relations

FIFTH EDITION

The
Politics of
International
Economic
Relations

FIFTH EDITION

Joan Edelman Spero

Jeffrey A. Hart
Indiana University

St. Martin's Press • **New York**

Sponsoring editor: Beth A. Gillett
Manager, publishing services: Emily Berleth
Senior editor, publishing services: Douglas Bell
Project management and graphics: York Production Services
Production supervisor: Dennis Para
Cover design: Patricia McFadden
Cover art: David C. Chen, Stockworks/Martha Productions, Inc.

Library of Congress Catalog Card Number: 94-74773

Manufactured in the United States of America.

1 0 9 8 7
f e d c b a

For information, write:
St. Martin's Press, Inc.
175 Fifth Avenue
New York, NY 10010

ISBN: 0-312-08476-5

Acknowledgments

Acknowledgments and copyrights are continued at the back of the book on page 430, which constitutes an extension of the copyright page.

To Michael, Jason, and Benjamin
JES

To Joan and Zachary
JAH

Contents

Preface

The first edition of *The Politics of International Economic Relations,* published in 1977, was written to fill a void in the study of international relations—the gap between international politics and international economics. Since 1977 that gap has narrowed significantly. International political economy has emerged as a new and increasingly prominent field in political science. Theoretical and empirical analyses of the politics of international economic relations appear regularly in professional journals and books. Although the most important bridge building has come from political scientists, economists are now also including political variables in their analyses and applying economic theory to the study of political behavior. At the same time, a new generation of students in a variety of fields is being made aware of the interrelationship of economics and politics and is learning to use and integrate the tools of both fields.

Much has happened since 1977 to reinforce this academic evolution. Above all, the turbulence in the world economy has highlighted the political dimension of international economic relations. The persistent problems of the dollar and other international currencies, the many trade disputes between the United States and its major trading partners, crises in world oil markets, and the continuing financial crises in the developing countries have obliged scholars to reexamine the assumptions that separated the disciplines of economics and political science for over a century.

The focus of analysis and organization in this book has not changed much since the first edition. This edition continues the tradition established in previous ones of discussing problems that are faced by the developing countries and the formerly Communist countries separately from those that primarily affect the industrialized capitalist countries. In this fifth edition, we have added new material that reflects the major changes in the international system since the end of the Cold War. Also in this new edition, we discuss and try to explain the increasing pragmatism of domestic and foreign economic policies in many parts of the Third World, but especially in the faster-growing developing countries. Finally, this edition adds new material on the growing gap between the poorest regions of the world and the richest ones.

The first four editions of this book were written by Joan Spero. Each new edition has reflected a different dimension of her professional experience. At the time the first edition appeared, she was assistant professor of political science at Columbia University. When the second edition was published in 1980, she was ambassador of the United States to the Economic and Social Council of the United Nations. The third edition was published in 1985, when she was senior vice president of international corporate affairs at American Express Company. When the fourth edition was published in 1989, Joan Spero was senior vice president and treasurer at American Express. This book has benefited, in her view, from her experiences in the academic, governmental, and business worlds. Joan

Spero is currently Under Secretary of State for Economic, Business, and Agricultural Affairs.

While this new edition of *The Politics of International Economic Relations* reflects Joan Spero's experience as a senior policy maker in the Clinton administration, it was not written as an official statement of U.S. Government policy, but, rather, as a continuation of the analytical approach of the first four editions. The opinions and views expressed are those of the author and are not necessarily those of the Department of State.

The fifth edition was written jointly by Joan E. Spero and Jeffrey A. Hart, a professor of political science at Indiana University. Hart has also served for short periods in governmental positions. In 1980, he was a professional staff member of President Carter's Commission for a National Agenda for the Eighties. Hart was an internal contractor for the Congressional Office of Technology Assessment in 1985–1986 and has collaborated since 1987 with members of the Berkeley Roundtable on the International Economy (BRIE), including Michael Borrus, Laura D'Andrea Tyson, currently chair of the National Economic Council, and Stephen Cohen. He echoes Joan Spero's sentiments about the intellectual benefits of combining academic and nonacademic pursuits.

We owe a debt of gratitude to Jeffry Frieden for reading and providing comments on the entire manuscript and to the following individuals for their review of portions of the current edition: Jack Bielasiak, Catherine Gwin, and Stephen Kobrin. We would also like to thank the following reviewers for their time and efforts: M. Mark Amen, University of South Florida; Steve Chan, University of Colorado at Boulder; John A. C. Conybeare, University of Iowa; Patricia Davis, University of Notre Dame; C. Roe Goddard, American Graduate School of International Management; Stephan Haggard, University of California, San Diego; Edward D. Mansfield, Columbia University; Renee Marlin-Bennett, The American University; Curtis Peet, Bowling Green State University; David M. Rowe, The Ohio State University; and Veronica Ward, Utah State University. Extensive research assistance for this edition was provided by Sangbae Kim and Khalil Osman, both graduate students at Indiana University. Previous editions benefited from research assistance provided by Kristin Brady, Stephen Gaull, Christiana Horton, Deirdre Maloney, and Kathleen McNamara. The following individuals provided advice on drafts of previous editions of the book: Andrew Bartels, Toby Gati, Lisa Lamas, Charles Levy, Edward Morse, Richard O'Brien, and John Sewell.

In addition, we would like to thank the College Division of St. Martin's Press and its fine editorial staff, including Don Reisman, Beth Gillett, and Kimberly Wurtzel, for supporting this revision of the text. Our thanks, as well, to Dolores Wolfe and the staff of York Production Services.

Joan E. Spero
Jeffrey A. Hart

About the Authors

Joan E. Spero was appointed in 1993 by President Bill Clinton as Under Secretary of State for Economic, Business, and Agricultural Affairs. She has played a central role in the Clinton administration's foreign economic policy and has participated directly in many of the events discussed in this book: the reshaping of the Bretton Woods institutions such as the International Monetary Fund and World Bank; the completion of the Uruguay Round and the creation of the World Trade Organization; the launching of new regional economic initiatives through the Asia Pacific Economic Cooperation forum, the Summit of the Americas, and the New Transatlantic Agenda; the transition of former communist countries into participants in the institutions and economic system of the West. As the senior economic official in the Department of State, she advises Secretary of State Warren Christopher on international economic policy and leads the work of the State Department on issues ranging from investment and aviation negotiations to bilateral relations with key partners such as Japan and the European Union. She has also been a central player in the Middle East peace process, fostering economic development, cooperation, and prosperity as the basis for a lasting peace.

Ms. Spero received her doctorate in political science from Columbia University and taught international politics and economics there from 1973 to 1979. In 1980 she was named U.S. Ambassador to the United Nations Economic and Social Council by President Jimmy Carter. From 1981 to 1993 she was an executive at the American Express Company where her last position was Executive Vice President for Corporate Affairs and Communications.

Jeffrey A. Hart is Professor of Political Science at Indiana University, Bloomington, where he has taught international politics and international political economy since 1981. He began his teaching career at Princeton University from 1973–1980. He was a professional staff member of the President's Commission for a National Agenda for the Eighties from 1980–1981. Hart worked at the Office of Technology Assessment of the U.S. Congress in 1985–1986 as an internal contractor and helped to write its report, *International Competition in Services* (1987). He was visiting scholar at the Berkeley Roundtable on the International Economy, 1987–1989. His publications include *The New International Economic Order* (1983) (with Stephen Woolcock and Hans Van der Ven), *Interdependence in the Post Multilateral Era* (1985), *Rival Capitalists* (1992), and scholarly articles in *World Politics*, *International Organization*, *The British Journal of Political Science*, and *The Journal of Conflict Resolution*.

The Politics of International Economic Relations

FIFTH EDITION

1

The Management of International Economic Relations since World War II

During and after World War II, governments developed and enforced a set of rules, institutions, and procedures to regulate important aspects of international economic interaction. For nearly two decades, this order, known as the **Bretton Woods Regime,** was effective in controlling conflict and in achieving the common goals of the states that had created it. There were three political bases for the Bretton Woods system: (1) the concentration of power in a small number of states, (2) the existence of a cluster of important interests shared by those states, and (3) the presence of a dominant power willing and able to assume a leadership role.[1]

The concentration of both political and economic power in the developed countries of North America and Western Europe enabled them to dominate the Bretton Woods system. They faced no challenge from the Communist states of Eastern Europe and Asia, including the Soviet Union, which were isolated from the rest of the international economy in a separate international economic system. Although the less-developed countries (LDCs) were integrated into the world economy, they had no voice in management because of their political and economic weakness. Finally, Japan, weakened by the war and lacking the level of development and the political power of North America and Western Europe, remained subordinate and outside the management group for much of the Bretton Woods era. The concentration of power facilitated the economic system's management by confining the number of actors whose agreement was necessary to establish rules, institutions, and procedures and to carry out management within the agreed-upon system.

Management was also made easier by a high level of agreement among the powerful on the goals and means of the international economic system. The

1

foundation of that agreement was a shared belief in **capitalism** and **liberalism.** The developed countries relied primarily on market mechanisms and private ownership.

They also agreed that the liberal economic system required governmental **intervention.** In the postwar era, government has assumed responsibility for the economic well-being of its citizens, and employment, stability, and growth have become important subjects of public policy. The **welfare state** grew out of the Great Depression, which created a popular demand for governmental intervention in the economy, and out of the theoretical contributions of the **Keynesian** school of economics, which prescribed governmental intervention to maintain adequate levels of employment.

For the international economy, the developed countries favored a liberal system, one that relied primarily on a free market with the minimum of barriers to the flow of private trade and capital. The experience of the 1930s, when proliferation of exchange controls and **trade barriers** led to economic disaster, remained fresh in the minds of public officials. Although they disagreed on the specific implementation of this liberal system, all agreed that an open system would maximize economic welfare.

Some also believed that a liberal international economic system would enhance the possibilities of peace, that a liberal international economic system would lead not only to economic prosperity and economic harmony but also to international peace.[2] One of those who saw such a security link was Cordell Hull, the U.S. secretary of state from 1933 to 1944. Hull argued that

> unhampered trade dovetailed with peace; high **tariffs,** trade barriers, and unfair economic competition, with war . . . if we could get a freer flow of trade—freer in the sense of fewer discriminations and obstructions—so that one country would not be deadly jealous of another and the living standards of all countries might rise, thereby eliminating the economic dissatisfaction that breeds war, we might have a reasonable chance of lasting peace.[3]

A belief in governmental intervention and cooperation at the international level also evolved from the experience of the 1930s. The failure to control beggar-thy-neighbor policies, such as high tariffs and competitive devaluations, contributed to economic breakdown, domestic political instability, and international war. Harry D. White, a major architect of the Bretton Woods system, summarized the lesson that was learned:

> The absence of a high degree of economic collaboration among the leading nations will . . . inevitably result in economic warfare that will be but the prelude and instigator of military warfare on an even vaster scale.[4]

To ensure economic stability and political peace, states agreed to cooperate to regulate the international economic system.

The common interest in economic cooperation was enhanced by the outbreak of the Cold War at the end of the 1940s. The economic weakness of the

West, it was felt, would make it vulnerable to internal Communist threats and external pressure from the Soviet Union. Economic cooperation became necessary not only to rebuild Western economies and to ensure their continuing vitality but also to provide for their political and military security. In addition, the perceived Communist military threat led the developed countries to subordinate their economic conflict to their common security interests.

The developed market economies also agreed on the nature of international economic management, which was to be designed to create and maintain a liberal system. It would require the establishment of an effective international monetary system and the reduction of barriers to trade and capital flows. With these barriers removed and a stable monetary system in place, states would have a favorable environment for ensuring national stability and growth. The state, not the international system, bore the main responsibility for national stability and growth. Thus the members of the system shared a very limited conception of international economic management: regulation of the liberal system by removing barriers to trade and capital flows and creating a stable monetary system.

Finally, international management relied on the dominant power to lead the system. As the world's foremost economic and political power, the United States was clearly in a position to assume that responsibility of leadership. The U.S. economy, undamaged by war and with its large market, great productive capability, financial facilities, and strong currency, was the dominant world economy. The ability to support a large military force plus the possession of an atomic weapon made the United States the world's strongest military power and the leader of the Western alliance. The European states, with their economies in disarray owing to the war, their production and markets divided by national boundaries, and their armies dismantled or weakened by the war, were not in a position to assume the leadership role. Japan, defeated and destroyed, was at that time not even considered part of the management system.

The United States was both able and willing to assume the leadership role. U.S. policymakers had learned an important lesson from the interwar period. The failure of U.S. leadership and the country's withdrawal into **isolationism** after World War I were viewed as major factors in the collapse of the economic system and of the peace. U.S. policymakers believed that after World War II the United States could no longer isolate itself. As the strongest power in the postwar world, the United States would have to assume primary responsibility for establishing political and economic order. With the outbreak of the Cold War, yet another dimension was added to the need for American leadership. Without such leadership, it was believed, the economic weakness in Europe and Japan would lead to Communist political victories.

Furthermore, the Europeans and the Japanese—economically exhausted by the war—actively encouraged this U.S. leadership role. They needed American assistance to rebuild their domestic production and to finance their international trade. The political implications of U.S. leadership, therefore, were viewed as positive, because it was felt that U.S. economic assistance would alleviate domestic economic and political problems and encourage international stability. What the Europeans feared was not U.S. domination but U.S. isolation: the history of the late entry into the two world wars by the United States was fresh in their minds.

Throughout the Bretton Woods period, the United States mobilized the other developed countries for management and, in some cases, managed the system alone. The United States acted as the world's central banker, provided the major initiatives in international trade negotiations, and dominated international production.

This coincidence of three favorable political conditions—the concentration of power, the cluster of shared interests, and the leadership of the United States— provided the political capability equal to the tasks of managing the international economy. It enabled Europe and Japan to recover from the devastation of the war and established a stable monetary system and a more open trade and financial system that led to a period of unparalleled economic growth.

By the 1970s, however, the Bretton Woods system was in disarray, and the management of the international economy was gravely threatened. Changes in power, leadership, and the consensus on a liberal, limited system undermined political management.

Although the developed countries remained the dominant political and economic powers, states outside the group challenged their right to manage the system. The less-developed countries sought to increase their access to the management and, thus, to the rewards of the international economic system. The Soviet Union and the countries of Eastern Europe also sought greater participation in the international economy. That quest intensified with the breakup of the Soviet system beginning in the late 1980s.

More importantly, power shifted within the group of advanced industrial nations. In the 1960s, Europe experienced a period of great economic growth and dynamism in international trade. Six European countries had united in 1957 to form the **European Economic Community,** an economic bloc rivaling the U.S. economy and a potential political force. The six countries became fifteen by 1995 and the European Economic Community has now evolved into the **European Union (EU).**

Japan's **economic development** was even more spectacular. In the 1960s, Japan became a major world economic power and joined the developed countries' condominium. By the 1990s, Japan was a powerful economic competitor to both the United States and Europe.

In the 1970s, a weakened dollar and a weakening balance of trade undermined U.S. international economic power. In the early 1980s, a strong dollar paradoxically undermined U.S. economic power by hurting the ability of U.S. firms to compete in export markets. Even though U.S. economic growth was a bit higher in the early 1980s than it had been in the 1970s, and both unemployment and **inflation** stayed low, the United States suffered from "twin deficits" in both government spending and the **balance of payments.** The **debt crisis** of the 1980s and the problems of the United States in continuing to finance its global activities led to a series of power-sharing and burden-sharing arrangements with Europe and Japan.

Europe and Japan became more and more dissatisfied with the prerogatives that leadership gave the United States. The clearest example of this was the growing European and Japanese criticism of the dollar system and U.S. payments deficits. The United States, for its part, was increasingly dissatisfied with the costs of leadership. Whereas the Europeans and Japanese criticized U.S. deficits, the United States criticized their refusal to upwardly revalue their currencies against the dollar. As domestic economic problems emerged from the late 1960s onward, U.S. leaders increasingly began to feel that the costs of economic leadership outweighed its benefits.

The relaxation of security tensions in the early 1970s reinforced the changing attitudes toward American leadership, especially in Europe but also, to a lesser degree, in Japan. Détente and the lessening of the perceived security threat weakened the security argument for Western economic cooperation and U.S. leadership. Europe and Japan were no longer willing to accept U.S. dominance for security reasons, and the United States was no longer willing to bear the economic costs of leadership for reasons of security. By the 1990s, the end of the Cold War further undermined the security imperative for economic cooperation.

Though U.S. dominance was increasingly unsatisfactory for the United States as well as for Europe and Japan, no new leader emerged to fulfill that role. Europe, although economically united in a common market, lacked the political unity necessary to lead the system. West Germany and Japan, the two strongest economic powers after the United States, were unable to manage the system by themselves and, in any case, were kept from leadership by the memories of World War II.

Finally, by the 1970s, the agreement on a liberal and limited system, which was the basis of Bretton Woods, had weakened. The most vociferous dissenters from the liberal vision of international management were the less-developed countries. In their view, the open monetary, trade, and financial system perpetuated their underdevelopment and subordination to the developed countries. They sought to make that development a primary goal and responsibility of the system.

For many in the developed countries as well, liberalism was no longer an adequate goal of management. The challenge to liberalism in the developed countries grew out of its very success. The reduction of barriers to trade and capital enabled an expansion in international economic interaction among the developed market economies: larger international capital flows, the growth of international trade, and the development of international systems of production. As a result, national economies became more interdependent and more sensitive to economic policy and events outside the national economy. The problem was heightened because this sensitivity grew at a time when states were more than ever expected to ensure domestic economic well-being. Because of the influence of external events, states found it increasingly difficult to manage their national economies.

Interdependence led to two reactions and two different challenges to liberalism. One reaction was to erect new barriers to limit economic interaction and, with it, interdependence. An open international system, in the view of many, no longer maximized economic welfare and most certainly undermined national **sovereignty** and autonomy. Some argued that liberalism was no longer an adequate guide for policy in an increasingly tariff-free world economy, where **nontariff barriers (NTBs)** are deeply embedded in national economic policy and economic behavior is the main impediment to trade. Pressures grew for protetion and **managed trade,** and efforts to strengthen regional groupings, such as the EU and the North American Free Trade Agreement (NAFTA), grew. These regional groupings were not protectionist, although there were temptations to erect new barriers to extra-regional trade and investment flows while reducing the internal ones. By the 1990s it was clear that the most important regional groups had resisted those temptations. The revival of regional integration efforts in the 1980s and 1990s reinforced—rather than undermining—the liberal world economic order.

Another reaction was to go beyond liberalism, beyond the idea of a limited management to new forms of international economic cooperation that would manage interdependence. An open system, according to this viewpoint, maximized welfare but required, in turn, new forms of international management that would assume responsibilities and prerogatives formerly undertaken by the state. These views led to efforts to establish a regular series of international economic summits and attempts (mostly unsuccessful) to coordinate national macroeconomic policies. In the 1980s, new initiatives were taken to upgrade the multilateral trade regime with a new and more ambitious trade round—the Uruguay Round. The successful conclusion of the Uruguay Round in 1994 was evidence for the continued power of the idea of trying to manage interdependence.

In the 1980s, many developing countries took a more pragmatic approach to multilateral management, seeking to work within the prevailing regime rather than to establish a **New International Economic Order (NIEO).** In particular, those developing countries that moved rapidly toward industrialization—the so-called **Newly Industrializing Countries,** or **NICs**—sought to play a greater role within the system. They pursued export-oriented policies and became active participants in the General Agreement of Tariffs and Trade (GATT). For a time it seemed that these rapidly growing countries would also become more integrated into the world financial system, especially through their new access to private **capital markets**. However, the heavy borrowing of many NICs, particularly those in Latin America, led instead to the LDC debt crisis of the 1980s, which posed a threat not only to their development and political stability but also to the international financial system itself. In the 1990s, as developing countries regained access to growing world capital markets, the fragility of certain LDC economies created new vulnerabilities for the international financial system. Management of the role of the developing countries in the global financial system posed a challenge for both developed and developing countries.

Finally, changes in domestic and international policy in the two key Communist countries—the Soviet Union and the People's Republic of China—opened up the possibility of greater East-West economic interaction. Gorbachev's *perestroika*, or restructuring, sought to move the Soviet economy more in the market direction and to open up trade, finance, and investment relations with the West. It had the unforeseen result of hastening the Soviet Union's economic decline and helping to bring about the breakup of the Soviet empire. The end of communism in the former Soviet Union and Eastern Europe created new demands on the system for resource flows, economic interaction, and participation in management of the system. In contrast, China's economic reforms led to rapid growth. Expectations of political liberalization grew within China until the suppression of the student demonstrations in Tienanmin Square in 1989. Now China seems to have settled into a pattern of economic development typical of the earlier experience of other Asian NICs: export-oriented growth within a politically authoritarian system. The key question for the rest of the world was how and on what terms to integrate the formerly Communist countries and China into the world economy.

The main political problem facing the international economy, and a crucial problem of all international relations, is how new forms of political management will develop and whether those forms will be able to deal with the three key challenges of our time: (1) the continued political responsibility of governments for the economic welfare of their citizens in the face of increased globalization of the world economy, (2) the reduction of inequalities within and across nations in a context of increasing population growth and migratory flows, and (3) managing the transition of the formerly Communist countries to full participation in the world economy as capitalist market economies.

NOTES

1. On the idea of the need for a leader, see Charles P. Kindleberger, *The World in Depression, 1929–1939* (Berkeley and Los Angeles: University of California Press, 1973). Kindleberger's early speculations on this issue have resulted in an enormous number of works on what is now called "hegemonial stability theory (HST)." See the bibliography for citations of these works.

2. Kenneth Waltz, *Man, the State and War* (New York: Columbia University Press, 1969). For a discussion of how liberal ideas motivated U.S. foreign economic policy after World War II, see David P. Calleo and Benjamin M. Rowland, *America and the World Political Economy* (Bloomington: Indiana University Press, 1973). For a more recent work on this topic, see G. John Ikenberry, "Creating Yesterday's New World Order: Keynesian 'New Thinking' and the Anglo-American Postwar Settlement," in Judith Goldstein and Robert O. Keohane, eds., *Ideas and Foreign Policy: Beliefs, Institutions, and Political Change* (Ithaca, N.Y.: Cornell University Press, 1993).

3. Quoted in Richard N. Gardner, *Sterling-Dollar Diplomacy in Current Perspective: The Origins and Prospects of Our International Economic Order*, expanded ed. (New York: Columbia University Press, 1980), p. 9.

4. Quoted in Ibid, p. 8.

2

International
Money Management

In July 1944, representatives of forty-four nations met on an estate in Bretton Woods, New Hampshire, to create a new international monetary order. Foremost in their minds was the collapse of the international monetary system in the 1930s. In those years, **economic nationalism**—competitive **exchange rate** devaluations, formation of competing monetary blocs, and the absence of international cooperation—contributed greatly to economic breakdown, domestic political instability, and war. The goal at Bretton Woods was to establish an international economic system that would prevent another economic and political collapse and another military conflict. It was the international consensus that previous monetary systems that relied primarily on **market forces** had proved inadequate.[1] At Bretton Woods, officials were prepared to establish a publicly managed international monetary order.

U.S. policymakers involved in creating the new economic order had concluded that the failure of U.S. leadership was a major cause of the economic and political disaster. During World War II, U.S. leaders thus decided that the United States would have to assume the primary responsibility for establishing a postwar economic order. That order would be designed to prevent economic nationalism by fostering **free trade** and a high level of international interaction. A liberal economic system, ensured by international cooperation, would provide the foundation for a lasting peace. Thus, during two years of bilateral negotiation, the United States and the United Kingdom, the world's leading economic and political powers, drew up a plan for a new system of international monetary management.[2]

The Anglo-American plan, approved at Bretton Woods, became the first publicly managed international monetary order. For a quarter of a century, international monetary relations were stable and provided a basis for growing international trade, economic growth, and political harmony among the developed market economies. Then, in the 1970s, the Bretton Woods system collapsed under the strain of growing interdependence and weakening U.S. monetary power. Beginning in the 1970s, monetary management focused on efforts to maintain order and stability in international monetary affairs in an environment of increasing globalization of financial markets and the growing economic power of Japan, Europe, and the NICs.

In this chapter we shall examine monetary management in the period since World War II: the functioning and breakdown of Bretton Woods and international monetary relations in the post–Bretton Woods era. We will examine how nations have sought to provide the three central functions of an international monetary system: adequate liquidity, timely adjustment, and, most importantly, confidence in the soundness of the system.

Just as any national economy needs an accepted currency, so the international economy requires an accepted vehicle for investment, trade, and payments. Unlike national economies, however, the international economy lacks a central government that can issue currency and manage its use. Historically, this problem has been solved through the use of gold and national currencies. In the nineteenth and first half of the twentieth centuries, gold played a key role in international monetary transactions. Gold was used to back currencies; the international value of currency was determined by its fixed relationship to gold; and gold was used to settle international accounts.

The British pound was a supplement to gold. Based on the dominant British economy, it became the reserve, transaction, and intervention currency. After World War II, as we shall see, the U.S. dollar became the key international currency. Dollars were held as reserves by **central banks;** the dollar became the unit for international trade, investment, and finance; and dollars were used to intervene in exchange markets to maintain fixed exchange rates. Although the use of the dollar eventually became a central problem for managing the system, efforts to replace it, including the creation of an international money, failed.

An international monetary system must also have means for adjusting imbalances in international payments. In national economies, payments imbalances among regions are adjusted more or less automatically through movement of capital and through common fiscal and **monetary policies.** In international economic relations, disequilibria in payments can be settled by financing, by changing domestic economic policy to shift trade and investment patterns, by rationing the supply of foreign exchange through exchange controls, or by allowing the currency exchange rate to change. Effective adjustment can be promoted by international cooperation, but it requires above all alteration of domestic policies to achieve international solutions, a politically difficult task.

In the Bretton Woods era, adjustment was based on a fixed exchange rate system supplemented by financing, exchange controls, exchange rate changes, and adaptation of national policies. After Bretton Woods, the system was based on frequent exchange rate changes supplemented by financing and changes in national economic policies. The tension between international adjustment needs and domestic political requirements is a central dilemma of international monetary relations. For example, it is often necessary but politically difficult to implement policies that reduce governmental budget deficits and the rate of inflation in order to stabilize a country's exchange rate or to reduce the deficit in its balance of payments. Such policies generally result in lower growth rates and higher levels of unemployment in the short term even though they may result in higher rates of growth and employment in the long term.

This tension is accentuated by the globalization of world capital markets. It is tempting for democratically elected governments, for example, to put off the domestic economic reforms that are needed to defend a declining currency or to delay adjustments that might reduce the size of a balance of payments deficit because the necessary adjustments are likely to be politically unpopular. Yet, these adjustments often have to be made to prevent capital flight or attacks by speculators on the value of a national currency or some other disruptions created by the enhanced mobility of global capital.

The Original Bretton Woods Agreement

In actuality, the Bretton Woods system never functioned as the United States and the others who signed the agreement had planned. The new order was intended to be a system of limited management by international organizations. Two public international organizations, the **International Monetary Fund (IMF)** and the **International Bank for Reconstruction and Development (IBRD**, known as the **World Bank),** were, for the first time in history, to perform certain monetary functions for the international system.

The rules of Bretton Woods, set forth in the articles of agreement, provided for a system of fixed exchange rates. Public officials, fresh from what they perceived as a disastrous experience with floating rates in the 1930s, concluded that a fixed exchange rate was the most stable and conducive basis for trade. Thus, all countries agreed to establish the parity, or value, of their currencies in terms of gold and to maintain exchange rates within 1 percent, plus or minus, of parity. The rules further encouraged an open system, by committing members to the **convertibility** of their respective currencies into other currencies and to free trade.[3]

The IMF was to be the keeper of the rules and the main instrument of public international management. Under the system of weighted voting, the United States exerted a preponderant influence in that body. IMF approval was necessary for any change in exchange rates, and it advised countries on policies affecting the monetary system. Most importantly, it could advance credits to countries with payments deficits. The IMF was provided with a fund, composed of member countries' contributions in gold and in their own currencies. The original quotas were to total $8.8 billion. In the event of a deficit in the current account, countries could borrow from this fund for up to eighteen months and, in some cases, for up to five years.

Despite these innovations in public control, the original Bretton Woods agreement mainly emphasized national and market solutions to monetary problems. It was expected that national monetary reserves, supplemented when necessary by IMF credits, would finance any temporary balance of payments disequilibria. No provision was made for the creation of new reserves; new gold production was considered sufficient. In the event of structural disequilibrium, it was expected that there would be national solutions—a change in the value of the currency or an improvement by other means of a country's competitive position. Few means were given to the IMF, however, to encourage such national solutions.

The Bretton Woods planners expected that after a brief transition period—of no more than five years—the international economy would recover and the system would enter into operation. To facilitate the postwar recovery, the planners created another institution, the International Bank for Reconstruction and Development, or World Bank, to make loans that would facilitate a speedy postwar recovery and also to promote economic development.[4]

From 1945 to 1947, the United States actively pressed for implementation of the Bretton Woods system as originally conceived. The United States provided resources to the IMF and the World Bank and urged other countries to do likewise. To permit postwar recovery and facilitate the implementation of the Bretton Woods agreement, the United States gave financial assistance: $3 billion in relief funds and, more importantly, a $3.75 billion loan to Great Britain, which was expected to enable that country to complete its reconstruction and return the pound to convertibility.

By 1947, however, the United States concluded that the Bretton Woods system was not working and, in fact, that the Western system was on the verge of collapse. World War II, it became clear, had destroyed the European economic system, which had been based heavily on international trade. The sources of Europe's foreign earnings had been wiped out. Its productive capacity had been destroyed or disrupted; its overseas earnings had turned into debts; its shipping was decimated; and its payments deficit was large and growing. Western Europe was faced with vast import needs, not only for reconstruction but also for mere survival.[5]

The Bretton Woods institutions were unable to cope with this problem. The IMF's modest credit facilities were insufficient to deal with Europe's huge needs and, in any case, the IMF could make loans only for current-account deficits, not for capital and reconstruction purposes. A total of only $570 million, contributed initially by the United States, was actually available for World Bank lending. In addition, because the World Bank relied on U.S. financial markets to float its bonds, it was obliged to follow a conservative lending policy, making loans only when repayment was assured. By 1947, the IMF and the World Bank themselves admitted they could not deal with the system's economic problems.[6]

The economic crisis of 1947 was directly linked with political problems. Germany lay in ruins economically and politically. The governments of Italy and France, faced with pressures from powerful labor unions, were highly unstable. Britain, partly due to its economic difficulties, was withdrawing from India and Palestine and abandoning its political and security commitments to Greece and Turkey. More importantly, the Soviet Union seemed willing and able to take advantage of the West's economic plight and political instability to further its aim of territorial expansion in Europe. The Soviet Union had forcibly established Communist governments in the countries it occupied at the end of the war: Hungary, Romania, Poland, and Bulgaria, and it had pressured Iran and Turkey for territorial concessions. Communist guerrillas were making significant headway in Greece, and large Communist parties in the governments of Italy and France tried to take advantage of labor unrest. The Soviet Union also refused to cooperate with the Allies on a postwar settlement for Germany.

After 1947, because of these circumstances, the Bretton Woods system evolved from limited management by international organization to management by the United States.

Unilateral U.S. Management

From 1947 to 1960, the United States was both able and willing to manage the international monetary system. The strength of the U.S. economy, the lessons of the interwar period, and security incentives made U.S. leadership acceptable economically and politically at home. The Europeans and Japanese also accepted U.S. management. Economically exhausted by the war, they needed U.S. assistance to rebuild their domestic production, finance their international trade, and provide a setting for political stability. Thus, after 1947, the United States began to manage the international monetary system by providing liquidity and adjustment.

By 1947, it was clear that neither gold nor the pound could continue to serve as the world's money. Gold production was insufficient to meet the demands of growing international trade and investment. Because of the weakness of the British economy, the pound was no longer able to serve as the primary world currency. The only currency strong enough to be used to meet the rising demands for international liquidity was the dollar. The strength of the U.S. economy, the fixed relationship of the dollar to gold ($35 an ounce), and the commitment of the U.S. government to convert dollars into gold at that price made the dollar as good as gold. In fact, the dollar was better than gold, as it earned interest and could be used for trade and finance.

There was, however, a major stumbling block to the dollar's emergence as the world's key currency: a huge dollar shortage. The United States was running huge trade surpluses, and its reserves were immense and growing. For the system to work, it would be necessary to reverse this flow: the United States had to run a payments deficit. That is just what happened.

From 1947 until 1958, the United States encouraged an outflow of dollars, which provided liquidity for the international economy. Dollars flowed out through U.S. aid programs: the Truman plan for aid to Greece and Turkey, aid to underdeveloped countries, and, most important, the **Marshall Plan**, which from 1948 to 1952 gave sixteen Western European countries $17 billion in outright grants. U.S. military expenditures in NATO countries and for the war in Korea provided another source of dollar liquidity. Thus the dollar became the world's currency, and the United States became the world's central banker, issuing dollars for the international monetary system.

In addition to providing liquidity, the United States managed imbalances in the system. It facilitated short-term adjustment through foreign aid and military expenditures, which helped offset the huge U.S. trade surplus and the European and Japanese deficits. In addition, the United States abandoned the Bretton Woods goal of convertibility and tolerated European and Japanese trade protection and discrimination against the dollar. For example, the United States absorbed large volumes of Japanese exports while accepting Japanese restrictions against U.S. exports. It supported the European Payments Union, an intra-European clearing system that discriminated against the dollar, and it promoted European exports to the United States. Finally, the United States used the leverage of Marshall Plan aid to encourage devaluation of many European currencies to support national programs of monetary stabilization.

To encourage long-term adjustment, the United States nurtured European and Japanese trade **competitiveness**. Policies for economic controls on the defeated Axis countries were scrapped. Aid to Europe and Japan, including the Marshall Plan aid to Europe, was designed to rebuild productive and export capacity. In the long run it was expected that such European and Japanese recovery would benefit the United States by widening markets for U.S. exports.[7]

The system worked well. Europe and Japan recovered and then expanded. The U.S. economy prospered partly because of the dollar outflow, which led to the purchase of U.S. goods and **services.** Yet by 1960, the U.S.-managed system was in trouble.

Multilateral Management under U.S. Leadership

The economic foundation of the U.S. management of the international monetary system was confidence in the U.S. dollar. This confidence was based on the strength of the U.S. economy, the enormous U.S. gold reserves, and the commitment to convert dollars into gold. But ironically, the system also relied on a process that eventually undermined the very confidence on which the structure was built: the constant outflow of dollars from the United States. The U.S. deficit and the foreign holding of dollars provided sufficient liquidity for international transactions. If, however, the deficit continued, and if outstanding dollar holdings abroad became too large in relation to gold reserves, confidence in the dollar—and thus in the entire system—would be jeopardized.[8]

By 1958, the United States no longer sought a payments deficit. The European and Japanese recoveries were nearly complete. Balances of payments were improving, and official reserves were growing steadily. By the end of 1959, European and Japanese reserves equaled those of the United States. U.S. gold holdings, however, had fallen from $24.4 billion at the end of 1948 to $19.5 billion at the end of 1959. More importantly, dollars held abroad had risen from $7.3 billion in 1948 to $19.4 billion at the end of 1959. The excess of U.S. gold holdings over foreign dollar holdings had fallen from $18.1 billion to $0.5 billion. In 1960, for the first time, foreign dollar holdings exceeded U.S. gold reserves.[9] Private long-term capital outflow, caused to a great extent by direct investment abroad and foreign military and aid expenditures, led to payments deficits in 1950, 1953, and 1959 (see Figure 2-1).

The first run on the dollar, which occurred in November 1960 when speculators converted dollars into gold, signaled the end of the unilateral system of U.S. management. The dollar system did not collapse. The United States was still able to play a strong leadership role, and the dollar and its economy remained healthy. But the United States could no longer manage the system alone. Henceforth, it would be obliged to join in collective management, to seek the cooperation of other members of the system, and to make concessions.

At the end of the 1950s, the IMF, largely inactive during the period of U.S. unilateral management, began to play a more important role, largely by lending funds to Europeans and others to finance temporary payments disequilibria. Increases in the fund's quotas at this time facilitated the more active role. The principal functions of monetary management, however, were performed by a multilateral group of the major states. One important new form of multilateral management was central bank cooperation. Since 1930, European central bankers had

Figure 2–1   Balance on Current Account (balance of payments) of the United States, 1946–1962, in Current Dollars

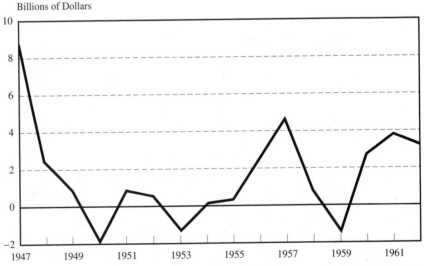

Billions of Dollars

Source: *Economic Report of the President* (Washington: U.S. Government Printing Office, January 1989), 424–425.

met together regularly at the Bank for International Settlements (BIS) in Basel, Switzerland, but the United States had never become a member and had never participated in their frequent meetings.[10] After the dollar crisis of 1960, however, high officials of the U.S. central bank, the Federal Reserve, joined the monthly meetings, although the United States did not join the BIS until 1994.

U.S. participation enabled the Basel group to control important aspects of the international monetary system. The bankers provided ad hoc crisis management by supporting currencies that came under pressure. The group also regulated the price of gold. In 1961, the bankers agreed to control gold speculation by centralizing gold dealings through a "gold pool," buying gold when it fell below $35 an ounce and selling it when it rose above that limit. The bankers also cooperated in exchange markets and began to play an important role in the burgeoning Eurocurrency market (see below) by investing, intervening, and accumulating information. Finally, the bankers regularly exchanged information about national policies affecting the international monetary system.

A second management system developed at this time was the Group of Ten, composed of finance ministers. The Group of Ten was formed in December 1961 when representatives of ten industrial countries—Belgium, France, Germany, Italy, the Netherlands, Sweden, Canada, Japan, the United Kingdom, and the United States—met to create the General Arrangements to Borrow, a $6 billion fund for exchange rate management that was under the control of its ten members.[11] It soon became a forum for discussion and exchange of information, a vehicle for negotiating monetary reform, as well as a mechanism for crisis management. In 1968, for example, the group stopped a dollar crisis and eased pressure on the U.S. gold supply by creating a two-tier gold system: a private market in which the price of gold could fluctuate freely and a public market in which the group agreed to sell one another gold at $35 an ounce. The Group of Ten was complemented by Working Party Three of the Organization for Economic Cooperation and Development (OECD), where finance officials discussed economic policies, exchanged information, and studied the operation and reform of the monetary adjustment process.

A series of bilateral arrangements between the United States and other members of the Group of Ten supported this multilateral management system. These arrangements included currency swap arrangements and standby credit lines to be used by central bankers for crisis management; special long-term U.S. bonds denominated in foreign currencies (known as Roosa bonds after their architect) that countries agreed to hold in lieu of converting dollars into gold; and German agreements to purchase U.S. military equipment and to continue to hold large amounts of U.S. dollars to offset the cost of U.S. troops stationed in Germany.

Finally, the United States sought to shore up the system by improving the U.S. balance of payments and reestablishing confidence in the weakening dollar. Unilateral U.S. efforts included an interest equalization tax on foreign securities designed to make borrowing in the United States less desirable and thus to reduce capital outflows, capital restraints on U.S. foreign investment, the tying of foreign aid, a decrease in duty-free tourist allotments, and programs to encourage U.S. exports. However, the United States was unwilling to alter its expansionary macroeconomic policies despite the pressures this put on its balance of payments.[12]

Multilateral management mechanisms not only prevented and contained currency crises but also achieved a major reform of the system. In the early 1960s, inadequate liquidity was seen as a crucial problem. Once the United States solved its balance-of-payments problems, as was expected, there would be a liquidity shortage and a need to provide alternative forms of international money. The problem of the future, it was believed, would not be too many dollars but too few.[13] In 1968, after five years of negotiations by the Group of Ten, an agreement was reached to create Special Drawing Rights (SDRs), artificial international reserve units created by the IMF, which could be used to settle accounts among central banks. Significantly, the new form of international liquidity would be managed not by the United States alone but by the Group of Ten jointly, for the Europeans were given a veto power on the creation of new SDRs.[14] The $6 billion of the new "paper gold" created was small compared with total world reserves at that time, close to $100 billion in 1970.[15] Nevertheless, for the first time in history, the international monetary system had an internationally created and managed asset.

The SDR agreement was the height of multilateral cooperation. Yet just at this point the system began to crack. Continuing currency crises in 1967 and 1968 heralded the eventual demise of the Bretton Woods monetary regime.

Breakdown of Bretton Woods

Several structural changes that emerged in the 1960s and early 1970s led to the breakdown of the Bretton Woods system. One change was the development of a high level of financial integration. The return to convertibility of the Western European currencies at the end of 1958[16] and of the Japanese yen in 1964 made possible the huge expansion of international financial transactions. Multinational banks became the vehicles for large international financial flows. Beginning in the 1960s, the number of multinational banks increased rapidly. In 1965, only 13 U.S. banks had branches abroad, but by the end of 1974 125 did. The assets of the U.S. banks' foreign branches rose from about $9 billion in 1965 to over $125 billion in 1974. Concomitantly, there was an expansion of foreign banks in the United States. The number of foreign branches and agencies in New York City, for example, rose from 49 in 1965 to 92 in 1974. The total assets of these branches and agencies in the same period rose from $5 billion to $29 billion, and by the end of 1974 foreign banks operating in the United States had total assets of $56 billion.[17]

Financial integration was also a result of the internationalization of production. Multinational corporations that controlled large liquid assets became sophisticated in moving their capital from country to country to take advantage of

interest rate spreads or expected exchange rate adjustments. In the 1960s and 1970s, as crises multiplied and risks increased, the movements of such capital became an important part of financial management.[18]

A final source of financial integration in this period was the Eurocurrency market. **Eurocurrencies** are national currencies—dollars, marks, francs, pounds, yen—held and traded outside their home country, primarily in Europe. For example, branches of U.S. banks or foreign banks in London accept dollar deposits and lend those deposits in the form of dollars. The Eurocurrency markets originated in the late 1950s, primarily with Eurodollars, and grew to huge proportions in the 1960s and 1970s, reaching almost $1 trillion by 1978 (see Figure 2-2).[19] The market flourished largely because it was controlled neither by state regulation nor by constraints of domestic money markets. It thus has been able to establish highly competitive interest rates that have attracted huge sums. Because it consists largely of short-term money, funds in the Eurocurrency market are highly mobile and highly volatile.[20]

These new forms of financial integration made possible huge international capital flows that put great strain on the international monetary system. In a fixed exchange rate regime, as we have seen, governments facing balance-of-payments disequilibria had several policy alternatives. If the disequilibrium was small or short-term, governments could finance the imbalance or impose exchange controls. If the disequilibrium was structural, they could either change the value of their currencies—devalue or revalue them—or alter domestic fiscal or monetary

Figure 2–2   The Growth of the Eurodollar and Eurocurrency Markets, 1964–1987

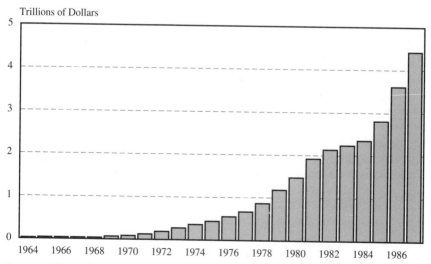

SOURCE: Morgan Guaranty Trust Company, *World Financial Markets,* various issues.

policy to restore balance. However, political leaders were often reluctant to take politically risky measures to address structural imbalances. The failure to resolve these disequilibria led to large speculative international capital movements. Efforts to intervene in exchange markets to prevent change were overwhelmed by rapid and massive international financial flows, which made it impossible to maintain the fixed value of currencies within a range of plus or minus 1 percent. Crises developed and governments were eventually forced to alter both exchange rates and national economic policies.

Financial integration also increasingly interfered with national economic management, especially with national monetary policy. Interest rates, for example, became a less-effective means of managing the national economic system. Low interest rates, used to stimulate an economy, can lead to an outflow of capital to countries with higher interest rates. In April and May 1971, a lowering of interest rates in the United States led to an outflow of capital. Conversely, high interest rates used to manage inflation may be defeated by capital inflows attracted precisely by those higher interest rates. Such was the case in Germany in 1969 and 1971. The need to defend fixed exchange rates in an interdependent system also interfered with domestic monetary management. Germany's attempts to deflate its economy and to control inflation were seriously hampered by the need to absorb large amounts of dollars to maintain the value of the deutsche mark.

For a long time, the United States was the one country that was not interdependent in this sense. U.S. national economic policy was not influenced by the international position of the dollar or by financial integration. Large capital flows had less effect on the huge U.S. economy than on the smaller European and Japanese economies. Furthermore, as long as other countries would absorb dollar outflows, the United States did not have to take domestic measures to balance international accounts. Thus in the 1960s the United States was able to rely on special balance-of-payments measures and avoid restrictive monetary or fiscal policy. Nevertheless, the U.S. economy was constrained by the international monetary system. By the late 1960s, the dollar was overvalued partly because of inflation induced by expenditures on the Vietnam War and partly because other countries had altered their exchange rates to account for inflation, even though the value of the dollar had not been altered. This overvalued dollar contributed to large investment outflows and led to declining exports and increasing imports (see Figure 2-3), which had an adverse impact on domestic economic performance.

The solution for any country, aside from the United States, in this position would have been to devalue the currency or deflate the economy to reestablish a competitive trade position. Neither was politically attractive. The United States was willing to have others revalue but did not want the domestic political problem of devaluing the dollar. Other countries holding vast sums of dollars and enjoying trade surpluses refused to allow a realignment of their currencies. The Europeans and the Japanese demanded instead a deflationary U.S. policy, arguing that the dollar outflow and the expansion of the U.S. economy were causing inflation abroad. This call for restraint was in direct conflict with U.S. domestic

Figure 2–3   U.S. Balance of Trade, 1946–1973 Current Dollars

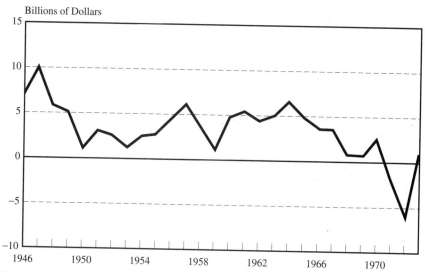

SOURCE: *Economic Report of the President* (Washington: Government Printing Office, January 1989), 424–425.

economic objectives as well as with President Nixon's political desires for reelection in 1972—and his desire to stimulate the U.S. economy in 1970 to provide a better setting for that election.

In addition to interdependence, increased pluralism also eroded monetary management. By the mid-1960s, the United States was no longer the dominant economic power it had been for almost two decades. Europe and Japan—with higher levels of growth, and per capita income approaching that of the United States—were narrowing the gap between themselves and the United States (see Figure 2-4). A more equal distribution of economic power led to a renewed sense of political power and to increasing dissatisfaction with U.S. dominance of the international monetary system and, in particular, with the privileged role of the dollar as the international currency. The Europeans and Japanese resented the prerogatives that the monetary system provided for the United States. They were concerned that U.S. domestic policies were undertaken with little or no regard for their international economic consequences and critical of the fact that the United States could carry out unlimited foreign expenditures for political purposes—military activities and foreign aid—without the threat of payments constraints. Such prerogatives of U.S. dominance were acceptable to a war-weary Europe and Japan confronting a hostile Soviet Union. They were less acceptable to a recovered and revitalized Europe and Japan faced with a less hostile neighbor.

The continuing decline of the dollar accentuated the problem of maintaining

Figure 2–4   GNP per Capita in Constant 1993 Dollars for the Five Largest Industralized Countries, 1962–1993

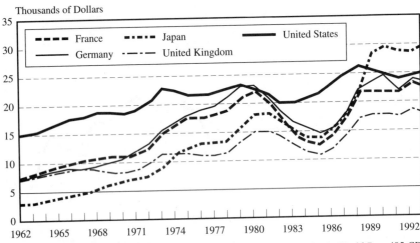

SOURCE: Calculated by the authors from GNP per capita data in World Bank, *World Data '95 CD-ROM* (Washington: World Bank, 1995); and CPI data in *Economic Report of the President* (Washington: Government Printing Office, 1995).

confidence in the system. Despite large and persistent deficits, it had seemed possible until 1965 that the dollar drain might be reduced or eliminated and that confidence in the system could be preserved. But the Vietnam conflict and the refusal of the Johnson administration to pay for both the war and its domestic social programs through taxation resulted in an increased dollar outflow to pay for the military expenses as well as in rampant inflation caused by a growing budget deficit, which led to further deterioration in the U.S. balance of trade (see Figure 2-3). By the end of the 1960s, large U.S. trade deficits seemed chronic.

The recovery of Europe and Japan also made monetary management more difficult. One example of this was the long and difficult negotiation over the SDR reform, which lasted five years and almost failed several times. By the time an agreement was reached, the problem of liquidity shortage, which it had been intended to solve, had been transformed into liquidity excess.

In short, financial integration grew faster than international management. New problems created by interdependence, including huge international capital flows, strained the fixed exchange rate system and interfered with national economic management. In the face of these problems, there was decreased cooperation, an absence of leadership, and, finally, a breakdown in management.

From 1968 to 1971, international monetary management was paralyzed. Despite the expansion of the bilateral swaps and the creation of new multilateral swaps, the central banks were unable to control the large currency flows and to contain currency crises. The Group of Ten was unable to move on further monetary reform and fell to bickering over currency realignment and national economic policies.

Most important, the United States abdicated monetary leadership and pursued a policy of "benign neglect." It let others defend the existing exchange rate system; permitted a huge foreign dollar buildup; and remained passive during currency crises. The United States also followed its domestic policies regardless of international consequences and disregarded the inflationary consequences of the huge dollar outflow in other parts of the system. And the United States no longer sought to mobilize the system for reform.

By late summer 1971, benign neglect was no longer a sustainable policy. In the spring and summer of 1971, there was a run on the dollar, and for the first time in the twentieth century, the United States showed a trade deficit (see again Figure 2-3). The U.S. gold stock declined to $10 billion versus outstanding foreign dollar holdings estimated at about $80 billion, inflation was rampant, and unemployment widespread. Political problems due to the economic situation led to pressure from all political quarters to do something.

On August 15, 1971, President Nixon—without consulting the other members of the international monetary system—announced a new economic policy: henceforth, the dollar would no longer be convertible into gold, and the United States would impose a surcharge of 10 percent on dutiable imports in an effort to force West Germany and Japan to revalue their currencies.[21] August 15, 1971, marked the end of the Bretton Woods period.

The shock of August 15 was followed by efforts by the Group of Ten under U.S. leadership to patch up the system of international monetary management. The first attempt was an agreement reached at the Smithsonian Institution in Washington in December 1971. The United States, feeling able to alter the rules and to improve its position, took a forceful leadership role in the negotiations. It used the import surcharge and dollar inconvertibility as weapons to force European and Japanese compromises, while at the same time agreeing to devalue the dollar. The Smithsonian agreement provided for a 10-percent devaluation of the dollar in relation to gold, a realignment of other exchange rates, and greater flexibility in rates that would float within a plus or minus 2.25 percent of parity, over twice the range of the Bretton Woods agreement.

The Smithsonian agreement was intended to be temporary and would give the participants time to negotiate long-term reform. In 1972, the Committee on Reform of the International Monetary System and Related Issues was established with the IMF to reform the international monetary system. Composed of the Group of Ten plus ten representatives of the developing countries, the so-called Committee of Twenty was charged with devising ways to manage world monetary reserves, establishing a commonly accepted currency and creating new adjustment mechanisms.

When President Nixon announced the agreement at the Smithsonian, he called it "the greatest monetary agreement in the history of the world." In fact, the Smithsonian agreement provided little more than temporary crisis control. It prevented deterioration in the system—a further hardening of trade restrictions, capital controls, and multiple exchange rates—but did not solve the fundamental problems of managing interdependence. The increased flexibility in and realignment of exchange rates were insignificant in the face of differing national policies and huge international capital flows. And the dollar, still the center of the system, remained inconvertible into gold.

"The greatest monetary agreement in the history of the world" lasted a little over a year. Soon massive currency flows led to new pressures on the Smithsonian rates, and national currency controls to hold back the pressure on the new rates proliferated. In June 1972, Britain and Ireland floated their currencies, and a new currency crisis began in January and February 1973. Even a second 10-percent devaluation of the U.S. dollar at that time could no longer save the fixed exchange rate system. By March 1973, all of the major world currencies were floating. Management was left to the market and in a minor way to central bankers who intervened in exchange markets on a somewhat cooperative basis to prevent extreme fluctuations.

The effort of the Committee of Twenty to achieve reform also was unsuccessful. The committee's reform plans centered on a system of stable but adjustable exchange rates and the provision of new forms of international liquidity. But while the committee debated, massive changes occurred in the international monetary system. Fixed exchange rates were replaced by the float. Inflation erupted, fueled by U.S. inflation combined with an enormous dollar outflow and worldwide commodity shortages. Different national rates of inflation made stability impossible and increased national desires for floating exchange rates to enable a degree of isolation from external inflation.[22]

Finally, while the committee debated, a handful of oil exporters engineered a dramatic rise in the price of petroleum (see Chapter 9). Within a year, the price of oil quadrupled. As a result, huge sums—an estimated $70 billion in 1974 alone—were transferred from the oil-consuming countries, primarily from the developed market economies, to the oil-producing states.[23] This price change created a major new problem of financial recycling. Under the ideal free-trade model, the surplus earnings of the oil-producing states would have been channeled back to the oil-consuming countries in the form of revenue from the import of goods and services from the oil consumers. But the transfer of resources to the oil-producing states had been too large for them to absorb. Despite huge development needs and arms expenditures, these states as a whole could not take in enough imports to make up for the loss to the consuming countries. In 1974, the current-account surplus of the oil-producing states was over $70 billion, and by 1980, a second round of precipitous oil price increases had pushed it above $114 billion.[24]

Many of the oil-consuming countries could not reduce their oil consumption sufficiently to eliminate their deficits or increase exports sufficiently to cover the gap. Thus they had to borrow to pay for their deficits, and the only sources for such borrowing were the countries with surpluses from oil earnings. This was the recycling problem that, less than a decade later, was transformed into the developing countries' external debt crisis (see Chapter 6).

After 1974, surpluses were recycled primarily through private banks, which accepted the deposits of the oil-exporting countries and lent these funds to the oil-importing countries. Smaller amounts were recycled through government securities and direct loans and investment by the oil-producing states and through international institutions (such as the IMF and the World Bank), which borrowed from the oil producers and made loans to the oil consumers. Thus the private system, especially the banking system, was the primary monetary manager. Throughout the 1970s, private banks remained the principal recyclers and, in the process, accumulated large Eurocurrency deposits and equally large international loan portfolios. Despite the effectiveness of reliance on the private market, it posed certain problems. The role of the private banks in recycling required increasing their ratio of assets (loans) to capital, thus bringing into question the financial stability of the banking system. Furthermore, many developing countries that borrowed heavily from commercial banks were eventually unable to service their loans. By the early 1980s, as we shall see, the resulting debt crisis raised serious questions about the strength of the international financial markets.

The float, inflation, and the monetary consequences of the oil crisis overwhelmed the Committee of Twenty. In January 1974, the committee concluded that because of the turmoil in the international economy, it would be impossible to draw up and implement a comprehensive plan for monetary reform.[25]

For a year and a half, the world focused on the overwhelming problem of coping with the immediate consequences of the oil shock: inflation, **recession,** and recycling. Then, in November 1975, heads of government of the major monetary powers—the United States, the United Kingdom, France, West Germany, Japan, and Italy—met at the French chateau of Rambouillet to decide on the framework for a new monetary system. This meeting was the first of what would become regular annual economic summits of the seven major industrial powers.[26] At the IMF meeting in January 1976, the final details were hammered out in the Second Amendment to the Articles of Agreement of the International Monetary Fund.

On paper, the Second Amendment seemed to signal a return to multilateral public management of the international monetary system. It called for an end to the role of gold and the establishment of the SDR as the principal reserve asset of the international monetary system. It legitimized the de facto system of floating exchange rates but permitted return to fixed exchange rates if an 85-percent majority approved such a move. And it called for greater IMF surveillance of the exchange rate system and management of national economic policies to promote a stable and orderly system.[27]

In reality, the monetary powers had not reformed the system of public management; they had merely codified the prevailing nonsystem. The Second Amendment did not resolve the problem of the dollar; its guidelines for managing exchange rates were undefined; its calls for appropriate national policies and national cooperation with the fund carried little obligation; its mechanisms for institutionalizing cooperation were fragile; and it was implemented in an unstable international economic environment. The Second Amendment signaled the beginning of a period characterized as much by national and regional as by multilateral management.

Management Dilemmas in the Post–Bretton Woods Era

The interdependent and more pluralistic international monetary system that has prevailed since 1976 has confronted several major management problems. One is the long-standing dilemma of the dollar. Despite continuing challenges to the dollar's credibility and persistent dissatisfaction abroad with U.S. economic policies, the U.S. dollar survives as the world's major currency. Throughout the 1970s and 1980s, foreign exchange constituted approximately 90 percent of official reserves excluding gold, and the dollar accounted for an average of 70 percent of official holdings of foreign exchange in those years.[28]

The dollar has retained its central role through this period despite widespread dissatisfaction with the dollar both when it is seen as excessively weak as in the late 1970s or as excessively strong as in the first half of the 1980s. As in the Bretton Woods system, the size of the U.S. economy and its highly developed financial markets as well as U.S. political stability make it desirable and feasible to use the dollar. The U.S. government continues to support the dollar's role while other countries with strong economies and stable polities have been reluctant to allow their currencies to play a central international role. For years, West Germany and Japan, fearing loss of control over their domestic economies, restricted their capital markets to make it difficult for foreigners to hold deutsche marks and yen. Efforts to enlarge the role of the SDR, including changing its valuation and raising interest rates, have been unsuccessful. SDRs account for less than 5 percent of official reserves.[29]

There has been, nonetheless, a shift away from the dollar as the exclusive reserve and transaction currency. In 1978, dollars accounted for 76 percent of official holdings of foreign exchange, while deutsche marks accounted for 11 percent and yen for 3 percent. By 1993, the dollar share had fallen to 61 percent while the deutsche mark had risen to 16 percent and the yen to 9 percent (see Figure 2-5). Holding and using currencies other than the dollar became more attractive in the 1980s and 1990s as the U.S. balance of payments weakened dramatically, while other countries, particularly Japan and Germany, accumulated payments surpluses. The expectation that the dollar would have to decline to reflect the worsening payments situation made it prudent to diversify currency holdings.

Furthermore, in the 1980s and 1990s a number of countries liberalized financial regulations making it easier for their currencies to be used and held abroad. Japan, for example, took a number of steps to internationalize the yen. It eliminated exchange controls, removed restrictions on Euro-yen activities of Japanese

Figure 2–5   The Dollar, the Deutsche Mark, and the Yen as Percentage of Total Foreign Currency Holdings, in 1978, 1986, and 1993

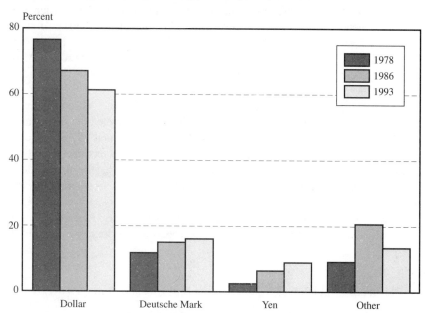

SOURCE: International Monetary Fund, *Annual Report 1987* (Washington: IMF, 1987), 58; and IMF, *Annual Report 1994,* 158.

institutions, and increased access of foreign financial institutions to Japanese capital markets. Importantly, these steps were taken under pressure from the United States to open up financial markets to foreign institutions and to allow the yen to become an international currency, and they were negotiated bilaterally with the United States.[30]

Floating exchange rates (as opposed to the fixed rates of Bretton Woods) are another central characteristic and major problem of the prevailing system.[31] Although most of the IMF's members maintain some form of fixed exchange rate, the world's major currencies float against one another. Proponents had argued that a float would provide for relative stability and rationality in exchange rates through the stabilizing effect of speculation. Prompt exchange rate changes, they contended, would result in more effective current-account adjustment. Trade deficits and inflation would lead to exchange rate depreciation, increased competitiveness of exports, and decreased competitiveness of imports, and this would thereby restore the trade balance. A float would also make possible greater autonomy for national policy in an era of interdependence, by freeing economic policy from external balance of payments constraints of maintaining a fixed exchange rate.

Floating exchange rates have operated effectively in several ways: They have not disrupted international trade and investment, as many critics feared, and they were probably the only system that could have endured the serious economic shocks of the 1970s and 1980s, including the oil and debt crises and inflation differentials. They also encouraged the long-term movement of exchange rate changes generally in a direction to correct payments imbalances. However, there have been several serious problems with the floating rate system. Exchange rates have been highly volatile, frustrating a smooth and rapid adjustment process. Most major currencies have been subjected to wide and often inexplicable fluctuations, especially in short-term rates (see Figure 2–6).

One reason for exchange rate movements lies in the emergence of globally integrated international financial markets. We have already noted the significance of the Eurocurrency markets that developed in the 1960s and 1970s and contributed to growing financial interdependence, and we have seen the end of the fixed exchange rates of Bretton Woods. In the 1980s and 1990s, the internationalization of financial markets increased exponentially, driven by several powerful forces.[32]

Most developed countries—the United Kingdom, France, Germany, Canada, Australia, and Japan—relaxed exchange controls, opened domestic markets to

Figure 2–6   Monthly Percent Change in Real Exchange Rates, 1960–1990

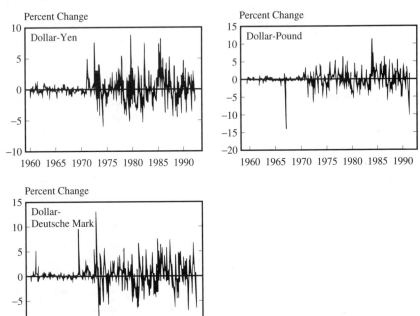

Source: Barry Eichengreen, *International Monetary Arrangements for the 21st Century* (Washington: Brookings Institution, 1994), 12.

foreign financial institutions, and removed some domestic regulatory barriers. As a result of deregulation, national financial markets became integrated into the global market enabling larger amounts of capital to flow more freely across national boundaries.

A revolution in telecommunications, information processing, and computer technologies made possible a vastly increased volume, speed, and global reach of financial transactions. Finally, the growing sophistication of financial players reinforced deregulation and the technological revolution. In the 1960s and 1970s, as we have noted, the multinational corporation, with its pool of funds and its worldwide borrowing needs, contributed to growing international financial flows. In the 1980s and 1990s, the concentration of capital in institutions, such as pension funds, money market funds, and insurance companies, reinforced the trend toward sophisticated, global management of large pools of capital. Professional managers of such funds, operating in an environment of volatile prices, exchange rates, and interest rates, were increasingly willing to move money across international boundaries to diversify risk and take advantage of market differentials.[33]

Whereas twenty years ago, international portfolio investments were used mainly by international banks and multinational corporations as a way of hedging against foreign exchange risks and differences in the rate of growth of different national markets, now individuals do the same thing via their investments in international mutual funds. About $903 billion were invested in foreign equities and assets in funds managed in Europe and the United States at the end of 1991.[34] By the end of June 1994, net international bank credit was $4.1 trillion, net Euronote placements were $331 billion, net international bond financing was $1.97 trillion, for a total of net international financing (which excludes double counting) of $5.65 trillion.[35]

As a result of these multiple forces, global financial markets exploded in size and became a major influence on the floating exchange rate system. World financial flows now exceed trade flows by a factor of at least 30 to 1.[36] By 1992, total cross-border ownership of tradable securities had risen to an estimated $2.5 trillion. Many of these assets were short-term holdings in foreign currencies and securities and therefore highly liquid investments. Net *daily* turnover in nine of the major national markets for foreign currency was estimated to be about $1 trillion.[37]

The emergence of a highly integrated world capital market facilitated enormous flows of international funds that respond as much to political risk and interest rate differentials as to trade balances. Thus, for example, high real American interest rates and the search for a political safe haven in the early 1980s attracted a large flow of capital into the United States (see Figure 4-5 in Chapter 4). These flows maintained, for a few years, the strength of the dollar despite the deteriorating U.S. current account position and the strengthening trade balances of other industrial countries, particularly Germany and Japan. In 1994, as we shall see, Mexico suffered a massive capital outflow due to a sudden loss of confidence in the Mexican government's economic policies and to concerns about political stability. As a result, the Mexican government was forced to allow the peso to be devalued and to implement domestic austerity policies.

Massive financial imbalances that have not been adjusted through market mechanisms are another problem of the prevailing monetary system. We have seen how the oil crises of the 1970s created a financial imbalance that swamped efforts to recreate a fixed exchange rate regime. So, in the 1980s the debt crisis and the massive U.S. budget and trade deficits created a serious adjustment problem.

As we have seen, a rapid increase in bank lending to developing countries was a major solution to the problem of recycling OPEC financial surpluses. In the period before 1979, the private system of recycling worked well. Lending helped promote the developing countries' productive capacities, maintained their growth, and, in turn, created demand for exports from the developed countries. LDC exports grew along with debt, enhancing their **debt service** ability. However, after the second oil crisis of 1979, debtor countries were hit hard by the increase in the price of oil; by restrictive monetary policies in the major industrial countries that led to record-high real interest rates and an increased debt service burden; and by world recession, which led to a plunge in commodity prices and in demand for LDC exports. Nonetheless, banks continued to lend and developing countries continued to borrow, building up a huge debt, which they were increasingly unable to service (see Chapter 6, which discusses international financial flows).

A crisis erupted in 1982 when Mexico announced that it was unable to service its debt. Mexico's external debt totaled more than $80 billion and included loans that accounted for a significant percentage of the largest U.S. banks' capital in 1982. And Mexico was just the tip of the iceberg. At the end of 1982, total LDC debt amounted to $831 billion.[38] The world's major private banks had significant exposure in developing countries. Default by the debtor nations thus could have had several serious consequences for the international monetary system: a collapse of confidence in the international banking system, possible illiquidity or insolvency of the banks, dangerous disruption of financial markets and—in a worst-case scenario—world recession or **depression.**

As we will see, the international financial community succeeded in containing the debt crisis of the 1980s through an ongoing series of reschedulings of both public and private debt. Some rapidly growing developing countries eventually regained access to world financial markets, but others remained heavily burdened by debt. Indeed, **debt rescheduling** actually led to an increase in outstanding LDC debt and thus in the potential management problem. By 1992, total outstanding long-term debt of LDCs had grown to $1.3 trillion.[39]

Unprecedented imbalances among the developed countries created an equally destabilizing situation. Despite expectations, the floating exchange rate system has not ensured effective current account adjustment and has not prevented the development of large, unsustainable external deficits and surpluses. In the 1980s, the United States accumulated two massive and unprecedented deficits—sometimes referred to as the "twin deficits" (see Figure 2-7). A large budget deficit was the result of lowering taxes without reducing government spending. The budget

Figure 2–7   The Twin Deficits in the United States, 1981–1993, in Current Dollars

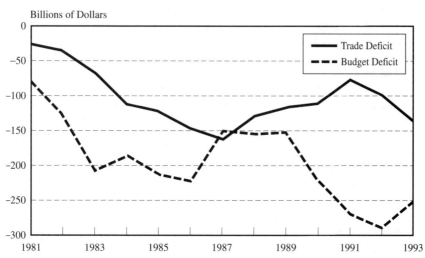

Billions of Dollars

SOURCE: *Economic Report of the President* (Washington: Government Printing Office, 1995), 365, 394.

deficit contributed to the trade and balance of payments deficits by increasing demand for imports and creating favorable conditions for capital inflows. Other causes of the trade deficit included an overvalued dollar; strong U.S. economic growth in comparison with other developed countries; lower demand in traditional markets for U.S. agricultural exports; the increased competitiveness of foreign companies even as the competitiveness of U.S. industry declined; the rise in protectionist barriers; and the Third World debt crisis, which lowered demand for U.S. exports (see Chapter 3).

The twin deficits of the 1980s called for adjustments in U.S. economic policies, which were not forthcoming. Improvements in the budget deficit were blocked by a political conflict between a president opposed to raising taxes and a Congress opposed to spending cuts; improvements in the trade deficit were hampered by the budget crisis as well as by the resistance of the administration to adopt domestic policies that would lead to devaluation of the dollar. Instead of adjusting, the United States used its unique position in the international monetary system to finance its deficits. As in the past, the central role of the dollar in the international financial system enabled the United States to more or less automatically finance its deficits through foreign capital inflows. In the 1980s, the amount of such financing dwarfed that of previous years. In 1986, the United States had a positive net international investment at market value of $136 billion. In 1989, the United States became a net debtor with a negative net investment position of $77 billion. By 1994, net investment was negative $584 billion.[40] Despite the changed U.S. international position, the dollar remained strong for the first half of the 1980s, buoyed by high real U.S. interest rates and the search for a political safe haven.

United States dependence on such capital inflows created a serious threat to the dollar, which remained the basis of the international monetary system. At some point, the trade deficit would undermine confidence in the U.S. currency and lead to a decline in the dollar. Furthermore, because much of the capital inflow sustaining U.S. imbalances was short-term, a loss in confidence could lead to a precipitous, free fall of the dollar and a serious shock to the system. By the 1990s, the domestic political consensus in the United States shifted toward greater willingness to address the problem of the budget deficit, and U.S. policy focused on the need for the United States to be competitive in international markets. U.S. domestic policy adjustments especially deficit reduction combined with international economic cooperation made it more likely that any decline of the dollar would lead to a soft, not a hard, landing.

Two mirror images of the U.S. trade deficit were the trade surpluses of Japan and West Germany (see Figure 2-8). By 1987, Japan had a trade surplus of $96.5 billion and Germany a surplus of $70 billion. By 1993, the Japanese trade surplus had grown to $141.4 billion, while the German trade surplus shrank to $42.1 billion, largely as a result of the integration with East Germany. Of growing importance also were the trade surpluses of the newly industrialized countries in Asia, such as Taiwan, which had a 1994 surplus of $12 billion and Korea with a 1988 surplus of $14.4 billion.[41]

Finally, the prevailing system has not, as was hoped, resolved the dilemma of interdependence. Even the United States, especially in recent times, has not been able to pursue national economic policies without regard to international constraints. Especially in the new world of global financial interdependence, autonomous national economic policymaking has proved illusory. Yet achieving the level of international cooperation necessary to maintain stability in the world monetary system has proved equally difficult because of domestic political constraint and because each nation still cherishes the illusion of autonomy.

The period since 1976 has been one of muddling through, characterized as much by national and regional management as by multilateral management. The monetary powers have cooperated to stabilize the system during periods of crisis and have periodically sought to coordinate economic policies in order to achieve long-term stability. Policy coordination has, however, been limited in scope and in success. Despite the growth of interdependence, national governments have been either unwilling or unable to adjust national economic policies to international economic needs.

Europe's Efforts to Build a Regional Monetary System

The most ambitious effort at international monetary cooperation since the collapse of the Bretton Woods system has been the European Monetary System

Figure 2–8   Balance of Trade of the Five Largest Industrial Nations, 1973–1993 in Current Dollars

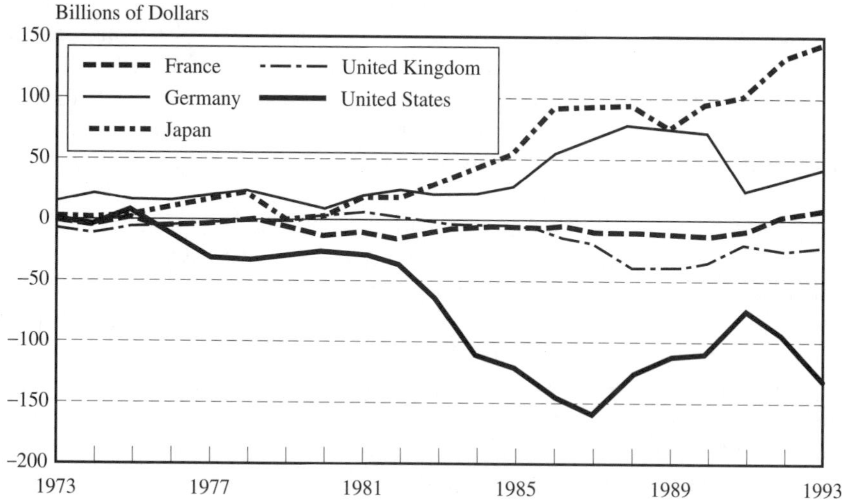

Billions of Dollars

SOURCE: International Monetary Fund, *International Financial Statistics Yearbook 1990,* (Washington: IMF, 1990), 140; and Organization for Economic Cooperation and Development, *OECD Economic Outlook,* 55 (Paris: OECD, June 1994).

(EMS).[42] Members of the European Union, with their high level of intra-EU trade and cross-border investments and their Common Agricultural Policy, which is based on common prices and relies on stable exchange rates, have an especially strong interest in stabilizing exchange rates among themselves.[43]

Discussions on stabilizing exchange rates in Europe began in the 1960s, shortly after the signing of the Treaty of Rome. Fissures in the Bretton Woods system along with early achievements in European economic integration were the main factors behind the initiation of these talks. They culminated in the Werner Report of 1970, which set forth detailed plans for monetary union. The recommendations of the Werner report were rendered moot by the collapse of the Bretton Woods system in 1972.

After 1972, the member states agreed to hold their currencies within a 2.25-percent band against one another while allowing this band to move within a 4.5-percent band against the dollar. The arrangement was called the "snake in the tunnel." In addition to the six member states of the European Economic Community, Britain, Ireland, and Denmark joined the snake in May 1972. Britain and Ireland left the snake in June 1972.

The snake was an attempt to reconstruct an international fixed rate monetary regime in the face of the collapse of Bretton Woods. It failed to accomplish that goal, however, or even the more limited one of jointly floating the EU member states' currencies against the dollar. Italy left the snake in February 1973 and

France in January 1974. The French returned briefly in mid-1975 only to leave permanently eight months later.

Part of the problem was the way in which the shock of higher world oil prices was transmitted within Europe. Britain became an oil exporter and needed flexibility to adjust its exchange rate to maximize the benefits of increased oil revenues. France was unable to keep inflation low enough and Italy to reduce its balance of payments deficit sufficiently to remain in the snake. They needed to devalue their currencies to maintain the international competitiveness of their export-oriented industries.

In December 1978, the Council of Ministers of the European Community agreed to create a "zone of monetary stability in Europe:" a system with fixed, although adjustable, exchange rates among the members and a floating rate with the outside world; the creation of a European Currency Unit (ECU), a basket of currencies serving as a basis for fixing exchange rates, a means of settlement and a potential future reserve asset; and a network of credit arrangements and plans for a future European Monetary Fund for financing payments imbalances and supporting the fixed rates. The EMS went into effect in March 1979.

At that time, all members of the EMS except the United Kingdom agreed to participate in the exchange rate mechanism (ERM) by maintaining fixed exchange rates with 2.25 percent fluctuation margins (except for the Italian lira, which was allowed to fluctuate within a wider 6-percent band). Fixed rates were to be maintained by convergent national economic policies and, when necessary, by intervention in currency markets financed by mutual lines of credit. The U.K.'s opposition to the ERM was both economic (based on the special role of the pound sterling as an international currency and as the currency of an oil exporter) and political (based on the need to subject its domestic economic policy to international constraints, especially to the policies of West Germany, which had the strongest economy and currency in the EMS).

During the first four years of the EMS, there were seven realignments of EMS currency values. These realignments devalued the lira and the franc relative to the deutsche mark by 27 and 25 percent respectively. This was a healthy development, given that the initial exchange rates for the lira and the franc had probably been set too high. Indeed, the next four years of the EMS witnessed only four more realignments, substantially smaller than the previous ones. After 1983, exchange rate variability within the EMS declined substantially, while monetary policies converged on virtually every dimension.[44] From January 1987 until September 1992, there were no realignments within the ERM, while Spain, the United Kingdom, and Portugal joined the ERM, and Finland, Sweden, and Norway explicitly linked their currencies to the ECU.

The success of the EMS was not complete, however. The European Monetary Fund, which was to have been a quasi-central bank and the institutional framework for the EMS, was not established. In 1989, central bankers agreed to the long-term objective of creating a European central bank but recognized that members would first have to harmonize economic and monetary policies over a period of years.[45] There were numerous realignments of rates, and fixed rates were made possible by exchange controls on weaker currencies. The Italian lira had wider than 6-percent fluctuation margins. Furthermore, despite growing internal support for EMS membership, the United Kingdom, Greece, and Portugal remained outside the EMS. Nevertheless, by fixing rates and forcing coordination of national economic policies, the EMS produced lower inflation and less misalignment of rates than would have occurred had unguided market forces prevailed. Finally, although the ECU had not, as intended, become a major reserve unit or a means of settlement between EU monetary authorities, it had established a permanent role in international financial markets as a major currency of denomination for banking and securities market transactions.

In 1986, the members of the EU committed themselves to deepening the integration process by passing the Single European Act (SEA). One of the provisions of the SEA undermined the institutions that had allowed the EMS to operate successfully. The SEA mandated removal of all obstacles to completing the internal market, including capital controls. Capital controls included a broad variety of measures affecting capital markets, including taxes on holdings of foreign currencies and regulations on how foreign currencies could be put to use. Capital controls allowed the central banks of EMS members to prevent speculation against their currencies in anticipation of realignments. Without these controls, in short, it would be impossible to continue with the EMS strategy of periodic realignments.[46]

As part of the process of implementing the SEA, therefore, a committee was appointed under the chairmanship of Jacques Delors, President of the Commission, to study the feasibility of creating a monetary union for Europe. The Delors Report was published in 1989, beginning a new round of negotiations that culminated in proposals for a three-stage process to achieve an Economic and Monetary Union (EMU) included in the December 1991 Maastricht Treaty.

In Stage One, the system was to remain more or less as it was in the late 1980s, with nine European currencies bound together by the ERM. Stage Two, begun on January 1, 1994, was to proceed further with liberalization of capital markets. The Council of Central Bank Governors was replaced by a new institution called the European Monetary Institute (EMI). Stage Three, which was to begin no later than January 1, 1999, would start with the dissolution of the EMI and its replacement by a European Central Bank. After 1999, then, there would be one European currency as well as a relatively autonomous, single supranational authority responsible for making monetary policy in the EU.[47]

Much of the politics of European monetary integration after 1991 centered on the preconditions for participation in the monetary union (see Table 2-1). All the members of the EU could not meet the preconditions by the original deadline (December 31, 1996), and it was unlikely that all of them would meet the preconditions by subsequent deadlines. Therefore it became increasingly likely that the EMU would be composed initially of a subset of EU member-states and that others would join if and when they were able to meet the convergence criteria.[48]

Table 2-1   Preconditions (convergence criteria) for Participation in the European Monetary Union

Variable	Target
Inflation rate	Less than or equal to 1.5 percent over rate of lowest three members
Interest rate on long-term government bonds	Less than or equal to 2 percent above rate of three members with the lowest inflation rates
Government budget deficit	Less than or equal to 3 percent of GDP
Outstanding government debt	Less than or equal to 60 percent of GDP
Currency exchange rate	Within ERM band for at least 2 years

Source: *Economic Report of the President* (Washington: Government Printing Office, 1994), 247.

The politics of European monetary integration was complicated by the unification of Germany and the subsequent currency crises of 1992–1993. East and West Germany were unified in 1990. Economic decisions made at the time of unification generated inflationary pressures that caused the German central bank, the Bundesbank, to raise interest rates. Higher German interest rates put pressure on the other members of the EMS to either raise their interest rates or unpeg their currencies to prevent an outflow of short-term capital investments to Germany.

In addition, on June 2, 1992, Denmark held a referendum on the Maastricht Treaty. The treaty was rejected by a slim majority of Danish voters. The Danish vote combined with German post-unification monetary policy changes set off a round of speculation affecting European currencies. The first to suffer was the Italian lira. Then the three currencies in the wide (6-percent) band of the EMS — the British pound, the Spanish peseta, and the Portuguese escudo—weakened. Pressure mounted again prior to the French referendum on Maastricht on September 20. On August 26, the pound fell to its ERM floor. On September 16, the British and Italian governments withdrew the pound and the lira from the ERM. Other ERM members intervened in support of their currencies, but the lira was devalued by 7 percent against other ERM currencies on September 13 and then later allowed to float. The pressure on the EMS did not end, however. Indeed, it actually intensified until the final crisis "put an end to Europe's policy of pegging exchange rates within narrow bands." After the temporary withdrawal of Germany in July from the EMS, European governments opted for widening the narrow band from 2.25 to 15 percent on August 2, 1993.[49]

The 1992–1993 crises illustrated the problems of managing a fixed exchange rate system in the face of political uncertainty and high international capital mobility.[50] Nevertheless, the commitment to European monetary union remained strong. Most EU member states saw monetary integration as the next essential step in Europe's growing economic integration. The predictability and simplicity of a fixed or single currency would facilitate trade and investment flows within the EU. A unified European market, in turn, was seen as promoting Europe's competitiveness in the global marketplace, especially vis-à-vis the United States and Japan. Thus large European firms operating in more than one European country have actively supported monetary integration and many political leaders argue that national interests can best be realized in a united Europe.[51]

U.S. Policy: Alternating between Unilateralism and Collective Management

While the EMS countries have pursued a zone of stability since the end of the Bretton Woods system, U.S. policy has been characterized by two conflicting strategies: (1) periodic efforts to improve the functioning of the system through multilateral cooperation and (2) resistance to the inevitable consequences of interdependence for U.S. domestic economic policy.

From 1977 to 1981, the Carter administration emphasized collective management of international economic relations. A principal objective in the early Carter years was to achieve world recovery from the recession of the mid-1970s through cooperation of the major industrialized countries. The U.S. strategy for global economic growth was based on the **"locomotive theory,"** which called for coordinated national economic policies and for countries with payments surpluses—that is, Germany and Japan—to follow expansionary policies that would serve as engines of growth for the rest of the world.

Collective management seemed to achieve some success in 1978 when Germany, France, and Japan agreed at the economic summit to pursue more expansionary policies, and the United States agreed, as a trade-off, on a program to curb inflation and energy consumption. The agreement seemed to be a major milestone, demonstrating that the world's economic powers were capable of coordinating national economic policies and that the United States could still be the driving force behind multilateral management.[52] However, the 1978 dollar crisis, which immediately followed the agreement, demonstrated that governments, especially the U.S. government, were still reluctant to alter domestic policies for international reasons. Then the oil crisis of 1979 and the fear of inflation led to the abandonment of the goal of economic stimulation.

The dollar crisis of 1978 followed a familiar pattern. More rapid growth and greater inflation in the United States than the rest of the world led to trade and current account deficits, plummeting confidence in the ability of the United States to pursue stringent economic policies and a continuing decline in the dollar. Initially, the United States resisted defending the dollar. Then, the government sought to resolve the problem through external policies and limited domestic policies: intervening in foreign exchange markets, doubling the swap network with West Germany, selling SDRs and gold, voluntary wage and price guidelines, and fiscal constraints.

Finally, the United States was forced to take major domestic and international measures. On November 1, 1978, President Carter announced a new restrictive economic and dollar defense program: a restrictive monetary policy, the mustering of $30 billion in foreign currencies for possible intervention in foreign exchange markets, a policy of active intervention in those markets, and an expansion of the sale of U.S. gold.[53] The package was a major departure in U.S. policy. For the first time since World War II, the United States altered domestic economic policy for international monetary reasons.

Initially, it seemed that the thrust of U.S. policy was permanently altered and that the United States had accepted its interdependence. In 1979, when the dollar again came under pressure, the Federal Reserve announced a major new policy designed to bring U.S. inflation under control. Before October 1979, the Federal Reserve had concentrated on raising or lowering interest rates through open market operations and raising or lowering the discount rate, the rate at which the Federal Reserve makes loans to member banks, as the principal policies for controlling the supply of money and credit. In 1979, the Federal Reserve turned, instead, to monetarism—that is, to managing the size of the nation's money supply. By focusing on the size and growth of certain monetary aggregates and by responding immediately to changes in the size of those aggregates, the Federal Reserve hoped to bring inflation under control and to return stability to the international monetary system.

In particular, the Federal Reserve under its new chairman, Paul Volcker, adopted a policy late in 1979 of increasing interest rates by rapidly tightening the money supply so as to reduce inflation. The prime rate for bank loans went up from 9.06 percent in 1978 to a peak of 18.87 percent in 1981 (see Figure 2-9),[54] as a result, and while inflation was reduced significantly, the higher interest rates of the late 1970s and early 1980s also created a serious recession (lowering the rate of economic growth and increasing unemployment), thus reducing the chances for reelection of Jimmy Carter.[55]

With the election of Ronald Reagan in 1981, the policy of combining international cooperation with domestic policy changes was altered to U.S. unilateralism in international monetary relations. Domestically, the Reagan administration combined the tight monetary policy and the monetarist approach, begun in 1979, with an expansionary fiscal policy known as **supply-side economics.**[56]

The United States pursued a tight monetary policy, based on strict adherence to monetary targets, in order to fight inflation. Yet at the same time, it raised expenditures, especially for defense, and—according to supply-side theory—reduced taxes in an effort to stimulate savings, investment, and growth.

The United States reverted to economic unilateralism in its international monetary policy. Departing from previous U.S. policy, the Reagan administration

Figure 2–9   Interest Rate (bank prime rate) and the Multilateral Trade-Weighted and Inflation-Adjusted Value of the Dollar, 1965–1994

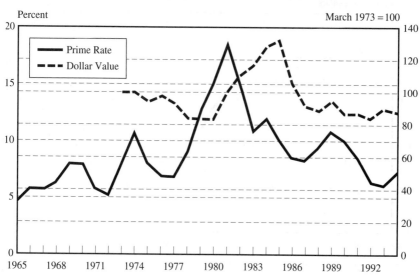

SOURCE: *Economic Report of the President* (Washington: Government Printing Office, 1995), 358, 402

officially rejected intervention in foreign exchange markets and ceased efforts to coordinate national economic policies. Although the impact of U.S. policies on the world economy was profound and often disruptive, the United States carried out its abrupt shift and continued to conduct its policies, not only without serious consultation, but also without taking into account their impact on other countries. The United States also conducted domestic economic policy without taking into account the international repercussions on the U.S. economy.

There were many beneficial effects of the new U.S. policies: inflation subsided, and as confidence grew, the dollar turned from a weak to a strong currency. But there were also heavy costs. The tight monetary policy of the United States drove interest rates at home and abroad to unprecedented high levels. High U.S. interest rates led to a dollar that was overvalued in trade terms and to dislocations in exchange markets (see Figure 2-10). Short-term capital flowed into the United States to take advantage of high interest rates.

Other developed countries were faced with difficult policy choices: raising their interest rates above the level warranted by their economic situation and thus avoiding an outflow of capital to the United States but dampening growth; keeping rates low and allowing capital to flow to the United States; or imposing capital controls. The decision of most was to avoid capital controls and raise interest rates. But in the end, they found themselves with the worst of both worlds:

Figure 2–10   Balance of Trade, 1973–1994, in Current Dollars

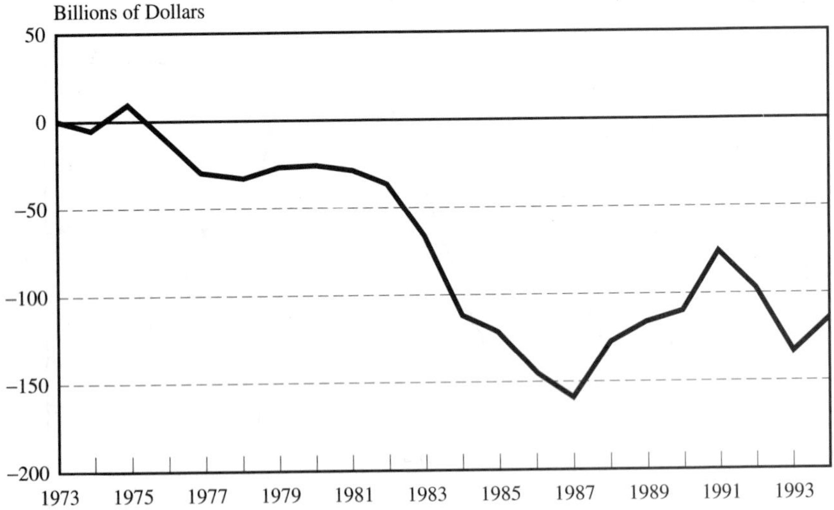

Billions of Dollars

SOURCE: *Economic Report of the President* (Washington: Government Printing Office, 1995), 394.

recession as well as capital outflows.[57] The consequences for the developing countries were far worse: declining exports and greater debt service costs, the recipe for the debt crisis. The repercussions on the United States were also serious. A high dollar plus world recession led to a decline in U.S. exports and massive merchandise trade deficits (see again Figure 2-10). The drop in U.S. exports in turn retarded American growth. The monetary system whose purpose was to foster trade and investment was now disrupting it.

Despite its unilateralism in exchange rate policy, the United States, as we shall see, was willing to cooperate in the management of the debt crisis (see Chapter 6). The debt crisis altered somewhat the U.S. attitude toward worldwide financial stability. At the time of the first major Mexican debt crisis (in 1982), the Federal Reserve eased its stringent monetary policy in order to lower worldwide interest rates; the United States became more willing to intervene in limited situations to smooth volatile foreign exchange markets; and, in a reversal of previous policy, the United States supported increases in IMF quotas in order to enable the fund to play a role in debt management.

Despite growing pressure from the other members of the system to restore some degree of multilateral monetary management, the United States continued to pursue a unilateral policy, arguing that the best thing the United States could do for the system would be to get its own house in order. United States monetary and fiscal policy remained out of balance and highly disruptive and the United

States did not believe it had to alter its policies to achieve stability in exchange markets. It was not until 1985, when economic dislocations became unsustainable politically and economically, that the United States returned to a more multi-lateral policy.

By 1985, a serious misalignment in world exchange rates had developed. The dollar had appreciated sharply due to the combination of tight monetary and loose **fiscal policies** in the United States and to conflicting rather than complementary policies in the major trading partners of the United States. From mid-1980 to mid-1985, the dollar appreciated 21 percent against the yen, 53 percent against the deutsche mark, and 49 percent against the pound.[58] Despite massive U.S. trade deficits, the dollar remained strong because of high U.S. interest rates, a growing U.S. economy, and confidence in U.S. political stability. Exchange markets were highly volatile owing to differing national economic performances, the globalization of financial markets, and the absence of coordinated government intervention in exchange markets. In large part because of the overvalued dollar, the U.S. trade deficit reached crisis proportions, politically as well as economically. Protectionist pressures arising from the trade deficit increased, finally forcing the United States to cooperate with other countries in a joint effort to manage exchange rates.

In a secret meeting held in September 1985 at the Plaza Hotel in New York, the United States ended its benign neglect and agreed with Japan, the United Kingdom, West Germany, and France to cooperate more closely in monetary management.[59] The participants agreed to work together on economic matters, especially intervention in exchange markets. The United States pledged to narrow its budget deficit by reducing spending, and the other participants agreed to pursue economic policies that would help ease the imbalances in the world economy and promote healthy growth with low inflation. The Plaza agreement was followed by coordinated exchange market intervention and interest rate reductions, which led to a more reasonable exchange rate for the dollar against currencies such as the yen and the deutsche mark (which meant all currencies of the EMS). The Plaza agreement marked the beginning of a new era in monetary management. Finance ministers of the world's monetary powers, recognizing the need to expand policy coordination, began meeting regularly to coordinate exchange rate intervention and to attempt—not always successfully—to coordinate economic policy as well.

The Plaza agreement was significant in another way: it marked the active entry of Japan into the world management system. Before 1985, Japan had been largely a passive member of the management system. Although Japan's economy and international trade had grown dramatically, the yen did not become fully convertible until 1980. By 1985, Japan's economic weight was second only to that of the United States. Today, Japan has the second largest market economy in the world, a currency whose international use is increasing significantly, and a massive financial surplus heavily invested abroad, especially in the United States.

Any efforts to stabilize the system and to coordinate economic policies would be meaningless without Japan.

Japan's new strength created new vulnerabilities, including the threat of closure of the trading system because of rising **protectionism,** especially in Japan's critical U.S. market; the uncertainty of financial investments due to a collapsing dollar; and increasing political pressure on Japan to open its markets, liberalize its financial system, and alter its domestic policies to help manage the world economy. Gradually, although reluctantly, Japan began to respond to its changed economic and political environment. From the time of the Plaza agreement, Japan played an active role in international monetary negotiations and in the efforts to agree on and implement appropriate domestic economic policies. Increasingly, international economic management hinged on the cooperation of the big three economic powers: the United States, West Germany, and Japan.

The new cooperative approach that began with the Plaza agreement was formalized at the May 1986 economic summit in Tokyo. There, the Group of Seven (G-7) not only reaffirmed the importance of cooperative intervention in exchange markets but also affirmed that close coordination of domestic economic policies was needed to stabilize the system.[60] The G-7 agreed to monitor the basic economic policies and performance of each country—inflation, interest rates, growth, unemployment, deficits, trade balance—and to recommend remedial action whenever the policy of one country was thought to be damaging others. The stated goal was to coordinate domestic economic policies to attain steady growth with a minimum of inflation.

But stated goals and policy action are quite different. International coordination of domestic fiscal and monetary policy remained elusive. While finance ministers and central bankers often agreed on appropriate policies, political constraints—the need for legislative approval and the reluctance to relinquish sovereignty over macroeconomic policy—limited actual coordination. Some steps were taken. In 1986, the United States passed legislation to slow the growth of the U.S. federal budget deficit. Germany and Japan took limited steps—lowering discount rates—to stimulate their economies to offset the decline in U.S. growth. But agreement could not be reached on the appropriate levels of U.S. budget cutting or of growth stimulation in Japan and Germany.

There were also disagreements on the appropriate exchange rate for the dollar. Japan and Germany feared a large decline of the U.S. currency would damage their trade as well as the value of their investments in the United States and argued that a significant dollar decline would upset financial markets. The United States, on the other hand, wanted to use the dollar decline to improve the trade imbalance and deflect congressional pressure for protectionist trade legislation and argued that a larger decline of the dollar would not upset capital inflows into the United States, needed to finance the trade and budget deficits. As disagreement persisted, cooperation in exchange market intervention broke down and exchange markets became unstable.

In February 1987, the world's monetary powers met at the Louvre in Paris to attempt once again to stabilize the international monetary system. Officials announced to the world that exchange rates had come into the proper relationship, and that they would oppose further substantial shifts and would cooperate to stabilize exchange rates at prevailing levels. The participants agreed on informal, flexible, and unannounced target ranges for intervention in exchange markets. At the Louvre, officials again sought to coordinate domestic policies. Germany and Japan agreed to take modest but significant steps to stimulate domestic demand, and the United States reaffirmed its commitment to reduce its budget deficit.[61]

The Louvre agreement was both a major step in the effort to establish international economic management and another example of the problem of coordinating economic policy. With one important exception, the G-7 did not live up to its stated commitments to coordinate policy. The German government, faced with a public that had a historical fear of inflation, was reluctant to pursue serious stimulative policies; and the U.S. Congress and administration were unable to agree on a significant **deficit** reduction package. Japan, however, did move toward stimulating domestic demand by pursuing a more expansionary fiscal policy and by reorienting from reliance on export-led growth to development of domestic demand.[62]

As G-7 cooperation disintegrated, private investors, fearing a dollar devaluation, reduced inflows of funds to the United States, forcing central banks to buy dollars to stabilize exchange rates and prevent a crash of the U.S. currency. As a result, the bond market began a severe decline; international equity markets collapsed in October 1987; and the dollar began what seemed like a free fall, declining 15.6 percent vis-à-vis the yen and 13.4 percent against the deutsche mark from September to the end of December.

The October crisis galvanized the key actors to make domestic economic policy changes. The United States eased monetary policy and Congress passed a limited deficit reduction bill, the Gramm-Rudman-Hollings bill; West Germany and other European countries lowered interest rates; and Japan's cabinet approved a stimulative budget. Finally, in December 1987, the G-7 announced that appropriate steps had been taken to stabilize exchange rates and that there should be no further significant shifts in the value of the dollar. They implemented massive coordinated action by central banks to stabilize the dollar and to signal their intent to the world. Throughout 1988, the G-7 met regularly and acted effectively to stabilize exchange markets. Cooperation in monetary policy increased and progress was made on the coordination of fiscal policy. Japan, in particular, successfully pursued a stimulative domestic economic policy. The United States made some limited progress in reducing its budget and trade deficit. As a result, exchange rates, including the dollar, stabilized. However, the long-term success of international monetary cooperation of the G-7 continued to depend on the ability of the key monetary actor, the United States, to pursue policies that would reduce its twin deficits.

Following the election of Bill Clinton in 1992, new stresses emerged in the international monetary system. The end of the Cold War and German reunification had temporarily reduced German trade surpluses and, in any case, the United States was able to achieve an overall trade surplus with Western Europe even though it maintained a bilateral deficit with Germany. For this reason, after 1990, American trade politics focused most heavily on the size of the U.S.-Japanese trade deficit and its relationship to the yen-dollar exchange rate. Despite major improvements in the **productivity** of U.S. firms and a fairly steady decline in the value of the dollar against the yen, U.S. exports to Japan grew much more slowly than imports from Japan.

Some economists argued that the only solution to U.S.-Japanese trade problems was to allow the yen to revalue upward still further against the dollar so that Japanese products, such as automobiles, would be less competitive with U.S. products.[63] Indeed, that was what happened in currency markets. In February 1993, the yen began to rise steadily against the dollar. By August, the new Japanese Prime Minister, Morihiro Hosokawa, was expressing concern over the rise of the yen and suggesting coordinated intervention by the G-7 in foreign exchange markets to stop it. The dollar continued to decline against the yen, however, and the yen/dollar issue became politicized in Japan. Major manufacturers like Toyota, Nissan, and Matsushita complained to the government and demanded action to halt the rise of the yen.[64]

The G-7 was unable to affect exchange rates. The size of global private capital markets dwarfed the funds available for G-7 monetary management and overwhelmed several efforts at intervention in currency markets. Clearly, only changes in domestic economic policy and performance could effectively alter currency relationships. The G-7 dialogue about monetary management increasingly focused not on managing exchange rates but on urging members to pursue appropriate macroeconomic policies and on organizing opportunistic intervention to stabilize currency markets.

In the face of this, the Clinton administration pursued two policy approaches. Domestically, it sought to improve U.S. macroeconomic fundamentals and to increase U.S. competitiveness through budget deficit reduction and deregulation. Due to deficit reduction legislation and strong economic performance, the U.S. deficit fell from $269.2 billion in fiscal year 1991 to $163.8 billion in fiscal year 1995.[65] Internationally, the administration focused on bilateral, regional, and multilateral trade initiatives as a way to reduce the trade deficit. Japan, for its part, sought to stimulate and deregulate its economy. But there were recurring political crises, and weak coalition governments were not up to the task of addressing Japan's serious structural problems.

While currency management remained limited, the United States and the G-7 were still able to provide leadership in crisis management. In late 1994, such a financial crisis developed in Mexico and threatened to spread internationally. In the early 1990s, Mexico seemed to have found the recipe for economic development. Domestic deregulation and privatization combined with liberalization of trade and investment led to rapid growth and a massive inflow of foreign direct and portfolio investment. Unlike the 1980s, flows to Mexico and other so-called emerging markets took the form not of bank lending but of borrowing from the world's rapidly growing securities markets. But in 1994 economic mismanagement in Mexico, and especially the maintenance of an overvalued currency and excess dependence on short-term capital inflows, combined with several political shocks, including an uprising in the south, the assassination of the leading presidential candidate, and the kidnapping of a prominent businessman, led to a collapse of confidence. Funds that had flowed so easily into Mexico now fled and the peso collapsed. The Mexican crisis led to significant pressures on the currencies and financial systems of other Latin American countries, most notably Argentina and Brazil, and disrupted markets from India to South Africa. From there, the crisis threatened financial markets worldwide.

In order to prevent further disintegration of the Mexican economy and the possible attendant political instability, the U.S. government stepped in with a $20 billion support package for Mexico and pressed members of the Bank for International Settlements to make available another $10 billion. The IMF agreed to an unusually large loan of $17.8 billion in return for an agreement by Mexico to implement a stiff **stabilization program.** Supported by this international safety net, the Mexican government implemented stringent fiscal and monetary policies that stabilized the exchange rate but caused a serious recession and weakened the domestic financial system. Stringent domestic policies and multilateral lending by the World Bank and IMF also shored up the Argentine financial system.

Having experienced in such a dramatic way the vulnerabilities created by the new global financial flows, the G-7 developed a plan at the 1995 economic summit in Halifax, Nova Scotia, for crisis prevention and management. The G-7 proposed that the IMF pursue more ambitious surveillance policies to prevent future crises. They also called for greater transparency—for greater disclosure of financial and economic information—on the part of IMF member states. They recommended the formation of an IMF Emergency Financing Mechanism and a doubling of General Arrangements to Borrow within the IMF to ensure that such funds would be adequate for the management of future crises. Finally, the G-7 called for further study of how international debt could be restructured to prevent future crises. In the 1980s, the IMF, together with key central banks, the main lending banks, and the debtor country's government could renegotiate debt. In the 1990s, an anonymous global financial securities market became a key actor difficult to incorporate in debt negotiations. The challenge to the international monetary system was to invent new ways of restructuring debt in this new environment.

Monetary Management in the 1990s

It remains to be seen whether states will muster the political will and skill to manage the system. Gone are those simpler days when the United States, along with the United Kingdom, could draw up a constitution for a world monetary order. In a world in which monetary power is more widely dispersed, management will depend not on the preferences of a dominant power but on the negotiation of several key powers, primarily the United States, Germany, and Japan. While monetary power is now more widely dispersed, it is not equally dispersed. The United States still remains the most powerful monetary actor and without an active U.S. role within the multilateral system, effective management is impossible.

Management will also be complicated by the conflict between interdependence and national sovereignty. Managing interdependence requires the coordination of national economic policies and the imposition of international discipline over policies that have always been the prerogative of national governments. The experience of the European Monetary System and the groping efforts of the G-7 to coordinate policy indicate both the need for and the difficulty of achieving such coordination. Numerous ideas for achieving coordination and stability have been proposed, ranging from managed floats to formulas for fixing exchange rates to a return to a modified **gold standard** or a standard based on a basket of commodities.[66] Ultimately, they all depend on the ability of countries to achieve adequate coordination of macroeconomic policies. Indeed, some believe that such coordination is impossible and that discipline and management are best left to the marketplace.

In a multilateral system, improvement in management will be slow. It will depend on trial and error and the development of common norms as opposed to formal agreements, as in the days of Bretton Woods or even the Second Amendment. Such a process is not necessarily bad, as formal agreements often do not work as planned. The Bretton Woods agreement, for example, never operated as the United States intended. But in the Bretton Woods period, there was a dominant power ready and able to step in and establish new rules for regulating conflict. Today, although the United States is still necessary, it is not sufficiently dominant to fulfill its earlier role. The danger in the present multilateral system is that with incomplete management, crises may go unregulated, cumulate, and become far more difficult and costly to resolve.

It is possible—although by no means certain—that states will develop the means not only of crisis management but also of crisis prevention. The consensus among the powerful on the need for cooperation and joint management persists in word if not always in deed. The leaders of the developed states have time and again stressed the necessity of interdependence and of cooperating to maintain economic prosperity and political stability. Mechanisms for consultation and policy coordination still operate, but what will be done with them remains to be seen.

NOTES

1. For earlier systems of management, see Robert Triffin, *The Evolution of the International Monetary System: Historical Reappraisal and Future Perspectives* (Princeton, N.J.: International Finance Section, Department of Economics, Princeton University, 1964); Stephen V. O. Clarke, *Central Bank Cooperation, 1924–1931* (New York: Federal Reserve Bank of New York, 1967); and Barry Eichengreen, *Golden Fetters: The Gold Standard and the Great Depression* (New York: Oxford University Press, 1992).

2. See Richard N. Gardner, *Sterling-Dollar Diplomacy in Current Perspective: The Origins and Prospects of Our International Economic Order* (New York: Columbia University Press, 1980), chs. 1 and 2; and Michael D. Bordo, "The Bretton Woods International Monetary System: A Historical Overview," and G. John Ikenberry, "The Political Origins of Bretton Woods," in Michael D. Bordo and Barry Eichengreen, eds., *A Retrospective on the Bretton Woods System: Lessons for International Monetary Reform* (Chicago: University of Chicago Press, 1993).

3. Richard N. Gardner, chs. 3–5, 7; J. Keith Horsefield, ed., *The International Monetary Fund, 1945–1965: Twenty Years of International Monetary Cooperation*, vol. 1 (Washington: International Monetary Fund, 1969), 10–118.

4. Edward S. Mason and Robert E. Asher, *The World Bank Since Bretton Woods* (Washington: Brookings Institution, 1973), 11–36.

5. See United Nations Economic Commission for Europe, *A Survey of the Economic Situation and Prospects of Europe* (Geneva: United Nations, 1948); and United Nations Economic Commission for Europe, *Economic Survey of Europe in 1948* (Geneva: United Nations, 1949).

6. Mason and Asher, *World Bank Since Bretton Woods*, 105–107 and 124–135.

7. For example, see Walter LaFeber, *The American Age: U.S. Foreign Policy at Home and Abroad*, vol. 2, 2nd ed. (New York: Norton, 1994), 479–482.

8. See Robert Triffin, *Gold and the Dollar Crisis: The Future of Convertibility* (New Haven: Yale University Press, 1960).

9. International Monetary Fund, *International Financial Statistics* (Washington: IMF, Supplement 1972), 2–3.

10. The Bank for International Settlements was a consortium of European central banks originally established in 1930 to implement a plan for rescheduling German reparations and to provide a forum for central bank discussion. The BIS now includes representatives of the central banks from other industrialized regions.

11. Switzerland joined in 1964, which made the Group of Ten in fact a group of eleven.

12. G. L. Bach, *Making Monetary and Fiscal Policy* (Washington: Brookings Institution, 1971), 111–150.

13. See Walter S. Salant et al., *The United States Balance of Payments in 1968* (Washington: Brookings Institution, 1963).

14. Stephen D. Cohen, *International Monetary Reform, 1964–1969* (New York: Praeger, 1970); and Fritz Machlup, *Remaking the International Monetary System: The Rio Agreement and Beyond* (Baltimore: Johns Hopkins University Press, 1968).

15. International Monetary Fund, *Annual Report 1972* (Washington: IMF, 1972), 28.

16. This was convertibility for nonresidents. Full convertibility came in 1961.

17. Richard A. Debs, "International Banking" (address delivered to the tenth annual convention of the Banking Law Institute, New York City, May 8, 1975), 3.

18. Sidney M. Robbins and Robert B. Stobaugh, *Money in the Multinational Enterprise: A Study in Financial Policy* (New York: Basic Books, 1973); and Lawrence B. Krause, "The International Economic System and the Multinational Corporation," *The Annals* 403 (September 1972): 93–103.

19. There are many theories regarding the origins of the Eurodollar market. For example, see Paul Einzig, *The Euro-Dollar System: Practice and Theory of International Interest Rates*, 4th ed. (New York: St. Martin's Press, 1970); and Geoffrey Bell, *The Eurodollar Market and the International Financial System* (New York: Wiley, 1973).

20. Now almost as important as Eurocurrency markets for generating international flows of short-term investment are the enormous pools of capital that are invested by the managers of equity and fixed-income assets funds, what are often called "mutual funds" in the United States. See further discussion of this below.

21. On the crisis, see Susan Strange, "The Dollar Crisis 1971," *International Affairs* 48 (April

1972): 191–215; and Joanne Gowa, *Closing the Gold Window: Domestic Politics and the End of Bretton Woods* (Ithaca, N.Y.: Cornell University Press, 1983).

22. Committee on Reform of the International Monetary System and Related Issues (Committee of Twenty), *International Monetary Reform: Documents of the Committee of Twenty* (Washington: International Monetary Fund, 1974), p. 8.

23. International Monetary Fund, *Annual Report 1975* (Washington: IMF, 1975), 12.

24. International Monetary Fund, *Annual Report 1983* (Washington: IMF, 1983), 21.

25. Committee on Reform, *International Monetary Reform*, pp. 216, 219.

26. See George de Menil and Anthony M. Solomon, *Economic Summitry* (New York: Council on Foreign Relations, 1983); Robert D. Putnam and Nicholas Bayne, *Hanging Together: The Seven-Power Summits* (Cambridge: Harvard University Press, 1984); and Joseph P. Daniels, *The Meaning and Reliability of Economic Summit Undertakings, 1975–1989* (New York: Garland, 1993).

27. International Monetary Fund, *Proposed Second Amendment to the Articles of Agreement of the International Monetary Fund: A Report by the Executive Directors to the Board of Governors* (Washington: IMF, March 1976).

28. International Monetary Fund, *Annual Report 1987* (Washington: IMF, 1987), 58, 60.

29. Ibid., 58.

30. See Edward J. Lincoln, *Japan: Facing Economic Maturity* (Washington: Brookings Institution, 1988), 210.

31. For example, see Group of Thirty, *The Problem of Exchange Rates: A Policy Statement* (New York: Group of Thirty, 1982); Henry C. Wallich, Otmar Emminger, Robert V. Roosa, and Peter B. Kenen, *World Money and National Policies* (New York: Group of Thirty, 1983); and John Williamson, *The Exchange Rate System* (Cambridge: MIT Press, 1983).

32. On internationalization, see *Recent Innovations in International Banking*, (Basel, Switzerland: BIS, April 1986); Maxwell Watson, Donald Mathieson, Russell Kincaid, and Eliot Kalter, *International Capital Markets: Developments and Prospects* (Washington: International Monetary Fund, February 1986); and Maxwell Watson, Russell Kincaid, Caroline Atkinson, Eliot Kalter, and David Folkerts-Landau, *International Capital Markets: Developments and Prospects*. (Washington: International Monetary Fund, December 1986).

33. Excellent documentation of this trend can be found in Barry Eichengreen, *International Monetary Arrangements for the 21st Century* (Washington: Brookings Institution, 1994), 65–66.

34. Tommaso Padio-Schioppa and Fabrizio Saccomani, "Managing a Market-Led Global Financial System," in Peter B. Kenen, ed., *Managing the World Economy: Fifty Years After Bretton Woods* (Washington: Institute for International Economics, 1994), 250.

35. Bank for International Settlements, *International Banking and Financial Market Developments* (Basel, Switzerland: BIS, November 1994), 1.

36. See *World Financial Markets*, September/October 1987; and Robert Wade, "Globalization and the State: What Scope for Industrial Policies," in Susanne Berger and Ronald Dore, eds., *Convergence or Diversity? National Models of Production and Distribution in a Global Economy* (Ithaca, N.Y.: Cornell University Press, forthcoming).

37. Eichengreen, *International Monetary Arrangements*, 60.

38. See World Bank, *World Debt Tables* (Washington: World Bank, 1988).

39. *World Debt Tables 1993–94: External Finance for Developing Countries*, vol. 1 (Washington: World Bank, 1993), p. 171.

40. *Economic Report of the President* (Washington: Government Printing Office, 1995), table B-103. This document was accessed via the Internet at http://www.access.gpo.gov/eop/ on March 7, 1996. Net international investment is calculated by subtracting the value of assets owned by foreign firms and individuals in the United States from the value of assets owned by U.S. firms and individuals abroad. The value of these assets can be calculated either on the basis of original cost or on current market value. The figures reported here are based on current market value.

41. The Korean trade surplus was only $2.9 billion in 1994. For Korean data, see *World Data '95 CD-ROM* (Washington: World Bank, 1995). For Taiwan, see Central Bank of China (R.O.C.), Economic Research Department, *Financial Statistics Monthly: Taiwan District of The Republic of China* (Taipei: Central Bank of China, October 1995), p. 170.

42. See Horst Ungerer et al., *The European Monetary System, 1979–1982*, Occasional Paper No. 19 (Washington: International Monetary Fund, 1983); Horst Ungerer et al., *The European Monetary System: Recent Developments*, Occasional Paper No. 48 (Washington: International Monetary Fund, 1986); Directorate General for Economic and Financial Affairs, EC, "The Creation of a European Financial Area," *European Economy*, No. 36 (Brussels: Commission of the European

Community, May 1988); and Daniel Gros and Niels Thygesen, "The EMS: Achievements, Current Issues and Directions for the Future," CEPS Paper No. 35 (Brussels: Centre for European Policy Studies, 1988).

43. This argument is made very convincingly in Jeffry Frieden, "Economic Liberalization and the Politics of European Monetary Integration" (University of California, Los Angeles, July 1993, unpublished manuscript). See also Barry Eichengreen and Jeffry Frieden, "The Political Economy of European Monetary Unification," in Barry Eichengreen and Jeffry Frieden, eds., *The Political Economy of European Monetary Unification* (Boulder, Colo.: Westview, 1994); and Jeffry Frieden, "The Impact of Goods and Capital Market Integration on European Monetary Politics," *Comparative Political Studies*, forthcoming.

44. See Susan M. Collins and Francesco Giavazzi, "Attitudes toward Inflation and the Viability of Fixed Exchange Rates: Evidence from the EMS," in Michael D. Bordo and Barry Eichengreen, eds., *A Retrospective on the Bretton Woods System: Lessons for International Monetary Reform* (Chicago: University of Chicago Press, 1993); Jürgen von Hagen, "Monetary Policy Coordination in the European Monetary System," in Michael U. Fratianni and Dominick Salvatore, eds., *Monetary Policy in Developed Economies* (Westport, Conn.: Greenwood Press, 1993); and Jürgen von Hagen and Michael Fratianni, "Policy Coordination in the EMS with Stochastic Asymmetries," in Clas Wihlborg, Michele Fratianni, and Thomas D. Willett, eds., *Financial Regulations and Monetary Arrangements After 1992* (New York: North Holland, 1991). Von Hagen argues that the EMS dampened inflation rates somewhat but possibly at the expense of lower growth rates. Von Hagen and Fratianni discuss the argument that the main function of the EMS was to better enable its members to absorb shocks from the world economy.

45. European Community, Committee for the Study of Economic and Monetary Union, *Report on Economic and Monetary Union in the European Community* (The Delors Report), (Brussels: European Community) April 12, 1989.

46. Barry Eichengreen, "European Monetary Integration," *Journal of Economic Literature* 31 (September 1993): 1328.

47. Jürgen von Hagen and Michele Fratianni, "The Transition to Monetary Union and the European Monetary Institute," *Economics and Politics* 5 (July 1993): 167–168; and Wayne Sandholtz, "Choosing Union: Monetary Politics and Maastricht," *International Organization* 47 (winter 1993): 1–39.

48. See Geoffrey Garrett, "The Politics of Maastricht," *Economics and Politics* 5 (July 1993): 105–123. Garrett argues that Germany favors the second path, sometimes called the "two-speed Europe" option.

49. Eichengreen, *International Monetary Arrangements*, 98.

50. Ibid., 100–101.

51. The arguments made here are consistent with those made by Jeffry Frieden and Wayne Sandholtz in previously cited work.

52. For discussion on the 1978 agreement, see de Menil and Solomon, *Economic Summitry*, 23–29, 47–48.

53. The restrictive monetary policy consisted of a record increase in the discount rate from 8.5 to 9.5 percent and the imposition of a reserve requirement on certificates of deposit. The "war chest" included enlarged swaps with the central banks of West Germany, Japan, and Switzerland; the issuance of U.S. Treasury securities denominated in foreign currencies; a drawdown in IMF reserves; and the sale of SDRs.

54. *Economic Report of the President* (Washington: Government Printing Office, 1994), 352.

55. On monetarism, see Milton Friedman and Anna Jacobson Schwartz, *A Monetary History of the United States 1867–1960* (Princeton, N.J.: Princeton University Press, 1963), the twelfth volume of a series, *Studies in Business Research*, published by the National Bureau of Economic Research.

56. See Bruce R. Bartlett, ed., *The Supply Side Solution* (Chatham, N.J.: Chatham House, 1983); Victor A. Canto et al., *Foundations of Supply-Side Economics: Theory and Evidence* (New York: Academic Press, 1983); Lawrence Robert Klein, *The Economics of Supply and Demand* (Baltimore: Johns Hopkins University Press, 1983); and Paul Krugman, *Peddling Prosperity: Economic Sense and Nonsense in the Age of Diminished Expectations* (New York: Norton, 1994), ch. 3.

57. See Kenneth King, *U.S. Monetary Policy and European Responses in the 1980s*, Chatham House Paper 16 (London: Routledge, 1982); and Sylvia Ann Hewlett, Henry Kaufman, and Peter B. Kenen, eds., *The Global Repercussions of U.S. Monetary and Fiscal Policy* (Cambridge, Mass.: Ballinger, 1984).

58. U.S. Department of Commerce, *U.S. Trade Performance in 1985 and Outlook* (Washington: Government Printing Office, 1986), 105–106.

59. On the period from the Plaza agreement to the Louvre agreement, see Yoichi Funabashi, *Managing the Dollar: From the Plaza to the Louvre* (Washington: Institute for International Economics, 1988).

60. The G-7 includes the United States, Japan, Germany, the United Kingdom, France, Canada, and Italy. Annual economic summits of the G-7 usually include representatives of the European Union.

61. Funabashi, 177–210.

62. See *Report of the Advisory Group on Economic Structural Adjustment for International Harmony* (chaired by Haruo Maekawa), submitted to Prime Minister Nakasone on April 7, 1986.

63. C. Fred Bergsten and Marcus Noland, *Reconcilable Differences? United States–Japan Economic Conflict* (Washington: Institute for International Economics, 1993). Bergsten was an adviser to the Clinton campaign; Noland joined the Council of Economic Advisers after the election.

64. George Melloan, "Global View: Trade Isn't War; Repeat, Trade Isn't War," *Wall Street Journal*, May 1, 1995, p. A15.

65. Economic Report of the President (Washington: Government Printing Office, 1996).

66. See John Williamson, The Exchange Rate System (Washington: Institute for International Economics, 1985); John Williamson and Marcus Miller, *Targets and Indicators: A Blueprint for International Coordination of Economic Policy* (Washington: Institute for International Economics, 1987); and International Monetary Fund, *Exchange Arrangements and Exchange Restrictions: Annual Report* 1987 (Washington: IMF, 1987).

3

International Trade and Domestic Politics

Trade policy is the stuff of domestic politics. Tariffs, quotas, and nontariff barriers are familiar issues for a broad range of economic groups, from farmers to manufacturers to labor unions to retailers. Because trade policy often determines prosperity or adversity for these groups, it is also the subject of frequent and often highly charged domestic political conflict.

In the United States, the Constitution accentuates the political conflict over trade policy by giving Congress the power to levy tariffs and regulate foreign commerce while at the same time giving the president authority in foreign policy. Conflict within Congress and between Congress and the executive branch is a central characteristic of U.S. trade policy. Because members of Congress are responsible to their constituents and, therefore, responsive to their economic concerns, there is often pressure within Congress for a trade policy that protects those special interests. Furthermore, the demands of relatively few interest groups directed at Congress may snowball into national trade policy, as occurred with the Smoot-Hawley Tariff Act of 1930, the most protectionist law of the century.[1]

While Congress tends to link trade policy with particular domestic interests, the U.S. executive branch often links trade policy with larger foreign policy and foreign economic goals. Thus, for example, since the 1930s, U.S. presidents have advocated open trade as the preferred economic policy, for broad economic and strategic reasons. Presidents, however, must have congressional approval for any agreement to reduce trade barriers. Yet the very process of approval raises the threat of interest group opposition. Presidents have tried to overcome this legislative constraint by asking Congress to delegate authority to the president to conclude trade agreements and to limit the need for subsequent congressional approval. Since 1934, Congress has regularly delegated such power for specifically limited periods of time and with specific constraints. A recent example of this was President Clinton's request in the spring of 1993 for "fast track" authority to negotiate the final terms for the Uruguay Round of the General Agreement on Tariffs and Trade (GATT).

Domestic politicization in the United States and throughout the world has been an important constraint on international management. In this chapter, we shall examine the evolution of trade management in the face of domestic political constraints.[2]

The Havana Charter

The same factors that led to the creation of a managed international monetary system after World War II also led to the first attempt to subject trade to systematic international control. Protectionism and the disintegration of world trade in the 1930s created a common interest in an open trading order and a realization that states would have to cooperate to achieve and maintain that order. The retreat into protectionism in the interwar period led not only to economic disaster but also to international war. In the postwar era, mechanisms for guarding against such economic nationalism and reducing and regulating restrictions on trade would have to be created. In the United States, policy was shaped by Secretary of State Cordell Hull, who was the major advocate of the liberal theory that open trade would lead to economic prosperity and international peace.[3]

The interwar experience also led to the willingness of the United States to lead the system. As the State Department explained:

> The only nation capable of taking the initiative in promoting a worldwide movement toward the relaxation of trade barriers is the United States. Because of its relatively great economic strength, its favorable balance of payments position, and the importance of its market to the well-being of the rest of the world, the influence of the United States on world commercial policies far surpasses that of any other nation.[4]

Despite the perception of a common interest in management and an open system and despite the willingness by the United States to lead the system, conflict within and across nations made it difficult to translate the generally perceived common goals into an international order for more open trade. The conflict between domestic politics and international management began with the negotiations for the Havana Charter, the first attempt to build a global legal regime for international trade. The charter was an essential part of the plan to create a new, internationally managed economic system in the postwar era and, like the rest of that plan, was a product of strong U.S. leadership.

U.S. efforts to create an open system dated from the Reciprocal Trade Agreements Act (RTAA) of 1934, a product of Cordell Hull's liberal vision. Under that act, the United States concluded numerous agreements reducing the high tariffs of the early 1930s.[5] During World War II, the United States obtained from its allies commitments to a postwar international commercial order based on the freeing of international trade. In 1945, the U.S. government presented a plan for a multilateral commercial convention to regulate and reduce restrictions on international trade.[6] The convention offered rules for many aspects of international trade—tariffs, preferences, quantitative restrictions, **subsidies,** state trading, international commodity agreements—and provided for an International Trade Organization (ITO), the analog of the International Monetary Fund in the area of trade, to oversee the system. In 1946, the United States called for an international conference to discuss this U.S. proposal and to implement a new trading order. The conference was held in Havana, and it produced the Havana Charter for the ITO, which was signed by all attendees in the fall of 1947 at the conclusion of the conference.[7]

Agreement on a new international order for trade, however, was more difficult to achieve than was agreement on a monetary order. The process of negotiating a postwar trade regime was very different from that of negotiating the postwar monetary regime. At Bretton Woods, the United States and the United Kingdom dominated the decision making and were able to arrive at an early compromise. They did not have to consult as widely with other nations concerning monetary arrangements after the war as they did with trade, except perhaps in setting up new international financial institutions like the International Monetary Fund and the World Bank. Since the new monetary system was to be based on the U.S. dollar and the British pound sterling, backed by gold, and there were no other candidates for key currencies, a U.S.-British compromise was sufficient. The two powers were less able to agree on trade, however, and, in any case, other countries' views had to be taken into account.

The United States initially advocated a multilateralization of the RTAA. Clair Wilcox, the head of the U.S. delegation in London during early negotiations with Britain for the ITO, explained U.S. policy in the following manner:

> Every nation stands to gain from the widest possible movement of goods and services. . . . That international trade should be abundant, that it should be multilateral, that it should be nondiscriminatory, that stabilization and trade policies should be consistent—these are propositions on which all nations, whatever their forms of economic organization, can agree.[8]

This meant the abolition of all **trade preference systems,**[9] but Britain initially insisted on maintaining its Imperial Preference System. At Bretton Woods, the United States and Britain agreed to disagree on this issue until after the end of World War II. At the trade conference in Havana in 1947, the less-developed countries in attendance (mostly from Latin America) demanded special trade provisions for the promotion of economic development in the new world trade regime. The Europeans pressed for a postwar system that permitted them to continue their preferential trading arrangements. In addition, the British delegation, influenced by the views of John Maynard Keynes, supported proposals for commodity agreements and other methods of stabilizing the export revenues of developing countries. The result was a document quite different from the one envisioned by U.S. negotiators like Clair Wilcox. In the end, the Havana Charter was a complex compromise that embodied in some ways the wishes of everyone, but in the end satisfied no one.[10]

Nevertheless, the charter might have become operational had it not been for domestic politics in the United States. Although the Roosevelt and Truman administrations had been strong advocates of a new trading order and had led the international system through the complex negotiating process, Congress prevented the United States from adhering to the Havana Charter. The traditionally high tariff policy of the Republican party; the opposition of both the protectionists, who felt that the charter went too far, and the liberals, who felt that it did not go far enough toward free trade; and the opposition of business groups that opposed compromises on open trade and at the same time feared increased governmental involvement in trade management coalesced in a majority against the United States' own charter. After delaying for three years, the Truman administration finally decided in 1950 that it would not submit the Havana Charter to Congress, where it faced inevitable defeat. Once the United States withdrew, the charter was dead.[11] Despite a prevailing norm of international cooperation and strong and persistent U.S. leadership, an agreement on international control of trade proved elusive.

Multilateral Management under U.S. Leadership

The demise of the Havana Charter meant that trade management would be more limited than was originally envisaged, although still quite close to the wishes of the United States. The consensus for an international trading order survived, embodied in the GATT, which also had been signed by attendees of the Havana conference in 1947, to provide a procedural base and establish guiding principles for the periodic multilateral tariff negotiations. In fact, the first trade "round" was held in Geneva in that same year. Intended originally to be a treaty operating under the umbrella of the ITO, the GATT, by default, became the world's trade regime.[12]

The GATT reflected the prevailing agreement on open trade: the economic consensus that open trade would allow countries to specialize according to the principle of **comparative advantage** and thereby achieve higher levels of growth and well-being, and the political consensus that a liberal trading regime would promote not only prosperity but also peace. The major rule for implementing free trade under the GATT was the principle of nondiscrimination. All of the contracting parties—that is, all member states—agreed to adhere to the **most-favored-nation (MFN)** principle, which stipulated that "any advantage, favor, privilege, or immunity granted by any contracting party to any product originating in or destined for any other country shall be accorded immediately and unconditionally to the like product originating in or destined for the territories of all other contracting parties."[13] The only exceptions to this general rule of equal treatment were for existing preferential systems and future **customs unions** and free-trade associations. A second element of nondiscrimination in the GATT was the provision for **national treatment,** a rule designed to prevent discrimination against foreign products after they enter a country. Under GATT rules, a country must give imports the same treatment as it gives products made domestically in such areas as taxation, regulation, transportation, and distribution.[14]

GATT also established an international commercial code with rules on such issues as **dumping** and subsidies. Dumping is defined as pricing "below normal market price,"[15] although in some nations, like the United States, the definition of dumping in national legislation is more elaborate. Antidumping restrictions are designed to prevent the use of **"predatory pricing,"** which allows the firms of one country to underprice the firms of other countries in order to increase their market power.[16] Subsidies are government payments made to domestic producers to offset partially their costs of producing and selling goods and services. Governments use subsidies to support weak firms just entering a new market as well as older firms suffering from intensified competition. Dumping and subsidies are often attacked politically as "unfair" trade practices, and hence the GATT needed to address this issue by including restrictions on them in the overall regime.[17]

One of the most important rules in the GATT's commercial code prohibited the use of quantitative restrictions, such as import quotas, except for temporary balance-of-payments or national security reasons. The GATT also provided a mechanism for resolving disputes under its commercial code.

There were, however, important departures from these rules. Provisions in the original GATT treaty and amendments made in the 1950s established a separate regime for agricultural trade. GATT rules on agriculture reflected the powerful political influence of agricultural groups and the resultant policies of government intervention to protect domestic prices and producer incomes and to ensure food security. GATT rules reflected, in particular, the domestic agricultural policies of the United States, which pressed for an international regime that would enable the United States to preserve its policy of production controls, **price supports,** export subsidies, and import protection implemented in the 1930s. Thus, for example, export subsidies on primary agricultural products were permitted as long as those subsidies did not interfere with established market shares, a concept alien to GATT rules for trade in other goods. GATT rules facilitated the use of quantitative restrictions in agriculture. In 1955, for example, the United States obtained a waiver under GATT rules that gave it special permission to impose quotas on agricultural products.[18]

There were also important gaps in the coverage of the GATT. Whereas the Havana Charter included provisions for economic development, commodity agreements, restrictive business practices, and trade in services, these were not included in the GATT. In addition, other topics not of great concern at the time, such as relations with state trading countries, were left undeveloped in the code. These departures from GATT norms and gaps in GATT coverage eventually became a major problem for the management of international trade. Finally, the

GATT's institutional mechanisms had important weaknesses. The dispute settlement mechanism was lengthy, allowed parties to delay or block decisions, and was not binding.[19]

In addition to establishing trade principles, the GATT provided a set of rules and procedures for what was to be the principal method of trade management in the postwar period: multilateral trade negotiations. The agreement contained a commitment to enter into such negotiations and provided guidelines for them. The most important rule was **reciprocity,** the concept that tariff reductions should be mutually advantageous.[20] Although not part of the original GATT, the **principal supplier procedure** by which negotiations were to take place among actual or potential principal suppliers—those nations accounting for 10 percent or more of a given product in world trade—also became a negotiating rule of the GATT.[21]

From a temporary treaty, the GATT became not only an established commercial code but also an international organization with a secretariat and a director general to oversee the implementation of its rules, manage dispute settlements, and provide a forum and support for multilateral trade negotiations. Whereas the GATT provided the framework for achieving trade liberalization, the United States put that framework into action. With the coming of the Cold War, Cordell Hull's vision of trade liberalization took on new significance as a key to a prosperous West and to Western security in the face of Soviet aggression. The great postwar economic strength of the United States and the lure of foreign markets were a further reason for U.S. interest in leading trade liberalization.

U.S. leadership was made possible by a new domestic approach to trade policy.[22] In order to avoid the pressure of special interest groups for protection, Congress delegated to the president, for a specific period of time, the authority to reduce tariffs by specific amounts without subsequent congressional approval. This congressional delegation of negotiating authority, begun in 1934 with the passage of the RTAA, was periodically renewed throughout the postwar period. Later, when nontariff barriers were negotiated, Congress agreed to consider proposals for their removal without allowing amendments and within a short time frame. This is called the "fast-track" negotiating authority. In addition, Congress created a quasi-judicial system of trade remedies that channeled grievances of specific industries to fact-finding agencies outside the Congress. Finally, the decision-making process in Congress was concentrated in two powerful committees that dominated trade policy and that supported a liberal trading order.[23]

In the two decades following World War II, the United States led the system by helping Europe and Japan rebuild production and by pushing for trade liberalization. In the early years, the Marshall Plan, or the European Recovery Program as it was officially known, was the tool of U.S. leadership in Europe. As we have seen, the United States played a key role in financing international trade and encouraging long-term European trade competitiveness through the Marshall Plan. The United States also used the plan as a lever to encourage regional trade liberalization in Europe. During the war and the immediate postwar period, significant barriers to trade had been erected throughout Europe, which underscored the trade restrictions in effect since the 1930s. The United States pushed actively for the liberalization of trade and payments among Western European countries and, in some cases, made available the funds for such liberalization, even though this conflicted with the larger U.S. goal of nondiscrimination on an international basis and even though regional liberalization sometimes involved direct discrimination against the United States.[24]

The United States also took an important leadership role with Japan. During the Occupation, the supreme commander for the Allied forces and his administration directly controlled Japanese trade and the Japanese monetary system. Until the 1960s, the United States helped the recovery and development in Japan by keeping the U.S. market open for Japanese goods while at the same time accepting Japanese protectionist policies, many of which had been instituted under the Occupation. The United States also supported Japanese membership in the GATT and urged the Europeans, unsuccessfully, to open their markets to Japanese exports.[25]

Finally, the United States took a leading role in multilateral trade negotiations. The idea of creating a more open system through negotiations to remove tariffs and other trade barriers had originated with the U.S. Reciprocal Trade Agreements Act of 1934, which had led to a series of bilateral negotiations. Tariff reductions in these negotiations were based on reciprocity (that is, on mutual advantage), a system that headed off potential domestic political opposition to tariff reduction within the United States. The reductions negotiated bilaterally were broadened under the most-favored-nation agreements that the United States had established with numerous countries under various commercial treaties.

In the postwar period, this procedure of bilateral negotiations was expanded to a series of multilateral trade negotiations conducted by the members of the GATT. The United States, with the world's largest economy and a huge share of international trade, was the essential motivating force in these negotiations. Because the United States was, in many cases, one of the world's principal suppliers, its participation was required under the GATT's negotiating rules. Because the U.S. market was so important, there was little possibility of achieving reciprocity in tariff negotiations without the United States. Most importantly, without U.S. initiatives, the negotiations would probably never have taken place. Initiatives by the United States were responsible for the eight major trade negotiations from the Geneva Round in 1947 to the Uruguay Round, which began in 1986 (see Table 3-1). The U.S. negotiators were necessary participants—mobilizing others, seeking compromises—in the actual negotiations.

Furthermore, throughout the 1940s and 1950s, the United States accepted limited benefits from the trade negotiations. Although tariffs were reduced on a reciprocal and mutually beneficial basis, U.S. trading partners gained more than the United States did. Because of European and Japanese exchange controls that persisted through the 1950s, the trade concessions had a limited effect on U.S. exports. Because the United States did not impose controls, Europe and Japan gained immediate benefits from the tariff reductions. The United States accepted

Table 3-1   Trade Negotiation Rounds

Year	Name of Round	Number of Participants
1947	Geneva	23
1949	Annecy	13
1950	Torquay	38
1956	Geneva	26
1960–1961	Dillon	26
1962–1967	Kennedy	62
1973–1979	Tokyo	99
1986–1993	Uruguay	125

SOURCE: *Economic Report of the President* (Washington: Government Printing Office, 1995), 205.

such asymmetrical benefits because of a commitment to European and Japanese recovery, because it expected to benefit from the reductions when the exchange controls were removed, and because it sought to maintain the momentum of establishing a more open trading system.

The system worked very well for the developed countries. Most quotas and exchange rate barriers were eliminated. Although restrictions remained in agricultural products, there was substantial liberalization of trade in manufactured products (see Figure 3-1).[26] The resulting rapid growth of world trade was an

Figure 3–1   Average U.S. Tariff Rates on Dutiable Imports, in Percentages, 1821–1993

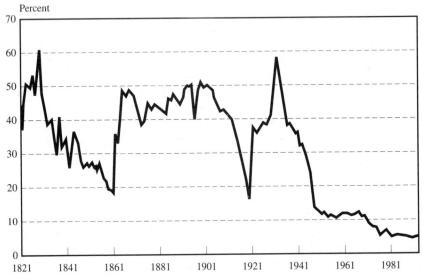

SOURCE: U.S. Department of Commerce, Bureau of the Census, *Historical Statistics of the United States;* and *Statistical Abstract of the United States* (Washington: Government Printing Office), various years.

Figure 3–2   Growth in World Exports, 1958–1993, in Constant 1993 Dollars

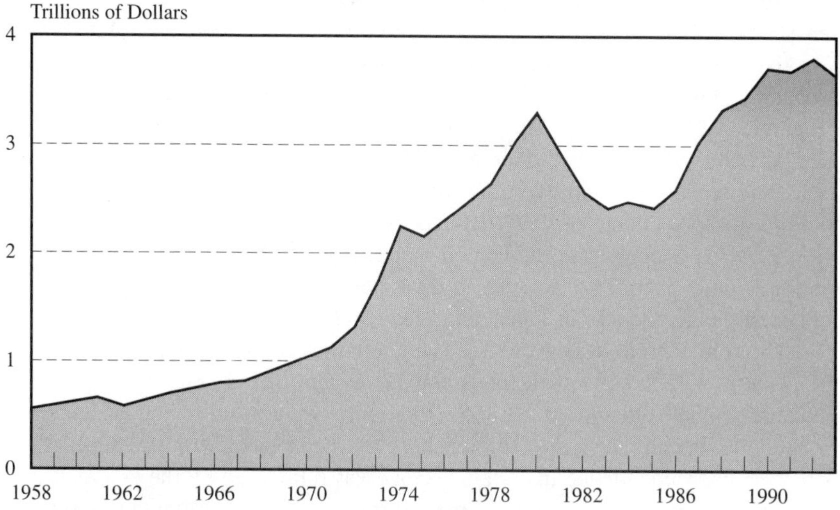

Trillions of Dollars

SOURCE: International Monetary Fund, *Direction of Trade Statistics, Yearbook* (various years); and *Economic Report of the President* (Washington: Government Printing Office, 1995).

important source of economic prosperity (see Figure 3-2). The high point of trade management of this period was the Kennedy Round, which culminated in 1967. Although states were unable to reach any significant agreement on agricultural trade, tariffs on nonagricultural products in the developed countries were reduced by about one-third.[27] After the Kennedy Round reductions, tariffs on dutiable, nonagricultural products were reduced to an average of 9.9 percent in the United States, 8.6 percent in the six EC (European Community) states, 10.8 percent in the United Kingdom, and 10.7 percent in Japan.[28] The overall reduction in tariffs for the first five trade rounds was 73 percent; for the Kennedy round alone it was 35 percent.[29]

Structural Change and Protectionism

After 1967, however, important changes in the international trading system began to emerge and to undermine the GATT system of management and the liberal international trading order created by the GATT. Over the next two decades, structural changes led to domestic political challenges to international management of trade and to new forms of protection. Governments sought, with only limited success, to stem the tide of protectionism and to modernize the international trading regime. Thus the conflict between national and international approaches to management—the same conflict we have seen in the international monetary system—came to plague international trade management.

As in the case of monetary relations, a central force for change was increased interdependence. Interdependence increased the level of political sensitivity to trade as trade came to affect more sectors and more jobs. After World War II, economic growth, trade liberalization, decreasing transportation costs, and broadening business horizons led to a surge in trade among the developed market economies.[30] Merchandise trade among the developed countries more than quadrupled between 1963 and 1973; increased over two-and-one-half times from 1973 to 1983; and grew more than two times again between 1983 and 1990.[31] From 1960 to 1992, the percentage of GDP derived from trade (exports plus imports) went from 9.6 to 21.9 percent in the United States, from 35.5 percent to 60 percent in Germany, and from 14.5 percent to 23.1 percent in France. Trade over GDP remained steady and low in Japan and steady and high in Britain (see Figure 3-3).

The role of trade was even greater in certain sectors. For example, in 1979, 5.5 percent of U.S. consumer goods and 12 percent of U.S. business equipment purchases came from abroad. By 1987, the figures for consumer goods had grown to about 12 percent, whereas foreign business equipment outlays exceeded 40 percent.[32] Interdependence in certain sectors was reinforced by the emergence of the global company, which sources parts from around the world. One example is the Boeing Company, which produces commercial jetliners. In 1980, imported parts accounted for 2 to 3 percent of airplanes produced by Boeing. By 1988, imported parts represented 28 percent of Boeing airplanes.[33]

Another dimension of trade interdependence was the growing convergence of the developed countries' economies. The rapid accumulation of physical and

Figure 3–3   Trade (exports + imports)/GDP, 1960–1992

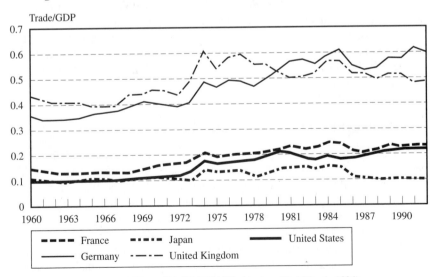

SOURCE: World Bank, *World Data '94 CD-ROM* (Washington: World Bank, 1994).

human capital, the transfer of technology, and the growing similarities of wages narrowed the differences in **factor endowments,** which are the basis for comparative advantage and trade. In 1970, for example, labor costs in the United States and West Germany were over twice the labor costs in Japan. By 1986, the costs were roughly equal.[34] Similarly, in 1970, U.S. manufacturing productivity was 58 percent greater than West Germany and 105 percent greater than Japan in 1970. By 1986, these figures had fallen to 20 percent and 2 percent, respectively (see Figure 3-4).[35]

U.S. **productivity** growth was somewhat stronger in the early 1990s than it was in the 1970s and 1980s, however. Average annual growth in total factor productivity of nonfinancial corporations was 2.7 percent for the 1991–1994 period—a marked improvement over the dismal 0.8 percent average growth rate of the previous four years.[36] Still, U.S. productivity growth was only slightly higher than that of its major trading partners during this period.[37]

Convergence altered the nature of comparative advantage, leading to more complex specialization and fostering the global company and intraindustry trade. Also, because of economic convergence, small changes in factor costs led to large

Figure 3–4   Total Factor Productivity Growth in Five Industrialized Nations, 1960–1992, in Percentages

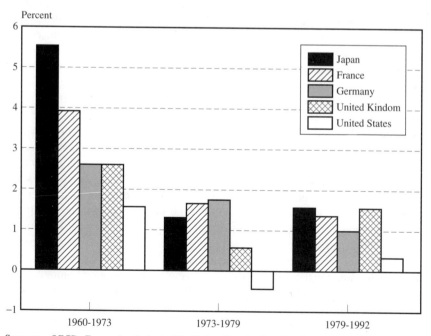

SOURCE: *OECD Economic Outlook 55* (Paris: Organization for Economic Cooperation and Development, June 1994).

shifts in competitive advantages and thus in trade, production, and employment—and to political reaction to those shifts.

A second change that increased protectionist pressures was the shift in competitiveness worldwide. Changes in factor endowments altered the competitive positions of several industries in the developed countries, including autos, steel, textiles, shipping, and consumer electronics. In some sectors, especially in industries like textiles and apparel where technology is stable and labor is a major factor in production costs, the shift favored the developing countries. Lags in capital investment in the developed countries plus rising labor productivity, lower labor costs, and aggressive export policies in some of the LDCs led to a shift in manufacturing from the industrialized nations to the newly industrializing countries (NICs), such as Taiwan, South Korea, Mexico, and Brazil.[38]

In other cases, because of differing levels of investment and research, of management effectiveness and labor productivity, as well as exchange rate changes, the shift occurred among the developed countries. The reasons for these shifts in competitiveness have become a subject of intense debate. In the United States, for example, debate has focused heavily on declining U.S. competitiveness vis à vis Japan, which has been evidenced by greater Japanese investment per employee, civilian **research and development (R&D)** spending, productivity growth, shares of world trade and production, and average growth of total gross fixed capital formation.[39]

The main economic manifestations of the relative decline in U.S. competitiveness were serious competition from imports in manufacturing industries, such as steel and motor vehicles, that had been the mainstays of the domestic economy.[40] By the 1980s, Japan was beginning to challenge high-technology industries in the United States and Western Europe, notably in electronics and specifically in the branch of electronics considered to be the most strategic—semiconductors.[41] The major political manifestation was increased pressure from these industries for protection. The combination of interdependence and changes in competitiveness made national economies more sensitive to external events and provoked domestic producers to mobilize for protection from foreign competition.

A third change contributing to protectionism were disruptions in the economic system in the 1970s and 1980s. Trade management from the end of World War II until the end of the Kennedy Round took place in an environment of unprecedented growth and stability. From 1960 to 1970, growth in the OECD countries averaged almost 5 percent per year, unemployment stood at 2.7 percent, and the volume of world trade grew at an average annual rate of 8.5 percent.[42] Throughout this period, the U.S. trade balance was strongly positive, providing the basis for a national consensus for liberalizing trade (see again Figure 2-3). In such an expanding world economy, economic groups were able to perceive the advantages of cooperation and trade liberalization.

In the 1970s and 1980s, these favorable conditions altered dramatically and contributed to the new protectionism. The 1970s was the era of **stagflation,** slow growth combined with rampant inflation. In the wake of the oil crisis, the developed countries' real GNP growth dropped to 2.7 percent between 1974 and 1979, while their inflation exploded to double digits, reaching a high of 13.4 percent in 1974.[43] Unemployment in the OECD countries increased to an average of 4.9 percent for the period 1974 to 1979.[44] Stagflation increased pressures on governments to adopt beggar-thy-neighbor policies such as trade restrictions (see Figure 3-5).

The floating exchange rate system also contributed to growing protectionism. In the 1970s, monetary problems led to trade measures designed to protect payments balances such as exchange controls and special duties. The breakdown in the system of fixed exchange rates also complicated the process of trade negotiations. In a fixed rate system, negotiators had been able to estimate the impact of agreements on their trade and payments. Under floating rates, such calculations were much more difficult. As a result of these economic changes, the value in dollar terms of world trade grew at an annual average of only 5 percent between 1975 and 1984 and only 3.2 percent between 1985 and 1994.[45]

In the early 1980s, deep recession put a brake on trade. Deflationary policies led to a steady decline in inflation from 12.9 percent in 1980 to 2.5 percent in 1986.[46] At the same time, growth came to a halt. The years 1980 to 1982 witnessed the lowest average growth rate—0.73 percent per year—of any three-year period since the end of World War II.[47] Unemployment rose to levels once thought politically unacceptable. By the end of 1983, recession had pushed total unemployment in the OECD countries to a record 8.5 percent.[48] Significantly, unemployment was concentrated in those industries with the highest levels of foreign competition. For example, in December 1982, when total U.S. unemployment reached its peak of 10.6 percent, unemployment in the auto industry stood at 23.2

Figure 3–5   Stagflation in the U.S. Economy, 1961–1980

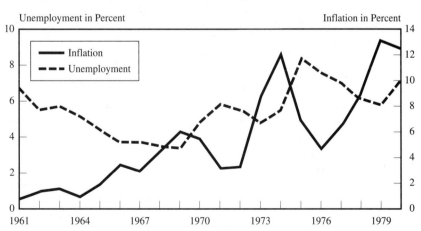

Source: *Economic Report of the President* (Washington: Government Printing Office, 1995), 320, 345.

percent, and in the primary metals (steel) industry, it was 29.2 percent.[49] Because of the recession, world trade stagnated. The growth of the volume of world trade slowed to 1.2 percent in 1980 and 0.8 percent in 1981, and it actually fell by 2.2 percent in 1982.[50]

By the second half of the 1980s, the economic environment for the industrialized countries improved. Growth rates increased somewhat, while inflation rates began to fall.[51] World trade began to resume its expansion (see again Figure 3-2). Because of labor market rigidities, however, unemployment remained high in most of Europe and the United States and persisted as a force for protection. In 1986, unemployment in the developed countries still stood at 8.3 percent, with U.S. unemployment at 7.0 percent, Japanese at 2.8 percent, and the EC at 11.2 percent.[52] In the 1980s, the exchange rate system emerged as a central problem for trade management. As we have seen, the misalignment of exchange rates was a major factor in the emergence of massive trade and payments imbalances. In particular, the overvaluation of the dollar and corresponding undervaluation of the yen and deutsche mark were a major cause of the U.S. trade deficit and the resultant rise in protectionism in the United States.

Pluralism

In the 1970s and 1980s, the rise of Japan and the European Union[53] and the relative decline of the United States complicated the system of trade management. Trade problems and a decline in power combined with growing protectionist pressures left the United States less willing and less able to lead the system. At the same time, the EU and Japan were not prepared to assume a leadership role. Absent strong leadership, management where power is more evenly shared proved a major challenge to the system.

Since 1958, the European Union has emerged as the world's largest trading bloc. The EU has established a customs union with free internal trade in goods, a common external tariff, and a common agricultural policy. Trade of EC countries has grown rapidly from 24.5 percent of total world trade in 1960 to 41.1 percent in 1990.[54] Trade among EU member states has grown even faster. Intra-EU trade as a share of total world trade increased almost threefold, from 8.4 percent in 1960 to 24.4 percent in 1990.[55] Intra-EU trade as a share of total EU member-state trade burgeoned from 34.4 percent in 1960 to 59.5 percent in 1990.[56]

In building this regional trading system, the EU has weakened the principle of nondiscrimination basic to the GATT—albeit with the blessing of the United States—and thus some day might pose challenges to liberalization of the larger international system. As we have argued earlier, however, so far the EU has resisted temptations to favor trade and capital flows within the Union at the expense of flows between the EU and the rest of the world. The continuing political fragmentation of the EU weakened its ability to act as the sole representative of Europe in international affairs, especially in traditional foreign policy areas (such as dealing with the civil war in Bosnia). But the EU represented all of its member states in trade negotiations and at international economic summits. So it can be argued that the EU, like other regional economic integration efforts (see the section on the new regionalism below), was still a building block for a liberal international economic order rather than an impediment.

The EU's first goal was to build a customs union with internal free trade and a common external tariff. Such customs unions are permitted as an exception to the GATT rules of nondiscrimination.[57] The European effort to establish such a union was supported by the United States, which, since the days of the Marshall Plan, actively encouraged a united Europe as a way of strengthening the West. When it looked as if the EU might increase trade discrimination, the United States, by initiating the Kennedy Round, sought to ensure that European integration would remain open and nondiscriminatory. The success of that round suggested that Europe would remain committed to multilateralism and liberalism. However, in the 1970s and 1980s, Europe showed signs of moving in the opposite direction.

The EU's Common Agricultural Policy (CAP) blocked imports into the community and artificially stimulated competition in other markets. The EU also entered into new preferential trading arrangements, which were explicitly outlawed under the GATT rule of nondiscrimination. Beginning in 1958 with an agreement with the then French colonies in Africa, the EU has negotiated preferential agreements with most of the Mediterranean Basin, much of Africa, and even with some developed countries of Western Europe. In the 1990s, many countries of Central and Eastern Europe became associated with the EU. The Union has viewed such agreements as aid to underdeveloped countries and as adjustments for the discriminatory effects of CAP. Although the preferences have not had so great a trade diversionary impact as CAP has—at least not for the developed market economies—the United States has viewed them as an important departure from the postwar agreement on nondiscrimination.[58]

The enlargement of the EU to its current membership of fifteen nation-states created further problems (see Table 3-2). This expansion not only increased the size of the agricultural protectionist regime and the existing preferential system but also became a force for the extension of EU preferences. Some of the European Free Trade Area (EFTA) countries, which for political reasons did not join the EU, as well as many Commonwealth countries, became linked with the EU through preferential trade agreements.

In the 1980s, EU attention focused on the new policy of completing the creation of a common internal market by 1992.[59] In 1985, the community announced a plan to remove over 300 nontariff barriers to intra-EU trade ranging from harmonizing standards to eliminating delays at borders to allowing cross border sales of services such as banking and insurance to tax harmonization. The thrust of the internal market program was decidedly liberal, based as it was on efforts to remove nontariff barriers to free trade.

However, as the Union worked toward its 1992 deadline, questions began to emerge about its impact on the multilateral trading system. Talk of "Europe for

Table 3-2   Member States of the European Union

Country	Member Since
Belgium	1957
France	1957
Germany	1957
Italy	1957
Luxembourg	1957
Netherlands	1957
Denmark	1973
Ireland	1973
United Kingdom	1973
Greece	1981
Portugal	1986
Spain	1986
Austria	1995
Finland	1995
Sweden	1995

SOURCE: *Economic Report of the President* (Washington: Government Printing Office, 1994), 247.

the Europeans" and "fortress Europe" raised concerns about increasing barriers to the outside world through, for example, extension of national protectionist policies to the Union as a whole or through harmonization of standards and regulations that would discriminate against non-European goods and services. Other questions concerned treatment of foreign firms that had invested in Europe and whether they would be considered "European" for purposes of cross-border sales of services and for government procurement.

The fears of many Americans in the 1980s about the creation of a "fortress Europe" were probably unjustified. The signing of the Maastricht Treaty in 1991 (see Chapter 2) and continued progress toward the goals established by both that treaty and the Single European Act of 1986 did not result in a more protectionist Europe. Changes in European institutions in the 1980s were aimed at making it easier for Europe to undertake the economic changes necessary for the region to maintain its international competitiveness in the face of growing competition from the United States and East Asia. The desire of Europe to be a player in markets for high-technology products, however, has resulted in some policies—such as the massive subsidies for the European civilian aircraft consortium, Airbus Industrie, and for the European electronics industry—that continue to bring it into conflict with the United States and Japan. In short, the worries about Europe shifted away from concerns about protectionism in trade policies to concerns about the use of "industrial policies" to favor European enterprises in international competition.

The rise of Japan as a force in the world economy and world trade has also complicated trade management. As late as 1960, Japan was a minor economic power, with a 3-percent share of world GNP. By 1992, Japan had become the second largest developed economy after the United States. Japan accounted for 15 percent of world GNP,[60] and for 5.6 percent of world trade, making it a trading power on a par with Germany.[61]

Behind this rapid change in position was the Japanese economic miracle: an annual real growth in GNP of 10 percent from 1950 to 1970. Starting from a position of relative technological backwardness, Japan achieved this remarkable growth rate through its ability to absorb and adapt foreign technology, the availability of labor due to the movement of people out of agriculture and a growing population, and heavy investment in manufacturing.[62] Government policies played a central role in the Japanese miracle. Targeted industries, such as steel, oil refining, petrochemicals, automobiles, aircraft, industrial machinery, electronics, and computers, were promoted through tax incentives as well as financing provided by government lending institutions and private savings encouraged by government policies.

Export expansion and import protection played a central role in government policy. Because of Japan's dependence on imports of raw materials and **capital goods** essential for growth, government plans and private industry strategies placed heavy emphasis on limiting "nonessential" imports and fostering exports.[63] Government provided industry with significant protection from import competition through tariffs and quantitative restrictions as well as administrative regulations, such as import licensing and import deposits. While the other developed countries were liberalizing trade through multilateral negotiations, Japan retained barriers on virtually all imports. At the same time, tax incentives, export financing assistance, and an undervalued yen encouraged Japanese exports. Finally, the government carefully controlled foreign investment.[64] Thus, in the 1950s and 1960s, Japan created an industrial base heavily biased against imports and oriented toward exports.[65]

After 1973, growth slowed due to the end of the process of technological catch-up, lower investment rates, and other factors, such as slower population growth and rising energy costs. Industrial development shifted from heavy industry, such as steel, to more sophisticated industries, such as automobiles and electronic products.[66] Nevertheless, Japan's average growth rate of 4.3 percent from 1974 to 1985 exceeded that of other industrial economies. In the 1970s, Japanese government policy also changed. Although the government still took a lead role in certain strategic sectors, such as computers, the role of government in industrial development began to decline as Japanese industry reached greater maturity.[67]

Beginning in 1970, Japan gradually liberalized trade policy. Quotas on many goods were eliminated; significant across-the-board tariff cuts were instituted; and the yen began to appreciate. Following the Tokyo Round, Japanese tariff barriers were roughly comparable to those of the United States.[68] Japan's strategy of export promotion, however, not only remained but also was reinforced by the oil crises of 1973 and 1978–1979, which accentuated Japan's sense of dependence on and vulnerability to imports of raw materials.

By the 1980s, Japan had become a source of trade friction due to the seemingly chronic Japanese merchandise trade surplus (see again Figure 2-9). Most visible was Japan's growing imbalance in trade with the United States, its principal trading partner. While the bilateral Japan-EU surplus grew from $9.9 billion in 1980 to $26.5 billion in 1993, its surplus with the United States grew from $7.3 billion in 1980 to $51 billion in 1993.[69]

The principal cause of the massive surplus was an imbalance in macroeconomic policies, particularly between the United States and Japan, which was reflected in capital flows and exchange rate relations. Japan maintained a high savings rate fostered by government policies, which dated from the era when Japan needed high levels of investment for economic development. However, because of slower growth and investment and a policy of government fiscal austerity, there was insufficient demand for these savings within Japan. As the Japanese government eliminated exchange controls and other limits on Japanese foreign investment, surplus yen began to flow abroad in response to demand, primarily from the United States. The U.S. savings rates were low, while demand for funds in the growing U.S. economy was too high to be satisfied from domestic sources alone. For much of the 1980s, U.S. business was investing heavily and the U.S. government was generating huge budget deficits that had to be financed. Japan provided much of that financing. The high value of the dollar against the yen between 1981 and 1985 made Japanese exports more competitive worldwide, especially in the United States.

Differing domestic demand was also an important dimension of the macroeconomic imbalance. As the United States stimulated its economy in the early 1980s, imports of consumer goods increased more than 150 percent from $34.4 billion in 1980 to $87.0 billion in 1987.[70] The Japanese were well positioned to take advantage of this surge in consumer demand. For decades, Japanese manufacturers had concentrated on export-led growth and on developing the U.S. market. Since the 1970s, they had focussed on developing products targeted at the U.S. consumer. Japanese automobiles and consumer electronic products, for example, were well designed for the U.S. market, of high quality, and, due to productivity improvements and a declining yen, increasingly price competitive. At the same time, because of slower growth and fiscal austerity, Japanese demand, especially demand for competitive U.S. machine tools and heavy equipment, was restrained.

These macroeconomic differences were accentuated by continuing barriers to imports and to inward foreign investment into Japan. With the exception of agriculture, most Japanese tariff and quota barriers had been removed. However, nontariff barriers deriving from the earlier era of cooperation between government and business remained a problem. Government procurement policies favored Japanese telecommunications and computer manufacturers. Regulation was used effectively to block imports. For example, patent approvals were delayed until Japanese producers became competitive. Inspections and approvals by foreign testing agencies were rejected by some ministries, and the process of regulatory approval was often long and not transparent. Industrial targeting, as in the case of computers, was still used to discriminate against foreign goods. In addition, private patterns of behavior, such as so-called *keiretsu* behavior—the preference of Japanese for dealing with other Japanese suppliers as well as the complex Japanese distribution system—formed barriers to foreign access to Japanese markets.[71] Some U.S. multinationals were rich enough and patient enough to pay the high price of cultivating the Japanese domestic market. IBM, Caterpillar, Xerox, McDonalds, Johnson & Johnson, CocaCola, and others were successful in establishing a firm foothold in Japan. For those U.S. firms that were smaller or less export oriented, overcoming these public and private barriers proved especially difficult.

As a result of this combination of factors, the bilateral U.S.-Japan trade imbalance soared in the 1980s. Even after the Plaza agreement of 1985 when the value of the dollar began to decline, Japanese surpluses continued to grow. In part this was due to the so-called J-curve effect, whereby the impact of a depreciation is initially an increase in a deficit as the cost of goods already contracted for import rises. Persistent depreciations of the dollar from 1985 to 1987 accentuated the J-curve effect and masked the turnaround in the physical volume and yen value of U.S.-Japan trade. Furthermore, the trade impact of dollar depreciation was reduced, because Japanese exporters, dependent on the U.S. market, increased prices less than the magnitude of the dollar depreciation in order to retain their market share. They were able to do this without cutting profit margins too much because of continuous improvements in production and distribution technologies.[72]

The political consequence of the Japanese trade surplus was increasing trade friction between Japan and its trading partners. Pressures grew for protection against Japanese imports and for action to open Japanese markets. In the West, the Japanese surpluses were often attributed not to macroeconomic imbalances but to unfair trade practices by Japan. Protectionist pressures were accentuated by the traditional Japanese export strategy of capturing market share. This strategy led to swift penetration of certain foreign markets, which led to equally swift foreign political reaction in such powerful sectors as semiconductors, telecommunications equipment, and automobiles. Finally, the slow process of decision making in Japan, where consensus must be formed before action is taken, exacerbated growing Western criticism of Japan as a free rider in the system.[73]

Growing Western exasperation seemed unfounded in Japan. From a Japanese perspective, the country had moved far and fast under Western prodding to liberalize trade. Under heavy pressure, Japan had opened up a variety of protected markets, such as telecommunications, cigarettes, beef, citrus, and airport construction. It had taken steps toward liberalization of its financial markets, opening the securities and trust banking business to foreigners.[74] Furthermore, Western governments subjected Japan to numerous highly protectionist **Voluntary Restraint Agreements (VRAs)**.[75] In the mid-1980s, under pressure from the West and from a revalued yen, Japan stimulated domestic demand and reduced its trade surplus somewhat. After the Plaza agreement, net exports measured in terms of physical volume and net receipts in yen declined (see Figure 3-6). Imports from the developing countries increased dramatically. As seen from Japan, foreign profligacy, especially U.S. macroeconomic policy and declining Western productivity and competitiveness, were the root of the problem.[76]

Finally, one of the most important developments in the 1970s and 1980s was the erosion of U.S. dominance of the international trading system and the related decline in U.S. support for a multilateral trade regime. While the United States remained the world's largest economy and largest trading power, it was no longer overwhelmingly preponderant as it was in the first two postwar decades. In 1950 the United States accounted for 26.1 percent of trade among developed market economies (which would have been 80 percent or more of world trade; by 1994 the United States accounted for only 14.1 percent of world trade.[77] Furthermore, after 1970 the United States began to experience what seemed to be chronic merchandise trade deficits. The huge and traditional (since 1893) U.S. merchandise-trade surplus turned in 1971 into a persistent and growing merchandise trade deficit (see again Figures 2-3 and 2-10). The traditional U.S. surplus with Japan turned into deficit in 1965, and its traditional surplus with Western Europe diminished and, depending on the relative macroeconomic situation, periodically became a deficit.

The erosion of U.S. trading dominance was accentuated by interdependence. Between 1970 and 1992, trade as a percentage of U.S. GDP rose from 8.7 percent to 21.9 percent (see Figure 3-3).[78] Interdependence was a new condition for the

Figure 3–6   Japan's Balance of Trade (exports – imports), 1960–1994, in Current Yen

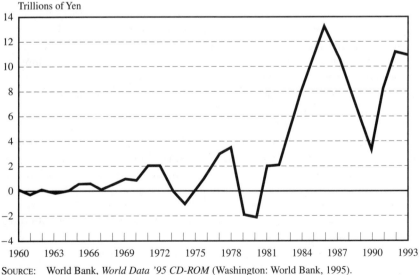

Trillions of Yen

SOURCE: World Bank, *World Data '95 CD-ROM* (Washington: World Bank, 1995).

United States. In contrast with Europe and Japan, whose economies had long been dependent on trade, international trade had been important but not vital to the United States because of its vast continental market. As the United States faced more competition at home and abroad, the political consensus for a multi-lateral, open trading regime led by the United States began to erode.

The decline of U.S. trade preponderance and the swelling trade deficit raised questions about U.S. international competitiveness. The ability of countries to compete in foreign trade depends on productivity, which, in turn, depends on investment in both physical and human capital as well as on research and development. While much of the deterioration of the U.S. trading position in the 1980s was attributable to the overvalued dollar, there were deeper problems created by several decades of sluggish productivity growth. Even though U.S. exports rebounded and regained some world market share following the devaluation of the dollar in 1985, the United States maintained a chronic balance-of-trade deficit through the mid 1990s.

Several indicators suggest a relative decline in U.S. competitiveness. While the United States still retains the highest absolute level of productivity, it has been losing ground relative to competitors. Total factor productivity—output per combined units of labor and capital—in the U.S. business sector has grown more slowly than that of other industrialized countries since the 1960s (see again Figure 3-4).[79] Since 1972, investment in relation to GDP increased only 3.1 percent in the United States—less than half the Group of Seven average of 7.1 percent—while in Germany it rose 33 percent, and in Japan, 24.6 percent.[80] While overall research and development expenditures in the United States have kept pace with those of other developed countries, much of that expenditure has been for military purposes. Nondefense research and development spending relative to GDP in the United States has increased only 3 percent since 1970, while that of Germany increased 31 percent and that of Japan 55 percent. In terms of patenting activity, the United States is also losing ground. Between 1963 and 1977, for example, 72.3 percent of the patents awarded in the United States were of U.S. origin; by 1991, this figure was only 53.4 percent.[81] Not all evidence suggests a U.S. decline, however. In terms of relative unit labor costs, Japan and Germany have increased from 1980 levels, while the United States has actually declined.[82] Furthermore, U.S. industry has adapted to changing competition by increasing automation, downsizing, mergers, and streamlining operations. Overall, evidence suggests the United States has lost some of its relative position, largely as a result of gains in Japan, Europe, and the Asian NICs.

Finally, in the 1970s and 1980s, U.S. support for multilateralism was further undermined by changes in the domestic political system that had developed to deflect protectionist pressures from special interest groups.[83] A series of congressional reforms weakened the power of the committees that had virtually exclusively controlled U.S. trade policy, while the growing importance of nontariff barriers imbedded in a variety of national policies meant that these committees that had traditionally controlled trade could no longer claim exclusive jurisdiction over trade issues. In addition, a quasi-judicial system established by the Congress, called the International Trade Commission, which was supposed to manage trade grievances, began to break down both under the weight of increasing numbers of petitions and because a series of presidents often rejected the commission's recommendations as leading to protectionism. The pressures then spilled back to the Democratic Congress, which came to feel that the Republican administration was rigid and uncooperative on trade policy. The result was increasing efforts by Congress to reform U.S. trade law to reduce presidential discretion and to oblige retaliation against countries found in violation of international trade agreements.[84]

As a result of these changes, domestic pressures for protection increased and became increasingly effective. As trade problems developed, more industries organized into special interest groups to put pressure on Congress and the executive for relief from foreign competition. Beginning in the late 1960s, following the Kennedy Round, vulnerable industries such as textiles, steel, electronics, and shoes began to put strong pressure on Congress to alleviate import competition. In 1970, organized labor officially shifted its policy from support for free trade to active lobbying for protection. Proposals for sectoral protectionist legislation increased in Congress and put pressure on the president to negotiate bilateral agreements outside the GATT to avert legislated quotas and tariffs. At the same time, U.S. industries facing barriers to market access abroad increasingly turned to the U.S. government for help in breaking down foreign barriers. As markets became increasingly global, many high-technology, export-oriented industries, such as microelectronics and supercomputer industries, chafed under restrictions on access to foreign markets. Their goal was to use access to U.S. markets as bargaining leverage to open up foreign markets.[85]

As the trade problem deepened and spread from sensitive industries to the entire economy in the 1980s, many U.S. industry, labor, and political leaders came to believe the United States was no longer benefiting from the system and was being subjected to unfair treatment by its trading partners and by the trading regime. Japan, in particular, was singled out as a country that benefited from the liberal trading order and access to U.S. markets while maintaining barriers to its own market.[86] Proposals for broad-based protectionist legislation increased in Congress. In 1988, Congress enacted omnibus trade legislation, which tightened U.S. trade law to give the president less discretion in case of unfair trade practices by foreign competitors and to require the executive branch to identify and achieve changes in the policy of countries that have unfair trade practices.[87]

In response to persistent congressional pressures, the Reagan, Bush, and Clinton administrations sought nonlegislative ways to resolve trade conflicts: voluntary export restraint agreements as in automobiles; negotiations to open overseas markets, such as the Market Opening Sector Specific (MOSS) talks, the Structural Impediments Initiative and the framework for a new economic partnership between the U.S. and Japan; and aggressive use of the U.S. trade provisions, which authorizes the U.S. government to retaliate against countries deemed not to be allowing U.S. exports fair market access.[88] Finally, the United States negotiated a broad-based bilateral trading agreement with Israel in 1986 and a major agreement with Canada in 1987. The U.S.-Canada Free Trade Agreement, which was signed in 1988, reduced a number of trade and investment barriers between the two countries, established rules on trade in services, and put in place a new dispute settlement mechanism between the two countries.[89]

The New Protectionism

The result of these structural changes in the global trading economy was a surge in protectionist policies in developed countries. The new protectionism took several forms.

One form was nontariff barriers (NTBs) to trade. In part, the NTB problem grew out of the very success of the GATT. The GATT had been designed to liberalize trade by removing quotas and tariffs. With the success of such liberalization in manufactured products, the major remaining barriers to trade were nontariff barriers such as government procurement policies, customs procedures, health and sanitary regulations, national standards, and a broad range of other laws and regulations that discriminate against imports or offer assistance to exports. Regional policy, agricultural policy, and consumer and environmental protection are other examples of nontariff measures that have trade-distorting consequences.

Furthermore, the success of the GATT in trade liberalization actually increased the use of nontariff barriers. Because governments can no longer use tariffs and quotas as tools of national economic policy, they have tried to insulate the domestic economy from international competition through a variety of national policies. States have used subsidies and tax preferences to help ailing industries, such as steel and shipbuilding. They have provided a variety of incentives for the development of new, technologically sophisticated industries, such as aerospace and computers. They have also used a combination of tax and financial incentives as well as requirements for local content, export performance, and technology transfer for foreign investors.

Countries now had to reduce nontariff trade barriers to maintain what had already been achieved, let alone continue the process of liberalization. However, the control of nontariff barriers was far more difficult than the regulation and removal of tariffs and quotas. Such policies were usually an integral part of national economic and social policies. Because they were often carried out for reasons other than trade protection, NTBs had traditionally been considered national prerogatives not subject to international negotiation. Nontariff barriers also posed practical negotiating problems. Because NTBs took many different forms and because many different governmental bodies had authority over them, it was not possible to use the same kinds of negotiating techniques that had proved to be successful in reducing tariffs.[90] The reduction of nontariff barriers required international agreements to coordinate and harmonize a broad range of policies, for which the GATT offered few guidelines.[91]

Another form of the protectionism that followed the reductions in tariffs negotiated in GATT trade rounds were voluntary restraint agreements (VRAs), also known as **voluntary export restraints (VERs).** VRAs were developed as a response to pressure for protection from import-sensitive industries. The GATT provided three principal forms of recourse for industries hurt by imports. If foreign competitors were dumping—that is, selling goods abroad at prices below those in the home market—countries were allowed to impose a duty to offset the dumping. Although antidumping laws were well developed both domestically and internationally, action could take a long time, and proving dumping cases could be difficult. The GATT also permitted countries to impose duties to offset foreign subsidies of exported products. Finally, the GATT permitted certain emergency measures known as safeguards. The GATT permitted governments to impose restrictions on fairly traded imports if an unforeseen surge in imports resulting from a trade concession caused or threatened serious injury to a domestic industry. Such safeguards had to be applied to all countries; protection had to be limited in time and be gradually removed; and importing countries had to adopt meaningful **adjustment policies.**

For several reasons, however, safeguards were rarely invoked directly. They had to be applied to all countries, whereas governments preferred to target certain suppliers for import controls. The GATT also required the importing country to grant compensatory concessions to all affected exporting countries. Furthermore, GATT did not clearly define "serious injury" and offered inadequate guidance— for example, on consultative procedures, duration, and adjustment—for implementing and regulating safeguards. Thus, governments turned increasingly to VRAs, which were outside the GATT framework.[92] They also increasingly moved toward the use of national antidumping laws, which were designed to be consistent with GATT rules for safeguards, to compensate for the absence of clear GATT rules in this area.

Under such agreements, which were usually bilateral and sometimes secret, low-cost exporters "voluntarily" restricted sales to countries where their goods were threatening industry and employment. There was a long history of such agreements. In the 1950s and 1960s, for example, the United States negotiated a number of voluntary export controls with Japan and many LDCs, under which exporters restricted their sales in the U.S. market. Two agreements—the Longterm Textile Arrangement of 1962 and the subsequent Multi-Fiber Arrangement of 1974—were negotiated multilaterally and within the GATT context (see Chapter 7). These earlier agreements were unusual steps, exceptions to normal GATT procedures. In the 1970s and 1980s, however, VRAs became an accepted mode of trade regulation.[93] VRAs proliferated in various sectors—textiles, steel, automobiles, electronics, and footwear—and covered trade among the industrial nations themselves.

In the United States, the typical pattern was a surge of imports, followed by massive filings of unfair trade actions, followed by pressure on Congress for protectionist legislation, followed, in turn, by a negotiated voluntary export restraint agreement as a way to reduce imports without resolving the legal cases and without legislating protection.

Steel was the first major industry subjected to VRAs among developed market economies. In 1968, faced with surging imports and under pressure from proposed legislation to limit steel imports, the Johnson administration negotiated VRAs with the European Union and Japan, which set specific tonnage limits on each for their steel exports to the United States.[94] In 1978, in response to new surges of imports and large number of antidumping cases, the Carter administration instituted the trigger price mechanism (TPM), which established a "fair value" reference price for steel based on Japanese production costs. All European and Japanese imports entering the United States below that price were presumed to be dumped and were subject to a fast-track antidumping investigation. By 1982, due to a rise in the dollar and renewed import competition, the TPM was on the rocks. Numerous trade actions against foreign producers and proposed legislation to cut imports forced the Reagan administration to negotiate VERs with not only the EU, Japan, and Australia but also Argentina, Brazil, Mexico, Korea, and South Africa.[95]

In the 1980s, VRAs among developed countries grew. The most important industry to be added to the list was automobiles, which account for 15 percent of world manufactured goods exports.[96] A surge in Japanese exports led to legal and political pressure to keep Japanese automobiles out of Western Europe and the United States. The first VRA on automobiles was in 1976 between the United Kingdom and Japan. The following year, France negotiated an agreement with Japan. In 1981, in response to proposed legislation to limit Japanese imports, the Reagan administration and Japan agreed to a VER. Agreements with West Germany, Canada, the Netherlands, Belgium, and Luxembourg followed.[97] By the latter half of the 1980s, VRAs had spread to high-technology sectors.

The GATT regime became increasingly irrelevant in the face of the new protectionism. The GATT had been designed to manage import restrictions, especially quantitative restrictions and tariffs, not nontariff barriers and voluntary export controls. Furthermore, countries often preferred politically negotiated bilateral solutions to the GATT's multilateral rules and procedures. Finally, with increasing government intervention in the economy, shifting comparative advantage and surplus capacity in many sectors, and frequent departures from GATT rules, many policymakers and analysts began to argue for a regime based on managed trade, not on the GATT principle of open trade. A managed-trade regime would recognize the reality, indeed the desirability, of government intervention in national economies to decide comparative advantage and intergovernmental agreements to shape international trade flows.[98] Proposals for such a regime ranged from an outright advocacy of tariff barriers as a tool of national policy[99] to proposals for global negotiations to allocate world production[100] to a set of regimes based on varying levels of government intervention, anywhere from managed trade in surplus sectors to free trade in the advanced sectors.[101]

New Issues

In addition to the new protectionism, trade management in the 1980s had to confront trade problems in sectors that had not yet been brought under GATT rules and process. One such challenge for the GATT was both old and new protectionism in agriculture. As we have seen, agriculture was subject to a separate GATT regime and did not benefit from the liberalization process of the postwar era.

National agricultural policies of most developed countries remained interventionist and protectionist. Since the 1930s, the U.S. government intervened in domestic agricultural markets to maintain agricultural prices and the income of U.S. farmers. It supported domestic prices by purchasing surplus commodities, production controls, and deficiency payments, and further managed the domestic market through export subsidies and import quotas. Japan's government, led by a political party that depended heavily on electoral support from farmers and also motivated by a deep concern for food security resulting from wartime shortages, had widespread import restrictions to maintain domestic agricultural prices above world price levels and to provide farmers with incomes comparable to nonfarmers.

The European Union maintained farm incomes through its Common Agricultural Policy (CAP). The CAP established common, artificially high internal prices, which it maintained through the purchase of surpluses and a flexible external tariff on agricultural imports, which ensured that imported products were more expensive than domestic products and that imported products could only assume the slack that the EU producers could not fill. Because the CAP had no production controls, high prices for agricultural products generated large food surpluses, which were exported with the help of export subsidies.[102]

Although protection was extensive, the exemption of agriculture from the rules of international trade did not become a serious problem until the 1980s. Conflict was limited because agricultural trade grew steadily, driven by economic growth, rising incomes, and improved diets. However, in the 1970s, burgeoning populations, inappropriate agricultural policies in developing countries and the Eastern bloc, unfavorable weather conditions, and overall global inflation led to a dramatic rise in the demand for food imports and in the price of agricultural products. Rising prices and expected long-term food shortages led both importing and exporting countries to increase production.[103] Favorable market conditions combined with government encouragement resulted in soaring food production.[104]

As production increased, world demand for agricultural products declined. Per capita food consumption grew at a slower rate; supply far outdistanced demand; world commodity markets collapsed; and agricultural producers in many developed countries faced the worst economic crisis since the 1930s. Governments that protected their domestic markets and maintained high domestic prices through a combination of domestic price supports, purchase of excess supplies, and import protection found themselves with growing mountains of surplus commodities. To reduce these surpluses, governments increased export subsidies and dumped agricultural products on the already strained international market. Export subsidies further depressed prices and had a serious negative effect on exporting countries such as Canada, Australia, and a number of developing countries that had relatively less intervention at home and that now faced greater competition abroad.[105] The budgetary costs of the agricultural trade war were also high. The costs of the CAP, estimated at $60 billion in 1986, created a budget crisis in the EU. United States expenditures for price and income support rose sixfold from 1982 to 1986, when they surpassed $26 billion.[106] Conflicts over agricultural policy increased. Even Japan, a large net importer of agricultural products, was criticized as never before for its protectionist policies.

GATT was unable to restrain the agricultural trade war, because domestic agricultural programs and export subsidies received special treatment under its rules. The combination of trade war and budgetary costs led countries for the first time in the postwar period to consider seriously multilateral negotiations that would change the GATT regime for agriculture and lead to reform of domestic agricultural policies.

In addition to agriculture, other sectors not adequately covered by the GATT raised important management issues in the 1980s. As the structure of international production and trade evolved, the developed countries tried to adapt the GATT to cover industries of increasing importance in international trade.

One challenge was posed by the growing importance of services in the national economies and international trade of the developed countries. Services, or invisibles, differ from goods in that they cannot be stored and, therefore, require some form of direct relationship between the buyer and seller. The international trade of services thus requires some form of commercial presence in foreign markets. Consumer services are provided directly to retail customers by such businesses as restaurants, hotels, and travel agencies and tend to be produced, sold, and consumed within the same market. Producer services—banking, securities trading, insurance, law, advertising, accounting, data processing—are used in the intermediate production of manufactured goods and other services and are more frequently traded internationally.

By the late 1970s, services in the United States accounted for two-thirds of the GNP and for more than 50 percent of the GNPs in twelve other developed countries. Within the service sector, producer services experienced particularly rapid growth.[107] As the economies of the developed countries matured, services came to play an ever greater role in the production and distribution of goods.[108] During the 1970s and 1980s, services also became a major factor in international trade among developed countries.[109] The liberalization of goods and capital markets created business opportunities for firms trading in services, while the revolution in telecommunications and computer technologies made possible the rapid transmission of data at long distance and enabled services to be offered across national boundaries. By 1993, for example, U.S. exports of services amounted to $297.1 billion, equivalent to 34.4 percent of U.S. exports.[110] Because of problems both in defining services and collecting data, worldwide exports of services are difficult to quantify with any degree of certainty. Many estimates put this figure around $600 billion.[111] Services account for between 20 percent[112] and 30 percent[113] of world trade.

Services trade grew despite widespread nontariff barriers. Many service industries, such as telecommunications, banking and insurance, and law and accounting, were highly regulated and often involved state-owned industry. Frequently, such regulation discriminated against foreign services providers by denying access to national markets or by imposing constraints on activities of foreign firms operating in domestic markets. Such barriers included discriminatory treatment of foreign firms in licensing and taxation; policies through which a section of the market was reserved for domestic industry; investment performance requirements; discriminatory government procurement; and government monopolies.[114] Barriers to trade in services had not been subject to the process of liberalization, because services were not covered by the GATT regime. Although there were efforts to establish liberalizing rules for such services as insurance in the OECD, by and large services have been outside the international trade regime.

As services grew in importance in the developed countries, service industries—particularly those in the United States and the United Kingdom—began to organize to press governments for adaptation of the trading regime to cover services. In the United States, for example, the service industry successfully pressed for a change in U.S. trade law to make trade rules and remedies applicable to services as well as goods.[115] As a result, services barriers began to receive greater attention in bilateral U.S. trade relations. The service sector in the developed countries also sought successfully to make the inclusion of services in the GATT a goal of the Uruguay Round of multilateral trade negotiations.

Intellectual property was another new trade issue.[116] The comparative advantage of many of the most competitive industries of the developed market economies became increasingly dependent on their advanced technology, which was expensive and time consuming to develop. Such technology could sometimes be easily and quickly copied and used to produce products at a much lower cost than that incurred by the developer, thus undermining the competitive ability of the firm that developed the technology. The cost of computer software, for example, derived largely from developmental costs. Yet such software could often be easily copied and sold at a price far below the cost to the developer. Similarly, the cost of developing pharmaceutical products is high, while drugs can be easily copied, produced, and sold below the cost to the developer.

For this reason, and to encourage the development of technology, most developed countries protect the developer of technology through patent, trademark, and copyright laws. However, intellectual property protection differed among the developed countries and frequently was nonexistent in developing countries. As high-technology firms increased in importance in trade and as their concern about intellectual property protection increased, they argued that "piracy"—the illegal copying of audio and video materials and computer software—

undermined their ability to compete internationally and, thus, disrupted trade. Because efforts to standardize and expand protection for intellectual property through the World Intellectual Property Organization (WIPO) did not lead to common rules and dispute settlement procedures, they and their governments argued that the GATT should be broadened to cover intellectual property issues.

Some developed countries also pressed for GATT rules to eliminate trade-restrictive and trade-distorting effects of government investment policies and practices.[117] Trade-related investment measures (TRIMs) included local content requirements, which required domestic sourcing; licensing requirements, which stipulated that an investor license production locally and often limit the amount of royalties; product mandating requirements, which obliged an investor to supply certain markets with specific products; trade-balancing requirements, which mandated arbitrary export or import levels; and export-performance requirements, which obliged an investor to export a percentage of its production.

Finally, concerns about the relationship between trade and the environment began to surface in the 1980s. Environmentalists worry that liberal international trade regimes can result in environmental "dumping"—that is the placement of the most environmentally destructive activities in countries with the least restrictive environmental regulations, thus forcing all other countries down to the standard set by the least environmentally conscious countries. Environmental issues played a role in the negotiations for a North American Free Trade Agreement, as we shall see in the next section. There was also some discussion at this time about the use of trade measures to restrict the importation of products that were obtained or produced with environmentally undesirable methods.

The most celebrated example of this was the attempt by the United States to restrict the importation from Mexico of canned tuna that had been obtained by the use of nets that many consumers in the United States considered to be inhumane. The nets in question did not permit dolphins to escape when the tuna were being hauled in. Since U.S. law mandated the use of nets that did not result in unnecessary dolphin deaths and since U.S. producers were not allowed to market tuna caught by the old method in the United States, the legal regime governing domestic tuna products was extended to imported products in the form of a total ban on the sale of those products. The Mexican government protested and took the case to the GATT. The GATT ruled against the United States in this case, provoking some environmentalists to assert that free trade and environmental protection were inherently incompatible.

Given the likely continued attention to problems of environmental degradation in the domestic politics of most industrialized nations, it is possible to predict with some confidence that debates about the linkages between trade and the environment are likely to figure importantly in future international trade negotiations. Agriculture, services, intellectual property, and the environment are just four of the more important new issues in the politics of international trade. Another set of issues are raised by the revival of interest in regional integration.

The New Regionalism

Another change in the trading system in the 1980s and early 1990s was the movement away from multilateralism toward bilateral and regional arrangements. As multilateral reform seemed to stall (see below on the Uruguay Round), many countries turned to alternative trade agreements. The EU, the largest regional trading bloc, continued to expand taking in the former EFTA countries and reaching agreements with many central and eastern European countries on association and possible eventual membership in the EU.

At the same time, the United States moved in the direction of regional agreements for the Americas and the Pacific Rim. In the spring of 1990, President Carlos Salinas de Gortari of Mexico proposed negotiations for a free trade area with the United States. Motivated not just by economic interest but also by the desire for a stable and prosperous southern neighbor, the U.S. government accepted. Negotiations, which also included Canada, began formally in June 1991. The stated aims of the North American Free Trade Area (NAFTA) were to "eliminate barriers to trade, promote conditions of fair competition, increase investment opportunities, provide adequate protection for intellectual property rights, establish effective procedures for . . . [resolving] . . . disputes, and to further trilateral, regional and multilateral cooperation."[118]

The NAFTA agreement signed in December 1992 was far-reaching. It extended many of the provisions of the U.S.-Canada Free Trade Agreement to Mexico and, in many aspects, went well beyond that earlier agreement. NAFTA provided for the elimination of tariffs and other trade barriers on manufactured goods, including such sensitive products as textiles, autos, and auto parts. It was intended gradually to eliminate tariffs and other trade barriers to agricultural trade. NAFTA also included significant agreements for liberalizing trade in services, including special provisions for land transportation and financial services that had previously been closed to foreign access in Mexico. It provided for a liberal investment regime that included national treatment for North American firms and elimination of performance requirements, and it opened a number of previously reserved sectors to foreign direct investment. The agreement also increased the level of intellectual property protection in Mexico. Finally, NAFTA extended the U.S.-Canadian dispute settlement system to all three countries.

NAFTA expanded the regional orientation of U.S. trade policy. At the same time, the agreement created an incentive for the completion of the Uruguay Round (see below). Furthermore, NAFTA became the opening shot in a major domestic U.S. debate linking trade issues with labor and environmental practices.

As trade with the NICs and other developing countries grew in the 1980s and 1990s, labor unions and their congressional supporters became concerned that labor practices such as the use of child and prison labor, and the denial of organizational rights to unions, gave developing countries a competitive advantage in labor-intensive production at the expense of American workers. Organized labor in the United States, and particularly their representatives in the AFL-CIO, saw linkages between trade agreements and foreign guarantees of labor rights as a way to advance the interests of their members internationally. Others supported this position because they opposed free trade generally and saw the debate over NAFTA as an opportunity to make their views known.

At the same time, environmental groups sought to use the national debate over NAFTA to advance their concerns. Some environmentalists viewed new trade agreements as opportunities to alter the environmental laws and practices of other countries. These environmentalists had previously supported congressional legislation that imposed trade sanctions on countries that violated international agreements for the protection of endangered species.

As a result of the new issues of labor and environment, securing ratification of NAFTA in the U.S. Congress was one of the more difficult tasks undertaken by the Clinton administration in its first year in office. Many in the president's own political party opposed the agreement because of concern about its effect on domestic employment. Others argued that free trade with Mexico would lead to further degradation of the environment, especially along the U.S.-Mexican border. As a candidate in 1992, Governor Clinton had criticized the agreement because it did not include labor and environmental provisions and vowed to negotiate additional agreements to cover these issues. As president in 1993, he reopened negotiations with Mexico and Canada to do so.

In the summer of 1993, the NAFTA agreement was modified to include new side agreements on environmental and labor practices. An agreement on the environment provided for the effective implementation of national environmental laws and cross-border cooperation to address pollution problems and to develop and finance border **infrastructure.** Another side agreement on workers' rights provided for the implementation of national labor laws and for cooperation on occupational, health, and safety standards, child labor, labor statistics, labor-management relations, and worker training.[119] Organized labor and some environmental groups continued to oppose even modified agreement, however. Congressional ratification of NAFTA in November 1993 was made possible only by bipartisan support for the agreement.

Following the ratification of NAFTA, a number of countries in the Western Hemisphere sought access to the new trade area. Many countries of Latin America and the Caribbean were already removing trade barriers among themselves. For example, Argentina, Brazil, Paraguay, and Uruguay formed a customs union known as Mercosur (Mercosul in Portuguese) and Mexico negotiated free trade agreements modeled loosely on NAFTA with Colombia and Venezuela. In December 1994, at the Summit of the Americas, a meeting of thirty-four democratically elected leaders of the hemisphere, the participants agreed to work toward a free trade area of the Americas by the year 2005.

Movement toward regional trade liberalization was also occurring in the Asian and Pacific region. In 1992, the six members of the Association of South East Asian Nations (ASEAN)—Brunei, Indonesia, Malaysia, Singapore, the Philippines, and Thailand—committed themselves to create a free trade area by

2003. Then in 1994, the Asia Pacific Economic Cooperation (APEC) Forum, consisting of eighteen countries bordering on the Pacific Ocean, agreed to work toward free trade and investment in the region by 2020.

Bilateralism also increased during this period. The U.S. and Japanese governments negotiated numerous bilateral accords under the MOSS, SII, and Framework agreements. These were multilateralized under the GATT's MFN rules. The EU entered into negotiations for agreements with a number of countries in the Mediterranean region.

As regional and bilateral arrangements proliferated, concern increased that the multilateral system might fragment into preferential trading blocs. While regional and bilateral agreements are appropriate ways to pursue the goal of free trade, they can become exclusive and trade-distorting if they are not constrained by a strong multilateral system. The future direction of the trading system thus depended on the ability of the major trading nations to modernize the GATT and to continue the process of multilateral liberalization.

The Tokyo Round

The Tokyo and Uruguay Rounds—the seventh and eighth rounds of multilateral trade negotiations—attempted to respond to the changed international trading system, to reform the postwar system of trade management by developing rules in new areas, and by addressing nontariff barriers to trade. The Tokyo Round, begun in 1973 and completed in 1979, started the process of trade reform.

The Tokyo Round of Multilateral Trade Negotiations (MTN) was the result of a U.S. initiative launched after the dollar crisis of 1971. Begun in 1973 in the midst of the oil crisis, deep recession, and rising protectionism, it took place in an economic and political environment less propitious than that of earlier trade negotiations. Nevertheless, its goals were more ambitious than those of earlier rounds. Previous negotiations sought to lower quotas and tariff barriers, primarily on nonagricultural products, and to implement GATT goals and rules. The Tokyo Round continued the pursuit of tariff reduction and also tried to regulate uncharted areas of international trade such as nontariff barriers; safeguards (i.e., the use of unilateral measures such as voluntary export restraint agreements); tropical products, which were of interest to developing countries; agriculture; and several sectors in which there were still unresolved problems.

In April 1979—six-and-a-half years after the first meeting in Tokyo—the multilateral trade negotiations were concluded.[120] Some of the goals of the participants had been achieved: tariffs on manufactured products were reduced; codes on certain nontariff barriers (NTBs) were drawn up; and changes were made in the application of GATT rules to the LDCs (see Chapter 7). Other efforts collapsed, including the liberalization of trade in agriculture and, most critically, the effort to regulate safeguards.

The most important outcome of the Tokyo Round was the progress made on regulating nontariff barriers to trade. The Tokyo Round agreement included several new codes that significantly modified the GATT system by extending trade management to nontariff barriers to trade. For example, the Code on Subsidies and Countervailing Duties was a step toward dealing with national industrial policies. The code recognized subsidies on manufactured products (but not raw materials) as nontariff barriers to trade. It allowed countries unilaterally to impose countervailing duties when a subsidy led to a material injury in the importing country and, with authorization from the other signatories, to impose such duties if subsidies led to injury to exports in third markets. A dumping code established comparable rules for antidumping measures. The Code on Government Procurement recognized government purchasing policies as NTBs and set rules for giving equal treatment to both national and foreign firms bidding for contracts from official entities. Although the number of government agencies covered by the code was small, it established an important precedent. Other codes covering product standards and customs valuation and licensing established rules for regulating these NTBs. The NTB codes not only established rules but also provided for surveillance and dispute settlement mechanisms. Each code set up a committee of signatories, some of which had powers only to consult (i.e., to oversee) and some of which were given dispute settlement authority.[121]

Despite the new departure signified by the NTB codes, there remained important limits to their effectiveness. Because the NTB codes applied only to the signatories, they diverged for the first time from the GATT principle of most-favored-nation status (MFN) or nondiscrimination. Whereas the developed countries signed and ratified the MTN codes, most of the developing countries were not convinced of their value and chose not to sign, thus leaving themselves open to discrimination that was legal under the GATT's rules. The codes were also incomplete. The Code on Subsidies and Countervailing Duties, for example, did not specify which forms of government intervention beyond direct export subsidies were to be considered trade barriers.[122] Even more serious was the failure to reach agreement on a safeguards code to bring rapidly proliferating VRAs under multilateral management. The pivotal, unresolvable issue in the safeguards negotiations was selectivity, the desire of some GATT contracting parties, most importantly the EU, to target safeguards measures instead of applying them on a MFN basis.[123]

The efforts to extend trade management to include agriculture also met with little success. The negotiations were unable to reconcile two opposing views of the purpose and nature of international control in agriculture. The United States, because of its competitive advantage in agriculture, advocated liberalization of agricultural trade including the modification of the European Union's CAP. The EU, on the other hand, urged the use of commodity agreements to stabilize world prices and long-term supply and refused to negotiate on the fundamentals of CAP. Japan was also unwilling to liberalize trade in agriculture. The result was thus minimal: an agreement to consult about certain agricultural problems, including those connected with meat and dairy products. The sectoral negotiations yielded only one important result: an agreement on civil aircraft that liberalizes trade in this industry. Finally, only limited progress was made on improving the GATT's dispute settlement mechanism. Thus, although the Tokyo Round agreement was an important step, it was only a limited one,[124] and it was to prove inadequate to stem the burgeoning protectionist pressures of the 1980s.

The Uruguay Round

Following the Tokyo Round, pressures on the GATT system increased. Departures from GATT rules, such as voluntary export restraints, grew; the agriculture trade war erupted; and trade conflicts became more frequent and more heated. Nevertheless, the postwar political consensus supporting open trade remained alive, if not well. The leaders of the developed countries used summit and OECD meetings to reiterate their commitment to open trade principles and to resolving specific conflicts, even as they negotiated managed-trade agreements. New forms of international dialogue were tried. Bilateral meetings, most notably between the United States and Japan, were used to try to resolve specific trade conflicts, and multilateral meetings, such as regular quadrilateral meetings of the United States, Japan, the European Union, and Canada, were begun to try to resolve systemic issues.

The precarious nature of the multilateral trading regime was revealed in 1982, when the GATT held its first ministerial meeting since the 1973 meeting that launched the Tokyo Round. The agenda of the meeting was ambitious: a review of the Tokyo codes on NTBs; action on GATT dispute-settlement procedures; continuation of the negotiations on a safeguards code; efforts to bring agriculture under the GATT regime; and consideration of new codes on trade in high technology and services. The meeting ended in failure. The ministers made virtually no progress on any issues under discussion and could pledge only to "make determined efforts" to ensure that their countries' trade policies were consistent with the GATT's rules.[125] Perhaps the most positive result of the ministerial meeting was the widening recognition that the international trading system faced collapse.

The following year, the Reagan administration, aided by the economic recovery in the United States, supported by the Prime Minister of Japan and the GATT secretariat, began a campaign to launch a new round of multilateral trade negotiations. Initially the EU, confronted with severe unemployment and recession, argued that the time was not right. However, in 1985, the world's trade officials agreed to launch a new round of multilateral trade negotiations and established a committee to develop an agenda. In September 1986, a special session of the GATT contracting parties meeting in Punta del Este, Uruguay, officially launched the negotiations, which came to be known as the Uruguay Round and set a target date of 1990 for their completion. The Uruguay Round negotiations began in 1987.

The ministerial declaration issued at Punta del Este instituted a standstill on new trade-restrictive or distorting measures and called for the elimination by the end of the Uruguay Round of measures inconsistent with the provisions of the GATT. The trade ministers also established fifteen negotiating groups that fell into four broad categories.

One group focused on issues that had been taken up in earlier negotiating rounds, including those (such as tariffs) that had long been on the GATT agenda as well as others (such as subsidies and safeguards) that had not been resolved satisfactorily in the Tokyo Round. Most important, and perhaps most difficult, among these issues were safeguards. As we have seen, the GATT rules on safeguards were ineffective and relatively easy to circumvent through new protectionist measures, such as voluntary restraint agreements (VRAs). Although the 1986 ministerial declaration called for "a comprehensive agreement on safeguards," the political difficulty of reaching such an agreement remained significant. As in the Tokyo Round, the central conflict centered on selectivity. The EU insisted on the need for selectivity. The United States advocated safeguards taken either on a most-favored-nation or "consensual selectivity" basis. The developing countries—for whom the safeguards negotiations were a top priority in the Uruguay Round—strongly advocated the most-favored-nation position.

A second set of negotiations focused on concerns of developing countries, such as tropical products, natural resource–based products, textiles, and clothing. Due to the increasingly active role of the developing countries in the GATT, successful completion of these negotiations was essential to their continued involvement in the GATT system (see Chapter 7).

A third set of negotiating groups had mandates to reform existing GATT rules or mechanisms. Dissatisfaction with existing GATT dispute settlement mechanisms had been mounting for years. Countries were able to delay or block resolution of a dispute; there was no effective mechanism for enforcing decisions or overseeing their implementation; and protection of third countries affected by the dispute was inadequate. The ministerial declaration at Punta del Este instructed the negotiating group on dispute settlement to "improve and strengthen the rules and procedures of the dispute settlement process." Negotiations moved rapidly in this negotiating group due to broad agreement on the need to expedite dispute settlement procedures and to the absence of any significant North-South division. By the end of 1988, negotiators had agreed on several measures to streamline procedures and speed up decisions in the dispute settlement process. These reforms were implemented on a provisional basis in 1989.

The negotiations on the functioning of the GATT system (FOGS) were intended to strengthen the role of GATT as an institution. The negotiating group focused on ways to enhance GATT surveillance of trade policies and practices; to improve the overall effectiveness and decision making of the GATT by involving ministers; and to strengthen the GATT's relationship with the IMF and World Bank. Because there was a significant degree of consensus on what needed to be done, negotiations on FOGS proceeded smoothly. By the end of 1988, agreement was reached on the establishment of a new trade policy review mechanism to examine and publicize national trade policies on a regular basis. Negotiators agreed to begin implementing this mechanism in 1989 rather than wait until the conclusion of the Uruguay Round.

Finally, some groups sought to broaden the scope of the GATT to cover nontraditional areas. One of the most significant and controversial decisions made at Punta del Este was the agreement to include the so-called new issues—services, intellectual property rights, and investment—in the round. The opposition to their inclusion was led by a small group of developing countries, which feared that GATT rules developed for the new issues could be used by the industrialized countries to overwhelm their fledgling industries and to undermine domestic policies that the developing countries considered critical to their national economic development. They argued that the Uruguay Round should concentrate instead on unfinished business from the Tokyo Round and on reform in areas where the GATT had clearly failed to impose adequate international discipline, such as safeguards, textiles, and agriculture. They also insisted that the GATT was not the appropriate forum for the new issues that, they argued, came under the purview of other organizations, such as WIPO for intellectual property or the United Nations for investment.

The industrialized nations stressed the need to modernize the GATT by broadening its scope to deal with new areas of trade. As in previous GATT rounds, the United States took the initiative in pushing aggressively for the inclusion of services, intellectual property rights, and investment in the Uruguay Round. The EU and Japan supported the U.S. position, but they were not entirely convinced of the wisdom of increasing the burden of the GATT at a time when so many longstanding problems had yet to be resolved. They also shared some of the concerns of the developing countries about the extent to which GATT rules in the new areas might impinge on their sovereignty in domestic regulation and government policy. In the case of investment in particular, they questioned the appropriateness of using the GATT as the forum for management. Finally, while there was a consensus among the developed countries about the principles that would cover some of the new issues (especially services and intellectual property), it proved difficult to come to agreement on specific details of the application of those principles.

Over the years considerable progress was made toward agreement on various matters under negotiation. Yet, by 1993, the Uruguay Round seemed headed toward failure. At the beginning of the talks, it looked as if the main conflict would be between the rich and poor nations. But as the 1980s wore on, most of the developing nations moved toward more **export-oriented development** strategies that depended upon an expansion of overseas markets which would only be possible with a new trade agreement. At the same time, important lines of cleavage developed among the industrialized nations. Disagreements over agricultural subsidies were the most contentious and almost resulted in the failure of the Uruguay Round. At the beginning of the Uruguay Round, the U.S. government ambitiously proposed phasing out all direct farm subsidies and farm trade protection within a decade. The Cairns group—a coalition of fourteen smaller producing nations from both developed and developing regions (including Argentina, Australia, Canada, Hungary, and Malaysia among others)—advocated a similar approach. The EU accepted the need to reduce subsidies, but viewed the U.S. proposal as highly unrealistic, advocating instead an approach that would allow it to maintain its Common Agricultural Policy. Japan also opposed the U.S. proposal, but generally tried to keep a low profile.

At a midterm review of the Uruguay Round in Montreal in December 1988, the agricultural disagreements, combined with similar ones in textiles, intellectual property, and safeguards, resulted in a suspension of talks until April 1989, when the United States and the EU agreed to procedural arrangements for continuing discussions on agriculture. The April 1989 understanding did not last long, however, and the stalemate over agriculture produced a total breakdown in talks at the GATT ministerial meeting in Brussels in December 1990. At the Brussels meeting, a compromise on agriculture was proposed by the Dutch and Swedish delegations. Their proposal was to cut border restrictions, domestic subsidies, and export subsidies by 30 percent over a five-year period from a 1990 base. The United States and the Cairns Group accepted the proposal as a basis for negotiations, but it was rejected by the EU, Japan, and South Korea.

Finally, in December 1991, GATT Director General Arthur Dunkel circulated a comprehensive draft agreement that he hoped would get the negotiations back on track. The Dunkel draft omitted elements of previous draft treaties, including commitments regarding tariffs, services trade, and government procurement. It was initially rejected by the EU because of the way it dealt with agricultural subsidies. It took two more years to negotiate a final agreement, but when it finally emerged, the Dunkel text "survived with surprisingly few changes."[126]

The last two years of the Uruguay Round negotiations were marked by continued disagreements on agriculture, increasingly within the EU. A series of reforms for the CAP were proposed in January 1991 by the Commissioner for Agriculture, Ray MacSharry, to reduce price supports while at the same time continuing to protect small farmers in Europe.[127] In May 1992, the Council of the EU reached agreement on the MacSharry proposals, thus easing somewhat the tensions behind the U.S.-European disputes over agricultural subsidies. The United States and the EU negotiated an accord in November 1992 at Blair House in Washington on agricultural subsidies, but the election campaigns of that year got in the way of concluding the agreement.

After taking office in 1993, the newly elected U.S. president, Bill Clinton, made the completion of the Uruguay Round a high priority for his administration, especially after securing ratification of NAFTA. Clinton asked for and received "fast-track" negotiating authority from Congress that expired on December 15, 1993. In addition, Clinton administration initiatives in convening a meeting to promote Asia Pacific Economic Cooperation (APEC) in Seattle, Washington, in November 1993 had the desired effect of raising fears in Europe that the United States would proceed without Europe if necessary to secure new arrangements for trade. U.S. initiatives, together with the appointment of Peter Sutherland as the new GATT secretary general, created the impetus for a successful resolution of the remaining differences between the United States and the EU.

Between December 1 and December 15, 1993, negotiations were conducted in earnest for the completion of the Uruguay Round. A number of breakthroughs occurred on agricultural subsidies. The Blair House accord had proposed a reduction of subsidies by 21 percent over six years. On December 6, the United States and the EU agreed to more limited subsidy reductions, even though the French delegation continued to hold out for even more limited action. The French government also threatened to veto the agreement if it did not provide protection for the European film, television, and financial services industries. The tiff over services was dealt with by deferring the deadline for negotiations, but the only way to satisfy the French government on the film and television industries and to secure agreement prior to the December 15 deadline was for the United States and the EU to agree to remove "audio-visual services" from the final draft of the GATT agreement. Director General Sutherland then declared the Uruguay Round successfully concluded on December 15. The agreement was signed by delegates from 124 countries on April 15, 1994, in Marrakesh, Morocco, and entered into force on January 1, 1995.

The agreement signed at Marrakesh was a 400-page document accompanied by roughly 22,000 pages of detailed tariff schedules. It provided for further cuts in tariffs, significant reductions in agricultural subsidies, elimination of textile and apparel quotas over ten years, new trade rules for services, intellectual property, and trade-related investment. It included new procedures for the settlement of disputes, and it established a new entity called the World Trade Organization (WTO) in Geneva, which would assume the functions of the old GATT Secretariat.

The Uruguay Round Agreement

The most comprehensive of all GATT trade agreements, the Uruguay Round agreement broke new ground in a number of areas. It improved market access in many sectors by reducing tariff and nontariff barriers. The agreement cut tariffs on manufactured products by over one-third. It provided for the gradual elimination of the Multi-Fiber Arrangement (MFA) under which quotas were imposed limiting developing country textile exports to developing countries. The Uruguay Round agreement also expanded the number of agencies and products covered by the government procurement code negotiated in the Tokyo Round.

The agreement also extended the world trade regime to agriculture in a meaningful way for the first time. While many agricultural barriers remained, the agreement improved market access for many agricultural products. It provided for the elimination of quotas and their replacement by tariffs (known as **tariffication**), which in turn could be reduced over time in a straightforward manner. The agreement also established limits on export and agricultural subsidies that distort trade.

The process of rules development begun in the Tokyo Round was expanded. Although the Uruguay Round agreement did not eliminate the use of antidumping laws as a nontariff barrier, it did improve the code on antidumping measures to improve transparency, and suggested new and better methods for measuring the extent of dumping and new procedural rules to prevent the abuse of national antidumping laws. The Round's Agreement on Subsidies and Countervailing Measures significantly improved the Tokyo Round code by expanding the list of prohibited practices, increasing the disciplines on subsidies, and broadening the coverage to all GATT members. The Uruguay Round also included an Agreement on Safeguards, which defined when countries may impose temporary restrictions to deal with surges in imports that threaten serious injury to a domestic industry.

The Uruguay Round also modernized the international trading system by establishing rules for new issues: services, intellectual property, and investment. The agreement applied the traditional rules of international trade, including national treatment and MFN, to services and provided for greater market access in many service sectors, including advertising, accounting, engineering, finance, information and computer services, and tourism. However, in telecommunications and financial services transport, for example, negotiators were unable to reach agreement and the negotiations remained open. The negotiations on trade-related intellectual property (TRIP) led to the establishment of comprehensive trade rules to protect copyrights, patents, trademarks, and industrial designs. The agreement incorporated national treatment and MFN and dealt with such problems as compulsory licensing. However, to satisfy the developing countries, it allowed for relatively long periods for phasing in the new rules.

The agreement on trade-related investment measures (TRIM) took a first step toward developing international rules on investment. It prohibited measures such as local content, trade balancing, and foreign exchange balancing requirements. The TRIM agreement was incomplete, however, because even though it did apply national treatment principles, it did not include MFN provisions and did not cover the important questions connected with right of establishment and investment incentives.

The Uruguay Round agreement modernized the GATT's procedures. For example, it improved the dispute settlement mechanism by making it faster and more decisive. It gave the newly created World Trade Organization new authority to monitor and enforce compliance with WTO rules and decisions. Under the agreement, the GATT was transformed from a treaty to a permanent organization, the WTO, thus filling the gap left by the failure of the Havana Charter's ITO. The agreement established a new structure, rules, and procedures for the WTO.[128]

Conclusion

The vitality of the multilateral and liberal trade regime will depend on the continuing development of effective forms of collective management. Central to a strong multilateral system is the effective implementation of the Uruguay Round Agreements and a strong World Trade Organization. A multilateral commitment to making new features in the WTO, like the dispute settlement mechanism, work successfully is key, as is the ability of the WTO to address new issues, like the relationship between trade and labor standards, trade and environment, and trade and competition policy. Major players must play by the rules if the multilateral system is to remain the cornerstone of the international trade regime. Economic power is now more dispersed than it was at the end of World War II. The United States as the largest (although no longer the dominant) member will have to continue to provide leadership for the system. This will be possible only if the United States can redress its trade imbalance, revitalize its competitiveness and thus resist protectionist pressures. At the same time, Europe and Japan must define new, more active roles in trade management. Europe will have to find the appropriate balance between looking inward toward creating an internal market and outward toward defending the multilateral trading system. Because of Japan's economic strength and its important role in world trade, it needs to work harder at reestablishing a reasonable balance of trade, as well as integrating itself better into the management of the international trading system. Collective management in forums like the annual economic summits of the G-7 countries can be used to avoid the sort of long-term feuds on trade that characterized the Uruguay Round. Finally, the global trade regime will need to adapt to the evolving role of new players (see Chapters 7 and 10). The rapidly growing NICs must assume greater responsibility for the effective functioning of the system. Furthermore, those developing countries, as well as the fledgling democratic regimes of the formerly communist countries, which have not yet fully joined the system, should be brought more fully into it.

NOTES

1. E. E. Schattschneider, *Politics, Pressures and the Tariff* (Englewood Cliffs, N.J.: Prentice-Hall, 1935). See also Robert A. Pastor, *Congress and the Politics of U.S. Foreign Economic Policy, 1929–1976* (Berkeley and Los Angeles: University of California Press, 1976); and Stephanie Ann Lenway, *The Politics of U.S. International Trade: Protection, Expansion and Escape* (Marshfield, Mass.: Pitman, 1985).

2. The analysis in this chapter concentrates on trade relations among developed market economies. For issues involving the underdeveloped countries, see Chapter 6 of this text; for East-West trade issues, see Chapter 10.

3. See, for example, Richard N. Gardner, *Sterling-Dollar Diplomacy in Current Perspective: The Origins and Prospects of Our International Economic Order* (New York: Columbia University Press, 1980), p. 9; and Walter LaFeber, *The American Age: U.S. Foreign Policy at Home and Abroad*, vol. 2, 2nd ed. (New York: Norton, 1994), 372–373.

4. Richard Gardner, *Sterling-Dollar Diplomacy*, 102.

5. LaFeber, *The American Age*, 374–375; Henry J. Tasca, *The Reciprocal Trade Policy of the United States* (Philadelphia: University of Pennsylvania Press, 1938); Kenneth A. Oye, *Economic Discrimination and Political Exchange: World Political Economy in the 1930s and 1980s* (Princeton: Princeton University Press, 1992), 91–102; and Carolyn Rhodes, *Reciprocity, U.S. Trade Policy, and the GATT Regime* (Ithaca, N.Y.: Cornell University Press, 1993), ch. 3.

6. U.S. Department of State, *Proposals for the Expansion of World Trade and Employment* (December 1945); and U.S. Department of State, *Suggested Charter for an International Trade Organization of the United Nations* (September 1946).

7. Gardner, *Sterling-Dollar Diplomacy*; Clair Wilcox, *A Charter for World Trade* (New York: Macmillan, 1949). The trade charter was not exclusively an American idea; British planners were also closely involved in the process. See E. F. Penrose, *Economic Planning for the Peace* (Princeton: Princeton University Press, 1953).

8. Quoted in Judith Goldstein, "Creating the GATT Rules: Politics, Institutions, and American Policy," in John G. Ruggie, ed., *Multilateralism Matters: The Theory and Praxis of an Institutional Form* (New York: Columbia University Press, 1993), 216.

9. A trade preference offers lower tariffs on imports from a specified country or group of countries. By its nature, a trade preference violates the principle of "most favored nation," a principle of nondiscrimination among trading partners in the setting of tariff levels.

10. See Gardner, *Sterling-Dollar Diplomacy*, chs. 8 and 17; Wilcox, *A Charter for World Trade*; Committee for Economic Development, Research, and Policy Committee, *The United States and The European Community: Policies for a Changing World Economy* (New York: CED, November 1971); and John H. Jackson, *The World Trading System: Law and Policy of International Economic Relations* (Cambridge: MIT Press, 1989), 32–34.

11. Gardner, *Sterling-Dollar Diplomacy*, ch. 17; and William Diebold, Jr., *The End of the ITO* (Princeton: International Finance Section, Department of Economics and Social Institutions, Princeton University, 1952).

12. Jackson, *The World Trading System*, 33.

13. Kenneth W. Dam, *The GATT: Law and International Economic Organization* (Chicago: University of Chicago Press, 1970), 392.

14. Ibid., 396–397.

15. Peter B. Kenen, *The International Economy*, 3rd ed. (New York: Cambridge University Press, 1994), 247. In the GATT commercial code, dumping is defined as pricing exported goods lower than in the domestic market of the exporting country.

16. Market power—usually created by having few or no competitors—allows firms to take advantage of the "rents" (supernormal profits) that accrue to monopoly or oligopoly producers.

17. The GATT commercial code originally addressed only export subsidies, not subsidies in general; ibid., p. 249.

18. Dale E. Hathaway, *Agriculture and the GATT: Rewriting the Rules* (Washington: Institute for International Economics, September 1987), 103–113; Judith Goldstein, "The Impact of Ideas on Trade Policy: The Origins of U.S. Agricultural and Manufacturing Policies," *International Organization* 43 (winter 1989): 31–71; and Judith Goldstein, *Ideas Interests, and American Trade Policy* (Ithaca, N.Y.: Cornell University Press, 1993).

19. Jackson, *The World Trading System*, 303.

20. For an interesting discussion of the evolution of thinking about reciprocity in U.S. trade policy, see Caroline Rhodes, *Reciprocity, U.S. Trade Policy, and the GATT Regime*, 8–12. See also Robert Keohane, "Reciprocity in International Relations," *International Organization* 40 (winter 1986), 1–28.

21. See Richard Blackhurst, "Reciprocity in Trade Negotiations under Flexible Exchange Rates," in John P. Martin and Alasdair Smith, eds., *Trade and Payments Adjustment under Flexible Exchange Rates* (London: Macmillan, 1979), 224.

22. For an analysis of the process of making trade policy during this period, see Raymond A. Bauer, Ithiel de Sola Pool, and Lewis Anthony Dexter, *American Business and Public Policy: The Politics of Foreign Trade* (Chicago: Aldine, Atherton, 1972).

23. I. M. Destler, *American Trade Politics: System Under Stress* (Washington: Institute for International Economics, 1986), 9–36.

24. William Diebold, Jr., *Trade and Payments in Western Europe: A Study in Economic Cooperation, 1947–1951* (New York: Harper and Row, 1952); Robert Triffin, *Europe and the Money Muddle: From Bilateralism to Near Convertibility, 1947–1956* (New Haven: Yale University Press, 1957); Hadley Arkes, *Bureaucracy, the Marshall Plan, and the National Interest* (Princeton: Princeton University Press, 1973); Imanuel Wexler, *The Marshall Plan Revisited: The European Recovery Program in Economic Perspective* (Westport, Conn.: Greenwood, 1983); and Daniel Verdier, *Democracy and International Trade: Britain, France, and the United States, 1860–1990* (Princeton: Princeton University Press, 1994), 203–213.

25. Robert S. Ozaki, *The Control of Imports and Foreign Capital in Japan* (New York: Praeger, 1972), 5–9; Warren S. Hunsberger, *Japan and the United States in World Trade* (New York: Harper and Row, 1964); and Theodore Cohen, *Remaking Japan: The American Occupation as New Deal* (New York: Free Press, 1987).

26. For example, see Gardner Patterson, *Discrimination in International Trade: The Policy Issues, 1945–1965* (Princeton: Princeton University Press, 1966); and Karin Kock, *International Trade Policy and the GATT, 1947–1967*, Stockholm Economic Studies XI (Stockholm: Almquist and Wiksell, 1969).

27. John W. Evans, *The Kennedy Round in American Trade Policy: The Twilight of the GATT?* (Cambridge: Harvard University Press, 1971), 282. For other studies of the Kennedy Round, see Ernest H. Preeg, *Traders and Diplomats: An Analysis of the Kennedy Round Negotiations Under the General Agreement on Tariffs and Trade* (Washington: Brookings Institution, 1970); and Thomas B. Curtis and John R. Vastine, *The Kennedy Round and the Future of American Trade* (New York: Praeger, 1971).

28. Robert E. Baldwin, *Non-Tariff Distortions of International Trade* (Washington: Brookings Institution, 1970), 1.

29. *Economic Report of the President* (Washington: U.S. Government Printing Office, 1995), 205.

30. Richard N. Cooper, *The Economics of Interdependence: Economic Policy in the Atlantic Community* (New York: McGraw-Hill, 1968), 59–80.

31. General Agreement on Tariffs and Trade, *International Trade, 1986–1987* (Geneva: GATT, 1987), 158; and General Agreement on Tariffs and Trade, *International Trade, 1990–1991*, vol. 2 (Geneva: GATT, 1991), 78.

32. Allen Sinai, "The 'Global' Factor and the U.S. Economy," *Economic Studies Series*, no. 27, Shearson Lehman Brothers (October 6, 1987), 1.

33. *New York Times*, May 5, 1988, p. 1.

34. Council on Competitiveness, *Competitiveness Index: Trends, Background Data, and Methodology* (Washington: Council on Competitiveness, 1988), Appendix II.

35. Ibid.

36. Information downloaded from the World Wide Web pages of the Bureau of Labor Statistics of the U.S. Department of Labor at http://stats.bls.gov. The specific document was entitled "Productivity and Costs: First Quarter 1995" and may also be found on the BLS gopher server at gopher://stats.bls.gov.

37. "Riding High: Corporate America Now Has an Edge Over Its Global Rivals," *Business Week*, October 9, 1995, 134. Despite the title, the data portrayed on p. 140 tell a different story.

38. See Richard Blackhurst, Nicolas Marian, and Jan Tumlir, *Adjustment, Trade, and Growth in Developed and Developing Countries*, GATT Studies in International Trade, no. 6 (Geneva: General Agreement on Tariffs and Trade, 1978); and William Diebold, Jr., "Adapting Economics to Structural Change: The International Aspect," *International Affairs* (London) 54 (October 1978): 573–588.

39. Paul R. Krugman and George N. Hatsopoulos, "The Problem of U.S. Competitiveness in Manufacturing," *New England Economic Review* (January/February 1987): 22; Organization for Economic Development and Cooperation, *OECD Economic Outlook*, 42 (Paris: OECD, December 1987), 41, 178; Stephen Cohen and John Zysman, *Manufacturing Matters* (New York: Basic Books, 1987), ch. 5; and Jeffrey Hart, *Rival Capitalists: International Competitiveness in the United States, Japan, and Western Europe* (Ithaca, N.Y.: Cornell University Press, 1992), ch. 1.

40. See Susan Strange, "The Management of Surplus Capacity: or How Does Theory Stand Up to Protectionism 1970s Style?" *International Organization* 33 (summer 1979): 573–588; Peter Cowhey and Edward Long, "Testing Theories of Regime Change: Hegemonic Decline or Surplus Capacity?" *International Organization* 37 (spring 1983): 157–188; and Hart, *Rival Capitalists*, 12–25.

41. Michael Borrus, *Competing for Control* (Cambridge, Mass.: Ballinger, 1990).

42. *Economic Report of the President* (Washington: Government Printing Office, 1988), 373, 374; and GATT, *International Trade, 1986–1987*, 10. Unemployment figures are for the G-7 countries.

43. *OECD Economic Outlook*, 42 (December 1987), 174, 184.

44. Ibid., 190.

45. International Monetary Fund, *World Economic Outlook* (Washington: IMF, October 1993), Statistical Appendix, table A21. The figures cited are based on averages of growth in world exports and imports.

46. *OECD Economic Outlook*, 42 (December 1987), 184.

47. Ibid., 174.

48. Ibid., 190.

49. U.S. Department of Labor, Bureau of Labor Statistics.

50. International Monetary Fund, *Annual Report, 1987* (Washington: IMF, 1987), 16.

51. *OECD Economic Outlook*, 42 (December 1987), 174, 184.

52. *OECD Economic Outlook*, 42 (December 1987), 5, 28.

53. From this point on, we will be using **European Union** or its acronym **EU** to refer to the what was called initially the European Economic Community (EEC) and then later the European Community (EC). We will revert to the older names and acronyms wherever that is historically appropriate or where to do otherwise would be confusing.

54. International Monetary Fund, *Direction of Trade Annual, 1960–1964*; IMF, *Direction of Trade Annual, 1970–1974*; and Gabriel Stern and Tamim Bayoumi, *Regional Trading Blocs, Mobile Capital, and Exchange Rate Coordination*, Bank of England, Working Paper Series no. 12, April 1993, 9.

55. Ibid.

56. Ibid.

57. See Jacob Viner, *The Customs Union Issue, Studies in the Administration of International Law and Organization*, vol. 10 (New York: Carnegie Endowment for International Peace, 1950).

58. John Ravenhill, *Collective Clientelism: The Lomҫ Conventions and North-South Relations* (New York: Columbia University Press, 1985); and Enzo R. Grilli, *The European Community and the Developing Countries* (New York: Cambridge University Press, 1993), ch. 4.

59. See Paolo Cecchini, ed., *The European Challenge, 1992: The Benefits of a Single Market* (Hants, England: Wildwood House, 1988); Lord Cockfield, *White Paper on Completing the Internal Market* (Brussels: Commission of the European Community, 1985); Jacques Pelkmans and Alan Winters, *Europe's Domestic Market*, Chatham House paper no. 43, Royal Institute of International Affairs (London: Routledge, 1988); Michael Calingaert, *The 1992 Challenge from Europe: Development of the European Community's Internal Market* (Washington: National Planning Association, 1988); Gary Clyde Hufbauer, ed., *Europe 1992: An American Perspective* (Washington: Brookings Institution, 1990); David R. Cameron, "The 1992 Initiative: Causes and Consequences," in Alberta M. Sbragia, ed., *Europolitics: Institutions and Policymaking in the "New" European Community* (Washington: Brookings Institution, 1992); Wayne Sandholtz and John Zysman, "1992: Recasting the European Bargain," *World Politics* 42 (1989): 95–128; and Wayne Sandholtz, *High-Tech Europe* (Berkeley: University of California Press, 1992).

60. Keizai Koho Center, *Japan 1987: An International Comparison* (Tokyo: Japan Institute for Social and Economic Affairs, April 30, 1987), 9; and World Bank, *World Development Report, 1994* (Washington: 1994).

61. International Monetary Fund, *Direction of Trade Statistics Yearbook, 1994* (Washington: IMF, 1994).

62. See Edward Denison and William Chung, "Economic Growth and Its Sources," in Hugh Patrick and Henry Rosovsky, eds., *Asia's New Giant* (Washington: Brookings Institution, 1976), 63–151.

63. Philip H. Trezise and Yukio Suzuki, "Politics, Government, and Economic Growth in Japan," in Patrick and Rosovsky, op. cit., 753–811; and Chalmers Johnson, *MITI and the Japanese Miracle* (Stanford, Calif.: Stanford University Press, 1982).

64. Mark Mason, *American Multinationals and Japan: The Political Economy of Japanese Capital Controls, 1899–1980* (Cambridge: Harvard University Press, 1992); and Dennis Encarnation, *Rivals Beyond Trade: America versus Japan in Global Competition* (Ithaca, N.Y.: Cornell University Press, 1992).

65. There is some controversy as to whether the Japanese case represents "export-led" growth or not. On this debate, see Lawrence B. Krause and Sueo Sekiguchi, "Japan and the World Economy," in Patrick and Rosovsky, op. cit., 397–410; and Shigeto Tsuru, *Japan's Capitalism: Creative Defeat and Beyond* (New York: Cambridge University Press, 1993), ch. 3.

66. Edward J. Lincoln, *Japan Facing Economic Maturity* (Washington: Brookings Institution, 1988), 14–68.

67. Ezra Vogel, *Comeback Case by Case: Building the Resurgence of American Business* (New York: Simon and Schuster, 1985); and Richard Samuels, *The Business of the Japanese State: Energy Markets in Comparative and Historical Perspective* (Ithaca, N.Y.: Cornell University Press, 1987).

68. C. Fred Bergsten and William R. Cline, *The United States-Japan Economic Problem* (Washington: Institute for International Economics, 1987), 53–119.

69. International Monetary Fund, *Direction of Trade Statistics Yearbook 1987* (Washington: IMF, 1987), 243, 245; *Direction of Trade Statistics Yearbook 1988* (Washington: IMF, 1988), 243; and *Direction of Trade Statistics Yearbook 1995* (Washington: IMF, 1995).

70. Bureau of Economic Analysis, *Survey of Current Business* (Washington: Department of Commerce, July 1984), 60; and *Survey of Current Business*, May 1988, 11.

71. On this subject, see Ronald Dore, *Flexible Rigidities* (Stanford, Calif.: Stanford University Press, 1986), 79; Michael Gerlach, *Alliance Capitalism: The Social Organization of Japanese Business Networks* (Berkeley, Calif.: University of California Press, 1989); Marie Achordoguy, *Computers, Inc. Japan's Challenge to IBM* (Cambridge: Harvard University Press, 1989); Robert Z. Lawrence, "Efficient or Exclusionist? The Import Behavior of Japanese Corporate Groups," *Brookings Papers on Economic Activity*, 1 (1991), 311–330; and Laura D'Andrea Tyson, *Who's Bashing Whom?* (Washington: Institute for International Economics, 1992), 56–57.

72. In recent years, the U.S. bilateral trade deficit with Japan has decreased with the devaluation of the dollar against the yen, especially after 1993, when the Clinton administration adopted a policy of not intervening in currency markets to support the dollar's value against the yen. The trade deficit was cut substantially but still remained high enough to continue to be a source of concern to both countries.

73. See Clyde V. Prestowitz, Jr., *Trading Places: How America Allowed Japan to Take the Lead* (New York: Basic Books, 1988); and Karel van Wolferen, *The Enigma of Japanese Power* (London: Macmillan, 1989).

74. C. Fred Bergsten and William R. Cline, *The United States–Japan Economic Problem* (Washington: Institute for International Economics, 1987), 53–119.

75. These are generally agreements to restrict exports, called voluntary export restraints (VERs). VERs were used to get around the GATT restrictions on quantitative import restrictions. VRAs were "voluntary" on the part of both the exporter and the importer and therefore did not violate GATT norms of reciprocity, whereas in actuality the effects of the VRAs were virtually indistinguishable from those of unilaterally imposed quantitative import restrictions. That is, they tended to raise the price of the goods subject to VERs in the country of destination because demand remained relatively constant while supply diminished.

76. See Makoto Kuroda, "Japan's Trade Surplus Is Declining Fast," *Amex Bank Review* 15 (March 24, 1988), 2–3.

77. International Monetary Fund, *International Financial Statistics Yearbook 1985* (Washington: IMF, 1985); and International Monetary Fund, *Direction of Trade Statistics Yearbook* (Washington: IMF, 1995), 3.

78. *International Financial Statistics Yearbook, 1985*; *International Financial Statistics*, April 1988 (Washington: IMF 1985 and 1988).

79. *OECD Economic Outlook*, 42 (December 1987), 41.

80. Council on Competitiveness, *Competitiveness Index*, Special Supplement, May 1988, 7.

81. National Science Foundation, National Science Board, *Science and Engineering Indicators* (Washington: Government Printing Office, 1993), 455.

82. *OECD Economic Outlook*, 42 (December 1987), 70.

83. See I. M. Destler, *American Trade Politics: System Under Stress* (Washington: Institute for International Economics, 1986).

84. This was the origin of the tightened antidumping and unfair trade laws of the 1970s and 1980s. See Stephen Woolcock, Jeffrey Hart, and Hans van der Ven, *Interdependence in the Postmultilateral Era* (Lanham, Md.: University Press of America, 1985). See also Richard Boltuck and Robert E. Litan, eds., *Down in the Dumps: Administration of the Unfair Trade Laws* (Washington: Brookings Institution, 1991); J. Michael Finger, ed., *Antidumping: How It Works and Who Gets Hurt* (Ann Arbor: University of Michigan Press, 1993); and Pietro S. Nivola, *Regulating Unfair Trade* (Washington: Brookings Institution, 1993).

85. On the politics of supporters of free trade, see I. M. Destler and John S. Odell, *Anti-Protection: Changing Forces in the United States Trade Politics* (Washington: Institute for International Economics, September 1987); and Helen V. Milner, *Resisting Protectionism: Global Industries and the Politics of International Trade* (Princeton: Princeton University Press, 1988).

86. Helen V. Milner and David B. Yoffie, "Between Free Trade and Protectionism: Strategic Trade Policy and a Theory of Corporate Trade Demands," *International Organization* 43 (spring 1989): 239–272.

87. See Prestowitz, *Trading Places*, op. cit.

88. Tyson, *Who's Bashing Whom?*, 58–66; and Edward J. Lincoln, *Japan's Unequal Trade* (Washington: Brookings Institution, 1990).

89. Geza Feketekuty, *International Trade in Services: An Overview and Blueprint for Negotiations* (Cambridge, Mass: Ballinger, 1988), especially ch. 9.

90. See the discussion of "tariffication" in the section above that deals with the Uruguay Round negotiations.

91. See William Diebold Jr., ed., *Bilateralism, Multilateralism and Canada in U.S. Trade Policy* (Cambridge, Mass.: Ballinger, 1988); Jeffrey J. Schott and Murray G. Smith, eds., *The Canada–United States Free Trade Agreement: The Global Impact* (Washington: Institute for International Economics, 1988); and Paul Wonnacott, *The United States and Canada: The Quest for Free Trade* (Washington: Institute for International Economics, 1987).

92. Robert E. Baldwin, *Non-Tariff Distortions of International Trade* (Washington: Brookings Institution, 1970); William Diebold, Jr., *The United States and the Industrial World: American Foreign Policy in the 1970s* (New York: Praeger, 1972), 123–140; J. M. Finger, H. K. Hall and D. R. Nelson, "The Political Economy of Administered Protection," *The American Economic Review*, 72 (1982): 452–466; Stanley D. Metzger, *Lowering Non-Tariff Barriers: U.S. Law, Practice and Negotiating Objectives* (Washington: Brookings Institution, 1974); and Jagdish Bhagwati, Protectionism (Cambridge: MIT Press, 1988), ch. 3.

93. See 97th Cong., 2d sess., *The Mercantilist Challenge to the Liberal International Trade Order*, a study prepared for the use of the Joint Economic Committee, Congress of the United States, December 29, 1982 (Washington: Government Printing Office, 1982), 8–31.

94. See Brian Hindley and Eri Nicolaides, *Taking the New Protectionism Seriously*, Thames Essay No. 34 (London: Trade Policy Research Centre, 1983); and Michael Borrus, "The Politics of Competitive Erosion in the U.S. Steel Industry," in John Zysman and Laura D'Andrea Tyson, eds., *American Industry in International Competition* (Ithaca, N.Y.: Cornell University Press, 1983).

95. Ingo Walter, "Structural Adjustment and Trade Policy in the International Steel Industry," in William R. Cline, Trade Policy in the 1980s, 497–500; Gary C. Hufbauer and Diane T. Berliner, and Kimberly A. Elliot, *Trade Protection in the United States: 31 Case Studies* (Washington: Institute for International Economics, 1986), 156, 176; Ingo Walter, "Structural Adjustment and Trade Policy in the International Steel Industry," in Cline, *Trade Policy in the 1980s*, 489.

96. Hufbauer et al., 170–173.

97. General Agreements on Tariffs and Trade, *International Trade 1986–1987*, 29.

98. See Robert B. Cohen, "The Prospects for Trade and Protectionism in the Auto Industry," in Cline, *Trade Policy in the 1980s* (Washington: Institute for International Economics, 1983), 527–563; Gary C. Hufbauer et al. 249–262.

99. See Paul R. Krugman, ed., *Strategic Trade Policy and the New International Economics* (Cambridge: MIT Press, 1986).

100. This is the view of the Cambridge Economic Policy Group; see their journal, the *Cambridge Economic Policy Review*.

101. Albert Bressand, "Mastering the World Economy," *Foreign Affairs* 16, no. 4 (spring 1983): 747–772.

102. By 1991, the CAP built up surpluses of over 20 million tons of cereals, 1 million tons of milk, and 750,000 tons of beef. Nicholas Hopkins, *Completing the GATT Uruguay Round: Renewed Multilateralism or a World of Regional Trading Blocs?*, Wilton Park Paper 61 (London: Her Majesty's Stationery Office, 1992), 9.

103. Robert B. Reich, "Beyond Free Trade," *Foreign Affairs* 16, no. 4 (spring 1983): 773–804. See also Stephen S. Cohen and John Zysman, *Manufacturing Matters: The Myth of the Post-Industrial Economy* (New York: Basic Books for the Council on Foreign Relations, 1987).

104. See Raymond Hopkins and Donald F. Puchala, eds., "The Global Political Economy of Food," *International Organization* 32 (summer 1978): entire issue.

105. Dale E. Hathaway, *Agriculture and the GATT: Rewriting the Rules* (Washington: Institute for International Economics, September 1987), 43.

106. See Robert L. Paarlberg, *Fixing Farm Trade: Policy Options for the United States* (Cambridge: Ballinger Publishing for the Council on Foreign Relations, 1988), 13–40.

107. David C. Mowery, *International Collaborative Ventures in U.S. Manufacturing* (Cambridge, Mass.: Ballinger, 1988); Steven S. Wildman and Stephen E. Siwek, *International Trade in Films and Television Programs* (Cambridge, Mass.: Ballinger, 1988); Lawrence J. White,

International Trade in Ocean Shipping Services (Cambridge, Mass.: Ballinger, 1988); Ingo Walter, *Global Competition in Financial Services: Market Structure, Protection, and Trade Liberalization* (Cambridge, Mass.: Ballinger, 1988); Thierry J. Noyelle and Anna B. Dutka, *International Trade in Business Services: Accounting, Advertising, Law, and Management Consulting* (Cambridge, Mass.: Ballinger, 1988); Jonathan David Aronson and Peter F. Cowhey, *When Countries Talk: International Trade in Telecommunications Services* (Cambridge, Mass.: Ballinger, 1988); and Daniel M. Kasper, *Deregulation and Globalization: Liberalizing International Trade in Air Services* (Cambridge, Mass.: Ballinger, 1988).

108. *Economic Report of the President* (Washington: Government Printing Office, 1988), 144.

109. See Ronald Kent Shelp, *Beyond Industrialization* (New York: Praeger, 1981); Thomas M. Stanback, Jr., Peter J. Bearse, Thierry J. Noyelle, and Robert A. Karasek, *Services: The New Economy* (Totowa, N.J.: Allanheld, Osmun, 1981); and Office of Technology Assessment, *Trade in Services: Exports and Foreign Revenues* (Washington: Government Printing Office, September 1986).

110. International Monetary Fund, *International Financial Statistics Yearbook, 1994* (Washington: IMF, 1994).

111. *International Financial Statistics Yearbook*, 1987, 701.

112. Coalition of Service Industries; British Invisibles Export Council, *Annual Report and Accounts 1986–1987* (London: British Invisible Exports Council, 1987), 34.

113. U.S. Department of Commerce, *U.S. Trade: Performance in 1985 and Outlook* (Washington: Government Printing Office, 1986), 2.

114. Coalition of Service Industries. Derived from IMF figures by Boston Economic Advisors, Inc.

115. See Spero, "Removing Trade Barriers"; and William Diebold, Jr., and Helena Stalson, "Negotiating Issues in International Services Transactions," in Cline, *Trade Policy in the 1980s*, 581–609.

116. U.S. Congress, *Trade and Tariff Act of 1984*, Public Law 98-573, October 30, 1984.

117. See Robert P. Benko, *Protecting Intellectual Property Rights: Issues and Controversies* (Washington: American Enterprise Institute for Public Policy Research, 1987); R. Michael Gadbaw and Timothy J. Richards, eds., *Intellectual Property Rights: Global Consensus, Global Conflict?* (Boulder, Color: Westview Press, 1988); and Helena Stalson, *Intellectual Property Rights and U.S. Competitiveness in Trade* (Washington: National Planning Association, 1987).

118. *Description of the Proposed North American Free Trade Agreement*, prepared by the governments of Canada, the United Mexican States, and the United States of America, August 12, 1992, 1.

119. Gary C. Hufbauer and Jeffrey J. Schott, *NAFTA: An Assessment* (Washington: Institute for International Economics, 1993).

120. Business Roundtable, "Negotiations on International Investment in the Uruguay Round: A Preliminary Statement," March 1988; and U.S. Trade Representative, *Submission of the United States to the Negotiating Group on Trade-Related Investment Measures* (Washington: Office of U.S. Trade Representatives, June 1987).

121. See U.S. Senate, Committee on Finance, *Trade Agreements Act of 1979, Report on H.R. 4537 to Approve and Implement the Trade Agreements Negotiated Under the Trade Act of 1974, and for Other Purposes*, 96th Cong., 1st sess. (Washington: Government Printing Office, 1979); Stephen D. Krasner, "The Tokyo Round: Particularistic Interests and Prospects for Stability in the Global Trading System," *International Studies Quarterly* 23 (December 1979): 491–531; and Thomas R. Graham, "Revolution in Trade Politics," *Foreign Policy* 36 (fall 1979): 49–63.

122. See U.S. Senate, Committee on Finance, MTN Studies No. 4, *MTN and the Legal Institutions of International Trade*, report prepared at the request of the Subcommittee on International Trade, 96th Cong., 1st sess. (Washington: Government Printing Office, 1979).

123. See Gary C. Hufbauer, "Subsidy Issues After the Tokyo Round," in Cline, *Trade Policy in the 1980s*, 327–361.

124. See Alan W. Wolff, "The Need for New GATT Rules to Govern Safeguard Actions," in Cline, *Trade Policy in the 1980s*, 363–391.

125. See John H. Jackson, "GATT Machinery and the Tokyo Round Agreements," in Cline, *Trade Policy in the 1980s*, 159–187.

126. Jeffrey J. Schott, *The Uruguay Round: An Assessment* (Washington: Institute for International Economics, 1994), 7.

127. Michele de Benedictus, Fabrizio De Filippis, and Luca Salvatici, "Nature and Causes of CAP: Changes in the 1980s and a Tentative Exploration of Potential Scenarios," in Giovanni Anania, Colin A. Carter, and Alex F. McCalla, eds., *Agricultural Trade Conflicts and GATT: New Dimensions in U.S.-European Agricultural Trade Relations* (Boulder, Colo.: Westview, 1994), 132–142.

128. Jeffrey J. Schott, *The Uruguay Round: An Assessment* (Washington: Institute for International Economics, November 1994).

4

The Multinational Corporation and the Issue of Management

A **multinational corporation (MNC)**[1] is "an enterprise that engages in **foreign direct investment (FDI)** and that owns or controls value-added activities in more than one country."[2] A firm is not really multinational if it just engages in overseas trade or serves as a contractor to foreign firms. There are a number of ways of assessing the degree of multinationality of a specific firm. For example, firms are considered to be more multinational if (1) they have many foreign affiliates or subsidiaries in foreign countries; (2) they operate in a wide variety of countries around the globe; (3) the proportion of assets, revenues, or profits accounted for by overseas operations relative to total assets, revenues, or profits is high; (4) their employees, stockholders, owners, and managers are from many different countries; and (5) their overseas operations are much more ambitious than just sales offices, including a full range of manufacturing and research and development activities.[3]

Multinational corporations finance some portion of their overseas operations by transferring funds from the country of the "parent" firm to the country of the "host" firm (usually an affiliate or subsidiary, but also possibly a joint venture with another firm). This transfer is called foreign direct investment (FDI). The purpose of the transfer is to own or control overseas assets. What precisely constitutes control is somewhat problematic. For practical purposes, most collectors of statistics on FDI consider an overseas investment to involve control only when the investor owns 10 percent or more of the equity (total stock) of the affiliate— on the assumption that investors owning less than 10 percent of equity have no control.[4] Even though a group of smaller investors can band together to control a firm, their investments will not generally be included in statistics on FDI. So there is a gray area between genuine FDI and foreign "portfolio investment"—investment that presumably does not involve direct control over overseas assets.[5]

Foreign direct investment is not a new phenomenon.[6] From the time that people began to trade with one another, they set up foreign commercial operations. Mediterranean traders like the Genoese and the Venetians established banking operations in distant locations as early as 1200 A.D. to finance the trade which their ships carried. Foreign commercial investment reached a high point in the development of the large mercantile trading companies, such as the British East India Company and the Hudson's Bay Company. Beginning in the eighteenth century, but more importantly in the nineteenth century, there was direct foreign investment in agriculture, mining, and manufacturing as distinct from the earlier forms of commercial investment. By the early 1890s, large U.S. manufacturing firms—like Singer Sewing Machines (the first large multinational corporation), American Bell, General Electric, and Standard Oil, to mention but a few—had large investments abroad. By 1914, according to one study, U.S. direct foreign investment amounted to an estimated $2.65 billion, 7 percent of the U.S. **gross national product (GNP)** of that time.[7]

In another sense, foreign direct investment *is* a new phenomenon. The nature and extent of international business have changed dramatically since 1945. After World War II, there was a major expansion in the investments of U.S. firms abroad. The new investments tended to be in manufacturing, whereas previous investments had been in agriculture, banking, retailing, and raw materials. Whereas the activities of U.S.-owned multinational corporations and their host countries were the focus of much attention in the 1960s and 1970s, in the 1980s debates over multinationals began to recognize the growing role in the world economy of the MNCs of Europe, Japan, and a number of NICs.

Business has become more genuinely global: the number of home and host countries and the number and variety of multinational firms has been increasing constantly. During the early 1990s, for example, at least 37,000 multinational parent firms controlled over 206,000 foreign affiliates.[8] The United States, for example, is now a host country for over 15,000 foreign affiliates. Even the formerly communist countries are now promoting inflows of FDI. The result is that globally oriented MNCs of various nationalities are increasingly influential players in the world economy. Now the controversy over MNCs tends to center around the globalization of world business rather than the promotion of U.S. imperial aims by U.S. multinationals. As businesses become more globally oriented while the global political system remains largely under the control of the governments of nation-states, the question of who is to regulate business globally has become an important concern in world politics.

In addition, the globalization of business may be linked to recent trends toward the construction of stronger regional trading and investment blocs (see Chapter 3). If nationally oriented firms can no longer compete successfully with globally oriented ones, then one way for the firms of smaller nation-states to make the transition to a global orientation is to promote regional economic integration. By doing so, however, they may be creating an alternative to globalization.

In this chapter we will concentrate on factors influencing FDI flows and the expansion of MNC activities among the industrialized countries. In Chapter 8, we will discuss FDI flows from the industrialized countries to the developing countries.

Common Characteristics of MNCs

Multinational corporations range from companies that extract raw materials to those that manufacture consumer goods such as soft drinks or high-technology products like computers to those that offer services such as insurance or banking. These multinational corporations differ not only in what they do but also in how they do it, their level of technology, their organizational structure, and the structure of the market for their products. Nevertheless, certain characteristics common to many multinational corporations can be used to describe this phenomenon and to identify the problems it creates.

Multinational corporations are among the world's largest firms. In 1992, the top twenty-five multinationals had sales over $25 billion each, and the largest—General Motors—had sales in 1993 of $134 billion. The sales of each of the top ten multinational corporations in 1992 were over $59 billion, more than the gross domestic product (GDP) of at least 100 countries. Indeed, General Motors' 1992 sales were larger than the GDP of all but the 21 largest national economies and well ahead of Denmark, Norway, Saudi Arabia, and Poland (see Table 4-1). These corporate giants also tend to compete in oligopolistic markets. Some are able to dominate markets because of their sheer size, others (even some small- and medium-sized firms) because of their access to financial resources, control of proprietary technology, or possession of a special, differentiated product.[9]

Multinational corporations are not simply large corporations that market their products abroad; they are firms that have sent abroad a package of capital, technology, managerial talent, and marketing skills to carry out production in foreign countries. In many cases, the multinational's production is truly worldwide, with different stages of production carried out in different countries. Marketing also is often international. Goods produced in one or more countries are sold throughout the world. Finally, multinational corporations tend to have affiliates in many countries. One analyst defined a multinational corporation as one with investments in six or more foreign countries and found that such firms accounted for 80 percent of all foreign subsidiaries of major U.S. corporations.[10]

The forms that multinational organizations take are various. Generally, foreign subsidiaries are directly owned by the parent through either sole ownership or joint venture with public or private groups. The **internalization theory** of multinational activity explains why firms may prefer direct foreign investment to alternative ways of doing international business like exporting and licensing.[11] It is generally less expensive for local firms to do business in their home markets than for foreign firms. The extra costs connected with doing business abroad must be offset by advantages that a particular foreign firm may have, such as manage-

Table 4-1   Countries and Corporations: A Ranking by GDP and Sales, 1992–1993

Rank	Country/Firm	GDP/Sales (billions of dollars)
1	United States	5,920
2	Japan	3,670
3	Germany	1,789
4	France	1,320
5	Italy	1,223
6	United Kingdom	903
7	Spain	575
8	China	506
9	Canada	494
10	Russian Federation	387
11	Brazil	360
12	Mexico	329
13	Netherlands	320
14	Republic of Korea	296
15	Australia	295
16	Switzerland	241
17	Argentina	229
18	Sweden	221
19	Belgium	219
20	India	215
21	Austria	185
22	General Motors (U.S.)	134
23	Indonesia	126
24	Denmark	124
25	Norway	113
26	Saudi Arabia	111
27	Thailand	110
28	Iran	110
29	Ford Motor (U.S.)	109
30	South Africa	104
31	Turkey	99.6
32	Exxon	97.8
33	Royal Dutch Shell (United Kingdom/Netherlands)	95.1
34	Ukraine	94.8
35	Finland	93.9
36	Toyota (Japan)	85.3
37	Poland	83.8
38	Portugal	79.6

Table 4-1 *Continued.*

Rank	Country/Firm	GDP/Sales (billions of dollars)
39	Hong Kong	77.8
40	Israel	69.8
41	Hitachi (Japan)	68.6
42	Greece	67.3
43	IBM (U.S.)	62.7
44	Matsushita (Japan)	61.4
45	Venezuela	61.1
46	General Electric (U.S.)	60.8
47	Daimler-Benz (Germany)	59.1
48	Malaysia	57.6
49	Mobil (U.S.)	56.6
50	Nissan (Japan)	53.8
51	British Petroleum (UK)	52.5
52	Phillipines	52.5
53	Samsung (South Korea)	51.4
54	Philip Morris (U.S.)	50.6
55	IRI (Italy)	50.5
56	Siemens (Germany)	50.4
57	Colombia	48.6
58	Singapore	46
59	Volkswagen (Germany)	46.3
60	Chrysler (U.S.)	43.6
61	Ireland	43.3
62	Toshiba (Japan)	42.9
63	United Arab Emirates	42.5
64	Pakistan	41.9
65	Unilever (United Kingdom/Netherlands)	41.8
66	New Zealand	41.3
67	Chile	41.2
68	Nestle (Switzerland)	38.9
69	Myanmar	37.8
70	Elf Aquitaine (France)	37
71	Honda (Japan)	35.8
72	Algeria	35.7
73	Hungary	35.2
74	ENI (Italy)	34.8
75	Fiat (Italy)	34.7
76	Sony (Japan)	34.6
77	Texaco (U.S.)	34.4

Table 4-1   *Continued.*

Rank	Country/Firm	GDP/Sales (billions of dollars)
78	Puerto Rico	34
79	Egypt	33.6
80	NEC (Japan)	33.2
81	DuPont (U.S.)	32.6
82	Chevron (U.S.)	32.1
83	Philips (Netherlands)	31.7
84	Daewoo (South Korea)	30.9
85	Procter & Gamble (U.S.)	30.4
86	Belarus	30.1
87	Renault (France)	30
88	Nigeria	29.7
89	Fujitsu (Japan)	29.1
90	Mitsubishi Electric (Japan)	28.8
91	Kazakhstan	28.6
92	Morocco	28.4
93	Asea Brown Boveri (Switzerland)	28.3
94	Hoechst (Germany)	27.8
95	Alcatel Alsthom (France)	27.6
96	Mitsubishi Motors (Japan)	27.3
97	PEMEX (Mexico)	26.6
98	Czech Republic	26.2
99	Mitsubishi Heavy (Japan)	25.8
100	Peugeot (France)	25.7

SOURCES: World Bank, *World Development Report 1994: Infrastructure for Development* (Washington: World Bank, 1994); and "The World's Largest Industrial Corporations," *Fortune* July 15, 1994.

rial or marketing techniques or new production processes, that are internal to the firm. Companies cannot rely on open market mechanisms if they wish to profit from developing that knowledge. It is difficult to price intangible assets like knowledge, and it is often difficult and costly to negotiate and enforce contracts connected with the transfer of that knowledge. As a result, the company "internalizes" the market by setting up a foreign subsidiary that can ensure maximum control over the use of firm-specific knowledge. If the success of the firm depends crucially on controlling its internal knowledge advantages, the firm will insist upon maintaining 100-percent control of its subsidiaries abroad.

Joint ventures and *licensing* are other options available to multinationals wanting to do business abroad. In a joint venture, the various partners own less than 100 percent of the equity of the joint venture firm. There may be a majority owner with more than 50 percent ownership, or all the owners may be minority owners. The owners typically select a management team made up of representatives of all the owner firms to run the joint venture. Licensing involves the granting of usage rights for the intellectual property—for example, patents, copyrights, and trademarks—of the licensee to the licensing firm in exchange for some sort of payment. In certain countries, joint ventures and licensing are the only avenues available to MNCs who wish to participate in the local economy, due to the restrictive investment policies of host governments.

Another option that has become more common recently in certain industries is the *strategic alliance*. Strategic alliances are partnerships between separate, sometimes competing, companies. When the companies are from different countries, they are called international strategic alliances. The companies are drawn together because each needs the complementary technology, skills, or facilities of the other; nonetheless, the scope of the relationship is strictly defined, leaving the companies free to compete outside the relationship. A strategic alliance may be formally ratified in the form of a joint venture, but companies are increasingly using other ways to work together with other firms. The purposes of the alliances range from joint research and development to designing industry standards to sharing distribution or marketing networks in a way that both benefits the companies and reduces their risks. One of the catalysts for these arrangements has been the rapidity of technological change and the skyrocketing costs of development, especially in high-technology sectors. Another has been the perceived need to compensate for disadvantages that individual firms have in competing with larger and more integrated firms or alliances.[12]

Decision making for multinationals tends to be centralized, though management structures vary from company to company, and policy control emanates from the parent company when the international aspects of a firm's business become important. The classic evolution of international investment has been from semi-independent foreign operations to the integration of international operations within a separate international division to the integration of international operations within the whole company. As a result, although multinational corporations have decentralized many decisions to the local level, key decisions involving foreign activities, such as the location of production facilities, distribution of markets, location of research and development facilities, long-range planning, and especially capital investment, tend to be made by the parent company.[13]

Yet another organizational characteristic is the integration of production and marketing on an international scale. Production may take place in different stages in several different countries, and the final product may be marketed in still other countries. The European Ford Escort, for example, includes parts from fifteen different countries, which are assembled in the United Kingdom and Germany and then sold throughout Europe. Integrated production and the need for central decision making and **central planning** are made possible by central control and central management. Central control and management of geographically dispersed activities are made easier by the use of modern computing and telecommunications technologies.

Multinationals often are mobile and flexible. Some are tied to specific countries by the need for raw materials or by a large capital commitment. Others, however, are able to shift their operations across national boundaries for the purposes of company profits, markets, security, or survival. As part of their effort to transcend national borders, many multinationals try to create global staffs that are drawn from many countries to serve in yet others. As part of their effort to gain and protect their knowledge in strategically important areas, they recruit skilled personnel and make corporate allies wherever they can find them. Mobility and flexibility are thus increasingly an advantage that globally oriented MNCs have over more locally or even nationally oriented firms.

The special characteristics of multinational corporations can cause conflict with states, and their international scope has been known to create political problems. Most importantly, multinational corporations may seek goals or follow policies that are valid from the firm's international perspective but that are not necessarily desirable from the national perspective.[14] The policies and goals of multinational corporations may conflict with the policies and goals of the states in which they operate. There is also a related jurisdictional problem. Legally, multinational corporations have many different national identities and are therefore subject to many different jurisdictions. Because no one entity or country is responsible for overall jurisdiction and because jurisdiction is often unclear, it is sometimes difficult for states to exert legal control over resident multinational corporations, even if they are domestically owned.

Trends in FDI and Other MNC Activities

The spread of multinational corporations, and especially of U.S. multinationals, has been characteristic of the contemporary world economy. From 1971 to 1992, the stock of U.S.-owned direct investment abroad measured by book value rose from $86.2 billion to $423.2 billion.[15] Direct investment by other developed countries, though smaller than U.S. investment, also rose sharply. From 1971 to 1992, the stock of direct investment by West Germany rose from $7.3 billion to $186 billion, that of the United Kingdom from $16.2 billion to $259 billion, and that of Japan from only $4.4 billion to $251 billion (see Figure 4-1).

Total annual outflows of FDI rose from around $12 billion in 1970 to over $171 billion in 1992, down from a peak of $222 billion in 1990 (see Figure 4-2). Growth in outflows tapered off after the deepening of the world debt crisis in the early 1980s, but resumed rapid growth after the mid 1980s. The downturn in the early 1990s was due to the decline in outflows of Japanese FDI and the U.S. economic recession that began in 1990 (more on this below). The aggregate trend in inflows of FDI worldwide mirrored that of outflows for the most part (see Figure 4-3). Note that while industrialized nations were by far the main sources and destinations of FDI outflows, developing nations greatly increased their share of total FDI inflows in the early 1990s (see Figures 4-2 and 4-3).

Figure 4-1   Outward Stock of Direct Foreign Investment in Current Dollars, 1960–1992

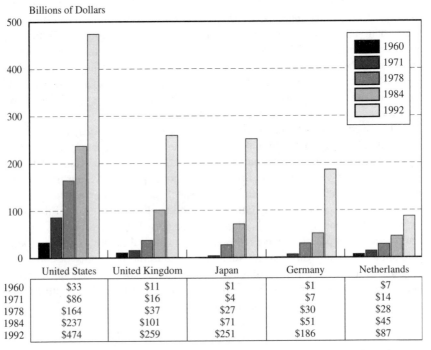

Billions of Dollars

	United States	United Kingdom	Japan	Germany	Netherlands
1960	$33	$11	$1	$1	$7
1971	$86	$16	$4	$7	$14
1978	$164	$37	$27	$30	$28
1984	$237	$101	$71	$51	$45
1992	$474	$259	$251	$186	$87

SOURCE: Center on Transnational Corporations, *Transnational Corporations in World Development: Trends and Prospects* (New York: United Nations, 1988), 518–526; and United Nations Conference on Trade and Development, *World Investment Report 1994* (New York: United Nations, 1994), 14.

The FDI outflows and inflows of the five largest industrialized economies fluctuated widely in recent years. All five large industrialized economies experienced rapid increases in outbound FDI in the 1980s. Japanese outflows, in particular, rose very rapidly and then declined rapidly after 1990 (see Figure 4-4). In marked contrast, inflows of FDI to Japan were low relative to those going into other large industrialized countries. FDI inflows to the United States increased rapidly during the 1980s, as did those to the United Kingdom, reflecting the efforts of Japanese firms to establish economic beachheads in North America and Europe in a time of movement toward a more regionalized world trading system (see Figure 4-5). European FDI flowed into the United States (and vice versa) for the same reason.

Canada, which traditionally has had widespread and high levels of foreign investment, represents the most extreme case of an industrialized country that was dependent on inflows of FDI. Average annual inflows of FDI into Canada were $979 million between 1982 and 1987. Inflows increased to $7.6 billion in 1990 and rose slightly to $7.8 billion in 1992.[16] At the end of 1973, companies whose

Figure 4-2 Outflows of FDI from Industrialized and Developing Nations, 1970–1992, in Current Dollars

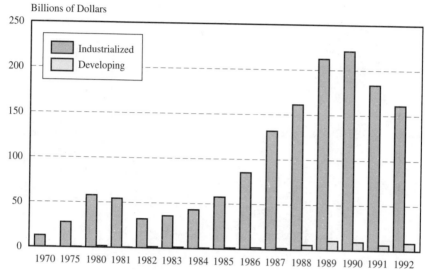

SOURCES: Center on Transnational Corporations, *Transnational Corporations in World Development: Trends and Prospects* (New York: United Nations, 1988), 503–510; UNCTAD, *World Investment Report, 1993: Transnational Corporations and Integrated International Production* (New York: United Nations, 1993), 234–247; UNCTAD, *World Investment Report, 1994: Transnational Corporations, Employment and the Workplace* (New York: United Nations, 1994), 409.

equity was controlled abroad accounted for 58 percent of the capital in Canadian manufacturing, 75 percent in petroleum and natural gas, 58 percent in other mining and smelting, and 34 percent of all other industries outside agriculture and finance. By 1987, even though those figures had declined, they were still quite high: 48 percent in manufacturing, 74 percent in petroleum and natural gas, 40 percent in other mining and smelting, and 26 percent of all industries outside agriculture and finance.[17] In 1984, 20 percent of Canada's GNP was accounted for by branches of subsidiaries of foreign multinationals.[18] The ratio of FDI inflows to gross fixed capital formation rose from 3.7 percent during the 1986–1990 period to 7.2 percent in 1992.[19]

MNC penetration is noteworthy, although less extensive, in Europe. In the early eighties, foreign multinationals in the United Kingdom accounted for 19 percent of industrial output and 15 percent of industrial employment. At the same time, foreign-owned enterprises in West Germany accounted for 26 percent of industrial production, and in France, for 25 percent. Capital stock of foreign affiliates accounted for approximately 13 percent of GNP in the United Kingdom, 5 percent in Germany, and 3 percent in France during the same period.[20] Annual inflows of FDI into the European Union averaged $19 billion in 1982–1987. Inflows increased to $109 billion in 1990, dropping off to around $82 billion in

Figure 4-3   Inflows of FDI to Industrialized and Developing Countries, 1970–1992, in Current Dollars

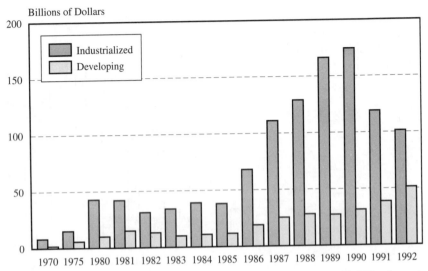

SOURCE: Center on Transnational Corporations, *Transnational Corporations in World Development: Trends and Prospects* (New York: United Nations, 1988), 503–510; UNCTAD, *World Investment Report, 1993: Transnational Corporations and Integrated International Production* (New York: United Nations, 1993), 234–247; UNCTAD, *World Investment Report, 1994: Transnational Corporations, Employment and the Workplace* (New York: United Nations, 1994), 409.

Figure 4-4   FDI Outflows from the Five Largest Industrialized Countries in Current Dollars, 1965–1993

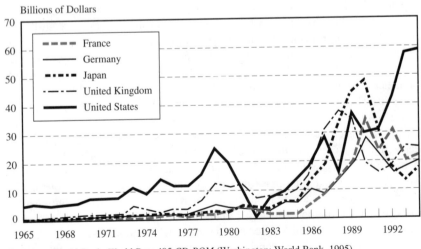

SOURCE: World Bank, *World Data '95 CD-ROM* (Washington: World Bank, 1995).

Figure 4-5   FDI Inflows into the Five Largest Industrialized Countries in Current Dollars, 1965–1993

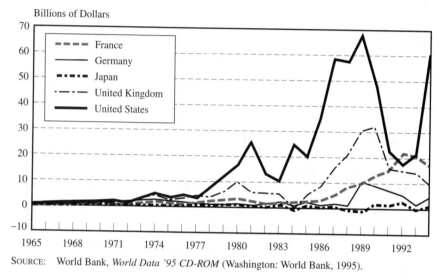

SOURCE: World Bank, *World Data '95 CD-ROM* (Washington: World Bank, 1995).

1992.[21] While the United States accounted for the largest share of non-European FDI inflows, the U.S. share declined steadily in the 1980s and the Japanese share increased rapidly.[22]

Investment in the United States by European and Japanese corporations increased greatly in the 1980s. Whereas in the early 1960s, the stock of foreign direct investment in the United States was negligible, by 1980 the United States had about $83 billion in foreign direct investment, and by 1992 this had grown to $420 billion. In 1970, the stock of direct foreign investment into the United States was only about 20 percent of U.S. direct investment abroad. By 1992, that figure was about 86 percent.[23] In the late 1980s, the flow of FDI into the United States exceeded the outflow for the first time in U.S. history.

There were several reasons for the increased interest of foreign corporations in investment opportunities in the United States. One was the increased size and aggressiveness of non-U.S. firms while the European and Japanese economies grew rapidly. Another was that the decline of the dollar in the 1970s and the late 1980s brought down the cost of acquiring U.S. firms, making them more attractive to foreign corporations. This circumstance coincided with corporate restructuring in the United States, which left many companies up for sale, and with the search by U.S. surplus trading partners for safe places to invest their money. A further incentive to invest in the United States was growing trade frictions and protectionist pressures in such vulnerable sectors as electrical equipment and automobiles. Thus production in the United States itself guaranteed continued access to the huge U.S. market. And finally, foreign investors have been attracted to the huge U.S. market and by the [relative] political stability of the United States, especially compared with that of many developing countries and even many European nations.

One interesting new dimension of foreign investment in the United States was the influx of foreign banks and securities firms, which were attracted to the United States by their multinational clients who had already settled there, by profits to be made in U.S. financial markets, and by the low cost of acquiring U.S. banks. The growth of Japanese banks was particularly important in the 1980s, keeping pace with the spread of Japanese business and foreign investment. Japan was the world's leading capital exporter by the end of the 1980s, and the United States was one of its favorite sites for investment.

Approximately 45 percent of Japanese offshore equity investment went to the United States in 1987, amounting to $14.7 billion. It increased by $9.3 billion in 1988, $2.3 billion in 1989, and $4.3 billion in 1990. These investments were not merely in manufacturing: nonmanufacturing investments, especially trade, sales, banking, finance, insurance, and real estate, made up 70 percent of Japanese foreign investment in North America by March 1988.[24]

Japanese financial institutions have challenged U.S. supremacy in the banking and securities areas. In 1985, Japanese banks overtook U.S. banks as the world's biggest lenders.[25] Although only one of the top ten banks in the world measured by assets was Japanese in 1978, twelve of the top fourteen were Japanese by the end of 1986,[26] and four of the top ten securities firms ranked by capital were Japanese.[27] The assets of Japanese banks grew from 25 percent of the total assets of the largest fifty banks in 1980 to 57 percent in 1989, but dropped to 46 percent in 1990.[28]

Japanese overall FDI outflows reached a peak of $48 billion in 1991, but then declined by 36 percent in 1991 and again by 44 percent in 1992 to a level of $17 billion. Japanese investors divested many of their U.S. holdings in the early 1990s and the flow of Japanese FDI into the United States declined from a peak of $30.6 billion in 1990 to $13.9 billion in 1992.

To summarize, one of the big changes after 1980 was the increased role of Europe and Japan in generating outflows of FDI. All three major industrialized regions rapidly increased their FDI outflows, but one major industrialized country, Japan, stood out as attracting considerably lower inflows than the others. Europe and the United States considered this to be evidence that there continued to be significant barriers to FDI inflows in Japan, even though the Japanese government had dismantled most legal barriers. Accordingly, in the 1990s, both the U.S. government and the EU put increasing pressure on the Japanese government and industry groups to open the Japanese economy to inflows of foreign direct investment.[29]

Explaining the Rapid Growth in MNC Activity

There are a number of theories about the factors that have contributed to the enormous expansion of the MNC activity in the past three decades. Clearly, changes in technology and organizational sophistication created the possibility of expansion. The development of new communications technologies, cheaper and more reliable transportation networks, and innovative techniques of management and organization have made possible the kind of centralization, integration, and flexibility that are the hallmark of the successful MNC. But these were merely enabling factors. The question remains as to why we have seen such a great expansion of MNC activity since the end of World War II.

One answer would be to stress the importance of government policies.[30] Some governments—particularly powerful governments like that of the United States—actively encouraged multinational expansion. The progressive elimination of restraints on capital flows made expansion of direct investment possible. The reduction of tariffs made direct investment more attractive. Governments directly subsidized FDI outflows by providing various forms of insurance for international investments. The United States, for example, created the Overseas Private Investment Corporation (OPIC) in 1961 to insure U.S. firms against some of the risks involved in direct investment.[31] Canadians and Europeans created incentives to attract inflows of foreign investment.[32] Although the U.S. federal government has not officially courted foreign investment, in recent years individual states have taken the lead, even competing with one another for foreign manufacturing plants.[33]

But, again, government policy changes alone would not have resulted in the expansion of MNC activity described above. Foreign investment, after all, is the result primarily of decisions made by private firms. Theories about FDI that do not take into account the firm-level incentives to invest overseas are not likely to be very helpful in explaining the trends described above. We turn, therefore, to a set of theories that deal with this very issue.

Internalization Theory

Internalization theory, as mentioned briefly above, contends that firms expand abroad in order to "internalize" activities in the presence of market imperfections just as they expand domestically for similar reasons. The particular market imperfections that create incentives for internalization are represented in the idea of transaction costs. Transaction costs arise when markets cannot produce desired results. For example, when the costs of concluding long-term contracts with an external firm are higher than the costs of establishing a new internal unit to accomplish the same purpose, then it can be said that the market for long-term contracts is imperfect and generates high transaction costs.[34]

There are both natural and artificial reasons for market imperfections. Long-term contract markets are inherently difficult to organize and prone to high transaction costs. Similarly, it is frequently difficult to put an accurate price on technologies when licensing them or otherwise transferring them to another firm. There are problems of asymmetry of knowledge between the buyer and seller that make such markets notoriously tricky. Often sellers require buyers to sign "nondisclosure agreements" to protect their intellectual property before explaining what the technology does in the first place. It is no wonder that buyers often perceive these transactions to have high costs and that they sometimes try to avoid them by creating their own technologies or by buying companies that own the technologies they need (both forms of internalization). Sellers are equally wary, mainly because they do not wish to lose control over knowledge that may provide them with important competitive advantages.

Market imperfections of this sort may be considered artificial to the extent that they are at least partly the result of government policies. Markets for information are frequently faulty, but trade barriers or lax government enforcement of intellectual property rights may create higher than normal transaction costs for firms considering alternatives to foreign direct investment, and thus may help to motivate them to internalize those costs by investing abroad.[35]

John Dunning has expanded upon internalization theory by suggesting that three conditions must be met before a firm will be able to compete with local firms despite the disadvantages of being foreign: (1) it must have market power that derives from ownership of some specialized knowledge, (2) it must consider the particular foreign location advantageous for new investments relative to alternative locations including its home market, and (3) it must prefer FDI over exporting and licensing by the usual internalization logic. This expansion on internalization theory is called the *OLI model*, where OLI stands for ownership, location, and internalization.[36]

The OLI model has become the most widely accepted theory of direct foreign investment among economists.[37] Nevertheless, there are other theories that attempt to explain some aspects of MNC behavior and/or MNC/host country relationships that are somewhat different from and not entirely compatible with the OLI model.

Product Cycle Theory

The **product cycle theory** argues that firms expand abroad when their principal products become "mature" in domestic markets. During the initial or rapid growth stage of product commercialization the firm attempts mainly to respond to domestic demand. As growth tapers off, the firm may begin to look for new sources of demand in export markets. Eventually, domestic demand begins to fall as the market is saturated, new firms begin to challenge the earlier entrants to the market, and the firm looks for ways to protect its revenues and profits by establishing foreign subsidiaries with lower factor costs so as to remain competitive in the home market and/or better market access to foreign markets. As overall demand for the product moves toward zero, the firm will try to move on to new products or attempt to create new advantages by altering the product (see Figure 4-6).[38] The product cycle theory was designed to explain changes over time in FDI on the part of manufacturing firms, and was never put forward as a general theory of MNCs or FDI. Nevertheless, it adds something to OLI theory by positing a reason for changes over time in firm-specific ownership advantages.

Figure 4-6   Product Cycle Theory

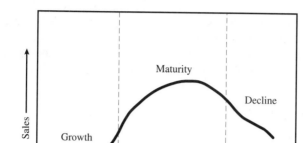

Source: Raymond Vernon, "International Investment and International Trade in the Product Cycle," *Quarterly Journal of Economics* 80 (May 1966): 190–207.

Obsolescing Bargain Theory

A close relative of product cycle theory is the theory of the obsolescing bargain. In **obsolescing bargain theory**, a firm that has invested in a host country starts with a good bargaining position with the host country's government because of firm-specific advantages such as superior technology, access to capital markets, and access to final product markets. An excellent example of this would be the initial negotiations between American oil companies and host governments in the Middle East in the 1920s. U.S. firms were able to win favorable "concessions" for the right to drill for petroleum in the new oil fields. Once the firm has made an investment, however, the bargaining advantage may slowly shift to the host country. The technology may mature and become more easily accessible to the host country's firms, and the host country may learn how to gain better access to global capital markets and to final product markets. It then attempts to negotiate more favorable terms with the foreign investor.

Oligopoly Theory

The **oligopoly theory** of foreign investment contends that firms move abroad to exploit the **monopoly** power they possess through such factors as unique products, marketing expertise, control of technology and managerial skills, or access to capital.[39] In the battle for profits and market share, firms engaged in oligopolistic competition may move abroad as part of their overall competitive strategy. They may move aggressively to exploit a new foreign market in the hope that this action will give them a permanent advantage over their competitors. Conversely, a company whose competitors have just entered a foreign market might be forced to go international defensively, in order to block their opponent's move or at least prevent the competitor from gaining a survival-threatening advantage.

The oligopoly theory is consistent with the OLI model in that the OLI model asserts that a firm must have some sort of market power derived from firm-specific advantages (usually based on the firm's special knowledge). Many oligopolistic industries are populated with precisely this type of firm. What oligopoly theory adds to the OLI model is the idea that the timing of entry into specific foreign markets may depend upon the timing of entry of a given firm's competitors.

The Tariff-Jumping Hypothesis

Another important hypothesis about FDI flows deals with the attempt by MNCs to jump over tariff or nontariff barriers by establishing foreign subsidiaries. The **tariff-jumping hypothesis** has been used recently to explain the increased willingness of Japanese and U.S. MNCs to invest in Ireland and the United Kingdom. Because Ireland and the UK are members of the European Union, investing in those two countries may provide improved access to all the members of the EU. As a result, the data appear to indicate that non-European MNCs seem more than usually interested in investing in those two countries. The tariff-jumping hypothesis, again, is consistent with the OLI model because the existence of the European Union, with its high external tariffs and low internal ones, gives a locational advantage to relatively low-wage countries within the EU.[40]

Barrier-jumping is also posited as an explanation for the rapid increase in FDI flows from Japan to the United States. This is particularly true of Japanese investments in automobile production in the United States. The first big jump in Japanese FDI in autos occurred in 1981, the year in which a VER was negotiated to limit Japanese exports. Investments continued during the 1980s on the assumption that the U.S. market would be closed to Japanese imports unless they were replaced with local production. As a result, Japanese production capacity in the United States increased from zero in 1980 to approximately 1.6 million units per year in 1990 (see Figure 4-7).[41]

The Importance of the Home Country

More recent theorizing about the behavior of MNCs stresses the importance of the home country environment. Marked differences in the behavior of MNCs from different home countries—for example, U.S. firms versus Japanese firms—suggest that the way in which the home country structures its domestic economy has an important impact on the way in which domestic firms internationalize their business activities, despite the fact that most economic theories of MNC behavior seem to imply that the home country context should be largely irrelevant. While there is a certain convergence in the behavior of firms from different home countries over time in terms of the way they deal with questions of organizing export activities, local production, R&D, and marketing,[42] firms of different nationalities retain important distinctive characteristics that are strongly affected by the home environment. For example, Japanese firms belong to confederations

Figure 4-7   Exports versus Local Production of Automobiles in the United States by Japanese Firms, 1980–1990

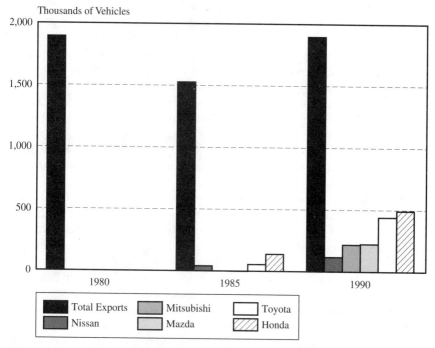

SOURCE: Japan Automobile Manufacturing Association.

of allied firms called **keiretsu.** When Japanese firms go abroad, they try to sustain their ties with other *keiretsu* firms at home and abroad, even when this might not be entirely rational from a short-term economic perspective.[43] U.S. firms, in contrast, are not as likely to develop long-term relationships with other firms, even though they are quite willing to nurture short-term partnerships.

The Consequences of MNC Activity

Modern governments have given high priority to the public policy goals of **economic efficiency,** growth, and improvement in the standard of living. In evaluating the impact of multinational corporations on developed market economies and determining the management problems raised by multinationals, one must examine the effect of those firms on economic performance. This is not a simple task, however, because it is somewhat difficult to separate out the effects of FDI and other MNC activities from those of other variables on a given country's economic performance. For most macroeconomists, for example, capital investment is capital investment no matter who owns it or where it comes from. Empirical studies of the impact of increases in FDI inflows, therefore, have to consider what might have happened to domestic investment levels in the absence of increased inflows. Similar points could be made about transfers of new technology or efforts to raise the skill levels of local MNC employees.[44] Nevertheless, there have been some efforts to study empirically the consequences of MNC activity.

Proponents of multinational corporations argue that FDI is a mechanism for increasing economic efficiency and stimulating growth. By transferring capital, technology, and know-how and by mobilizing idle domestic resources, multinational corporations (argue their advocates) increase world efficiency, foster growth, and thereby improve welfare.[45] To be more specific, the potential gains from FDI fall into two main categories. First, FDI may facilitate trade in goods and services by allowing firms to compensate for market imperfections by engaging in international intrafirm trade. Second, FDI may generate positive external economies that benefit firms and other economic actors that are not directly engaged in FDI.[46]

It is difficult to measure the actual gains from trade associated with FDI, but there are strong indications—for example, that FDI flows are associated with increasing levels of trade. That is, even when MNCs invest in overseas production facilities to service foreign markets, some of that overseas investment generates demand for exports from the home country. A hypothetical example would be the establishment of an automobile assembly plant by a U.S. MNC in Belgium. Until the firm locates Belgian (or European) suppliers of automobile components, it is quite likely the firm would continue to purchase components from U.S. companies for its Belgian operations. Even when local suppliers are substituted for initially imported components, there will continue to be a demand for goods and services that the firm thinks it can get only from the home country.

In other words, the same factors that create incentives for FDI also create incentives for intrafirm trade. In 1988, for example, Japanese subsidiaries in the United States purchased over four-fifths of their imports from their parent companies in Japan and exported over three-fifths of their exports to the same companies. In the same year, intracompany trade between U.S. parent firms and U.S.-owned foreign affiliates accounted for over two-fifths of total U.S. imports and over one-third of total U.S. exports.[47] As a result of the increase in FDI flows and MNC activity, a large and growing proportion of world trade in manufactures, more than 30 percent, is accounted for by MNC affiliates. A growing share of the total MNC-generated trade is intrafirm trade.[48]

It is possible, however, that external economies are more important than gains from trade, since FDI tends to generate more rapid growth in overseas production and sales than in exports (with some notable exceptions). Measuring the extent of external economies is difficult in general, and therefore not much research has been undertaken in this area. One method that has been used is to examine changes in productivity, export performance, and research effort of locally oriented domestic firms after the entry of foreign firms.[49] Some additional clues about externality gains can be obtained from analyses of inflows of FDI into specific countries and industries.

For example, suppose that there had never been any Japanese investment in local production of automobiles in the United States and that U.S. auto firms had succeeded in getting higher trade barriers against Japanese firms to reduce competition from Japan. Then consumers would have lost by not being able to purchase the relatively inexpensive but high quality automobiles produced by Japanese firms, and U.S. firms would not have been forced to upgrade the quality of their products and the efficiency of their plants to match those of Japanese producers.[50] The end result would have been a decline in the overall international competitiveness of the U.S. auto industry. Thus Japanese inflows of FDI in automobiles in the 1980s may have been good for U.S. competitiveness.

It is important to remember, however, that the United States generally has low barriers to trade. As a result, incentives for firms located there to become internationally competitive are higher than those for firms located in countries with high barriers to trade. Thus one would not expect FDI inflows into the latter to have positive effects on their international competitiveness. Similarly, one would not expect the externality-based benefits of FDI inflows to be as great in countries with relatively low levels of human capital development as in countries, like the United States, with relatively high levels of human capital.[51] This suggests that there may be a stronger basis for concern about the possible negative effects of FDI inflows in developing countries than in industrialized countries (see Chapter 8). Nevertheless, even in industrialized countries there are important concerns about the effects of MNC activities.

Critics of multinational corporations believe that inflows of FDI may reduce efficiency and stifle growth in host countries. Because MNCs tend to be oligopolistic, they may be able to predate domestic firms, limit their own production, maintain artificially high prices, and thus earn oligopoly rents. If the rents are not reinvested locally, but rather are extracted via profit repatriation, then the country might have been better off limiting the entry of MNCs or limiting the repatriation of profits, because domestic firms would have been more likely to reinvest such rents domestically. In addition, critics argue that MNCs may actually hinder national growth and economic prosperity by absorbing local capital instead of providing new capital, by applying inappropriate technology, by creating "bad" (low-skill and low-wage) jobs instead of "good" (high-skill and high-wage) jobs, by doing research in the home country instead of in the host country, and by employing expatriate, not indigenous, managers. Most of these criticisms can be tested empirically and most of the available evidence suggests that they are not correct, but there are a few areas where the criticisms seem to have some validity.[52]

MNCs in Canada and Europe

Over the years, much research has been devoted to the question of the effects of FDI on economic performance on specific countries or regions.[53] Most studies of the economic impact of multinational corporations on their host developed market economies conclude that their overall effect is positive. One such case is

Canada. Because of its significant penetration, foreign investment has been an important public issue in Canada and the subject of several official and semiofficial studies and much private scholarly examination. Most of these studies have concluded that foreign investment has favorably affected the Canadian economy.[54]

One of the earlier reports, although critical of foreign investment, concluded that direct foreign investment, especially U.S. investment, was a key factor in Canadian economic development generally and an important factor specifically in capital formation, export promotion, and the balance of payments. Furthermore, the report concluded, it was important that this investment was direct and not portfolio investment, for direct investment brought not only financial resources but also a package of product, technology, management, and market access. The report noted that there were problems with direct foreign investment, that it may have stunted the domestic Canadian capital market and damaged the initiatives of local entrepreneurs, but it concluded that "the host country typically benefits and often substantially from foreign direct investment."[55]

Similar conclusions have been reached in Europe. The 1981 Caborn report adopted by the Parliament of the European Community, which called for greater regulation of multinational corporations, found that multinational enterprises raise the level of world economic activity and have "favorable impacts on productivity, growth rates and overall level of employment, on the dissemination of new products and processes and also of managerial know-how."[56] Other benefits cited in studies of individual European economies include improvements in balance of payments, research and development, the level of technology, and increased dynamism.[57]

Despite indications of overall benefits from multinational corporations, such investment is not without costs for the host state. Costs are incurred because behavior that is rational for the corporation may be less beneficial to the host country. Several concerns have been revealed in public and private studies.[58] The fear of technological dependence is one. Although access to advanced technology is one of the primary economic benefits of multinational corporations for the host developed countries, that access may stifle domestic research and development. The concentration of research and development in the home state may discourage research and development activities in the host state and result in the subordination of the host to technology controlled from abroad. There is a related concern that host states may pay excessive costs for imported technology, because the control of technology by a multinational enables the parent to charge a monopoly **rent** for its use.[59] A similar concern arises concerning management skills. The transfer of managerial talent to host countries can be a source of efficiency and growth, but the use of foreign managers may also deny nationals opportunities to use and develop their skills.

Yet another concern grows out of the multinational corporations' oligopolistic character. The entrance of foreign competitors may stimulate domestic competition and thus encourage efficiency, but it may also reduce competition and threaten existing domestic industries. Even such market dominance by multinational corporations may be beneficial if it brings with it new technologies and other economic efficiencies. But if it does not introduce such improvements, it may decrease efficiency. Special concern is voiced by states when multinational corporations acquire existing national firms. Acquisition may give the firm access to capital, technology, and other resources and thereby improve its performance, but it may simply indicate a transfer of ownership, adding no new efficiencies.

Some concern has been expressed regarding the import orientation of multinational corporations. An official Canadian study, known as the Gray report, found that subsidiaries in Canada preferred to seek supplies and services within the company, as opposed to within the country. This preference for importing from the parent may provide the highest-quality goods and services, but it may retard the development of Canadian manufacturing and service sectors and thus limit the spillover effect that foreign investment has on the rest of the Canadian economy.[60] Other concerns have been voiced regarding export policy. Although the evidence suggests that multinational corporations have an equal or better export record than their domestic counterparts do, the practice of restricting exports and limiting markets of individual subsidiaries is not unknown in multinational corporations. Finally, there is concern connected with the multinational corporations' balance-of-payments impact. The consensus of economists is that balance-of-payments effects of MNCs are minor in comparison with macroeconomic factors such as the growth rate of the economy, changes in exchange rates, and the like, but critics continue to argue that MNCs contribute to trade deficits because of their greater propensity than domestic firms to import needed inputs.

In evaluating the problems created by the conflict between multinational corporations and their host states over economic efficiency, growth, and welfare, one must go beyond economic analyses. Equally important is the way in which the host country's citizens view the impact of multinationals on the national economy.

A survey of public opinion in Western Europe was conducted in 1974 and 1976 and involved nearly thirteen thousand people in the nine countries that were then members of the EC. The poll revealed that although many Europeans were critical of multinationals, they generally believed that multinationals have a positive economic impact. Foreign investment was seen as a modernizing force that keeps prices down, aids economic development, and improves business methods. Still, many Europeans were concerned about the disruptive effects that multinationals might have on the international monetary system and, especially, about the multinationals' ability to shift production without regard to the consequences for the home country.[61] Among national elites, opinions varied: business people and senior civil servants were the most favorable; politicians, academics, and clergy were more circumspect; and trade unionists, students, and youth leaders were generally critical.[62]

Another study showed that elites in Canada and Europe considered national income effects, balance-of-payment effects, and employment effects to be of most concern in terms of the economic effects of multinationals. The overall impact on national income was generally considered positive for the host nation, although opinion on the balance-of-payment effects was more divided, tending toward the negative. Opinion was also divided on employment effects of multinationals. Although most agreed that foreign companies paid higher wages, they also felt that other benefits for workers were worse.[63]

In sum, the multinationals' economic impact on the host economy seems generally positive, and the public generally perceives that positive impact. Yet there are real economic concerns in specific areas. The important issue for the developed host countries is not whether foreign investment is economically worthwhile but whether it is possible to increase the benefits and decrease the costs associated with foreign direct investment.

For much of the 1960s and 1970s, examination of the effect of multinational corporations focused on the host states, with the implicit assumption that the home state was the recipient of economic benefits. In recent years, however, the assumption that multinational corporations are good for the home economy has come under fire. Some analysts and influential interest groups in the United States, particularly labor union representatives, feel U.S. direct foreign investment has had a negative effect on the U.S. economy by favoring foreign investment over foreign trade and production in the United States, exporting jobs instead of goods, allowing tax revenues to escape, and impairing domestic economic development by sending capital abroad instead of using it at home. Although these arguments have increasing political significance, several studies of the impact of foreign investment on the U.S. economy reveal that investment has not taken place at the expense of domestic investment, trade, or employment.[64]

Indeed, the politics of multinational corporations within the industrialized countries increasingly involves debates over what should be done to assist domestically owned MNCs to become more internationally competitive. Some political actors favor extensive interventions on the part of the government to promote specific firms and industries—sometimes called *industrial policy*, but also referred to as *technology policy* when it involves more focused assistance for the creation and commercialization of new technologies. These proponents often argue in favor of interventions to counter the industrial policies of others, especially Japan and the Asian NICs. Others oppose such interventions as being contrary to the norms of the multilateral trading system, difficult to carry out in the new globalized world economy because the national identity of MNCs is becoming somewhat less clear, and generally ineffective in promoting the interests of the nation.

National Economic Control

A second area of potential multinational-state conflict in developed countries is the interference of multinational corporations in the national control of the economy. As developed states have sought to manage their economies to improve economic efficiency, growth, and welfare, concern about external constraints on that control by multinational corporations has emerged.

The concern with national control is clearly revealed in studies of elite and public attitudes toward foreign investment. In a survey of European public opinion, most of the negative views on multinationals centered on fears that they might erode the national control of the economy.[65] Many respondents saw major differences between U.S. and European multinationals: corporations based in the United States were viewed as typically powerful, dynamic, and well organized but also uncontrollable and morally suspect; whereas multinationals based in Europe were seen as socially committed, humane, and loyal as business partners.[66] Various studies of Canadian attitudes reveal that the most adverse feeling toward multinational corporations involved the loss of control. Canadians generally believe that there is a trade-off between the economic benefit of multinational corporations and their adverse effect on control over national affairs.[67]

The sense of lost control reflects, in part, an intangible feeling that as a result of foreign investment, decisions crucial to the national economy are made outside the nation. The perception is not that these decisions are adverse, just that they are made elsewhere. The tendency of multinational corporations to centralize decisions in the parent suggests that the fears that decision making shifts from host to investing country are often justified. Interestingly, the intangible fear of loss of decision making may not be related to the level of foreign investment. Canadians, who have a vast amount of foreign investment, are no more concerned than are the English, who have much less. The French, with a low level of investment, on the other hand, evidence a high level of concern. The fear of lost control seems to be related more to different national expectations regarding the need for independence than to the actual threat to that independence.[68]

The fear of lost control of sensitive industries is particularly acute. Countries, including the United States, have always been concerned about foreign ownership of such sectors as communications, transportation, and finance. Increasingly, public officials feel that industries with a large influence on the economy, such as the automotive or petroleum industries, or those in the vanguard of scientific and technological development, such as computers or electronics, should remain under national control.[69] Such concern emerged in the United States in 1987 when the Japanese company, Fujitsu Ltd., tried to acquire an 80-percent share in Fairchild Semiconductor Corporation, a pioneering firm in the industry and a large supplier of computer chips for the U.S. military which had fallen upon bad times. Various U.S. government officials argued strongly that the sale ought to be blocked on national security grounds. Ironically, Fujitsu was proposing to buy the 80-percent share that already belonged to another foreign firm, the French company Schlumberger, Ltd. Apparently the concern of government officials was not simply that it was foreigners who wanted to buy Fairchild, but that it was the Japanese in particular, with whom U.S. semiconductor competition has been particularly fierce. In this case, the issue never came to decision because Fujitsu withdrew its offer as a result of the controversy. Since that time, however, as foreign investment in the United States has increased, public opinion has been increasingly wary of foreign investors, especially in the sensitive high-technology industries.

Whereas multinational corporations have often played an important role in achieving national goals, there is a concern that they are less responsive to national economic planning than are domestically owned firms operating primarily in the national market.[70] The concern is, first, that activity rational for an international firm may not be in tune with that planned for the national economy and, second, that the multinational has the capacity to circumvent mechanisms for implementing national plans. Because multinational corporations have access to outside financing, they are not as dependent as domestic industry is on national governmental finance and thus may not respond to governmental incentives to invest in certain industries or certain regions. Because they have fewer links with the national economy and polity, it is feared, multinational corporations are less likely to cooperate voluntarily with national planning goals.

The Gray report, for example, expressed a concern that multinational corporations might interfere with the Canadian government's goal of increasing investment in manufacturing and discouraging overdevelopment of resource extraction. The report pointed out that foreign fabricating and manufacturing firms that integrate vertically backwards to obtain secure supplies of natural resources are less likely to respond to Canadian needs and economic capabilities because their raison d'être is shaped heavily by their committed investment elsewhere.[71]

A greater concern is that multinational corporations may evade national taxation. Through its central control of pricing, the multinational corporation can take profits in countries where taxes are low and avoid showing profits and paying taxes in those countries where taxes are high. Because transactions of subsidiaries of the same multinational are not arm's length transactions—that is, not determined by free-market prices—the central decision-making unit can artificially fix the prices of those transactions. These so-called **transfer prices** can be manipulated to minimize taxes.[72] A multinational can, for example, inflate the price of imports or decrease the value of exports among affiliated companies in order to minimize the earnings of a subsidiary in a high-tax country. This issue emerged in the United States when certain states proposed using a "unitary tax" formula for computing state taxes of multinational corporations. The purpose of the unitary tax is to prevent multinationals from manipulating transfer prices to their own benefit. Rather than taxing the company on its state revenues, the state would tax it according to a complex formula based on its world-wide earnings. This provoked a strong reaction, particularly from Japanese and British corporations, who threatened to stop investing in states that used unitary tax formulas.[73]

A controversy over California's unitary tax led to the U.S. Supreme Court's 1994 decision on a lawsuit filed by Barclays Bank of the United Kingdom in 1984 and another by Colgate-Palmolive in 1986 arguing that the California system was unconstitutional. On June 20, 1994, the Court voted 7-2 in favor of California's right to keep the unitary tax. If the Court had voted against California, the state would have had to refund approximately $2 to $4 billion in taxes already collected under the law and return to a system of taxation based on the assumption of "arms length" relationships between MNC parents and local subsidiaries.

The California legislature decided in 1986 and 1993 to modify the unitary tax law to make it elective. State authorities realized that the system was creating disincentives for inflows of new FDI and recognized that it was quite difficult to administer because of wide variations in national accounting practices, fluctuations in international exchange rates, and lack of full cooperation from foreign MNCs in tax audits.[74] So while the ruling of the U.S. Supreme Court paved the way for other states to adopt unitary taxes, California was slowly but surely jettisoning the idea.

Another dimension of interference in national control is in what one author called the "national order."[75] Multinational corporations, it is charged, are less bound by national social codes and economic relationships. Thus the links between business and government that exist in Europe and in Japan and that are a tool for national economic management may be more tenuous and less effective between national governments and foreign multinationals.[76]

Another aspect of the national order is labor-business relations. It has been argued that foreign multinationals have followed labor policies inimical to national labor policies. It has been charged that they are more willing than national firms, for example, to discharge employees and are less willing to consult employees in making decisions that will affect them.[77] Europe is particularly sensitive to this because of its commitment to labor rights and employment protection, but these concerns have also surfaced in the United States. In 1988, the British construction company Beazer tried to buy Koppers, a Pittsburgh-based construction materials and chemicals company. In order to stir up public opposition to the takeover, Koppers' management successfully played up fears that Beazer, as an insensitive foreign company, would close the plant or fire workers.

Interference by Home Governments of Multinationals

Another dimension of the problem of control is not the threat from the multinational itself but from the multinational's home government to the host country, primarily the threat from the United States to the host countries of U.S. multinational corporations. Such interference occurs when U.S. laws are applied beyond U.S. borders through subsidiaries of the multinational corporation (MNC).[78]

One area of U.S. interference has been through extraterritorial application of U.S. export controls. The Trading with the Enemy Act of 1917, the Export Control Act of 1949, and its successors, the Export Administration Acts of 1969 and 1979, were used by the U.S. government to control dealings of foreign affiliates of U.S. corporations.[79] The Trading with the Enemy Act empowered the president to regulate all commercial and financial transactions by U.S. citizens with foreign countries or nationals in time of war or national emergency. The act was invoked to prohibit all trade with Cuba, North Korea, North Vietnam, and, until recently, China. The Export Control and Export Administration acts gave the executive branch the authority to "prohibit or curtail" all commercial exports, including technical know-how, to Communist or other specified countries from U.S. companies or their foreign subsidiaries on the basis of national security, foreign policy, or short supply. Because U.S. courts held the parent firm criminally liable for the acts of its foreign affiliates, there was a great incentive for multinational corporations to cooperate with these U.S. regulations.

There have been cases in which the United States has blocked U.S. subsidiaries' transactions abroad that were legal under the laws of the host country. In 1982, in a highly politicized episode, the United States ordered U.S. multinational corporations operating abroad to comply with a U.S. embargo on the export of high-technology products to the Soviet Union for use in the construction of a natural gas pipeline from the Soviet Union to Western Europe. The sanctions, originally promulgated in December 1981, following the imposition of martial law in Poland, were extended in June 1982 to subsidiaries of U.S. companies abroad and foreign companies working under U.S. license. The embargo applied to technology that had been purchased when there were no controls on exports from the United States. The incident provoked a serious conflict between the United States and its European allies, who saw the U.S. action as a unilateral and retroactive application of extraterritorial jurisdiction. Some European governments issued formal orders requiring the resident companies to honor the contracts, and when the companies complied, the United States imposed penalties on them, including the revocation of all export licenses.[80]

The U.S. government, however, has not always prevailed. Resistance by the French government and courts led the United States to withdraw its restriction on the sale of trucks made in France by a U.S. firm to the People's Republic of China. And after five months, the U.S. decision to extend the pipeline embargo to foreign subsidiaries of U.S. corporations and licenses was reversed following an agreement by the North Atlantic Treaty Organization (NATO) allies to study East-West trade. Numerous other cases suggest that the U.S. government is often willing to accede when foreign governments insist.[81]

Another area of U.S. (as well as EC and West German) interference has been through antitrust legislation. The Sherman and Clayton acts seek to prevent restraint of competition both within the United States and in U.S. import and export trade. The U.S. courts have asserted a wide-ranging extraterritorial jurisdiction of these laws, including application to the subsidiaries of U.S. multinational corporations. The fact that a U.S. corporation is a parent of a foreign subsidiary has been held sufficient for jurisdiction by U.S. courts. On this basis, the U.S. government has attempted to force, not always with success, disclosure of information by foreign subsidiaries. It has forced U.S. parents to divest themselves of foreign affiliates or to alter the behavior of their affiliates, even though that ownership or behavior was legal under the host country's laws. United States courts, for example, forced a U.S. beer company to divest itself of a subsidiary in Canada and obliged American parents to order their subsidiaries to cease to operate in a radio **cartel** in Canada, even though this cartel had been approved by the Canadian government.

In another case, U.S. courts claimed jurisdiction in a private antitrust claim against foreign companies joining in a uranium cartel outside the United States and with the expressed consent of their governments. But instead of the defendant firms, the relevant governments, including Canada and the United Kingdom, appeared in court and argued that the United States could not exercise jurisdiction because it had provoked the cartel by embargoing the use of foreign-origin uranium in U.S. nuclear reactors; because the cartel was, as a result, created as a matter of government policy; and because laws outside the United States do not regard cartel formation as unlawful. The court not only rejected these arguments but also criticized the governments for appearing in place of the firms. Largely in reaction to the uranium case, the United Kingdom enacted legislation to block such action by foreign governments.[82]

Finally, there has been intervention through U.S. balance-of-payments policies. In the 1960s, the U.S. government tried to improve its balance of payments by asking U.S. corporations to limit their new foreign investment in developed countries, to increase the amount of foreign investment financed by borrowing abroad, and to increase the return of earnings and short-term assets from their foreign affiliates. This had a serious impact on investment abroad, particularly in Europe, where the policy threatened to dampen economic growth, hurt the balance of payments, and dry up local capital markets when U.S. corporations borrowed on local capital markets instead of borrowing in the United States. The capital restraints were ended in the 1970s following the emergence of the float and the improvement in the U.S. balance-of-payments position. Given the internationalization of capital markets in the 1980s, it is unlikely that similar controls could be imposed today.[83]

The U.S. government also used U.S. multinational affiliates to pressure South Africa to end its apartheid policy. The Comprehensive Anti-Apartheid Act of 1986 prevented U.S. companies and their foreign branches from providing new loans to the South African government or engaging in new investment in South Africa. Canada, the European Community, the Commonwealth nations, and the Nordic nations passed similar laws prohibiting new investment, and the Nordic countries and Australia and Canada did not allow new bank loans. Congress considered but did not enact stricter legislation, such as requiring mandatory disinvestment by U.S. multinationals or imposing a full-trade boycott on South Africa.

In addition to federal actions directed at ending apartheid, many U.S. state and local governments took a strong stance against apartheid by enacting partial or total disinvestment policies, prohibiting investment of state-run funds in companies that did business in South Africa, or refusing to make purchases from or give contracts to firms that did business in South Africa. Although the state and local governments were not in a position to mandate that U.S. companies withdraw from South Africa, their laws forced multinationals to choose between their U.S. business and their South African business.

Federal, state, and local laws were successful in inducing U.S. corporations to leave South Africa. From 1984 to 1988, for example, 141 U.S. companies withdrew their equity investments from South Africa (although some of these maintained other economic links). It is unlikely that the actions of the United States or those of the other countries that supported the economic embargo against the South African apartheid regime were responsible by themselves for bringing about the end of apartheid, but it is significant that Nelson Mandela was quick to acknowledge its importance after his election to the presidency of the post-apartheid regime. Also, it is noteworthy that so many governments considered manipulation of their multinationals to be a legitimate means of undermining apartheid in South Africa.

In conclusion, the potential for the home country to interfere with MNC activities abroad is very real. If one considers the volume of transactions carried out by multinational corporations, however, the number of actual threats of home country interference is relatively small. Home governments of industrialized nations appear to have adopted a policy of avoiding interference in the activities of MNC affiliates, except in unusual circumstances.

Multinationals and the National Political Process

One final but important area in which multinational corporations may interfere is in the politics of the home and host states. As with any corporation in the home or host country, the multinational is a potentially powerful political actor that can, and at times does, seek to influence law and public policy and that does have an impact on the political environment. The nature and significance of the multinational corporation's effect on national politics in developed countries are areas that have not been sufficiently examined and about which little is known.

There are several ways in which multinational corporations might attempt to influence politics in host countries. In the most extreme case, they might overthrow an unfriendly government or keep a friendly regime in power. They might intervene in elections through legal or illegal campaign contributions or take action to support or oppose particular public policies. Finally, multinational corporations might influence the national political culture—that is, shape public political values and attitudes. In all of these actions, the firm may act on its own, at the instigation or with the support of the home government.[84]

In the case of Canada, the Gray report, which considered these possibilities, concluded that multinational corporations have little direct impact on Canadian public policy. The influence of foreign investment, according to that study, was in shaping alternatives available to Canadian decision makers. For example, because of the structure of Canadian industry and the fact that some firms are foreign controlled, public policy is limited in its efforts to rationalize industry.[85] The U.S. Senate Subcommittee on Multinational Corporations found that multinational corporations have engaged in legal and illegal payments in developed countries, but the subcommittee did not suggest just how such payments influenced public policy.[86]

Multinational corporations may also affect public policy in the home state. One study of U.S. foreign policy found that the direct influence of any particular corporation is likely to be balanced by countervailing powers, even though corporate groups may shape policy. The most important influence, the study concluded, was the ability of business generally to influence the political consensus from which U.S. foreign policy is drawn. The predominance of the liberal approach to international economic relations is an example of this intangible yet significant influence.[87]

A somewhat different view emerged from the hearings of the Senate Subcommittee on Multinational Corporations held in 1975. These hearings suggested that multinational corporations at times become an important part of the dynamic of U.S. foreign policymaking by initiating demands, providing information, and at times cooperating in the execution of policy. Another impression is that multinational corporations at times follow policies independent of, and perhaps in contradiction to, official governmental policy.[88]

Another effect of multinational corporations on national politics is through their influence on social structure. One study suggested that multinational corporations are altering both national and international class structures, creating new social, economic, and political divisions. According to the study, there is a new class structure emerging that consists of a transnational managerial class favoring a liberal international economic order; a large class of established labor with secure employment and status in their local communities, which has been the primary object and beneficiary of social legislation and economic management; and a group of social marginals that has not been integrated into the new industrial society and that suffers the system's social costs. The study found that this new class structure, shaped by the multinational enterprise, will create new social conflicts not suited to control by presently established institutions.[89]

In conclusion, concern has risen in recent years, and with that concern, conflict has been generated over the multinational corporation. The regulation of multinational corporations, however, has not become such a highly politicized and controversial issue in the Western system as it has in the Third World. Although some believe that multinational corporations should be managed to maximize benefits, there is a general perception of the importance of international investment. The former prime minister of Canada, Pierre Trudeau, offered this explanation:

> I don't worry over something which is somewhat inevitable, and I think the problem
> of economic domination is somewhat inevitable, not only of the United States over
> Canada but perhaps over countries of Europe as well . . . These are facts of life, and

they don't worry me. I would want to make sure that this economic presence does not result as I say in a real weakening of our national identity. I use that general expression too. The way in which I do that is to try and balance the benefits against the disadvantages. It is obvious if we keep out capital and keep out technology, we won't be able to develop our resources and we would have to cut our standard of consumption in order to generate the savings to invest ourselves and so on... Each country wants to keep its identity or its sovereignty, to speak in legal terms. It has to instantly make assessments, and when we make assessments it is to try and select those areas which are important for our independence, for our identity.[90]

International Regimes for Foreign Direct Investment

Compared with the control of money and trade, the international management of FDI has been extremely limited and relatively informal.[91] One reason for the absence of an international regime for FDI is that the devising of international rules for multinational corporations has only recently become an issue in international economic relations. The need for monetary and trade orders became clear as a result of the crisis of the 1930s, which was a crucial force behind the establishment of the postwar management mechanisms. In investment, however, no such international crisis and no consensus have arisen in the West. It was not until the 1960s that MNCs became an issue in international politics and even then, they were more important for North-South politics than for relations among the industrialized countries (see Chapter 8). The fear of economic costs and loss of national control caused by the growth in FDI in the industrialized countries has been balanced for the most part by the perception of economic benefits.

One factor shaping these generally positive perceptions of multinational corporations is the dominant liberal philosophy of the governments and globally oriented business interests in the industrialized world. FDI, like other international financial flows and trade, is viewed by these individuals as economically rational and beneficial. The role of large corporations in politics is not seen as dangerous in countries where domestic corporations play such roles. This general receptivity to international capital affects reactions to multinational corporations. It is interesting that the principal dissent comes from labor leaders in all of the industrialized countries and from the governments of France and Japan, two countries that were slow to embrace the idea of the MNC and which actively fostered partnerships between the government and domestic firms in the pursuit of national economic development.[92]

Another reason for the limited perceived threat has been the power relationship between the multinational corporations and the governments of the developed countries. In the developed countries, the multinational corporation is not perceived as a major threat to governmental power. Whereas firms can influence economic performance and interfere with a nation's economic management, they cannot undermine the authority of these powerful, sophisticated governments.

Although multinational corporations control sensitive sectors, they do not, except in Canada, loom so large in the national economy that governments feel they must acquiesce to their strength. Furthermore, Western governments possess not only the expertise—lawyers, accountants, economists, business experts—to regulate multinational corporations but also the confidence that they can devise means for control.

Yet another reason for the limited perception of threat in the West is that virtually all industrialized nations have their own multinational corporations. The position of the governments of the developed market economies as both home and host moderates their desires to restrict multinational corporations, for any restriction would limit the expansion of their own MNCs. Reinforcing this limited concern over foreign investment in the late 1970s and early 1980s was the troubled economic scene in the West, one of the more prominent features of which has been a decline in new capital formation. There has thus been a reluctance to question the source of any new capital investment.

A final dimension of the limited threat and lack of international control of multinational corporations is the absence of U.S. interest in such management. Concern about foreign investment in the United States, especially by the Japanese, has been rising. Nevertheless, U.S. perception of a need for management, crucial to the development of a formal regime, has not existed in the field of international investment. The lack of perceived problems for U.S. political and economic systems, the dominant liberal ideology, and the political significance of the large multinational corporations in U.S. politics has made U.S. leadership more interested in promoting than controlling foreign investment.

As multinationals have become more important and better understood, the trend toward liberalizing regulations on multinationals has been echoed throughout the Northern states, as we will see in the following discussions of national, regional, and international management.

National Management

Most efforts to control multinational corporations in the present international system occur within the host country. Although policy in developed market economies has been receptive to foreign investment, there have been some attempts to regulate foreign corporations to maximize economic benefits and to minimize the loss of control.

The most important form of regulation is the control of initial capital investment. States have sought to restrict key sectors for national investment and to regulate the degree of foreign ownership or control in sectors open to foreign investment. Although all countries have some form of key sector control—transportation, communications, and defense industries are commonly restricted industries—few of the developed market economies have comprehensive regulations or even a clear national policy regarding foreign investment.[93]

For many years, Japan followed a comprehensive, restrictive policy.[94] In investment as well as trade, Japan's public philosophy and governmental policy differ from those of other Western countries. Postwar policy was originally based on the Foreign Exchange Control Law of 1949 and the Foreign Investment Law of 1950, which provided governmental authority to screen all new foreign investment, with a view to limiting that investment, and to prevent the repatriation of earnings and capital of foreign investors. Government policy was highly restrictive. New foreign investment was limited to a few industries, and within those industries, foreign ownership was limited to no more than 49 percent. When purchasing existing industry, foreigners were limited at most to a 20 percent ownership of unrestricted industries and a 15 percent interest in the many restricted industries.

While restricting direct foreign investment, Japan tried to obtain the benefits of multinational corporations by purchasing advanced technology through licensing agreements instead of acquiring technology through foreign control. As a result of these comprehensive, restrictive policies, FDI inflows into Japan have been quite low (see again Figure 4-5). Also, most foreign MNC affiliates are joint ventures in which the foreign partner owns 50 percent or less of the venture.

Starting in 1967, as Japan's balance of payments strengthened and foreign pressure for liberalization increased, Japanese policy changed somewhat. The number of restricted industries was reduced, and 100-percent foreign ownership was permitted in many industries in May 1973. In 1980, the Japanese government passed a new Foreign Exchange Control Law. This legislation liberalized foreign exchange controls, removed formal entry restrictions on foreign direct investment (with the exception of twenty-two industries, including agriculture, forestry, fisheries, mining, petroleum, leather, and leather manufactures) and permitted 100-percent foreign control through new investment or acquisition.

In the mid-1980s, Japan relaxed controls in the financial services sector, allowing foreign institutions to obtain securities and trust bank licenses and encouraging the Tokyo Stock Exchange to open membership to foreigners. There remains a review process through the Committee on Foreign Exchange and Other Transactions in the Ministry of Finance, which evaluates foreign investment according to criteria such as effects on national security, impacts on domestic enterprise in the same or related business, smooth performance of the national economy, reciprocity with the home country of the investor, and the need for approval for capital export transactions. One of the most effective barriers to foreign investment is the *keiretsu* system that can effectively restrict inward foreign investment. Many Japanese financial and industrial firms hold each other's stock as part of their keiretsu obligations, a policy promoted by the Japanese government since World War II to prevent hostile takeovers of any sort, including foreign acquisitions.[95] Finally, though the Japanese government has allowed some liberalization, it has always retained the power to restrict foreign investment at any time at its own discretion.

On the other hand, the Japan External Trade Organization (JETRO), once an export-promoting organization, has been turned into an investment-attracting organization; and the Japan Development Bank is now providing favorable rates on loans to foreign investors. As a result of liberalization, foreign investment in Japan has risen, although Japan still has very low levels of foreign investment inflow in comparison with those of other OECD countries (see again Figure 4-5).[96] Similarly, the Ministry of International Trade and Industry (MITI) has become a defender of the "internationalization" of the Japanese economy, even while it remains a promoter of the interests of Japanese firms in world trade. MITI understands that in order for Japanese exports and outbound foreign investments to expand in the long run, Japan will have to become more open to imports and inbound FDI. Thus MITI pushes Japanese business and the rest of the Japanese government in the direction of making it easier for non-Japanese firms and individuals to set up business in Japan.[97]

Canada also drew up a policy for regulating the inflow of foreign investment in the seventies. The Canadian Foreign Investment Review Act of 1972 established the Foreign Investment Review Agency (FIRA) to screen virtually all new direct foreign investment in Canada. Its coverage was comprehensive (including new businesses), most acquisitions, the expansion of existing foreign-owned firms into nonrelated businesses, and change of foreign ownership. As a matter of national policy, FIRA refused takeovers in the fields of broadcasting, rail and air transportation, newspapers, nuclear energy, and banking. Evaluation of the benefit to Canada of foreign investment was determined by criteria such as contribution to employment, new investment, exports, processing of raw materials, purchase of supplies in Canada, access to sophisticated technology, improved productivity, and competition, as well as the degree of Canadian equity participation.

FIRA also insisted that foreign investors fulfill performance requirements in return for permission to invest in Canada. These commitments included import substitution requirements, export targets, research and development expenditures to be made in Canada, local equity participation guarantees, and exclusive production-in-Canada arrangements. Many investors were deterred by such requirements from making application to FIRA.[98] Others complied. But FIRA's restrictions brought a negative reaction from the United States, which in 1982 filed a complaint with the GATT, charging that FIRA's performance requirements were illegal. In 1983, a GATT panel found that Canadian requirements forcing companies investing in Canada to buy a certain proportion of their goods and services in Canada were illegal under GATT but that its export performance requirements were compatible with GATT.[99]

In 1984, the Foreign Investment Review Act was replaced by the Investment Canada Act, which was designed to promote, rather than discourage, foreign investment. Foreign investment is still screened, but only those investments exceeding C$5 million and C$50 million for direct and indirect investments respectively are subject to the screening procedure, greatly decreasing the number of foreign investments subject to review. The stated purpose of the review is to ensure that the investment be "of net benefit to Canada."[100] Under the U.S.-Canada Free Trade Agreement signed by the two countries in 1989, U.S. firms were given even greater opportunities for Canadian investment, because indirect acquisitions would eventually be exempted from any review, and the threshold for review of direct acquisitions would be raised.[101] U.S. firms wishing to make major investments in Canada still must have their proposals reviewed (which is not the case for Canadian firms investing in the United States), but the likelihood of rejection has continued to decrease. These developments were reinforced and generalized to include Mexico with the signing of the North American Free Trade Agreement (NAFTA) in 1992.

Other states also screen inbound investment. Britain and France rely on an ad hoc consideration of applications for new direct foreign investment. Investments that might create foreign dominance of an important economic sector, damage national research and development, interfere with official plans for industrial rationalization, or create excessive concentration are reviewed by the appropriate ministries or agencies. There are no formal statutory guidelines for evaluating foreign investment, other than national antitrust and competition laws,[102] but in practice, judgments tend to favor investments that benefit employment, balance of payments, research and development, and exports; create new enterprises instead of acquiring existing firms; encourage national management at both the national and the parent level; and fit in with governmental plans for industrial reorganization.

In general, investment policy in the mid-1960s was restrictive, but since then many countries have become highly receptive to foreign investment.[103] The United Kingdom, for example, has been traditionally favorable to foreign investment, and, under the Conservative government since 1979, it has abandoned any government planning role, preferring to leave investment decisions to the operation of a free market. In 1985 the government of the United Kingdom permitted a merger between Westland, a British helicopter manufacturer, and the U.S. company United Technologies, despite strong pressure to favor the development of a Euro-consortium to strengthen European air industry cooperation. In 1988, the Swiss chocolate company, Nestlé, was allowed to buy Rowntree (a British candy producer) despite strong nationalistic protests. Nonetheless, even in a fundamentally liberal environment, such as Great Britain's, the desire for a national presence, or even a national champion in certain industries, has occasionally prevailed. When British Caledonian Airways was up for sale in 1987, both the Scandinavian carrier SAS and British Air made a bid for control. The government subtly discouraged SAS by declining to guarantee retention of route licenses; the British Air bid succeeded, allowing it to expand significantly its size and route capacity, providing England with a strong national airline carrier to compete in the post-1992 internal market.

U.S. controls on foreign investment have traditionally been limited to the International Investment and Trade in Services Act (IITSA) of 1976, which established a mechanism to monitor foreign investment, and the International Emergency Economic Powers Act of 1977, which empowers the president to block foreign acquisitions of U.S. companies or compel divestiture of an already acquired domestic company if he determines there is an extraordinary threat to the national security, foreign policy, or economy. Various other sectoral controls limit foreign investments in areas such as aviation, atomic energy, and communications.

As foreign investment in the United States increased dramatically in the eighties, more attention was given to regulation. The Bryant Amendment to the Omnibus Trade Bill of 1988, which was defeated, would have required foreign investors to file certain proprietary information with the Department of Commerce for public disclosure. Another amendment to the 1988 trade bill (section 721, also known as the **Exon-Florio amendment** after its sponsors Senator J. James Exon and Representative James J. Florio) extended the scope of the IITSA to prohibit mergers, acquisitions, or takeovers of U.S. firms by foreign interests when such actions are deemed a threat to the national security of the United States. After lapsing for technical reasons in the fall of 1990, the Exon-Florio authority was reinstated in August 1991 and made a permanent part of U.S. law.[104]

The job of implementing the Exon-Florio amendment was given to an interagency committee called the Committee on Foreign Investment in the United States (CFIUS), which is chaired by the secretary of the treasury and includes representatives from the departments of State, Defense, Commerce, and Justice, as well as the Office of Management and Budget, the Office of the U.S. Trade Representative, and the Council of Economic Advisers. CFIUS investigates any transaction that falls under the statute and then makes a recommendation to the president, who then makes the final decision on whether to invoke the law.

The first CFIUS investigation under the Exon-Florio amendment was conducted in late 1988 and early 1989. It involved the proposed takeover of the silicon wafer division of the Monsanto Corporation by a German chemical firm, Hüls AG. While some members of the committee wanted to bar the purchase, the government negotiated an agreement with Hüls whereby the purchase would be approved if the company agreed to maintain production of wafers and continue research and development in the United States.[105]

Up to mid-1994, the CFIUS received 750 notifications of transactions, conducted fifteen investigations, and blocked only one purchase. Five proposals were withdrawn during review, however, including the proposed acquisition of a U.S. machine tool manufacturer by a major Japanese firm called FANUC. A particularly contentious case was the takeover of a U.S. firm called Semi-Gas, which produced ultrapure industrial gases used in semiconductor manufacturing, by Nippon Sanso, a Japanese firm.[106] This deal was particularly sensitive because Semi-Gas had been a collaborator with U.S. semiconductor and electronics firms in an R&D consortium[107] called Sematech (short for semiconductor manufacturing technology). Sematech had been part of a U.S. effort to reestablish technological leadership in semiconductors, having lost out in some key semiconductor areas to Japan in the early 1980s. What bothered many people was that U.S. tax dollars had been spent to raise the technological capabilities of firms like Semi-Gas, and it did not seem to make sense, therefore, to allow Japanese firms to reap the benefits.

The Exon-Florio amendment was amended further in 1993 to prevent (1) foreign acquisition of U.S. firms with contracts with the U.S. departments of Defense and Energy worth more than $500 million and (2) awarding of U.S. government contracts involving "top secret" information to firms controlled by foreign governments. The new law also empowered CFIUS and other government agencies to review proposals for investments in high-technology areas deemed "critical" not just for national security reasons but also for U.S. competitiveness. The open-ended nature of these provisions made it possible for the U.S. government to begin screening a much broader range of inward flows of FDI.

Motivating these recent efforts was increasing economic nationalism. There is a growing concern in the United States over excessive dependence on foreign capital to finance growth, and a vocal minority would like to see even stricter limits on foreign investment.[108] Proponents of this minority view argue that the United States is sacrificing its long-term competitiveness by becoming dependent on Japanese and other foreign technology. In the automobile sector, for example, there are many American-Japanese joint ventures in which the production of sophisticated parts takes place in Japan and the final product is assembled in the United States. Some fear that the United States is losing its production capability in this process, its companies reduced to "screwdriver factories" where the high-technology parts are made abroad and the workers are only capable of producing low-technology parts and assembling all the pieces. In Japan, it is argued, workers are learning sophisticated production techniques that will allow them to become the unchallenged champions in automobile production in a short time.[109] Antiforeign sentiment lies below the surface of the U.S. consciousness, but some U.S. companies are discovering that it can be easily stirred and are using this knowledge as a tool for trying to prevent foreign takeovers of their companies.

Nonetheless, the prevailing view in the United States still defends the benefits of foreign investment for the United States and would like to see a more liberal economic environment for foreign investment here and abroad. Judging by the actions of most U.S. states, one would assume that foreign investment is highly desirable. State governors are competing intensely at times to attract new foreign manufacturing plants. In return for the jobs and the economic stimulus of the new plants, they are willing to offer tax incentives, regulatory breaks, and other inducements. This has been taken to such a degree that a backlash has developed, in which U.S. companies argue that they are being discriminated against by their own local governments, which favor foreign companies and allow them to produce in the United States much less expensively than U.S. companies. It remains to be seen which of these two opposing points of view will prevail; but there is no doubt that the United States is facing an important new wave of protectionism and economic nationalism that is not likely to disappear in the near future.

Aside from imposing entry requirements, countries may also attempt to manage the behavior of multinational corporations once established in their state. The ability to control the multinational corporations' behavior is crucial to management, because it involves activities that affect national economic performance and national control, such as taxation, labor policy, capital movements, and competition policy. Indeed, governments in the developed countries closely regulate the operations of those firms—both national and multinational—operating within their borders. However, with some exceptions, the developed countries' governments have not sought to impose special or differential regulation on the operation of multinational corporations. Controls on intracorporate capital flows and intracompany charges, for example, would be difficult to apply, could provoke retaliation, and could act as a deterrent to foreign investment, which is viewed positively in the developed market economies. Furthermore, governments in the developed countries have the administrative and legal capacity to control the MNCs through legislation, regulation, and administrative practice, which applies to domestic as well as foreign corporations. Finally, the principle of *national treatment*—a GATT rule specifying that foreign-owned enterprises are to be treated no less favorably than are domestically owned enterprises—acts as a deterrent to discrimination against MNCs. Although national treatment is not universally accepted and is inconsistently applied, it is embodied in certain bilateral treaties such as the friendship, commerce, and navigation treaties with the United States and in the multilateral codes of the OECD (page 138) and thus serves as a constraint on government policy. Exceptions to national treatment do exist in the areas of government subsidies, government purchasing, work permits and immigration policy, and participation in industry groups that set sectoral policy.

Governments have also applied informal pressure on firms to fulfill certain "performance requirements" in areas such as plant or export expansion and to adhere to national labor practices. They have carefully monitored foreign investors' adherence to national tax legislation and foreign exchange laws. As governments, especially in Europe, have expanded their intervention in the national economy through law and regulation, foreign investors have been increasingly obliged to adopt practices—for example, labor relations policies— consistent with those of the host country. Finally, where there has been a conflict of law or policy between the host and the home state, as in the case of the U.S. extraterritorial application of export controls, the governments of the host countries have insisted on asserting their jurisdiction over the resident MNCs. As we have already discussed, several European countries required resident companies to ignore U.S. restraints on pipeline exports to the Soviet Union.[110]

Finally, there have been increasing attempts in the major home country, the United States, to regulate home country MNCs. Concerns with balance-of-payments deficits led to capital controls; organized labor expressed concern over export of jobs and the tax "loopholes" enjoyed by multinational corporations; and the Senate Subcommittee on MNCs in the mid-1970s revealed a broad range of potential foreign policy problems posed by multinationals. In 1977, Congress enacted legislation to prohibit the use of bribery and illicit payments for political purposes by U.S. corporations operating abroad. And in the late 1970s and early 1980s, several U.S. states, in an effort to raise new revenues and to offset the ability of multinational corporations to select the state or country of lowest taxation, enacted unitary tax legislation that taxed both foreign and domestic corporations on their worldwide income instead of on income earned in that particular state. The result was an outcry from Japan and Europe, alleging violation of tax treaties that eliminated double taxation.

Because the developed market economies have been unwilling to restrict too severely the multinational corporations, many have tried to minimize their costs in other ways. Many states and regions, such as the EC, have tried to strengthen their domestic industry. Such policies, as part of broader industrial policies, include governmental encouragement and support of industrial concentration and rationalization of national industry, research and development, maintenance of key industries or companies, and development of national capital markets and national managerial skills. Methods include governmental financial assistance, tax preferences, government participation in industry, encouragement of mergers, financing of research and training programs, and "buy national" procurement policies. Within the European Community, many of these policies are being made illegal, which has discouraged the growth of "national champions." Nonetheless, in certain industries, such as defense, strong domestic suppliers have been encouraged (i.e., GEC-Marconi in the United Kingdom and Matra in France), and in other instances steps have been taken to strengthen individual countries' competitive positions in preparation for the creation of the internal market in 1992 (see Chapter 3). The Spanish government, for example, encouraged mergers of Spanish banks in order to prevent local market dominance by non-Spanish banks after 1992. But the main emphasis within the European Community is on promoting certain competitive pan-European "sunrise" industries to fight U.S. and Japanese dominance (see section on regional management).

In addition to national policy, interest in some broader form of management has emerged from time to time.

Regional Management

Regional common markets and free trade areas have provided new opportunities for regional management of multinational corporations. Within the context of such agreements there is room for substantial control or liberalization of investment policies.

One potentially important forum for the multilateral management of multinational corporations is the EU. A European solution figures prominently in the European critics' analysis of foreign multinational investment in Europe.[111] Two approaches to regional policy have been suggested. One approach, prevalent in the seventies, was to develop European Union regulations to limit the autonomy of MNCs in areas of frequent national conflict such as labor relations. The other approach has been the Union's encouragement of large European corporations, capable of competing globally with U.S. and Japanese corporations in high-technology sectors. The control function has not been developed as far as expected, in part because of the liberal, pro-business climate of Europe in the 1980s. Instead, the emphasis has been on the second approach in an effort to close the high-technology gap before the internal market is completed in 1992. However, it is possible that the control issues will reemerge as a priority, especially if the political left grows stronger in Europe.

European regional management faces major obstacles.[112] In addition to political opposition on some of these issues, a more basic problem concerns the authority of the EU to pass binding regulation on its member countries. Members of the community have consistently refused to delegate to the EU any national authority for regulation of industrial policy. A French proposal in 1965 for community regulation of foreign investment was rejected by the other members, who opposed a restrictive policy. In 1973, the European Commission proposed a number of community regulations regarding MNCs, including the protection of employees in event of a takeover and cooperation in monitoring MNC activities. The Caborn report, adopted by the European Parliament in 1981, called for maximizing the positive effects of multinational corporations and minimizing their negative effects by "the establishment of an appropriate framework of countervailing power at the international level through legislation, guidelines, codes, and multilateral agreements, and through greater cooperation and exchange between states."[113] Specifically, it recommended binding EU regulations in the areas of information disclosure, transfer pricing, and merger controls.

Although no specific directives aimed at non-EU investment were passed until 1993 (see below), the European Union moved ahead on several directives that would shape foreign as well as EU corporations' practices and address some of the concerns mentioned in the Caborn report. The most important areas have been accounting and information disclosure and antitrust policy, especially merger control. A number of directives—the EU form of legislation—in the area of company law are designed to increase the transparency of the activities of large conglomerates. The Seventh Company Law Directive, adopted in 1983, called for the consolidation of financial reporting to enable a fair review of the business as a whole. The First and Fourth directives had already specified the type of information to be published in public companies' accounts. The draft of the Ninth Directive would oblige groups of companies to define and publish the relationships between parents and subsidiaries and increase the rights of subsidiaries against the parent. The draft of the Thirteenth Directive would lay down rules for the conduct of takeover bids, particularly with regard to information disclosure.

Another area of concern was the promotion of greater participation and consultation rights for employees. The proposed Fifth Company Law Directive, to harmonize the structure of EU public companies, includes a provision for employee participation at the board level. Another proposed directive, known as the Vredeling proposal, called for greater consultation between management and labor regarding company policy and plans.[114] Though interest in these proposed laws stagnated because of liberalization and deregulation in the early 1980s, they were revived after 1993.

The Union's industrial policy was considerably strengthened in the 1980s. Industrial policy was designed initially to build EU industrial champions to counter U.S. and Japanese industrial and technological dominance. The Single European Act, which came into force in 1987, added a chapter to the EEC Treaty (the Treaty of Rome) entitled "research and technological development," which stated that "the Community's aim shall be to strengthen the scientific and technological basis of European industry and encourage it to become more competitive at [sic] international level."[115] This was to be realized through EU financial support for basic R&D, the opening up of national public sector procurement contracts, technical standardization, and the removal of fiscal and legal barriers to joint ventures and other forms of cooperation. A number of jointly funded research consortia were established in the areas of telecommunications, manufacturing technology, and information technologies and a steady increase in the number of intra-European mergers and joint ventures occurred. It soon became evident, however, that European MNCs needed to be able to construct alliances with non-European firms in certain important areas in order to be globally competitive. European laws and practices tended to reflect that necessity in the 1990s.

The Union made it clear that, while it wished to maintain a liberal policy toward trade and inward investment, it did not intend to allow foreign companies to reap the greatest benefit from the unified internal market. This meant that a degree of Union preference for European firms would continue to prevail and that foreign-based multinationals would not have the same access to EU programs as local companies, unless some reciprocity was recognized in the multinationals' home countries. This policy was taken up by the United States in the late 1980s and early 1990s with the establishment of such R&D consortia as Sematech, the HDTV Grand Alliance, and the U.S. Display Consortium. Even Japan began to invite the participation of foreign MNCs in its advanced R&D efforts during this period.

There was no Union policy specifically to regulate inward foreign investment, although individual EU states had their own regulations. However, Union action could be taken to disallow state financial inducements that acted as subsidies for foreign investors or to refuse to allow goods produced with less than an acceptable local content to circulate freely in the Union. This would curtail the operations of so-called "screwdriver plants," which simply assembled foreign-made components within the EU and thereby avoid external tariffs. In 1988, for example, France received permission from the EU to block the import of 300,000 television sets that were produced by Japanese companies but assembled in the EU. France claimed that these televisions did not qualify as European because of the high foreign content.

Mergers and joint ventures were permitted under European competition laws. After 1989, two separate laws governed joint ventures: Article 58 of the Treaty of Rome and the Merger Regulation of 1989. The Merger Regulation governed joint ventures that affected market structure significantly, while Article 58 covered all other joint ventures. Until the passage of the Merger Regulation, MNCs were not legally restricted in their decisions on European joint ventures. After 1989, however, all new joint ventures, including those that involved non-European MNCs, had to be approved by the European Commission.[116]

Another regional management issue in Europe was a directive of the European Commission concerning European works councils. Under this directive, all MNCs operating in Europe with 1,000 or more workers in more than one EU country were required to set up pan-European works councils to inform and consult their employees on key decisions. When the Maastricht Treaty came into effect on November 1, 1993, European legislation could no longer be vetoed by a single member state in the European Council, requiring instead three governments to be opposed. Until that time, Britain had blocked the directive by exercising its veto power. According to a study published by the European Employers' Union (UNICE), about 1,200 companies would be affected. Most foreign and some European MNCs opposed the legislation on the grounds of increased cost and reduced managerial flexibility. European unions and some MNCs supported the measure. Compagnie des Machines Bull, Thomson CSF, Grundig AG, Digital Equipment Corporation, Xerox Corporation, and IBM all set up some form of information and consultation procedure in anticipation of the new law.[117]

In addition to regional management through the EU, which is the best known and most complex regional internal market existing today, recent steps have been taken to create other regional areas for trade and investment liberalization. New Zealand and Australia have had a free-trade area for many years, and have just strengthened it through the Closer Economic Relationship agreement to include substantial liberalization of investment and harmonization of regulatory barriers. NAFTA and the U.S.-Canada Free Trade Agreement have similar provisions, which increase cross-border competition in manufacturing by eliminating most tariffs and enable service industries, such as banks and insurance companies, to compete directly for business in the three countries. Previously, for example, U.S. financial institutions were not allowed to own more than 25 percent of federally regulated Canadian-controlled financial institutions, and Canadian companies were not allowed to offer Canadian government securities in the United States. Both of these policies have been changed under the U.S.-Canada Free Trade Agreement.

International Management

International regulations and agreements have tended to encourage the expansion of multinational corporations. Western international law enacted before World War II offered protection for foreign investment. The traditional law of prompt, adequate, and effective compensation in the case of nationalization and various patent and copyright conventions was designed for this purpose, and the postwar agreements reinforced this general trend.[118] The IMF's provisions regarding currency convertibility allow the repatriation of capital and earnings and thus facilitate the international flow of capital. The GATT's tariff reductions smooth international production and transfers within the multinationals. In addition, the OECD's Code on Liberalization of Capital Movements establishes the norms of nondiscrimination between foreign and domestic investors within a country, freedom of establishment, and freedom of transfer of funds.

Although there has been some marginal international regulation through various international agencies and international conventions, whose authority covers certain aspects of multinational operations,[119] there were until the 1970s few attempts to manage multinational corporations at an international level, and most of those attempts failed.

One such effort died with the Havana Charter.[120] The management of international investment had not been a part of the U.S. scheme for a new postwar economic order. Ironically, in response to strong pressure from U.S. business groups, the U.S. delegation at Geneva in 1947 proposed a draft article on foreign investment. The article, intended to codify the prevailing Western liberal attitude toward foreign investment and the rights of capital-exporting countries, provided for protection against nationalization and discrimination. Once the matter was placed on the negotiating agenda, however, its character quickly changed. The less-developed countries, led by the Latin American states, were able to redefine the proposed article to protect not capital exporters but capital importers. Provisions of the Havana Charter allowed capital-importing countries to establish national requirements for the ownership of existing and future foreign investment and to determine the conditions for further investments. The inclusion of the investment provisions was a major reason for the opposition of U.S. business to the Havana Charter and for its eventual failure. The GATT, its successor, contained no provisions for investment. However, an agreement on trade-related investment measures was part of the Uruguay Round (see Chapter 3).

Throughout the 1950s and early 1960s, a do-nothing attitude prevailed. Attempts to write international foreign investment laws, such as the United Nations' Economic and Social Council efforts in the 1950s and those of GATT in 1960 on restrictive business practices, surfaced but led nowhere.[121]

In the late 1960s, as concern increased, more comprehensive proposals for a system of international control were drawn up. The most far-reaching proposals called for a body of international law under which multinational corporations would be chartered and regulated and for an international organization to administer these regulations.[122] Other proposals advocate the development of a GATT for investment.[123] This intergovernmental general agreement would consist of a few fundamental concepts of substance and procedure on which there might be a general international consensus and would establish an agency to investigate and make recommendations about the creation or infringement of rules (much as the GATT organization has done). Such an agency would not have compulsory authority, but it would have the power to publicize its findings and thus appeal to public opinion.

Although such a comprehensive, self-sufficient supranational body or even GATT-like Code for Investment seem unlikely, other options are available. These include amending existing WTO agreements, drawing up a separate agreement committing its signatories to apply WTO principles to investment, or prosecuting investment issues that are trade related through the WTO dispute resolution framework in order to set precedents covering investment. The United States participated in the Uruguay Round agreements that dealt with trade-related investment measures (TRIMs) (see Chapter 3). Although limited, the TRIMs agreement was a landmark in multilateral investment management, both because it integrated investment into the new WTO and because its emphasis was on encouraging investment flows. These included local content requirements, local equity requirements, technology transfer or export requirements, remittance restrictions, and incentives.

The OECD has been another forum for devising a regime for international investment. In 1976, largely in response to pressure from both less-developed and developed countries, the developed market states agreed on a voluntary code of conduct for multinational corporations. One factor leading to the OECD agreement was the new interest of the U.S. government and U.S. business in such an international code. Public revelations of corporate bribery and illegal political activity created domestic pressures for regulating U.S. corporations. U.S. firms sought to deter, through an international agreement, congressional legislation and to internationalize any constraints placed on them.

The stated goal of the OECD code is to maximize international investment. It suggests guidelines for corporate behavior, such as greater disclosure of information, cooperation with the laws and policies of host governments, less anticompetitive behavior and fewer improper political activities, respect for the right of employees to unionize, and cooperation with governments in drawing up voluntary guidelines for corporate behavior. As part of the multinational agreement, the OECD countries further agreed on guidelines for government policy regarding multinational corporations, including nondiscrimination against foreign corporations, equitable treatment under international law, respect for contracts, and government cooperation to avoid beggar-thy-neighbor investment policies. Finally, the developed countries agreed to establish consultative procedures to monitor and review the agreed-upon guidelines. Although the OECD code is voluntary and its guidelines are often deliberately vague, it is a step toward the development and implementation of international norms.[124]

The OECD agreed in 1979 on a Model Tax Convention, which deals with transfer pricing. This convention attempted to establish an "arm's length principle" to prevent transfer pricing that takes advantage of tax havens—geographic zones with much lower than average tax levels—by shifting profits toward the tax haven. The arm's length principle compares prices used in intrafirm transactions with those that might be used between unrelated firms. If there is a major discrepancy, then the intrafirm prices violate the arm's length principle. While this is by no means a perfect resolution of the problems posed by transfer pricing, it probably helps to prevent the most blatant abuses. In a report published in 1994, the OECD reaffirmed its commitment to the arm's length principle.[125]

In 1995, the twenty-five members of the OECD began negotiations on new rules for international investment called the Multilateral Agreement on Investment. The agreement was designed to increase investment flows by clarifying the rights of foreign investors, eliminating barriers to investment, and creating a venue for dispute settlement. The members of the OECD asked outsiders to consider joining the agreement.[126]

Another limited international solution was offered by the United Nations. Largely as a result of the pressures from the Third World Countries, in 1974 and 1975 two new organizations were established within the United Nations system: the Center on Transnational Corporations (CTC), which gathered and generated information on multinational corporations, and also the intergovernmental United Nations Commission on Transnational Corporations (UNCTC), which acted as a forum for considering issues related to multinational corporations, for conducting inquiries, and for supervising the center. The commission's activities focused on the development of an international code of conduct for multinational corporations. Because the commission was such a large, public governmental forum and because the positions of the member countries differed (thirty-three were developing countries, five were socialist, and ten were developed market economies), the bargaining process was tedious and often confrontational. After well over a decade, the negotiations on a code of conduct remained deadlocked on a number of issues. Most difficult were the definition of a transnational corporation—with the developed market countries wanting to include state-owned transnationals of the Eastern bloc and the socialist states not wanting to accept this definition—as well as the demand of the developed market economies for assurances on the treatment of MNCs by host governments in return for concessions governing the MNCs' behavior. In the 1980s, as interest shifted from controlling to encouraging foreign investment, the code negotiations languished.

The CTC attempted to remedy the dearth of information on multinationals by studying their operations and effects, offering technical advice to member countries, and making policy recommendations to the commission. In the process, the center has commissioned and compiled information on multinationals and has made available services to countries whose lack of information could place them at a negotiating disadvantage with foreign corporations.[127] When the United Nations was restructured in the early 1990s, the UNCTC was disbanded.[128]

Other steps have been taken in the United Nations toward regulating various MNC activities. The United Nations Conference on Trade and Development (UNCTAD) formulated a code in 1980 on restrictive business practices that establishes principles and rules for controlling anticompetitive behavior, such as abuse of market power or restraint of competition. Other agreements have been reached concerning consumer protection, and transborder data flows. Negotiations are taking place in various parts of the United Nations system on technology transfer and international patent agreements.[129]

One final form of international management of multinational corporations involves not a unified and centralized order but, rather, a complex system of bilateral or multilateral negotiations among states, possibly leading to a series of agreements on specific matters or to methods for mediating conflicts. Conflicting national laws, in such areas as taxation, antitrust regulations, patents, export controls, and balance-of-payments controls, may be harmonized through such negotiation. In the area of taxation, for example, the OECD has written a draft convention containing proposals regarding many issues of taxation. Although never implemented, the treaty has guided subsequent bilateral negotiations and treaties among the developed market economies.[130]

Another bilateral approach might be the establishment of arbitration, adjudication, or simply consultation procedures that would accompany regulations or take the place of regulations when rules cannot be agreed upon. Although the World Bank has set up such an organization, called the International Center for the Settlement of Investment Disputes (ICSID), very few nations have recognized it, and few disputes have been submitted to it. It is possible, however, to create institutions or processes to which countries or companies and countries desiring a solution can turn. Such commissions existed in the socialist states to manage state-corporate disputes, and NAFTA and the U.S.-Canada Free Trade Agreement include provisions for a dispute settlement panels to resolve trade disputes and to continue reviewing each country's trade remedy laws.

In conclusion, the international management of multinational corporations has focused on promoting foreign direct investment. Not until the 1970s were there any significant attempts to establish rules of conduct, and even then the political impetus came largely from the developing countries. Despite some international tension and national uneasiness regarding multinational corporations, there is no dominant perception of a common interest in control in the developed market economies or in the one country that might mobilize the system for common action—the United States. Until there is a change in this international consensus, the international control of multinational corporations will remain limited. Thus the international politics of FDI in the coming years is not likely to focus on international regimes but rather on national and regional policies.

NOTES

1. Multinational corporations (MNCs) are also referred to as multinational enterprises (MNEs), transational corporations (TNCs), and transnational enterprises (TNEs).

2. John H. Dunning, *Multinational Enterprises and the Global Economy* (Reading, Mass.: Addison-Wesley, 1992), 3. Increasingly, a firm can come to resemble a multinational corporation by negotiating international cooperation agreements (ICAs) with firms in other countries, instead of

engaging in foreign direct investment. So the most important prerequisite for calling a firm multinational is no longer the ownership of overseas assets but rather direct participation in overseas value-added activities. We are indebted to Stephen Kobrin for his comments on this point.

3. Ibid.

4. The 10-percent cutoff has been adopted by the Organization for Economic Cooperation and Development as a standard for measuring FDI. Unfortunately, only the United States and Japan abide by the OECD standard. See DeAnne Julius, *Global Companies and Public Policy: The Growing Challenge of Foreign Direct Investment* (London: Royal Institute of International Affairs, 1990), 16.

5. Edward M. Graham and Paul R. Krugman, *Foreign Direct Investment in the United States*, 3rd ed. (Washington: Institute for International Economics, 1995), 9–11.

6. This chapter focuses on direct foreign investment in the developed market economies; see Chapter 8 for a discussion of investment problems in North-South relations.

7. Mira Wilkins, *The Emergence of Multinational Enterprise: American Business Abroad from the Colonial Era to 1914* (Cambridge: Harvard University Press, 1970), 201; Alfred D. Chandler Jr., *The Visible Hand: The Managerial Revolution in American Business* (Cambridge: The Belknap Press of Harvard University Press, 1977); and Alfred D. Chandler, *Scale and Scope: The Dynamics of Industrial Capitalism* (Cambridge: The Belknap Press of Harvard University Press, 1990).

8. United Nations Conference on Trade and Development, *World Investment Report, 1994: Transnational Corporations, Employment and the Workplace* (New York: United Nations, 1994), 3.

9. See Stephen Hymer and Robert Rowthorn, "Multinational Corporations and International Oligopoly: The Non-American Challenge," in Charles P. Kindleberger, ed., *The International Corporation* (Cambridge: MIT Press, 1971), 57–91.

10. Raymond Vernon, *Sovereignty at Bay: The Multinational Spread of U.S. Enterprises* (New York: Basic Books, 1971), 11.

11. The internalization theory is based on work done by Ronald H. Coase on the theory of the firm. See Coase's "The Nature of the Firm," *Economica* 4 (1937): 386–405. Stephen Hymer, in *The International Operations of National Firms: A Study of Direct Foreign Investment* (Cambridge: MIT Press, 1976), emphasizes the market imperfections—such as high transaction costs—that allow multinationals to realize monopoly or oligopoly rents. Oliver Williamson has taken Coase's and Hymer's work further in two books: Oliver Williamson, *Markets and Hierarchies* (New York: Free Press, 1975); and Oliver Williamson, *The Economic Institutions of Capitalism: Firms, Markets and Relational Contracting* (New York: Free Press, 1985). John Dunning has managed to synthesize these different approaches in a theory that will be discussed at greater length below.

12. On joint ventures, see Richard E. Caves, *Multinational Enterprise and Economic Analysis* (Cambridge, England: Cambridge University Press, 1982) and David C. Mowery, ed., *International Collaborative Ventures in U.S. Manufacturing* (Cambridge: Ballinger, 1988). On strategic alliances, see Bernard M. Gilroy, *Networking in Multinational Enterprises: The Importance of Strategic Alliances* (Columbia: University of South Carolina Press, 1993); Peter F. Cowhey and Jonathan D. Aronson, *Managing the World Economy: The Consequences of Corporate Alliances* (New York: Council on Foreign Relations Press, 1993); Refik Culpan, ed., *Multinational Strategic Alliances* (New York: International Business Press, 1993); and Lynn K. Mytelka, ed., *Strategic Partnerships: States, Firms and International Competition* (Rutherford, N.J.: Fairleigh Dickinson University Press, 1991).

13. Louis T. Wells, Jr., "The Multinational Enterprise: What Kind of International Organization?" in Robert O. Keohane and Joseph S. Nye, Jr., eds. *Transnational Relations and World Politics* (Cambridge: Harvard University Press, 1972): 97–114; John M. Stopford and Louis T. Wells Jr., *Managing the Multinational Enterprise: Organization of the Firm and Ownership of the Subsidiaries* (New York: Basic Books, 1972); and Stefan H. Robock et al., *International Business and Multinational Enterprises* (Homewood, Ill.: Irwin, 1977): 399–450.

14. See Vernon, *Sovereignty at Bay.*

15. *Survey of Current Business*, August 1987 (Washington: Government Printing Office, 1987). Note that these figures are cited at book value, which means that they represent the historical value of the investments—that is, what they cost at the time of acquisition with no adjustment for inflation or changing market values since then. This means that the U.S. investments, which were generally made earlier, are undervalued. Although the increase in other countries' foreign direct investment is significant, the contrast would not be as sharp if all investments were measured at current market value.

16. United Nations Conference on Trade and Development (UNCTAD), *World Investment Report 1994* (New York: United Nations, 1994), 409.

17. A. E. Safarian, *Governments and Multinationals: Policies in the Developed Countries* (Washington: British-North American Committee, 1983), 14; Steven Globerman, "Canada," in John H. Dunning, ed., *Multinational Enterprises, Economic Structure and International Competitiveness* (New York: Wiley, 1985); and Michael J. Twomey, *Multinational Corporations and the North American Free Trade Agreement* (Westport, Ct.: Praeger, 1993), 78.

18. John Dunning and John Cantwell, *IRM Directory of Statistics of International Investment and Production* (New York: New York University Press, 1987), table A-8.

19. UNCTAD, *World Investment Report 1994*, 421.

20. Ibid.

21. UNCTAD, *World Investment Report 1994*, 409.

22. V. N. Balasubramanyam and David Greenaway, "Economic Integration and Foreign Direct Investment: Japanese Investment in the EC," *Journal of Common Market Studies* 30 (June 1992): 175–193; Yoko Sazanami, "Determinants of Japanese Foreign Direct Investment: Locational Attractiveness of European Countries to Japanese Multinationals," *Revue Économique* 43 (July 1992): 661–670; and Stephen Thomsen and Stephen Woolcock, *Direct Investment and European Integration* (London: Royal Institute of International Affairs, 1993): 63–65.

23. *Survey of Current Business*, August 1987, tables 9 and 10. The 1992 percentage was calculated by the authors from data reported in the UNCTAD *World Investment Report 1994*.

24. Japan Economic Institute, "Japan's Fiscal 1987 Foreign Direct Investment," *JEI Report* no. 23B (June 17, 1988), 9–13.

25. Randall Jones, "Japan's Role in World Financial Markets," *JEI Report* no. 42A (November 14, 1986).

26. "The Top 500 Banks in the World," *American Banker* (July 26, 1988): 34; and United Nations, *Transnational Corporations in World Development: Trends and Prospects* (New York: United Nations, 1988), 114.

27. United Nations, *Transnational Corporations in World Development: Trends and Prospects* (New York: United Nations, 1988), 119.

28. Martin Carnoy, "Multinationals in a Changing World Economy: Whither the Nation-State?" in Martin Carnoy, Manuel Castells, Stephen S. Cohen, and Fernando H. Cardoso, *The New Global Economy in the Information Age: Reflections on Our Changing World* (University Park: Pennsylvania State University Press, 1993), 52. In recent years, Japanese banks have been hurt by losses in real estate and other types of investments. The general doldrums of the Japanese economy in the early 1990s diminished the role of Japanese banks in the world economy.

29. On this topic, see Dennis Encarnation, *Rivals Beyond Trade: America Versus Japan in Global Competition* (Ithaca, N.Y.: Cornell University Press, 1992); and Mark Mason, *American Multinationals and Japan: The Political Economy of Japanese Capital Controls, 1899–1980* (Cambridge: Harvard University Press, 1992).

30. For a general analysis, see Thomas L. Brewer, "Government Policies, Market Imperfections, and Foreign Direct Investment," *Journal of International Business Studies* 24 (first quarter 1993): 101–120. See also United Nations Center on Transnational Corporations, *Government Policies and Foreign Direct Investment*, UNCTC current studies, series A, no. 17 (New York: United Nations, 1991).

31. Charles Lipson, *Standing Guard: Protecting Foreign Capital in the Nineteenth and Twentieth Centuries* (Berkeley: University of California Press, 1985), 242–248.

32. For national incentives, see Stephen E. Guisinger, *Investment Incentives and Performance Requirements* (New York: Praeger, 1985); Earl H. Fry, *The Politics of International Investment* (New York: McGraw-Hill, 1983), 127–160; and Organization for Economic Cooperation and Development, *Investment Incentives and Disincentives and the International Investment Process* (Paris: OECD, 1983).

33. Susan and Martin Tolchin, *Buying into America: How Foreign Money Is Changing the Face of Our Nation* (New York: Times Books, 1988); and James Moses, *State Investment Incentives in the USA* (London: Economist Publications, 1985).

34. Williamson, *Markets and Hierarchies*, 4.

35. Thomas L. Brewer, "Government Policies, Market Imperfections, and Foreign Direct Investment," 104.

36. Dunning, *Multinational Enterprises and the Global Economy*, ch. 4.

37. See, for example, Wilfred J. Ethier, "The Multinational Firm," *Quarterly Journal of Economics* 101 (November 1986), 805–833.

38. Vernon, *Sovereignty at Bay*, 65–77; and Raymond Vernon, "The Product Cycle Hypothesis in a New International Environment," *Oxford Bulletin of Economics and Statistics* 41 (1979), 255–267.

39. See Stephen H. Hymer, *The International Operations of National Firms: A Study of Direct Foreign Investment* (Cambridge: MIT Press, 1976); and Charles P. Kindleberger, *American Business Abroad: Six Lectures on Direct Investment* (New Haven: Yale University Press, 1969), 1–36.

40. John Lunn, "Determinants of U.S. Direct Investment in the E.E.C.," *European Economic Review*, 13 (January 1980): 93–101; Claudy G. Culem, "The Locational Determinants of Direct Investments among the Industrialized Countries," *European Economic Review*, 32 (April 1988): 885–904; and Patrick J. O'Sullivan, "An Assessment of Ireland's Export-Led Growth Strategy via Foreign Direct Investment," *Weltwirtschaftliches Archiv*, 129 (1993): 139–158.

41. Ryuhei Wakasugi, "Is Japanese Foreign Investment a Substitute for International Trade?" *Japan and the World Economy* 6 (1994): 45–52.

42. Evidence for this convergence in the behavior of foreign MNCs in the United States can be found in Edward M. Graham and Paul R. Krugman, *Foreign Direct Investment in the United States*, 3rd ed. (Washington: Institute for International Economics, 1995).

43. Robert Z. Lawrence, "Efficient or Exclusionist? The Import Behavior of Japanese Corporate Groups," *Brookings Papers on Economic Activity*, 1 (1991): 311–341; Richard Florida and Martin Kenney, "Transplanted Organizations: The Transfer of Japanese Industrial Organization to the United States," *American Sociological Review* 56 (June 1991): 381–398; and Michelle Gittelman and Edward Graham, "The Performance and Structure of Japanese Affiliates in the European Community," in Mark Mason and Dennis Encarnation, eds., *Does Ownership Matter? Japanese Multinationals in Europe* (Oxford: Clarendon Press, 1994).

44. On this point, see Dunning, *Multinational Enterprises and the Global Economy*, 281–283.

45. See Harry G. Johnson, "The Efficiency and Welfare Implications of the International Corporation," in Kindleberger, *The International Corporation*, 35–56; Kindleberger, *American Business Abroad*.

46. Graham and Krugman, *Foreign Direct Investment in the United States*, 57.

47. Encarnation, *Rivals Beyond Trade*, 28.

48. Dunning, *Mutlinational Enterprises and the Global Economy*, 386, 408–411.

49. An example of this sort of work is Ann Harrison, "The Role of Multinationals in Economic Development: The Benefits of FDI," *Columbia Journal of World Business* 29 (winter 1994): 7–11. The work reported was done in developing countries but could have been as easily done in industrialized countries.

50. Graham and Krugman, *Foreign Direct Investment in the United States* 59; and James P. Womack, Daniel T. Jones, and Daniel Roos, *The Machine That Changed the World: The Story of Lean Production* (New York: Rawson Associates, 1990), especially 86.

51. See Eduardo Borenzstein, José de Gregorio, and Jon-Wha Lee, *How Does Foreign Direct Investment Affect Economic Growth?*, Working Paper No. 5057, (Cambridge, Mass.: National Bureau of Economic Research, March 1995).

52. See Stephen Hymer, "The Efficiency (Contradictions) of Multinational Corporations," *American Economic Review*, 60 (May 1970), 441–448; Graham and Krugman, *Foreign Direct Investment in the United States*, 59–66.

53. A good summary can be found in Dunning, *Multinational Enterprises and the Global Economy*, chs. 10–16.

54. See Royal Commission on Canada's Economic Prospects, *Final Report* (Ottawa: Queen's Printer, 1958); Task Force on the Structure of Canadian Industry, *Foreign Ownership and the Structure of Canadian Industry* (Ottawa: Privy Council Office, 1968); and *Foreign Direct Investment in Canada* (The Gray Report) (Ottawa: Information Canada, 1972). For private studies, see Charles A. Barrett, *The Future of Foreign Investment in Canada* (Ottawa: Conference Board of Canada, 1984); and A. E. Safarian, *Foreign Direct Investment: A Survey of Canadian Research* (Montreal: Institute for Research in Public Policy, 1985). For a somewhat more skeptical view, see Steven Globerman, *U.S. Ownership of Firms in Canada* (Montreal and Washington: Canadian-American Committee, 1979). For a critical analysis, see Kari Levitt, *Silent Surrender: The Multinational Corporation in Canada* (New York: St. Martin's Press, 1970).

55. Task Force, *Foreign Ownership and the Structure of Canadian Industry*, 37.

56. (Caborn Report) European Communities, European Parliament, Working Documents 1981–1982, *Report on Enterprises and Governments in Economic Activity*, Doc. 1-169/81 (May 15, 1981), 5.

57. Giles Y. Bertin, "Foreign Investment in France," in Isaiah A. Litvak and Christopher J. Maule, eds., *Foreign Investment: The Experience of Host Countries* (New York: Praeger, 1970), 105–122; Dunning, "Multinational Enterprises and Nation States," 406–408; John H. Dunning, "The Role of American Investment in the British Economy," *Political and Economic Planning*, Broadsheet No. 508 (February 1969); and Stephen Young, *Foreign Multinationals and the British Economy* (New York: Croom Helm, 1988).

58. See Task Force, *Foreign Ownership and the Structure of Canadian Industry*, and *Foreign Direct Investment in Canada*; United Nations, *Transnational Corporations in World Development*; Jack N. Behrman, *National Interests and the Multinational Enterprise: Tensions Among the North Atlantic Countries* (Englewood Cliffs, N.J.: Prentice-Hall, 1970), 32–84; Jean-Jacques Servan-Schreiber, *The American Challenge* (New York: Atheneum, 1968); and Susan and Martin Tolchin, *Buying into America*.

59. On this point, see Johnson, (Note 45) "The Efficiency and Welfare Implications of the International Corporation."

60. Task Force, *Foreign Direct Investment in Canada*, 183–211.

61. Georges Peninou et al., *Who's Afraid of the Multinationals? A Survey of European Opinion on Multinational Corporations* (Hampshire, England: Saxon House, 1978), 59–62.

62. Ibid., 93–97.

63. John Fayerweather, "Elite Attitudes Toward Multinational Firms" in J. Fayerweather, ed., *Host National Attitudes Toward Multinational Corporations* (New York: Praeger, 1982).

64. See Cooper, *The Economics of Interdependence*, 98–103; and Robert G. Gilpin, Jr., *U.S. Power and the Multinational Corporation: The Political Economy of Foreign Direct Investment* (New York: Basic Books, 1975). For an evaluation of the impact of U.S. multinationals' overseas activities on the United States, see C. Fred Bergsten, Thomas Horst, and Theodore Moran, *American Multinationals and American Interests* (Washington: Brookings Institution, 1978); Robert Stobaugh et al., *Nine Investments Abroad and Their Impact at Home* (Boston: Division of Research, Harvard Graduate School of Business Administration, 1976); Richard T. Frank and Richard T. Freeman, *Distributional Consequences of Direct Foreign Investment* (New York: Academic Press, 1978); and AFL-CIO, 16th Constitutional Convention, *Resolution on International Trade and Investment*, October 1985. A more recent study by Martin Feldstein suggests that each dollar of outbound FDI reduces domestic investment by about a dollar and the domestic capital stock by between 20 and 38 cents. See Martin Feldstein, *The Effects of Outbound Foreign Investment on the Domestic Capital Stock*, National Bureau of Economic Research Working Paper #4668, March 1994.

65. Peninou et al., *Who's Afraid of the Multinationals?* 59–62. See also Joseph La Palombara and Stephen Blank, *Multinational Corporations in Comparative Perspective* (New York: The Conference Board, 1977), 6–8.

66. Peninou et al., *Who's Afraid of the Multinationals?* 69–70.

67. J. Alex Murray and Lawrence Le Duc, "Changing Attitudes Toward Foreign Investment in Canada," in John Fayerweather, *Host National Attitudes Toward Multinational Corporations* (New York: Praeger, 1982), 216–235.

68. John Fayerweather, "Elite Attitudes Toward Multinational Firms: A Study of Britain, Canada, and France," *International Studies Quarterly* 16 (December 1972): 472–490.

69. For example, see the analysis of French attitudes toward sensitive industries in Allan W. Johnstone, *United States Direct Investment in France: An Investigation of the French Charges* (Cambridge: MIT Press, 1965), 32–34.

70. See Behrman, *National Interests and the Multinational Enterprise*, 69–84.

71. Task Force, *Foreign Direct Investment in Canada*, 428.

72. Organization for Economic Cooperation and Development, *Transfer Pricing and Multinational Enterprises: Three Taxation Issues* (Paris: OECD, 1984); Alan M. Rugman and Lorraine Eden, eds., *Multinationals and Transfer Pricing* (New York: St. Martin's Press, 1985); and Roger Y. W. Tang, *Transfer Pricing in the 1990s: Tax and Management Perspectives* (Westport, Conn.: Quorum Books, 1993).

73. Dunning, *Multinational Enterprises and the Global Economy*, 509.

74. George Graham, "U.S. Tax Move Alarms Multinational Groups," *Financial Times*, August 15, 1995, p. 4; Jonathan Schwarz, "Survey of World Taxation," *Financial Times*, February 24, 1995, p. 35; and "The Unitary Tax Escape," *The Fresno Bee*, July 6, 1994. On the difficulty of administering the California unitary tax, see General Accounting Office, *Tax Policy and Administration: California Taxes on Multinational Corporations and Related Federal Issues* (Washington: Government Printing Office, August 10, 1995).

75. Behrman, *National Interests and the Multinational Enterprise*, 73–76.

76. See Hart, *Rival Capitalists*, especially chs. 2 and 3.

77. See Wolfgang Streeck, "Lean Production in the German Automobile Industry? A Test Case," in Suzanne Berger and Ronald Dore, eds., *Convergence or Diversity? National Models of Production and Distribution in a Global Economy* (Ithaca, N.Y.: Cornell University Press, forthcoming).

78. See Behrman, *National Interests and the Multinational Enterprise*, 88–127.

79. See, for example, Michael Mastanduno, *Economic Containment: CoCom and the Politics of East-West Trade* (Ithaca, N.Y.: Cornell University Press, 1992); and William J. Long, *U.S. Export Control Policy: Executive Autonomy versus Congressional Reform* (New York: Columbia University Press, 1989).

80. Bruce Jentleson, *Pipeline Politics: The Complex Political Economy of East-West Energy Trade* (Ithaca, N.Y.: Cornell University Press, 1986); Beverly Crawford, *Economic Vulnerability in International Relations: East-West Trade, Investment, and Finance* (New York: Columbia University Press, 1993), ch. 5; and Angela Stent, *From Embargo to Ostpolitik: The Political Economy of West German-Soviet Relations* (New York: Cambridge University Press, 1981).

81. Behrman, *National Interests and the Multinational Enterprise*, 104–113.

82. Mark R. Joelson, "International Antitrust: Problems and Defenses," *Law and Policy in International Business* 2 (summer 1970): 1121–1134.

83. John B. Goodman and Louis W. Pauly, "The Obsolescence of Capital Controls? Economic Management in an Age of Global Markets," *World Politics* 36 (October 1993): 50–82; and John Conybeare, *U.S. Foreign Economic Policy and the International Capital Markets: The Case of Capital Export Controls, 1963–74* (New York: Garland, 1988).

84. See similar possibilities outlined in Task Force, *Foreign Direct Investment in Canada*, 301–306; Pat Choate, *Agents of Influence: How Japan Manipulates America's Political and Economic System* (New York: Simon and Schuster, 1990).

85. Task Force, *Foreign Direct Investment in Canada*, 305–307.

86. See U.S. Senate, 93rd Cong., 1st and 2nd sess., and 94th Cong., 1st and 2nd sess., *Multinational Corporations and United States Foreign Policy*, hearings before the Subcommittee on Multinational Corporations of the Committee on Foreign Relations (Washington: U.S. Government Printing Office, 1975).

87. Dennis M. Ray, "Corporations and American Foreign Relations," *The Annals*, 403 (September 1972), 80–92.

88. For a discussion of International Telephone & Telegraph, see U.S. Senate, *Multinational Corporations and United States Foreign Policy*; see also Jerome Levinson, "The Transnational Corporations and the Home Country," in *Conference on the Regulation of Transnational Corporations*, February 26, 1976 (New York: Columbia Journal of Transnational Law Association, 1976), 17–22.

89. Robert W. Cox, "Labor and the Multinationals," *Foreign Affairs*, 54 (January 1976), 344–365.

90. In John Fayerweather, *Foreign Investment in Canada: Prospects for National Policy* (White Plains, N.Y.: International Arts and Sciences Press, 1973), 32.

91. For an excellent discussion of this subject, see Charles Lipson, *Standing Guard: Protecting Foreign Capital in the Nineteenth and Twentieth Centuries* (Berkeley: University of California Press, 1985).

92. See Hart, *Rival Capitalists*, chs. 2 and 3.

93. For a good summary of national approaches to the management of foreign direct investment, see Linda M. Spencer, *American Assets: An Examination of Foreign Investment in the United States* (Arlington, Va.; Congressional Economic Leadership Institute, 1988), 19–27. See also Earl H. Fry, op. cit. and OECD, *Investment Incentives and Disincentives*.

94. See M. Y. Yoshino, "Japan As Host to the International Corporation," in Kindleberger, *The International Corporation*, 345–369; Lawrence B. Krause, "Evolution of Foreign Direct Investment: The United States and Japan," in Jerome B. Cohen, ed., *Pacific Partnership: United States–Japan Trade: Prospects and Recommendations for the Seventies* (Lexington, Mass.: Lexington Books for Japan Society, 1972), 149–176; Noritake Kobayashi, "Foreign Investment in Japan," in Litvak and Maule, *Foreign Investment: The Experience of Host Countries*, 123–160; Mark Mason, *American Multinationals and Japan: The Political Economy of Japanese Capital Controls, 1899–1990* (Cambridge: Harvard University Press, 1992); and Dennis J. Encarnation, *Rivals Beyond Trade: America versus Japan in Global Competition* (Ithaca, N.Y.: Cornell University Press, 1992).

95. Robert Z. Lawrence, "Japan's Low Level of Inward Investment: The Role of Inhibitions on Acquisitions," in Kenneth A. Froot, ed., *Foreign Direct Investment* (Chicago: University of Chicago Press, 1993).

96. See Japan Economic Institute, "Recent Trends in U.S. Direct Investment in Japan," Report No. 23A (June 15, 1984), and "Foreign Direct Investment in Japan" Annual Updates for 1985 (August 16, 1985), 1986 (October 10, 1986) and 1987 (April 17, 1987), *JEI Report* (Japan Economic Institute, Washington). See also Dennis Encarnation, "American-Japanese Cross-Investment: A Second Front of Economic Rivalry" in Thomas McCraw, ed., *America versus Japan* (Boston: Harvard Business School Press, 1986).

97. In July 1995, the United States and Japan concluded an investment agreement under which the Japanese government undertook to promote FDI inflows into Japan by giving foreign investors access to Japanese government finance and by promoting access zones and joint research facilities.

98. FIRA rejected only 10 percent of the proposals submitted for review between 1974 and 1985, but if one considers proposals that were withdrawn prior to review or firms that were deterred from going through the process at all, the rejection rate was probably closer to 25 percent. See Rod B. McNaughton, "U.S. Foreign Direct Investment in Canada, 1985–1989," *The Canadian Geographer* 36 (summer 1992), 181–189.

99. See Safarian, *Governments and Multinationals*, 14–20. For a critical review of FIRA, see Christopher C. Beckman, *The Foreign Investment Review Agency: Images and Realities* (Ottawa: Canadian Conference Board, 1984).

100. On Investment Canada Act, see *Investment Canada, Annual Report 1986-87* (Minister of Supply and Services Canada, 1987); and Thorne, Ernst and Whinney, Canada's Investment Canada Act: An Executive Summary (Toronto: Thorne, Ernst and Whinney, 1986).

101. See A. E. Safarian, "The Canada-U.S. Free Trade Agreement and Foreign Direct Investment," *Trade Monitor* no. 3, May 1988, C.D. Howe Institute, 16ff.; Earl Fry and Lee H. Radebaugh, *The Canada/U.S. Free Trade Agreement: The Impact on Service Industries* (Provo, Ut.: Brigham Young University, 1988); Jeffrey Atik, "Fairness and Managed Foreign Direct Investment," *Columbia Journal of Transnational Law* 32 (1994); 1–42; and *The Canada-U.S. Free Trade Agreement* (Ottawa: Department of External Affairs, 1987).

102. On the role of the British Monopolies and Mergers Commission in approving foreign acquisitions, see Edward Graham and Michael Ebert, "Foreign Direct Investment and U.S. National Security: Fixing Exon-Florio," *The World Economy* 14 (September 1991): 256–261.

103. Charles Torem and William Laurence Craig, "Developments in the Control of Foreign Investment in France," *Michigan Law Review* 70 (December 1971): 285–336; Safarian, *Governments and Multinationals*, 20–24.

104. Graham and Krugman, *Foreign Investment in the United States*, 126.

105. Ibid., 129.

106. Ibid., 129–130.

107. An R&D consortium is an effort, usually jointly funded by a government together with a number of private firms who are members of the consortium, to share the costs of developing a new commercial technology. Japan pioneered this form of collaborative research and was particularly successful in the semiconductor industry with its VLSI (very large scale integrated [circuits]) program between 1976 and 1979.

108. See Tolchin, *Buying into America* and Robert B. Reich, "Corporation and Nation," *The Atlantic*, May 1988, 76.

109. Robert Reich and E. Mankin, "Joint Ventures with Japan Give Away Our Future," *Harvard Business Review* no. 2 (March-April 1986): 78–86. Reich, currently Secretary of Commerce in the Clinton administration, changed his views on this subject in subsequent publications, including *The Work of Nations* (New York: Knopf, 1991).

110. See Cynthia Day Wallace, *Legal Control of the Multinational Enterprise* (The Hague: Martinus Nijhoff, 1982); and John Robinson, *Multinationals and Political Control* (New York: St. Martin's, 1983).

111. See Schreiber, *The American Challenge*.

112. See J. J. Boddewyn, "Western European Policies Toward U.S. Investors," *The Bulletin* (March 1974) 45–63; Raymond Vernon, "Enterprise and Government in Western Europe," in Raymond Vernon, ed., *Big Business and the State: Changing Relations in Western Europe* (Cambridge: Harvard University Press, 1974), 3–24; and Behrman, *National Interests and the Multinational Enterprise*, 161–172.

113. Caborn report, p. 7.

114. For an analysis that argues that the EC has imposed significant controls on MNCs, see Robinson, *Multinationals and Political Control*. For a survey of European Community initiatives and their status, see *Business Guide to EC Initiatives* (Brussels: American Chamber of Commerce in Belgium, 1988).

115. Article 130f (1), "Treaty Establishing the European Economic Community (as amended by the Single European Act, July 1, 1987)," *Treaties Establishing the European Communities* (Luxembourg: Office for Official Publications of the European Communities, 1987), 239.

116. Alyssa A. Grikscheit, "Are We Compatible? Current European Community Law on the Compatibility of Joint Ventures with the Common Market and Possibilities for Future Development," *Michigan Law Review* 92 (February 1994): 968–1033.

117. Denise Claveloux, "Pending Social Legislation Means Big Changes to How EC Does Business," *Electronics*, November 8, 1993, 13; and "Unions Love Maastricht," *The Economist*, December 4, 1993, 54.

118. See Lipson, *Standing Guard*, 132–133.

119. For example, the International Civil Aviation Organization (ICAO), the International Labor Organization (ILO), and the World Health Organization (WHO).

120. See Clair Wilcox, *A Charter for World Trade* (New York: Macmillan, 1949), 145–148.

121. United Nations Economic and Social Council, *Report of the Ad Hoc Committee on Restrictive Business Practices* (New York: United Nations, 1953); and General Agreement on Tariffs and Trade, *Decisions of the Seventeenth Session* (Geneva: GATT, December 5, 1960), 17.

122. See George W. Ball, "Cosmocorp: The Importance of Being Stateless," *Columbia Journal of World Business*, 2 (November-December 1967): 25–30.

123. Paul M. Goldberg and Charles Kindleberger, "Toward a GATT for Investment: A Proposal for Supervision of the International Corporation," *Law and Policy in International Business*, 2 (summer 1970): 195–323.

124. Organization for Economic Cooperation and Development, *International Investment and Multinational Enterprises* (Paris: OECD, 1976). Experience with the OECD guidelines to date indicates that they may indeed have some impact on the operations of multinationals within member states. See, for example, R. Blanpain, *The Badger Case and the OECD Guidelines for Multinational Enterprises* (Deventer, the Netherlands: Kluwer, 1977). For OECD reviews, see OECD, *National Treatment for Foreign Controlled Enterprises in OECD Member Countries* (Paris: OECD, 1978); OECD, *International Direct Investment: Policies, Procedures and Practices in OECD Member Countries* (Paris: OECD, 1979); and OECD, *Controls and Impediments Affecting Inward Direct Investments in OECD Countries* (Paris: OECD, 1987).

125. Organization for Economic Cooperation and Development, *Transfer Pricing Guidelines for Multinational Enterprises and Tax Administrations* (Paris: OECD, 1994).

126. Eduardo Lachica, "OECD Nations Ask Outsiders to Join Investment Treaty," *The Wall Street Journal*, November 9, 1995, p. A17.

127. For a compendium of the center's publications, see United Nations, Center on Transnational Corporations, *Bibliography on Transnational Corporations* (New York: United Nations, 1988). The center's periodical, *CTC Reporter*, carries summaries and announcements of the center's work.

128. The CTC, which had been based in New York, was absorbed into the United Nations Conference on Trade and Development (UNCTAD) in Geneva. Fortunately, UNCTAD has continued to publish the data on FDI and MNC activities that were previously published by the CTC.

129. Black, Blank, and Hanson, *Multinationals in Contention*, 221–225; Werner Feld, *Multinational Corporations and U.N. Politics: The Quest for Codes of Conduct* (Elmsford, N.Y.: Pergamon Press, 1980); Debra Lynn Miller, "Panacea or Problem? The Proposed International Code of Conduct for Technology Transfer," *Journal of International Affairs* (spring-summer 1979): 43–62.

130. See Seymour J. Rubin, "The International Firm and the National Jurisdiction," in Kindleberger, *The International Corporation*, pp. 179–204 and 475–488.

5

The North-South System and the Possibility of Change

The management problems of the North-South system are quite different from those of the Western system. For the interdependent system of developed market economies, the crucial issue is whether it is possible to achieve the necessary political capability at the national, regional, and global levels to ensure that international economic relations continue to result in mutually beneficial outcomes while also modernizing (although not drastically altering) the international economic institutions that have been in place since World War II. The North-South system is separate from, but also embedded in, the Western system. It is separate because the rules of the North-South system reflect the much lower income levels and resource bases of the developing countries. It is embedded because the countries of the North (actually the West) have veto power over important changes in the system. The main question for the North-South system is whether it is possible to change the system so that more than a small number of developing countries benefit from it.

In the Western system, control is facilitated by a perceived common interest in the system. In the North-South system, there is less perception of a common interest. The developed market economies feel that the North-South system, although perhaps not perfect, is legitimate, because it benefits them and because they have significant decision-making authority. The Southern states tend to feel that both the Western and the North-South systems are illegitimate because they have not enjoyed a large enough share of the economic rewards. From their viewpoint, neither system has adequately promoted their economic development. Also, they feel that their interests are not properly represented in these international economic regimes.

One of the key sources of Southern grievances with the North-South system is the inability of the South to reduce the gap in average incomes between itself and the North. Average income, as measured by gross national product (GNP) divided by the total population (GNP per capita), was $21,960 in the 38 high-income countries, $2,440 in the 113 middle-income countries, and $390 in the 56 low-income countries in 1992. The total population of the three groups of countries in that year was 808 million, 1.4 billion, and 3.2 billion, respectively. The gap in average incomes appears to have increased between 1982 and 1992 (see Figure 5-1).[1]

Global income is distributed quite unequally, and inequality may be increasing. The share of world income for the richest 20 percent of the global population rose from 70 percent to 85 percent from 1960 to 1991; the share of the poorest 20 percent declined from 2.3 percent to 1.4 percent during the same period.[2] Average annual growth in nominal GDP between 1974 and 1992 was 5.5 percent in the low-income countries, 1.1 percent in the middle-income countries, and 2.6 percent in the high-income countries (see Figure 5-2).[3] While economic growth rates were higher on the average in the South than in the North in recent years, high population growth rates and the relatively low income base of the South prevented economic growth from making much of an impact on the standard of living of the South's people, with the notable exception of a small number of very fast-growing countries. It is a hopeful sign, of course, that the two largest low–income countries—China and India—have experienced rapid growth in recent years.

Figure 5-1   GNP per Capita, Atlas Method, for Low-, Medium-, and High-Income Countries, 1982–1992, in Current Dollars

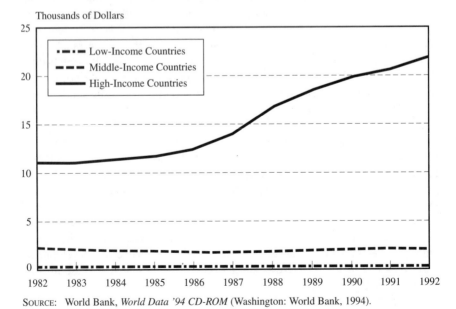

SOURCE: World Bank, *World Data '94 CD-ROM* (Washington: World Bank, 1994).

Figure 5-2   Growth in Nominal GDP in Low-, Middle- and High-Income Countries, 1974–1992, in Percentages

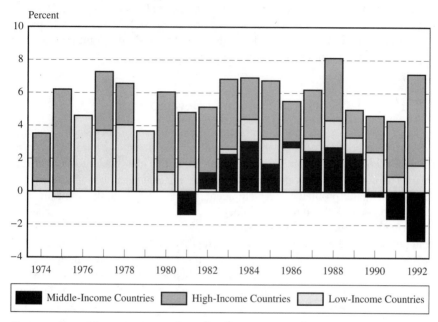

SOURCE: World Bank, *World Data '94 CD-ROM* (Washington: World Bank, 1994).

The management processes of the North-South system are quite different from those of the Western system. In the West, there is a relatively highly institutionalized system consisting of international organizations, elite networks, processes of negotiation, agreed-upon norms, and rules of the game. Although power is unequally distributed in the West, all members have access to both formal and informal management systems. In North-South relations, in contrast, there is no well-developed system with access for all. The South has been regularly excluded from the formal and informal processes of system management. North-South relations are controlled by the North as a subsidiary of the Western system. Understandably, the North perceives this structure as legitimate, whereas the South generally perceives it as illegitimate.

Since the end of World War II, developing countries have persistently sought to change their dependent role in international economic relations. As we shall discuss, their efforts to achieve growth and access to decision making have varied over time and from country to country. Southern strategies have been of three main types: (1) attempts to delink themselves from some aspects of the international economic system, (2) attempts to change the economic order itself, and (3) policies designed to maximize the benefits from integration into the prevailing system. These strategies have been shaped to a significant degree by the central question of whether it is possible to achieve growth and development within the prevailing international economic system. The dominant liberal philosophy argues that such development is not only possible but also most likely under a liberal economic regime. Two contending approaches—Marxist (and neo-Marxist) theories and **structuralism**—challenge the liberal analysis and argue that the system itself is at the root of the development problem.

Liberal Theories of Economic Development

Liberalism—especially as embodied in classical and neoclassical economics—is the dominant theory of the prevailing international economic system. Liberal theories of economic development argue that the existing international market structure provides the best framework for Southern economic development.[4] The major problems of development, in this view, lie in the domestic economic policies of the developing country, which create or accentuate market imperfections, reduce productivity of land, labor, and capital, and intensify social and political rigidities. The best way to remedy these weaknesses is through the adoption of market-oriented domestic policies. Given appropriate internal policies, the international system—through increased levels of trade, foreign investment, and foreign aid flows—can provide a basis for more rapid growth and economic development.

Trade, according to liberal analyses, can act as an engine of growth. Specialization that is consistent with national comparative advantages increases income levels in all countries engaging in free or relatively open trade. Specialization in areas where the factors of production are relatively abundant promotes more efficient resource allocation and permits economic actors to apply more effectively their technological and managerial skills. It also encourages higher levels of capital formation through the domestic financial system and inflows of FDI. Private financial flows from developed countries can be used to fund investment in infrastructure and productive facilities. In addition, foreign aid from developed market economies, although not a market relationship, is believed to help fill resource gaps in less-developed countries by, for example, providing capital, technology, and education. Finally, specialization in the presence of appropriate antitrust enforcement can stimulate domestic competition and improve international competitiveness simultaneously.

From the liberal viewpoint, the correct international Southern strategy for economic development is to foster those domestic changes necessary to promote foreign trade, inflows of foreign investment, and the international competitiveness of domestic firms. In practice, this means the reversal of policies that hinder trade and investment flows, such as high tariffs and restrictions on FDI inflows, and the adoption of policies that increase domestic levels of competition—for example through the privatization of state enterprises, deregulation of overregulated markets, and other domestic reforms.

Marxist and Neo-Marxist Theories of Development

Marxist and neo-Marxist theories take a view that is opposite to that of the international market system.[5] Southern countries, it is argued, are poor and exploited because of their history as subordinate elements in the world capitalist system. This condition will persist for as long as they remain part of that system. The international market is under the control of monopoly capitalists whose economic base is in the developed economies. The free flow of trade and investment, so much desired by liberals, enables the capitalist classes of both the developed and underdeveloped countries to extract the economic wealth of the underdeveloped countries for their own use. The result is the impoverishment of the masses of the Third World.

Trade between North and South is an unequal exchange, as control of the international market by the monopolies/oligopolies headquartered in the developed capitalist countries leads to declining prices for the raw materials produced by the South and rising prices for the industrial products produced by the North. Thus the **terms of trade** of the international market are biased against the South.[6] In addition, international trade encourages the South to concentrate on backward forms of production that prevent development. The language of comparative advantage used by liberal free-traders masks their desire to maintain an international division of labor that is unfavorable to the South.

Foreign investment further hinders and distorts Southern development, often by controlling the most dynamic local industries and expropriating the economic surplus of these sectors through the repatriation of profits, royalty fees, and licenses. According to many Marxists, there is a net outflow of capital from the South to the North. In addition, foreign investment contributes to unemployment by establishing capital-intensive production, aggravating uneven income distribution, displacing local capital and local entrepreneurs, adding to the emphasis on production for export, and promoting undesirable consumption patterns.

Another dimension of capitalist creation and perpetuation of underdevelopment is the international financial system. Trade and investment remove capital from the South and necessitate Southern borrowing from Northern financial institutions, both public and private. But debt service and repayment further drain Third World wealth. Finally, foreign aid reinforces the Third World's distorted development, by promoting foreign investment and trade at the expense of true development and by extracting wealth through debt service. Reinforcing these external market structures of dependence, according to some Marxists and neo-Marxists, are clientele social classes within the underdeveloped countries. Local elites with a vested interest in the structure of dominance and a monopoly of domestic power cooperate with international capitalist elites to perpetuate the international capitalist system.

Because international market operations and the clientele elite perpetuate dependence, any development under the international capitalist system is uneven, distorted, and, at best, partial. For most Marxists and neo-Marxists, the only appropriate strategy for development is revolutionary: total destruction of the international capitalist system and its replacement with an international socialist system. They differ on whether it is possible to achieve this revolutionary ideal on a national basis or whether it is necessary for the revolution to be global, but they agree that revolutionary change is the only way to achieve true development in the South.[7]

The Structuralists

Structural theory, which has had a significant influence on the international economic policy of the South, falls between liberalism and **Marxism.**[8] Structuralist analysis, like Marxist analysis, contends that the international market structure perpetuates backwardness and dependency in the South and encourages dominance by the North. According to this view, the market tends to favor the already well endowed and to thwart the less developed. Unregulated international trade and capital movements will accentuate, not diminish, international inequalities, unless accompanied by reforms at the national and international levels.

The structural bias of the international market, according to this school, rests in large part on the inequalities of the international trading system. Trade does not serve as an engine of growth as asserted by the liberals but actually widens the North-South gap. The system creates declining terms of trade for the South. Income inelasticity of demand for the primary product exports of the less-developed countries (increased income in the North does not lead to increased demand for imports from the South) and the existence of a competitive international market for those products lead to lower prices for Third World exports. At the same time, the monopoly structure of Northern markets and the rising demand for manufactured goods lead to higher prices for the industrial products of the North. Thus, under normal market conditions, international trade actually transfers income from the South to the North.[9]

Structuralists also argue that international trade creates an undesirable dual economy. Specialization and concentration on export industries based on comparative advantages in agriculture or the extraction of raw materials by the Southern economies do not fuel the rest of the economy as projected by the liberals. Instead, trade creates an export sector that has little or no dynamic effect on the rest of the economy and that drains resources from the rest of the economy. Thus, trade creates a developed and isolated export sector alongside an underdeveloped economy in general.

Foreign investment, the second part of the structural bias, often avoids the South, where profits and security are lower than in the developed market economies. When investment does flow to the South, it tends to concentrate in export sectors, thereby aggravating the dual economy and the negative effects of trade. Finally, foreign investment leads to a net flow of profits and interest to the developed, capital-exporting North.

The structuralist prescription for promoting economic development in the

South focuses on four types of policy changes: (1) **import-substituting industrialization (ISI);** (2) increased South-South trade and investment; (3) regional integration; and (4) population control. Structuralists assert that it is the specialization of Third World countries in the production and export of raw materials and agricultural commodities that hurts them in world trade because of the declining terms of trade for those products. Therefore the South needs to diversify away from agriculture and raw materials toward manufacturing and services activities. To do this, it may need to adopt high tariffs initially to encourage the establishment of domestic manufacturing facilities. This is the essence of import substitution.

Second, the South needs to reduce trade barriers among the developing countries in order to compensate for the generally small size of their domestic markets and to achieve economies of scale similar to those enjoyed by the industrialized nations of Europe, Asia, and North America. The best way to do this is to foster regional integration agreements among the developing countries, not unlike the ones that helped to bring prosperity to Western Europe after World War II. Increased South-South trade would be advantageous not just in adding to total world demand for exports from the South but also in allowing developing countries to develop technologies appropriate for the South, to counter the power of Northern MNCs, and to increase generally the competitiveness of businesses headquartered in the South.

Finally, structuralists like Raúl Prebisch and W. Arthur Lewis recognized that a key problem that had to be addressed was the depressing effect of rapid population growth on the average wages of Third World workers. If population growth could be reduced by appropriate population control policies, then it would be easier to achieve high standards of living for the impoverished masses of the South. Politically, this was the least popular part of the structuralist policy agenda, but it has received greater attention in recent years.

Contrasting Marxist and Structuralist Perspectives

Although the structuralist analysis of the international market is similar to the Marxist analysis in its stress on the negative effects of the declining terms of trade of the developing countries, the two theories diverge on a critical point. Structuralist theory argues that the international system can be reformed, that the natural processes can be altered. Although the various theorists differ on preferred reforms—foreign aid, protection, access to Northern markets—they all believe that industrialization can be achieved within a reformed international market and that such industrialization will narrow the development gap.

Marxist theories, on the other hand, contend that the capitalist system is immutable, that it will defend itself, and that the only way to change it fundamentally is through revolution: destruction of the international capitalist system and its replacement with an international socialist system. Marxists explain the impossibility of reform in two ways.

One explanation is that developed capitalist economies are unable to absorb the economic surplus or profits generated by the capitalist system of production.[10] Capitalist states cannot absorb their rising surplus internally through consumption, because the worker's income does not grow as fast as capitalist profits do. To prevent unemployment and the inevitable crisis of capitalism resulting from overproduction and underconsumption, the developed market economies invest excess capital in and export excess production to the underdeveloped countries. Another way to absorb the rising surplus and prevent the crisis of capitalism, according to some, is to invest in the military at home, which in turn leads to pressure for expansion abroad. By absorbing economic surplus, foreign expansion prevents or at least delays the collapse of the capitalist system. Thus, dominance, dependence, and imperialism are essential and inevitable dimensions of capitalism.

A second explanation of the necessity of capitalist imperialism derives from the North's need for Southern raw materials.[11] According to this argument, capitalist economies depend on Southern imports, and the desire to control access to those supplies leads to Northern dominance.

Weaknesses in the Three Perspectives

Empirical examination reveals important weaknesses in all three perspectives. We will start with the Marxist approach. Although some economic ties with the South are important to the developed countries, they are for the most part not crucial to the North's economic well-being. Indeed, as we shall discuss, the problem for the less-developed countries may be that they are not important enough for the North.

First, the underconsumption arguments of the Marxists are weak, because the developed market economies are able to absorb their economic surplus. While the developed economies have had difficulties maintaining aggregate demand at acceptable levels, they have managed the problem internally through modern economic policies: income redistribution, fiscal and monetary policy, and public and social expenditures—what has come to be called the "welfare state." Although the developed countries have had serious economic problems—sluggish growth, surplus industrial capacity, inflation—these cannot be adequately explained by underconsumption theories.

Second, foreign investment, especially in less-developed markets, is not of vital importance to the developed market economies, as illustrated by the case of the United States, the principal foreign investor. Foreign investment is a relatively small percentage of total U.S. investment. In 1992, U.S. outward FDI was $34.8 billion, or 3.8 percent of total investment in fixed capital for that year (see Figure 5-3). In 1992, U.S. stock in overseas FDI amounted to $474 billion, whereas its total investment was in the trillions of dollars. Furthermore, the South is not the main area of U.S. foreign investment and is, in fact, declining in importance. In 1991, the developing countries accounted for 25 percent of all U.S.

Figure 5-3   U.S. FDI Outflows Compared with Domestic Fixed Capital Investments, 1965–1992, in Current Dollars

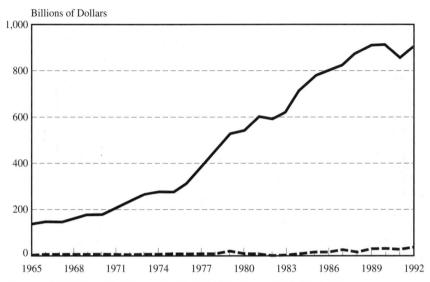

SOURCE: World Bank, *World Data '94 CD-ROM* (Washington: World Bank, 1994).

direct foreign investment, whereas the developed market economies accounted for 74 percent. In 1960, U.S. direct foreign investment in the South accounted for 35 percent, versus an investment of 61 percent in the developed market economies (see Figure 5-4).[12]

Moreover, income from the developing countries is not of vital economic importance to the United States. In 1991, Southern earnings accounted for 40 percent of total U.S. earnings on foreign direct investment, about 9.3 percent of total business earnings, and an infinitesimal part of its total GNP.[13] Although Southern investment is a small part of total foreign investment, returns for many years were greater in the less-developed countries. In 1982, the rate of return on U.S. investments in the Third World was 15.8 percent, as compared with an 8.2 percent return in the North.[14] This situation was reversed in 1986–1988. For example, in 1986, the rate of return on investments in industrialized countries was 17.5 percent, while it was 11.8 percent in the developing countries. The rate of return on investments in developing countries once again exceeded that on investments in industrialized countries in 1989 (see Figure 5-5).[15] In sum, U.S. investment in and earnings from the developing countries are significant but hardly crucial to the overall U.S. economy.

Trade with the South as a whole is also not of overwhelming economic importance to the North. In 1993, exports from developed to developing countries accounted for 28.8 percent of exports of the developed market economies, of

Figure 5-4   Percentage of U.S. Outflows of FDI to Industrialized and Developing Countries, 1960–1990

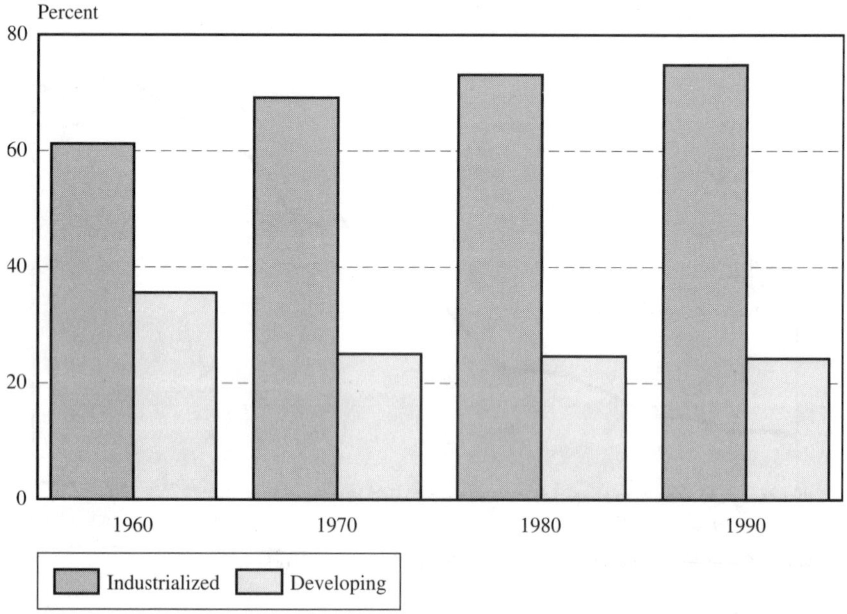

Percent

SOURCE: *Statistical Abstract of the United States* (Washington: Government Printing Office, various years).

which 12.9 percent was exports to oil-exporting LDCs. In the same year, imports of the developed countries from the LDCs were 28.1 percent of total imports of which 17.9 percent was from oil exporters.[16] The minor overall importance to the United States of trade with the South is demonstrated by the fact that in 1992, U.S. exports to developing countries represented only 3.1 percent of the U.S. GNP.[17]

In sum, the case for dependence as a necessary outlet for capitalist surplus is not sustainable. The underdeveloped countries provide significant earnings for the developed market economies and are important investment and export outlets, but they are not crucial for the survival of the North. The available data suggest that the economic importance of the South for the North has declined overall in the decades since World War II, with the notable exception of dependence of the North on petroleum exports from the South (see Chapter 9).

But Northern dependence on Southern raw materials is also limited. Raw materials in general are not as significant as Marxist theory suggests, and, where they are significant as with oil, raw material dependence may work to the detriment of the developing countries, not to their advantage. The United States, and to a greater extent the Europeans and Japanese, depend on the import of certain

Figure 5-5   Rate of Return on U.S. Foreign Investments in Industrialized and Developing Countries, 1982–1989, in Percentages

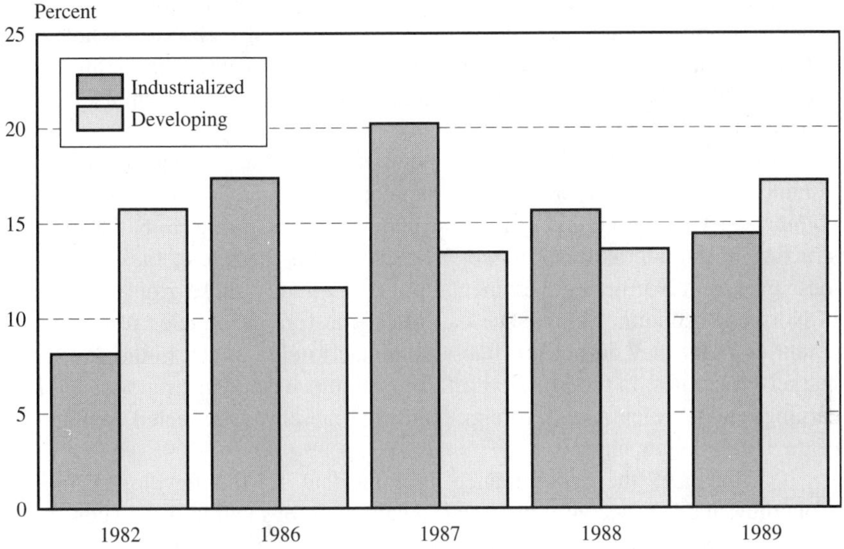

Percent

| Industrialized |
| Developing |

Source: *Survey of Current Business* (Washington: Department of Commerce, August, 1990), 60.

raw materials, but in only a few cases are the major suppliers of these materials Southern countries.[18] Furthermore, foreign dependence is declining as growth in overall consumption of raw materials declines due to changing growth patterns, conservation, technological improvements, and substitution.

In conclusion, the arguments that dominance and exploitation of the South are necessary for the capitalist economies as a whole do not stand the empirical test. The South is important but not vital.

There is, however, the Marxist argument that dependence, although not important to the capitalist economies as a whole, is necessary for the capitalist class that dominates the economy and polity.[19] According to these theories, capitalist groups, especially those managing the multinational corporations, seek to dominate the underdeveloped countries in their quest for profit. Because these groups control the governments of the developed states, they are able to use governmental tools for their class ends.

To evaluate this theory, it is necessary to determine whether the capitalist class as a whole has a common interest in the underdeveloped countries, even though most capitalists do not profit, as has been shown, from foreign trade and investment. Arthur MacEwan argues that the entire capitalist class has an interest in dominance and foreign expansion, including those capitalists having no relation to or profit from such expansion.[20] This is true, he explains, because there is a common interest in expansion that maintains the system as a whole. Yet the preceding analysis of the macroeconomic importance of the Third World suggests that the less-developed countries are not economically necessary to the North and that certain Northern groups, such as the petroleum industry, enjoy most of the benefits of economic ties with the South. Thus, the capitalist class as a whole does not have an interest in the South and in dominance, because only a small percentage of that class profits from dominance and because the system itself is not dependent on dominance.

A stronger argument is that some powerful capitalists, such as the managers of multinational corporations, have a crucial interest in the South and in Northern dominance. Clearly, certain firms and certain groups profit from the existing structure of the international market. The question is the role of these firms and these groups in Northern governmental policy. Certainly, those groups interested in Northern economic dominance can affect the foreign policies of developed countries.[21] But they do not inevitably dominate foreign policy in the developed market economies. In the Middle East, for example, despite the importance of oil earnings and petroleum, U.S. foreign policy has not always reflected the interests of the U.S. oil companies.[22]

On balance, then, dominance is important to the developed market economies and is especially important to certain groups within those economies. But dominance is neither necessary nor inevitable. Under the right political circumstances, change is possible. The problem is that the South has only limited ability to demand change from the North. Economically underdeveloped and politically fragmented, the South has limited leverage on the North. As we shall discuss, because the South is not vital for the North, the developed countries need not respond to Southern demands for change.

The Marxist perspective is not alone in having some difficulties in reconciling theory with evidence. The liberal perspective has trouble explaining a number of empirical anomalies as well. For example, neoclassical trade theory, as embodied in the Hecksher-Ohlin (H-O) theory of international trade, explains trade in terms of differences in comparative advantages across countries. Comparative advantages are determined by the relative abundance or lack of key factors of production (e.g., labor, land, and capital). But, "nearly half of the world's trade consists of trade between industrialized countries that are similar in their factor endowments."[23] If H-O theory were correct, then most of the world's trade would be North-South trade instead of North-North trade.

One way that neoclassical theories have tried to deal with this anomaly is by examining the effects of trade barriers on North-South trade.[24] Another is to relax the assumptions of H-O theory concerning declining returns to scale and the existence of competitive markets.[25] Yet another is to provide separate explanations of inter- and intra-industry trade.[26] Each approach has its merits, but there is still no overarching theory of trade that satisfactorily explains recent patterns in world trade.

In addition, liberals have problems explaining why countries with strongly interventionist governments, like Japan and South Korea, have done so well at promoting exports. According to the liberal orthodoxy, countries with governments that maintain a hands-off approach to promoting international competitiveness are more likely to end up with internationally competitive firms than those with interventionist governments.

Finally, despite the arguments of liberals for several decades that there should not be a long-term trend toward declining terms of trade for the developing countries, the evidence appears rather to support the contentions of both Marxists and structuralists that such a downward trend exists.

The main criticism of the structuralists, besides the one just mentioned concerning the lack of solid evidence for declining terms of trade, have to do with the relative ineffectiveness and undesirability of import substitution as a development strategy. We deal with this criticism in the next section.

Development Strategies

Since the end of World War II, developing countries have pursued several different strategies in an effort to alter their dependence. In finance, trade, investment, and commodities, they have sought greater rewards from the greater participation in the international economic system. Over the years, those strategies have alternated between seeking to change the system and seeking to accommodate to it.

During the formative period of Bretton Woods, those developing states that were independent—primarily the Latin American countries—attempted to incorporate their goal of economic development and their view of appropriate international strategies for development into the North's plans for the new world economic order. The political and economic weakness of the developing world at this time doomed their efforts. At Bretton Woods, they sought, and failed, to ensure that development—meaning development for both industrial and developing countries—would have the same priority as reconstruction did in the activities of the new International Bank for Reconstruction and Development. At Havana, they argued for modification of the free-trade regime: for the right to protect their infant industries through trade restrictions such as import quotas and for permission to stabilize and ensure minimum commodity prices through commodity agreements. Some LDC interests, such as the right to form commodity agreements and to establish regional preference systems to promote development, were, in fact, included in the Havana Charter. But these provisions were lost when the charter was not ratified and the GATT took its place.[27]

In the 1950s and 1960s, developing countries abandoned these first efforts to shape the international system and turned inward. Faced with an international regime that they believed did not take their interests into account and that excluded them from management, developing countries turned to policies of diversification and industrialization via import substitution. The stress on industrialization was reinforced by the preoccupation of developing countries with decolonization and by the belief that the end of colonial political exploitation would foster economic development.

In this period, the main development strategy was import substitution. Developing countries protected local industry through tariffs, quantitative controls, and multiple exchange rates, and they favored production for local consumption over production for export. Governments became actively involved in promoting economic development, largely by channeling resources to the manufacturing sector. Import substitution did not mean total isolation from the international system. Trade with the North continued to flow. Developing countries also encouraged inflows of foreign direct investment, especially in manufacturing, as a way of fostering domestic productive capacity. As a result, there was a major movement of multinational corporations into developing countries. LDCs also tried with some success to persuade developed countries to provide foreign aid for development. As decolonization swept the Third World and competition with the Soviet Union shifted to the South, aid became a useful political tool in the Cold War as well as a way for colonial powers to retain links with their former colonies. During this time, aid became a regular feature of North-South relations.

Toward the end of this period, elements of a new strategy began to emerge. Import substitution gradually came to be seen as a failure. High tariff barriers that were supposed to be temporary became more or less permanent, thanks to the successful lobbying of domestic interests that wanted the barriers kept high. Import substitution therefore created uncompetitive industries while at the same time weakening traditional exports. The foreign investment that jumped over the high tariff barriers of the Third World came to be seen as a threat to sovereignty and development. Foreign aid and regional integration proved inadequate to ensure economic growth. Instead of relying on domestic change, developing countries began to argue that only changes in the international system could promote development. As independent developing countries became more numerous, they began to meet with each other and to develop plans for changing the prevailing international economic regime. The hope was that such common action would increase the bargaining leverage of the South and enable the less-developed countries to negotiate that change with the North.

In the 1960s, developing countries gradually began to work together to press for changes in the system. They created the Group of Seventy-Seven (G-77) to act as a permanent political bloc to represent developing country interests in U.N. forums. In Third World conferences and United Nations forums where the South commanded a majority, the G-77 pushed through declarations, recommendations, and resolutions calling for economic reforms.[28]

The developing countries achieved some largely procedural changes. They persuaded the GATT to include economic development as one of its goals. The United Nations established the United Nations Conference on Trade and Development (UNCTAD), which the South intended to be its international economic forum. UNCTAD provided the developing countries with a new economic doctrine that followed the ideas of the structuralists. As UNCTAD's first secretary general, Raúl Prebisch argued that what was needed was a redistribution of world resources to help the South: restructuring of trade, control of multinational corporations, and greater aid flows.

The strategy of seeking to change the international system reached its apex in the 1970s with the South's call for a New International Economic Order (NIEO).[29] The NIEO grew out of the threat and the promise of the economic crises of the 1970s. The combination of food shortages, the rapid increase in the price of oil, and a recession in the developed countries undermined growth prospects in much of the South and made developing countries desperate for change. At the same time, the success of the oil-producing and oil-exporting countries in forcing changes in the political economy of oil held out the prospect of new leverage on the developed countries. Developing countries sought to use their own commodity power and to link their interests with OPEC, their fellow members of the G-77, to demand changes in the global economic system. The NIEO included a greater Northern commitment to the transfer of aid and new forms of aid flows; greater control of multinational corporations and greater MNC transfer of technology to developing countries; and trade reforms including reduction of developed country tariff barriers and international commodity agreements.

Success of the NIEO depended on Southern unity, the credibility of the commodity threat, and the North's perception of vulnerability. It foundered on all three. Southern unity was weakened by the differential impact of the food, energy, and recession crises; by the growing gap between the NICs and the least-developed countries; and by traditional regional and political conflicts. The credibility of the commodity threat was undermined by the inability to develop other OPECs, by OPEC's unwillingness to link the oil threat to G-77 demands in any meaningful way, and by declining demand for Southern raw materials. And, in the end, the North did not perceive any significant vulnerability to Southern threats. The North was willing to enter into a dialogue about changing the international economic system—as in the 1975 to 1977 Conference on International Economic Cooperation (CIEC)—but it was unwilling to make any substantive changes.

By the 1980s, developing countries had effectively abandoned the hope of reforming the international system and were once again thrown back on their own resources. The recessions and debt restructurings of the 1980s made the industrialized countries even less responsive to demands for systemic change and less willing to dispense foreign aid. The failure of the NIEO led developing nations to pursue different routes to development.

The G-77 survived as a bargaining group in the United Nations, but Southern unity became increasingly irrelevant to the development strategy of most Southern states. The developing countries were increasingly fragmented. A number of countries in Asia achieved rapid growth largely by integrating into the system, welcoming foreign investment, and exporting manufactured products to developed countries. Other advanced developing countries, such as Brazil and

Mexico, relied on a relatively closed internal market.[30] The interests of these countries increasingly departed from those poorer countries, especially in Africa, which existed at the poverty line and relied on foreign assistance for survival. Even the NICs were divided. Those in Asia became concerned about growing protectionism in the United States; others, especially Latin American countries that had borrowed heavily from commercial banks, faced the debt crisis; others such as Mexico and Venezuela faced the collapse of oil prices and the growing conflicts within OPEC.

The debt crisis of the 1980s played an important role in the rethinking of development strategies that occurred during the decade. The need to generate new sources of exports to service the debts accumulated in the 1970s created enormous incentives to adopt export-oriented development strategies and to jettison, or at least modify significantly, the import substitution policies of the past. Indebted countries that were unable to increase exports had to adopt governmental austerity measures that generally hurt the poorest part of the population the most. The success of the Asian NICs and the failure of protectionist and statist policies led to a rethinking of effective strategies for development and to the adoption of liberal domestic and international economic policies. Some faster-growing countries in the South also began to experience problems of environmental degradation. In the 1980s, people of the South began to flow North in unprecedented numbers in search of greater political freedoms and economic opportunities. Some entered the North legally, others illegally. Debt, environmental concerns, and migration issues dominated the North-South agenda by the end of the 1980s as a result.

The issue for developing countries, as the end of the twentieth century has approached, has remained little different than it was in 1945: whether it was possible to achieve growth and development within the prevailing system and, if so, how. While the North was not prepared to make major changes in the system to help the South, it was willing to transfer funds and to offer advice and encouragement for adopting export-led growth development strategies. Furthermore, the North was increasingly interested in Southern markets and concerned about preventing further degradation of the global environment and reducing the flow of Southern peoples to the North. This concern was clearly evidenced in the U.S. debate over NAFTA. It remained to be seen whether these new Northern preoccupations were enough to overcome the deep divisions between the two groups of countries.

NOTES

1. The World Bank defined low-income countries as those countries with per capita income less than $675; middle-income as those with per capita income in the $675 to $8,355 range; and high-income as those with per capita income higher than $8,355. See World Bank, *World Tables 1994* (Washington: World Bank, 1994) 748, for the list of countries in each category.

2. United Nations Development Program, *Human Development Report* 1994 (New York: Oxford University Press for the UNDP, 1994), 35.

3. World Bank, *World Data '94 CD-ROM* (Washington, D.C.: World Bank, 1994).

4. For examples of liberal theory, see Gottfried Haberler, *International Trade and Economic Development* (Cairo: National Bank of Egypt, 1959); Ragnar Nurkse, *Equilibrium and Growth in the World Economy* (Cambridge: Harvard University Press, 1961); Walt W. Rostow, *The Stages of Economic Growth: A Non-Communist Manifesto* (Cambridge, England: Cambridge University Press, 1962); Walt W. Rostow, *Politics and the Stages of Growth* (Cambridge, England: Cambridge University Press, 1972); Gerald M. Meier, *International Trade and Development* (New York: Harper and Row, 1963); Gerald M. Meier, ed., *Pioneers in Development* (New York: Oxford University Press, 1984); Harry G. Johnson, *Economic Policies Toward Less Developed Countries* (New York: Praeger, 1967); and Jagdish Bhagwati, *Essays in Development Economics: Wealth and Poverty*, vol. 1, and *Dependence and Interdependence*, vol. 2 (Cambridge: MIT Press, 1985). For an interesting overview of the literature, see Walt W. Rostow, *Theorists of Economic Growth from David Hume to the Present* (New York: Oxford University Press, 1990).

5. For examples of Marxist and neo-Marxist perspectives, see Samir Amin, *Accumulation on a World Scale* (New York: Monthly Review Press, 1974); Samir Amin, *Unequal Development: An Essay on the Social Formations of Peripheral Capitalism* (New York: Monthly Review Press, 1976); Paul A. Baran, *The Political Economy of Growth* (New York: Monthly Review Press, 1968); Fernando H. Cardoso and Enzo Faletto, *Dependency and Development in Latin America*, trans. Marjory Mattingly Urquidi (Berkeley: University of California Press, 1979); Arghiri Emmanuel, *Unequal Exchange: A Study of the Imperialism of Trade* (New York: Monthly Review Press, 1972); Andre Gunder Frank, *Capitalism and Underdevelopment in Latin America*, rev. ed. (New York: Monthly Review Press, 1969); Harry Magdoff, Imperialism: *From the Colonial Age to the Present* (New York: Monthly Review Press, 1978); Dan W. Nabudere, *The Political Economy of Imperialism* (London: Zed Press, 1977); Theotonio Dos Santos, "The Structure of Dependence," in K. T. Fann and Donald C. Hodges, eds., *Readings in U.S. Imperialism* (Boston: Porter Sargent, 1971); and Immanuel Wallerstein, *The Capitalist World Economy* (Cambridge, England: Cambridge University Press, 1979). See also "Facing the 1980s: New Directions in the Theory of Imperialism," a special issue of the *Review of Radical Political Economics*, 11 (winter 1979).

6. This is a view shared by non-Marxist theorists as well. See the section below on structuralist approaches.

7. This brief summary does considerable violence to the richness and diversity of views within the Marxist and neo-Marxist schools. For more nuanced summaries, see Fernando H. Cardoso, "The Consumption of **Dependency Theory** in the United States," *Latin American Research Review* 7 (fall 1977): 7-24; Raymond Duvall, "Dependence and Dependencia Theory," *International Organization* 32 (winter 1978): 51–78; Ronald Chilcote, "Dependence: A Critical Synthesis of the Literature," *Latin American Perspectives* 1 (spring 1974): 4–29; and Gabriel Palma, "Dependency: A Formal Theory of Underdevelopment or a Methodology for the Analysis of Concrete Situations of Underdevelopment," *World Development* 6 (1978): 881–924.

8. For examples of structuralist theory, see Gunnar Myrdal, *Rich Lands and Poor: The Road to World Prosperity* (New York: Harper and Row, 1957); Raúl Prebisch, "Commercial Policy in the Underdeveloped Countries," *American Economic Review* 49 (May 1959): 251–273; Raúl Prebisch, *The Economic Development of Latin America and Its Principal Problems* (New York: United Nations, 1950); W. Arthur Lewis, *The Evolution of the International Economic Order* (Princeton: Princeton University Press, 1978); and Johan Galtung, "A Structural Theory of Imperialism," *Journal of Peace Research* 8 (1971): 81–117.

9. This is the essence of the argument put forward by Raúl Prebisch, one of the most influential advocates of the structuralist perspective. See Joseph L. Love, "Raúl Prebisch and the Origins of the Doctrine of Unequal Exchange," *Latin American Research Review* 15 (1980): 45–72.

10. Paul A. Baran and Paul M. Sweezy, *Monopoly Capital: An Essay on the American Economic and Social Order* (New York: Monthly Review Press, 1966). These authors define economic surplus as "the difference between what a society produces and the costs of producing it" (p. 9). For a critical analysis of the concept, see Benjamin J. Cohen, *The Question of Imperialism: The Political Economy of Dominance and Dependence* (New York: Basic Books, 1973): 104–121.

11. See, for example, Pierre Jalée, *Imperialism in the Seventies*, trans. R. and M. Sokolov (New York: Third World Press, 1972).

12. U.S. Department of Commerce, Bureau of the Census, *Statistical Abstract of the United States 1974* (Washington: Government Printing Office, 1974), 781; and *Statistical Abstract of the United States 1993* (Washington: U.S. Government Printing Office), 801.

13. U.S. Department of Commerce, *Survey of Current Business* (August 1990), 60.

14. U.S. Department of Commerce, *Survey of Current Business* (August 1988): 45; (July 1988): 86.

15. U.S. Department of Commerce, *Survey of Current Business* (August 1988): 45.

16. International Monetary Fund, *Direction of Trade Statistics, Yearbook 1994* (Washington: IMF, 1994), 10, 16.

17. International Monetary Fund, *Direction of Trade Statistics Yearbook, 1994* (Washington: IMF, 1994), 420.

18. Commodity Research Bureau, *1986 CRB Commodity Yearbook* (Jersey City, N.J.: CRB, 1986).

19. See Arthur MacEwan, "Capitalist Expansion, Ideology and Intervention," *Review of Radical Political Economics* 4 (spring 1972), 36–58; and Thomas Weisskopf, "Theories of American Imperialism: A Critical Evaluation," *Review of Radical Political Economics* 6 (fall 1974), 41–60.

20. MacEwan, "Capitalist Expansion."

21. See U.S. Senate, *Multinational Corporations and United States Foreign Policy*, hearings before the Subcommittee on Multinational Corporations of the Committee on Foreign Relations, 93rd Cong., 2nd sess. (Washington: U.S. Government Printing Office, 1975).

22. On this question, see Stephen Krasner, *Defending the National Interest* (Princeton: Princeton University Press, 1978); G. John Ikenberry, *Reasons of State: Oil Politics and the Capacities of American Government* (Ithaca, N.Y.: Cornell University Press, 1988); and Daniel Yergin, *The Prize: The Epic Quest for Oil, Money and Power* (New York: Simon and Schuster, 1991).

23. Elhanan Helpman and Paul Krugman, *Increasing Returns, Imperfect Markets, and International Trade* (Cambridge: MIT Press, 1985), 2.

24. See, for example, James R. Markusen and Randall M. Wigle, "Explaining the Volume of North-South Trade," *Economic Journal* 100 (December 1990): 1206–1215.

25. This is the approach suggested by the work of Helpman and Krugman and other strategic trade theorists.

26. See Edward E. Leamer, *Sources of International Comparative Advantage: Theory and Evidence* (Cambridge: MIT Press, 1984).

27. See Richard Gardner, *Sterling Dollar Diplomacy* (Oxford: Clarendon Press, 1956); Robert Hudec, *The GATT Legal System and World Trade Diplomacy* (New York: Praeger, 1975); and Janette Mark and Ann Weston, "The Havana Charter Experience: Lessons for Developing Countries," in John Whalley, ed., *Developing Countries and the Global Trading System, Vol. 1, Thematic Studies for a Ford Foundation Project* (Ann Arbor: University of Michigan Press, 1989).

28. Branislav Gosovic and John G. Ruggie, "On the Creation of the New International Economic Order," *International Organization* 30 (spring 1976): 309–346; Robert A. Mortimer, *The Third World Coalition in International Politics*, 2nd ed. (Boulder, Colo.: Westview, 1984), ch. 3; and Marc Williams, *Third World Cooperation: The Group of 77 in UNCTAD* (New York: St. Martin's Press, 1991), 78.

29. Robert Rothstein, *Global Bargaining: UNCTAD and the Quest for a New International Economic Order* (Princeton: Princeton University Press, 1979); Jeffrey Hart, *The New International Economic Order: Conflict and Co-operation in North-South Economic Relations 1974–77* (New York: St. Martin's Press, 1983); Craig Murphy, *The Emergence of the NIEO Ideology* (Boulder, Colo.: Westview, 1984); and Stephen D. Krasner, *Structural Conflict: The Third World Against Global Liberalism* (Berkeley: University of California Press, 1985).

30. Stephan Haggard, *Pathways from the Periphery* (Ithaca, N.Y.: Cornell University Press, 1990); Alice H. Amsden, *Asia's Next Giant: South Korea and Late Industrialization* (New York: Oxford, 1989); and Robert Wade, *Governing the Market: Economic Theory and the Role of Government in East Asian Industrialization* (Princeton: Princeton University Press, 1990).

6

International Financial Flows

The effort of the South to obtain financial capital for development is a central theme in North-South relations. Developing countries, short of their own funds, traditionally turned to capital surplus countries for private funds in the form of bank loans and the purchase of bonds to finance infrastructure and productive facilities. In the nineteenth century, for example, British capital helped build U.S. railroads and industry; and in the first half of the twentieth century, foreign capital flowed to Latin America to finance industrialization. In the first twenty-five years of the Bretton Woods era, public funds for development were more important than private lending in North-South financial relations. Foreign aid, virtually nonexistent before World War II, came to account for a large portion of financial transfers to developing countries in the 1950s and 1960s. Then, in the 1970s and early 1980s, private financial flows reemerged as commercial banks in the developed countries financed public works and private industry in many developing countries. This was followed by a global debt crisis that temporarily stemmed the flow of new private bank loans to the Third World. Public flows resumed their growth during the debt crisis, partly to compensate for the interruption of private flows. In the late 1980s and early 1990s, private flows resumed to the most creditworthy developing countries. Private bank loans did not play as large a role in this period as they had in the 1970s. Instead, much of the increased flow of private capital to the South came from new sources such as international mutual funds. The other developing countries continued to depend heavily on public flows. In this chapter, we examine the evolution of financial flows, both public and private, in North-South relations.

Foreign Aid and the Postwar Order

Although foreign aid was one of the most innovative developments in North-South relations in the Bretton Woods era, it was not part of the original postwar vision of the developed countries. To be sure, the International Bank for Reconstruction and Development (IBRD), also known as the World Bank, was established along with the IMF as one of the two international institutions of the Bretton Woods system. Recognizing the massive needs for financing and the disruption of capital markets after the war, the founders of Bretton Woods set up this unique public multilateral institution to finance the rebuilding of war-torn countries and the development of members of the Bank. With capital provided by member states, the World Bank was to borrow in private capital markets and make loans at market rates to cover the foreign exchange needs of borrowing countries.

After the war, the less-developed countries sought to ensure that development would have the same priority as reconstruction and that they would have access to World Bank financing. However, the developed countries that dominated the World Bank unanimously agreed that European postwar reconstruction would be the first priority for the Bank. Furthermore, the United States and other developed countries rejected the developing country argument that public capital was needed for economic development. In the view of the North, a combination of domestic capital and new funds from trade expansion was the appropriate route to growth. External capital, where necessary, would have to be private and would be obtained by promoting foreign direct investment and by trade liberalization, which would improve export opportunities for investors. In those rare cases where public external financing might be appropriate, financing was to be limited in amount and offered on market or hard, not concessional or soft, terms.[1] Thus, in its first five years, one-half of World Bank lending went to European reconstruction and development; the other half was extended to developing countries on hard terms.[2]

Northern policy on bilateral aid closely resembled that in international forums. In the early postwar period, the United States was the only country able to transfer significant resources to the less-developed countries. The rhetoric at this time suggested that bilateral aid for development would be a major aspect of U.S. foreign policy. In the famous "Point Four" of his inaugural address in 1949, President Harry S Truman called for "a bold new program . . . for the improvement and growth of underdeveloped areas."[3] The reality, however, was different. Emphasis was to be on self-help; where external capital was needed, it was to be primarily private; and where private capital was unavailable, external financing was to come primarily from the World Bank. United States economic aid was very limited. The Export-Import Bank gave market-term loans for financing U.S. trade, and the technical assistance program offered a small number of grants. Between 1950 and 1955, bilateral overseas development aid (that is, public transfers of funds directly from one country to another) from all of the developed market countries averaged $1.8 billion a year, and multilateral flows amounted to $100 million a year.[4]

The Link between Aid and Foreign Policy

In the mid-1950s, Northern policies shifted. One reason was the emergence of the less-developed countries as increasingly active, albeit weak, actors in international relations. In the two decades following World War II, much of Africa and

Asia achieved political independence. By 1965, 85 out of 118 members of the United Nations were developing countries. As the less-developed countries became more numerous, they also became more outspoken and somewhat more united and specific in their demands for international economic reform, including more financial aid. Gradually, the newly independent countries began to coordinate policies within the U.N. system and to meet together in international conferences of developing countries where they formulated common demands on the North.

The emergence of the new Third World became significant when the United States and the Soviet Union decided to make the developing world an arena of competition in the Cold War. Following the Communist takeover of China in 1949 and the Korean conflict of 1950, the United States began a program of military assistance to developing countries bordering the Soviet Union and the People's Republic of China and to certain Middle Eastern countries.[5] After Stalin's death in 1953, the Soviet Union for the first time contributed to United Nations technical assistance programs, entered into trade agreements with Southern countries, and provided financial assistance to Egypt, India, Syria, Indonesia, and Afghanistan. Then, in 1956, Soviet Premier Nikita Khrushchev announced that competition with the West would be expanded to the less-developed countries.[6]

The Soviet Union's threat to the West's position of dominance in the developing world led the United States for the first time to conclude that economic assistance to the South could be a powerful tool in the Cold War.[7] One influential study expressed well the U.S. view:

> A comprehensive and sustained program of American economic assistance aimed at helping the free underdeveloped countries to create the conditions for self-sustaining growth can, in the short run, materially reduce the danger of conflict triggered by aggressive minor powers, and can, say in two to three decades, result in an overwhelming preponderance of societies with a successful record of solving their problems without resort to coercion or violence. The establishment of such a preponderance of stable, effective and democratic societies gives the best promise of a favorable settlement of the Cold War and of a peaceful, progressive world environment.[8]

According to economic analysis at the time, the growth of the less-developed countries was constrained primarily by insufficient capital investment, which was in turn limited by insufficient savings and/or foreign exchange. External financial assistance, it was argued, would fill this resource gap. Capital flows plus technical assistance to improve the use of both domestic and external capital would create the conditions for self-sustaining economic growth. Economic growth, in turn, would provide a constructive outlet for nationalism, foster social progress, develop political leadership, and encourage confidence in the democratic process.[9] Aid would serve U.S. foreign policy by "help[ing] the societies of the world develop in ways that will not menace our security—either as a result of their own internal dynamics or because they are weak enough to be used as tools by others."[10] This focus on foreign aid as part of U.S. political and security policy has been a central theme in U.S. aid policy throughout the post-war era.

France and the United Kingdom, motivated both by security concerns and by the desire to maintain political and economic relationships with their former colonies, adopted similar policies.[11] As a result, bilateral foreign aid programs expanded dramatically. The United States established the Development Loan Fund (DLF) in 1958 and rapidly increased its size. Major new aid programs for Latin America were drawn up after Vice President Richard M. Nixon was stoned and mobbed in his car on a trip to Latin America in 1958 and after the Cuban Revolution of 1960. Between 1961 and 1969, $4.8 billion was sent from the United States to Latin America. Overall, annual U.S. aid increased from $2.0 billion in 1956 to $3.7 billion in 1963.[12] British aid doubled from $205 million in 1956 to $414 million in 1963, and French aid rose from $648 million in 1956 to $863 million in 1963.[13] Between 1960 and 1962, new development aid authorities were created in Canada, Japan, the United Kingdom, Denmark, Sweden, and Norway.

Multilateral aid also increased. As Europe recovered from the war, World Bank lending shifted to developing countries, and the Bank's capital was increased to allow greater lending. In 1956, World Bank members created the subsidiary International Finance Corporation (IFC) to promote private investment in developing countries. In 1960, the International Development Agency (IDA) was established as a separate institution closely integrated with the World Bank with a mandate to make soft or highly concessional loans. In 1958, the United States, reversing its long-standing opposition, agreed to the establishment of the Inter-American Development Bank and provided $350 million of the bank's initial capital of $1 billion.[14] African and Asian development banks followed in 1964 and 1966, respectively.

Thus aid emerged in the 1950s and 1960s as a new form of international economic interaction. Never before in history had states voluntarily transferred funds on concessional terms to other countries; never before had multilateral institutions played such a role in economic relations. While aid thus ushered in a new form of international relations, it did not, as we shall examine, change the balance of economic power between North and South.

Stagnation of Aid

Although aid became a regular feature of North-South economic relations, Northern political support for public financial assistance to developing countries was uneven and the flow of aid proved to be somewhat erratic. Between 1960 and 1970, total aid flows from all the industrialized countries remained roughly constant in real terms.[15] Most European countries regularly increased their aid as their economies strengthened. Germany and Japan became major donors in the late 1950s and 1960s, in part because of reparation payments after the war and partially as a reflection of their high domestic growth rates. The Nordic countries and the Netherlands, motivated by a sense of moral responsibility, provided dramatic increases in aid flows throughout the 1960s and 1970s.

At the same time, however, official development assistance from the United States, the United Kingdom, and France declined. United States aid, for example, declined from $3.5 billion in 1967 to $3.0 billion in 1973, but in real resource value (constant 1967 dollars), it fell to $2.0 billion.[16] In 1973, U.S. overseas development aid fell to a postwar record low of $2.97 billion.[17]

One reason for the shift in U.S. aid policy was disillusionment after a period of high expectations about the link between aid and foreign policy. The heavy emphasis of the U.S. aid program on the foreign policy benefits of foreign assistance led to disappointment when the political and security goals of economic assistance were not realized. The long and frustrating war in Vietnam played an important role in this dissatisfaction. Aid did not lead, as predicted, to economic development, democratic government, and political stability. Growth was uneven, instability seemed to increase with development, and aid did not necessarily win friends and influence people.[18] Meanwhile, the cost of aid grew, and willingness to assume such costs decreased in the face of growing U.S. external payments and budget deficits and the cost of the war in Vietnam.[19]

The South's political and military significance to the United States also diminished. As the strategic relationship between the United States and the Soviet Union stabilized and the superpower conflict moderated, "winning" or "losing" Third World allegiances was still important to each side, but they both discovered that it was difficult to win friendship through economic assistance. The South also began to look less suitable as a testing ground for rival forms of political and economic organization. The South was insufficiently democratic for the West to use it as a site for proving the general viability of **democracy;** it was insufficiently socialist for the East to use it as a showcase for **socialism.** Proportionally greater amounts of shrinking United States aid were devoted to a few militarily strategic countries: India, South Vietnam, and Indonesia in the early 1970s, and later on Egypt, Israel, and Central America. At the same time, a shrinking share of development aid went to needy but less strategically important countries.

The link between foreign aid and foreign policy also became less important for France and the United Kingdom.[20] Although sub-Saharan Africa remained important for French prestige and economic benefit, its significance for French security disappeared, and its role in French foreign policy generally declined. Similarly, as Britain cut its military commitments east of the Suez Canal and moved toward a more Atlantic-oriented foreign policy, its political and security motivations for aid to the Commonwealth faded.

Overall aid flows stagnated in the 1960s as European and Japanese increases in aid flows were offset by decreases in aid from the United States, the United Kingdom, and France. Furthermore, after 1960 the South was increasingly burdened with debt service on earlier public financial flows. From 1965 to 1969, the rise in debt service payments on the official and officially guaranteed loans to eighty less-developed countries exceeded the rise in gross flows of new capital aid. As a result, the net transfer of resources fell slightly during this period.[21]

The **stagnation**, and in some cases decline, in aid flows also disillusioned Southern governments. A few developing countries, such as Myanmar (then called Burma), rejected aid and turned to other self-help policies.[22] Most developing countries tried to increase the amount and improve the conditions of aid by acting together to negotiate with the developed countries. In the early 1960s, they expanded their earlier coordination by forming the Group of Seventy-Seven (G-77), a united Southern bloc, to improve their bargaining position and to confront the North with common demands for changes in the international economic system (see Chapters 5 and 7). Acting primarily in the United Nations, they sought to increase aid flows by pressing the Northern countries to transfer first 1.0 percent and then 0.7 percent of their respective GNPs to developing countries. They also proposed improvements in the terms of aid: more soft loans and grants, longer duration of loans, easing the debt burden, and ending the policy of tying aid to purchases in the donor country.[23] Finally, the Group of Seventy-Seven sought to limit Northern control by increasing the multilateral component of aid and by making aid transfers more automatic. One such proposal was to allocate newly created SDRs (Special Drawing Rights) to underdeveloped countries, the IDA, or regional development banks.[24]

The strategy of Southern unity was largely unsuccessful. Although the North (with the exception of the United States) eventually agreed to transfer 0.7 percent of its GNP to developing countries, with the exception of a few small but wealthy European donors this goal has not been met. Unfortunately for the South, none of the largest donors of aid came close to the 0.7 percent goal (see Figure 6-1). The developed countries also rejected other reform proposals including the SDR-aid link.

Financial Flows in the 1970s: Politicization and Privatization

The 1970s witnessed two important developments in the North-South financial relationship: the politicization and the privatization of financial flows. On the one hand, the issue of aid flows became highly politicized as Southern countries confronted developed countries with demands for a new international economic order. At the same time, the share of aid in total flows from North to South declined due to a massive surge in private commercial bank lending to certain developing countries (see Figure 6-2).

The setting for the political confrontation over aid was the commodity crises of the 1970s. The rapid increases in the price of food and oil in the early 1970s were major shocks for many developing countries, in some cases stimulating rapid growth for commodity exporters and in other cases drawing away scarce resources for vital food and energy imports. These shocks created new needs and greater demands for economic aid in the developing countries while at the same time undermining the political support for aid in the developed countries. The

Figure 6-1   Bilateral Official Development Assistance (ODA) by the Five Largest Industrialized Countries, Selected Periods between 1950 and 1988, in Constant 1987 Prices

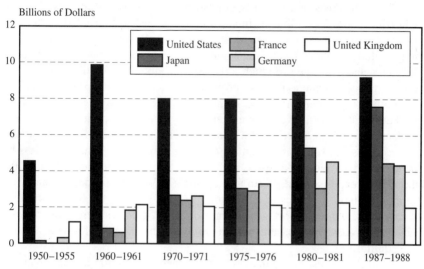

SOURCE: Stephen Browne, *Foreign Aid in Practice* (New York: New York University Press, 1990), 40–41.

Figure 6-2   Total Net Resource Receipts of Developing Countries from All Sources, 1956–1973, in Current Dollars

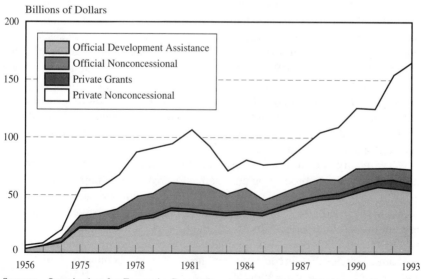

SOURCE: Organization for Economic Cooperation and Development, *Development Cooperation* (Paris: OECD, 1995), 58–59; and earlier issues.

crises posed a major threat to Southern economies but weakened the South's ability to address the threat, because they affected the South in different ways and thereby accentuated the divisions among the developing countries.

The food crisis had its roots in postwar development strategies aimed at industrialization. Development funds were channeled to industry and agricultural prices kept low to feed the growing urban population. The resulting neglect of agriculture in many developing countries reached catastrophic proportions in the 1970s and continued to touch large areas of the Third World in the 1980s. Southern food production in the postwar era has not kept up with a rapidly expanding population.[25] In Asia, application of agricultural technology developed during the green revolution and effective government policy improved the production of wheat and rice. But South America and especially Africa, where coarse grains and starch roots remain the basic staple diet, were helped less by the green revolution. As a result, parts of the South became dependent on the agricultural exports of the North to meet the gap between production and consumption. These increases in agricultural imports strained the South's balance of payments, and food shortages and nutritional deficiencies were a natural consequence of austerity measures adopted to bring the balance of payments back into equilibrium.

Until the 1970s, major increases in Northern production and international food aid helped fill the supply and foreign exchange gap. But in the early seventies, a decline in Northern food production led to a sharp rise in world food prices, severe food shortages, and balance-of-payments crises for many Southern states. From 1970 to 1980, the cost of developing country imports of agricultural products rose 20 percent annually.[26] As food stocks fell and prices rose, the volume of Northern food aid was greatly reduced.

After 1975, there appeared to be improvements in the food crisis. For humane reasons and out of self-interest, the developed countries sought to improve the world's food system. After 1973, both bilateral and multilateral food aid increased, and from 1973 to 1981, overall food aid quintupled in current prices and doubled in constant prices.[27] In 1974 the International Fund for Agricultural Development (IFAD), with initial funding of $1 billion, was created to provide aid for agricultural development in the poorest countries. Overall food production in the developing countries rose and the cost of cereal imports as a percentage of export earnings dropped.[28]

The reality, however, was less promising. In much of the South, improvements in agricultural production and food aid were offset by population increases. Although Asia achieved a 21-percent increase in per capita production between 1975 and 1985, South American per capita output increased only 6.9 percent in the same period.[29] In Africa, the food crisis actually worsened in the late 1970s and 1980s because of the combination of a rapidly growing population, economic policies that discouraged food production by keeping food prices low, and poor soil management. From the early 1970s to the early 1980s, per capita food production in Africa declined about 1.1 percent per year. As a result, Africa's food import bill rose 17 percent in 1982 to $1 billion, an amount equivalent to the total U.S. aid program in Africa.[30] A sub-Saharan crisis in 1984–1985 provoked a huge outpouring of emergency aid, but the underlying problems of inadequate agricultural production and of antiagriculture government policies in countries did not change. Finally, the willingness of developed countries to support non-emergency food aid programs decreased.

The second crisis for the South in the 1970s was that of oil and energy. Price increases that took the cost of a barrel of oil from $1.80 in 1971 to over $35 in 1981 threatened development in countries without oil resources and caused new divisions within the South between oil exporters and importers, and between oil importers able to obtain commercial loans and those dependent on aid. The rising price of oil and oil-related products, such as petrochemical fertilizers, caused the current account deficit of LDC oil importers to increase from $11.3 billion in 1973 to $46.3 billion in 1975, and to $89.0 billion in 1980.[31] A secondary effect of the oil crisis was severe recession in the North. The resultant decrease of prices and quantities of imports from the South further aggravated the balance-of-payments crisis. Finally, even the oil exporters were not exempt from negative effects of the oil crisis. Certain countries, such as Mexico and Nigeria, mismanaged their new revenues, overborrowed while they were prosperous, and were badly hurt when oil prices eventually declined.

Middle-income oil importers financed current account deficits and maintained their growth by borrowing from private commercial banks. This borrowing from private financial markets was a major development in North-South financial flows. It marked the beginning of what seemed to be a new era for development finance but turned out to be the onset of the world debt crisis.

The new borrowing of developing countries was made possible by changing policies of commercial banks. Until the late 1960s, less-developed countries, with their slow growth and bad credit records, appeared as undesirable markets for Northern banks. Thus, bank lending to the developing countries was limited primarily to short-term trade finance. In the late 1960s and early 1970s, however, many banks from the OECD countries became attracted to the profits in international markets. With rapid growth and rising exports, many developing countries appeared capable of servicing increased debt. As a result, banks were willing to expand from short-term trade finance to longer-term project lending. Interest in lending to developing countries was reinforced by the inflow of petrodollar deposits following 1973 that left banks with vast amounts of funds available for lending and only limited markets for such lending in the slowly growing developed countries. Finally, bank lending was actively encouraged by the governments of developed countries, which saw it as a mechanism for petrodollar recycling (see Chapter 2).

With an ample supply of petrodollars on deposit, massive demand from the LDCs, and official encouragement from the OECD governments, bank flows to LDCs surged. Large loans were made at floating interest rates calculated at a percentage over the interbank lending rate and were syndicated or divided up among many banks. From 1973 to 1975, oil-importing developing countries' annual borrowing from private financial institutions went from $6.5 billion to $14.2 billion. By 1978, the annual flows reached $19.5 billion, and in 1981, they peaked at $35.7 billion.[32] By 1977, the total private debt of the developing countries reached $141 billion; by 1981, it had increased to $293 billion.[33]

In the 1970s, the rapid growth of bank lending did not pose a problem for developing country borrowers. Lending helped expand productive capacity and maintained growth, even after the first oil shock. From 1973 to 1980, middle-income oil importers achieved an average annual GDP growth of 5.7 percent, whereas the industrial countries' GDP grew at only 2.8 percent per year.[34] Furthermore, because developing countries' exports increased, their ability to service debt remained strong. Finally, debt service was eased by inflation, which meant that real interest rates were low or negative.

Not all countries, however, had access to private financial markets. Low-income developing countries, unable to borrow from banks, remained dependent on concessional flows. Fortunately, although overall aid flows did not rise by much after the first oil shock, flows to the low-income countries—especially from multilateral agencies and OPEC—did increase and helped offset the effects of the oil price rise (see Figure 6-3).

The external shocks of the 1970s proved very damaging to the prospects for development in the low-income countries and even for the maintenance of exist-

Figure 6-3 Bilateral and Multilateral Official Development Assistance (ODA) by Groups of Donor Countries, 1956–1993, in Current Dollars

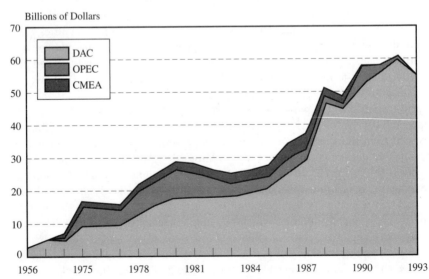

SOURCE: Organization for Economic Cooperation and Development, *Development Cooperation* (Paris: OECD, 1995), 58–59; and earlier issues.

ing levels of real per capita income. Higher oil costs combined with recession drained foreign exchange and forced a curtailment of imports necessary for development and survival. The decrease in energy consumption meant a drop in overall production and consumption, which were already precariously low. For the low-income countries, any hope for growth hinged on increasing the real value of their Official Development Assistance (ODA).

In the face of these crises, the South sought to increase public financial flows to the developing countries and to make those flows more automatic. The major strategy of the 1970s was Southern unity and confrontation. In the 1960s, the developing countries had tried with little success to increase their bargaining strength and to obtain greater concessions from the North by acting as a bloc in negotiating with the developed countries. With the onset of the oil crisis of the 1970s, the South felt that it had obtained new leverage in negotiating with the North and tried to use that leverage to obtain a variety of structural changes, including more aid on better terms.

Ironically, the actions of the oil-producing states—which posed a severe threat to the South—also served as a force for Southern unity and cooperation. One effect was psychological. The ability of a unified OPEC (Organization of Petroleum Exporting Countries) to attain significant rewards from the North demonstrated the potential effectiveness of Southern unity in bargaining with the North. It also created, at least temporarily, a sense of Southern solidarity.

The oil crisis, too, held out the hope of a new bargaining chip for the South. The oil-producing countries could hurt the North by withholding petroleum or raising prices, or they could offer the North inducements such as energy agreements or an energy dialogue. If the oil-producing states remained part of the Southern bloc, then the oil stick or the oil carrot could be linked to demands for systemic reform, and the balance of power could be altered. Some oil-producing states, especially Venezuela and Algeria, encouraged the linkage of Southern development demands with raw materials threats or inducements. However, others, in particular the Persian Gulf states, played little or no role in the Southern group and had no interest in using their oil weapon for broader purposes.

In the heady days following OPEC's initial success, the South boldly tried to force systemic reform on the North. In the spring of 1974, the Group of Seventy-Seven issued a call for a new international economic order that included changing the system of financial flows (see Chapters 5 and 7). The Declaration and Action Programme on a New International Economic Order (NIEO) called for a link between SDR allocation and development finance, the implementation of the 0.7-percent-of-GNP goal for industrial country foreign aid established by the United Nations, and greater participation by the less-developed countries in IBRD, IDA, and IMF decision making.[35] Throughout the 1970s, the developing countries consistently urged the realization of the new international economic order in their multilateral negotiations with the developed countries.

The North, itself a victim of the energy and recession crises, firmly resisted the South's efforts to create the NIEO. Southern stridency and Northern resistance increased the contentiousness of relations in this period. The South was able to force the North to discuss the concept of reform at the United Nations and other multilateral forums, but it was not able to make the North actually negotiate for systemic change, nor was the South able to play its oil card to force the North to respond. The OPEC countries, in the end, were not willing to link the price and availability of oil to the NIEO.

Because of Southern pressure and the Northern desire to alleviate the crises of the 1970s, however, there was some improvement in financial flows, especially multilateral flows, to the South. As has been noted, food aid increased. The IMF was also gradually adapted to respond to the developing countries' problems. Several temporary mechanisms were created to deal with balance-of-payments crises following the two oil shocks: an oil facility was created in 1974 to finance the payments deficits caused by the increase in petroleum prices; a trust fund was financed by the sale of IMF gold; the Supplementary Finance Facility was created in 1979 to help alleviate serious payments imbalances; and an enlarged access policy allowed countries with protracted and structural balance-of-payments problems to borrow larger percentages of their quotas. There were also permanent changes in the IMF that benefited the developing countries: the Extended Fund Facility was created in 1974 to make money available for longer periods and in larger amounts than the usual IMF drawings, and the Compensatory Finance Facility, which helps countries suffering from severe drops in primary commodity prices, was enlarged and extended to cover cereal imports.[36]

As the United States and other developed countries gave increasing emphasis to multilateral aid, the World Bank also expanded in the 1970s. In addition to its traditional support for infrastructure projects, the bank began to make loans for basic human needs projects, including the development of subsistence farming, minimally adequate housing, and rudimentary health care.[37] In the late 1970s, the bank increased its lending for energy development. In response to the second oil crisis, it launched structural adjustment lending, a form of medium-term balance-of-payments support to enable countries to adapt the structure of production to prevailing world conditions, especially to changes in the cost of energy and food.[38] Finally, the bank sought to promote commercial lending to developing countries through cofinancing: mixed projects combining private and World Bank funding.[39]

Another success of the 1970s was the ability of the oil-importing developing countries to obtain aid from the new rich: the oil producers.[40] Throughout the 1970s, the attempt to obtain aid from the oil exporters was an important and successful strategy of the South. Significant OPEC financial flows explain in part Southern acquiescence to the increase in oil prices that devastated their economies. The old poor appealed to the new rich on the basis of Third World solidarity, and their history of common action and shared problems made the oil producers receptive to some of the South's demands. In the 1970s, because major oil producers were unable to absorb their new wealth, they found it relatively easy to assist in development finance. During that time, the North also looked to the oil producers for development finance. New IMF facilities and IFAD, for example, were based in part on financing by OPEC members.

Although the South was unable to achieve its vision of a new international economic order based in part on increased aid flows and significant changes in decision making, there were important changes in financial flows during the 1970s: greater concessional flows to the low-income developing countries; more multilateral aid; and a new source of aid from OPEC.

The Aid and Debt Crises of the 1980s

While the promise of public and private financial flows was great at the end of the 1970s, that promise had turned sour by the mid-1980s. The combination of recession and new conservative governments in the North in the early 1980s increased the focus on nonconcessional flows and private market solutions and decreased the flow of aid. Two additional external shocks hit the developing countries between 1979 and 1981. First, the second oil crisis of 1978–1979 caused a surge in the price of oil to a high of $35 in 1981 (see Chapter 9). Second, anti-inflationary policies in the developed countries and a steep recession (see Chapter 2) caused a precipitous drop in commodity prices and an adverse shift in the LDCs' terms of trade (see Chapter 7). A related problem for indebted countries was the rapid rise in international interest rates that resulted from the efforts of the U.S. Federal Reserve after 1979 to reduce inflation in the United States. Higher interest rates meant that indebted countries had to work harder to repay the interest on their loans. In short, a series of changes in the world economic situation turned private bank flows into the debt crisis. As a result, total financial flows to developing countries (concessional and commercial) fell greatly (see Figure 6-2).

Although a handful of developing countries were able to increase their exports of manufactured products to the North, demand for most of the South's products stagnated. The industrial recession also intensified protectionist pressures that further limited the export of manufactured goods. At the same time, the rise in the value of the dollar reduced commodity prices and increased the cost of many LDC imports denominated in dollars. Anti-inflationary policies combined with fiscal deficits in the developed countries led to unprecedented high interest rates and a resultant rise in the burden of debt servicing. Finally, these international shocks were aggravated by expansionary domestic economic policies in many of the LDCs: increased government spending to maintain growth rates exacerbated both fiscal and trade deficits.

The effects of these shocks were an increase in the trade deficit of developing countries from $22.2 billion in 1979 to $91.6 billion in 1981; increases in interest payments from $24.3 billion in 1979 to $41.8 billion in 1981; and a current account deficit that rose from $31.3 billion in 1979 to $118.6 in 1981. By

1981, interest payments almost offset new private lending. By 1982, when the debt crisis struck, interest payments exceeded new lending by $3.5 billion.[41]

With the recession of the early 1980s, domestic political opposition to foreign aid expenditures grew in the North. At a time of domestic unemployment and—at least in the United States—a cutback in domestic welfare programs, increased or even constant expenditures on foreign aid were politically impossible. Opposition to foreign aid was reinforced by an ideological challenge to economic aid as a route to development and a tool of foreign policy. Conservative governments elected to power in the 1980s in the United States and the United Kingdom argued that foreign aid had only a limited role to play in the development process. According to the view of the Reagan and Thatcher governments, economic recovery and development in both the developed and the developing countries had to be based on a return to free-market principles. The developing countries above all had to provide incentives and commercial opportunities for private enterprise, both domestic and foreign. Economic aid would be limited in amount, would not compete with private efforts, and would have as its main purpose the support of private enterprise and free markets. According to this view, much foreign aid—especially aid from multilateral institutions—did not meet these criteria.

In the 1980s, foreign economic aid also lost much of its political rationale, at least for the United States. With a strong East-West defense orientation, the Reagan administration was more interested in increasing its defense budget, in offering military assistance instead of foreign aid for development, and in granting bilateral rather than multilateral aid.

From 1980 to 1983, these economic and political changes led to another decline in multilateral aid, although levels still remained higher than in the late 1970s. The United States reduced its contributions to the International Development Agency, cut back on its commitment to IFAD, resisted capital increases in the World Bank, and dragged its heels on increasing IMF quotas. The United States also pushed for changes in the use of multilateral aid. It vetoed projects such as government funding of alternative energy sources which, it contended, could be privately financed. It argued that countries like India and China should not benefit from concessional funds because they could go to private markets for capital. Finally, the United States sought to attach conditions to aid flows so that they would promote private enterprise and investment capital. In the United Kingdom, the Thatcher government also decreased its official development assistance by almost 38 percent during this period, both bilaterally and multilaterally.

As a result of the recession's pressures, aid from the OECD countries actually fell from $27.3 billion in 1980 to $25.6 billion in 1981, before rebounding in 1982 to $27.9 billion. From 1980 to 1981, U.S. aid fell from $7.1 billion to $5.8 billion, then rose in 1982 to $8.3 billion. In constant prices, however, OECD and U.S. aid continued to decline.[42]

While overall aid stagnated, bilateral aid became increasingly defense oriented instead of development oriented. In 1973, 22 percent of U.S. bilateral aid was
for political/strategic purposes, and 78 percent was for development. By 1985, 67
percent of the total was for political/strategic purposes, and 33 percent was for
development assistance.[43] The changing political economy of oil (see Chapter 9)
also undermined OPEC's interest in aid transfers. Beginning in 1980, OPEC aid
decreased in absolute amounts, as a percentage of GNP, and as a percentage of
total official development assistance. From 1980 to 1985, total OPEC aid fell by
more than 50 percent, from $8.7 billion to $3.0 billion (see again Figure 6-3).

By the mid- to late-1980s, however, some concessional aid was restored.
New surplus countries, such as Japan, began extending more aid to the developing countries. As Japan's trade and financial surplus soared, it came under pressure from the United States to recycle those surpluses in part to developing countries. The United States saw this as a way to alleviate pressures on the United
States for aid flows. At the same time, Japanese leaders sought to define a greater
world role for Japan. They perceived that leadership in the Third World was a role
that Japan could assume without threatening the United States and without taking
on military responsibilities forbidden under Japan's constitution and unacceptable to the Japanese public. Thus, Japanese aid increased significantly, from $3.1
billion in 1981 to $11.3 billion in 1993, terms were eased, and the scope of recip-
ients broadened.[44]

In 1987, Japan announced a program to recycle a part of its current account
surpluses to the developing countries through bilateral loan programs and multilateral institutions. A total of $67.2 billion was disbursed under the program,
which ended in June 1992. A new program called the "Funds for Development
Initiative" was proposed to succeed it in June 1993. The goal for the new program
was to provide between $120 and $125 billion in official flows to the South over
five years. Both plans channeled the funds through the Exim Bank of Japan,
OECD yen loans, and multilateral development banks.[45]

Despite budgetary problems, the United States became more receptive to the
need for some concessional flows in particularly hard-hit areas such as sub-
Saharan Africa and also as a means of promoting "growth with adjustment" as a
way out of the debt crisis under the **Baker Plan.** Following the announcement of
the Baker Plan in 1985, the United States approved a $75 billion increase in the
World Bank's authorized capital; agreed to fund a new World Bank agency, the
Multilateral Investment Guarantee Agency (MIGA), to insure foreign direct
investment in developing countries; and provided new funds for the concessional
lending arm of the World Bank, the International Development Agency (IDA).
However, the lopsided distribution of U.S. aid to strategic countries was not
changed.

While both concessional and nonconcessional resources declined in real
terms during the 1980s, by the end of the 1980s both resumed their upward trend
(see Figure 6-2). Total net resources flowing to the developing countries reached

Figure 6-4   Net Official Development Assistance (ODA) by Donor Country in 1993 in Current Dollars

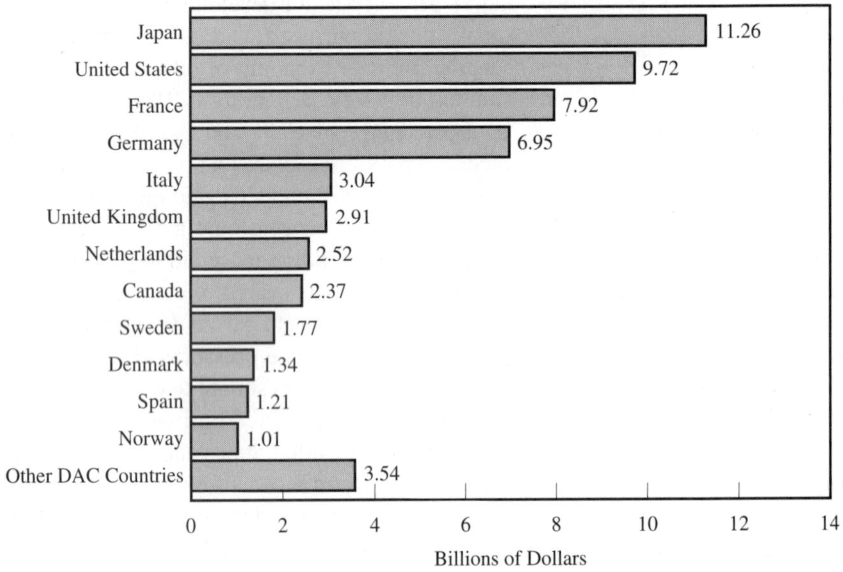

a postwar peak of $168.7 billion in 1993. ODA, however, declined from its post-war peak of $59.5 billion in 1992 to $55 billion in 1993.

One significant change over time was the growing importance of aid from Europe and Japan. In 1988, Japan overtook the United States as the largest donor of aid. In 1993, Japanese ODA was $11.3 billion while U.S. ODA was $9.7 billion (see Figure 6-4). The distribution of recipients across the major donor countries reflected a specialization of donors in aid to particular regions. The Europeans tended to provide aid to African countries and the formerly communist countries, the United States was the main aid donor to the Middle East (mainly Egypt and Israel) and Latin America, while Japan focused most of its aid efforts in Asia (see Figure 6-5).

The Impact of Aid

After more than a thirty years of concessional flows, it was possible to assess the impact of foreign aid.[46] From an economic standpoint, the reviews were mixed but positive. The bottom line was that aid helped certain countries enormously, usually for short periods of time, but did not have much effect on the general problem of global poverty and inequality. Indeed, a few economists purported to show that aid could not have such an effect even if it was intended to do so.[47]

Figure 6-5   Destinations by Region of Official Development Assistance (ODA) from the Five Largest Industrialized Countries, 1992–1993, in Percentages

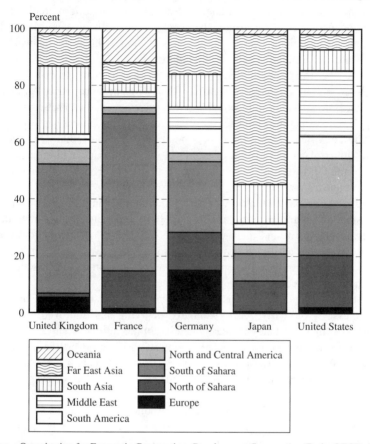

SOURCE: Organization for Economic Cooperation, *Development Cooperation* (Paris: OECD, 1995), table 45.

Overall growth of developing countries was significant. The GDP of the low- and middle-income countries grew at an annual rate of 5.2 percent between 1970 and 1980 and 2.9 percent between 1980 and 1993. In contrast, the GDP growth rate for high-income countries was only 3.2 percent between 1970 and 1980 and 2.9 percent between 1980 and 1993.[48] In per capita terms, this growth was less dramatic. From 1965 to 1986, per capita GNP rose at an annual rate of 2.9 percent in the less-developed countries versus 2.3 percent in the industrialized countries.[49] From 1980 to 1993, average annual growth in per capita GNP in the low- and middle-income countries was only 0.9 percent.[50] Growth also aggravated the unequal distribution of income in much of the South, where national income remained or became even more concentrated in the hands of a few. In general, measures of income distribution within the developing countries worsened between 1960 and the 1990s.[51]

Growth rates were also very uneven, leading to greater differentiation among developing countries. One group, the newly industrializing countries (NICs), experienced phenomenal growth and became important players on the world economic stage. A number of factors, including foreign aid, led to self-sustaining growth in the four "Asian tigers"—South Korea, Taiwan, Hong Kong, and Singapore—and in Mexico and Brazil. By the 1970s, these countries "graduated" from concessional flows and were able to tap private capital markets. Another set of upper-middle-income countries that bridged the development gap was the oil-exporting countries. Other LDCs, most notably China and India, which account for two-thirds of the population of the developing countries, had important successes in the fields of food self-sufficiency and growth. These and other middle-income countries maintained fairly strong growth rates.[52]

Other developing countries, however, including many African nations and others such as Myanmar, Bangladesh, and Haiti, experienced no growth during this period or even found themselves worse off. These low-income developing countries were the hardest hit by the commodity crises, especially in food and energy. Furthermore, they had virtually no access to commercial credit, which made them almost completely dependent on aid.

There is still a tremendous gap between rich and poor (see Chapter 5). Nonetheless, by the early 1980s, standards of living had improved universally. Importantly, life expectancy increased and infant mortality decreased significantly. Moreover, the proportion of people living in absolute poverty in noncommunist developing countries decreased by a third between 1960 and 1980.[53] Unfortunately, as we shall see, the crises of the 1980s halted, or even reversed, that process.

Aid was only one of many factors that produced these results. Concessional flows seem to have made a positive contribution to GNP growth, but their role is difficult to quantify. Although aggregate data show little or no correlation between aid and growth for developing countries as a whole, individual country studies show clearer correlations. It appears that aid can add significantly to growth in individual countries, particularly when accompanied by other sensible development policies. One study estimates that significant amounts of aid used reasonably efficiently can add 0.6 percent to 1.5 percent to the annual growth rate of a developing country.[54] On the other hand, aid is ineffective when applied through misguided donor or recipient programs or when other structural domestic barriers counteract its effect.

Aid contributed in important ways to growth in certain countries such as Pakistan, South Korea, and Taiwan, which received massive aid inflows. Even in these cases, however, aid had a positive impact because of other factors such as effective private initiatives.[55] On the other hand, in some countries, such as Mexico and Thailand, growth took place without significant aid.[56] Finally, there are cases of countries such as Bangladesh that received significant amounts of foreign aid but whose growth rates were still far below average.

Quality of life, including health, would certainly be worse in most developing countries had it not been for substantial medical and poverty-alleviation aid. In many cases, aid has been responsible for real increases in health and welfare. Unfortunately, in some cases aid has merely prevented bad situations from becoming worse.

In general, aid strategies have improved as practitioners have learned more about development. Many disappointing episodes in the early days resulted in later, more sophisticated, realistic, and carefully planned strategies. For example, the early efforts at rapid industrialization were replaced by greater recognition of the role of agriculture in development. Early emphasis on aggregate growth was tempered by concern for poverty alleviation, meeting basic human needs, and equity. At the same time, individual project lending was supplemented with comprehensive structural lending, and greater emphasis on free-market solutions. Most recently, planners have recognized the importance of analyzing the environmental impact of new projects.[57]

Finally, aid has had a political as well as an economic impact. The aid policies of most Northern states have reinforced their economic links with recipient countries and occasionally have given them extra leverage in their relations with the South. The United States, for example, has used aid to discourage the expropriation of existing investment. An amendment to the Foreign Assistance Act of 1962 stipulated that U.S. aid must be withheld in the event of nationalization or expropriation without prompt, adequate, and effective compensation.[58] Many donor countries have also encouraged new foreign investment by providing information, sharing the costs of investment surveys, and guaranteeing such investment against risk. Aid also supports trade links by encouraging the use of donor goods, especially through tied aid, and discouraging the development in some cases of competing industry.[59]

Aid is frequently used to influence economic policies in recipient countries.[60] The United States, for example, places economic conditions on aid that shapes monetary and fiscal policy, investment policy, and international economic policy, such as exchange rate and nationalization policy. Through the supervision of aid projects, the aid bureaucracies in all countries have become involved in decision making in recipient countries. Such economic influence occurs in multilateral aid programs as well. The World Bank, for example, has used its aid to promote market-oriented reforms in developing countries.[61]

Aid can also be used to support the preferred internal and external policies of the recipient governments. The United States, for example, has given emergency support in economic crises to the Philippines in 1987 and to Mexico in 1982, 1988, and 1995. Also, the withdrawal or threatened withdrawal of aid has been used to express disapproval of or opposition to internal and external policies. The United States withheld aid from Haiti in 1987, from Panama in 1988, and from Nigeria in 1994. And, reflecting the political/security focus of the U.S. foreign aid program, assistance has been used to promote foreign policies, such as granting basic rights and supporting countries in conflict with the Soviet Union (for example, Pakistan).[62]

Aid has not always enhanced the North's bargaining power. The degree of Northern dominance through aid varied not only in some "objective" measurement of Northern influence but also in the eye of the beholder. Scholars in the North have argued about whether aid was given for altruistic reasons and without political strings; or whether it was given primarily for political or strategic reasons. There is evidence for both perspectives. Others have argued that the effects of aid on the recipients were nil or even counterproductive. The recipients, on the other hand, often felt that aid constituted not influence but unwanted intervention in national policy.[63]

The Onset of the Debt Crisis

One of the major developments in financial flows to the developing countries in the 1980s was the dramatic change in private flows. The rise in the price of oil (see Chapter 9), combined with restrictive monetary policies in the major industrial countries, led to record-high real interest rates and world recession. As a result, the LDC debtor nations faced declining terms of trade—plunging commodity prices and a threefold increase in the price of oil—and falling export volumes.

By 1982, external LDC debt was 264 percent above 1975 levels. The highly indebted countries, consisting of (in order of exposure), Brazil, Mexico, Argentina, Venezuela, Nigeria, Philippines, Yugoslavia, Morocco, Chile, Peru, Colombia, Ivory Coast, Ecuador, Bolivia, Costa Rica, Jamaica, and Uruguay, by 1982 had outstanding debt 305 percent higher than in 1975.[64] Borrowing from private commercial sources accounted for an ever greater portion of total debt (see Figure 6-6), rising from 60 percent of the highly indebted countries' debt in 1975 to 76 percent by 1982.

Because of rising interest rates, developing countries also faced sharp increases in the cost of servicing their greatly increased debt. By 1982, the debt service ratio, measured by the dollar value of interest and principal amortization payments as a percentage of the dollar value of exports, rose to 21 percent for all debtors and to 38.8 percent for the highly indebted countries.[65]

Before 1979 borrowing had been for relatively long terms of three to five years. But as lenders became cautious in 1979 to 1981, they turned increasingly to short-term credits, which made the borrowers much more vulnerable to a change in the lenders' willingness to continue the flows. Significantly, in many, although not all, cases, this new lending was used for consumption, not for increases in productive capacity. In some countries, including Argentina, Venezuela, and Mexico, some lending was dissipated in capital flight.

A few critics warned of danger. But the ease of adjustment in the 1970s to

Figure 6-6   Long-Term Debt Outstanding by Groups of Indebted Countries, 1970–1993, in Current Dollars

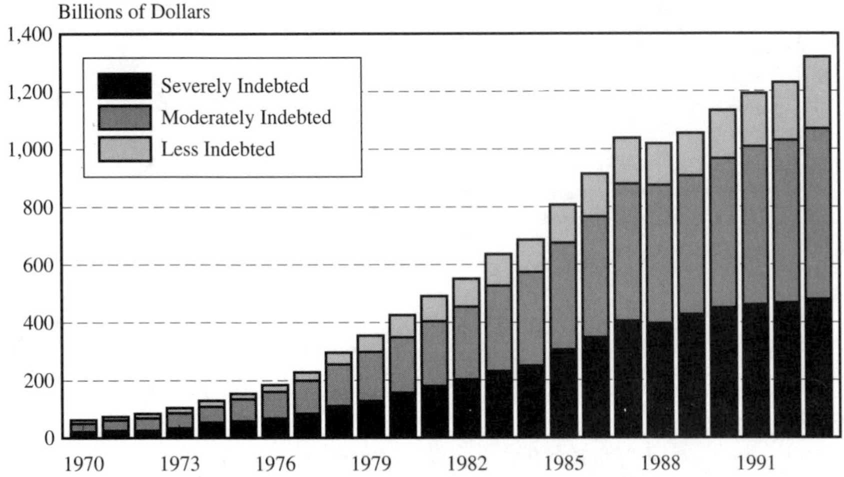

SOURCE: World Bank, *World Data '95 CD-ROM* (Washington: World Bank, 1995).

increased lending to developing countries, inaccurate predictions about world recovery and declining interest rates, plus the system's ability to manage earlier debt reschedulings with no lasting consequences for the international system, led to complacency on the part of bankers and government officials in both the developed and less-developed countries. The system was set for crisis.

The first signs of the increasingly fragile structure of international debt came in 1981 and early 1982. Argentina's decision to suspend payments on its $37 billion in external debt following its defeat by Britain in the 1982 Falklands war lowered confidence in the capital markets, which responded by shortening maturities and demanding repayment of some short-term obligations. A number of countries found themselves in a severe liquidity squeeze.

More important than the Argentine payment suspension was the announcement of the Mexican government in August 1982 that it would be unable to service its foreign debt. Mexico's ambitious growth policies had resulted in an overheated and increasingly inflationary economy and surging budgetary and trade deficits (see Figure 6-7). The weakening world oil market (see Chapter 9) reduced the value of Mexico's oil exports, which comprised three-fourths of its total export earnings; higher interest rates and growing debt drove up the annual cost of debt service; the greatly overvalued peso led to a surge in Mexico's imports; and the situation was aggravated by capital flight.[66] An upcoming presidential election made the government particularly unwilling to take far-reaching measures to avert a crisis. One month after the July 1982 election, a financial panic erupted.

**Figure 6-7   Trade Balances of Brazil and Mexico in
Current Dollars, 1960–1994**

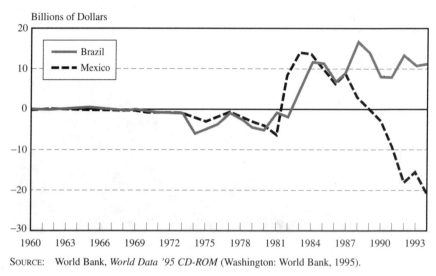

SOURCE: World Bank, *World Data '95 CD-ROM* (Washington: World Bank, 1995).

The Mexican debt crisis of 1982 posed a major challenge to the world's financial system. Until then, external debt problems like Mexico's had been rare and had generally involved relatively small amounts of commercial bank borrowings. By contrast, Mexico's external debt totaled more than $85 billion and included loans that accounted for a significant percentage of the capital of the largest U.S. banks in 1982. Moreover, Mexico was just the tip of the iceberg. At the end of 1982, loans to Argentina, Brazil, Mexico, Venezuela, and Chile alone amounted to over $260 billion. Brazil by itself had borrowed $91 billion.[67] The world's major private banks, especially U.S. banks, had significant exposure in these countries.[68]

In the developed countries, the LDC debt crisis was treated primarily as a threat to the international financial system. Defaults by debtor nations could have led to a collapse of confidence in the international banking system, possible illiquidity or insolvency of the banks, dangerous disruption of the financial markets, and, in a worst-case scenario, world recession or depression.[69] As a Federal Reserve Bank study later put it: "International bankers and policy makers faced a threat of financial disorder on a global scale not seen since the Depression."[70] Central bankers, finance ministers, and heads of government, determined to prevent any such danger to the international financial system, cooperated to manage the crisis. The United States played an important leadership role in mobilizing international management. In the process, the central banks and the IMF also assumed significant roles.

Within two days of the 1982 crisis, the United States forwarded to Mexico $2 billion in prepayments for oil and in credits for the purchase of U.S. agricultural products. It also helped arrange a $1 billion bridging loan from a group of central banks acting through the BIS. The principal foreign creditor banks agreed to postpone debt service fees for three months. Under pressure from the United States, Mexico and the IMF began negotiations for a longer-term arrangement. Thus the immediate crisis was averted.

In November 1982, Mexico and the IMF reached an accord. In exchange for $3.84 billion in IMF credits between 1983 and 1985, Mexican authorities agreed to carry out a strict austerity program that included reducing the budget deficit, limiting public sector external borrowing, and reducing or eliminating subsidies and public works projects. Significantly, the IMF refused to conclude its agreement until the commercial banks agreed to lend an additional $5 billion to Mexico. This was the first time that the IMF insisted on large complementary financing from banks as an essential element of an IMF lending agreement. At the same time, the Mexican government, acting on behalf of all Mexican borrowers and its private creditors, agreed to begin negotiations to postpone debt repayments and lengthen repayment timetables.[71]

As bank lending to developing countries abruptly halted after August 1982, the debt crisis spread rapidly through Latin America and the rest of the developing world. By December 1982, Brazil, with $91 billion in foreign debt, was in trouble. By the end of 1983, Brazil, almost all the other Latin American countries, and a number of African countries had rescheduled their debts.[72] By the end of 1983, more than twenty-five countries around the world, with a combined outstanding bank debt of more than $200 billion, had gone into arrears.

Debt Crisis Management

Mexico became the model for managing these debt crises. Each country was handled separately as its debts came due or as it fell into arrears, according to what came to be called the case-by-case approach. Although the process thus varied from country to country, a pattern of crisis management emerged. The debt problem was handled as a temporary liquidity problem that could be managed through domestic austerity programs, rescheduling debt payments, and some new lending. The key elements of debt management became negotiation of a loan from and an economic stabilization agreement with the IMF, debt rescheduling with commercial banks, and new public and private lending.

Reaching agreement with the IMF on a loan and a domestic austerity program—a condition of IMF borrowing—became a central part of debt rescheduling. Although its loans were small compared with total indebtedness, the IMF provided a vehicle for imposing and surveying national economic policies deemed necessary for debt repayment. The IMF could hold up its lending and all rescheduling if a debtor did not agree to certain policies. It could also hold up disbursements of monies if a country did not meet agreed-upon economic commitments.

In this first period of the debt crisis from 1982 to 1984, IMF economic programs focused on austerity policies. Budget deficits were to be reduced through spending restraint, reduced subsidies, and higher taxes. External imbalances were to be improved by slowing domestic demand, raising the volume of exports, and cutting the prices of tradable products. Inflation was to be controlled by tight monetary policy, competitive exchange rates, positive real interest rates, limits on wage increases, and fiscal austerity. These changes were expected to enable debtor countries to overcome what was seen as a temporary liquidity problem, so they could service their debts and return to normal access to commercial credit markets.

A second central element of debt rescheduling was an agreement between creditor banks and the debtor government. The banks were represented by an advisory committee, a group of lead banks with significant financial exposure in the country, which had to reach agreements not only with the debtor but also with other smaller creditor banks. The debtor government represented all domestic debtors. Negotiations focused on new terms and conditions of outstanding medium- and long-term loans. Short-term trade credits by and large were serviced and not rescheduled, while other short-term loans were rescheduled in many cases. Repayment schedules were extended, grace periods given on principal repayment, and rates adjusted. But debtors were always expected to service debts fully, and no debt relief such as reduction of interest or principal was provided.

Creditor banks were also expected to provide new financing for debtor countries. The commitment of new lending by creditor banks to a debt-plagued country became an essential element of any debt-rescheduling package. Central banks and the IMF became deeply involved in pressing creditors to continue lending to debtor countries. Indeed, in what has been called coerced lending, the central banks and the IMF virtually required private banks to commit additional funds to debtor countries, according to a quota allocation system based on each bank's exposure in the country.[73]

Finally, creditor governments, whose various credit-granting institutions, such as export credit agencies, had outstanding loans to debtor countries, themselves had to reschedule. This was done through the Paris Club of government creditors, which negotiated as a group with debtor countries. The Paris Club handled virtually all debt rescheduling for poorer debtors such as those in Africa that were never able to borrow significantly from commercial banks and whose debt was owed mostly to government entities.[74]

From 1982 to 1984, the strategy of debt management through austerity, rescheduling, and new lending seemed to work. Cooperation among key parties in developing a system of crisis management averted the feared world financial crisis. Through the IMF, concerted lending by commercial banks, and ongoing trade finance, monies continued to flow to debtor countries, enabling them to make interest payments to banks. Debtors, following IMF-imposed policies, reduced their budget deficits by cutting back on public and private investment. For the heavily indebted countries, the rate of growth in investment was minimal in 1981 at only 0.4 percent and fell by 13.1 percent in 1982, 21 percent in 1983, and by 2.1 percent in 1984. In the same period, real growth in imports, including capital equipment for development projects or parts for manufactured products for export, grew at a rate of 2.3 percent in 1981, then fell by 14.1 in 1982, by 20.4 in 1983, and by 1.1 percent in 1984.[75] Largely by restraining imports, the major debtors generated large trade surpluses that brought them close to current account balance. For example, by suppressing domestic demand and encouraging non-oil exports, Mexico went from a $7 billion deficit on current account in 1982 to a $5 billion surplus in 1983. Brazil's trade surplus increased from $800 million in 1982 to $6.5 billion in 1983 and in 1984 even higher exports led to a small current account surplus (see again Figure 6-7).[76]

Following the initial crises, some improvements were made in the debt management system. Initially, debt reschedulings covered only one year, so frequent reschedulings became regular events. In 1984, Mexico and its creditors reached the first multi-year rescheduling agreement (MYRA), which lasted four years, provided for a fourteen-year final maturity, lower interest rates, monitored by the banks of Mexico's economic performance over the long term, and the banks' right to refuse to proceed with a second phase of rescheduling if Mexico did not meet its economic targets. The Mexican agreement became a model for other MYRAs.

The creditor governments also ensured that the IMF had adequate resources to continue its crisis management role. Not surprisingly, the debt crisis placed serious financial strains on the Fund and decreased its resources. In 1983, members agreed to increase IMF quotas by almost 50 percent. At the same time, the Group of Ten agreed to increase the General Arrangements to Borrow (GAB) and to allow IMF members other than the Group of Ten access to GAB credits if their problems seriously threatened the international monetary system.[77] Finally, the breathing room created by debt management gave creditor banks time to reduce their exposure to developing country debtors by increasing their capital and restraining further lending to LDCs.

Despite these successes, the first phase of debt management neither resolved the debt problem nor brought it under adequate long-term control. Indeed, the strategy actually undermined the long-term ability of the indebted countries to service their debts. Austerity policies, which dramatically reduced domestic demand and imports, also brought growth to a halt. Cutbacks in investment and imports removed catalysts for growth. Devaluations designed to improve balance-of-payments adjustment made it more costly in local currency to service external debt and aggravated the fiscal problems of the government, which had to purchase foreign exchange for debt service.

A few debtor countries—particularly Korea and Turkey—made quick structural adjustments and resumed growth. Most, however, fell into recession. Most seriously affected were the highly indebted countries. Real GDP growth for the highly indebted group fell by 0.4 percent in 1982 and by 2.9 percent in 1983 before rising by 1.9 percent in 1984—half the rates of the 1960s and 1970s, and barely faster than population growth.[78]

Because GDP and exports grew slowly or not at all, the debt service capacity of the major countries did not improve. Furthermore, because of concerted lending and increased loans from the IMF and World Bank, long-term debt outstanding increased further from $391 billion in 1982 to $454 billion in 1985 (see again Figure 6-6). From 1982 to 1985, the ratio of debt to GNP for the highly indebted countries rose from 32.4 to 49.5. Although the debt service ratio (total debt service to exports of goods and services) for these countries improved due to falling interest rates, it became clear that the debt crisis was more than a temporary liquidity problem.

In September 1985, the United States took the lead in calling for a new debt strategy. In a speech to the annual meeting of the World Bank and IMF, Treasury Secretary James Baker recognized that normal access of LDC debtors to commercial lending could only be restored through growth.[79] He proposed a three-part plan to restore growth in fifteen of the most heavily indebted countries and to complement the ongoing country-by-country debt restructuring efforts.

First, debtor governments would implement market-oriented structural changes to remove economic inefficiencies that were seen as impediments to growth. Reforms included trade liberalization such as reducing tariffs and quotas; financial liberalization such as improved access for foreign direct investment; deregulation, including reducing subsidies, interest rate controls and exchange rate regulations; and privatization of state-owned industry. Second, the Baker Plan called on commercial banks to provide $20 billion in new loans over three years. Finally, the multilateral development banks, particularly the World Bank, were to increase disbursements by $3 billion per year. Increased World Bank structural adjustment lending was to facilitate domestic reform. The combination of economic reforms and new financial flows was expected to lead to a growth in output and exports and, eventually, to a return to solvency and access to credit markets.

The Baker plan, however, did not lead to a resurgence of growth. While countries such as Mexico, Chile, and Uruguay pursued structural adjustment policies, others such as Brazil, Argentina, and Peru did not implement significant reforms. Efforts to carry out structural reforms were limited by political constraints. Fragile democratic regimes in countries like Brazil and Argentina found it difficult to implement reforms because of opposition from important political constituencies. In addition, there were real differences of opinion within all of these countries about the desirability of market-oriented as opposed to government-led approaches to growth.[80]

Economic reality also left little room for maneuvering. Inadequate tax systems left countries dependent on tariffs for revenue and made widespread tariff reduction difficult. Financial liberalization was set back by increased government demands on the banking system for debt financing and by persistent financial crises. Despite fiscal austerity, public sector deficits remained large because foreign debt service constituted such a large share of government expenditures—about 30 percent in many countries.[81] Public deficits contributed to high inflation and high interest rates, which, in turn, worsened the debt service burden because they tended to result in currency devaluations. Anti-inflation programs were over-whelmed by fiscal imbalances.[82] Large public financing needs squeezed out private savings while high interest rates and the uncertainty created by high and unstable inflation rates damaged investors' confidence.

External conditions were also unfavorable. Growth in the developed countries slowed; there was a persistent weakness in nonoil commodity prices; and turmoil in OPEC led to a sharp drop in oil prices after 1985. As a result, the overall terms of trade moved sharply against the major debtors from 1985 to 1987, falling at an average annual rate of 6.7 percent.[83] Lower inflation and lower interest rates in the industrial countries were not enough to offset the decline in the terms of trade.

Finally, the financial inflows prescribed by the Baker Plan were not forthcoming. Commercial banks continued to lend large amounts of new money to the major debtor countries as part of rescheduling agreements. By 1988, they had largely met the $20 billion target of new loans set by the Baker Plan. However, due to debt servicing by LDCs to banks, net commercial bank flows to debtor countries were actually negative. In 1986, LDC debtors had a net outflow to commercial banks (Figure 6-8). Public financial flows were a mixed picture. World Bank commitments to the highly indebted countries met the Baker Plan target, increasing from $9.2 billion in 1981–1982 to $12.9 billion in 1986–1987. Net transfers, however, told a far different story. In 1986, net trans-

Figure 6-8   Net Credit and Loan Flows from the International Monetary Fund to the Developing Countries in Current Dollars, 1987–1994

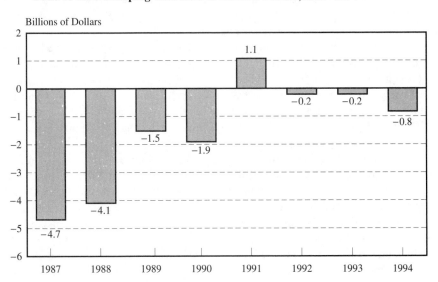

SOURCE: International Monetary Fund, *World Economic Outlook* (Washington: IMF, 1995), 167.

fers were far short of the $3 billion per year goal and in 1987 they were actually a negative $0.6 billion.[84]

Critics argued that World Bank flows should have been even greater and that the Bank should have played a more active role in promoting financial flows. Bank officials, on the other hand, pointed out that lending was constrained by the economic crisis in the debtor countries, which left them short of matching funds to invest in new projects and unwilling or unable to implement structural adjustment programs. They also pointed out the growing limits on World Bank lending imposed by a shortage of capital.

IMF net flows to the heavily indebted countries actually declined. In 1983, the Fund transferred $6.5 billion to these countries, providing an important offset to the contraction of private flows. In 1986 and 1987, IMF net resource transfers to the heavily indebted countries were negative. In 1987, repayments to the Fund exceeded new disbursements by $4.7 billion; this reverse flow declined abruptly in 1989 to $1.5 billion, but remained negative while decreasing gradually through 1994.[85] In response to criticism, the Fund pointed out that the reverse flow occurred, in part because of repayments for the heavy outflows during the early years of the debt crisis and in part because debtors had not implemented economic reforms required for IMF lending.[86]

While some improvements were made after 1985, the Baker Plan did not fulfill its goal of achieving sustained growth in major debtor countries. Table 6-1 presents various indicators for this period. After recovering briefly in 1985, investment stagnated and actually declined in 1988. Exports of goods as a percentage of GDP declined while imports remained largely constant. Real GDP growth for the group rose only 2.4 percent per year for the period 1985 to 1988. Per capita growth was lower, averaging 1 percent per year. Per capita consumption levels fell and poverty levels increased.

Total long-term debt for the seriously indebted countries rose from $442 billion in 1985 to around $570 billion in 1987 and stayed at around that level through 1992 (see Figure 6-6). The average proportion of debt to GNP for the seriously indebted countries rose from 68.3 percent in 1982 to 163.7 percent in 1989. It dropped in 1990 to 160.4 percent but then rose again to 172.5 percent in 1992 (see Figure 6-9). Average debt service as a percentage of exports peaked at 33.2 percent in 1986 and then dropped (see Figure 6-10).

Some modifications were made in an effort to improve the working of the Baker Plan. An increase in World Bank capital authorized in 1988 was intended to enable bank flows to continue and possibly increase. In 1987, Secretary Baker endorsed the "menu approach" of different techniques to reduce the overall level of debt. Included on the menu were devices developed both by markets and by governments. One of the first developments was a debt swap market through which creditors exchanged debt with each other as a way of balancing exposure to certain countries or of balancing debt maturities. A secondary market for the sale of debt at a discount also developed and many banks used the market to dis-

Table 6-1 Highly Indebted Countries and the World Economy, 1980–1988

	1980	1981	1982	1983	1984	1985	1986	1987	1988[1]
Economic Growth Indicators				PERCENTAGE REAL CHANGE					
Industrial Country Output	1.3	2.0	-0.4	2.8	4.5	3.1	2.7	3.3	3.9
World Trade[2]	1.3	2.4	-1.0	3.0	9.9	4.0	2.6	4.3	7.5
HIC GDP[3]	5.6	0.6	-0.4	-2.9	1.9	3.7	3.4	1.7	2.0
HIC Investment[3]	9.4	0.4	-13.1	-21.0	-2.1	4.5	1.9	0.8	-2.9
HIC per Capita Consumption[3]	3.4	0.3	-2.2	-4.1	-1.7	0.2	2.6	-1.4	-0.6
HIC Exports[3]	1.1	-6.6	0.0	5.0	9.3	2.2	0.7	0.4	6.4
HIC Imports[3]	8.2	2.3	-14.1	-20.4	-1.1	-1.6	4.0	-1.7	2.0
				BILLIONS OF U.S. DOLLARS					
Total External Debt	289.0	351.0	391.0	422.0	438.0	454.0	482.0	527.0	529.0
Net Flows to HICs	28.6	43.7	34.6	19.1	13.3	6.0	4.5	6.2	7.6
Net Resource Transfers to HICs	8.8	18.3	3.7	-9.9	-19.9	-26.5	-25.8	-21.8	-31.1

[1]Preliminary estimates.
[2]Volume.
[3]Constant 1980 U.S. dollars

SOURCE: World Bank, *World Debt Tables* (Washington: World Bank, 1988), p. xvii.

Figure 6-9   Average Debt/GNP for the Seriously Indebted Countries, 1970–1992, in Percentages

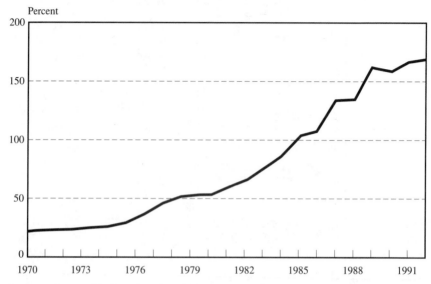

SOURCE: Computed by the authors from World Bank, *World Data '94 CD-ROM* (Washington: World Bank, 1994).

Figure 6-10   Average Debt Service as a Percentage of Exports of Goods and Services, Severely Indebted Countries, 1970–1992

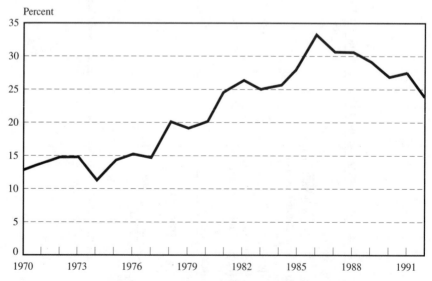

SOURCE: Computed by the authors from World Bank, *World Data '94 CD-ROM* (Washington: World Bank, 1994).

Figure 6-11   Secondary Market Prices for Selected Countries, March 1986–September 1992*

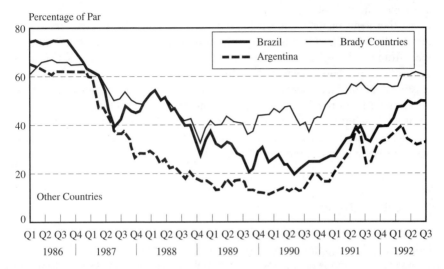

*Weighted by commercial debt outstanding. Brady countries are Costa Rica, Mexico, Phillipines, Uruguay and Venezuela. Other countries are Algeria, Bolivia, Bulgaria, Chile, Congo, Côte d'Ivoire, Ecuador, Egypt, Honduras, Hungary, Morocco, Nicaragua, Peru, Poland, and Senegal.
SOURCE: Euroweek, LDC Debt Report, Salomon Brothers, and World Bank.

pose of LDC debt. By 1988, the average price of LDC debt was below fifty cents on the dollar (see Figure 6-11).

Debt-equity swaps were also on the menu. These involved the exchange of bank debt for equity investments in debtor countries and required debtor government participation. A creditor bank might swap debt on its own behalf or sell debt to an investor at a discount. The bank or the investor exchanged the debt for local currency at the debtor central bank at a rate below full face value but above the amount the investor paid the bank. The currency was then used to make a local equity investment. The commercial bank thus reduced its debt exposure by selling it or turning it into a real asset; the debtor country lowered its debt and promoted new investment; and the investor obtained favorable financing for investment.

Some countries, especially Chile and Mexico, used debt-equity swaps to reduce overall debt. Most LDCs, however, controlled such swaps in order to minimize various problems. Swaps could be inflationary if a country simply created local currency to finance them. So, monetary policy was used to offset swaps, and the amount of swaps allowed has been limited. There was also a question whether investment would have taken place anyway at less cost for the debtor government. Thus, countries have restricted the type of investment eligible for swaps. And debt-equity swaps also raised political issues about control of the national econ-

omy traditionally associated with foreign investment. For this reason, some countries did not allow swaps and others have periodically closed the swap window,
as Mexico did in 1988.

Other items on the menu were exit bonds made available to creditors as part
of a rescheduling. Exit bonds gave creditors a lower rate of interest but exempted
them from providing new money as part of concerted lending packages. One vari-
ation of an exit bond developed by the Mexican government offered to swap
existing debt for fixed interest bonds whose principal was collateralized by a U.S.
government bond purchased by the Mexican government. Overall, these menu
items were helpful in reducing the debt service burden, but only at the margins.
Despite the Baker Plan and the menu modification, debtor economies stagnated
and the system continued to lurch from crisis to crisis.

Debt Fatigue

By 1987, the debt crisis had entered a new phase characterized by debt
fatigue and disintegrating cooperation among the participants. The first sign of
change came from the debtor countries. Initially, debtor governments had, by and
large, been willing participants in the debt management system developed after
1982. Their cooperation stemmed partly from a sense of responsibility for solving their problems and partly from lack of leverage with the creditor banks and
governments. The major source of LDC leverage would have been to threaten or
actually to default on their debt. But unless they acted simultaneously, default
would have damaged their economies more than those of the creditors.
Furthermore, the case-by-case approach acted as an effective deterrent to cooperation among debtor countries. When one country faced financial problems and
was in the midst of rescheduling, other countries had just concluded agreements
with creditors and were in no mood to reopen the debate. Sequential rescheduling negotiations in which each debtor government sought to take advantage of its
own special situation discouraged cooperation or even sharing information
among debtors.

As slow or no growth persisted and the debt burden grew, social and political tensions within debtor countries rose, and dissatisfaction with the system
emerged. With access to credit markets an elusive goal, economically painful and
politically difficult policies designed to satisfy creditors became less acceptable.
As early as 1984, the newly elected Argentine government resisted a proposed
IMF austerity program as unduly severe economically and a threat to the fragile
democratic political consensus and threatened to refuse to pay the interest on its
debt. At the same time, Argentina joined with other Latin American debtor countries in the so-called Cartagena Group to make specific proposals for easing the
debt service burden, including limiting debt payments to a "reasonable" percentage of export earnings and relaxing IMF austerity programs by giving priority to
economic growth.[87] In 1985 the newly elected government in Peru announced it

would limit its debt service to 10 percent of exports. These actions, however, had little impact on the debt management system. Argentina was discouraged by Brazil and Mexico and eventually signed an agreement with the IMF; Peru was treated as a pariah by both creditors and debtors; and the Cartagena group did not become a debtor cartel.

By 1987, however, conditions had changed. Bolivia, Costa Rica, the Dominican Republic, Ecuador, and Honduras had unilaterally suspended all or part of their debt service. Most important, Brazil, in the first challenge to the system by a major debtor, suspended payments on its $110.5 billion of medium- and long-term debt. The Brazilian moratorium was designed to obtain better terms including some form of debt relief in its debt-rescheduling negotiations. A Brazilian default would have forced creditor banks to suffer substantial losses and could have started a chain reaction among debtor governments.

Rather than improving its leverage, however, the moratorium weakened Brazil's ability to extract concessions from creditor banks and governments. Banks throughout the developed world responded to Brazil's action by increasing their reserves for possible losses on LDC loans. Having gradually increased their equity capital after 1982, banks were better able to withstand the losses to earnings that resulted from this action. The banks thus called Brazil's bluff and demonstrated that banks were more willing to suffer earnings losses than to give in to Brazil and to the precedent of debt relief. Banks also reduced trade credit lines and delayed disbursement of loans. Some countries, especially the United States, put pressure on Brazil to return to the fold. Brazil also received little support from other debtors. A summit meeting of Latin America's major debtors called for lower interest rates and reduction in debt-service payments but led to no common action. One year after declaring its moratorium, Brazil reentered negotiations with creditor banks and eventually concluded a new rescheduling agreement.

Although Brazil's moratorium was unsuccessful, it demonstrated growing debtor dissatisfaction with the debt management system. This dissatisfaction was increasingly used by opposition parties in debtor countries that based their electoral platforms on debt relief. For example, in 1988, debt was a major issue in elections in Mexico, where the opposition party that advocated debt relief offered a serious challenge to the previously dominant governing party, and in Venezuela, where the winning candidate advocated debt relief.[88]

There was restiveness among creditor banks as well. While debtors had been divided and unable to form a debtor cartel, creditors had been united from the beginning through the advisory committees, which were a form of creditor cartel. Now, creditor unity had begun to weaken. Small and regional banks and even some larger banks, which did not see long-term future business in the debtor countries, sought to limit or reduce their lending to LDC debtors. Most set aside significant reserves for losses on LDC loans. Some sold all or part of their portfolios at a discount in the debt market. These banks resented being called upon to make new loans to debtor countries at a time when the actual value of loans in the secondary market was below face value and when prospects for a return to solvency seemed dim. It became increasingly difficult for the lead creditor banks and governments to persuade these banks to provide new money as part of the restructuring packages. Pressure on big banks increased, not only from reluctant creditors and from the secondary market where loan values were significantly discounted, but also from the stock markets where values of the major banks with exposure in developing countries were depressed because of the LDC debt overhang. Following the increases in reserves in 1987, more banks became interested in reducing lending to LDC debtors and many major lenders sold debt in the secondary market.

Finally, banks from different countries took different positions in the restructuring negotiations. For example, differences in regulatory and tax treatment between countries led banks to have different positions on setting up reserves against potential losses on LDC loans, and this led to opposing views on concessions to debtor countries. Debt-restructuring packages became harder to negotiate because of the divisions among banks and raised concern that overall new flows would decline. In 1988, the World Bank predicted that commercial bank lending would fall far short of the private sector financing needed by the debtor countries;[89] an organization representing banks from around the world announced that private flows would not meet the demand;[90] some bankers began to call for a new strategy involving debt relief and greater involvement by creditor country governments;[91] and members of Congress offered plans to reduce debt service.[92]

Despite growing pressures, the United States continued to insist on the viability of the Baker Plan and to oppose any form of debt relief. The Reagan administration argued that the strategy allowed banks to reduce exposure to LDC debt, helped stabilize the financial system, and made it possible, given favorable conditions, for the debtors to grow and to reduce debt through the menu approach. In the administration's view, it was inappropriate and politically infeasible for creditor country governments to ask taxpayers to "bail out" the banks or the LDC debtors.

In the face of initial U.S. opposition, other industrial countries also began wavering in their support of the U.S. government. Britain, France, and Germany supported debt relief for the poorest debtors in Africa whose debt was largely to governments. In 1987, with U.S. acquiescence, they approved the creation of an Expanded Structural Adjustment Fund in the IMF to provide greater funds for the least-developed countries to adjust to market changes. Despite U.S. resistance, the heads of state at the 1988 Toronto Summit agreed on a plan to alleviate the debt-service burden for the poorer sub-Saharan African countries. The plan gave these debtors various options for lowering interest rates, stretching out repayments, and actual forgiveness of debt to developed country governments. This was the first recognition of a need for debt relief.

Also at the Toronto Summit, and later at the 1988 World Bank/IMF meeting, the Japanese government called on the Group of Seven to develop new forms of debt relief for middle-income debtors. The Japanese offered a proposal for the exchange of debt for securities and for a central role for the IMF. The Japanese proposal for a new approach to debt management was part of its efforts to develop a new role as a world power in developing countries and complemented its new aid initiatives.[93]

By the end of 1988, the need for revision of the Baker Plan was increasingly clear. The World Bank said that the time had come for the international debt strategy to enter a new phase. As the Bank put it: "The declining interest of commercial banks in sovereign risk lending to highly indebted countries coupled with the continued uncertainties arising from the debt overhang may be a signal that it is time to rework the 1985 consensus."[94] The challenge described by the Bank was to develop new ways for debtor countries both to restructure their economies and to obtain adequate funds to renew investment and thus development over the long term. At risk was not only economic development for the developing countries but also economic benefits for the developed countries that exported large amounts to debtor countries. Also at stake, as the Mexican election and the elections in other Latin American countries revealed, was the political stability of democratic regimes in many debtor countries.

One of the first initiatives of the new administration of President George Bush was to face up to these realities. In December 1988, even before his inauguration, President-elect Bush announced "a whole new look" on U.S. policy toward the world's debtor countries.[95] As the Bush administration worked to develop a new approach, pressure for change increased. The new Mexican president called for debt reduction in his inaugural address in January and, then, in March rioting and hundreds of deaths followed the imposition of austerity measures by the newly elected Venezuelan government, which demonstrated dramatically the political threat.[96]

In March 1989, Treasury Secretary Nicholas Brady announced a new LDC debt strategy.[97] Although it was vague on many details, the strategy called for a shift in emphasis from new lending to debt reduction by banks and stated that World Bank and IMF resources should be available to debtor countries with sound economic reform policies for use in encouraging debt reduction. Bit by bit, details on the **Brady initiative** began to emerge. First, it became clear that debt reduction would be added to a menu of options that still included new money from banks. In terms of debt reduction, the United States proposed mostly voluntary exchanges of old debt for new bonds: either bonds paying market rates but exchanged for bank loans at a discount, or bonds paying sharply reduced interest but exchanged at par value. It was envisaged that the principal and at least one year of interest on the new bonds would be secured by a country's existing reserves or funds from IMF or World Bank loans. The Treasury proposal also envisioned lending by international financial institutions to countries to buy back debts at secondary market prices.

Support for the Brady initiative came promptly from Japan, which pledged $4.5 billion in loans to be provided in parallel with IMF and World Bank loans.

Many of the debtor countries also welcomed the Brady initiative, seizing on the hope for substantial reductions in their bank debts. However, other industrial countries, particularly the United Kingdom and Germany, remained wary and expressed concern that the Brady initiative was transferring risks from the private sector to the public. Other analysts, while welcoming the new direction in policy, worried that the Brady initiative did not go far enough fast enough to turn around the economic and political situation in the debtor countries.

Implementation of the Brady initiative was left to negotiations between banks and specific debtor countries. Negotiations over Mexican debt provided the first test case. After months of stalled talks between Mexico and bank representatives, a new debt reduction agreement was reached in late July 1989, under pressure from Secretary Brady and with the assistance of U.S. officials. The agreement, which followed the main points for debt resolution set out by Brady earlier in the year, covered $54 billion of the $69 billion owed by Mexico to private banks. The Mexican plan specified three options for the banks: (1) swapping old loans in return for thirty-year bonds paying interest at the same rate as the old loans but valued at 35 percent less than the old loans; (2) swapping old loans for thirty-year bonds with the same value, but with a lower, fixed interest rate; or (3) agreeing to lend new money (or recycle interest received from Mexico) for four years, at levels equal in amount to 25 percent of the bank's exposure. In return, the agreement called for a guarantee of the interest payments on the bonds for eighteen months, to be financed by funds from the IMF, the World Bank, Mexico, and Japan.[98]

The Mexican agreement was seen by many as a new departure, for it represented the first time that private banks accepted debt forgiveness and voluntarily reduced debt levels. It was estimated that the agreement would bring $2.5 billion of new money into the Mexican economy over a four-year period, and would reduce Mexico's interest payments, estimated at $9.6 billion in 1989, by $1.5 billion a year.[99] The involvement of the two international organizations—the IMF and the World Bank—and the Japanese participation in the process were also seen as positive precedents for further debt negotiations. However, it was uncertain to what degree the agreement would help resolve Mexico's long-term economic problems. Critics of the agreement called for a more ambitious program, asserting that radical levels of debt reduction (some argued for total debt forgiveness) were necessary to resolve the crisis. Without adequate relief, argued the critics, Mexican growth would continue to stagnate, capital flight would persist, and Mexico would be unable to attract needed foreign direct investment.

It was not clear whether the revised Mexican formula of 1989 could be applied to other debt-burdened nations whose economies were not as strong as Mexico's. The amount of debt reduction needed for countries such as the Philippines might be too large to negotiate successfully. Securing the large amounts of money needed for collateral financing of other debt reduction agreements would be problematic. Finally, the Mexican agreement represented a delicate balance between voluntary, private negotiations and government intervention. A comprehensive resolution to the debt crisis that used the Mexican example as its model would be difficult without strong leadership by public officials in bringing lenders and borrowers to agreement.

Following the Mexican experience, numerous other debtor countries restructured their commercial bank debt and issued Brady bonds. Restructuring of bank debt was linked with macroeconomic stabilization and broad structural reform in debtor countries. The IMF and World Bank, strongly supported by the United States and other bilateral lenders, conditioned their lending on adoption of sound macroeconomic policies such as deficit reduction and on economic restructuring programs including domestic deregulation, privatization, trade liberalization, and more open investment policies. Gradually, the economies of debtor countries stabilized and they returned to a pattern of growth.

From Debt Crisis to Emerging Markets

The successful implementation of macroeconomic and structural adjustment policies plus debt restructuring itself enabled a number of debtor countries to return to a state of creditworthiness in the 1990s. At the same time, securities markets were exploding in size and becoming global (see Chapter 2). Participants in those markets are professional managers of mutual funds, insurance companies, pension funds, and proprietary funds of banks and securities firms. These professional managers seek high returns, have a greater appetite for risk, and are willing to invest abroad to diversify their portfolios and achieve higher yields. In the first half of the 1990s, as the developed countries experienced sluggish growth, weak demand for funds and low interest rates, the rapidly growing and newly creditworthy developing countries appeared as attractive investments. Thus was born the phenomenon of "emerging markets." Whereas once, only banks lent to developing countries, now equity and debt of a number of developing countries and their domestic firms could be issued, sold, and traded in global financial markets. For example, in 1987, only 0.5 percent of foreign portfolio investment form industrial countries went to emerging markets; by 1993, that figure was 16 percent.[100] In 1990, net portfolio investment in developing countries was $6.2 billion; by 1993, it was $88.3 billion.[101]

The premier emerging market was Mexico. Between 1982 and 1988, the Mexican economy suffered from stagflation: virtually zero growth and high inflation. Between 1988 and 1992, however, the Mexican economy grew at an annual average rate of 3.5 percent. Inflation was reduced to 15 percent by 1992. The government succeeded in reducing its spending and in raising revenues by privatizing state enterprises. Mexico joined the GATT in 1986 and subsequently reduced both tariff and nontariff barriers to imports as part of a shift toward an export-oriented development strategy. The peso was pegged against the dollar at a fixed rate to signal the government's intent to rein in inflation and to reduce uncertainty about exchange rates with North America. The announcement of the signing and ratification of the North American Free Trade Agreement (NAFTA) helped to cement the confidence of both domestic and foreign investors in the overall health of the Mexican economy. From 1990 to 1993, Mexico received $94 billion in net capital inflows, about one-fifth of all such flows to developing countries. Net portfolio investment in Mexico, which averaged a negative $1.1 billion from 1983 to 1989, rose to $4.5 billion in 1990 and to $28.4 billion in 1993. These inflows enabled Mexico to increase its foreign exchange reserves and created a boom on the Mexican stock market. The foreign inflows also enabled the government to maintain a fixed exchange rate between the dollar and the peso, which was both a way of fighting inflation and a sign of the strength of the Mexican economy.

In 1994, a combination of economic and political events ended this favorable situation, especially the ability of the Mexican government to maintain a fixed peso/dollar exchange rate. Confidence in Mexico was undermined by signs of political instability. A rebellion broke out in the southern state of Chiapas in January and flared off and on over the year. In March, just five months before the presidential elections, the candidate of the ruling PRI party was assassinated. In September, one month after the election of the new PRI candidate, Ernesto Zedillo, just as the political situation seemed to be stabilizing, the secretary general of the new PRI was assassinated.

At the same time, the situation in world capital markets was changing. U.S. investments became more attractive as the Federal Reserve raised interest rates to prevent inflation. In 1994, net inflows of portfolio investment into Mexico fell to $7.8 billion. As a result, it became more costly and more difficult for the Mexican government to finance its fiscal and trade deficits. No longer able to finance its deficits in pesos, and, unwilling to change its economic policies before a critical election, Mexico began to issue *tesobonos*, short-term debt securities denominated in pesos but indexed to the dollar. Instead of devaluing the peso, the government gradually depleted its foreign exchange reserves in a futile effort to maintain what it saw as the symbol of its economic and political strength.

By the end of the year, the situation had become untenable. Portfolio investors once enamored of Mexico as an emerging market left in droves. Interest rates rose dramatically, stock prices plummeted, and the peso-dollar exchange rate came under considerable speculative pressure. On December 20, 1994, the Mexican government devalued the peso and on December 22 allowed it to float against the dollar. The peso crisis immediately affected the equity markets of other Latin American countries, notably those of Argentina and Brazil, and created speculative pressures on their currencies as well.

The U.S. government quickly recognized the threat that the peso crisis posed not only to international financial markets and the international monetary system, but also to the economy and political system of its southern neighbor. It led in the mobilization of an international rescue package to stabilize the Mexican economy and, thereby, the international financial system. The first step was an $18 billion international credit package including $9 billion from the United States, which was accompanied by the announcement of a stabilization plan by Mexico. Markets continued to deteriorate, however. The Clinton administration then proposed a loan guarantee program but was forced to withdraw this proposal when it met with opposition from the newly elected, Republican-controlled Congress. Finally, the United States led in the development of a loan package of $50 billion, including up to $20 billion of loans and guarantees from the United States and $18 billion from the IMF. The announcement of this loan package was accompanied by development of a new economic plan by the Mexican government, which included substantial increases in government revenues, spending cuts, and curbs on wage increases. As in the 1980s, Mexico found itself once again obliged to pursue a domestic austerity program which, while promoting confidence in financial markets, caused a severe recession at home. By the end of 1995, the financial situation had almost returned to normal. The success of the Mexican stabilization program plus new loans from the World Bank and IMF helped to stabilize the financial turmoil in Argentina and Brazil.

Following the Mexican crisis, the G-7 countries led by the United States worked to devise ways to prevent and manage future crises of this dimension. Learning from the Mexican experience that the best way to prevent crises is for borrowing countries to follow appropriate national policies, the G-7 agreed that the IMF should develop an early warning system by enhancing its surveillance: that is, its review and critique of national policies. They agreed that it should find ways to make more information public in a timely manner to help financial markets operate effectively. They also agreed to create an emergency lending facility in the IMF and to expand the resources available in the General Arrangement to Borrow (GAB) in the event of a crisis. Finally, unlike the debt crisis of the 1980s, when the IMF and the creditor governments worked with the lending banks and the debtor governments to restructure loans, the international financial institutions and creditor government realized that they had no mechanisms for restructuring debt held by millions of investors who owned securities issued by debtor countries and companies. Thus they agreed to explore how it might be possible to restructure or otherwise work out such debt in the future.

Following U.S.-led support for Mexico at the Halifax economic summit in the summer of 1995, markets remained stable but cautious. Mexico used the money borrowed from the United States to pay off its maturing *tesobonos*. Eventually, the tide was stemmed and Mexico was able to borrow again on international capital markets, albeit at high interest rates. The Mexican crisis illustrated both the promise and the dangers for countries availing themselves of the new financial resources made possible by the rapid increases in capital flows to emerging markets. Countries that borrowed heavily but did not simultaneously pursue appropriate domestic policies were at grave risk because of the potential for rapid outward movements of capital.

The Impact of the Debt Crisis on
Third World Strategy

The cumulative effect of the oil price increases of the 1970s, the debt crises of the 1980s, and the rapid growth of the emerging markets in the 1990s, was a growing differentiation among groups of Third World countries—oil producers versus oil consumers, NICs versus less industrialized countries, highly indebted versus less indebted countries, and so on. As the strains among these groups intensified, and as the stalemate with the North persisted, the South's solidarity and sense of direction began to crack.

The developing countries deemphasized their earlier proposals for changes in international economic regimes (like the NIEO) and focused, instead, on the need for immediate action to alleviate the South's most pressing problems. In a variety of forums—meetings of UNCTAD, the nonaligned movement—they called for expanded lending and more structural adjustment lending by the World Bank; an increase in IMF quotas; allocations of new SDRs to developing countries; easing of IMF conditionality; new IMF lending facilities; and increases in official development assistance.[102]

The North, they argued, should respond in its own self-interest. In an interdependent world, economic vitality in the North was intimately linked with Southern growth, which needed to be reactivated through financial flows to and trade with the Third World. Specifically, argued the South, the debt crisis posed a serious problem for Northern banks, Northern economies, and the entire international financial system. It was thus imperative for the developed countries—and in their own self-interest—to devise new mechanisms to ensure financial flows to developing countries.

The developed countries rejected the South's program. Budget problems placed severe limits on their ability and willingness to make even modest concessions to the developing countries. Furthermore, the North, and especially the United States, argued that the developing countries would benefit from growth in the North and from domestic reforms in the South, and that special measures such as those proposed by the South were inappropriate and, indeed, counterproductive.

Finally, the North's rejection reflected a new strategy for negotiating with the developing countries. From the very beginning, the North had never wanted to negotiate with the South as a bloc. The program of the group was more radical than that of individual developing countries. In the Northern view, their policies had become increasingly divorced from political reality, and their tone had become increasingly strident. The North, pointing out the diversity among the developing countries, had always preferred to deal with the South bilaterally or regionally.

Indeed, throughout the era of Southern unity, the Northern states continued to feel that the real business of dealing with the South took place in bilateral relations or in multilateral forums such as the IMF, the World Bank, and the GATT, in which the South did not act as a bloc. The unity of the South during the 1960s and 1970s had forced the North to negotiate with it as a bloc in United Nations forums. The crises of the 1970s and 1980s fragmented the South and made it politically possible for the North to move negotiations back to more predictable forums.

The debt crisis reinforced this Northern strategy of returning to safer negotiating forums. The differential impact of the crisis, combined with the concern about the potential for a debtors' cartel, led the North to follow successfully a policy of negotiating with the debtor countries on a case-by-case basis. The debt crisis also shifted the focus of North-South interaction. In the 1960s and 1970s, the politics of financial flows centered on concessional flows and flows to the most needy. With the onset of the debt crisis, the issue shifted to the size of nonconcessional flows. Concessional flows increased to low-income countries who were unable to benefit from nonconcessional flows. They also increased to countries who were cut off from those flows because of problems of servicing their debt. But the basic problem that Northern policymakers thought they had to solve was how to get the flow of nonconcessional funds to resume the rapid growth it had enjoyed between 1973 and 1982.

The political attention of the developed countries thus turned to debt rescheduling, balance-of-payments lending to the debtor countries, and ways to enable the debtor countries to resume some level of economic growth so that they could repay their debts and avert political instability. Attention focused on the more advanced developing countries whose potential debt defaults posed a serious threat to the developed market economies. Thus the debt crisis further fragmented the South and weakened the least-developed countries that were not eligible for major private commercial lending.

The Future of Aid and Financial Flows

As a result of the crises of the 1970s and 1980s, the future of international financial flows to developing countries is uncertain. There was a dramatic resumption of the growth of nonconcessional flows from the mid 1980s until the Mexican peso crisis of 1994. Latin America especially benefited from this resumed growth. A new development during this period was an unprecedented increase in portfolio investments, stemming partly from the rationalization and deregulation of Southern equity markets and partly from the desire of many Northern investors to benefit from the rapid growth of some Southern economies.

The Third World was becoming increasingly differentiated between groups of fast-growing and slow-growing economies. The fragmentation of the South meant that certain Southern countries—and especially the more creditworthy NICs and indebted countries—were in a better position than the rest to obtain private financing from the developed countries. The other countries of the South were hurting for both private and public capital flows. Thus, financial flows reinforced the growing differentiation of the South. Some Third World countries— Brazil, Taiwan, and South Korea, for example—appeared increasingly likely to cross the economic gap between themselves and the North and graduate to full status as industrialized countries, but a large group of developing countries were falling behind. One of the more important results of the economic disorder of the 1970s and 1980s, therefore, was not the end of the Third World or of Southern dependence on the North but the emergence of a Fourth World—a disparate group of poorer and slower-growing countries.

The South's continuing political and economic weakness, and fragmentation, as well as competing demands on the North's resources because of internal economic problems and shifting Northern diplomatic strategies caused by the end of the Cold War, undermined the political basis for aid flows. In the 1990s, aid budgets in most of the developed countries came under pressure. As governments moved to reduce budget deficits, they were forced to make cuts in domestic programs making it politically impossible to sustain existing levels of foreign aid. In such a budget tightening environment, donors demanded better domestic policies from aid recipients: less wasteful spending on the military, more democratic governance policies, and policies to promote domestic market economies.

Although the debt crisis temporarily turned commercial flows into a financial drain on most LDC debtors, however, both concessional and nonconcessional flows had resumed by the late 1980s, albeit with somewhat greater caution and selectivity on the part of private lenders. New kinds of private investments began to flow South in the late 1980s, some of which were to cause problems because of their focus on short-term results.

Nevertheless, there were some counter-balancing forces. There was a crisis of conscience growing out of the recognition of the desperate plight of the least-developed countries. The problems of sub-Saharan Africa in the 1980s, for example, led to special aid measures for that region. Temporary relief measures such as food aid and some balance-of-payments assistance for the poorest of the Southern states were adopted. But a heightened sense of moral responsibility in the North for alleviating poverty in the South, as the postwar history of aid demonstrates, was a weak reed on which to base Southern demands for greater resource transfers. Such reactions were usually ephemeral and clearly not the basis for any major shift in aid.

A more sustained source of optimism could be found in the balancing effect of the increasing variety of donors that participated in resource transfers to the South. As the United States and the United Kingdom pulled back on Third World aid beginning in the 1960s, the Nordic countries and others in Western Europe increased their aid. As the majority of the North felt the impact of the recession caused by the oil crisis in the 1970s, OPEC donors helped to make up the difference. When the United States faced budgetary and payments deficits in the 1980s, Japan and Western Europe became more willing and able to take up some of the financial burden of transferring resources to the Third World. By 1988, Japan had become the world's largest single aid donor. By the 1990s some of the newly prosperous NICs were beginning programs of assistance—largely technical assistance—to other developing countries. Although this diversification of donors did not guarantee the long-term stability or growth of concessional aid, it reduced some of the risks for developing countries who depended on continued aid flows.

Perhaps the greatest potential source of change in Northern attitudes was the growing perceived importance of achieving access to the domestic markets of the faster-growing Southern economies. Markets in the Third World, especially in the newly industrialized countries, were expanding rapidly and becoming increasingly important for Northern exports. The percentage of Northern merchandise exports going to the developing countries rose from 23 percent in 1973 to 28 percent in 1980.[103] As a result of the debt crisis, exports from industrial countries to developing countries fell from 30 percent of all exports in 1981 to 22.6 percent in 1987. After hovering around 23 percent until 1990, they rose again to 28.8 percent in 1993.[104] Although the threat of global financial collapse subsided as banks increased their equity capital, diversified their loan portfolios, sold off debt on secondary markets, and set up reserves for LDC loan losses, the continuing LDC debt exposure remained a threat to the strength of many commercial banks.[105] Many indebted developing countries were able to continue to service their debts to Northern banks and attract further flows from Northern investors because they were able to achieve and maintain high rates of economic growth. The next chapter (Chapter 7) focuses on the debate over the role of governmental development strategies in making that growth possible.

Another hopeful sign was the increased awareness in both the North and the South of the need to manage global resources. Shortages of food, raw materials, energy, and private capital affected the North as well as the South after 1973. Although the effects of post-1973 economic disorder in the North were less severe than in the South, they created a general interest in improving the system. During the Reagan and Bush administrations, for example, the desire of the U.S. government to improve the performance of global financial markets eventually led to a greater willingness to intervene and to support multilateral management of the debt crisis. Similarly, the Reagan administration led the fight to establish a treaty to protect the ozone layer of the upper atmosphere. Global concerns about protecting the environment in the 1980s resulted in calls for improved North-South cooperation. International environmental cooperation was likely to benefit both the North and the South and to require the participation of certain Southern states in establishment of new regimes. The South was likely to benefit in the long run from the growing recognition that the North could not solve many of its environmental problems without cooperation from the South.

NOTES

1. On early financing priorities for the World Bank, see Henry J. Bitterman, "Negotiation of the Articles of Agreement of the International Bank for Reconstruction and Development," *The International Lawyer* 5 (January 1971): 59–88; and Edward S. Mason and Robert E. Asher, *The World Bank Since Bretton Woods* (Washington: Brookings Institution, 1973), 1–35.

2. Mason and Asher, *World Bank Since Bretton Woods*, 178–179.

3. U.S. Department of State, "The Inaugural Address of the President," *The Bulletin* 20 (January 30, 1949): 125.

4. Goran Ohlin, *Foreign Aid Policies Reconsidered* (Paris: Organization for Economic Cooperation and Development, 1966), 66.

5. See "Military Assistance and the Security of the United States, 1947–1956," a study prepared by the Institute of War and Peace Studies of Columbia University, in U.S. Senate, *Foreign Aid Program*, a compilation of studies and surveys under the direction of the Special Committee to Study the Foreign Aid Program, 85th Cong., 1st sess. (Washington: U.S. Government Printing Office, 1957), 903–969.

6. See Marshall I. Goldman, *Soviet Foreign Aid* (New York: Praeger, 1967), 60–167; and Robert S. Walters, *American and Soviet Aid: A Comparative Analysis* (Pittsburgh: University of Pittsburgh Press 1970), 26–48.

7. Several official and unofficial reports at this time showed that there was a link between U.S. security and Southern economic development. See *Report to the President on Foreign Economic Policies* (Washington: Government Printing Office, 1950); International Development Advisory Board, *Partners in Progress: A Report to the President* (March 1951); U.S. Mutual Security Agency, Advisory Committee on Underdeveloped Areas, *Economic Strength for the Free World: Principles of a U.S. Foreign Development Program,* a report to the director for mutual security (Washington: Government Printing Office, 1953).

8. U.S. Senate, *Foreign Aid Program*, 1957, 20.

9. See Max F. Millikan and Walt W. Rostow, *A Proposal: Key to an Effective Foreign Policy* (New York: Harper, 1957), 34–38.

10. Ibid., 39. For an analysis of the role of aid in political development, see Robert A. Packenham, *Liberal America and the Third World: Political Development Ideas in Foreign Aid and Social Science* (Princeton: Princeton University Press, 1973).

11. See Ohlin, *Foreign Aid Policies Reconsidered*, 27–36. See also Teresa Hayter, *French Aid* (London: Overseas Development Institute, 1966); and Overseas Development Institute, *British Aid—A Factual Survey* (London: Overseas Development Institute, 1963–1964).

12. Organization for Economic Cooperation and Development, *Flow of Financial Resources to Less-Developed Countries, 1956–1963* (Paris: OECD, 1964), 19.

13. Ibid.

14. David A. Baldwin, *Economic Development and American Foreign Policy* (Chicago: University of Chicago Press, 1966), 204.

15. See Walt W. Rostow, *Eisenhower, Kennedy, and Foreign Aid* (Austin: University of Texas Press, 1985), 88–89.

16. Organization for Economic Cooperation and Development, *Development Cooperation 1974 Review* (Paris: OECD, 1974).

17. Ibid., 133.

18. Samuel P. Huntington, *Political Order in Changing Societies* (New Haven: Yale University Press, 1968), 1–92.

19. See Samuel P. Huntington, "Foreign Aid for What and for Whom," *Foreign Policy* 1 (winter 1970–1971): 161–189; and Samuel P. Huntington, "Does Foreign Aid Have a Future?" *Foreign Policy* 2 (spring 1971): 114–134.

20. On French and British aid during this period, see Teresa Hayter, *French Aid* (London: Overseas Development Institute, 1966), and Bruce Dinwiddy, ed., *European Development Policies: The United Kingdom, Sweden, France, EEC and Multilateral Organizations* (London: Praeger Publishers for the Overseas Development Institute, 1973).

21. United Nations Conference on Trade and Development, *Debt Problems of Developing Countries* (New York: United Nations, 1972), 1.

22. See "The Policy of Self-Reliance: Excerpts from Part III of the Arusha Declaration of February 5, 1967," *Africa Report* 12 (March 1967): 11–13; and Henry Bienen, "An Ideology for Africa," *Foreign Affairs* 47 (April 1969): 545–559. On Burma, see Mya Maung, *Burma and Pakistan: A Comparative Study of Development* (New York: Praeger Publishers, 1971); and David I. Steinberg, Burma: A Socialist Nation in Southeast Asia (Boulder, Colo.: Westview Press, 1982).

23. United Nations Conference on Trade and Development, *Towards a New Trade Policy for Development* (New York: United Nations, 1964), 79–89; and United Nations Conference on Trade and Development, *Towards a Global Strategy of Development* (New York: United Nations, 1968), 32–44.

24. See Y. S. Park, *The Link Between Special Drawing Rights and Development Finance*

(Princeton: Princeton University, Department of Economics, International Finance Section, September 1973).

25. On the food crisis, see Raymond Hopkins and Donald Puchala, eds. "The Global Political Economy of Food," *International Organization* 32 (summer 1978); and World Bank, *World Development Report 1986*, ch. 4.

26. Food and Agricultural Organization, *Commodity Review and Outlook 1981–1982* (Rome: FAO, 1982), 4.

27. Organization for Economic Cooperation and Development, *Development Cooperation: 1983 Review* (Paris: OECD, 1983), 136.

28. Ibid., 135.

29. Robert L. Paarlberg, "U.S. Agriculture and the Developing World," in *Growth, Exports and Jobs in a Changing World Economy: Agenda 1988* (New Brunswick, N.J.: Transaction Books, 1988).

30. Henry Bienen, "The United States and Sub-Saharan Africa," in John P. Lewis and Valeriana Kallab, eds., *U.S. Foreign Policy and the Third World: Agenda 1983* (New York: Praeger for the Overseas Development Council, 1983), 77. See also Carol Lancaster, "Africa's Economic Crisis," *Foreign Policy* no. 52 (fall 1983): 149–166.

31. International Monetary Fund, *Annual Report*, 1983 (Washington: IMF, 1983), 33.

32. Ibid., 33.

33. World Bank, *World Debt Tables: External Debt of Developing Countries* (Washington: World Bank, 1983), xiii.

34. World Bank, *World Development Report 1988* (New York: Oxford University Press, 1988), 37.

35. "Declaration and Action Programme on the Establishment of a New International Economic Order," in Guy F. Erb and Valeriana Kallab, eds., *Beyond Dependency: The Developing World Speaks Out* (New York: Praeger, 1975), 193–194.

36. See John Williamson, *The Lending Policies of the International Monetary Fund* (Washington: Institute for International Economics, 1982); and Stephan Haggard, "The Politics of Adjustment: Lessons from the IMF's Extended Fund Facility," in Miles Kahler, ed., *The Politics of International Debt* (Ithaca, N.Y.: Cornell University Press, 1986).

37. See Robert L. Ayres, *Banking on the Poor* (Washington: Overseas Development Council, 1983). For a highly critical study of the World Bank, see Teresa Hayter, *Aid as Imperialism* (Harmondsworth, England: Penguin Books, 1971).

38. See G. K. Helleiner, "Policy-Based Program Lending: A Look at the Bank's New Role," in Richard E. Feinberg and Valeriana Kallab, eds., *Between Two Worlds: The World Bank's Next Decade* (New Bruswick, N.J.: Transaction Books, 1986).

39. Richard E. Feinberg, "Bridging the Crisis: The World Bank and U.S. Interests in the 1980s," in Lewis and Kallab, eds., *U.S. Foreign Policy and the Third World: Agenda 1983*, 141–149.

40. Andre Simmons, *Arab Foreign Aid* (Rutherford, N.J.: Fairleigh Dickinson University Press, 1981); Robert A. Mertz, *Arab Aid to Sub-Saharan Africa* (Munich, Germany: Kaiser, 1983); and Gerd Nonneman, *Development, Administration, and Aid in the Middle East* (New York: Routledge, 1988).

41. World Bank, *World Development Report 1983*, 182; OECD, *Development Cooperation: 1983 Review*, 52.

42. John W. Sewell and Christine E. Contee, "U.S. Foreign Aid in the 1980s: Reordering Priorities" in John W. Sewell, Richard E. Feinberg, and Valeriana Kallab, eds., *U.S. Foreign Policy and the Third World: Agenda 1985–1986*, 99.

43. Organization for Economic Cooperation and Development, *Development Cooperation: 1987 Review* (Paris: OECD, 1987), 327.

44. On increased Japanese lending and aid, see Toshihiko Kinoshita, *Japan's Current "Recycling Measures": Its Background, Performance, and Prospects*, Export-Import Bank of Japan, 1988 (mimeo); Margee M. Ensign, *Doing Good or Doing Well? Japan's Foreign Aid Program* (New York: Columbia University Press, 1992); Alan Rix, *Japan's Foreign Aid Challenge: Policy Reform and Aid Leadership* (New York: Routledge, 1993); Robert M. Orr Jr., *The Emergence of Japan's Foreign Aid Power* (New York: Columbia University Press, 1990); and Shafiqul Islam, ed., *Yen for Development: Japanese Foreign Aid and the Politics of Burden-Sharing* (New York: Council on Foreign Relations, 1991).

45. World Bank, *World Debt Tables 1993–94: External Finance for Developing Countries*, vol. 1 (Washington: World Bank, 1993), 16.

46. For excellent overviews of aid, see Robert Cassen and Associates, *Does Aid Work? Report to an Intergovernmental Task Force* (Oxford: Clarendon Press, 1986). This study was commissioned by the Development Committee of the World Bank and the IMF. See also John P. Lewis and Valeriana Kallab, eds., *Development Strategies Reconsidered* (New Brunswick, N.J.: Transaction Books, 1986); Sarah J. Tisch and Michael B. Wallace, *Dilemmas of Development Assistance: The What, Why, and Who of Foreign Aid* (Boulder, Colo.: Westview, 1994); Joan M. Nelson, *Global Goals, Contentious Means: Issues of Multiple Aid Conditionality* (Washington: Overseas Development Council, 1992); Joan M. Nelson and Stephanie J. Eglinton, *Encouraging Democracy: What Role for Conditional Aid?* (Washington: Overseas Development Council, 1992); and Stephen Browne, *Foreign Aid in Practice* (New York: New York University Press, 1990). For a critical view of the role of aid, see Peter Bauer, *Equality, the Third World, and Economic Illusion* (Cambridge: Harvard University Press, 1981).

47. See, for example, Rob Vos, "Aid Flows and the International Transfer Problem in a Structuralist North-South Model," *Economic Journal* 103 (March 1993): 494–508.

48. World Bank, *World Development Report 1995* (Washington: World Bank, 1995), 165.

49. Ibid., 223.

50. *World Development Report 1995*, 163.

51. Irman Adelman, "A Poverty-Focused Approach to Development Policy," in Lewis and Kallab, *Development Strategies Reconsidered*, 53.

52. World Bank, *World Development Report 1988*, 224–225.

53. Adelman, "A Poverty-Focused Approach," 52–53. Absolute poverty level is defined in World Bank terms as below an annual per capita income of less than US $50 in constant 1960 dollars.

54. Cassen, *Does Aid Work*, 24–25.

55. Irving Brecher and S. A. Abbas, *Foreign Aid and Industrial Development in Pakistan* (Cambridge: Harvard University Press, 1972); Gustav F. Papenek, *Pakistan and Development: Social Goals and Private Incentive* (Cambridge: Harvard University Press, 1967); Irma Adelman, ed., *Practical Approaches to Development Planning: Korea's Second Five-Year Plan* (Baltimore: Johns Hopkins University Press, 1969); and Neil H. Jacoby, *U.S. Aid to Taiwan* (New York: Praeger, 1966).

56. Roger D. Hansen, *Mexican Economic Development: The Roots of Rapid Growth* (Washington: National Planning Association, 1971).

57. John P. Lewis, "Overview: Development Promotion: A Time for Regrouping," in Lewis and Kallab, *Development Strategies Reconsidered*, 3–46.

58. This amendment is called the Hickenlooper Amendment. See Paul Sigmund, *Multinationals in Latin America: The Politics of Nationalization* (Madison: University of Wisconsin Press, 1980), 8–10.

59. See Joan M. Nelson, *Aid, Influence, and Foreign Policy* (New York: Macmillan, 1968), 69–90. On aid tying, see Organization for Economic Cooperation and Development, "Aid Tying and Mixed Credits," in *Twenty-five Years of Development Cooperation* (Paris: OECD, 1985), 241–250.

60. For an early discussion of this subject, see Klaus Knorr, *The Power of Nations* (New York: Basic Books, 1975), ch. 16.

61. See Gerald K. Helleiner, "Policy-Based Program Lending," and Joan M. Nelson, "The Diplomacy of Policy-Based Lending," in Feinberg and Kallab, *Between Two Worlds*; and Miles Kahler, "External Influence, Conditionality, and the Politics of Adjustment," in Stephan Haggard and Robert R. Kaufman, eds., *The Politics of Economic Adjustment: International Constraints, Distributive Conflicts, and the State* (Princeton: Princeton University Press, 1992).

62. Howard Wriggins, "Political Outcomes of Foreign Assistance: Influence, Involvement, or Intervention?" *Journal of International Affairs* 22 (1968): 217–230; and Joan M. Nelson and Stephanie J. Eglinton, *Encouraging Democracy: What Role for Conditional Aid?* (Washington: Overseas Development Council, 1992).

63. International Monetary Fund, *World Economic Outlook* (Washington: IMF, April 1984), 205; David H. Lumsdaine, *Moral Vision in International Politics: The Foreign Aid Regime 1949–1989* (Princeton: Princeton University Press, 1993); Brian Smith, *More Than Altruism: The Politics of Private Foreign Aid* (Princeton: Princeton University Press, 1990); and Sarah J. Tisch and Michael B. Wallace, *Dilemmas of Development Assistance: The What, Why, and Who of Foreign Aid* (Boulder, Colo.: Westview, 1994), ch. 3.

64. World Bank, *World Debt Tables* (Washington: World Bank, 1988), 5, 30.

65. World Bank, *World Development Report* (New York: Oxford University Press, 1988), 31.

66. William R. Cline, "Mexico's Crisis, the World's Peril," *Foreign Policy* no. 49 (winter 1982–1983): 107–120; Jeffry Frieden, *Debt, Development and Democracy: Modern Political*

Economy and Latin America, 1965–1985 (Princeton: Princeton University Press, 1991), ch. 6; and Robert R. Kaufman, Carlos Bazdresch, and Blanca Heredia, "Mexico: Radical Reform in a Dominant Party System," in Stephan Haggard and Steven B. Webb, eds., *Voting for Reform: Democracy, Political Liberalization, and Economic Adjustment* (New York: Oxford University Press for the World Bank, 1994).

67. World Bank, *World Debt Tables 1985–1986* (Washington: World Bank, 1985), 254, 274, 278, 326, 358.

68. For statistical evidence about bank exposure, see data from an IBCA Banking Analysis as cited in the *Financial Times*, January 5, 1989, p. 15.

69. On systemic problems, see Jack M. Guttentag and Richard Herring, *The Lender of Last Resort Function in an International Context*, Essays in International Finance (Princeton: International Finance Section, Princeton University, 1983).

70. Edward J. Frydl and Dorothy M. Sobol, "A Perspective on the Debt Crisis, 1982–1987," in Federal Reserve Bank of New York, *Seventy-Third Annual Report* (New York: Federal Reserve Bank of New York, 1988), 5.

71. "Mexico under the IMF," *The Economist*, August 20, 1983, 19–20. See also Karin Lissakers, "Dateline Wall Street: Faustian Finance," *Foreign Policy* no. 51 (summer 1983): 160–175; and M. S. Mendelsohn, *Commercial Banks and the Restructuring of Cross-Border Debt* (New York: Group of Thirty, 1983).

72. E. Brau and R. C. Williams, with P. M. Keller and M. Nowak, *Recent Multilateral Debt Restructuring with Official and Bank Creditors* (Washington: International Monetary Fund, December 1983).

73. See Jack Guttentag and Richard Herring, *The Current Crisis in International Banking* (Philadelphia: University of Pennsylvania, Wharton Program in International Banking and Finance, October 1983); Charles Lipson, "Bankers' Dilemma: Private Cooperation in Rescheduling Sovereign Debts," in Kenneth A. Oye, ed., *Cooperation Under Anarchy* (Princeton: Princeton University Press, 1986); and Charles Lipson, "International Debt and International Institutions," in Miles Kahler, ed., *The Politics of International Debt* (Ithaca, N.Y.: Cornell University Press, 1986).

74. See Peter M. Kelleo with Nessanke E. Weerasinghe, *Multilateral Official Debt Rescheduling Recent Experience* (Washington: International Monetary Fund, May 1988).

75. World Bank, *World Debt Tables* (Washington: World Bank, 1988), xvii.

76. Frydl and Sobol, "Perspective on the Debt Crisis," 19.

77. International Monetary Fund, *Annual Report, 1983* (Washington: IMF, 1983): 87–88.

78. World Bank, *World Debt Tables* (Washington: World Bank, 1988), xvii.

79. "Statement of the Honorable James A. Baker III before the Joint Annual Meeting of the International Monetary Fund and the World Bank, Seoul, Korea," *Treasury News* (October 8, 1985).

80. For an overview, see Stephan Haggard and Steven B. Webb, "Introduction" in Haggard and Webb, *Voting for Reform.*

81. Jeffrey Sachs and Harry Huizinga, "U.S. Commercial Banks and the Developing-Country Debt Crisis," *Brookings Papers on Economic Activity*, 2 (Washington: Brookings Institution, 1987), 560.

82. See World Bank, *World Development Report 1988* (Washington: World Bank, 1988), 55–71.

83. Ibid., 192.

84. Ibid., 30.

85. Ibid.; and International Monetary Fund, *World Economic Outlook 1995* (Washington: IMF, 1995), 167.

86. See International Monetary Fund, *World Economic Outlook 1988*, (Washington: IMF, April 1988).

87. Roger Lowenstein, "After Cartagena: Latin Debtors Hope for New Remedies," *Wall Street Journal*, June 25, 1984, 31.

88. The Venezuelan candidate, Carlos Andrés Pérez, reversed his position on this issue after taking office.

89. World Bank, *World Development Report 1988*, 3.

90. *Investors Daily*, September 14, 1988, p. 14.

91. See, for example, "Third World Debt: A Reexamination of Long-Term Management: Report of the Third World Debt Panel of the Economic Policy Council of UNA-USA," September 7, 1988 (New York: United Nations Association of the United States, 1988).

92. One proposal called for banks to forgive 3 percent of interest and principal over a three-year period. See Senator Bill Bradley, "The Debt Crisis as a U.S. Job Crisis," speech delivered to the National Press Club, Washington, July 24, 1986. Other proposals would create a debt-restructuring facility to buy LDC loans at a discount and to lower debt service. See U.S. Congress, *Omnibus Trade and Competitiveness Act of 1988*, PL 100-418 (Washington: Government Printing Office, August 23, 1988), Sec. 3111-3113; and James D. Robinson III, "A Comprehensive Agenda for LDC Debt and World Trade Growth," *The Amex Bank Review Special Papers*, No. 13 (March 1988).

93. "Statement by the Hon. Satoshi Sumita, Governor, the Bank of Japan and Alternate Governor of the Fund and the Bank for Japan at the Joint Annual Discussion," Press Release 12, September 27, 1988, IMF/The World Bank Group.

94. World Bank, *World Debt Tables 1988*, xi.

95. "Bush Backs U.S. Shift on World Debt," *New York Times*, December 20, 1989, B10.

96. The demonstrations were followed two years later by an unsuccessful coup d'état. See Andrés Serbin, Andrés Stambouli, Jennifer McCoy, and William Smith, eds., *Venezuela: La democracia bajo presión* (Caracas: Editorial Nueva Sociedad, 1993).

97. "Statement of the Honorable Nicholas F. Brady to the Brookings Institution and the Bretton Woods Committee Conference on Third World Debt," *Treasury News* (Washington, March 10, 1989).

98. "Relief from Washington as Brady Plan Passes Its Test," *Financial Times*, July 25, 1989, p. 3. See also "Brady's Mexican Hat-Trick," *The Economist*, July 29, 1989, 61–62.

99. *The Economist*, July 29, 1989, 61; and "Mexico Pins Hopes on Debt Agreement," *Wall Street Journal*, July 25, 1989, p. A-15.

100. International Monetary Fund, *International Capital Markets Developments: Prospects and Key Policy Issues* (Washington: IMF, May 8, 1995), 5–6.

101. Ibid., 4.

102. See Overseas Development Institute, *UNCTAD VI: Background and Issues*, Briefing Paper No. 4 (London: Overseas Development Institute, 1983).

103. World Bank, *World Bank Development Report 1984* (Washington: World Bank, 1984), 15.

104. International Monetary Fund, *Direction of Trade Yearbook 1988* (Washington: IMF, 1988), 8; and International Monetary Fund, *International Direction of Trade 1994* (Washington: IMF, 1994), 10.

105. William Seidman, Chairman, Federal Deposit Insurance Corporation, "Import of LDC Debt Situation on Financial Condition of the FDIC." Testimony before the Committee on Banking, Finance, and Urban Affairs, U.S. House of Representatives, January 5, 1989.

7

Trade and Development Strategies

Most Southern economies are highly dependent on trade with the North. Export earnings constitute a large share of their GNP, and imported goods are crucial to their development. Yet many developing countries believe that the international market has not promoted their development and that they have been excluded from the trade management system established by the North. Since World War II, the developing countries have pursued three distinct but not necessarily exclusive strategies to achieve their goals of development and independence: (1) delinking from the international trading system, (2) seeking to force changes in the system, and (3) integrating into the prevailing regime.[1]

Isolation from the Postwar Trading Order

In constructing the postwar trading order, the wartime and postwar planners from the North assumed that a system based on free trade would benefit both developed and developing countries. In their view, free trade would lead to the most efficient and profitable use of national **factors of production,** increase national income and foreign exchange earnings, attract foreign private capital, and thus stimulate Southern development.[2]

The Southern states felt, however, that free trade threatened their strategy of import substitution, which was based on promoting domestic industrial development behind protective walls. The economic rationale for this development policy was the infant-industry argument that protection from foreign competition for an initial stage would allow domestic industrial producers to begin manufacturing for the domestic market. Once the infant stage was completed, protection could be removed and free trade resumed.[3] Such temporary protection had historically been a route to development in the North and, it was hoped, would help Southern industrialization and development as well. Such protection also appealed to the developing countries as a way of saving precious foreign exchange by decreasing imports.[4]

Thus, in the negotiations leading up to the Havana Charter, the Southern countries argued that their developing country status required special treatment under the free-trade rules proposed by the North. They sought exemptions from the new rules, including the ability to use import quotas and tariffs to protect **infant industry,** to establish new preferential trading systems, and to enter into commodity agreements to stabilize and ensure minimum commodity prices. They also wanted to obtain tariff concessions from developed countries without having to offer concessions in return.[5]

Because the North wanted approval by the developing countries for the new trade charter, the South was able to achieve some limited modifications in the Havana Charter, especially a new chapter that recognized the special needs of developing countries. In order to promote economic development, developing countries could increase bound (i.e., legally negotiated) tariffs, impose quantitative restrictions or quotas on imports, establish regional preference systems, and enter into commodity agreements. However, these exceptions to free trade could be taken only with the prior approval of the ITO (International Trade Organization) and/or the parties to trade agreements involved and had to follow restrictive guidelines.[6]

The inclusion of the developing countries' concerns into the system ended with the death of the Havana Charter. The General Agreement on Tariffs and Trade (GATT), which replaced the charter as the constitution of the new trading order, was designed as an interim measure and included none of the provisions for development that the South had fought to include in the Havana Charter. All that was left was a GATT article that authorized a country under certain restricted conditions to use tariffs and quantitative restrictions to assist economic development or deal with payments imbalances.[7]

The GATT's negotiating process also effectively excluded the developing countries from the international management of trade. The GATT's reciprocity rule stated that all trade concessions had to be mutual. But the South, with its small markets, had little to exchange for concessions in its favor. The GATT followed the technique of negotiating trade concessions among the importing countries and principal suppliers of any particular item. Because there were no principal suppliers, many products of interest to the developing countries, such as raw materials, were left out of the GATT negotiations. Even when the developing countries were the principal suppliers, they were unable to put products or issues of interest to them on the agenda, because the South represented only a minority of the GATT membership and power. The developing countries were also hampered by the lack of staff and resources to sustain difficult and sophisticated trade negotiations with the powerful developed countries.

Thus the GATT was a rich man's club. By the end of the 1950s, its thirty-seven members included twenty-one developed countries and only sixteen developing countries. While virtually all the developed nations were members, many developing countries, including Argentina and Mexico, did not join the GATT. Those Southern countries that did join did not participate actively in the multilateral trade negotiations. GATT tariff negotiations reduced barriers to manufactured goods of interest to developed countries while barriers to exports of concern to developing countries were generally left intact. Because Southern products were not covered in tariff negotiations, developing countries were not legally bound to lower tariffs on manufactured goods and actually raised tariffs on these products. In addition, most developing country members used the GATT's balance-of-payments exemptions to protect their markets.[8]

The primary strategy of developing countries in this period was to insulate themselves from the international market and to pursue industrialization through import substitution. Many developing countries, particularly those in Latin America, either continued the protection introduced before or during the war or established new protectionist barriers in an attempt to develop an internal market for domestic production. Very high rates of protection for domestic industry were ensured through tariffs that were sometimes several hundred percent or more, exchange controls, multiple exchange rates for different products, import licensing, and outright bans on the importation of goods produced domestically.[9] Protection provided powerful incentives for the development of local production to replace imports by providing an assured market and by channeling domestic savings into industry through increased industrial profits.[10]

From Import Substitution to Trade Expansion

Import substitution fostered some industrialization, but often at a high price. The new industries were often inefficient and their output costly and uncompetitive. Faced with small domestic markets, unsuccessful efforts at regional integration, and strong competition abroad, most developing countries could not achieve adequate scales of production to build efficient industries. Furthermore, policies that encouraged the importation of capital-intensive production technologies discouraged the growth of demand for labor and thus had only a minor effect on employment levels.

Import substitution also often created a balance of payments deficit. Production of high-cost domestic manufactures came at the expense of both export-oriented manufacturing and traditional agricultural exports. Furthermore, high tariff barriers for manufactured imports did not necessarily decrease total imports but, rather, changed the composition of imports. Instead of importing finished products, Southern countries now imported raw materials, parts, and capital goods.[11] New systems of licensing and currency exchange controls created new rigidities in Southern economies that discouraged competition and promoted inefficiency.[12] Foreign multinationals tried to jump over the high tariff barriers for assembled products by establishing assembly plants, which tended to increase imports of components without expanding exports.

Industrialization through import substitution also damaged agriculture. New investment in agriculture was limited; real earnings declined as industrial profits rose; and income inequalities between agriculture and industry were exacerbated. As a result, people began to leave the countryside for the town, but the new industry in the cities could not absorb the burgeoning urban population. Thus unemployment and income inequalities worsened.[13]

By the end of the 1950s, the governments of many Southern states concluded that their international trade and economic development policies could not be based on import substitution alone and would have to focus on export expansion. They came to believe that focusing on export growth while continuing to protect domestic markets could maximize efficiency of production and increase earnings and foreign exchange available for development, much as the liberals had always argued. According to a number of influential spokespersons for the developing countries, most notably Raúl Prebisch, such benefits could not occur without a restructuring of the international trading system, because the existing system prevented export growth.

First, there was, Prebisch claimed, a long-term deterioration in the South's terms of trade.[14] The prices of raw materials exported by the developing countries were declining in relation to the prices of manufactured products imported from the developed countries. Because of trade unions and monopoly markets in the developed market economies, it was argued, increased productivity in manufacturing in the North was absorbed by higher wages and profits and did not lead to a fall in the price of manufactures. On the other hand, because of unemployment and the absence of labor organization in the developing countries plus the existence of a competitive international market for Southern raw materials, increased productivity in primary products led not to increased wages or profits but to a decline in prices. The terms of trade also turned against the South because of demand in the North for **primary products** from the South was inelastic with respect to income and consequently an increase in the production of raw materials led to a decline in prices rather than to an increase in consumption. Finally, the prices of Southern products tended to fall because of the increased production of synthetics and substitutes—for example, polyester fabrics replacing cotton cloth—in the North.

The structural decline in terms of trade for primary producers was aggravated by Northern protectionist policies. According to the South, the development of competitive, mechanized Northern agriculture through protectionist systems, the development of domestic mineral extraction under protectionist national security policies, and Northern taxes on tropical foodstuffs accentuated the declining position of commodity exports. Another problem of the international market, according to the South, was the inherent instability of commodity prices. In their view, fluctuations in prices and thus in export earnings hindered investment and disrupted development planning.

The empirical evidence on the declining terms of trade thesis is mixed. The original research by Prebisch and his associates was strongly challenged in the 1950s and 1960s for using inappropriate measures of the terms of trade and being dependent on time periods that were most likely to yield the expected results.

Figure 7-1   Average Terms of Trade for Groups of Developing Countries, 1965–1991 (1987=100)

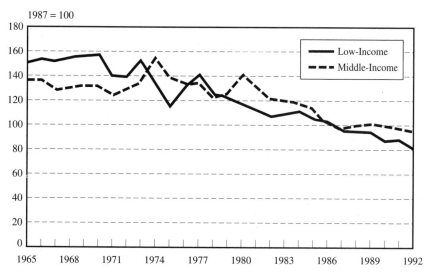

SOURCE: Computed by the authors from World Bank, *World Data '94 CD-ROM* (Washington: World Bank, 1994).

Subsequent research on the relative prices of primary commodities (including fuels) versus those of traded manufactures indicate a long-term decline of about 36 percent between 1900 and 1986, or about 0.5 percent per year.[15] Just for the purposes of illustration, Figure 7-1 displays the average terms of trade for two groups of developing countries between 1965 and 1992. There is a downward trend for both groups.

Finally, the South felt that its real potential to export manufactured products was constrained by Northern dominance of the international market. The head start of the North, which gave the developed countries established positions in international markets, as well as Northern protection prevented the expansion of Southern manufactured exports. The South was particularly critical of Northern protectionist measures (for example, the practice of imposing a higher tariff on intermediate or finished products than on raw materials). Such "cascading" tariffs meant that the effective rate of protection of the finished product was much higher than the nominal rate was. Differential tariffs favored the import of raw materials from the developing countries, discouraged the import of processed or semi-processed products, and thus discouraged the development of Southern industry. Unusually high tariffs or import quotas were imposed on many Southern manufactures, such as textiles, footwear, and leather goods, that competed effectively with Northern industries. Where there were no tariff or quantitative restrictions, the North often forced "voluntary" export restraint agreements on Southern states.[16] Such nontariff barriers as health standards, labeling requirements, and customs procedures posed difficult hurdles for the Southern states with their lack of marketing expertise and experience.[17]

These constraints on developing country exports were reflected in the South's diminished role in international trade. The Southern share of world exports dropped from 31.6 percent in 1950 to 21.4 percent in 1960. In the same period, the trade of the developed market economies grew from 60.4 percent of total world exports to 66.8 percent, and the socialist states went from 8.0 percent of total world exports to 11.8 percent. Between 1950 and 1960, exports from the developed countries grew 8.7 percent, whereas those of the developing countries grew only 3.5 percent.[18]

The proportion of exports of primary goods (including unprocessed raw materials and agricultural commodities) as compared with manufactured goods in the total exports from developing countries declined from 74.2 percent in 1970 to 41.6 percent in 1990 (see Figure 7-2). This is partly a function of the success of import substitution policies in creating the basis for industrialization in the Third World; but it is also a reflection of the rapid growth of manufactured exports from a relatively narrow subset of developing countries who turned toward export-led development strategies. Even though the composition of exports of developing countries shifted away from raw materials and commodities toward manufactured goods, the terms of trade still deteriorated for the Third World as a whole.[19]

As the South turned from isolation to trade expansion, exclusion from the GATT's trade-management system became unacceptable, and Southern political pressure for a change in the GATT system increased. At Third World conferences and at the United Nations and within the GATT itself, developing states pushed

Figure 7-2   Composition of Exports of Developing Countries, 1970–1990, in Percentages

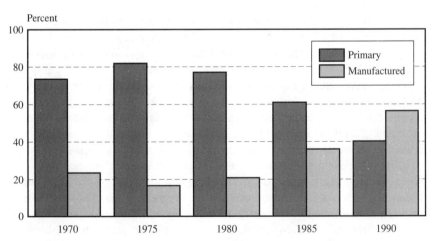

SOURCE: United Nations, *International Trade Statistics Yearbook*, various years.

for greater consideration of their trade problems. Southern pressure was reinforced by the independence of many colonial states and by the expansion of the Cold War to the developing world. As part of its new initiatives in the South, the Soviet Union proposed an international conference on trade and the creation of a world trade organization outside the GATT. The North persuaded the South to reject the Soviet proposal in favor of reform within the GATT.

For the developed countries, reforming the GATT meant little more than studying the problems of developing countries. In 1957, the contracting parties of the GATT appointed a panel of experts to examine the problems of Southern trade. The panel's report, published in 1958, focused on the problems of trade in primary products: Northern trade barriers, the deterioration in the price of exports from the developing countries, and Southern import-substitution policies. The panel also noted that tariff barriers to Southern manufactured exports remained higher than tariffs on developed country exports despite GATT liberalization.[20] The report led to the 1958 GATT Programme for the Expansion of International Trade, and to the establishment of a GATT committee to consider problems of Southern exports of primary products and manufactured goods and to make recommendations for the expansion of Southern export earnings.

Developing countries used this new committee and the ongoing trade rounds to push for better access to Northern markets through unilateral concessions from developing countries, including a standstill on tariff and nontariff barriers for exports of Southern states, elimination of quantitative restrictions inconsistent with the GATT rules, duty-free entry for tropical products, elimination of customs duties on primary products important to the trade of developing countries, reduction and elimination of customs tariffs on semiprocessed and processed Southern exports, and reduction by the North of internal taxes and revenue duties on products produced primarily or wholly in Southern states. The Northern countries, however, were prepared to agree only to a set of goals, not a policy commitment.[21] The developing countries, frustrated with the realities of trade and with the structure of management, turned to a new strategy: changing the GATT not from within but through an assault from without.

Unity and Confrontation

Beginning in 1961, the South developed a united front to press the North for changes in trade management and in the operation of the international trading system. In Third World conferences and in the United Nations General Assembly, where the South commanded a majority, the developing countries pushed through their demands for trade and other economic reforms. A key plank in the Southern platform was a call for an international conference on trade and development. Confronted with the South's persistence and growing unity plus its increasing numerical control of the General Assembly, the North agreed to convene a United Nations Conference on Trade and Development (UNCTAD), which was held in 1964.[22]

The Southern countries then focused on achieving trade reform through UNCTAD. They formed the Group of Seventy-Seven (G-77), named for the cosponsors of the Joint Declaration of the Developing Countries made to the General Assembly in 1963.[23] The declaration spelled out for the first time its common goals for trade reform:

> The existing principles and patterns of world trade still mainly favor the advanced parts of the world. Instead of helping the developing countries to promote the development and diversification of their economies, the present tendencies in world trade frustrate their efforts to attain more rapid growth. These trends must be reversed.[24]

In order to make international trade "a more powerful instrument and vehicle of economic development,"[25] the G-77 offered a series of goals for UNCTAD, ranging from the improvement of institutional arrangements to the progressive reduction and early elimination of all barriers and restrictions impeding Southern exports (without reciprocal concessions on their part), to increased exports of primary products to the developed countries, and the stabilization and establishment of fair prices.[26] The G-77, which retained its original name but which came to include 131 states by 1995,[27] became a permanent political group representing Southern interests within the UN system.

UNCTAD also became a permanent United Nations organization in 1964.[28] Its doctrine, which has served as a basis for united G-77 action, was developed by UNCTAD's first secretary-general, Raúl Prebisch.[29] In UNCTAD's structuralist analysis of North-South relations, the world is divided into a center, or the developed countries, and a periphery, or the developing countries. The market works against the developing countries because of the long-term structural decline in Southern terms of trade and because of Northern protectionist policies that discriminate against Southern exports. As a result, the South has "a persistent tendency toward external imbalance," what Prebisch called the "trade gap." Unless measures are taken to counteract the structural bias against the South and to fill the trade gap, argues UNCTAD, the underdeveloped countries will not be able to meet reasonable growth targets.

Despite the creation of UNCTAD, the united Southern front did not greatly alter the management of trade or the operation of the international market. Maintaining Southern unity proved difficult. Many cleavages—political and ideological, differing levels of development, and different relations with Northern states—divided the South. Although there had been no problem reaching agreement on common general goals, these differences made it difficult to reach agreement on specific, short-term policies. The cleavages also tended to prevent the group from establishing priorities and contribute to the accumulation and escalation of demands, which politicized conflict and confrontation with the North and prevented serious bargaining.[30] The South was also weakened by a united front of Northern opposition to the creation of a powerful UNCTAD, unwillingness to treat UNCTAD as a legitimate negotiating forum, and insistence on dealing with trade issues in the GATT. The South's marginal economic importance, its declining importance as an area of superpower competition, and its own internal divisions enabled the North to defeat, weaken, or ignore the South's proposed resolutions. Thus the South was unable to achieve its goals of a change in institutional structure, increased exports of Southern manufactures, and improvement in Southern commodity trade.

Despite opposition from the North, the South was able to obtain the establishment of UNCTAD as a permanent organization within the framework of the United Nations. UNCTAD also led to changes in the GATT. Faced with an attempt to replace the GATT as the principal forum for trade management, the North agreed to add to the GATT agreement a new section on trade and development, Part IV, which came into operation in 1965.[31] It called on states to refrain from increasing trade barriers against products of special concern to the developing countries, to give priority to the reduction and elimination of such barriers, and to implement a standstill on internal taxes on tropical products. More important, Part IV provided for exceptions to the free-trade rules for the developing countries: It eliminated the rule of reciprocity in trade negotiations and accepted commodity agreements to stabilize and ensure more equitable prices. Finally, the new section called for joint action to promote trade and development, which was the basis for establishing a Trade and Development Committee in the GATT to work on the elimination and reduction of trade barriers.

The institutional changes in UNCTAD and the GATT had little impact. UNCTAD cannot compel its members to take action: It can only make proposals and create public pressure on the members to comply. Part IV of the GATT is similarly nonbinding. The continued weakness of the developing countries in the GATT was evidenced during the Kennedy Round negotiations of 1964 to 1967 (the first trade negotiation that followed the implementation of Part IV). Although developing countries participated for the first time in an active way and although their participation was encouraged by the developed countries, the results of the round for the South were slim. Restrictions against Southern manufactures, such as textile products and clothing, remained higher than the norm; agricultural protectionism, including that on tropical products, remained intact; and quantitative restrictions and nontariff barriers continued to limit Southern exports generally.[32]

The South's limited ability to change Northern policy was revealed again in the case of Southern demands for a scheme to expand the industrial exports of developing countries.[33] Growth of manufactured exports, it was argued, could not be achieved alone by eliminating obstacles such as tariffs and quotas. It would also be necessary to give industrial exports from developing countries preferential access to Northern markets (that is, lower tariffs for the products of developing countries than for those of the developed countries). Preferences would help Southern industries overcome the problem of high initial costs of infant industries and, by opening larger markets, would enable them to achieve economies of scale, lower their costs, and eventually compete in world markets without preferences.[34]

Following years of conflict over the concept of a **generalized system of preferences (GSP)**, agreement was reached in 1968 on the principle of establishing a preferential scheme, and in 1971, the GATT authorized the preference scheme through a waiver of its most-favored-nation requirement. However, there were important limits on GSP schemes implemented by the Northern states.[35] Because the North was unable to agree on a common general system, individual states adopted similar but different schemes. These individual preference schemes have been temporary—for example, the U.S. scheme, passed in 1975, lasted for ten years and had to be renewed by Congress. The main schemes have been subject to ceiling limitations on the quantity or value of any particular import receiving preferences. In addition, many products have been excluded from preferential treatment including many import-sensitive goods for which the South enjoys a comparative advantage.[36] Geographical coverage is also uneven. For example, Taiwan was included in the U.S. scheme but not in that of the EC. The developed countries have also reserved the right to refuse to grant preferences to any state they choose, although only the United States has actually taken such action in the case of OPEC.[37]

Furthermore, evidence suggests that only a few countries, including South Korea and Hong Kong, have benefited from GSP and that these countries could have competed in international markets without any preferences.[38] The strategy of the more industrialized developing countries in international discussions of preferences has been on broadening the applicability of preferences to their manufactured exports, arguing that incomplete coverage is a form of nontariff barrier to Third World exports. The counterstrategy of the North has been to argue for "graduation"—which includes the ending of trade preferences for the more industrialized developing countries. The least-developed countries export few goods that enable them to make effective use of the preference schemes, so they have little at stake in this particular debate. And ironically, the GATT's success in general trade liberalization tends to eliminate the difference between preferential treatment and general treatment and to erode the advantages of preferences.[39]

The story of commodity schemes, the third Southern demand, was shorter and even less successful.[40] Commodities represent a huge share of Southern exports and foreign exchange earnings. In 1978, for example, over 80 percent of the South's export earnings came from primary commodities.[41] In 1992, 47 percent of the South's export earnings came from primary commodities.[42] The problems of commodity trade are numerous: price fluctuations that affect foreign exchange earnings; Northern protectionism and discriminatory tax policies; and competition from synthetics and substitutes.[43] Southern proposals to UNCTAD have been equally numerous: commodity agreements to stabilize prices and to establish remunerative and equitable prices; compensatory finance schemes to ease earnings fluctuations; the liberalization of Northern protection against Southern commodities; and aid for products facing competition from substitutes and synthetics. Until the oil crisis of 1973 and its aftermath, the North successfully resisted all such proposals.[44]

In sum, Southern unity and confrontation without further leverage proved to be weak bargaining tools. The UNCTAD "victories" led to only minor revisions in Southern dependence. The result was more frustration and hostility from the developing world.

Commodity Power and the
New International Economic Order

Suddenly, in the early 1970s, OPEC's ability to seize control of the international oil system suggested that Southern producers could pose a serious threat to the North by withholding or threatening to withhold supplies of raw materials (see Chapter 9). At the time, it seemed that the North was becoming dependent on a variety of raw material imports from the South. While overall consumption was rising, high-grade Northern supplies of many materials were being depleted, and extraction in the North was becoming increasingly expensive. Because supplies in the developing countries were plentiful and production costs were low, demand for raw material imports from the developing countries was increasing.[45]

An economic boom in the developed countries at the end of the 1960s and the beginning of the 1970s led to a surge in Northern demand for raw materials from the developing countries. Inflation and the uncertainties of floating exchange rates led to a shift of speculative funds into commodities, further increasing demand and creating price increases and supply shortages. Furthermore, as the oil crisis demonstrated, the North's ability to ensure access to supplies through political and military action was weakened by the end of colonialism and the waning influence of the West in Third World governments. Not surprisingly, many developing countries concluded that the North was now vulnerable to commodity threats.

The credibility of the threat was enhanced by a growing Southern ability to control access to their raw materials. New, skilled cadres in many Southern states had acquired expertise in the raw materials industry and in world commodity market conditions and operations (see Chapter 8). Greater national control over raw material production facilitated the control of supplies. Moreover, as frustration with the North grew, the South's political leaders become more willing to use these new skills to manipulate raw material supplies.

The South's discovery of commodity power led to a new period in North-South relations. Southern states united to use aggressively the commodity weapon and other economic and political resources at their disposal to persuade the North to restructure the international economic system (for commodity cartels, see Chapter 9). At Third World Conferences in 1974, 1975, and 1976, the G-77 drew up a coordinated program for a new international economic order (NIEO). The Declaration and Action Programme on the Establishment of a New International Economic Order adopted in 1974 by a special session of the General

Assembly reflected the South's new sense of power. The declaration proclaimed that the present international economic order is in direct conflict with current developments in international political and economic relations.

> The developing world has become a powerful factor that makes its influence felt in all fields of international activity. These irreversible changes in the relationship of forces in the world necessitate the active, full and equal participation of the developing countries in the formulation and application of all decisions that concern the international community.[46]

While the Southern program for the new international economic order touched all areas of international economic interaction, the South placed special emphasis on trade reform. It called for a reduction in Northern tariff barriers on a nonreciprocal basis, improvement in the preference schemes implemented by the developed countries, more effective adjustment assistance in the developed countries to ease the cost of more imports in the developing countries and to defuse political opposition, and international commodity agreements. A central element of the Southern program was a proposed Integrated Programme for Commodities that was to consist of an international agency and a common fund of $6 billion to support the prices of ten commodities.[47]

The ability of the developing countries to change the old economic order depended in part on Southern unity. The South stood a much better chance of forcing the North to make concessions if it could link its various potential commodity threats and, in particular, the oil threat, the inducement of an international agreement on oil prices, or if OPEC's considerable financial power could be linked to other Third World demands. However, unifying this heterogeneous group of states continued to be a difficult task. The impact of rising oil prices on the oil-importing developing countries and the growing economic divergence between the newly industrialized countries (NICs) and the other developing countries were particularly divisive.

Nevertheless, the South demonstrated a surprising degree of cohesion. Over a decade of common action gave the group an understanding of how to conduct international negotiations. In this period, some oil producers, Algeria and Venezuela in particular, played a leadership role in mobilizing a common Southern front and linking the oil issue to other Third World demands. The credibility of the South's threat to the North was enhanced by the projections of most resource economists at this time that demand for developing country raw materials would rise due to the rapid growth in consumption of durable goods and the depletion of known mineral resources.[48] A minority view at the time argued that oil was the exception, that commodity power was a short-term phenomenon based on temporary shortages, and that even if there were scarce resources producers would not be able to coordinate their actions as OPEC had to threaten the North (see Chapter 9).[49]

Because of the perceived seriousness of the commodity threat, coupled with Northern concerns about growing financial linkages with the developing countries, the tremendous financial power of the capital-surplus oil exporters, and a growing interest in Southern markets, the developed countries were willing to enter into negotiations with the South on the issue of a new international economic order. Thus they agreed to several special sessions of the United Nations General Assembly to discuss the NIEO and they supported special producer-consumer negotiations.

European countries that were more vulnerable to supply interruption were the most receptive to the NIEO demands. The EC, for example, agreed to the first Lomé Convention between the Community and forty-six associated African, Caribbean, and Pacific (ACP) states. The agreement increased aid to the ACP states and gave them a greater voice in aid management; provided for preferential access for ACP products to EC markets without reciprocal advantages for EC products; and created a compensatory finance scheme, STABEX, to stabilize the export earnings of the associated states from twelve key commodities.[50]

The United States—more self-sufficient and, thus, less vulnerable to external supply control—felt that the developed market economies should not make impetuous bargains with the South based on what it saw as a temporarily unfavorable situation. In the view of U.S. policymakers, the only threat came from the oil-producing states. When the Southern oil consumers recognized that OPEC was damaging their economies, the United States believed they would turn on the oil producers. The cyclical factors that led to temporary Northern vulnerability would eventually disappear and commodity prices would fall.

As the 1970s wore on, the North did come to feel less vulnerable. The oil countries, in particular the Gulf states, were not willing to use their leverage on behalf of other developing countries. Furthermore, as raw material prices began to decline, it became clear that the rise in commodity prices in the 1970s was a cyclical and not a structural phenomenon. Finally, developing countries were unable to unite to create cartels similar to OPEC.

The various negotiations on the establishment of a new international economic order (held in the 1970s) revealed the limits of Southern power. One example was the Conference on International Economic Cooperation (CIEC), which met from 1975 to 1977. It linked Northern interest in an energy dialogue with OPEC (see Chapter 9) to G-77 desires for negotiations on other raw materials, finance, and development as well as energy. The results of CIEC were meager: an agreement in principle to establish a common fund for commodity-price stabilization, a promise by the North to redouble its efforts to reach the 0.7-percent-of-GNP aid target, and a pledge by the North to give $1 billion to the least-developed countries. The common fund was eventually adopted by UNCTAD in 1980 but never implemented because of an inadequate number of ratifications. The 0.7-percent target was not reached. And the $1 billion for the least-developed countries had, by and large, already been committed. The conference was unable to reach agreement on the key issues of oil price and supply and international monetary reform.[51]

The G-77 also used UNCTAD to put forth programs for NIEO demands. The main UNCTAD effort focused on the proposal for an Integrated Programme on Commodities. It called for the negotiation of international commodity agreements (ICAs) for raw materials exports important to developing countries and the establishment of a common fund to stabilize the prices of developing country commodities.

ICAs are accords among producers and consumers designed to stabilize or increase the price of particular products. They may be of three types or combinations thereof: (1) *buffer-stock schemes*, such as that of the International Tin Agreement, whereby price is managed by purchases or sales from a central fund at times of excessive fluctuation; (2) *export quotas*, such as those used by the International Coffee Agreement, whereby price is managed by assigning production quotas to participating countries in order to control supply; and (3) *multilateral contracts*, whereby the importing countries contract to buy certain quantities at a specified low price when the world market falls below that price and the exporting countries agree to sell certain quantities at a fixed price when the world market price exceeds the maximum.

UNCTAD's efforts to implement international commodity agreements foundered on the traditional problems of ICAs. Producers who would like to use ICAs to raise prices and consumers who want only to stabilize prices often have difficulty agreeing on objectives. When they have been able to reach agreement, ICAs have been plagued by such problems as temptations to cheat when prices rise, variations of price and supply among different qualities of the same commodity, encouragement of using substitutes, the difficulty of imposing drastic production or export reductions, the high cost of financing buffer stocks, and the political and financial difficulty of managing an ICA when there is a long-term downward trend in commodity prices. Moreover, most Northern governments oppose ICAs as inefficient, encouraging waste and the misallocation of resources, helpful to only a few developing countries, and actually damaging to others faced with higher prices due to ICAs.[52] Despite UNCTAD efforts, few ICAs—tin, sugar, coffee, cocoa, natural rubber, and tropical timber—have been negotiated. Most of these date back to the 1960s and are not a result of UNCTAD's efforts. Only the rubber and tropical timber agreements were formally concluded under UNCTAD and the latter provides only for cooperation and consultation on product and market development, conservation and reforestation, not on price stabilization.[53]

UNCTAD's common fund never saw the light of day.[54] Following Northern resistance to the South's proposed $6 billion fund, UNCTAD eventually agreed in 1980 on a less ambitious $400 million plan. However, the agreement never received the ratifications needed to set it into operation.

Although the Southern vision of the new international economic order was never implemented, there were some additional limited achievements in the 1970s. One was the establishment of compensatory financing facilities that attempted to stabilize or increase the export earnings of developing countries by compensating them when the fall in the price of a commodity leads to a decline in export earnings. A Compensatory Financing Facility created by the IMF in

1963 was greatly expanded in 1975, 1979, 1988, 1990, and again in 1993. It allowed IMF members to borrow from the fund in excess of their regular quota limits when commodity prices and thus export earnings fell below normal levels.[55] Another compensatory financing facility was the EEC STABEX scheme set up under the Lomé Convention of 1975. It established a fund to pay the associated ACP states compensation when the market price for certain commodities fell below a certain level. Wealthier associated states received an interest-free loan, whereas the poorest states received a grant.[56]

The developing countries also achieved some success in the GATT's Tokyo Round of multilateral trade negotiations that took place from 1975 to 1979.[57] Their main goal was to obtain what came to be known as "special and differential treatment" that would exempt developing countries from the GATT's rules on reciprocity and most-favored-nation obligations. During the Tokyo Round, the developing countries succeeded in obtaining a series of agreements that built the principle of special and differential treatment of developing countries into the GATT rules. These agreements gave permanent legal authorization for GSP preferences and preferences in trade between developing countries. They also authorized "more favorable" treatment for developing countries on nontariff barriers and special favorable treatment for the least-developed developing countries.[58]

As a balance to special and differential treatment, the developed countries insisted on the inclusion of a "graduation clause" in the GATT articles. It set forth the principle that as Southern countries reached higher levels of development, preferential treatment would be withdrawn and countries would be expected to assume the full rights and obligations of the GATT.[59] The developing countries, especially the NICs, unsuccessfully opposed this principle, which they saw as a device that the North could use to withdraw preferential treatment unilaterally whenever the developing countries began to threaten the Northern economies. One problem with the graduation provision was that it included no criteria or standards for graduation.

In addition to this amendment of the GATT, developing countries were able to obtain special and differential provisions in the various codes negotiated during the Tokyo Round. For example, Southern countries were permitted under the government procurement code to rely on domestic purchases when they were necessary to protect infant industries and balance-of-payments positions. Similarly, standards code did not bind Southern countries when its provisions conflicted with development, financial, and trade needs. And the subsidies code excused developing countries from most obligations.[60]

The developing countries achieved little else in the Tokyo Round. The failure to reach agreement on a safeguards code (on safeguards, see Chapter 3) left in place many of the new Northern protectionist policies such as VERs. As the target of many of these policies, the developing countries had particularly sought strict rules governing the application of safeguard measures; explicit criteria of actual, not potential, injury to producers in importing states; and controls on selectivity—that is, the ability of individual exporters to be singled out and subjected to safeguard actions. The developing countries were dissatisfied with the results of the Tokyo Round, and many chose not to ratify the code agreements.

By the close of the 1970s, the South's strategy based on unity, commodity power, and the NIEO had reached a dead end. While the G-77 continued to call for its vision of a new international economic order in the United Nations and UNCTAD, developments in the international market were changing the South's bargaining power and creating a very different economic order.

The New Order for the 1980s

Trade between the developed and developing countries underwent several changes that altered the politics of North-South trade in the 1980s. Despite the predictions of experts that the world faced a future of ever-diminishing raw materials, the soaring commodity prices of the mid-1970s turned out to be a cyclical phenomenon. If anything, the long-term trend seemed to be a decline and not an increase in the growth of world demand for raw materials. In the 1970s and 1980s, rates of growth of GNP in the developed countries fell from the rapid rates of the 1960s, thus slowing demand for commodities. Demand also declined as output in the Northern states shifted from manufacturing, which requires raw materials, to services, which use far fewer raw materials (see Chapter 3). The dramatic rise in prices in the 1970s encouraged conservation, greater recycling, and the substitution of traditional materials by synthetics or by technology and energy-intensive materials. This decline in demand growth combined with a new capacity created by investment during the commodity shortages of the 1970s led to excess capacity, oversupply, and weakening of prices.[61]

Prices of non-oil commodities of developing countries fell by 24 percent between 1980 and 1986. They recovered somewhat, rising 14 percent between 1986 and 1988, but then fell again by 16.6 percent between 1989 and 1993.[62] From 1985 to 1992, the terms of trade fell by 10 percent for the low-income developing countries, by 4, 2, and 0 percent, respectively, for the lower-middle, middle, and upper-middle income developing economies.[63] From 1980 to 1986, the industrial countries' terms of trade *improved* by 9 percent.[64]

The decline in commodity prices seriously affected the poorest of the developing countries who still relied heavily on commodity exports. For example, the value of Zambia's exports, over 90 percent of which are copper, declined by over one-half between 1980 and 1985. In the same period, Liberia's export earnings, largely from iron ore and rubber, and Bolivia's earnings, largely from tin, declined by nearly 40 percent.[65] Although cyclical factors may boost demand for certain raw materials and while certain developing country exporters may benefit from shifts in demand for commodities, commodity power will not be an effective bargaining tool for the South.

While many of the poorest developing countries were caught in the collapse of commodity prices, others were developing strong manufacturing capabilities and increasing their exports of manufactured products. In the 1970s, export-oriented industrialization policies of a number of developing countries began to bear fruit. Lower labor costs in labor-intensive industries, such as textiles and shoes, and production innovations often acquired from the North, as in the case of steel, enabled certain developing countries to compete successfully in Northern markets.

From 1970 to 1992, the share of manufactured goods in exports from the developing countries almost doubled, reaching 52 percent of the total value of their exports in 1986, up from 27 percent in 1970.[66] By 1993, Southern manufactured exports accounted for 32 percent of world manufactured exports.[67] Southern manufactures also came to represent a large share of Northern imports. Between 1963 and 1987, Southern manufactures increased from 4 to 13 percent of their share of industrial country manufactured imports.[68] By 1990, 32 percent of U.S. imports of manufactured products came from developing countries, up from 15 percent in 1972. In 1990, Japan obtained 44 percent of its manufactured imports from the South, up from 18 percent in 1972.[69]

The principal beneficiaries of this change in the structure of trade were the newly industrializing countries (NICs), especially the "four tigers" of East Asia—South Korea, Taiwan, Singapore, and Hong Kong.[70] In the 1950s and early 1960s, the East Asian NICs, with the exception of Hong Kong, had followed successful import substitution policies. Domestic production of consumer nondurables replaced imports, resulting in a period of rapid growth. However, in the 1960s and 1970s, import substitution reached its limits. Expansion into machinery and consumer durables would have required extending protection and investment into more capital-intensive sectors; the costs of deepening import substitution would have been high given the small domestic markets in these countries; and domestic industries would not have been able to take advantage of economies of scale without expanding into foreign markets.

The four tigers also realized they needed the foreign exchange earnings to import essential goods. Poorly endowed with natural resources, they needed foreign exchange to pay for raw materials imports. For South Korea and Taiwan, which were receiving extensive foreign assistance, export earnings would eventually have to replace foreign aid as a source of financing. However, import substitution discriminated against export sectors. Protection raised the cost of imported inputs essential for many export industries and thus decreased the export competitiveness. In addition, import substitution was often accompanied by overvalued currencies that increased the price of exports.

The switch to export-led growth policies did not mean eliminating all protection. All the tigers except Hong Kong retained many import tariffs and quantitative restrictions. Outward-oriented policies did mean eliminating the bias against exports: maintaining realistic exchange rates that did not discriminate against exports, reducing import barriers for inputs to the export sector, as well as removing any other export disincentives such as export taxes. In South Korea, Taiwan, and Singapore, outward-oriented policies also involved government promotion of exports through favorable credit terms for exporters, tax incentives, undervalued exchange rates that decrease export prices, encouragement of foreign investment in export industries, and direct subsidies for targeted sectors. Government intervention has been criticized for targeting certain sectors, such as the heavy and chemical industries in South Korea, which have been relatively less successful than industries that were "chosen" by the markets. However, general export incentives clearly aided the competitiveness of the NICs. Exports also increased through "offshore assembly" or "sourcing" arrangements, whereby multinational companies were encouraged to invest for export (see Chapter 8).[71]

These strategies have led to a dramatic increase in exports. The four tigers' share of world trade increased from around 2 percent in 1960 to 9.3 percent in 1993.[72] The four tigers alone account for over 60 percent of the manufactured exports from developing countries. With the addition of several other middle-income countries such as Brazil, Mexico, and Argentina, the share of the NICs of manufactured exports from developing countries has reached almost 75 percent.[73] The four tigers' share in OECD imports of manufactured goods increased from 1.3 percent in 1964 to 7.1 percent in 1993.[74] More importantly, outward-oriented strategies have resulted in higher growth rates than inward-oriented policies (see Figure 7-3).[75]

The success of the four tigers, however, created strong pressures for protection. In the 1980s, the United States, which in 1986 absorbed 38 percent of the four tigers' exports of manufactured goods and 34 percent of all their exports, removed GSP privileges from these countries, limited imports of textiles, footwear, and steel and other items, and put pressure on the Asian NICs to allow their currencies to appreciate vis-à-vis the dollar.[76] The United States also put pressure on South Korea and Taiwan to remove domestic protection and open their markets to U.S. goods and services. In the 1990s, this pressure was directed toward other Asian countries also experiencing rapid export growth, including the People's Republic of China.

The trade problems of the Asian NICs were characteristic of North-South trade relations generally. Southern manufactured imports posed a significant threat to important industrial sectors with high concentrations of employment in the North and thus provoked powerful political pressures for protection. As a result, North-South trade in manufactures was increasingly subjected to trade barriers, especially voluntary export restraints.

The classic example was textiles.[77] The South has a comparative advantage in significant portions of the textile industry, which are labor-intensive and require simple technology. Those same segments of the textile industry, however, represent an important share of the GDP and employment of the developed countries. Furthermore, the textile industry tends to be geographically concentrated and well organized politically, making it a powerful force in domestic trade politics in all the developed countries.

In 1962, as the LDCs became competitive in Northern textile markets, the members of the GATT negotiated the Long-Term Arrangement (LTA) regarding

Figure 7-3   Growth Rates of Forty-One Developing Countries Grouped by Trade Orientation

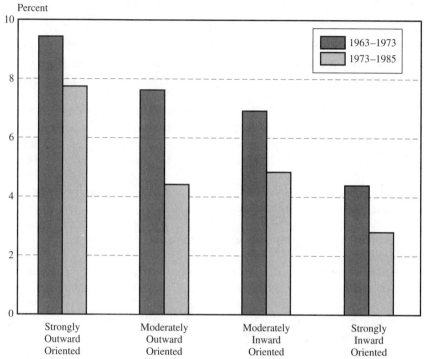

Note: Averages are weighted by each country's share in the group total for each indicator of the trade groups.

SOURCE: World Bank, *World Development Report 1987* (New York: Oxford University Press, 1987), 84.

international trade in cotton textiles that allowed for such departures from the GATT as quotas on textile imports and regulation of market share. Restrictive bilateral agreements were then negotiated within the framework of the LTA. In 1974, when LDCs had become competitive in artificial fibers and wool, the GATT contracting parties concluded the Arrangement Regarding International Trade in Textiles, known as the Multi-Fiber Arrangement (MFA). It creates a multilateral framework for restricting trade in textiles, under which specific bilateral controls are negotiated. Over the years, MFA agreements have been regularly extended and made more restrictive, by broadening the coverage and lowering the growth in market share of the LDCs. By 1986, 61 percent of Southern exports of textile yarn and fabrics and 78 percent of Southern exports of clothing were subjected to import restrictions.[78] Originally intended as temporary safeguard measures, the textile agreements became firmly entrenched institutionally, and significantly limited textile exports of the LDCs.[79]

The case of textiles was repeated, in less comprehensive but equally perni-cious ways, in many other sectors. Voluntary export restraints (VERs) increas-ingly restricted Southern access to Northern markets. Forty-seven percent of all export restraint arrangements in place in 1987 applied to exports from develop-ing countries.[80]

As a result of the new importance of manufactures and new forms of pro-tectionism, the trade policy of the LDCs focused more and more on access to the markets of the developed countries in general and on controlling VERs in partic-ular. A new safeguards agreement in the GATT became a high priority concern for the South in the Uruguay Round. The increasing importance of manufactured exports also raised the graduation issue. As the NICs became more competitive in a variety of manufactured products, the Northern governments claimed that they no longer deserved special privileges such as GSP or special and differential treat-ment in the GATT. In several forums, the North began to demand that the NICs graduate and assume the same commitments and responsibilities in the interna-tional trading system as the developed countries had.

In the 1970s, the South became not only an important exporter of manufac-tured products to the North, but it also became a more important market for the developed countries. From 1973 to 1981, the developing countries' share of the merchandise exports from the developed countries rose from 17 to 26 percent. Owing to the onset of the debt crisis, the share of the developing countries in total merchandise exports from the developed countries fell to only 18 percent in 1990.[81] In 1993, 42.5 percent of U.S. exports went to developing countries, up from 37 percent in 1980 and 29 percent in 1973.[82]

The LDC debt crisis demonstrated the significance of Southern trade for the North. In an effort to generate foreign exchange to service their debt, developing countries reduced imports through austerity policies, rationing of foreign exchange, and import restrictions. Imports by the highly indebted countries grew at an average of 5.5 percent from 1973 to 1980 and fell by 6.3 percent per year on average between 1980 and 1987.[83] From 1980 to 1987, total U.S. exports increased 8 percent, but exports to Latin America dropped 19 percent; worldwide U.S. exports of manufactured goods fell 23 percent, but manufactured exports to Latin America fell 32 percent.[84] At the same time, in order to increase foreign exchange earnings, debtor countries tried to export more to the North, thus aggra-vating protectionist pressures. United States imports from the heavily indebted countries increased by 18 percent between 1980 and 1987.[85]

The New Pragmatism

The new realities of the 1980s altered the trade strategy of the developing countries. The South's demand for a new international economic order was undermined by the collapse of commodity power, including the OPEC threat; by deep cracks in the G-77's solidarity, as several advanced developing countries were integrated into the existing international economic order; and by the weak-ened economic position of the South, especially the debt crisis. Meanwhile, the North was becoming both more protectionist at home and more insistent on mar-ket-oriented policies abroad. As we have seen, one of the main elements of Northern policies for developing country debtors was the implementation of domestic market-oriented reforms and international liberalization (see Chapter 6). The South's main bargaining chip in such a situation was to persuade the North that maintenance of world economic stability and prosperity depended on improving the lot of the developing countries.

The new forces of the 1980s also called into question the effectiveness of the South's preferred forums for management, especially UNCTAD and the United Nations. The South continued to use these forums to call for a new international economic order, but in the 1980s the G-77 focused instead on more pragmatic measures to deal with the South's economic crisis. According to the South, the world economic crisis called for special measures to promote global recovery, especially measures to assist the South, which was most seriously affected by the crisis. In trade, this would mean greater access for the South to the markets of the North: dismantling protectionism, halting subsidy and dumping investigations, suspending countervailing and antidumping duties, implementing structural adjustment policies, expanding the GSP, and offering favorable treatment to the developing countries for trade in services. In commodities, the G-77 called for less radical reforms than it had in the 1970s: interim commodity agreements to help stabilize commodity prices until ICAs could be negotiated; expansion of the IMF's buffer stock financing facility and compensatory financing facility; a new compensatory financing facility to cover the export-earnings shortfalls of coun-tries dependent on commodity exports; and assistance in processing, marketing, transporting, and distributing Southern commodities.[86]

Although the South moved away from its more extreme NIEO proposals in the 1980s, it did not move far enough for the North. In the view of the developed market countries, the principal measures to be taken by the international commu-nity were those that would preserve the liberal international trading and financial system. What the South called emergency measures—for instance, interim com-modity agreements—looked like fundamental deviations from the liberal order to the North. Thus, in the 1980s, the North-South dialogue in the United Nations system increasingly became a dialogue of the deaf. UNCTAD meetings produced only meager results.[87] And G-77 efforts in the United Nations General Assembly to launch a set of global negotiations led nowhere.[88]

As the strategy of confrontation and the NIEO collapsed, developing coun-tries shifted their focus to the GATT. One reason for the shift was the pressure of the developed countries, especially the United States, for a new round of multi-lateral negotiations. As the 1980s progressed, frustration with the existing trade regime grew in both the industrialized countries and the developing countries (see Chapter 3). Developed countries wanted a new multilateral trade round to bring agriculture and the so-called "new" areas of trade (services, intellectual property rights, and investment) under GATT discipline. There was also a growing sense of alarm at the proliferation of protectionist measures both outside of and in violation of the GATT rules. The United States, in particular, became convinced that without significant reform of the GATT rules and procedures, the GATT system would become increasingly divorced from economic reality and would ultimately collapse.

The dramatic export success of the newly industrialized countries was another motivation behind the drive for a new multilateral trade round. As concern mounted over the NICs' deepening penetration of U.S. and European markets, the industrialized countries accused the NICs of "free riding" on the international system by continuing to take advantage of the special treatment accorded developing countries by the GATT and by GSP programs despite overwhelming evidence that they had now become internationally competitive exporters. The industrialized countries insisted that the time had come for the NICs to "graduate" from developing country status (and the attendant benefits) and to be fully integrated into the GATT system, thereby becoming subject to obligations consonant with their new economic stature. As part of this push for "graduation," in January 1989 the United States removed the four tigers of Asia from the list of nations eligible for GSP privileges.

The industrialized countries also complained that the NICs engaged in unfair trade practices, ranging from export subsidies and dumping to restrictions on foreign imports and direct investment. The developed countries, especially the United States, also criticized the NICs for maintaining undervalued currencies that served to promote exports. Consequently, the number of bilateral trade disputes and unilateral trade actions initiated against these countries by the United States and by EC member states rose dramatically. The United States instituted trade negotiations with Korea and Taiwan over access to their markets for cigarettes, beef, beer, wine, and insurance. The EC entered into negotiations with Korea over the lack of patent protection.

While most concern focused on the NICs, developed countries also increased pressure on the non-NIC developing countries to liberalize their domestic trade and economic regimes, arguing that protectionist policies and demands for "special and differential" treatment made little economic sense. This change in approach was most evident in the growing emphasis of the World Bank and the IMF on the need for developing countries to undertake "structural" market-oriented economic reforms. A parallel approach was evident in the U.S. determination to use a new trade round to circumscribe the definition and application of "special and differential" treatment, to reform the GATT provision permitting developing countries to institute trade restrictions for "balance of payments" reasons, and to persuade developing countries to bind—and perhaps reduce—a substantial portion of their tariff schedules.

At the same time, the developing countries had become increasingly dissatisfied with what they regarded as the meager gains of previous trade rounds. Although, as we have discussed, some developing countries had participated in the GATT negotiations, most had chosen to take a passive rather than active role, largely out of the conviction that the GATT—as a "rich man's club"—had little to offer poor countries with no substantial political or economic leverage. Since tariff reductions agreed to in the GATT were applied on a most-favored-nation (MFN) basis, developing countries felt they could reap the benefits of the GATT negotiations without necessarily participating. Furthermore, since most developing countries played a very small role in international trade, they had little incentive to engage in pragmatic bargaining and preferred to take an ideological stance marked by North-South confrontation, as discussed earlier in this chapter.

By the late 1980s, however, developing countries had become more dependent than ever on trade, and their stake in the maintenance of a liberal international trading regime had risen proportionately. In 1970 the ratio of exports to gross domestic product in developing countries was 11 percent. By 1993, that ratio had grown to 22.4 percent.[89] A handful of countries—the NICs—had become highly successful exporters in a relatively short time, and other developing countries were eager to follow in their footsteps. Given the failure of the inward-looking economic policies of the past, the example of successful export-led growth of the NICs, and the continuing commodity and debt crises, the developing countries were forced to reevaluate their development strategies. Slowly but surely, a number of developing countries began reforming their domestic economic policies, liberalizing their trade regimes, and shifting toward a more export-oriented growth strategy.[90]

The importance of actively participating in the GATT was underlined by rising protectionism against developing country exports. Between 1981 and 1986, the EC, Japan, and the United States collectively increased the application of "hard-core" nontariff barriers from 19 to 21 percent of their imports from developing countries, compared to an increase from 13 to 16 percent for imports from other industrialized countries (see Figure 7-4). If we look at individual export sectors, the figures are even more telling. Nontariff barriers were applied by the industrial market economies to 55 percent of iron and steel imports and 31 percent of manufactures imports (nonchemicals) from developing countries, including 80 percent of clothing imports, and 27 percent of footwear imports.[91]

Market access thus became a priority trade issue for the developing countries in the 1980s and 1990s. Despite market access problems in Japan and Europe, the primary focus of this fear was the United States, which for many developing countries was by far their largest export market. As the United States continued to toughen its trade laws and as nontariff barriers continued to multiply, many developing countries came to view the GATT as their only chance of imposing discipline on U.S. trade policy and ensuring continued access to U.S. markets. This view was reinforced by the negotiation of NAFTA, which some countries saw as an indication that the United States was turning away from multilateralism. The European Community's renewed efforts after 1985 to achieve full economic integration similarly provoked fear that the GATT system was on the verge of disintegrating into protectionist regional and bilateral trading blocs.

Figure 7-4   Imports by Industrialized Countries and Regions from the Developing Countries Facing Nontariff Barriers, 1986

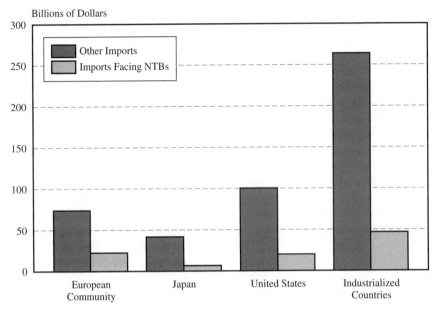

Billions of Dollars

Legend:
- Other Imports
- Imports Facing NTBs

Categories: European Community, Japan, United States, Industrialized Countries

SOURCE: UNCTAD database on trade control measures as cited in Sheila Page, *How Developing Countries Trade* (New York: Routledge, 1994), 57.

Developing countries also hoped that the Uruguay Round would force Japan to offer greater access to its markets.

Finally, by the mid-1980s there was greater recognition of the diversity of interests among developing countries and the problems that posed for the traditional bloc approach to relations with the North. At one extreme were the NICs, some of which seemed on the verge of joining the exclusive club of industrialized nations. At the other extreme were the least developed of the developing countries, clinging to the frayed margins of the international trading system. In the middle lay a wide range of countries at different levels of economic development, each differing in its degree of export dependence, in comparative advantage, and in its political and social objectives. In the face of such diversity, many developing countries came to believe that their interests would best be served by a pragmatic rather than ideological or bloc approach to negotiations in the GATT.

Initially the developing countries resisted the call by the developed countries for a new trade round and argued that instead of discussing new issues, the GATT talks should focus on old, unresolved issues. For example, Brazil proposed addressing the elimination of nontariff barriers and the Multi-Fiber Arrangement, liberalization in trade of tropical products, restraint in the use of antidumping and subsidy actions, and an improved dispute settlement mechanism.[92] Using the threat of nonparticipation in the round to bargain for greater attention to Southern concerns, the LDCs achieved some concessions such as a special negotiating group and a commitment to an early agreement on tropical products. With these concessions in hand, they concurred in the 1986 agreement to launch the Uruguay Round and entered the negotiations determined to be active participants in the GATT process. While only seventeen developing countries had joined the GATT in the twenty years up to 1987, between 1987 and 1994 twenty-nine developing countries joined the organization.

The most active and cooperative developing country participants in the negotiations were those that believed they had a great deal at stake: most of the NICs and developing countries from the next tier, such as the ASEAN nations. A handful of countries chose to pursue a hard line, making traditional G-77 demands, for example, for unqualified "special and differential" treatment. The hard-line countries were led by Brazil and India, which had large domestic markets and continued to rely on import substitution and included others that felt they would lose from liberalization.

Although many developing countries were reluctant to mar the appearance of Southern unity in international forums, they frequently chose to pursue a more pragmatic strategy in domestic, bilateral, and regional policies. Believing that only those who played the game had any chance of winning concessions, they worked with developing and industrialized countries alike in an effort to reach agreements on issues of importance to them. As a result, despite clear differences in priorities between the industrialized and developing countries, the Uruguay Round negotiations did not split along North-South lines. Instead, coalitions developed along issue lines which, in contrast to early rounds, often included both industrialized and developing countries. One pivotal coalition was the so-called "Cairns group" of thirteen agricultural exporting nations—nine of them developing countries—that was organized in 1986 to pressure the United States and the EC to find a solution to the problem of excess production and subsidization of agricultural products. Many other North-South informal groupings developed in the course of the negotiations on issues as varied as nontariff barriers, dispute settlement procedures, trade in services, tariffs, and tropical products.

Since the most important goal of the developing countries was increased access to industrialized country markets, they tended to focus their efforts in the Uruguay Round negotiations on such issues as enforcing the standstill and rollback of protectionist measures agreed to at the beginning of the trade round; bringing agriculture and textiles under GATT discipline; strengthening safeguards and discipline over "gray area" measures; eliminating nontariff barriers to trade; tightening GATT rules (e.g., the antidumping code) to limit the ability of developed countries to invoke their trade laws against alleged offending nations; and reforming the dispute settlement mechanism and other GATT procedures in order to improve surveillance and enforcement. The developing countries continued to insist on special treatment in recognition of their development needs, although a number of them indicated a willingness to be flexible on the precise form taken by such special treatment.

Concerning the so-called "new" issues under negotiation (services, intellectual property, and investment), the majority of developing countries were either lukewarm or hostile. They saw services, intellectual property, and investment negotiations as efforts aimed at changing developing country policies in areas not appropriately covered by the GATT. Only a handful of countries (the Asian NICs) expressed a qualified willingness to consider entering into agreements on these topics—and that was primarily because they suspected that they would be better off entering into multilateral agreements than being subjected to bilateral pressure from the developed countries, especially the United States. All the developing countries insisted that any concessions on the "new" issues would be linked to progress made on the more traditional issues of importance to them.

The strategy of pragmatic engagement led to important achievements for developing countries in the Uruguay Round (see Chapter 3).[93] Ninety-one developing countries participated in the negotiations, far more than in previous rounds, and their participation was more active and wide-ranging than ever before. As a result, they made important progress toward their goal of market access. For example, the Uruguay Round agreement provided for elimination over a ten-year period of quotas on textiles negotiated under the Multi-Fiber Arrangement, thus ending over thirty years of managed trade in textiles. The new regime for agricultural products that brought agriculture into the system of trade liberalization reflected the efforts of the developing country members of the Cairns group. And tariff cuts on a variety of tropical and natural resource–based industrial products benefited developing countries.[94]

Developing countries also benefited from the development of new trading rules. The elimination of voluntary export restraints and import surveillance measures through the safeguards code was a significant achievement. In 1992, approximately 10 percent of all LDC exports to developed countries were covered by such gray area measures.[95] In addition, the new rules on antidumping stood to benefit developing countries who are often the subjects of such actions. Finally, LDCs were able to gain special treatment, enabling them to use subsidies for development, and held off a number of demands of developed countries in the new issues. For example, they insisted on and achieved long phase-in periods for implementation of intellectual property rules and resisted pressure to significantly open their financial services markets. While they made important gains, the task remained unfinished, both in gaining greater access to the markets of the developed countries and in reforming their own economies to meet the challenge of international markets.

Beyond the Uruguay Round

The Uruguay Round negotiations thus were a landmark in the role of developing countries in the international trading system. Having concluded that the traditional strategies of import substitution and North-South confrontation had yielded few concrete benefits, the developing countries pursued more pragmatic policies and sought greater engagement in international trade. As forums traditionally preferred by the South such as UNCTAD became increasingly irrelevant, the South shifted its attention elsewhere, especially after 1995 to the new World Trade Organization (WTO). Previous nonmembers of the GATT, including China, Taiwan, and Vietnam, entered into negotiations for membership in the WTO. As a result of their achievements in the Uruguay round, developing countries now had a greater stake in the successful implementation of the round. In particular, developing countries were expected to be strong advocates of using the WTO's new rules and dispute settlement mechanisms as tools to defend themselves against Northern protectionism.

As part of the new pragmatism and the shift toward export-led growth strategies, and as a complement to their greater activism in multilateral negotiations, developing countries also pursued more aggressive regional trade strategies. Until the 1990s, regional integration in the South had not, for the most part, resulted in much growth in intraregional trade (see Table 7-1 and Figure 7-5). Now, with many countries adopting policies of unilateral tariff reductions in connection with their acceptance of the need to expand exports, there are fewer problems of pursuing regional integration than there were in the days of import substitution. An example of this was the new customs union formed by Argentina, Brazil, Paraguay, and Uruguay called Mercosur (Mercosul in Portuguese). Chile joined Mercosul in 1996.

In addition, a number of developing countries attempted to strengthen their trade ties with the North. Mexico did so in pushing for the North American Free

Table 7-1   Important Regional Groupings of Developing Countries

Region	Name	Short Name/Acronym
The Caribbean and Latin America	Latin American Integration Association	LAIA
	Andean Group	
	Central American Common Market	CACM
	Southern Cone Common Market	Mercosur
	Caribbean Common Market	CARICOM
Africa	Arab Maghreb Union	UMA
	Economic Community of Central African States	ECCAS
	Economic Community of West African States	ECOWAS
	West African Economic Community	CEAO
	Southern African Development Community	SADC
Asia	Association of South-East Asian Nations/AFTA	ASEAN/AFTA

Figure 7-5   Intratrade as a Percentage of Group Exports in a Variety of Regional Economic Organizations, 1970–1992

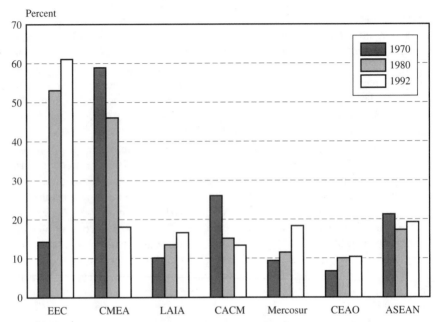

SOURCE: United Nations Conference on Trade and Development, *Handbook of International Trade and Development Statistics 1993* (Geneva: UNCTAD, 1993), 38–39

Trade Agreement (NAFTA). In 1995, NAFTA members began negotiations with Chile regarding that country's accession to the agreement. The EU agreed to enter into negotiations to expand its system of free trade agreements to a number of countries in the Mediterranean basin.

At the summit of the Americas in late 1994, the countries of the Americas including the United States and Canada agreed to begin discussions intended to lead to a free trade agreement of the Americas by the year 2005. Similar developments occurred in the Pacific region. The members of the Association of South-East Asian Nations (ASEAN)—Brunei, Indonesia, Malaysia, the Philippines, Singapore, Thailand, and Vietnam—agreed to form the ASEAN Free Trade Area (AFTA), with the goal of eliminating barriers and achieving free trade by the year 2003. Then in 1994, the Asia Pacific Economic Cooperation (APEC) forum, whose members included both developing (e.g., ASEAN, Korea, China, and Taiwan) and developed (e.g. the United States, Japan, and Australia) countries, agreed to achieve free trade and investment in the region, with developed countries achieving that goal by 2010 and developing countries by 2020 (see Chapter 3).

Finally, the poorest countries and regions of the South maintained special preferential trading relationships with countries and groups in the North. The special EC-ACP relationship has been maintained in a succession of Lomé Agreements.[96] In the 1980s, the United States passed trade legislation and negotiated a series of bilateral treaties giving the countries of the Caribbean Basin preferential access to U.S. markets.

The South's search for bargaining leverage in all of these forums will continue to be tested as it attempts to persuade the North that it is in the self-interest of the industrialized countries to make changes that will help the developing countries export, earn more, service their debts, and provide markets for Northern products. Strong protectionist pressures in both traditional manufacturing sectors and agriculture will make it difficult, although not impossible, for Northern governments to respond credibly to the South's demands. This task is made somewhat easier for the South by the growing importance to Northern multinational corporations of their operations in the South for serving global markets (see Chapter 8).

As developing countries pursued engagement and trade liberalization, the disparity between the Third and Fourth Worlds became more apparent. Some developing countries were able to grow rapidly enough to approach the per capita income levels of the North. Singapore, Taiwan, and Korea, for example, experienced steady growth in their per capita income between the 1960s and the 1990s. Some of these high-growth developing countries joined organizations like the OECD in recognition of their new status.[97] As the number of NICs grew, however, many developing countries remained mired in debt, dependent on exports of agricultural commodities and raw materials, and trapped in poverty. One major question for the period beyond the Uruguay Round, therefore, was what could be done to help these countries escape the vicious circle of poverty. The 1990s will continue to test the relationship between trade and development, and the outcome will profoundly affect the future of the international system.

NOTES

1. There is a close correspondence between the three strategies and the strategic options discussed in Albert Hirschman, *Exit, Voice, and Loyalty: Response to Decline in Firms, Organization, and States* (Cambridge: Harvard University Press, 1970).

2. Clair Wilcox, *A Charter for World Trade* (New York: Macmillan, 1949), 141.

3. Economic Commission for Latin America, *The Economic Development of Latin America and Its Principal Problems* (Lake Success, N.Y.: United Nations, 1950); and Economic Commission for Latin America, *Theoretical and Practical Problems of Economic Growth* (New York: United Nations, 1951).

4. Ian Little, Tibor Scitovsky, and Maurice Scott, *Industry and Trade in Some Developing Countries: A Comparative Study* (London: Oxford University Press for the OECD, 1970), xvii–xxii, 1–29. For an example of the economic argument underlying import substitution policies, see Gunnar Myrdal, *An International Economy* (New York: Harper and Row, 1969), 275–284.

5. Wilcox, *A Charter for World Trade*; and Williams Adams Brown, Jr., *The United States and the Restoration of World Trade* (Washington: Brookings Institution, 1950), 97–104, 152–158.

6. Wilcox, *A Charter for World Trade*, 140–167; and Brown, *The United States*, 178–180, 203–211, 217–222.

7. Only four less-developed countries—Ceylon (Sri Lanka), Cuba, Haiti, and India—sought and obtained permission to impose quantitative restrictions under Article 18. The limitations imposed by the contracting parties, however, destroyed much of the benefit of their use. Article 18 was revised in 1955 to provide a greater possibility for withdrawal or modification of concessions previously made and to enable the use of quantitative restrictions for balance-of-payments reasons. But once again, the many safeguards included rendered it of little use to the South. Sidney Wells, "The Developing Countries, GATT and UNCTAD," *International Affairs* 45 (January 1969), 65–67; and Karin Kock, *International Trade Policy and the GATT, 1947–1967* (Stockholm: Almqvist and Wiksell, 1969), 227–232.

8. Steffan B. Linder, "The Significance of GATT for Underdeveloped Countries," in *Proceedings of the United Nations Conference on Trade and Development,* 5 (1964), 502–532; and Robert Hudec, *Developing Countries in the GATT Legal System* (London: Trade Policy Research Center, 1987), 24.

9. Although it was not permitted under GATT, the South was able to follow protectionist policies under IMF rules, which allowed quantitative restriction for balance-of-payments reasons, or under GATT waivers, or because they were not members of GATT.

10. Little et al., *Industry and Trade in Some Developing Countries,* 1–29. For the Latin American experience with protection, see Economic Commission for Latin America, *The Process of Industrial Development in Latin America* (New York: United Nations, 1966), 21–35.

11. For the limits of import substitution, see Little et al., *Industry and Trade,* 1–29; and United Nations Conference on Trade and Development, *Toward a New Trade Policy for Development,* Report by the Secretary-General (New York: United Nations, 1964), 21–22.

12. Anne O. Krueger and Constantine Michalopoulos, "Developing-Country Trade Policies and the International Economic System," in Ernest H. Preeg, ed., *Hard Bargaining Ahead: U.S. Trade Policy and Developing Countries* (New Brunswick, N.J.: Transaction Books, 1985), 40–45.

13. World Bank, *World Development Report, 1986* (New York: Oxford University Press, 1986), ch. 4.

14. See United Nations Conference on Trade and Development, *Toward a New Trade Policy for Development.* For a summary of Prebisch's argument and the arguments of the critics of the theory of declining terms of trade, see A. S. Friedeberg, *The United Nations Conference on Trade and Development of 1964: The Theory of the Peripheral Economy at the Centre of International Political Discussions* (Rotterdam: Rotterdam University Press, 1969), 33–67.

15. David Sapsford, Prabirjit Sarkar, and Hans W. Singer, "The Prebisch-Singer Terms of Trade Controversy Revisited," *Journal of International Development* 4 (May-June 1992): 318.

16. One of the most flagrant examples of restrictive export agreements was the Long-Term Arrangement Regarding International Trade in Cotton Textiles, which was negotiated in the GATT. The North, in particular the United States, forced the less-developed exporters (as well as Japan) to agree to "voluntarily" limit their cotton textile exports with the threat that the alternative—national import quotas imposed by national legislatures—would be worse. Later, the cotton agreement was expanded to a Multi-Fiber Arrangement.

17. For the Southern view of trade barriers, see United Nations Conference on Trade and Development, *Toward a New Trade Policy for Development*; and United Nations Conference on Trade and Development, *Toward a Global Strategy of Development* (New York: United Nations, 1968). For other analyses, see Harry G. Johnson, *Economic Policies Toward Less Developed Countries* (New York: Praeger, 1967), 78–110; and Alexander J. Yeats, *Trade Barriers Facing Developing Countries* (London: Macmillan, 1979).

18. Economic Commission for Latin America, *Economic Survey 1969* (New York: United Nations, 1969), 61–62.

19. Sapsford, Sarkar, and Singer, "The Prebisch-Singer Terms."

20. *Trends in International Trade: A Report by a Panel of Experts* (Geneva: The Contracting Parties to the General Agreement on Tariffs and Trade, October 1958). The experts were Roberto de Oliveiro Campos, Gottfried Haberler, James Meade, and Jan Tinbergen.

21. Kock, *International Trade Policy,* 235–244; and Hudec, *Developing Countries,* 39–46.

22. For a history of events leading up to UNCTAD I, see Cordovez, "The Making of UNCTAD"; Friedeberg, *The United Nations Conference on Trade and Development of 1964*; and Charles L. Robertson, "The Creation of UNCTAD," in Robert W. Cox, ed., *International Organization: World Politics* (London: Macmillan, 1969), 258–274.

23. For an analysis of the Group of Seventy-Seven, see Branislav Gosovic, *UNCTAD, Conflict*

and Compromise: The Third World's Quest for an Equitable World Economic Order Through the United Nations (Leiden, the Netherlands: A. W. Sijthoff, 1972), 271–292. For a discussion of Southern unity, both in the Group of Seventy-Seven and UNCTAD, see Robert L. Rothstein, *Global Bargaining: UNCTAD and the Quest for a New International Economic Order* (Princeton: Princeton University Press, 1979), 118–122; and Jeffrey A. Hart, *The New International Economic Order* (New York: St. Martin's Press, 1983), 145–146.

24. United Nations General Assembly, *Official Records: Eighteenth Session*, Supplement No. 7 (A 5507), 24.

25. Ibid.

26. Ibid., 25.

27. *Yearbook of International Organizations 1995/96*, vol. 1, edited by the Union of International Associations (Munich, Germany: K.G. Saur Verlag, 1995), 665.

28. Gosovic, *UNCTAD, Conflict and Compromise*, 271. On UNCTAD see Joseph S. Nye, "UNCTAD: Poor Nations' Pressure Group," in Robert W. Cox and Harold K. Jacobson, *The Anatomy of Influence: Decision Making in International Organization* (New Haven: Yale University Press, 1973), 348–349.

29. For a statement of the UNCTAD doctrine, see United Nations Conference on Trade and Development, *Toward a New Trade Policy for Development* and *Toward a Global Strategy of Development*.

30. See Gosovic, *UNCTAD, Conflict and Compromise*, 279–286, on Southern cleavages and 293–301, for the Northern bloc within UNCTAD. There is also a group composed of the socialist states of Eastern Europe, known as Group D. For an analysis of bargaining within the Northern bloc over commodity issues, see Rothstein, *Global Bargaining*, 123–125.

31. On the addition of Part IV generally, see Kenneth W. Dam, *The GATT: Law and International Economic Organization* (Chicago: University of Chicago Press, 1970), 236–244; and Hudec, *Developing Countries in the GATT Legal System*, 56–60.

32. United Nations Conference on Trade and Development, *The Kennedy Round, Estimated Effects on Tariff Barriers: Report by the Secretary General of UNCTAD*, Parts I and II (New York: United Nations, 1968); and International Bank for Reconstruction and Development and International Development Agency, *Annual Report 1968* (New York: IBRD and IDA, 1968), 33–34.

33. For a history of the issue of preferences, see Gosovic, *UNCTAD, Conflict and Compromise*, 65–93; and Tracy Murray, *Trade Preferences for Developing Countries* (New York: Wiley, 1977), ch. 1. For a study of U.S. policy, see Ronald I. Meltzer, "The Politics of Policy Reversal: The American Response to the Issue of Granting Trade Preferences to the Developing Countries, 1964–1967" (Ph.D. diss., Columbia University, 1975).

34. United Nations Conference on Trade and Development, *Toward a New Trade Policy for Development*, 65–75.

35. For the details of the various preference schemes, see United Nations Conference on Trade and Development, *Operations and Effects of the Generalized System of Preferences: Fourth Review* (New York: United Nations, 1979).

36. United Nations Conference on Trade and Development, *Proceedings of the United Nations Conference on Trade and Development, Third Session* (April 13 to May 21, 1972), vol. 2, *Merchandise Trade* (New York: United Nations, 1973), 104–140; Tracy Murray, "How Helpful Is the Generalized System of Preferences to Developing Countries?" *Economic Journal* 83 (June 1973): 449–455; U.S. Code, *Congressional and Administrative News*, 93rd Cong., 2nd sess., 1974, vol. 2 (St. Paul: West Publishing, 1975), 2398-2399; and U.S. House of Representatives, Committee on Ways and Means, 98th Cong., 2nd sess., *Summary of Provisions of H.R. 3398, Trade and Tariff Act of 1984* (Washington: Government Printing Office, 1984).

37. U.S. Congress, House, Committee on Ways and Means, *Report to the Congress on the First Five Years' Operation of the U.S. Generalized System of Preferences (GSP)*, 96th Cong., 2nd sess. (Washington: Government Printing Office, 1980). See also, Pitou van Dijck, "Toward a Global System of Trade Preferences among Developing Countries," in Hans Linnemann, ed., *South-South Trade Preferences: The GSTP and Trade in Manufactures* (London: Sage, 1992), 53–60; and John Madeley, *Trade and the Poor: The Impact of International Trade on the Developing Countries* (New York: St. Martin's Press, 1993), 61–63. The GSTP is the Global System of Trade Preferences.

38. Rolf J. Langhammer and Andre Sapir, *Economic Impact of Generalized Tariff Preferences* (London: Trade Policy Research Centre, 1987).

39. For an analysis of the effects of tariff reductions on GSP, see Thomas B. Birnberg, "Trade

Reform Options: Economic Effects on Developing and Developed Countries," in William R. Cline, ed., *Policy Alternatives for a New International Economic Order: An Economic Analysis* (New York: Praeger, 1979), 234–239.

40. For histories of the commodity issue, see Gosovic, *UNCTAD, Conflict and Compromise*, 93–114; Carmine Nappi, *Commodity Market Controls: A Historical Analysis* (Lexington, Mass.: Heath, 1979); F. Gerard Adams and Jere R. Behrman, *Commodity Exports and Economic Development* (Lexington, Mass.: Lexington Books, 1982); and Alfred Maizels, *Commodities in Crisis: The Commodity Crisis of the 1980s and the Political Economy of International Commodity Policies* (Oxford: Clarendon Press, 1992).

41. Independent Commission on Development Issues, *North-South: A Program of Survival* (Cambridge, Mass.: MIT Press, 1980), 141.

42. World Bank, *World Development Report 1994* (New York: Oxford University Press, 1994), 191.

43. For background on the problems the commodity market poses for developing countries, see David L. McNicol, *Commodity Agreements and Price Stabilization* (Lexington, Mass.: Heath, 1978), 15–24; and Alton D. Law, *International Commodity Agreements* (Lexington, Mass.: Heath, 1975), ch. 1.

44. Gosovic, *UNCTAD, Conflict and Compromise*, pp. 99–101.

45. World Bank, *Commodity Trade and Price Index 1986* (New York: Oxford University Press, 1986), tables 5 and 16.

46. "Declaration and Action Programme on the Establishment of a New International Economic Order," in Guy F. Erb and Valeriana Kallab, *Beyond Dependency: The Developing World Speaks Out* (Washington: Overseas Development Council, 1975), 186. For another summary of NIEO proposals, see Branislav Gosovic and John G. Ruggie, "On the Creation of a New International Economic Order," *International Organization* 30 (spring 1976): 309–345.

47. The mechanisms for increasing and stabilizing prices were to include buffer stocks, a common fund for financing such stocks, multilateral purchase and supply agreements for particular commodities, and compensatory finance. For details on the Integrated Programme for Commodities, see United Nations Conference on Trade and Development, "An Integrated Programme for Commodities and Indexation of Prices," in Karl P. Sauvant and Hajo Hasenpflug, eds., *The New International Economic Order: Confrontation or Cooperation Between North and South?* (Boulder, Colo.: Westview, 1977), 85–102. For an analysis of the negotiations surrounding the program, see Rothstein, *Global Bargaining*, part I; and Hart, *The New International Economic Order*, 36–40.

48. See, for example, C. Fred Bergsten, "The Threat from the Third World," *Foreign Policy* 11 (summer 1973): 102–124; C. Fred Bergsten, "The New Era in World Commodity Markets," *Challenge* 17 (September-October 1974): 34–42; and Donella H. Meadows et al., *The Limits to Growth: A Report for the Club of Rome's Project on the Predicament of Mankind* (New York: Universe Books, 1972).

49. See, for example, Stephen D. Krasner, "Oil Is the Exception," *Foreign Policy* 14 (spring 1974): 68–84; and Raymond Mikesell, "More Third World Cartels Ahead?" *Challenge* 17 (November-December 1974): 24–27.

50. This first Lomé Convention was renewed and revised in 1979 and 1984. Negotiations on Lomé IV began in 1990. See Isebill V. Gruhn, "The Lomé Convention: Inching Toward Interdependence," *International Organization* 30 (spring 1976): 240–262; and John Ravenhill, "What Is to Be Done for the Third World Commodity Exporters? An Evaluation of the STABEX Scheme," *International Organization* 38 (summer 1984); 537–574. For background on Lomé II, see Carol C. Twitchett, "Lomé II Signed," *Atlantic Community Quarterly* 18 (spring 1980): 85–89; and Jonathan Fryer, "The New Lomé Convention: Marriage on the Rocks but No Separation," *International Development Review* 1 (1980): 53–54.

51. For details of this analysis, see Jahangir Amuzegar, "Requiem for the North-South Conference," *Foreign Affairs* 56 (October 1977): 136–159.

52. Johnson, *Economic Policies Toward Less Developed Countries*, 137–149.

53. In 1985, one of the most effective and long-lasting ICAs, the International Tin Agreement, collapsed when the tin buffer stock ran out of funds. For background on the various ICAs, see Nappi, *Commodity Market Controls*, 61–83. On the International Rubber Agreement, see Ursula Wassermann, "UNCTAD: International Rubber Agreement, 1979," *Journal of World Trade Law* 14 (May-June 1980): 246–248; and *UN Report* (January 20, 1984), 5–6.

54. For background on the common fund, see Nappi, *Commodity Market Controls*, ch. 6; Paul

D. Reynolds, *International Commodity Agreements and the Common Fund* (Lexington, Mass.: Heath, 1978); Jock A. Finlayson and Mark W. Zacher, *Managing International Markets: Developing Countries and the Commodity Trade Regime* (New York: Columbia University Press, 1988), ch. 2; and Gamani Corea, *Taming Commodity Markets: The Integrated Program and the Common Fund in UNCTAD* (New York: St. Martin's Press for Manchester University Press, 1992).

55. The facility originally allowed countries to access 25 percent of the quota. It was later increased to 83 percent of the quota for shortfalls in export earnings or for an increase in the price of cereal imports with a combined access limit of 105 percent. In 1988, a contingency mechanism was added to provide additional funding in response to adverse external developments. Borrowers must repay the fund within a five-year period, when, it is expected, the cyclical decline of prices will have been reversed. See International Monetary Fund, *Annual Report 1994* (Washington: IMF, 1994), and previous years.

56. John Ravenhill, *Collective Clientelism: The Lomé Convention and North-South Relations* (New York: Columbia University Press, 1985).

57. For background on the Southern countries and the Tokyo Round, see Bela Belassa, "The Developing Countries and the Tokyo Round," *Journal of World Trade Law* 14 (March-April 1980): 93–118; Thomas R. Graham, "Revolution in Trade Politics," *Foreign Policy* 36 (fall 1979): 49–63; Stephen D. Krasner, "The Tokyo Round: Particularistic Interests and Prospects for Stability in the Global Trading System," *International Studies Quarterly* 23 (December 1979): 491–531; and Hudec, *Developing Countries in the GATT Legal System*, 71–102.

58. General Agreement on Tariffs and Trade, *The Tokyo Round: Report by the Director-General of GATT* (Geneva: GATT, 1979); and Hudec, *Developing Countries in the GATT Legal System*, 85.

59. On the graduation issue, see Isaiah Frank, "The Graduation Issue for the Less Developed Countries," *Journal of World Trade Law* 13 (July-August 1979): 289–302.

60. GATT, *The Tokyo Round*, 166–177.

61. Raymond F. Mikesell, "The Changing Demand for Industrial Raw Materials," in John W. Sewell, Stuart K. Tucker, and contributors, *Growth, Exports, and Jobs in a Changing World Economy: Agenda 1988* (New Brunswick, N.J.: Transaction Books, 1988), 139–166.

62. International Monetary Fund, *World Economic Outlook 1988* (Washington: International Monetary Fund, 1988), 141; and United Nations, *World Economic and Social Survey 1994* (New York: United Nations, 1974), 72–73.

63. World Bank, *World Development Report 1994* (Washington: World Bank, 1994), 186–187.

64. *World Development Report 1988*, 242–243.

65. Mikesell, "The Changing Demand for Industrial Raw Materials," 140, 155; and Finlayson and Zacher. *Managing International Markets*, 4–5.

66. *World Development Report 1994*, 191.

67. *World Development Report 1993*, 14.

68. General Agreement on Trade and Tariffs, *International Trade 1987–1988* (Geneva: GATT, 1988), table AC3.

69. GATT, *International Trade*, various issues.

70. See Organization for Economic Cooperation and Development, *The Newly Industrializing Countries: Challenge and Opportunity for OECD Countries* (Paris: OECD, 1988); Lawrence B. Krause, *Introduction to Foreign Trade and Investment: Economic Growth in the Newly Industrializing Asian Countries* (Madison: University of Wisconsin Press, 1985), 22; Neil McMullen and Louis Turner, with Colin L. Bradford, *The Newly Industrializing Countries: Trade and Adjustment* (London: Allen and Unwin, 1982); and David Yoffie, *Power and Protectionism: Strategies of the Newly Industrializing Countries* (New York: Columbia University Press, 1983).

71. The key works are cited in Chapter 5, note 30.

72. IMF, *World Economic Outlook 1988*, 80; and IMF, *Direction of Trade Statistics 1994*, 2, 4.

73. Albert Fishlow, "Making Liberal Trade Policies Work in the 1980s," in Roger Hansen, ed., *U.S. Foreign Policy and the Third World, Agenda 1982* (New York: Praeger, 1982), 56–57.

74. OECD, *The Newly Industrializing Countries*, 19; and World Bank, *World Development Report 1995*, 193.

75. Other factors have been crucial to the East Asian NICs' success. The four tigers all have a highly educated and skilled workforce that is highly disciplined and motivated. The four also have high savings rates, which has provided the credit for investment and enabled them to avoid heavy external borrowing. To the extent that they relied on foreign borrowing, it was usually channeled into

export sectors that provided the foreign exchange necessary to service the debt. In addition, during the early stages of their industrialization, authoritarian regimes in South Korea, Singapore, and Taiwan allowed the political elites greater freedom to determine economic policies, resulting in greater continuity of economic policies. These countries had either undergone land reform or never had a landed class, and so they did not have political pressure from an entrenched privileged class. In addition, the political legitimacy of these governments rested heavily on their economic success. Economic growth has led to a decrease in absolute poverty, a more equitable income distribution, and an improvement in living conditions that has eased political pressures and promoted important democratization in both South Korea and Taiwan. These governments also felt insecure surrounded by Communist countries and believed that economic strength would increase their independence and security. In addition, under authoritarian governments, trade unions had limited bargaining authority and minimum wages were discouraged, which kept wages from increasing significantly.

76. GATT, *International Trade 1987–1988*, tables A14-A17.

77. Martin Wolf, "Managed Trade in Practice: Implications of the Textile Arrangements," in William R. Cline, ed., *Trade Policy in the 1980s* (Washington: Institute for International Economics, 1983), 455–482.

78. World Bank, *World Development Report 1987* (New York: Oxford University Press, 1987), 142.

79. Wolf, "Managed Trade in Practice," 468–469.

80. United Nations, *World Economic Survey 1988* (New York: United Nations, 1988), 34.

81. GATT, *International Trade 1987–1988*, table AA10; and *International Trade 1990–1991*, table A2.

82. *Economic Report of the President 1988* (Washington: Government Printing Office, 1988), 367; and IMF, *Direction of Trade Statistics 1994*, 420.

83. World Bank, *World Development Report 1988*, 197.

84. U.S. Department of Commerce, *Highlights of U.S. Export and Import Trade* (Washington: Government Printing Office, various issues).

85. GATT, *International Trade 1987–1988*, table AA-7.

86. United Nations Conference on Trade and Development, *The Buenos Aires Platform: Final Document of the Fifth Ministerial Meeting of the Group of 77* (March 28–April 9, 1983) (New York: United Nations, 1983).

87. United Nations Conference on Trade and Development, *Report of the United Nations Conference on Trade and Development on its Sixth Session* (June 6–July 2, 1983) (New York: United Nations, 1983).

88. See Jagdish N. Bhagwati and John Gerard Ruggie, eds., *Power, Passions, and Purpose: Prospects for North-South Negotiations* (Cambridge: MIT Press, 1984).

89. International Monetary Fund, *International Financial Statistics, Supplement on Trade Statistics, No. 15* (Washington: IMF, 1988): 50–51; and World Bank, *World Data '95 CD-ROM* (Washington: World Bank, 1995).

90. The shift was incremental rather than dramatic, however, since the domestic political influence of the export sector—although growing throughout the decade—remained minimal in most countries. As one analyst put it, the political balance between trade-liberalizing and trade-protectionist forces is the critical "knife's edge" on which national trade policy turns.

91. UNCTAD Database on Trade Control Measures.

92. Carlos Luiz Marone and Carlos Alberto Primo Braga, "Brazil and the Uruguay Round" (paper presented at the Conference on the Multilateral Trade Negotiations and Developing Countries, Washington, September 15–18, 1988).

93. See also International Monetary Fund, *The Uruguay Round: Economic Implications* (Washington: IMF, July 15, 1994).

94. IMF, *The Uruguay Round*, 6, 9.

95. Ibid., 10.

96. ACP nations are concerned however, that their benefits have been diluted by privileges the EC has given to other developing countries on certain items, such as on tropical products, during the Uruguay Round negotiations. They also fear they will lose other benefits as the EC moves toward a unified market and standardizes the individual preferential arrangements each country has with the former colonies.

97. In 1994, Mexico joined the OECD and Korea applied for membership.

8

Multinational Corporations in the Third World

The issue of managing multinational corporations was of great concern in the developing countries until the debt crisis of the 1980s.[1] Since that time, the developing countries have come to accept the growing presence of MNCs as a necessary evil, at worst, and as a contribution to the development process, at best. Multinational corporations may have greater power in the South than in the North, and there is some evidence that the costs of hosting multinationals have been greater in the developing world than in the industrialized world.

A number of developing countries have sought to implement public policies that can shift the perceived imbalance of power between host government and foreign corporations and to regulate multinational corporations in order to capture more of the benefits of foreign direct investment. Like the countries of the North that have tried to do this, however, they have found it increasingly difficult to influence the activities of MNCs as the world economy becomes more globalized. In particular, multinational corporations control access to certain advanced technologies that are necessary for global competitiveness. The developing countries may be more technologically dependent on MNCs than the industrialized countries because they have fewer resources to devote to creating indigenous alternatives.

Power: The Local Economy

The importance of foreign direct investment in the South varies from country to country. In some states, it is relatively insignificant, whereas in others it plays a key role. Multinational corporations have tended to concentrate their investments in a few developing countries. Ten countries alone accounted for 72.3 percent of all private foreign investment flows to the South between 1981 and 1992.[2] In these countries, in particular, foreign investment possesses considerable power.

FDI inflows into the Third World have tended to go disproportionately to Asia and Latin America (see Figure 8-1). The inflows into Asia accelerated in the late 1980s and early 1990s. They went primarily to Malaysia, Singapore, and China (see Figure 8-2). In Latin America, the primary destinations for FDI inflows were Argentina, Brazil, and Mexico, the three largest economies in the region (see Figure 8-3). FDI flows to two Asian NICs, Taiwan and South Korea,

Figure 8-1   Inflows of FDI by LDC Region, 1975–1992, in Current Dollars

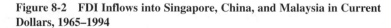

SOURCE: Sheila Page, *How Developing Countries Trade* (New York: Routledge, 1994), 104.

Figure 8-2   FDI Inflows into Singapore, China, and Malaysia in Current Dollars, 1965–1994

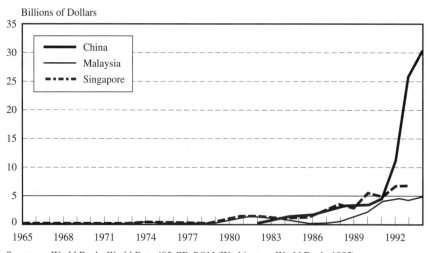

SOURCE: World Bank, *World Data '95 CD-ROM* (Washington: World Bank, 1995).

Figure 8-3   FDI Inflows into Argentina, Brazil, and Mexico in Current Dollars, 1965–1994

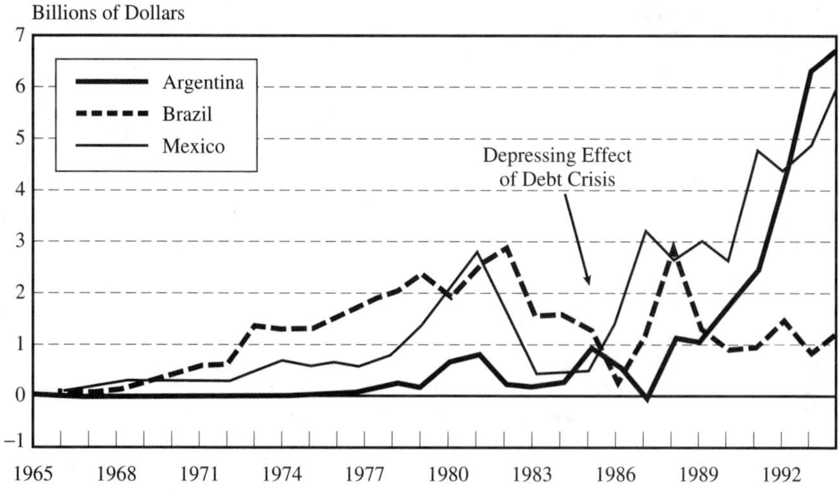

Billions of Dollars

SOURCE: World Bank, *World Data '95 CD-ROM* (Washington: World Bank, 1995).

have been historically quite low, since both countries have strongly favored domestically owned enterprises over MNCs in their development policies, but have increased rapidly in recent years (see Figure 8-4).

The power of multinational corporations grows out of their structural position within the relatively small and underdeveloped economies of many Southern states.[3] Because agricultural and service sectors still account for much of the gross national product of the developing countries, the multinational corporations may play a relatively small part in their total GNP. But foreign investment often accounts for a large share of critical sectors.

Historically, Northern firms controlled the South's extractive sector, long the key to development. Multinationals, for example, controlled oil in the Middle East, copper in Chile and Zambia, and bauxite in Jamaica and Guyana. In many cases, even when the ownership and control of production was transferred from multinational corporations to state-owned companies, the developing countries often remained dependent on the multinationals for processing, shipping, marketing, and distributing their raw materials. For example, in 1980, despite widespread nationalization of the petroleum industry in the developing countries, 43 percent of all crude oil produced outside North America and the socialist countries was either produced or purchased by the seven major international oil companies, and 24 percent was produced or purchased by smaller international oil companies or trading companies.[4] In 1982, 46 percent of the world's bauxite capacity, 50 percent of its alumina capacity, and 45 percent of its aluminum capacity were owned by six large multinational corporations.[5]

A second and newer sector of Northern control is manufacturing. Since

**Figure 8-4   FDI Inflows into Korea and Taiwan in
Current Dollars, 1965–1994**

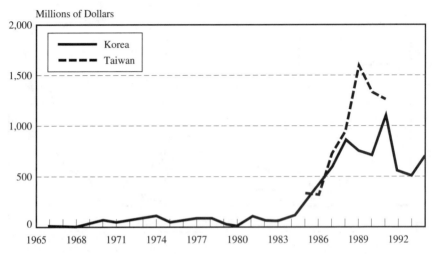

SOURCE: World Bank, *World Data '95 CD-ROM* (Washington: World Bank, 1995); and United
Nations Conference on Trade and Development, *World Investment Report* (New York: United
Nations, 1994), 14.

World War II, the developing countries have sought to expand their industrial sector as a primary means of development and have offered incentives for investment
in manufacturing. The multinational corporations have often taken the lead in
these new growth sectors. Foreign investment is growing most rapidly in manufacturing and is thus moving to dominate certain sectors of the new Southern
industry. In 1988, for example, foreign affiliates control 32 percent of production,
32 percent of exports, and 23 percent of the employment of Brazil's manufacturing sector. In Singapore, foreign affiliates control 63 percent of production, 90
percent of exports, and 55 percent of employment in manufacturing.[6]

Foreign firms also represent a significant percentage of the largest and most
powerful firms in Southern economies. Foreign investment in the Third World
generally is found in industries dominated by a small number of large firms. For
example, U.S. foreign investment is found in such highly concentrated industries
as petroleum, chemicals, transportation, insurance, food products, electronics,
and machinery.[7] The large firms that dominate such industries have more power
to control supply and price than do firms in more competitive industries. Thus the
oligopolistic structure of foreign investment means that significant economic
power is concentrated in the hands of a few large foreign firms.[8]

Power: Local Government

Such a situation of economic dominance, however, need not mean the
removal of decision making from national control. In principle, Southern governments could assert the control necessary to retain decision making at home. Host

state laws could be passed to regulate multinational corporations, and host governments could impose restrictions on multinational corporations when investment agreements are negotiated. To impose such controls, Southern governments could use the one important bargaining advantage they possess: control over access to their territories.[9] Control over access to resources that the multinational wants—local raw materials, labor, and markets—could be used by developing countries to impose controls on foreign investors.

In practice, however, the bargaining advantage of control over access is offset by the bargaining tools of the multinational corporation. The foreign investor often controls resources such as capital, technology, and access to foreign markets that the developing countries need for development. The South's desire for the benefits of foreign direct investment—for example, the ability to exploit a valuable raw material deposit or the possibility of expanding industrialization through new factories—poses a dilemma to policymakers in those countries. On the one hand, officials want to regulate the multinationals so as to maximize national benefits and minimize national costs. But on the other hand, they do not want to make regulation so restrictive that it will deter potential investors.

Related to the desire to regulate and the fear of overregulating is the problem of uncertainty.[10] Before a foreign investment is actually made, potential investors are uncertain about the operation's eventual success and final cost. For example, a corporation proposing to explore for and develop oil in a developing country cannot be certain of the ultimate success of the project until it has prospected and built up an extracting capability—that is, until it has determined whether oil will be discovered and at what price. Similarly, a corporation proposing to manufacture sewing machines for a local foreign market may not be able to determine the potential of that market and the final costs of production. Another risk faced by the corporation is the political instability in Third World host states and the uncertainty of the effect of political change and possible turmoil on investment. For foreign investors, such uncertainties serve to reduce the attractiveness of the local factors of production and the local market and thus weaken the hand of the host country (see the discussion of the obsolescing bargain in Chapter 4).

Another factor weakening the bargaining power of the developing countries is the absence of competition for investment opportunities. The availability of alternative sources of raw materials and cheap labor elsewhere can diminish the bargaining ability of any one Southern state. At times, the oligopolistic nature of multinational corporations—the fact that few companies dominate the industry and that those companies may collaborate with one another to decrease competition—can also weaken the hand of the developing countries.[11]

Furthermore, even if a country resolves the dilemma in favor of regulation, there remain constraints on the country's ability to carry out regulatory policies. The ability of Southern governments to control multinational corporations is shaped by the availability of the skilled persons necessary to draft and enforce laws and to negotiate agreements to regulate foreign investment. Without skilled lawyers, financial experts, and specialists in the particular businesses that the state seeks to regulate, Third World governments are no match for the multinational corporation.

Another governmental problem has been the ability of multinationals to intervene in the host state's domestic political process to advance their corporate interests. Multinational corporations are able to use their resources in legal or even illegal political activities in host countries. Tactics such as public relations activities, campaign contributions, bribery, and economic boycotts are available to the corporation. In their ability to intervene in domestic politics, multinational corporations are, in one sense, no different from national corporations; the problem they pose is not in the area of foreign investment but in their ability as private institutions to influence the government.

There are, however, several characteristics of multinational corporations that distinguish them from national corporations and that make their participation in host politics a problem for the Southern states. Because multinational corporations are foreign-owned, they are not considered legitimate participants in the national political process. Their interests may not necessarily be those of the host state; their policies may, in varying degrees, reflect their own corporate interests or the interests of their home state. For these reasons, numerous countries have barred foreign firms from political activities. Political participation by multinational firms carries the connotation and, at times, the reality of a challenge to national sovereignty. In addition, multinational corporations bring many resources to their political activities. Their financial resources and international structure can be powerful political tools.

Multinational corporations also can derive great power from their relationship with the "home" government, the government of the country in which their parent firm has its headquarters. Investment in Southern states tends to be highly concentrated according to the home country. United States investment, for example, is predominant in Latin America, whereas French investment is dominant in the former French colonies in sub-Saharan Africa.[12] In the home country, these giant corporations often play a powerful political role. The ability of a multinational to pressure its home government to take certain actions and follow specific foreign policies to influence host governments adds to the imbalance between southern governments and multinational corporations.[13]

In sum, because of their powerful position within the Third World's economies and vis-à-vis the Third World's governments, multinational corporations can affect economic efficiency and welfare and influence politics in Southern host countries. The crucial question then, is, how have these corporations used their power?

Efficiency, Growth, and Welfare

Proponents argue that foreign investment has a positive effect on Southern economic development.[14] Such investment fills resource gaps in developing countries and improves the quality of factors of production. One of the most important contributions is capital. Multinational corporations bring otherwise unavailable financial resources to the South through the firm's own capital and its access to international capital markets. Figures indicate that an important share of the flow of capital to developing countries comes from foreign investment. In the 1960s and 1970s, foreign direct investment accounted for approximately 15 percent of total flows, averaging $7 billion a year. These flows declined relatively in the early 1980s due partly to the inflow of other forms of foreign investment (see Chapter 6). Nonetheless, in 1992, foreign direct investment flows to developing countries reached approximately $23.7 billion, which represented 14.9 percent of the total flows to developing countries.[15]

Fourth, new foreign investments may help to increase the level of overall domestic investment. A recent cross-national study of 69 developing countries found that foreign investment increases of a dollar resulted in increases in total investment of between $1.50 and $2.30.[16]

Multinational corporations also contribute crucial foreign exchange earnings to the developing world through their trade effect. First, the marketing skills and knowledge of foreign markets of the multinational corporations and their competitive products, it is argued, generate exports and thus increase the foreign exchange earnings of the host countries. Foreign affiliates of multinational corporations have contributed to the growing role of developing countries in world trade (see Chapter 7). For example, foreign affiliates of U.S. firms in developing countries more than doubled their share of world trade between 1966 and 1983. In Latin America, U.S. affiliates outperformed domestic industries as exporters.[17] Furthermore, the manufacture for the local market of products that otherwise would have been imported also saves precious foreign exchange.

A second crucial resource gap filled by the multinational, according to proponents of foreign investment, is technology. The desire to obtain modern technology is perhaps the most important attraction of foreign investment for developing countries. Multinational corporations allow Southern states to profit from the sophisticated research and development carried out by the multinational and to make available technology that would otherwise be out of the reach of developing countries. Foreign firms train local staff, stimulate local technological activities, and transfer technology throughout the local economy.[18] Thus technology improves the efficiency of production and encourages development.

Third, say proponents, foreign investment improves the quality of labor in the South. It provides needed managerial skills that improve production, and it creates jobs and trains workers. Multinationals are depending less on expatriate labor and providing more opportunities for local professionals to manage and operate their facilities. The rapidly growing service sector, in particular, promotes the development of high-level skills in its local workforce.

Supporters contend, finally, that multinational corporations have a positive impact on welfare. The creation of jobs, the provision of new and better products, and programs to improve health, housing, and education for employees and local communities, it is thought, improve the standard of living in the Third World.

This positive view of the role of multinational corporations in growth, effi-ciency, and welfare has been challenged by critics of the multinationals. In the 1970s, a new body of critical analysis of multinational corporations emerged. It argued that, at best, those policies adopted because they are best for the multina-tional are not necessarily best for the subsidiary or the host state and that, at worst, the multinational exploits developing countries and perpetuates depen-dence.[19]

Multinational corporations, explain these critics, do not bring in as much foreign capital as their proponents suggest. The financing of foreign investment is done largely with host-country, not foreign, capital.[20] For example, between 1958 and 1968, U.S. manufacturing subsidiaries in Latin America obtained 80 percent of all their financing locally, through either borrowing or subsidiary earn-ings.[21] Furthermore, according to the critics, multinational corporations, because of their strength, often have preferred access to local capital sources and are able to compete successfully with and thus stifle local entrepreneurs. Critics contend that such local financing is often used to acquire existing nationally owned firms. One study of the Mexican economy revealed that 43 percent of U.S. multination-al corporations entered Mexico by acquiring existing firms and that 81 percent of these firms were formerly owned by Mexicans.[22] And in Brazil, 33 percent of U.S. multinational corporations began operations in Brazil by acquiring local firms. In the late 1960s and early 1970s, acquisitions accounted for 50 percent of the new multinational affiliates in Brazil, 63 percent of which were formerly owned by Brazilians.[23]

Some critics believe that foreign investment in developing countries actual-ly leads to an outflow of capital. Capital flows from South to North through prof-its, debt service, royalties and fees, and manipulation of import and export prices. Such reverse flows are, in themselves, not unusual or improper. Indeed, the rea-son for investment is to make money for the firm. What certain critics argue, how-ever, is that such return flows are unjustifiably high. They point to the fact that, in the seventies, profits in developing countries were substantially higher than profits in developed market economies. The average return on book value of U.S. foreign direct investment in the developed market economies between 1975 and 1978 was 12.1 percent, whereas the average return in developing countries was 25.8 percent.[24]

Furthermore, contend the critics, profits represent only a small part of the effective return to the parent. A large part of the real return comes from the licens-ing fees and royalties paid by the subsidiary to the parent for the use of technol-ogy controlled by the parent. In 1972, the payment by foreign affiliates for the use of technology accounted for 30 percent of total dividend income and 60 percent of all income from manufacturing received by U.S. parent corporations.[25] Critics do not argue that subsidiaries should not pay the parent for research and devel-opment costs incurred by the parent that eventually benefit the subsidiary. Rather, the critics contend that the subsidiaries in developing countries pay an unjustifi-ably high price for technology and bear an unjustifiably high share of the research and development costs. The monopoly control of technology by the multinational corporation enables the parent to exact a monopoly rent from its subsidiaries.[26] And the parent chooses to use that power and to charge inordinately high fees and royalties to disguise high profits and avoid local taxes on those profits, according to the critics.

Yet another mechanism of capital outflow—of disguising profits and evading taxes—identified by critics is trade. Much of the trade by multinational subsidiaries in developing countries is intracompany trade. Often, subsidiaries located in developing countries are obliged by agreements with the parent to purchase supplies from and to make sales to the parent.[27] The parent thus is able to manipulate the price of such intracompany imports and exports—the transfer price—to benefit the firm (see the discussion of this topic in Chapter 4). Critics of multinational corporations argue that firms have used transfer prices to underprice exports and overprice imports, thereby invisibly shifting profits from the South to the North.[28] In one study of an extreme case, it was argued that the overpricing of pharmaceutical imports into Colombia amounted to $3 billion.[29]

The negative effects of such decapitalization would be limited if, in the process of removing capital, the multinational corporations made a significant contribution to local development. Critics contend that the contribution of multinational corporations is limited or negative. Technology, they feel, is not the great boon for the South that the proponents of multinational corporations suggest. The high cost of technology has already been mentioned. Another criticism is that the importation of technology stunts the development of local technological capabilities.[30] Yet another problem is the appropriateness of technology. Although some foreign investment has entered the South to take advantage of abundant Southern labor and thus has contributed to employment, some multinational corporations bring advanced, capital-intensive technology developed in and for developed countries that does not contribute to solving the problem of unemployment in developing states.[31] Energy-intensive technology imported from the North may contribute to balance of payments problems for Third World energy-importing countries and may accentuate existing problems of pollution and resource depletion.

Critics also argue that multinational corporations do not benefit Southern labor. They make only a small contribution to employment, and they discourage local entrepreneurs by competing successfully with them in local capital markets by acquiring existing firms, by using expatriate managers instead of training local citizens, and by hiring away local skilled workers.[32] Finally, the trade benefits from the multinational corporations, according to the critics, are limited by restrictive business practices. Written agreements between parent and subsidiary may include clauses confining exports and requiring subsidiaries to produce only for the local market. Management policy, similarly, may hold down subsidiary production and marketing.[33]

In sum, say the critics, multinational corporations create a distorted and undesirable form of growth. They often create highly developed enclaves that do not contribute to the expansion of the larger economy. These enclaves use capital-intensive and energy-intensive technology that employs few local citizens; acquire supplies from abroad, not locally; use transfer prices and technology agreements to avoid taxes; and send earnings back home. In welfare terms, the benefits of the enclave accrue to the home country and to a small part of the host population allied with the corporation.

Not only does the enclave not contribute to local development, say the critics, but it often hinders it.[34] In other words, the MNC-dependent economy develops at the expense of the local economy and thus of local welfare. It absorbs local capital, removes capital from the country, destroys local entrepreneurs, and creates inappropriate consumer demands that turn production away from economically and socially desirable patterns.

Empirical studies examining the economic impact of multinational corporations on the developing countries appear to indicate that while inflows of FDI have a generally positive effect on economic growth, the extent of the impact depends on other variables. The impact of foreign investment varies from country to country, from sector to sector, from firm to firm, and from project to project. One important country-level variable that influences the aggregate impact of FDI flows is the level of human capital development in the host country. FDI flows have a more strongly positive effect on economic growth in countries that have made significant investments in education and worker training than in countries that have not done this.[35] Another important finding is that MNCs do not tend to create "pollution havens" in the Third World but that they do tend to use capital-intensive technologies and to raise the wages of local workers. Finally, there is empirical evidence to suggest that genuine technology transfer is quite limited, except in the case where the MNC has been able to maintain at least majority control over its subsidiaries.[36] This last finding suggests that it is not wise for the governments of developing countries to require MNCs to give up majority control of their subsidiaries to domestic joint venture partners if they want to receive the benefits of technology transfer.

The principal effect of the criticism of multinationals that began in the 1970s was to alter, for a time, the political reality of foreign investment in the developing countries. After the 1970s, most Third World governments no longer assumed that foreign investment would automatically promote development. As a result, they tried to regulate that investment to maximize the rewards and minimize the costs to the host economy.[37] By the 1980s, however, they began to question their own efforts in this regard, partly because of pressures from the industrialized countries to liberalize their economic systems but also because of increasing evidence that some of their regulatory efforts had failed to have the desired results. This was part of a larger process of questioning earlier beliefs about the desirability of pursuing economic development through import substitution policies.

National Political Process

The evidence suggests that multinational corporations have at times intervened in political processes in their host states in the Third World. While most foreign investors do not become actively involved in host country politics, some multinational corporations have taken both legal and illegal actions within host states to favor friendly governments and oppose unfriendly governments, to obtain favorable treatment for the corporation, and to block efforts to restrict corporate activity. They have engaged in such legal activities as contributing to political parties, lobbying with local elites, and carrying out public relations campaigns.[38] They have also engaged in illegal activities (illegal contributions to political parties),[39] bribes to local officials,[40] and refusals to comply with host laws and regulations.[41] They have also used such extralegal methods as international boycotts to pressure an unfriendly government.[42]

Multinational corporations have also used their power in the politics of the home state to obtain foreign policies favorable to corporate interests. They have helped shape the liberal world vision that the U.S. government has sought to implement since World War II and that has favored foreign direct investment. They have worked for specific legislation, such as the Hickenlooper amendment, which empowered the U.S. government to cut off aid to any country nationalizing U.S. investments without compensation; the Gonzalez amendment, which required the United States to vote against any multilateral bank loan to a nationalizing country; the Overseas Private Investment Corporation, which insured foreign investment in many Southern countries; and the trade legislation which withdrew Generalized System of Preferences (GSP) tariff benefits from any country that expropriated U.S. companies without compensation.[43] At times, corporations have gone beyond influencing legislation to seek governmental support for their opposition to unfavorable regimes in specific host countries.[44]

Not only have corporations sought to shape home government policy, but they have also served as tools of that policy. For example, in 1988 the United States used multinationals to put pressure on the Panamanian government of General Manuel Noriega by forbidding subsidiaries and branches of U.S. companies to issue any direct or indirect payments to the Noriega government. In the 1980s, it encouraged foreign investment to move to Jamaica following the change from a restrictive to a more open regime under Prime Minister Edward Seaga. However, multinational corporations do not necessarily advance the foreign policy of their home government. For example, foreign oil companies operating in Angola actively opposed U.S. sanctions on the Angolan government because the sanctions conflicted with their own interests.

One of the most notorious examples of interference in host country politics that served as a catalyst for host country policies to restrict multinational corporations was the intervention of the International Telephone & Telegraph Company in Chile in the early 1970s.[45] From 1970 to 1972, ITT actively sought, first, to prevent the election of Salvador Allende as the president of Chile and, once Allende was elected, to engineer his overthrow. In the process, ITT not only resorted on its own to a variety of illegal or extralegal activities but also tried to involve the U.S. government in both open and clandestine activities against Allende and was solicited by the U.S. government to serve as an agent of its policy.

The main reason for ITT's political intervention was concern that Chiltelco, ITT's profitable telephone company, would be nationalized without compensation if the Marxist candidate, Allende, won the 1970 Chilean election for president. As a result, ITT gave funds to conservative Chilean newspapers opposing Allende. It also tried unsuccessfully to get help from the U.S. Central Intelligence Agency in channeling funds to the conservative candidate opposing Allende. When Allende was elected, ITT conferred with the CIA on ways to destabilize his government. At one point, the company drafted an eighteen-point program of economic and political disruption to be carried out by the U.S. government and other multinational corporations. Included in the program were restricting public and private credit, boycotting Chilean copper, delaying fuel delivery and shipments of small arms and ammunition, and instituting an anti-Allende propaganda campaign and CIA activity. In March 1972, newspaper reports of ITT's attempts to overthrow Allende led to a Senate inquiry that revealed the extent of the company's intervention.[46] On the next day, the Allende government broke off negotiations with ITT regarding compensation for Chiltelco.

The intervention of ITT into Chilean politics is not an example of the typical behavior of multinational corporations in Southern states; most multinational corporations do not pursue such ruthless politics of intervention. But there have been enough examples of intervention to suggest that multinational corporations are in a position to exercise political influence and may use that position to favor what the companies perceive corporate interest to be. In that sense, multinational corporations have posed real or perceived threats to the autonomy of Southern political processes.

Management of Foreign Investment by Less-Developed Countries

In the 1950s and 1960s, most developing country governments encouraged foreign investment and placed few restrictions on the operation of foreign investors in their states. By and large, developing countries accepted the prevailing international liberal regime based on national treatment; prompt, adequate, and effective compensation in the event of expropriation; and the right of foreign investors to appeal to their home country governments for assistance. Latin America was the exception. Since the turn of the century, Latin American countries have adhered to the **Calvo Doctrine,** which asserts the right of host nations to nationalize foreign investments and make their own determination of what constitutes fair compensation; thus they reject the right of foreign investors to appeal to their home governments for help. Even in periods when foreign direct investment has been actively encouraged in Latin America, the Calvo Doctrine has been maintained.[47] In the 1970s, many Southern governments adopted the Latin American position, altering their open-door policies.

A shift in public attitudes toward foreign investment was an important factor behind this change. As nationalist sentiment developed in the late 1950s and 1960s, the multinational corporation came to be seen as a threat to economic and political independence.[48] Furthermore, the development process increased demands for improved economic welfare, housing, transportation, and jobs.[49] To satisfy these new pressures and to preserve their own political power, some Southern elites turned against the multinational corporation.[50] Opposition to multinational corporations became a politically useful and powerful platform for those elites.

In the 1970s, exposés of political intervention by multinational corporations in Southern politics outraged Southern publics and led to a new spurt of anti-multinational opinion. The ITT scandal played an important catalytic role in public mobilization against multinational corporations. The initial revelations led to a U.S. Senate inquiry into multinationals in general, which revealed other instances of their intervention in politics.[51] Publicity regarding ITT and Chile also led to a unified Southern outcry against multinational corporations and to a United Nations investigation of them.[52]

The new critical economic analysis that pointed out the detrimental effects of foreign investment also contributed to changing public attitudes toward multinational corporations. As one critic of multinational corporations observed:

> Serious and competent economists can make a strong case against a permissive attitude toward private foreign investment and thus bring respectability even to attitudes originally based upon an unthinking, emotional reaction.[53]

A second factor behind the new policies toward multinational corporations was a shift in power from the multinational to the host government. One reason for the change in the power relationship was what one analyst called the "learning curve."[54] Over the years, host governments developed significant expertise in monitoring and regulating foreign investment. They trained cadres in the legal, financial, and business skills necessary to regulate foreign subsidiaries. This movement up the learning curve made it possible for host governments to develop the laws and bureaucratic structures for managing multinational corporations.[55]

By the same token, the MNCs themselves began to learn how to deal with Third World hosts in order to counter the loss of initial bargaining advantages. They created joint ventures with local entrepreneurs, started new projects that appealed to local preferences, financed new investments with local capital, learned more about the local political system, and so forth, in order to counter the maneuvers of local nationalist forces. These countermeasures, while useful in many cases, were often insufficient to stop or slow down the growth of the political power of nationalist coalitions.

Decreasing uncertainty also contributed to the shift in power. Analysts have pointed out that a distinction must be made between the bargaining position of a host country vis-à-vis a potential investor and its bargaining position vis-à-vis an investor who has already made a significant and successful investment in its country.[56] When a country is seeking investment, it is in a weak bargaining position. Foreign investors are uncertain about the success of the proposed operation and its final cost. To overcome these uncertainties and to attract investment, host countries must follow permissive policies regarding investment. But once a foreign investment is made and is successful, the bargaining relationship changes, and the power of the host country increases. The host country now has jurisdiction over a valuable multinational asset. As uncertainty decreases, the host government comes to regret and resent earlier permissive policies and agreements. The operation's success leads the host government to seek revision of agreements with foreign investors, whereas the company's financial commitment and interest weaken its bargaining position and ability to resist new terms for operation.

A third factor contributing to the power shift was the increasing competition for investment opportunities in the South. The greater numbers of countries with major multinational corporations meant that Southern states had more alternatives in choosing foreign investors. These alternatives are important at the level of individual investments, allowing greater competition and thus better terms for the host countries. They are also important in that they allow the Southern states to diversify investment away from one traditionally dominant Northern home state. Thus, for example, Japanese multinationals have emerged as an alternative to U.S. firms in Latin America, and U.S. companies have in turn emerged as an alternative to French firms in Africa.[57]

This shift in power from foreign investor to host government has clearly been the case in raw materials, such as copper and oil, where host-government policy has evolved from permissive policies to attract investment, to more strict application of local laws in such areas as taxation and labor policy once the foreign investment has been successful, and to eventual ownership of equity or direct involvement in business decision making on such matters as price or supply.[58] It is less clear whether the shift in power applies to manufacturing. Some analysts argue that it is more difficult for developing countries to control global manufacturing firms with worldwide production and worldwide marketing, because local subsidiaries remain dependent on the parent for supplies, capital, technology, and markets.[59]

In the 1970s, these various forces of change led to new Southern attempts to regulate multinational corporations. As discussed, one such abortive effort was launched in the United Nations (see Chapter 4). Part of the Southern plan for the New International Economic Order (NIEO) was an attempt to bring multinational corporations under international control. In 1974, the United Nations made two major statements on the NIEO: the Declaration of the Establishment of the New International Economic Order and the Charter of Economic Rights and Duties of States. Both documents asserted the full sovereignty of each nation over its natural resources and all economic activities including the right of nationalization. The Declaration of the Establishment of the NIEO made no reference to any compensation, and the Charter simply said that any compensation should be "appropriate." Although the United Nations did establish a Center on Transnational Corporations, the attempt to draw up an international code of conduct proved impossible. The real effort to control multinational corporations came at the national level and, in the case of the Andean Common Market (ANCOM, whose original members were Bolivia, Chile, Colombia, Ecuador, Peru, and Venezuela at the regional level).[60]

The most publicized Southern attempts to manage multinational corporations have been nationalizations of local subsidiaries. Peru's government, for example, nationalized the International Petroleum Corporation, various banks, and the fishmeal and fish oil industry.[61] Chile and Zambia have taken over their copper industries,[62] and many oil-producing states have nationalized their oil industries.[63] Expropriation, although highly visible, is not the main method of Southern management or the prevailing trend of Southern attempts at control. In fact, after reaching a peak in 1975, nationalization declined dramatically (see Figure 8-5).[64]

More important than well-publicized nationalizations were new laws, regulations, and bureaucratic structures designed to strengthen governmental control and to increase the host country's share of the economic rewards from foreign investment.[65] Attempts to manage the multinational corporation through such laws and policies varied from country to country and within countries from industry to industry. Nevertheless, certain trends emerged.

Governments often put strict limits on the entry of new investment. Many countries enacted investment laws limiting the sectors in which foreign investment is permitted. Banking, communications, transportation, and public utilities are commonly reserved for national ownership. Restrictions were also placed on the amount of equity that foreigners may hold in local companies. For example,

Figure 8-5   Expropriation Acts by Year

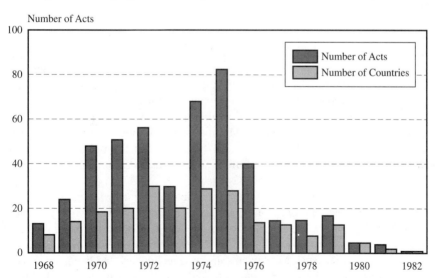

SOURCE: *UNCTC Reporter,* No. 25, as cited in John Madeley, *Trade and the Poor* (New York: St. Martin's Press, 1993), 91.

Mexico's foreign investment law of 1973 banned foreign investment entirely in sectors like those mentioned above and confined foreign equity and management control to 49 percent or less in many other sectors, including mineral exploitation, automobile manufacturing, and petrochemical by-products. One-hundred percent ownership was only allowed in a limited number of sectors: nonelectric equipment and machinery, electronics, machine tools, electronic machines and appliances, biotechnology, transportation equipment, chemicals, and hotels.[66] Several states also controlled the takeover of nationally owned firms by multinational corporations. Mexico, for example, required prior authorization before allowing a foreign investor to acquire 25 percent of the capital stock or 49 percent of the fixed assets of a nationally owned firm and gave Mexican investors a chance to make the purchase in place of the foreigner. In 1989 Mexico's restrictions on foreign investment were relaxed.[67]

Some countries sought with varying degrees of success to reduce the level of existing foreign investment. In the ANCOM Uniform Code on Foreign Investment, reserved sectors were to be closed not only to new but also to existing foreign investment. Foreign firms operating in reserved sectors were to offer at least 80 percent of their shares for sale to national investors.[68] ANCOM's effort foundered due to the conflicts among its member states and the difficulty of implementing such strict divestiture procedures. India was more successful in its divestitive efforts. Between 1977 and 1980, India reduced foreign ownership in almost four hundred companies by requiring the issue of shares to the Indian public.[69]

Through these sectoral and equity restrictions and reinforced by new domestic abilities to enforce these restrictions, governments sought to encourage new forms of foreign participation—joint ventures, licensing agreements, management contracts, and turnkey arrangements—to replace total or majority ownership. The goal was to "unbundle" the foreign investment package: to separate technology, managerial skills, and market access from equity and control.[70] As a result, joint ventures, production sharing, and technical assistance agreements became more common, and many multinational corporations accepted less than majority ownership of affiliates in developing countries.[71] By the early seventies, 38 percent of the affiliates of U.S.-based corporations in developing countries were co-owned or minority-owned. Multinationals based in other countries have shown even more flexibility: by the late sixties, the proportion of minority-owned affiliates of corporations based in Europe was 49 percent, and that of other (primarily Japanese) corporations was 82 percent.[72]

Developing countries also sought to regulate behavior by the multinationals after entry. Restrictions on profit and capital repatriation were widely implemented throughout the developing world. The Andean Group, for example, limited remittances of profits and capital to 20 percent of registered investments. A number of countries, such as Mexico, supervise technology and licensing agreements.[73] Some countries require registration and greater disclosure of such information as capital structure, the technology used and restrictions on its use, and reinvestment policies.[74]

An additional control technique relies not on restrictions but on positive incentives. Inducements, such as tax advantages or exemptions from import restrictions, have been used to encourage companies to invest in new fields or to use new technologies, to invest in export industries and in developing regions of the country, and to increase sectoral competition. Brazil has relied on such positive tools of public policy to manage multinational corporations. In the 1970s the Brazilian Industrial Development Council distributed incentives to foreign investors to regulate them and direct their investments into desirable sectors of the economy.[75]

Another technique is the support of state-owned industry. In many industries with high barriers to entry, government-owned enterprise is the only viable national alternative to foreign investment. In both Mexico and Brazil, for example, state-owned corporations have been formed in such basic industries as petroleum, steel, finance, utilities, and transportation.[76] Significantly, the emphasis on state-owned industry as a strategy for balancing foreign investment contributed to greater borrowing from foreign commercial banks in order to invest in national industry.[77]

A final method of control was the producer cartel (see Chapter 9). Various exporters of raw materials—particularly oil, copper, and bauxite—tried to manage multinational corporations by cooperating to increase prices as well as the national share of profits and national ownership. Until now, only OPEC, the oil producers' cartel, has used this technique successfully.

The 1980s: The New Pragmatism

In the 1980s, the Southern strategy of control and confrontation shifted toward more pragmatic policies toward multinational corporations. Although developing countries continued to closely monitor and control the activities of foreign investors, multinational corporations gradually came to be seen less as a threat and more as a potential opportunity for promoting growth and development.[78]

The new pragmatism was the result of several converging forces. The decline in foreign direct investment flows to developing countries played an important role. Restrictive policies enacted in the 1960s and 1970s deterred some direct investment and led foreign investors to turn to nonequity arrangements as a way of gaining access to LDC markets.[79] Particularly troublesome for potential investors were controls on remittances of earnings. Depressed economic conditions and low rates of return in most developing countries during the 1980s were an important factor in the decline in investment flows. For example, rates of return on U.S. foreign direct investment in Latin America fell from 18.8 percent in 1980 to 2.4 percent in 1983 before rising to 10.8 percent in 1985. Rates of return on U.S investment in other developing countries fell from 41.3 percent in 1980 to 22.5 percent in 1983 and to 18.6 percent in 1985.[80] The debt crisis further discouraged investment by making capital repatriation from many developing countries difficult or impossible. These unfavorable conditions in developing countries contrasted with rapid growth, rising rates of return, and few restrictions on foreign investment in many developed countries.

As a result, multinational corporations shifted their investment toward the developed countries and away from developing countries. Between 1982 and 1985, the share of foreign direct investment flowing to developing countries fell from 30.2 percent to 23.3 percent. The largest drop came in Latin America, where foreign direct investment fell from 14.4 percent of total world investment flows in 1982 to 9.1 percent in 1985.[81] In contrast, flows of investment to the rapidly growing countries of Asia were unchanged. Foreign investors were attracted by the large domestic markets in countries such as China, Indonesia, and Thailand; skilled, low-cost labor and well-developed infrastructure for export-oriented manufacturing, as in Hong Kong, Malaysia, Singapore, and Taiwan; petroleum and other natural resources, as in Indonesia and Malaysia; and generally more favorable policies regarding foreign investment in certain countries.[82]

The debt crisis was another factor leading to a shift in LDC attitudes toward foreign direct investment. (On debt, see Chapter 6). Ironically, the ready availability of bank capital in the 1970s had enabled developing countries to adopt the restrictive policies that contributed to the fall in direct investment flows in the 1980s. As we have seen, in the 1970s, commercial bank flows replaced both direct investment and foreign aid as a source of development finance for many middle-income Southern countries. In the 1980s, however, the debt crisis increased the attractiveness of foreign direct investment as a source of capital for growth. As a result of the crisis, both foreign and domestic sources of capital for investment were channeled to debt service. While foreign banks continued to lend to debtor countries, usually under pressure from their governments and the IMF, new lending was devoted to debt service and not investment. Although they were important borrowers from the World Bank, the middle-income debtors were no longer major recipients of foreign aid that had been redirected to the least-developed countries. In addition, domestic sources of capital were consumed by foreign debt service. As discussed, due to the debt crisis, investment and with it growth in the highly indebted countries collapsed. Increasingly, foreign direct investment emerged as one of the few possible sources of needed foreign capital and foreign exchange. Furthermore, unlike debt service, earnings on foreign investment are related to the success of an investment project, not to the vagaries of international interest rates.

More receptive policies toward foreign investment were also part of the prescription of developed countries and multilateral institutions for resolving the debt crisis. Improved access for foreign direct investment was one of the pillars of the Baker Plan for more liberal policies in debtor countries. A more positive approach to foreign investment was also fostered by the World Bank. The Bank's structural adjustment lending encouraged the easing of restrictions on foreign investment, and the Bank established a Multilateral Investment Guaranty Agency (MIGA) to insure and, thereby, promote direct investment in developing countries. In Pakistan and other nations, the World Bank has encouraged governments to allow private foreign investors to build and operate major infrastructure facilities, such as power plants and highways. These projects are occasionally even owned by the foreign investors, but eventually ownership and operation of the facilities is transferred back to the government or to local private enterprises. Furthermore, debt-equity swaps that were part of the menu for reducing commercial bank debt involved exchanging financial debt for foreign equity investment.

At the same time, developed countries generally took a more aggressive role on the issue of access for foreign investment to the markets of developing countries. The U.S. Trade and Tariff Act of 1984, for example, broadened the definition of barriers to market access to include investment as well as trade barriers, and the United States used the trade approach to push for access to markets for U.S. firms. In addition, the developed countries pushed for new investment provisions as part of the Uruguay Round (see Chapter 3).

This encouragement to open their policies and be more receptive to foreign investment fit well with the change in development strategies of many Southern countries. In the 1980s, many developing countries shifted from state-led investment to private-sector investment strategies. The clearest manifestations of this new approach were the privatization policies of several developing countries. In an effort to promote more efficient and competitive industry and to reduce the financial burden on government budgets, many developing countries divested a number of state-owned companies to the private sector.

Privatization policies complemented the new emphasis on export-led growth. As discussed, in this period many developing countries turned to the type of export-led development strategy that had been successful in the Asian NICs (see Chapter 7). In several of the NICs, promotion of foreign investment in the export sector was part of the export-led growth strategy. These countries attracted foreign direct investment in the export sector through export processing zones (EPZs) or by contractually requiring foreign firms to export in return for the right to invest (see below). Also related to the new emphasis on export-led growth was the growing interest of developing countries in obtaining access to modern technologies. Desire for advanced technology increased LDC receptivity to MNCs, the major holders of such technology.

These various forces converged in more liberal policies toward foreign direct investment. The new liberalism did not reverse established restrictive policies. Countries continued to control the entry and operations of foreign investors; most laws, regulations, and institutions put in place to control foreign investment remained; while countries opened up some sectors, such as those that exported or involved high technology, they maintained tightly closed policies in others (for example, the service sector); and the liberalization trend applied more to Asia and Africa than to Latin America where long-held concern about foreign investment inhibited change. Nevertheless, there was a clear trend toward encouraging foreign direct investment by reducing restrictions placed on the entry and operations of multinational corporations and by streamlining procedures and offering incentives to foreign investors.

New investment laws and policies adopted in the 1980s removed a variety of restrictions placed on foreign investors. A number of developing countries, including Korea, Mexico, and the ANCOM members, increased the number of sectors open to foreign investment. The opening tended to be in high-technology or export-oriented industries. In some countries, existing laws were implemented more flexibly. For example, IBM was given an exemption from Mexico's stringent limitation on foreign control of the informatics sector in order to set up a wholly owned subsidiary to produce microprocessors in Mexico. In return, IBM accepted a number of obligations regarding, for example, location of research and development in Mexico and exports from Mexico.[83] Similarly, in Brazil, the government's informatics policy, which excluded foreign firms from the small computer market, was attacked and greatly weakened in the late 1980s.[84] Privatization actions also involved foreign investors and not infrequently involved debt-equity swaps. Argentina allowed foreign private participation in petroleum extraction and telecommunications. In the case of telecommunications, foreign participation was financed in part with a debt-equity swap. Brazil sold part of its steel industry to foreign interests. Chile allowed foreign investors to use debt-equity swaps to buy stock in a state holding company. And the Philippines permitted foreign banks to convert their loan exposures into equity in its National Steel Company.[85]

Controls on operations were also eased in many developing countries. For example, Algeria eliminated requirements that the local partner exercise control, and ANCOM removed restrictions on profit remittances. Policies requiring gradual divestiture, in Mexico and ANCOM for example, were relaxed. Restrictions on operations were relaxed in certain preferred sectors. Venezuela and others, for example, exempted foreign investment in electronics, informatics, and biotechnology from limitations on reinvestment of profits, remittances, repatriation of capital, and divestiture requirements.[86] A number of developing countries, such as Algeria, India, Indonesia, Korea, Mexico, and the Philippines, also simplified administrative procedures for approving foreign direct investment. Finally, certain socialist countries, such as Ethiopia, Mozambique, North Korea, and China, passed new laws making foreign investment possible, primarily through joint ventures. China's liberalization policy was the most dramatic. Starting from scratch in 1979, China developed a foreign investment regime and implemented a policy that attracted a significant number of foreign corporations.[87]

A number of other developing countries have set up EPZs, which encourage investment for production of goods for export by making imports and exports free from tariffs or other trade restraints as well as through such techniques as providing infrastructure facilities for manufacturing and offering streamlined regula-

Table 8-1	Export Processing Zones (EPZs) by 1990		
	Number of Countries with an EPZ	*Number of EPZs in Operation*	*Persons Employed*
Africa	12	24	202,300
Asia and the Pacific	23	99	2,991,900
The Caribbean and Latin America	28	85	1,073,700
Total	63	208	4,267,900

SOURCE: John Madeley, *Trade and the Poor: The Impact of International Trade on Developing Countries* (New York: St. Martin's Press, 1993), 68.

tory and administrative procedures. Their use has grown dramatically in recent years. While only ten developing countries had EPZs in 1970, at least 63 Southern countries had them by 1990 (see Table 8-1). Although EPZs are designed for both foreign and domestic producers, many foreign firms have invested in EPZs as a way of gaining access to low-cost labor for the production of such labor-intensive goods as electronics and textiles. Export processing zones have clearly helped promote the export of manufactured products.[88]

As national policies became more accommodating, international efforts to control multinationals also shifted from hostility to greater cooperation. One important contributing factor was the rise of FDI *outflows* from the NICs, especially in Asia.[89] By the early 1990s, some developing countries had a growing stake in ensuring the access of their MNCs to other markets. A growing number of Southern countries, primarily in Africa and Southeast Asia, signed bilateral investment treaties (BITs) with developed countries. These treaties are designed to promote foreign investment by providing certain protections and a predictable foreign investment regime. They generally establish terms for entry of foreign investment; basic standards of treatment, such as national treatment or most-favored-nation treatment; conditions for nationalization and forms of compensation; rules for transfer of profits and capital repatriation; and dispute settlement mechanisms.[90] The Multilateral Investment Guarantee Agency (MIGA) was set up under the World Bank to guarantee private investment in developing countries against noncommercial risks, such as currency transfer, expropriation, breach of contract, war, and civil disturbance. Guarantees are contingent upon MIGA's judgment about the economic soundness and development validity of the investment as well as the approval of the host government.[91]

Meanwhile, negotiations for a United Nations Code on Transnational Corporations, originally conceived at the time of the NIEO, languished and seemed increasingly irrelevant. As attitudes toward foreign investment changed, Southern interest in the code declined. Developed countries remained adamantly opposed to the code and pushed instead for negotiations on investment under GATT (see Chapters 3 and 7). However, developing countries still wanted to maintain national sovereignty and to control entry and operations of foreign investors and thus strongly resisted negotiating investment issues, even the so-called trade-related investment measures (TRIMs) in the Uruguay Round. In the end, they accepted TRIMs because they were part of a package deal that included concessions from the industrialized countries on agriculture, textiles, and safeguards.

The Future: Cooperation or Conflict?

In the 1980s, there was clearly a shift in Southern attitudes toward multinational corporations. Developing countries became less confrontational and more concerned about promoting desired forms of investment. Nevertheless, for many developing countries, particularly those in Latin America and South Asia, deeply held concerns about the economic and political consequences of foreign investment remained.[92]

Views were equally mixed in the North. For many investors in the industrialized countries, the climate for investment in many developing countries continued to appear inhospitable or overly risky. Despite liberalization of policies toward inward FDI, access and operations in some countries remained overly constrained from their point of view. Increasingly, the developing countries had to compete with the formerly communist countries for available FDI. In some cases, as in India versus China, the communist country was better able than the noncommunist one to convince potential foreign investors that there would be fewer restrictions. The risk of economic downturns brought on by debt and currency crises reduced the flow of FDI to certain recipients. While interest in investment in the rapidly growing countries of Asia and Latin America remained high, the depressed economic conditions in most of the rest of the Third World remained a deterrent to investment.

Thus the events of the 1980s left unclear whether the hostile relationship between the LDCs and the MNCs had changed fundamentally or whether there was only a temporary truce based on the exigencies of debt and economic recession. Nevertheless, the globalization of the world economy had reached a point where few countries in the South could afford to say no to the multinationals. In the late 1980s and early 1990s, most developing countries had made their peace with foreign investment and were soliciting greater flows as part of their new, more outward-looking development strategies.

NOTES

1. The terms *foreign investment* and *multinational corporation* are used interchangeably in this chapter. Because much, although not all, foreign investment in less-developed countries is made by multinational corporations, this usage should not interfere with the analysis made and the conclusions reached.

2. United Nations Conference on Trade and Development, Division on Transnational Corporations and Investment, *World Investment Report 1994: Transnational Corporations,*

Employment and the Workplace (New York: United Nations, 1994), 14. The countries, in declining order of cumulative flows, are China, Singapore, Mexico, Malaysia, Brazil, Hong Kong, Argentina, Thailand, Egypt, and Taiwan.

3. For a similar analysis of two countries, see Richard S. Newfarmer and Willard F. Mueller, *Multinational Corporations in Brazil and Mexico: Structural Sources of Economic and Noneconomic Power*, report to the Subcommittee on Multinational Corporations of the Committee on Foreign Relations, 94th Cong., 1st sess. (Washington: U.S. Government Printing Office, 1975).

4. United Nations Commission on Transnational Corporations, *Transnational Corporations in World Development: Third Survey* (New York: United Nations, 1983), 197.

5. Ibid., 210.

6. United Nations Commission on Transnational Corporations, *Transnational Corporations in World Development: Trends and Prospects*, (New York: United Nations, 1988), 159.

7. Newfarmer and Mueller, *Multinational Corporations in Brazil and Mexico*, 25–27; and United Nations Conference on Trade and Development, *Restrictive Business Practices: The Operations of Multinational Enterprises in Developing Countries, Their Role in Trade and Development*, a study by Raymond Vernon (New York: United Nations, 1972), 3.

8. Gary Gereffi and Richard S. Newfarmer, "International Oligopoly and Uneven Development: Some Lessons from Industrial Case Studies," in Richard S. Newfarmer, ed., *Profits, Progress and Poverty: Case Studies of International Industries in Latin America* (Notre Dame, Ind.: University of Notre Dame Press, 1985), 385–442.

9. For an analysis of control over access, see Samuel Huntington, "Transnational Organizations in World Politics," *World Politics* 25 (April 1973): 333–368.

10. See Raymond Vernon, "Long-Run Trends in Concession Contracts," *Proceedings of the American Society for International Law*, sixty-first annual meeting (Washington: American Society for International Law, 1967), 81–90; and Theodore H. Moran, *Multinational Corporations and the Politics of Dependence: Copper in Chile* (Princeton: Princeton University Press, 1974), 157–162.

11. This applies particularly to collusion by the major international oil companies; see Chapter 9.

12. UNCTC, *Transnational Corporations in World Development: Third Survey*, 336–342.

13. See Dennis M. Ray, "Corporations and American Foreign Relations," in David H. Blake, ed., *The Annals of the American Academy of Political and Social Science: The MNC* (Philadelphia: 1972), 80–92.

14. See, for example, Harry G. Johnson, "The Efficiency and Welfare Implications of the International Corporation," in Charles P. Kindleberger, ed., *The International Corporation: A Symposium* (Cambridge: MIT Press, 1970), 35–56; Lester B. Pearson, *Partners in Development: Report of the Commission on International Development* (New York: Praeger, 1969), 99–123; United Nations Conference on Trade and Development, *The Role of Private Enterprise in Investment and Promotion of Exports in Developing Countries*, report prepared by Dirk U. Stikker (New York: United Nations, 1968); and Herbert K. May, *The Effects of United States and Other Foreign Investment in Latin America* (New York: Council for Latin America, 1970).

15. Organization for Economic Cooperation and Development, *Development Cooperation 1993: Efforts and Policies of the Members of the Development Assistance Committee* (Paris: OECD, 1993), 65. Please note that the UNCTAD estimates for FDI inflows to the developing countries in 1992 were considerably higher: $51.5 billion. See UNCTAD, *World Investment Report 1994* (New York: United Nations, 1994), 409.

16. Eduardo Borenszstein, José De Gregorio, and Jong-Wha Lee, *How Does Foreign Direct Investment Affect Economic Growth?* (Cambridge, Mass.: National Bureau of Economic Research, Working Paper No. 5057, March 1995), 3.

17. UNCTC, *Transnational Corporations in World Development: Third Survey*, 161–162. For a careful review of this subject, see Sheila Page, *How Developing Countries Trade* (New York: Routledge, 1994), ch. 6.

18. Ibid., 180–183.

19. Leading critics include Celso Furtado, for example, *Obstacles to Development in Latin America* (Garden City, N.Y.: Doubleday, 1970); Stephen Hymer, for example, "The Multinational Corporation and the Law of Uneven Development," in Jagdish N. Bhagwati, ed., *Economics and World Order: From the 1970s to the 1990s* (New York: Macmillan, 1972), 113–140; Ronald Muller, for example, *Global Reach: The Power of the Multinational Corporations* (New York: Simon and Schuster, 1974), written with Richard J. Barnet; Constantine V. Vaitsos, for example, *Intercountry Income Distribution and Transnational Enterprises* (Oxford, England: Clarendon Press, 1974); and

Fernando Henrique Cardoso, for example, *Dependencia and Development in Latin America* (Berkeley and Los Angeles: University of California Press, 1979), written with Enzo Faletto. An excellent summary of both critical and "neoconventional" perspectives on multinational corporations, as well as a case study of the Nigerian experience, is Thomas Biersteker, *Distortion or Development? Contending Perspectives on the Multinational Corporation* (Cambridge: MIT Press, 1978). See also Theodore H. Moran, "Multinational Corporations and Dependency: A Dialogue for Dependistas and Non-Dependentistas," *International Organization* 32 (winter 1978), 79–100.

20. Sidney M. Robbins and Robert Stobaugh, *Money in the Multinational Enterprise: A Study of Financial Policy* (New York: Basic Books, 1972), 63–71; R. David Belli, "Sources and Uses of Funds of Foreign Affiliates of U.S. Firms, 1967–68," *Survey of Current Business* (November 1970): 14–19; Grant L. Reuber, *Private Foreign Investment in Development* (Oxford, England: Clarendon Press, 1973), 67; Sanjaya Lall and Paul Streeten, *Foreign Investment, Transnationals and Developing Countries* (London: Macmillan, 1977); and L. E. Westphal, Y. W. Ree, and G. Pursell, "Foreign Influences on Korean Industrial Development," *Oxford Bulletin of Economics and Statistics* 41 (November 1979): 359–388.

21. Ronald J. Muller, "Poverty Is the Product," *Foreign Policy* 13 (winter 1973–1974): 85–88.

22. Newfarmer and Mueller, *Multinational Corporations in Brazil and Mexico*, 67–72.

23. Ibid., 121–125.

24. *Survey of Current Business* 57 (August 1977): 39; *Survey of Current Business* 59 (August 1979): 22.

25. Newfarmer and Mueller, *Multinational Corporations in Brazil and Mexico*, 17.

26. See Johnson, "The Efficiency and Welfare Implications of the International Corporation"; Walter A. Chudson, *The International Transfer of Commercial Technology to Developing Countries* (New York: United Nations Institute for Training and Research, 1971); and Lynn K. Mytelka, "Technological Dependence in the Andean Group," *International Organization* 32 (winter 1978): 101–139.

27. Vaitsos, *Intercountry Income Distribution and Transnational Enterprises*, 42–43.

28. Ibid., 44–54.

29. For a general discussion of transfer pricing, see the sources cited in note 44 in Chapter 4.

30. Constantine V. Vaitsos, "Foreign Investment Policies and Economic Development in Latin America," *Journal of World Trade Law* 7 (November-December 1973): 639; and Albert O. Hirschman, "How to Divest in Latin America and Why," *Essays in International Finance* (Princeton: International Finance Section, Department of Economics, Princeton University, November 1969), 5–6.

31. For a Mexican case study, see Fernando Fajnzylber and Trinidad Martínez Tarragó, *Las empresas transnacionales: expansión a nivel mundial y proyección en la industria mexicana* (Mexico City: Fondo de Cultura Económica, 1976).

32. The International Labor Organization has commissioned a number of studies on the employment impact of foreign direct investment in host developing countries. See, for example, Norman Girvan, *The Impact of Multinational Enterprises on Employment and Income in Jamaica* (Geneva: ILO, 1976); Juan Sourrouille, *The Impact of Transnational Enterprises on Employment and Income: The Case of Argentina* (Geneva: ILO, 1976); Sung-Hwan Jo, *The Impact of Multinational Firms on Employment and Income: The Case Study of South Korea* (Geneva: ILO, 1976); and *Technology Choice and Employment Generation by Multinational Enterprises in Developing Countries* (Geneva: ILO, 1984).

33. United Nations, *Multinational Corporations in World Development: Third Survey*, 195; Vaitsos, *Intercountry Income Distribution and Transnational Enterprises*, 54–59; and United Nations Conference on Trade and Development, *Restrictive Business Practices* (New York: United Nations, December 1969), 4–6.

34. For statistical evidence to this effect, see Michael B. Dolan and Brian W. Tomlin, "First World–Third World Linkages: External Relations and Economic Development," *International Organization* 34 (winter 1980): 41–64.

35. Borensztein, De Gregorio, and Lee, *How Does Foreign Direct Investment Affect Economic Growth?*, 12.

36. Gerald K. Helleiner, "The Role of Multinational Corporations in the Less Developed Countries' Trade in Technology," in Edward K. Y. Chen, ed., *Technology Transfer to Developing Countries* (New York: Routledge for UNCTAD, 1994), 52; and Ann Harrison, "The Role of Multinationals in Economic Development," *Columbia Journal of World Business* 29 (winter 1994): 7–11.

37. For analyses of recent empirical studies see UNCTC, *Transnational Corporations in World Development*, 132–237; and Theodore H. Moran, ed., *Multinational Corporations: The Political Economy of Foreign Direct Investment* (Lexington, Mass.: Lexington Books, 1985).

38. For an interesting case study, see Adalberto J. Piñelo, *The Multinational Corporation As a Force in Latin American Politics: A Case Study of the International Petroleum Company in Peru* (New York: Praeger, 1973).

39. Gulf Oil, for example, contributed $4 million illegally in South Korea. See *New York Times*, May 17, 1975, p. 1.

40. Bribes have been made, for example, by United Brands in Honduras for favorable tax treatment, and in arms and airplane sales, such as those of the Northrop Corporation in Saudi Arabia and Brazil. See Yerachmiel Kugel and Gladys Gruenberg, *International Payoffs: Dilemma for Business* (Lexington, Mass.: Heath, 1977).

41. See, for example, Piñelo, *The Multinational Corporation*, 17–25; and Neil H. Jacoby, Peter Nehemkis, and Richard Eells, *Bribery and Extortion in World Business* (New York: Macmillan, 1977).

42. The control of international markets, for example, made possible the boycott by the major international oil companies of Iranian oil in 1951–1953 that contributed to the overthrow of Premier Muhammed Mossadegh.

43. The Hickenlooper amendment was passed in October 1964 (Public Law 88-633, 78 Stat. 1009, Sec. 301). The Gonzalez amendment was passed as part of a general appropriations bill for multilateral banks in January 1974. See Anthony Sampson, *The Sovereign State of ITT* (New York: Stein and Day, 1973). On the Overseas Private Investment Corporation, see U.S. Senate, 93rd Cong., 1st sess., *The Overseas Private Investment Corporation: A Report to the Committee on Foreign Relations, United States Subcommittee on Multinational Corporations, October 17, 1973* (Washington: U.S. Government Printing Office, 1973).

44. See, for example, accounts of the role of the United Fruit Company in the United States in the overthrow of President Jacobo Arbenz of Guatemala, in Richard J. Barnet, *Intervention and Revolution: The United States in the Third World* (New York: World Publishing, 1968), 229–232; David Wise and Thomas B. Ross, *The Invisible Government* (New York: Random House, 1964), 165–183; U.S. Senate, Committee on Foreign Relations, Subcommittee on Multinational Corporations, 93rd Cong., 1st sess., *The Overseas Private Investment Corporation, A Report with Additional Views* (Washington: Government Printing Office, 1974); and the careful analysis of the role of U.S. multinationals in the ouster of President Salvador Allende of Chile in Paul E. Sigmund, *Multinationals in Latin America: The Politics of Nationalization* (Madison: University of Wisconsin Press, 1980), ch. 5.

45. Sigmund, *Multinationals in Latin America*, ch. 5.

46. U.S. Senate, *Multinational Corporations and United States Foreign Policy*, vol. 1.

47. Sigmund, *Multinationals in Latin America*, 20–23.

48. For an analysis of economic nationalism, see Harry G. Johnson, "A Theoretical Model of Economic Nationalism in New and Developing States," *Political Science Quarterly* 80 (June 1965): 169–185. See criticism by Vaitsos, "Foreign Investment Policies," 632. For evidence of this rising nationalism, see Jorge Dominguez, "National and Multinational Business and the State in Latin America" (paper presented at the annual meeting of the American Political Science Association, Washington, 1979). See also Richard L. Sklar, *Corporate Power in an African State: The Political Impact of Multinational Mining Companies in Zambia* (Berkeley and Los Angeles: University of California Press, 1975).

49. Samuel P. Huntington, *Political Order in Changing Societies* (New Haven: Yale University Press, 1968).

50. Moran, *Multinational Corporations and the Politics of Dependence: Copper in Chile*, 164–166.

51. See U.S. Senate, *Multinational Corporations and United States Foreign Policy*.

52. See United Nations, *Multinational Corporations in World Development and Report of the Group of Eminent Persons to Study the Impact of Multinational Corporations on Development and on International Relations* (New York: United Nations, 1974).

53. Edith Penrose, "The State and the Multinational Enterprise in Less-Developed Countries," in John Dunning, ed., *The Multinational Enterprise* (London: Allen and Unwin, 1971), 230. For the role of the new economic analysis in Chile, see Moran, *Multinational Corporations and the Politics of Dependence: Copper in Chile*, 57–88.

54. Moran, *Multinational Corporations and the Politics of Dependence: Copper in Chile*, 164.

55. Ibid.; and Alfred Stepan, *The State and Society: Peru in Comparative Perspective* (Princeton: Princeton University Press, 1978), 235.

56. Vernon, "Long-Run Trends in Concession Contracts"; and Moran, *Multinational Corporations and the Politics of Dependence: Copper in Chile,* 157–162.

57. UNCTC, *Transnational Corporations in World Development: Third Survey,* 18–19.

58. Vernon, "Long-Run Trends in Concession Contracts."

59. See Gary Gereffi and Richard S. Newfarmer, "International Oligopoly and Uneven Development: Some Lessons from Industrial Case Studies," in Newfarmer, *Progress, Profits, and Poverty,* 432. See also Newfarmer and Mueller on Mexico, in their *Multinational Corporations in Brazil and Mexico,* 59. In addition, once established in the host economy, multinational corporations form alliances with domestic groups and thereby actually improve their bargaining position vis-à-vis the local government.

60. Even ANCOM resolutions must be enacted nationally.

61. On International Petroleum Corporation, see Piñelo, *The Multinational Corporation.*

62. Moran, *Multinational Corporations*; and Sklar, *Corporate Power in an African State.*

63. For oil and other minerals, see Raymond F. Mikesell, ed., *Foreign Investment in the Petroleum and Mineral Industries: Case Studies of Investor-Host Country Relations* (Baltimore, Md.: Johns Hopkins University Press, 1971). Two interesting studies of nationalizations in developing countries are by Stephen J. Kobrin, "Foreign Enterprise and Forced Divestment in LDCs," *International Organization* 34 (winter, 1980): 65–88; and David A. Jodice, "Sources of Change in Third World Regimes for Foreign Direct Investment, 1968–1976," *International Organization* 34 (spring 1980): 177–206.

64. UNCTC, *Transnational Corporations in World Development: Trends and Prospects,* 315.

65. For a summary of the policies of various developing host countries toward foreign investment, see UNCTC, *Transnational Corporations in World Development: Trends and Prospects,* 261–298. A good summary of the problems that developing countries face in controlling foreign enterprises and a case study of Peru is in Stepan, *The State and Society: Peru in Comparative Perspective,* 230–289.

66. Rosemary R. Williams, "Has Mexico Kept the Promise of 1984? A Look at Foreign Investment Under Mexico's Recent Guidelines," *Texas International Law Journal* 23 (1988): 417–441. See also Sandra F. Maviglia, "Mexico's Guidelines for Foreign Investment: The Selective Promotion of Necessary Industries," *The American Journal of International Law* 80 (1986): 281–304. For a review of Venezuelan foreign investment regulations, see Robert J. Radway and Franklin T. Hoet-Linares, "Venezuela Revisited: Foreign Investment, Technology and Related Issues," *Vanderbilt Journal of Transnational Law* 15 (winter 1982): 1–45.

67. Ana Maria Perez Gabriel, "Mexican Legislation Affecting the Maquiladora Industry," in Khosrow Fatemi, ed., *The Maquiladora Industry: Economic Solution or Problem?* (New York: Praeger, 1990), 214–216; and Patricia A. Wilson, *Exports and Local Development: Mexico's New Maquiladoras* (Austin, Texas: University of Texas Press, 1990), ch. 1.

68. Chile withdrew from ANCOM in 1976 rather than impose restrictions on foreign investment. See Dale B. Furnish, "The Andean Common Market's Common Regime for Foreign Investments," *Vanderbilt Journal of Transnational Law* 5 (spring 1972): 313–339; Robert Black, Stephen Blank, and Elizabeth C. Hanson, *Multinationals in Contention: Responses at Governmental and International Levels* (New York: The Conference Board, 1978): 174–184; and Roger Fontaine, "The Andean Pact: A Political Analysis," *The Washington Papers* 5, no. 45 (Beverly Hills, Calif.: Sage, 1977).

69. United Nations, *Transnational Corporations: Third Survey,* 60–61.

70. Charles Oman, *New Forms of International Investment in Developing Countries* (Paris: OECD, 1983).

71. United Nations, *Transnational Corporations: Third Survey,* 102–122.

72. Ibid., 229.

73. Lacey and Garza, "Mexico—Are the Rules Really Changing?" 572–573.

74. Ibid.

75. See, for example, Business International Corporation, *Investment, Licensing and Trading Conditions Abroad: Brazil* (New York: Business International, 1973).

76. Newfarmer and Mueller, *Multinational Corporations in Brazil and Mexico,* 55, 112, 150; Peter Evans, *Dependent Development: The Alliance of Multinational, State, and Local Capital in*

Brazil (Princeton: Princeton University Press, 1979); and Peter Evans, *Embedded Autonomy: States and Industrial Transformation* (Princeton: Princeton University Press, 1995).

77. Jeffry Frieden, "Third World Indebted Industrialization: International Finance and State Capitalism in Mexico, Brazil, Algeria and South Korea," *International Organization* 35 (summer 1981): 407–431.

78. UNCTAD, *World Investment Report 1994*, pp. xxviii–xxxiv. For a skeptical view on this, see Alvin G. Wint, "Liberalizing Foreign Direct Investment Regimes: The Vestigial Screen," *World Development* 20 (October 1992): 1515–1529.

79. UNCTC, *Transnational Corporations in World Development: Trends and Prospects*, 67–71.

80. Ibid., 82.

81. Ibid., 76.

82. Ibid., 82–83.

83. Ibid., 269; and Van R. Whiting, Jr., *The Political Economy of Foreign Investment in Mexico: Nationalism, Liberalism, and Constraints on Choice* (Baltimore, Md.: Johns Hopkins University Press, 1992), ch. 8.

84. Jorg Meyer-Stamer, "The End of Brazil's Informatics Policy," *Science and Public Policy* 19 (April 1992): 99–110; Emanuel Adler, *The Power of Ideology: The Quest for Technological Autonomy in Argentina and Brazil* (Berkeley: University of California Press, 1987), ch. 10; and Evans, *Embedded Autonomy*.

85. UNCTC, *Transnational Corporations in World Development: Trends and Prospects*, 264–265.

86. Ibid., 269.

87. Ibid., 76–78.

88. Ibid., 169–173; and John Madeley, *Trade and the Poor: The Impact of International Trade on Developing Countries* (New York: St. Martin's Press, 1993), 68. See also, Jeffrey A. Hart, "Maquiladorization as a Global Process," in Steve Chan, ed., *Foreign Direct Investment in a Changing Global Economy* (New York: Macmillan, 1995).

89. Hans Jansson, *Transnational Corporations in Southeast Asia: An Institutional Approach to Industrial Organization* (Brookfield, Vt.: Edward Elgar, 1994); and Sanjaya Lall, ed., *New Multinationals: The Spread of Third World Enterprises* (London: Wiley, 1983).

90. UNCTC, *Transnational Corporations in World Development: Trends and Prospects*, 332–337.

91. Ibid., 348.

92. On Indian attitudes toward FDI, see Peter Evans, *Embedded Autonomy*; and Joseph M. Grieco, *Between Dependency and Autonomy: India's Experience with the International Computer Industry* (Berkeley: University of California Press, 1984).

9

Oil, Commodity
Cartels, and Power

The most successful effort of Southern countries to alter their dependent relationship with the North was the common action of OPEC (Organization of Petroleum Exporting Countries) in seizing control over the world's oil markets. By acting together in a producer **cartel**, the Southern oil-exporting states were able to increase not only their economic rewards but also their political power. OPEC's success led to efforts to form other Southern commodity cartels. But the OPEC model would prove difficult to reproduce, and even OPEC eventually confronted the inevitable limitations of a producer cartel.

The Dependency System of International Oil

For most of the twentieth century, the international oil system was controlled by a producer cartel. Until 1973, that cartel consisted of an oligopoly of international oil companies.[1] The "seven sisters"—five American (Standard Oil of New Jersey, now known as Exxon; Standard Oil of California, now known as Chevron; Gulf, now part of Chevron; Mobil; and Texaco), one British (British Petroleum), and one Anglo-Dutch (Royal Dutch-Shell)—first gained control of their domestic oil industries through **vertical integration**—that is, by controlling all supply, transportation, refining, marketing operations, as well as exploration and refining technologies.

In the late nineteenth century, the oil companies then in existence began to move abroad and obtain control of foreign supplies on extremely favorable terms.[2] After World War I, the seven formed joint ventures to explore foreign oil fields, and eventually in the 1920s they began to divide up sources of supply by explicit agreements. They were thus able to divide markets, fix world prices, and discriminate against outsiders.[3] Northern political dominance of the oil-producing regions—the Middle East, Indonesia, and Latin America—facilitated the activities of the oil companies. Governments provided a favorable political and military environment and actively supported the oil companies owned by their nationals.

In bargaining with the oil companies, the less-developed countries were confronted by an oil oligopoly supported by powerful Northern governments as well as by uncertainty about the success of oil exploration and the availability of alternative sources of supply. It is not surprising that the seven sisters obtained concession agreements that gave them control over the production and sale of much of the world's oil in return for the payment of a small fixed royalty to their host governments.[4]

Beginning in the late 1920s and continuing through the Great Depression, oil prices tumbled despite the efforts of the seven sisters to stabilize markets. At that time, the United States was the largest producer in the world and exported oil to Europe and elsewhere. Efforts at the government level (including not only the U.S. federal government but more significantly the largest producer state, Texas) succeeded where the seven sisters could not in regulating production in order to create a price floor. Thus, the Texas Railroad Commission emerged as the single most significant political force in the international oil industry.

Changes in this system began to emerge in the decade following World War II. In the 1950s, relatively inexpensive imported oil became the primary source of energy for the developed world. Western Europe and Japan, with no oil supplies of their own, became significant importers of oil. In 1950, U.S. oil consumption outdistanced its vast domestic production, and the United States became a net importer of oil. In the host countries, growing nationalism combined with the great success of oil exploration led to dissatisfaction with concession agreements and to more aggressive policies. In these years, the host governments succeeded in revising concession agreements negotiated before the war. They redefined the basis for royalty payments and instituted an income tax on foreign oil operations. They also established what at the time was considered a revolutionary principle: the new royalties and taxes combined would yield a fifty-fifty division of profits between the companies and their respective host governments.[5] As a result, profits accruing to host governments increased significantly. The per-barrel payment to Saudi Arabia, for example, rose from $0.17 in 1946 to $0.80 in 1956–1957.[6]

Nonetheless, the seven sisters, also known as the majors, continued to dominate the system. By controlling almost all the world's oil reserves outside the Communist states (e.g., production at the wellhead, refining and transportation, and marketing), they were able to manage the price of oil.

The seven sisters maintained control, in part, by preventing incursions by competitors. The majors blocked other companies from entering upstream operations such as crude oil exploration and production outside North America by locking in concession agreements with many oil-rich areas and by the long lead times required for finding and developing oil in territory unclaimed by the majors. Outsiders were also deterred from competing with the seven sisters downstream—that is, in refining, transportation, and marketing operations. Not having their own crude oil supplies, independent refiners had to purchase oil from the majors, who were also their competitors. But the majors deliberately took their profits at the less-competitive and lower-taxed upstream level by charging a high price for crude oil as compared with the final product. The small profits for downstream operations discouraged new entrants.

The management of the price of oil was facilitated by the highly inelastic demand for oil. Because there are no readily available substitutes and because it is difficult to decrease consumption, an increase in the price does not greatly decrease the demand for oil in the short run. Thus, if companies can maintain a higher price for oil, they will not lose sales volumes and so will reap high profits.

Thus, in the 1950s and 1960s, the seven sisters controlled supply by keeping out competitors and by a series of cooperative ventures: joint production and refining arrangements, long-term purchase and supply agreements, joint ownership of pipelines, and some joint marketing outside the United States. They also refrained from price competition. Price management by the majors was designed to keep the price of oil economically attractive but also low enough to discourage competing forms of energy, including nuclear energy. Developed country governments did not resist this price management. Europeans added a tax on petroleum in order to protect the domestic coal industry, because lower oil prices would have increased oil consumption at the expense of the politically powerful coal companies and coal miners. In the United States, higher oil prices were supported by the domestic oil industry that needed protection from lower international prices to survive and, as we shall discuss, eventually obtained that protection.[7]

Finally, the dominance of the seven sisters was backed by political intervention. One extreme example occurred in the early 1950s when the government of Iran sought a new agreement with the Anglo-Iranian Oil Company, a predecessor of British Petroleum, and nationalized the company's assets in Iran. The British government became actively involved in the negotiations, imposed an economic embargo on Iran, and threatened military intervention. After trying unsuccessfully to mediate between Britain and Iran, the United States worked with opposition parties and the shah to overthrow the Iranian government. A new concession was soon negotiated under which the U.S. companies replaced Anglo-Iranian.[8]

However, as OPEC would later discover, it is difficult to maintain a producer cartel in the long run. Over time, changes in the international oil industry, the oil-producing states, and the oil-consuming developed countries undermined the dominance of the seven sisters.[9] The oligopolistic structure of the international oil industry was weakened by the entrance of new players. Competition increased both upstream, as new players sought concessions to explore for and produce crude oil, and downstream, as more refineries were built and competition grew in markets for refined oil. Starting in the mid-1950s, companies previously not active internationally obtained and successfully developed concessions in existing and new oil-producing regions such as Algeria, Libya, and Nigeria. In 1952, the seven majors produced 90 percent of crude oil outside North America and the Communist countries, and by 1968 they still produced 75 percent.[10]

As new production by new producers came on line, the seven sisters were no longer able to restrict supply and maintain the price of oil at the old level. By the end of the 1950s, production increases outdistanced the growth in consumption. United States quotas on the import of foreign oil aggravated the problem. Quotas were instituted in 1958 ostensibly for national security reasons: to protect the U.S. market from lower-priced foreign oil in order to ensure domestic production and national self-sufficiency. In fact, quotas also helped domestic U.S. producers that could not have survived without protection.[11] The quotas effectively cut off the U.S. market for the absorption of the new supplies produced abroad. As a result, in 1959 and 1960, the international oil companies lowered the posted price of oil, the official price used to calculate taxes. This act was to be a key catalyst for producer-government action against the oil companies.

Changes in the oil-producing states also weakened the power of the oil company cartel. In addition to changing elite attitudes, improved skills, and less uncertainty, the emergence of new competitors was critically important in increasing the bargaining power of the host governments. In negotiations with the oil companies, producer states obtained larger percentages of earnings and provisions for relinquishing unexploited parts of concessions.[12] As a result, the oil-producing governments, especially large producers such as Libya and Saudi Arabia, increased their earnings and began to accumulate significant foreign exchange reserves. Monetary reserves further strengthened the hand of the oil producers by enabling them to absorb any short-term loss of earnings from an embargo or production reduction designed to increase the price of oil or to obtain other concessions.

At the same time, host governments began to cooperate with each other. Infuriated by the price cuts of 1959 and 1960 that reduced their tax receipts, five of the major petroleum-exporting countries—Iran, Iraq, Kuwait, Saudi Arabia, and Venezuela—met in 1960 to discuss unilateral action by the oil companies. At that meeting, the five decided to form an Organization of Petroleum Exporting Countries to protect the price of oil and the revenues of their governments.[13] In its first decade, OPEC expanded from five to thirteen members, accounting for 85 percent of the world's oil exports.[14] Initially, the new organization had little success. OPEC's influence depended on the ability of its members to cooperate to reduce production and thus to force a price increase. Although OPEC tried, it was unable to agree on production reduction schemes. Nevertheless, the individual oil-producing states succeeded in increasing their revenues. The posted price of oil was never again lowered. And the oil-producing states gradually expanded their experience in cooperation. But not until the 1970s, when other conditions became favorable, would OPEC become an effective tool of the producer states.[15]

Finally, the Western consuming countries became vulnerable to the threat of supply interruption or reduction. As oil became the primary source of energy and as U.S. supplies diminished, the developed-market economies became increasingly dependent on foreign oil, especially from the Middle East and North Africa. By 1972, Western Europe derived almost 60 percent of its energy from oil, almost all of which was imported. Oil from abroad supplied 73 percent of Japan's energy needs. And 46 percent of U.S. energy came from oil, almost one-third of which was imported. By 1972, 80 percent of Western European and Japanese oil imports came from the Middle East and North Africa. By 1972, even the United States relied on the Middle East and North Africa for 15 percent of its oil imports.[16] This economic vulnerability was accentuated by declining political influence in the oil-producing regions and by the absence of individual or joint energy policies to counter any manipulation of supply.

The Process of Change: From Negotiation to Unilateral Power

In the 1970s, OPEC took advantage of these changes and asserted its power as a producer cartel. Favorable international economic and political conditions plus internal cooperation enabled the oil-producing states—especially the Arab oil producers—to take control of prices and, then, to assume ownership of oil investments.

The OPEC revolution was triggered by Libya,[17] a country that had definite negotiating advantages: it supplied 25 percent of Western Europe's oil imports;[18] certain independent oil companies relied heavily on Libyan oil and were more vulnerable than the majors in Libya; and Libya had large official foreign exchange reserves. After Colonel Muammar al-Qaddafi seized power in 1969, the new radical government demanded an increase in the posted price of and the tax on Libyan oil. When the talks with the companies stalled in 1970, the government threatened nationalization and a cut in oil production. It targeted the vulnerable Occidental Petroleum, which relied totally on Libya to supply its European markets. Shortly after production cuts were imposed, Occidental, having failed to gain the support of the majors, capitulated, and the other companies were forced to follow. The settlement provided for an increase in the posted price of and the income tax on Libyan oil. The Libyan action revealed the vulnerability of the independent oil companies like Occidental and the unwillingness of the Western governments or the majors to take forceful action in their support.

At a meeting in December 1970, OPEC called for an increase in the posted price of and income taxes on oil. The companies, seeking to avoid a producer policy of divide and conquer, agreed to negotiate with all oil-producing countries for a long-term agreement on price and tax increases. The governments of the oil-consuming states, although increasingly concerned, allowed the companies to manage relations with the oil producers.[19] Following threats to enact changes unilaterally and to cut off oil to the companies in February 1971, the companies signed a five-year agreement that provided for an increase in the posted price of Persian Gulf oil from $1.80 to $2.29 per barrel, an annual increase in the price to offset inflation, and an increase in government royalties and taxes. In return, the companies received a five-year "commitment" on price and government revenues. In April 1971, a similar agreement, but with a higher price, was reached with Libya. After the devaluation of the dollar in 1971 and 1972 and thus of the real price of oil, the producers demanded and received a new agreement that provided for an increase in the posted price of oil and continuing adjustment to account for exchange rate changes. The price of Persian Gulf oil rose to $2.48.

No sooner had the issue of price and revenue been settled than OPEC requested a new conference to discuss nationalization—that is, control over production. A December 1972 agreement among Saudi Arabia, Qatar, Abu Dhabi, and the companies provided a framework: government ownership would start at 25 percent and rise gradually to 51 percent by 1982. Individual states then entered into negotiations with the oil concessionaires.

The final negotiation between the oil producers and the oil companies took place in October 1973. Despite their successes, the oil producers were dissatisfied. Although surging demand for oil drove up the market price, the posted price remained fixed by the five-year agreements. Thus, the oil companies, not the oil producers, benefited. Furthermore, the companies were bidding for new government-owned oil at prices above those of the five-year agreements.

Finally, increasing inflation in the West and continuing devaluation of the dollar lowered the real value of earnings from oil production. Economic conditions were favorable to OPEC. Because of rapidly rising demand and shortages of supply, the developed market economies were vulnerable to supply interruption. Thus, when OPEC summoned the oil companies for negotiations, they came. Negotiations began on October 8. The oil producers demanded substantial increases in the price of oil; the companies stalled; and on October 12 the companies requested a two-week adjournment of talks to consult with their home governments.

The adjournment was not for two weeks but forever. Political as well as economic conditions now enhanced the bargaining position and escalated the demands of the most powerful oil producers: the Arab states. The fourth Arab-Israeli war had begun on October 6, just two days before the oil talks began. A common interest in supporting the Arab cause vis-á-vis Israel and the supporters of Israel in the consuming states was a force for unity of the Arab members of OPEC in their economic confrontation with the companies and the consumers. On October 16, the Organization of Arab Petroleum Exporting Countries (OAPEC) unilaterally increased the price of their crude oil to $5.12.[20] Other oil producers followed. On December 23, OPEC unilaterally raised the price of Persian Gulf oil to $11.65.

After the autumn of 1973, oil prices were controlled by OPEC. Operating in a market where supplies were limited and demand high, the producers negotiated among themselves to determine the posted price of oil and the production reductions needed to limit supply and maintain price. The key to reducing supply was the role of the major reserve countries and large producers. Saudi Arabia and Kuwait were willing to support the cartel by themselves, absorbing a large part of the production reductions necessary to maintain the price. The role of these two countries was facilitated by the tight oil markets, which meant that price could be managed when necessary by only limited production reductions. Power over price was quickly translated into equity control. All the major oil-producing states signed agreements with the oil companies for immediate majority or total national ownership of subsidiaries located in those states. In the long run, as we shall see, the abrupt movement of control over production from the seven sisters to OPEC would prove to be the real revolution of the 1970s oil crisis.

The monopoly control of oil by OPEC, the unity of the producers, and tight market conditions undermined the position of the oil companies. Furthermore, the companies had little incentive to resist. They were able in most cases to pass the price increases along to consumers and thus did not suffer financially from the loss of control over price. Although no longer either the arbiters of supply and price or the owners of oil concessions, the seven sisters and their many smaller relatives still played a vital role in the international oil scene. As holders of technology and markets, they were needed by the newly powerful producer governments. As their holdings were nationalized, they became vital service contractors to the producer states. Still, it was a far cry from the days when the companies divided up the producing regions among themselves and obtained control of the world's oil for almost nothing.

With the decline of the companies, the Northern consumer governments tried but failed to agree on a common policy toward the producers. The United States urged Western Europe and Japan to form a countercartel that would undermine producer solidarity by presenting a united front and by threatening economic or military retaliation. The Europeans and Japanese—more dependent on foreign sources of oil, less interested in support for Israel, and somewhat fearful of U.S. dominance—instead advised cooperation with the producers. A consumer conference in early 1974 failed to reconcile these opposing views. The only agreement was to establish an International Energy Agency (IEA) to develop an emergency oil-sharing scheme and a long-term program for the development of alternative forms of energy. France, the strongest opponent of the U.S. approach, refused to join the IEA and urged instead a producer-consumer dialogue.

After the conference, consumer governments went their own ways. The United States tried to destroy producer unity by continuing to press for consumer unity and the development of the IEA. The Europeans sought special bilateral political and economic arrangements with the oil producers and resisted consumer bloc strategies. In late 1974, a compromise was reached between the United States and France. The United States obtained France's grudging acceptance of the IEA, although France still refused to join, and France obtained the grudging support of the United States for a producer-consumer dialogue. The Conference on International Economic Cooperation (CIEC), begun in 1975 (see Chapter 7), constituted a recognition, if not a total acceptance, by the United States and the other consumers that they could not alter the power of the producer states over the price of oil and that what they could seek at best was some conciliation and coordination of common interests. Even that coordination proved elusive. In 1977, the CIEC and the effort to achieve a forum for a producer-consumer dialogue failed.

OPEC Management

For five years the management of the international oil system was carried out by OPEC under the leadership of Saudi Arabia. Saudi dominance of OPEC's production and Saudi financial strength enabled that country to manage the oil cartel virtually singlehandedly. Saudi Arabia accounted for close to one-third of OPEC's production and exports, controlled the largest productive capacity and the world's largest reserves of petroleum, and possessed vast financial reserves (see Figure 9-1).

In periods of excess supply, as during the recession of 1975, Saudi Arabia maintained the OPEC price by absorbing a large share of the necessary production reductions. The burden of such reductions was minimal because of the country's huge financial reserves and because even its ambitious economic development and military needs could be more than satisfied at a lower level of oil exports. In periods of tight supply, Saudi Arabia increased its production to pre-

Figure 9-1   Production of Crude Petroleum by OPEC Countries in Millions of Barrels per Day, 1970–1994

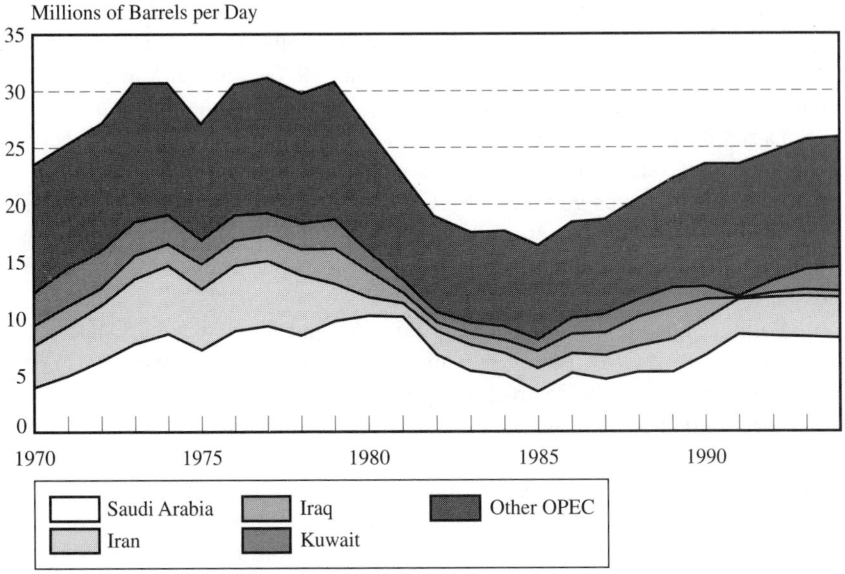

SOURCE: Department of Energy, Energy Information Agency, via the World Wide Web at http://www.eia.doe.gov.

vent excessive price rises. With a small population, limited possibilities of industrial development, and the world's largest oil reserves, Saudi Arabia's future is dependent on oil. Furthermore, with its financial reserves invested largely in the developed countries, it has a stake in the stability of the international economic system.

Thus, although the Saudis want a price of oil that is high in terms of Saudi Arabia's cost of production (less than $1 per barrel), they do not want a price high enough to jeopardize the future of an oil-based energy system and the viability of the world economy. The Saudi view is shared by other Gulf states who, with the Saudis, form the moderate camp in OPEC.

The Saudis were willing and able to threaten or actually to raise production to prevent the price increases desired by other OPEC members favoring a more hawkish strategy on oil prices. These countries, which traditionally have included Iran, Iraq, Venezuela, and Nigeria, have large populations, ambitious development plans, and smaller reserves and, therefore, they seek to maximize their oil revenues in the short term. For example, in 1975, OPEC, over Saudi opposition, approved an immediate 10-percent and subsequent 15-percent price increase. Saudi Arabia and the United Arab Emirates (UAE) split with the other OPEC members, announced a 5-percent increase, and greater production. By June, they had forced the rest of OPEC to limit the price increase to an acceptable 10 percent. In 1978, when oil markets eased, the Saudis maintained the price by absorbing the majority of reductions of production, exports, and earnings. And in 1979 and 1980, when supplies became tight once again, the Saudis increased production to try to prevent a price explosion.

In addition to Saudi policy, a propitious environment contributed to the stability of the international oil system. In the mid-1970s, recession in the OECD countries, combined with conservation efforts arising from the increase in price, led to a stabilization of demand for oil (see Figure 9-2). Indeed, demand for crude oil was about the same in 1992 as it was in 1973. At the same time, the supply of oil was steady and even growing. OPEC production as determined by the Saudis was steady: There were no serious efforts to constrict the supply in order to push up the price. And new sources of oil—from the North Sea, Alaska, Mexico—were coming on line (see Figure 9-3).

Political conditions in both the producing and the consuming states also enhanced stability. OPEC states, pursuing ambitious economic development programs, were spending their earnings at a rapid rate. Between 1974 and 1978, their combined current-account surpluses actually declined, from $35.0 billion to $5.2 billion.[21] As a result, the oil states had an interest in maintaining production, and therefore earnings, at a high level. In addition, key OPEC states friendly to the West, in particular Saudi Arabia and Iran, were responsive to Western concerns about the dangers of economic disruption from irresponsible management of the price and supply of oil.

The Western countries remained divided and acquiescent and, as time went on, increasingly complacent. Their inability to carry out a major restructuring of energy consumption rapidly was not cause for alarm, because the system seemed

Figure 9-2   World Primary Energy Use in Exajoules, 1950–1992

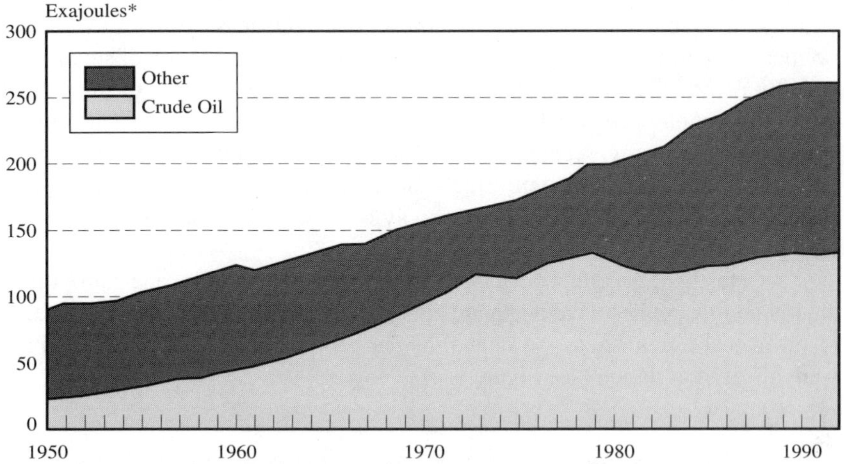

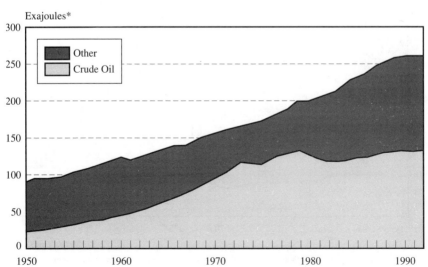

*Exajoules = 10^{18} joules. (A joule is a unit of measurement of energy equivalent to 1 watt of power, occurring for 1 second. The joule is approximately equivalent to 1/4 caloric or .001 BTU (British thermal unit). There are 3.6 million joules in a kilowatt hour).

Note: Includes biomass, the burning of wood, charcoal and other biologically based fuels for energy.
SOURCE: British Petroleum, *BP Statistical Review of World Energy* (London: 1993) and electronic database (London: 1992), and Worldwatch estimates contained in Worldwatch Institute, *Worldwatch Database Diskette 1995* (Washington: Worldwatch Institute, 1995).

Figure 9-3   OPEC and Non-OPEC Oil Production in Millions of Barrels per Day, 1970–1994

SOURCE: Department of Energy, Energy Information Agency, via the World Wide Web at http://www.eia.doe.gov.

to have stabilized at an acceptable level of price and supply. Furthermore, Western foreign policies—the U.S. policy of developing and relying on special relations with Saudi Arabia and Iran, and the European and Japanese policies of general political support for the oil producers—seemed to promise security of supply and stability of price. The Saudi rulers, safe on their throne, friendly to the United States (except on Arab-Israeli issues), and cognizant of their new responsibilities to the world economy, seemed to have OPEC well in hand. The government of the shah of Iran, also apparently stable and reliable, was more hawkish on price than the Saudis but more reliable on supply because it was not directly involved in the Arab-Israeli dispute.

As a result of the effective and moderate Saudi management and a propitious environment, supplies were adequate, and after the beginning of 1974, the price of oil in real terms actually dropped, as the periodic price increases by OPEC were offset by inflation (see Figure 9-4).

The Second Oil Crisis: A System Out of Control

By 1978, however, the political and economic environment had become highly unstable, and the ability and willingness of the Saudis to manage the price

Figure 9-4   Real Price of Oil, 1950–1993, in Constant 1993 Dollars per Barrel

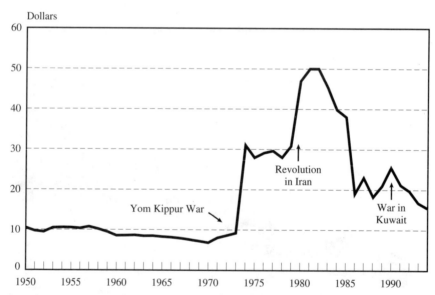

SOURCES: British Petroleum, *BP Statistical Review of World Energy* (London: 1993) and electronic database (London: 1992); Worldwatch estimates based on ibid., and on Department of Energy, Energy Information Administration, *Monthly Energy Review February 1994* (Washington: Government Printing Office, 1994).

and to ensure the supply of oil had diminished. By the end of the 1970s, the demand for oil imports increased as Western economies moved out of the 1974–1975 recession, as the initial shock effect of the price rise wore off, and as complacency set in with the real decline in the price of oil. While demand increased, the world's supply of oil fell. Iran had sharply curtailed its production. Saudi Arabia was willing to increase its production in the short run, but it kept output below capacity and suggested that it would not increase production ceilings in the future. And Kuwait announced plans to decrease its production.

By the end of 1978, the international oil system was once again vulnerable to disruption. World oil supplies were only barely adequate; any slight decrease in supply or increase in demand would precipitate a world shortage and put serious upward pressure on prices. If a supply reduction or demand increase were small, Saudi Arabia might be able to fill the gap and stabilize the system. But if the shifts were large, even the Saudis might not be able to control the system.

The event that created a world shortage of oil and disorder in world oil markets was the 1978 revolution in Iran. At the beginning of 1978, Iran exported 5.4 million barrels of oil a day, about 17 percent of total OPEC exports. At the end of 1978, as part of a successful effort to depose the shah, oil workers cut off all oil exports from that country. By the spring of 1979, the loss of Iranian oil had been to a great extent offset by increased production in the other oil-producing states. Saudi Arabia, for example, increased its production from about 8.3 million barrels per day in 1978 to about 9.5 million barrels in 1979.[22] However, the effect on oil markets of the loss of Iranian oil could not be completely offset. The crisis led not only to a shortage of supply during the latter part of 1978 and early part of 1979 but also to a greater demand for oil, as consumers tried to augment stocks to protect against anticipated future shortfalls in supply. The result of this perceived shortage and rapid scrambling for stocks was again escalating prices and turbulence in the world oil markets.

The first signal of that turbulence came at the December 1978 OPEC meeting. At that time, OPEC agreed to gradually implement price increases amounting to an effective increase of 10 percent for 1979, a rate above the expected Western inflation rates and therefore the first real increase in the price of oil in five years.

This new price, however, did not hold. The Iranian revolution set off panic in the **spot market** for oil, which spilled over into the long-term contract markets. Most crude oil was then sold by long-term contract between the oil-producing countries and the oil companies at a price determined by OPEC. Oil not under long-term contract was sold in spot markets where the price fluctuates according to market conditions. In 1978 and 1979, those conditions were very tight, creating severe upward pressure on the spot market prices. In early 1979, spot prices rose as much as $8.00 above the OPEC price of $13.34 for Saudi Arabian light crude, their chief traded oil. The differential between the OPEC price under long-term contract and the higher spot price benefited the oil companies, which were able to purchase contract oil at relatively low prices. Many OPEC members, unwilling to allow the companies to benefit from such a situation, put surcharges above the agreed OPEC price on long-term contract oil and even broke long-term contracts in order to sell their oil on the spot markets. Despite its production increases and its refusal to add surcharges, Saudi Arabia was unable by itself to restore order to the world oil markets.

In March 1979, OPEC confirmed that the system was out of control. Instead of gradually implementing the price increase agreed in December 1978, OPEC announced it would immediately implement a 14.5 percent increase. More importantly, OPEC decided that its members would be free to impose surcharges on their oil. The surcharges, which many members immediately instituted, demonstrated that even OPEC and the Saudis were unable to control the price of oil. Furthermore, the OPEC members sought to maintain the tight market, which favored price increases, by agreeing to decrease their production as Iran returned to the oil export market. Despite an agreement by International Energy Agency members to reduce oil consumption by 5 percent for 1979, there was little consumers could do in the short run to stabilize the system. In July 1979, OPEC raised the price again. As the oil minister of Saudi Arabia explained, the world was on the verge of a "free for all" in the international oil system.[23]

By the middle of 1980, the free-for-all appeared to be coming to an end. High levels of Saudi production and stable world consumption led to an easing of markets. In this climate, Saudi Arabia and other OPEC moderates sought to regain control over prices, reunify price levels, and develop a long-term OPEC strategy for gradual, steady price increases geared to inflation, exchange rate changes, and growth in the developed countries. In September 1980, OPEC discussed the long-term strategy and planned to continue deliberations at a summit meeting of heads of state in November 1980.

But the plan was destroyed by the outbreak of war between Iraq and Iran. On September 22, 1980, Iraq launched an attack on Iran's oil-producing region, and Iran's air force in turn attacked Iraq's oil facilities. The result was a halt in oil exports from these two countries and a reduction in world supplies by an estimated 3.5 million barrels per day—roughly 10 percent of world oil exports. The war dashed all hopes for stability in world oil markets. The OPEC summit was postponed indefinitely, and pressure began to build in the spot market. In December 1980, OPEC members set a new ceiling price of $33 a barrel and spot prices reached $41 a barrel.

The loss of Iraqi and Iranian oil was offset by a high level of world oil stocks, increased production by other Gulf states of an estimated 1 to 1.5 million barrels per day, and the sluggish demand caused by recession and the efforts of members of the International Energy Agency to dissuade companies from entering the spot market in precautionary panic buying, as they had done in 1979. Although such factors prevented panic and chaos, pressure on the spot prices was inevitable, as those countries that had relied on Iraq for oil imports turned to the spot market. As the hostilities continued, spot-market prices gradually rose, thus putting further pressure on long-term prices. Furthermore, damage to the oil production and export facilities in both countries raised questions about oil supplies even after the cessation of hostilities.

As the market conditions disintegrated, the foreign policies of the West, particularly that of the United States, were substantially weakened. The special relationship of the United States with Iran under the shah became one of hostility under the new Islamic government. Even the relationship of the United States with Saudi Arabia seemed threatened. The Camp David agreement between Israel and Egypt had led to a cooling of Saudi-U.S. relations. For the Saudis, the overthrow of the shah, the inability of the United States to keep him in power or even to prevent the holding of U.S. hostages raised doubts about the value and reliability of U.S. support. The events in Iran and an internal insurrection in Mecca in 1980 also raised the specter of internal political instability for both Saudi Arabia and the United States, which Tehran was seeking to foster.

Unstable market conditions and political uncertainty gave rise to widespread pessimistic predictions about the stability of oil prices and the availability of oil in the future. At the height of the second oil shock, experts predicted continuing chronic shortages and periodic interruptions in the supply of oil, at least through the end of the century, by which time alternative energy sources would supposedly be more fully developed. It was also predicted that OPEC market management would keep the price of oil rising approximately 2 percent faster than the rate of inflation.[24] Few observers of the international oil situation in the late 1970s foresaw the profound changes that were to take place as the world moved into the 1980s, changes that not only undermined the ability of the oil oligopoly to manage the price of oil but also threatened the very institutional survival of the OPEC cartel.

OPEC in Decline: The World Oil Glut

OPEC's problems in the 1980s stemmed from its success. The cartel's ability to increase the price of oil eventually transformed the world oil market. The demand for oil fell, non-OPEC production grew, and as a result, a long-term surplus emerged, putting sustained downward pressure on prices. Moreover, the excess supply made it more difficult, if not impossible, for OPEC to manage prices, as it had in the previous decade.

The transformation of the international oil scene was due, in part, to declining demand. Total oil consumption in the industrial countries fell by an estimated 10 percent between 1980 and 1984, after having risen almost continuously for decades.[25] Worldwide recession and slow rates of growth in the major consuming countries contributed substantially to this decline. There was also a structural change in consumption patterns. Price increases led to a greater substitution of other fuels for oil, especially in the developed market countries, which rapidly expanded their consumption of coal, natural gas, and, in some countries, nuclear energy. Higher oil prices also stimulated energy conservation and structural adjustment, which were reinforced by government regulations and incentives. Price controls had cushioned the U.S. economy from the effects of the oil-price increases, encouraging imports and discouraging domestic exploration. The removal of controls precipitated a reduction in imports and permanently altered the structure of demand in the United States.[26] In response to the high oil prices, energy efficiency increased. Automobiles became more fuel efficient and homes were better insulated. It is estimated that industry in the noncommunist developed countries improved its energy efficiency by a massive 31.1 percent between 1973 and 1982.[27]

Along with the fall in demand, higher oil prices also attracted new suppliers to the international market. OPEC's management task became considerably more difficult, as the OPEC countries lost a substantial portion of their share of world production to non-OPEC producers. OPEC's share of the world oil market fell from 63 percent in 1973 to 48 percent in 1979 to 33 percent in 1983 (see again Figure 9-3).[28] Non-OPEC production in the oil-exporting developing countries—especially Mexico and, to a lesser extent, China, Egypt, and Malaysia—rose steadily, from 2.8 million barrels per day in 1973 to 7.5 million barrels per day in 1983 (see Figure 9-5). In the developed countries, several large reservoirs of new

Figure 9-5   Oil Production in China, Egypt, Malaysia, and Mexico in Thousands of Barrels per Day, 1970–1994

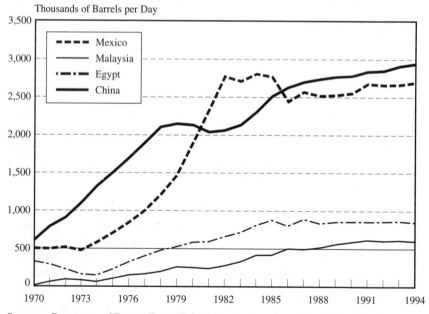

Thousands of Barrels per Day

SOURCE: Department of Energy, Energy Information Agency, via the World Wide Web at http://www.eia.doe.gov.

Figure 9-6   Oil Production in Norway, the United Kingdom, and the North Sea in Millions of Barrels per Day, 1970–1994

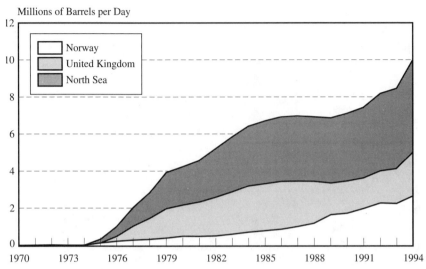

Millions of Barrels per Day

Norway

United Kingdom

North Sea

SOURCE: Department of Energy, Energy Information Agency, via the World Wide Web at http://www.eia.doe.gov.

oil came into full operation, most notably in the North Sea, which made Norway and Britain players in the international oil game (see Figure 9-6). In addition, the former Soviet Union increased its production and exports in order to boost its foreign exchange earnings (see Figure 9-7).[29]

Meanwhile, higher energy prices stimulated increased domestic oil production in the industrialized importing countries. Higher prices and price decontrol in the United States promoted greater investment in the petroleum sector and encouraged new oil companies to enter the market, exploring for new crude sources as well as developing new purchase and distribution lines.[30] As a result of conservation, adjustment, and increased domestic production, the noncommunist developed countries reduced their total demand for imported oil by 40 percent, decreasing their reliance on foreign oil from two-thirds of total consumption in 1979 to less than half in 1983.[31]

Trends in the developing countries were different from the experience of the developed countries. Oil consumption in the developing countries as a whole expanded by approximately 7 percent a year from 1973 to 1979, attributable to relatively high rates of economic growth, generally low domestic oil prices, a lack of oil substitutes, and a limited capacity for conservation. After the second oil shock, however, oil consumption in the developing world rose much more slowly, with most of the increase in consumption attributable to the net oil-exporting countries.[32] A few oil-importing developing countries were able to expand their

Figure 9-7   Petroleum Production in Russia and the Former Soviet Union in Millions of Barrels per Day, 1970–1994

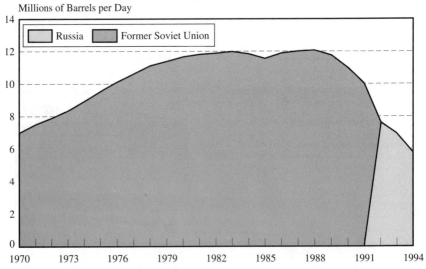

SOURCE: Department of Energy, Energy Information Agency, via the World Wide Web at http://www.eia.doe.gov.

domestic oil production. Brazil increased its production by 50 percent between 1973 and 1983, and India raised its output fivefold (see Figure 9-8).

Downward pressure on oil prices from the sharp drop in demand and the rise in non-OPEC production was exacerbated by an unprecedented drawdown of oil inventories by the international oil companies. Companies had built up their reserve stocks to their highest levels ever during the uncertainties of the 1979–1980 oil shock. Lower oil prices, high interest rates that raised the cost of holding inventories, and, most important, the growing realization that the sluggish world demand for oil was the result of long-term changes in demand patterns and not merely a cyclical phenomenon led to a massive reduction in inventories.[33]

Shifting supply and demand depressed oil prices. On the spot market, prices fell from $40 per barrel in 1980 to $30 per barrel at the end of 1982, further lowering long-term contract prices.[34] As a result, the GNP of the OPEC countries as a whole fell every year during this period. Although Saudi Arabia and some of the high-income OPEC countries were able to maintain positive trade balances, the current-account surpluses of many OPEC members disappeared, constraining their development plans, imports, and, for heavily indebted countries like Nigeria and Venezuela, payment of debt-service obligations.[35] The fall in demand imposed a particularly heavy burden on Saudi Arabia, which, in its informal role as OPEC's market manager, was forced to reduce its production drastically, from a peak of 9.9 million barrels per day in 1980 to less than 5 million barrels per day by 1983, in order to defend OPEC's prices. Saudi oil revenues fell from a peak of $102 billion in 1981 to $37 billion in 1983. The Gulf countries also reduced their production in support of the Saudi price stabilization effort. As a result, Kuwait's oil revenues fell from a 1980 peak of $19 billion to $9.8 billion in 1983, and the United Arab Emirates oil revenue declined from $18 billion to $11 billion during the same period.[36]

The changing pattern of oil production and consumption increased OPEC's management problems and undermined the cartel's cohesion. As we have seen, the factors that set the stage for OPEC's success in the 1970s had changed by the 1980s. Whereas the demand for oil had been inelastic in the 1970s, conservation and interfuel substitution increased elasticity by the 1980s. Whereas the oil supply seemed inelastic in the 1970s, by the 1980s, new sources had diminished much of the cartel's original advantage as the main source of the world's oil. New non-OPEC suppliers also made the cartel's management more difficult. Finally, as the tight supply eased and prices fell, political differences within the cartel further undermined OPEC's capacity for joint action. Excess supply gave rise to enormous strains within OPEC, and the hardship exacerbated traditional conflicts between those OPEC members seeking to maximize their short-term revenues in order to boost imports and hasten development plans and those like Saudi Arabia

Figure 9-8   Oil Production in Brazil and India in Thousands of Barrels per Day, 1970–1994

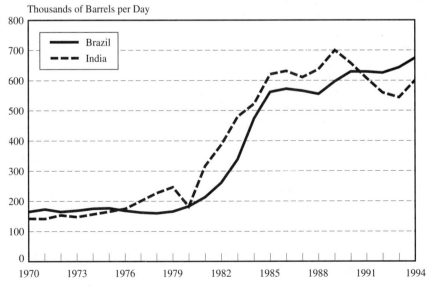

Source: Department of Energy, Energy Information Agency, via the World Wide Web at http://www.eia.doe.gov.

and the Gulf states wanting to maintain foreign dependence on OPEC oil for as long as possible by limiting the price increases.

Eventually, OPEC became a victim of the classic cartel problem: cheating. The first episode of cheating occurred between 1981 and 1983. In 1981, several OPEC members—in particular Algeria, Iran, Libya, Venezuela, and Nigeria—undercut the cartel's price-management system by producing over their prescribed ceiling, offering price discounts, and indirectly cutting prices through extended credit terms, barter deals, and the absorption of freight costs by the seller. As long as Saudi Arabia was willing to shore up prices by restraining its own production, these countries were able to violate OPEC's rules without creating a collapse of prices. The Saudis, however, became more and more bitter about having to sacrifice in the face of rampant cheating by their fellow cartel members. Not only were they losing foreign exchange earnings, they were also facing reduced supplies of natural gas that is produced in conjunction with oil and on which the Saudi economy had become dependent.

The expanded volume of oil traded on the spot market after 1978 made it more difficult for OPEC to monitor its members' oil transactions and thus aggravated OPEC's price-management problem. With new non-OPEC sources of supply, greater availability of cheaper oil from OPEC cheaters, slackened demand, and less fear of rising prices, the oil companies saw less need for long-term contracts and more often met their supply needs through the spot market. Whereas in 1973 over 95 percent of all oil was traded on long-term contracts, by 1983 at least 20 percent of the world's oil was traded on the spot market.[37]

The situation was aggravated by continuing disputes over national production allocations within OPEC. Iran, in particular, pressed to maintain or increase its market share at the expense of Saudi Arabia. The Gulf states were reluctant to agree to any production quota unless there was some agreement to end price discounting. Several cartel meetings failed to produce any consensus for dealing with the rampant cheating.

By early 1983, Algeria, Libya, Iran, and Nigeria were selling oil as much as $4 below the $34 OPEC price. Increasingly impatient, Saudi Arabia and its Gulf allies threatened to lower their prices to undercut the cheaters. The threat of a price war was serious. A price collapse would have had severe effects on growth, development plans, military expenditures, and domestic political stability in virtually all of the OPEC member countries. For indebted oil exporters like Mexico, Venezuela, Nigeria, and Indonesia—and their creditor banks—a sharp drop in prices could have precipitated bankruptcy and a worldwide financial crisis. Other exporters like the United Kingdom, Norway, and the Soviet Union would also suffer from a price fall, as would the oil and banking industries in the United States.

In January 1983, an emergency OPEC meeting collapsed because of the running feud over the distribution of the quotas and price discounting. The international oil markets reacted almost immediately. Spot market prices fell, oil companies began depleting their inventories, and producers came under increasing pressure to reduce their long-term contract prices. The Soviet Union reduced its prices, as did the smaller non-OPEC producers like Egypt. More significantly, the British and Norwegian oil companies proposed to reduce the price of North Sea oil. Meanwhile, Saudi Arabia and the other Gulf producers continued to threaten to cut their prices if some agreement were not concluded.

Finally, in March 1983, OPEC members hammered out an agreement that signaled major changes in the oil-management system. For the first time in the cartel's history, OPEC reduced the price of oil, from $34 per barrel to $29 per barrel. To maintain this price, the members agreed for the first time to a concerted production reduction scheme that limited OPEC output to 17.5 million barrels per day and allocated production among the members. Saudi Arabia formally accepted the role of "swing producer" and committed to adjust its output to support the newly agreed-upon price.[38]

Oil Price Wars

The new production reduction scheme slowed but did not stop the long-term decline in OPEC's power as a price-setting cartel. Sluggish demand and increasing production by countries outside OPEC continued to put downward pressure on oil prices. Domestic economic problems and financial shortages tempted members to break ranks by reducing prices and expanding production to obtain more revenues. As non-OPEC production grew and as non-OPEC producers such as Norway and the United Kingdom lowered prices below that of OPEC, it became more and more difficult for the cartel to reach agreement on production ceilings and quotas among members. In 1984, OPEC lowered the price to $28 per barrel, reduced its production ceiling to 16 million barrels per day, and lowered individual production quotas. Despite OPEC's production allocation scheme, virtually all of the decline in output was absorbed by Saudi Arabia. While other OPEC members either maintained or increased their output, Saudi production declined dramatically. By August 1985, Saudi output had fallen to 2.5 million barrels per day, less than one-fourth of its production in 1980–1981.[39] Saudi foreign exchange earnings suffered a steep decline and the drop in oil production once again impinged on domestic requirements for natural gas.

In the second half of 1985, Saudi Arabia abandoned the role of swing producer. In order to increase its production and restore its market share, Saudi Arabia abandoned selling crude oil on the basis of official OPEC prices and instituted "netback" sales contracts—a market-responsive price formula based on the value of products into which its oil was refined. Once this happened, OPEC was no longer able to manage the price of oil. In December 1985, OPEC recognized the inevitable. It abandoned the system of fixed official selling prices and concerted production reductions. For the first time since the seven sisters agreed to set prices, the oil cartel agreed to allow prices to be determined by the market.

Largely due to the dramatic increase in Saudi production, OPEC output

soared by almost one-third in 1986. The result was volatility and a sharp fall in
the price of oil. Spot-market prices fell from between $27 to $31 per barrel in
November 1985 to between $8 to $10 per barrel in July 1986.[40] The collapse of
oil prices led to a parallel drop in the value of oil exports to their lowest level
since 1973.

Pressure to restore concerted production reductions and higher prices built
both within and outside OPEC. In mid-1986, OPEC agreed to interim production
reductions and quotas. Then, in December, the cartel reached agreement on new
production reductions and quotas and on a new fixed export price of $18 per bar-
rel. Supply control was helped by a slight decline in non-OPEC production due
both to voluntary production restraint by non-OPEC exporters and to the shut-
down of some high-cost production, especially in the United States. As a result,
spot market prices rose to $17 to $19 per barrel in 1987.[41] Once again, the cartel
pulled back from a price war and reestablished market discipline and prices,
albeit at a lower level.

Nonetheless, economic and political conflicts continued to threaten OPEC's
ability to implement concerted production reductions. The traditional split
remained between hawks like Iran and Iraq, which sought to maximize oil earnings in the short term, and moderates like Saudi Arabia and the Gulf countries,
which sought to maximize oil earnings over the long-term. This conflict was complicated by an internal civil war over quota allocations. Although a number of
OPEC members felt their quota allocations were unfair, the cartel was hopeless-
ly divided and unable to revise the existing agreement. Thus, a number of members resumed cheating by producing over their quotas. The key was the United
Arab Emirates, a Gulf state that has a small population and no pressing revenue
needs and that thus should have fallen in the camp of the moderates. However, the
UAE believed its quota was unfair and in 1988 began pumping twice its allocation. As concerted supply restraint weakened, prices of oil slipped downward.

Another important problem grew out of the Iran-Iraq war. It was a sign of
the change in the oil markets that the bombing of oil tankers and shipping facilities in the Persian Gulf did not lead to a run-up in oil prices during the 1980s. The
spare capacity of the other OPEC and non-OPEC oil producers, public stocks in
consuming countries, as well as the oil-sharing arrangement of the International
Energy Agency cushioned any potential threat.

It was the end of the Iran-Iraq war that posed a threat to oil prices. During
the war, Iraqi demands for an increase in its quota met implacable resistance from
Iran, which insisted on maintaining its second place in OPEC quotas (behind
Saudi Arabia) and refused to allow its enemy to improve its relative position.
Resolution of the conflict was deferred during the war by leaving Iraq out of the
allocation scheme. As long as the war limited the ability of both Iran and Iraq to
pump oil, the Iraq-Iran conflict did not threaten OPEC's supply management.
However, the cease-fire between the two agreed in mid-1988 posed a serious
threat to OPEC's ability to control oil supplies. Iraq was in the process of significantly expanding its production capacity. Both countries faced higher revenue

needs for rebuilding and resuming economic development after the lengthy war, and both felt justified in producing more because of postwar needs and because of their reduced production during the war. However, because of the mutual distrust and antagonism arising from the war, OPEC was initially unable to negotiate a new allocation scheme.

At this point, Saudi Arabia intervened. Faced with cheating by the UAE, new demands by Iran and Iraq, and the seemingly intractable Iran-Iraq stalemate, Saudi Arabia followed the strategy that it had pursued before. It increased production in an effort to force other OPEC members to resume discipline. OPEC output rose from an estimated 18.5 million barrels per day to an estimated 22.5 million barrels per day. The glut of Saudi oil led to a fall in oil prices to $13 to $14 per barrel by late 1988. In real terms, oil prices were below the 1974 level. The decline in prices hurt the finances of all oil exporters; put severe pressure on indebted oil exporters such as Nigeria, Mexico, and Venezuela; and contributed to political instability in Algeria. By November, action by Saudi Arabia and Kuwait had forced OPEC to agree on a new production agreement to limit production to 18.5 million barrels per day and raise prices to $18 per barrel. Iran received its old share allocation and agreed to allow Iraq to return to the OPEC system with a quota equal to its own. Iraq's increase came at the expense of other cartel members, especially Saudi Arabia, whose quotas were decreased. The question was whether the agreement would hold and for how long, especially if and when the export capacity of both Iran and Iraq increased substantially.

The events of the 1980s thus led to a major change in OPEC's power as a price-setting cartel. Sluggish demand, sustained oversupply, competition from outsiders, economic temptations to break ranks by reducing prices and increasing production, and internal political conflicts undermined the role of the oil-producing cartel. Saudi Arabia could offset some cheating by other members but was no longer willing or able to single-handedly manage the cartel by playing the role of the swing producer.

In the absence of OPEC discipline, some cartel members protected themselves from price competition by buying refining and marketing operations in the major oil-consuming countries. During the 1980s, a number of OPEC members—Venezuela, Libya, Kuwait, Saudi Arabia, and the United Arab Emirates—acquired downstream operations in the United States and Western Europe. Moving downstream was intended to protect crude oil exporters when prices fall, because it guaranteed an outlet for oil and because prices for refined products fell less than prices for crude oil. As these OPEC members developed refining and marketing capacity, their oil operations came to resemble the large, integrated oil companies that once dominated the oil system (see Figure 9-9). They found themselves in even greater conflict with other OPEC members that remained dependent on crude oil exports for revenues and sought therefore to maximize oil earnings in the short term. The downstream diversification strategy, therefore, further weakened OPEC.

Figure 9-9 Top Ten Petroleum Firms by Product Sales in 1992, in Millions of Barrels per Day

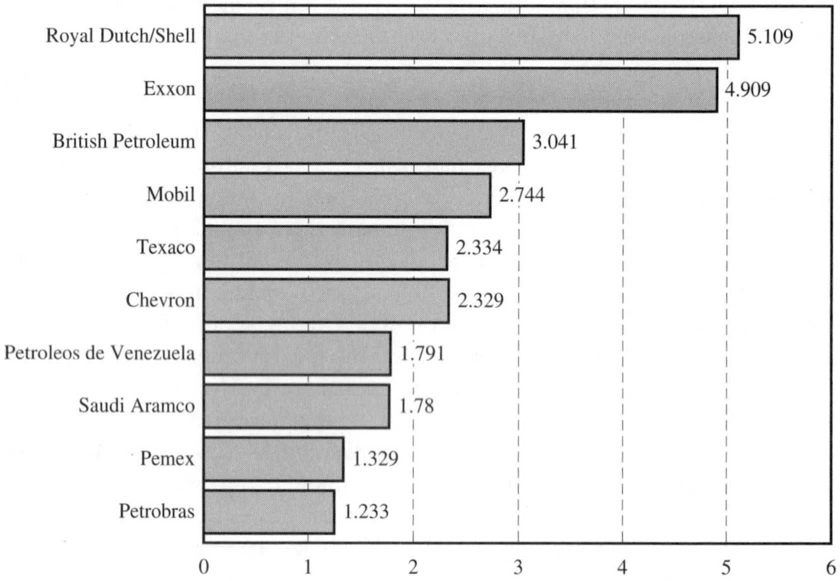

Royal Dutch/Shell	5.109
Exxon	4.909
British Petroleum	3.041
Mobil	2.744
Texaco	2.334
Chevron	2.329
Petroleos de Venezuela	1.791
Saudi Aramco	1.78
Pemex	1.329
Petrobras	1.233

SOURCE: United Nations, *World Economic and Social Survey 1994* (New York: UN, 1994), 143.

The Gulf War

Differences among OPEC members over the price of oil and production quotas necessary to manage the price were a major factor in the invasion of Kuwait by Iraq in August 1990. Concern about the consequences of that invasion for world oil markets was a central reason for the strong reaction of the United States, Saudi Arabia, and their allies. In 1989 and 1990, Iraq and Kuwait were on opposite sides of a significant conflict within OPEC. Iraq emerged from its war with Iran facing severe limits on its ability to produce and export oil. Huge debts made it impossible for Iraq to borrow funds to rebuild its oil production and export facilities. These constraints combined with its desperate financial situation led Iraq to advocate a policy of maintaining high prices within OPEC through greater member discipline. Kuwait took the opposite position. With a large production capacity of 2.5 million barrels per day and large reserves of 100 billion barrels, Kuwait, like Saudi Arabia, advocated lower prices as a way of discouraging production by alternative suppliers of petroleum and investment in alternative energy sources. Because Kuwait was not as influential within OPEC as Saudi Arabia, it did not feel as much responsibility for maintaining the organization's effectiveness.

Thus, Kuwait refused to go along with the production quota assigned to it by OPEC in the late 1980s of 1.15 million barrels per day. Cheating by Kuwait and the United Arab Emirates was addressed at an OPEC meeting in November 1989. At this meeting, Kuwait's quota was increased to 1.5 million barrels per day and the UAE was exempted from abiding by its quota. The new agreement did not hold, however, and oil prices declined from $20 per barrel in January to $17.75 per barrel in March 1990. In May, OPEC held an emergency meeting in an effort to decrease total production and increase prices. Saudi Arabia agreed to lower its production, pushing up the price by about $1 per barrel, but, according to Iraq, Kuwait refused to comply with OPEC limits. In the ensuing months, oil prices continued to fall to under $17 per barrel. Iraq claimed with increasing vehemence that Kuwait was deliberately undermining the Iraqi economy by overproducing, and that it was, in addition, siphoning oil from a disputed field on the border of the two countries. President Saddam Hussein began massing troops along the Iraqi-Kuwaiti border. A last ditch effort by OPEC to resolve the dispute collapsed in July, and on August 2 Iraq invaded Kuwait.[42]

The Iraqi invasion led to a spike in the price of oil to nearly $40 per barrel by October 1990. The invasion also led to a swift reaction by both producers and consumers of oil. The United States led the formation of a broad international coalition that included Saudi Arabia, numerous Middle Eastern countries, France, and the United Kingdom. In October 1990, the coalition supported a U.N. resolution authorizing an embargo that would close all world oil markets to Iraqi exports. This embargo affected a flow of 4.3 million barrels per day of oil to world markets, about 7 percent of the world total. U.N. action combined with increased production by both OPEC and non-OPEC producers helped to reduce the impact of this very effective embargo on the rest of the world. In addition, the oil consuming members of the International Energy Agency released their strategic oil reserves in order to cushion the impact of U.N. embargo on world oil markets.[43] The coalition then sent military forces to the region and, on January 16, 1991, launched a military action that liberated Kuwait and led to a record one-day drop in oil prices. The allies did not succeed in toppling Saddam Hussein, however.

While numerous factors motivated the United States and its allies in reacting strongly to the invasion of Kuwait, concern about oil was one of the most important. Control of Kuwait would have put Iraq in a position to dominate the weakened OPEC. Control over Kuwait's petroleum reserves would have given Iraq control over a total of 200 billion barrels, about one-fifth of the world total of known commercial oil reserves. Combined Iraqi and Kuwaiti daily production capacity would have been around 5.5 million barrels per day, still below that of Saudi Arabia (8.5 million barrels per day) but large enough to give the Iraqi government significant market power. Furthermore, with control of strategic military positions in Kuwait and with its large army, Iraq would have been able to threaten other key oil producers in the region, including Saudi Arabia. Such dominance of world oil markets by a single country was unacceptable to both consumers and producers of petroleum and helped to explain the unique alliance that formed against Saddam Hussein. Following the war, due to Iraq's continuing ability to manufacture weapons of mass destruction and its refusal to agree to effective monitoring of its activities, the U.N. maintained sanctions on all exports to Iraq except for food and medical supplies and other humanitarian needs. The U.N. also maintained its embargo on exports of Iraqi oil.

The Future of OPEC

The Gulf War demonstrated that OPEC was no longer able to play in the 1990s the role of balancer and regulator of the international oil system that it had played in the 1980s. The divergent interests of OPEC members has made price and production management increasingly difficult despite the powerful position of Saudi Arabia. Even that dominant country began to face financial problems in the 1990s as the price of oil declined and the Saudi budget grew faster than the growth in oil revenues.

Furthermore, because OPEC's share of the world oil market was smaller in the 1990s than in the 1970s and 1980s, price management would increasingly require the cooperation of non-OPEC producers. Such cooperation could not be guaranteed, however, since many non-OPEC producers, like the United Kingdom, Norway, and Mexico, continued to pursue independent strategies. In Mexico, the NAFTA treaty, which opened up sectors of the oil industry to foreign investment, combined with the aftermath of the 1994 peso crisis to make it difficult for the Mexican government to think of cooperating with OPEC to bolster oil prices.

Equally critical for the future of OPEC was the question of world demand and supply. In the 1980s and early 1990s, as the world supply of oil increased but OPEC's share decreased, the oil market became more like that of other commodities. That is, the oil market was subject to the sort of price volatility caused by temporary fluctuations in demand and supply that existed in world copper or bauxite markets, for example. Soaring oil prices in the 1970s led to a decline in demand in the 1980s due to conservation and substitution, and also to an increase in supply due to new exploration and production, resulting eventually in declining prices. Conversely, the lower price of oil in the 1980s encouraged greater consumption, discouraged investment in exploration and production, and contributed to the depletion of reserves that threatened to constrain supplies in the 1990s.

As the 1990s advanced, however, several new factors emerged. Growth in consumption, especially on the part of the rapidly growing NICs of Asia, continued unabated. However, possible new sources of supply—particularly in the oil-rich regions of the former Soviet Union (especially Kazahkstan, Azerbaijan, and Russia itself)—loomed on the horizon. Today, in the aftermath of the breakup of the Soviet Union, these regions may eventually open up to the kind of investment flows that are necessary to bring production capacity up significantly. But formidable legal, political, and financial barriers remain. Thus, it remains to be seen what role these countries will play not only in the supply but also in the politics of oil.

Other OPECs?

The success of the oil producers in the 1970s led to a revolution in the thinking of Southern raw material producers. Suddenly it seemed that producer cartels could bring the end of dependence. Producer organizations in copper, bauxite, iron ore, bananas, and coffee were either formed or took on new life after October 1973. In a variety of United Nations resolutions, the Third World supported the right of Southern exports to form producer associations and urged the North to "respect that right by refraining from applying economic and political measures that would limit it."[44]

Yet by the late 1970s the prospects for these new producer cartels seemed dim. None had succeeded in maintaining higher commodity prices in the face of depressed market conditions, most were fraught with internal dissension, and a few never even got off the ground. Still, it is worthwhile to examine both their potential and the reasons for their very limited successes. First, it is necessary to review the reasons for the success of the oil producers and thereby to develop a model for effective producer action.

Several market factors set the stage for OPEC's success in the 1970s. The demand for oil imports was high. Oil imports played an important and growing role as a source of energy in the North. Europe and Japan were dependent on foreign sources for oil. Even the once self-sufficient United States had become increasingly dependent on oil imports. In the medium term, the demand for oil and oil imports is also price inelastic. There are no readily available substitutes for petroleum, and there is no way to decrease consumption significantly. Thus an increase in the price of oil does not immediately lead to a noticeable decrease in demand.

Supply factors also favored OPEC in the medium term. The supply of oil is price inelastic; that is, an increase in its price does not lead to the rapid entrance of new producers into the market. Large amounts of capital and many years are required to develop new sources of oil. In addition, supply inelasticity was not relieved by the stockpiles of oil. In 1973, the developed countries did not have oil reserves to use even in the short run to increase supply and alleviate the effect of supply reductions.

Finally, at the time of the OPEC price increases, there was an extremely tight supply of oil in the international market. Rapidly rising demand in the consuming countries was not matched by rising production. As a result, a few important producers, or even one major producer, could be in a position to influence price by merely threatening to limit supply.

This economic vulnerability of consumers set the stage for OPEC's action. Several political factors, however, determined whether such action would take place, and an understanding of the behavior of interest groups helps explain the ability of the oil producers to take joint action to raise the price of oil.[45]

First, there is a relatively small number of oil-exporting countries. Common political action is more likely when the number of participants is so limited, as the small number maximizes all the members' perception of their shared interest and the benefits to be derived from joint action.

The oil producers were also helped by the experience of more than a decade of cooperation. OPEC encouraged what one analyst described as "solidarity and a sense of community."[46] It also led to experience in common action. Between 1971 and 1973, the oil producers tested their power, saw tangible results from common action, and acquired the confidence to pursue such action. This confidence was reinforced by the large monetary reserves of the major producers. The reserves minimized the economic risks of attempting some joint action such as reducing production or instituting an embargo. The reserves were money in the bank that could be used to finance needed imports if the joint effort to raise the price of petroleum was not immediately successful. According to one analyst, it enabled the oil producers to take a "long-term perspective," to adopt common policies in the first place, and to avoid the later temptation of taking advantage of short-term gains by cheating.[47]

The common political interest of the Arab oil producers in backing their cause in the conflict with Israel reinforced their common economic interest in increasing the price of oil. The outbreak of the 1973 war greatly enhanced Arab cohesiveness and facilitated the OPEC decision of October 16 to raise oil prices unilaterally.

Group theory suggests, however, that the perception of a common interest is often insufficient for common action. A leader or leaders are needed to mobilize the group and to bear the main burden of group action. Leadership was crucial to common oil-producer action. In 1973, the initiative by Arab producers in unilaterally raising prices made it possible for other producers to increase their prices. After 1973 the willingness and ability of Saudi Arabia to bear the major burden of production reductions determined the ability of producers to maintain higher prices.

Producer action was facilitated by the nature of the problem. Manipulating the price was relatively easy because it was a seller's market. Given the tight market, it was not necessary to reduce the supply significantly to maintain a higher price. Ironically, the international oil companies also helped joint-producer action. Producing nations were able to increase their price by taxing the oil companies. The companies acquiesced because they were able to pass on the tax to their customers.[48] Producing nations were also able to reduce the supply simply by ordering the companies to limit production. Increasing governmental control of the companies helped implement these reductions.

Finally, the success of the producers was assured by the absence of countervailing consumer power. The weakness of the corporations and the consumer governments was demonstrated by the Libyan success in 1970 and by subsequent negotiations. The disarray and acquiescence of the oil companies and the oil-consuming governments in 1973 sealed the success of the producing nations. Particularly important was the inability of the developed market economies to take joint action—in contrast with the group action of the producers—to counter the cartel.

In the aftermath of OPEC's success, several factors seemed to suggest that in the short term, and perhaps in the medium term, some producer cartels might succeed. In the near term, economic conditions were propitious for many commodities, particularly for those on which consuming states are highly dependent. The United States, for example, relies on imports of bauxite, tin, bananas, and coffee. Western Europe and Japan, less well endowed with raw materials, depend also on imports of copper, iron ore, and phosphates. Disrupting the supply of many of these commodities, particularly critical minerals, would have a devastating effect on the developed market economies.

In addition, over the short and medium terms, the demand for and supply of these commodities are price inelastic. As discussed earlier, with few exceptions, a price increase for these materials would not be offset by a decrease in consumption, which would lead to an increase in total producer revenues. Similarly, when supply is price inelastic, a rise in price will not immediately lead to the emergence of new supplies, because it takes time and money to grow new crops and exploit new mineral sources. It should be noted that for some critical raw materials, an inelasticity of supply can be cushioned by stockpiles, and developed countries have accumulated such supplies for strategic reasons. Nevertheless, although stockpiles can serve to resist cartel action over the short term, not all commodities can be stockpiled, and stockpiles in many commodities are generally insufficient to outlast supply interruptions that persist for more than a few months.

Tight market conditions favor producers in the short term. As demonstrated by the oil action, a seller's market facilitates cartel action by enabling one or a small number of producers to raise prices, as occurred in 1973–1974. At that time, the simultaneous economic boom in the North and uncertain currency markets that encouraged speculation in commodities led to commodity shortages and sharp price increases. The developed countries were particularly vulnerable to threats of supply manipulation, and the producer countries were in a particularly strong position to make such threats. For example, Morocco (phosphates) and Jamaica (bauxite) took advantage of this situation to raise prices.

In addition to these economic factors, several political conditions also favored producer action, again primarily over the short run. For many commodities—for example, bauxite, copper, phosphates, bananas, cocoa, coffee, natural rubber, and tea—relatively few Southern producers dominate the export market, and some of these producers have formed associations with the goal of price management. Several political developments made producer cooperation more likely in the mid-1970s. One was a new sense of self-confidence. The OPEC experience suggested to other producers that through their control of commodities vital to the North, they might possess the threat they had long sought. Thus, many Third World states felt that they could risk more aggressive policies toward the North.

Another new development stemmed not from confidence but from desperation. The simultaneous energy, food, recession, and inflation crises left most

Southern states with severe balance-of-payments problems. Some states may have felt that they had no alternative to instituting risky measures that might offer short-term economic benefits but that would probably prove unsuccessful or even damaging in the long run.

Reinforcing economic desperation was political concern. Political leaders, especially those in the Third World, tend to have short-run perspectives, as the maintenance of their power may depend on achieving short-term gains despite inevitable long-run losses.[49] However, this argument is directly opposite to the OPEC model for a successful producer cartel, wherein monetary reserves enabled the producing nations to take a long-term perspective, to risk short-term losses for long-term gains. In other cases, producers with huge balance-of-payments deficits may be moved to risk long-term losses for short-term gains. And as has been argued, the short-term maximization of revenues may in fact be rational action for the long-term view; that is, if producers feel that their short-term profits will be sufficient to achieve economic diversification and development, they may rationally pursue short-term gains.[50]

The emergence of leaders in some producer groups was yet another new development. Jamaica's unilateral action in raising taxes and royalties on bauxite production and Morocco's unilateral action to raise the price of phosphate altered the conditions for other bauxite and phosphate producers.

Finally, cooperation was sometimes made easier by the nature of the task of managing price and supply. In commodities such as bauxite and bananas, vertically integrated oligopolistic multinational corporations could be taxed according to the OPEC formula. In these and other commodities, production control was facilitated by increasing governmental regulation or ownership of production facilities.

With all of these factors working in favor of cartel success, why then were the raw-material producer associations so unsuccessful after 1974? Some of the reasons for the problems of cartels can be traced to the depressed economic conditions of the late 1970s and 1980s, whereas others are of a more general nature.

Although as we have noted, the demand and supply of many commodities are price inelastic over the short and medium terms, in the long run, the demand and supply are more elastic and thus less conducive to successful cartel action, as is illustrated by the OPEC experience of the 1980s. A rise in price above a certain level will generally lead to a shift in demand to substitutes. Aluminum will be substituted for copper; coffee will be replaced by tea. With time, it is also possible to develop new sources of supply for most commodities. New coffee trees can be planted; new mineral resources, including resources in the seabed, can be exploited. Of course, some of these new supplies may be relatively more expensive, as new production will often have to rely on costly technologies and lower-quality ores. Thus, it should be noted, new production may undermine a cartel, but it may have little effect on price.

Because of the long-term elasticity of demand and supply, the successful survival of a cartel generally depends on two complex factors. First, producers have to manage price so that it does not rise above a level that would encourage the use of substitutes. Such management requires sophisticated market knowledge and predictive ability. Because the threshold price may be lower than the preferred price for many producers, agreement on joint action may be quite difficult to achieve. Second, and equally difficult, the supply response from other producers must be managed. Currently existing cartels have been generally unable to manage successfully either prices or supply: price cutting among fellow cartel members has been common, and few producers have agreed to supply controls.

Despite some incentive for cooperation, there have been major problems in joint action. Although many commodities are supplied by a few producers, these producers often find they have more in conflict than in common. The copper producers, for example, are divided by political as well as economic differences. Moreover, although the foreign exchange crisis may encourage cooperation, it also may facilitate consumer resistance. Producing nations that have no reserves and that rely on the export of one commodity for the bulk of their foreign exchange earnings are not in a position to endure long-concerted corporate or consumer-government resistance. Furthermore, the temptation to take short-term profits from concerted action at the expense of longer-term gains is greater during a balance-of-payments crisis. And although the task of price management may be easy in some cases, as when there is a leader and multinational corporations are present, there are no such advantages for many commodity-producing nations.

One of the greatest barriers to producer cartels has been the task of managing supply. Few countries have a large enough share of production and large enough reserves to assume the kind of leadership role played by Saudi Arabia. No one country or small group of countries is able to bear the burden of supply reduction for the entire commodity group.

Without tight markets, then, supply can be controlled only through buffer stock schemes or export or production reductions—methods that are politically complex and economically costly. Many commodities are perishable and hence cannot be stored in a buffer stock, whereas other commodities require enormous buffer stocks and financing to maintain prices. Export and production reductions are equally difficult to accomplish. Export reduction without production controls poses the same problems of storing and financing as buffer stocks do. And agreements to reduce production are difficult to achieve, as OPEC's experience illustrates, and may be costly in terms of employment.

Perhaps the most devastating blow to the producer associations has been dealt by the stagnant—in some cases falling—demand for their commodities. In 1974 and 1975, as economic activity in the industrialized countries declined, the demand for industrial raw materials fell precipitously. Since then, there has been a steady decline in the Northern demand for Southern commodities (see Chapter 7).

Faced with reductions or slow growth in the demand for their commodities, the only hope for the producer associations is to reduce production and supply in order to maintain prices at desired levels. Yet, as we have indicated, most producing nations have found it politically or economically difficult to cut back production, and many cartel members have cut prices in order to increase their international competitiveness. The result has been a general oversupply of many raw materials and a drop in their prices that the cartels have been unable to counteract.

Bauxite, Bananas, and Copper

The problems of producer cartels as well as their potential benefits may be better understood by a brief examination of three attempts by commodity-producing organizations to increase prices: bauxite, bananas, and copper.

In 1974, Jamaica, confronted by rapidly rising import costs for food and petroleum, moved to increase its revenues from bauxite production and to alter its relationship with the six huge multinational companies that owned, processed, and marketed Jamaican bauxite.[51] Despite vigorous protests from the aluminum companies, taxes and royalties on bauxite production were raised, and the new taxes were based not, as before, on the tonnage of bauxite extracted but on the price of aluminum ingots on the North American market. This action increased by over sevenfold the amount collected by the Jamaican government in taxes and royalties on each ton of bauxite.[52] To prevent the companies from shifting production out of Jamaica, the aluminum firms were required to maintain the production levels established by the Jamaican government or to pay taxes on that level whether or not it was actually maintained. Finally, the Jamaican government negotiated long-term agreements with the aluminum companies, providing for increased local refining and government participation in ownership.

The Jamaican actions were followed by other Caribbean bauxite producers, and Jamaica played a leading role in establishing the International Bauxite Association (IBA) in March 1974. Within a few months, the IBA had a membership of eleven (Jamaica, Surinam, Guyana, the Dominican Republic, Haiti, Ghana, Guinea, Sierra Leone, Yugoslavia, Australia, and Indonesia), controlling nearly 85 percent of the noncommunist world's production of bauxite.

The outlook for IBA was optimistic. The consuming states were highly dependent on bauxite imports. None of the six largest consuming nations produced more than 50 percent of its bauxite needs, and most produced very little.[53] The United States, for example, imported 89 percent of its bauxite, and 86 percent of that came from Jamaica.[54] Furthermore, bauxite demand is price inelastic, in large part because the price of bauxite is only a small percentage of the price of aluminum, and most of the price relates to processing costs. Thus an increase in the price of the raw material does not lead to a major increase in the price of the finished product or, in turn, to a significant decrease in consumption. Supply is also price inelastic over the short and medium terms, as huge amounts of capital and many years are needed to develop new sources.

The structure of the market also favored the IBA. Bauxite is sold primarily among subsidiaries of large vertically integrated multinational aluminum corporations, and so the price is subject not to the market but to negotiation. Furthermore, the aluminum multinationals did not have strong incentives to resist pressure for price increases. Because the demand for bauxite, like the demand for petroleum, is inelastic, the multinational companies can pass on price to the end consumer. Thus, if the producing countries can develop bargaining advantages, they can renegotiate the price in their favor. Moreover, geographical and ethnic ties of several key producers—Jamaica, Surinam, and Guyana—facilitated cooperation among them. Perhaps most importantly, Jamaican leadership had demonstrated the benefits of cooperative action.

Despite these positive factors, the IBA's successes were limited. Differing economic and political interests among its members and the resulting lack of cohesiveness proved to be the cartel's central problem. The Caribbean countries, eager to increase prices, maximize government revenues in the short term, and increase national control over the bauxite and aluminum industry, pushed for common pricing and common export taxes. On the other hand, Guinea, in an effort to increase its market share, set its levy well below the Caribbean rate. Australia, as a developed country eager to increase its share of the market for bauxite and related products, did not cooperate in price setting efforts, in imposing a bauxite levy, or in nationalization. Equally troublesome was the rise of new producers outside the IBA. Moreover, a continued slump in the world aluminum market that began with the recession in the mid-1970s and continued into the 1980s, made it difficult for the IBA to act unilaterally to raise prices. Another long-term change was the emergence of substitutes for bauxite, such as new plastics that have been used in place of aluminum in the automobile and container industries.[55]

Differing interests of bauxite producers facilitated the development of new sources of supply. From 1974 to 1976, Australia and Guinea, with lower levels of taxation on bauxite exports than most IBA countries, rapidly increased their bauxite production at the expense of the Caribbean producers. Between 1973 and 1976, bauxite production in Jamaica, Surinam, and Guyana dropped more than 25 percent while production in Australia and Guinea rose by 74 percent. This trend away from the Caribbean and its high export levies continued. In 1973, 33 percent of world bauxite production was in Jamaica, Surinam, and Guyana; by 1976 this was down to 22 percent falling to 12 percent by 1988, whereas in the same period, the proportion of the world's bauxite mined in Australia and Guinea went from 29 percent to 45 percent and increased further to 51 percent by 1988. Brazil, which was not a member of the IBA, moved rapidly to increase its production. In 1976, Brazil accounted for only 1 percent of world production. By 1988, Brazil had increased its production ninefold, giving it 8 percent of world production.[56]

Yet another problem has been the relative decline of the role of the aluminum multinationals. Although they still dominate bauxite capacity and the international trade in bauxite, the six multinationals, somewhat like the seven sisters before them, have lost their downstream dominance of the market. For example, the control by the majors of noncommunist smelter capacity dropped from 80 percent in 1970 to 40 percent by 1982. By the mid-1980s, aluminum prices were being set by the market, not by the six multinationals. For the IBA, this meant that cartel management by way of taxing the multinationals was no longer possible.

As a result of these problems, the International Bauxite Association has largely given up hope of being the "bauxite OPEC" that some of its more militant members had hoped it would become. Instead, the IBA has concentrated on efforts to forge better relations with the aluminum-producing companies and to dispel the suspicions by the aluminum companies of the IBA that resulted from the association's cartel-like behavior during the 1970s. The focus of these efforts included an unsuccessful attempt by the IBA members to establish an international producer-consumer commodity agreement for bauxite under the auspices of UNCTAD.

In many ways, the situation of the banana producers resembles that of the bauxite exporters.[57] Banana production is highly concentrated, with five countries at the time accounting for 65 percent of the world's banana exports—Ecuador (19 percent), Costa Rica (16 percent), the Philippines (12 percent), Honduras (10 percent), and Panama (8 percent)—and the consuming countries are totally dependent on imports. Furthermore, the demand for bananas is price inelastic in the near term and, under certain conditions, in the long term, largely because, like bauxite, the price of the raw material is only a fraction of the price of the retail product. Temperature-controlled transportation, refining, and distribution account for most of the cost of bananas.[58] Thus, a large increase in the price of bananas does not lead to an equal increase in the retail price of bananas. If the price is not raised to such high levels that consumers turn to substitutes, demand will remain inelastic in the long run. Finally, supply is also inelastic in the short run.

Also as with bauxite, multinationals play a key role in the banana industry. Bananas are sold to subsidiaries of the same multinational corporation that owns and operates the banana plantations. These oligopolistic, vertically integrated multinational corporations are dependent on these sources of supply and are vulnerable because of expensive investments in transportation and refrigeration. Finally, because of their oligopolistic market position, the companies can pass on price increases to consumers without fearing a loss of markets to competitors. The banana-producing countries attempted to take advantage of these favorable conditions. In 1974, several Central American banana-producing countries and Colombia formed a union of banana-exporting countries and agreed to impose an export tax of $1.00 on each box of bananas. The effort failed. Only four countries—Colombia, Costa Rica, Honduras, and Panama—actually imposed a tax; only Panama imposed the agreed-upon $1.00 duty; and soon all reduced the duty sharply.

There were several reasons for the failure of the Unión de Paises Exportadores de Banana (UPEB). The multinational banana companies—United Brands, Standard Fruit, and Del Monte—fought back. They challenged the tax in local courts and refused to pay the government until the courts determined the legality of the duty. They stopped exports, cut production, destroyed crates of bananas, laid off workers, threatened not to reinvest after a hurricane in Honduras, and, in Honduras, resorted to bribery to obtain a tax reduction.[59]

Another problem was the refusal by Ecuador, the largest producer and the country with the greatest ability to expand its production, to join UPEB. Ecuador argued that the tax was not viable without concurrent production reductions and that, in any case, as an oil producer, it did not suffer from the oil price increase, which was UPEB's justification for its tax. Although Ecuador most probably acted out of self-interest, its decision did point out the important long-run problem of excess supply. Although the demand for bananas has grown, the supply has grown even more rapidly. Without some form of supply control, UPEB price rises would collapse. Because bananas are perishable, the form of control would have to be production reductions. Yet these are politically difficult to achieve. Even after catastrophic weather in 1982 destroyed a substantial proportion of the world's banana supply and sent prices soaring, it was clear that once the affected areas had recovered, oversupply conditions would again prevail. Against this backdrop, the UPEB members again attempted in 1983 to introduce more mechanisms to regulate the market through limits on new plantings, output controls, price harmonization, and export taxation. However, disagreements over the distribution of the burdens of these efforts continued. Although the Dominican Republic, Nicaragua, and Venezuela joined UPEB, Ecuador and the Philippines remained outside, and Colombia, although a member, did not collaborate closely with UPEB. As a result, UPEB, like the IBA, sought a producer-consumer agreement through the Food and Agricultural Organization of the United Nations, an effort that ended in failure due in part to UPEB internal dissension.

A third raw material group that has sought to carry out an OPEC strategy is the association of copper producers, CIPEC (Conseil Intergouvernemental des Pays Exportateurs de Cuivre). In June 1974 the group, which was formed in 1967, resolved "to control the declining price of copper on world markets."[60] To that end, CIPEC announced in November 1974 that its members would restrict monthly exports of copper by 10 percent and would not increase their inventories of refined copper. In April 1975, the export reduction was increased to 15 percent. All of this was to no avail. Copper prices continued to decline.

At first glance, several market factors would seem to have favored CIPEC. Although the United States then supplied 80 percent of its own copper needs through mining and recycling scrap, Europe imported 85 percent and Japan 86 percent of their respective total consumption.[61] Furthermore, import dependence was increasing. World copper consumption had risen rapidly, and with it imports had also risen. In 1950, for example, imports accounted for 41.1 percent of the industrial world's consumption, whereas in 1973, imports accounted for 51.5 percent of consumption.[62]

Demand is also price inelastic, at least in the short run. Because there are no readily available, adequate substitutes for copper, producers can increase their total earnings by increasing the price. Supply is also inelastic in the short run because of the cost and time involved in bringing new production on line. Moreover, copper stockpiles are usually quite limited.[63]

Several political factors also seemed conducive to CIPEC's success. CIPEC's four original members—Chile, Peru, Zambia, and Zaire—control 55 percent of the noncommunist world's copper exports. If other Third World producers had joined, CIPEC would have accounted for almost two-thirds of the world's exports.[64] In 1975 there was some movement toward expansion: Indonesia became a full member and Australia, Papua New Guinea, Mauritania, and Yugoslavia became associate members. In addition, because the governments of the principal members of CIPEC control all or a majority of production and all of the marketing of copper, they are in a position to carry out policies to control supply. Furthermore, the members had the experience of agreeing and carrying out export reductions in 1974 and 1975.

Despite these favorable conditions, CIPEC had little chance of increasing the price of copper.[65] In the long run, the demand for copper from CIPEC is highly elastic. New sources of raw copper are available, and so unless any increase in the price of copper is relatively modest, new supplies will be developed, including recycled copper. Also, unless any increase is limited, substitutes such as aluminum and plastics will be used.[66]

Finally, the demand for copper is relatively income elastic; that is, an increase in the growth rate of the developed countries will lead to an increase in the demand for copper, whereas a decline in growth will lead to a decline in demand. This elasticity was demonstrated by the rise in the price of copper during the economic boom of 1973–1974 and its precipitous drop during the recession of 1974–1975.[67] For producers, this means that except in times of boom in the developed market economies, copper is and will be in surplus supply. Thus, if producers wish to raise or even stabilize prices, they must develop schemes that will absorb huge quantities of copper or prevent its production in the first place. Small reductions such as the 15-percent export cutbacks of 1974–1975 are insufficient.

The problem of developing effective schemes to manage supply continues to be CIPEC's major challenge. One alternative would be to reduce production, but this would be difficult to accomplish, as non-CIPEC producers including the United States would not agree to such reductions and would take advantage of any price rises achieved by CIPEC reductions to increase their sales. One potential producer is the United States, which controls 27 percent of total world reserves and, thus, could disrupt the market. Furthermore, many CIPEC members themselves are not interested in production reductions. Because copper production is labor intensive, any reduction would lead to unemployment and, possibly, to social unrest and political problems for the producer governments. It is probably for this reason that the export reductions of 1974 and 1975 were not matched in most countries by production reductions. In addition, many CIPEC member governments are deeply in debt to foreign creditors and need the foreign

exchange they earn on copper exports. Chile and Peru, for example, have strenu-
ously opposed export reductions, and so CIPEC abandoned this tactic in 1977.[68]

Even if CIPEC could have agreed on how to reduce production or how to
finance a buffer stock, its members would have had difficulty in agreeing on a
common price, as production costs differ from country to country. Thus, what
looks like a low price for one producer would provide respectable profits for
another. Moreover, there are no common political interests to serve as an incentive for common CIPEC action. Indeed, there has been political conflict among
the members. Chile, in particular, has been politically isolated under the Pinochet
regime.

One scheme that CIPEC considered was a buffer stock. Under such a program, a central agency would buy copper when the price fell below an agreed-
upon floor and would sell it when it rose above that floor. However, because supply is generally way above demand, a buffer stock program would be prohibi-
tively expensive—one estimate suggested a cost of $5 billion, a sum clearly
beyond the capabilities of CIPEC.[69] Moreover, outside financing—from the
International Monetary Fund or OPEC, for example—was not available. (The
IMF offers assistance only to producer-consumer groups and OPEC showed little
interest in financing CIPEC.)

By the early 1980s, the chances of CIPEC's becoming an effective cartel
were even more remote. Far from exercising restraint, CIPEC members were maximizing production in spite of a continued slump in the world demand for copper
caused by the economic recession, which had affected the copper industry even
more than other commodities. Production by CIPEC members reached the point
that in 1983, the United States could impose import restrictions on copper to protect its own producers.[70] Chile and Peru, both with debt problems and both able to
produce copper efficiently enough to profit from increased copper sales even at
depressed world market prices, were the main source of overproduction. Less efficient producers like Zambia suffered more from depressed-market prices and thus
argued in CIPEC in favor of production restraints, but to no avail. This experience
further illustrates one of the reasons that CIPEC and other commodity-producer
associations failed to become effective cartels: divergent economic requirements
among their members. Like the IBA and UPEB, CIPEC turned to an unsuccessful
effort to manage copper prices through an international agreement between the
copper producers and the consumers.

There is a possibility that the producers might try joint action to increase the
price of commodity exports, if only out of sheer frustration and even against all
rational calculations. However, history suggests that these efforts will fail. In the
1980s, as a result of the continuing inability of commodity exporters to achieve
success through cartel action and because of the demonstrated effect of the waning of OPEC's power, developing country commodity exporters have increasingly directed their efforts toward improving their production and marketing capabilities. The producing countries have also sought to achieve other forms of commodity arrangements with consumers —for example, through international com-

modity agreements. Few of these arrangements have succeeded. However, they may gather greater support from the consuming countries in the future if there are short-run commodity shortages or disruptive markets that damage both developed and developing country producers.[71]

NOTES

1. See Morris A. Adelman, *The World Petroleum Market* (Baltimore: Johns Hopkins University Press, 1972); J. E. Hartshorn, *Politics and World Oil Economics: An Account of the International Oil Industry in Its Political Environment*, rev. ed. (New York: Praeger, 1962 and 1967); Edith T. Penrose, *The Large International Firm in Developing Countries: The International Petroleum Industry* (Cambridge: MIT Press, 1969); Anthony Sampson, *The Seven Sisters: The Great Oil Companies and the World They Made* (New York: Viking, 1975); Federal Trade Commission, *International Petroleum Cartel*, staff report to the Federal Trade Commission submitted to the Subcommittee on Monopoly of the Select Committee on Small Business, U.S. Senate, 82nd Cong., 2nd sess. (Committee Print No. 6) (Washington: Government Printing Office, 1952); and John M. Blair, *The Control of Oil* (New York: Pantheon, 1976).

2. See Zuhayr Mikdashi, *A Financial Analysis of Middle Eastern Oil Concessions: 1901–1965* (New York: Praeger, 1966); Charles Issawi and Mohammed Yeganeh, *The Economics of Middle Eastern Oil* (New York: Praeger, 1962), 24–40; and Daniel Yergin, *The Prize: The Epic Quest for Oil, Money, and Power* (New York: Simon and Schuster, 1991), chs. 1–6.

3. In 1928, for example, Shell, Standard Oil, and Anglo-Persian (the predecessor of BP) in order to bring order out of soft and volatile markets concluded the "As Is," or "Achnacarry," agreement to divide world markets and stabilize or determine world prices. In that same year a group of British, Dutch, U.S., and French companies agreed to divide up much of the old Ottoman Empire in the Red Line agreement. Also important was the basing-point pricing system that established a common price at several locations, or basing points, and standard, not actual, freight charges from the basing point to the destination. This system prevented low-cost producers from expanding their market share by reducing prices. See Penrose, *The Large International Firm*, 180–183. Apparently, there is some controversy about the success of the Achnacarry Agreement: see Yergin, *The Prize*, 264–265.

4. See Mikdashi, *A Financial Analysis*; Issawi and Yeganeh, *The Economics of Middle Eastern Oil*; Gertrude G. Edwards, "Foreign Petroleum Companies and the State in Venezuela," in Raymond F. Mikesell et al., eds., *Foreign Investment in the Petroleum and Mineral Industries* (Baltimore: Johns Hopkins University Press, 1971), 101–128; Franklin Tugwell, *The Politics of Oil in Venezuela* (Stanford: Stanford University Press, 1975); and Donald A. Wells, "Aramco: The Evolution of an Oil Concession," in Mikesell et al., *Foreign Investment in the Petroleum and Mineral Industries*, 216–236.

5. Wells, "Aramco: The Evolution of an Oil Concession."

6. Adelman, *The World Petroleum Market*, 207.

7. See, for example, Robert Engler, *The Politics of Oil: Private Power and Democratic Directions* (Chicago: University of Chicago Press, 1961).

8. Benjamin Shwadran, *The Middle East, Oil and the Great Powers* (New York: Council for Middle Eastern Affairs, 1955), 103–152; J. C. Hurewitz, *Middle East Politics: The Military Dimension* (New York: Praeger, 1969), 281–282; and Yergin, *The Prize*, ch. 23.

9. See Penrose, *The Large International Firm*, 248–263; Adelman, *The World Petroleum Market*, 196–204; and Yergin, *The Prize*, chs. 35–36.

10. Mira Wilkins, *The Maturing of Multinational Enterprise: American Business Abroad from 1914 to 1970* (Cambridge: Harvard University Press, 1974), 386–387.

11. See, for example, Engler, *The Politics of Oil*.

12. See note 4.

13. For a history of the OPEC countries, see Zuhayr Mikdashi, *The Community of Oil Exporting Countries: A Study in Governmental Cooperation* (Ithaca, N.Y.: Cornell University Press, 1972).

14. Zuhayr Mikdashi, "The OPEC Process," *Daedalus*, 104 (fall 1975): 203. The new members were Algeria, Libya, Qatar, the United Arab Emirates, Nigeria, Ecuador, Indonesia, and Gabon.

15. Mikdashi, *The Community of Oil Exporting Countries*, 196–207.

16. Joel Darmstadter and Hans Landsberg, "The Economic Background," *Daedalus*, 104 (fall 1975): 21.

17. On the evolution of events in Libya, see U.S. Senate Committee on Foreign Relations, *Multinational Corporations and United States Foreign Policy: Multinational Petroleum Companies and Foreign Policy*, hearings before the Subcommittee on Multinational Corporations, 93rd Cong., 1st and 2nd sess., Part 5 (Washington: Government Printing Office, 1974).

18. Organization for Economic Cooperation and Development, *Oil Committee, Oil Statistics: Supply and Disposal 1970* (Paris: OECD, 1971), 27. There were several reasons for the powerful Libyan position in the European market. The transportation of oil from Libya was much cheaper and safer than the transportation of oil from the Persian Gulf, which, with the closing of the Suez Canal, required a long trip around Africa. Furthermore, in 1970, there had been a decline in the supply of oil from Nigeria because of the civil war, and the pipeline that carried Saudi oil to the Mediterranean had been cut in Syria. Finally, Libyan oil was low in sulfur and therefore desirable for environmental reasons.

19. There was some consultation by the developed market states. The U.S. Department of Justice issued a waiver to oil companies under antitrust law, enabling them to cooperate in bargaining to resist unreasonable demands for higher prices. See U.S. Senate, *Multinational Corporations and United States Foreign Policy*, Part 5, 145–173. President Nixon then sent Undersecretary of State John N. Irwin to the Middle East to encourage governments to enter into joint negotiations with the companies. Secretary Irwin, however, capitulated to the demand of the shah of Iran for separate negotiations.

20. The Organization of Arab Petroleum Exporting Countries was formed by three Arab states—Kuwait, Libya, and Saudi Arabia—in 1968. It was expanded in 1970 to include Algeria, Abu Dhabi, Bahrain, Dubai, and Qatar.

21. International Monetary Fund, *Annual Report 1979* (Washington: IMF, 1979), 16, 27.

22. National Foreign Assessment Center, *International Energy Statistical Review* (Washington: Central Intelligence Agency, November 28, 1979), 2.

23. Anthony J. Paris, "OPEC Lifts Price 9%: At Least Five Members to Add Surcharges," *New York Times*, March 28, 1979, p. 1.

24. Edward L. Morse, "An Overview: Gains, Costs and Dilemmas," in Joan Pearce, ed., *The Third Oil Shock: The Effects of Lower Oil Prices* (London: Royal Institute of International Affairs, 1983), 3.

25. International Monetary Fund, *World Economic Outlook 1984: A Survey by the Staff of the International Monetary Fund* (Washington: IMF, April 1984), 128.

26. Morse, "An Overview," 8.

27. Leonard Silk, "The Painful Shift to Costly Oil," *New York Times*, September 28, 1983, D1.

28. IMF, *World Economic Outlook 1984*, 133.

29. Ibid., 130–133.

30. Morse, "An Overview," 4.

31. IMF, *World Economic Outlook 1984*, 128.

32. Ibid., 129–131.

33. Ibid., 134.

34. Ibid., 135.

35. Morse, "An Overview," 14–15.

36. IMF, *International Financial Statistics 1984* (Washington: IMF, August 1984).

37. Louis Turner, "OPEC," in Pearce, *The Third Oil Shock*, 85.

38. Ibid.

39. International Monetary Fund, *World Economic Outlook 1986* (Washington: IMF, April 1986), 151.

40. International Monetary Fund, *World Economic Outlook 1987* (Washington: IMF, April 1987), 98.

41. Ibid., 99.

42. *The First Oil War: Implications of the Gulf Crisis for the Oil Market* (Oxford, England: Oxford Institute for Energy Studies, August 1990).

43. U.S. Department of Energy, Energy Information Agency, *The U.S. Petroleum Industry: Past as Prologue, 1970–1992* (Washington: Government Printing Office, October 1, 1993), 57.

44. Guy F. Erb and Valeriana Kallab, eds., *Beyond Dependency: The Developing World Speaks Out* (New York: Praeger, 1975), 206.

45. The following analysis is to a great extent influenced by the theory of collective action developed by Mancur Olson, *The Logic of Collective Action: Public Goods and the Theory of Groups* (Cambridge: Harvard University Press, 1965 and 1971).

46. Mikdashi, *The Community of Oil Exporting Countries*, 196–207.

47. Stephen D. Krasner, "Oil Is the Exception," *Foreign Policy* 14 (spring 1974): 78–79.

48. See Raymond F. Mikesell, "More Third World Cartels Ahead?" *Challenge* 17 (November-December 1974): 24–26, on the OPEC method of taxing multinational corporations.

49. John E. Tilton, "Cartels in Metal Industries," *Earth and Mineral Sciences* 44 (March 1975): 41–44.

50. Harry G. Johnson, *Economic Policies Toward Less Developed Countries* (New York: Praeger, 1967), 136–162.

51. The six are the Aluminum Company of America, Alcan Aluminum Ltd., Reynolds Metals Company, Kaiser Aluminum and Chemical Corporation, Anaconda Company, and Revere Copper and Brass Company.

52. Carmine Nappi, *Commodity Market Controls* (Lexington, Mass.: D. C. Heath, 1979), 123.

53. Anthony Edwards, *The Potential for New Commodity Cartels: Copying OPEC, or Improved International Agreements?* QER Special No. 27 (London: Economist Intelligence Unit, September 1975), 41.

54. *Commodity Yearbook 1980*, 77. The crucial position of Jamaica in the U.S. market is based on its large production (it is the world's largest producer after Australia and is the largest exporter in the Third World), the low-cost transportation of Jamaican bauxite to U.S. markets, and the low-cost production in Jamaica.

55. Steven Kendall Holloway, *The Aluminum Multinationals and the Bauxite Cartel* (New York: St. Martin's Press, 1988), 79–82.

56. U.S. Department of the Interior, *Bureau of Mines, Minerals Yearbook 1986* (Washington: Government Printing Office, 1987), 24; *Minerals Yearbook 1982*, 21; *Minerals Yearbook 1977–1978*, 108; and *Minerals Yearbook 1975*, 243.

57. This discussion involves Latin American producers. The other producers, former British and French colonies, have special agreements with developed countries that guarantee markets and provide price supports and financial aid. See Edwards, *The Potential for New Commodity Cartels*, 37.

58. L. Emil Kreider, "Banana Cartel? Trends, Conditions, and Institutional Developments on the Banana Market," *Inter-American Economic Affairs* 31 (autumn 1977): 8; and Edwards, *The Potential for New Commodity Cartels*, 36.

59. Edwards, *The Potential for New Commodity Cartels*, 36–37, for example.

60. K. W. Clarfield et al., *Eight Mineral Cartels* (New York: Metals Week, McGraw-Hill, 1975), 57.

61. *Metal Statistics 1968-1978* (Frankfurt: Metallgesellschaft Aktiengesellschaft, 1979), 29–36.

62. Joseph C. Wyman, *Perspective on Copper* (New York: Research Group of Reynolds Securities, February 1975), 6.

63. Edwards, *The Potential for New Commodity Cartels*, 52.

64. Raymond F. Mikesell, *The World Copper Industry* (Baltimore: Johns Hopkins University Press, 1979), 20–23.

65. See Chibuzo Nwoke, *Third World Minerals and Global Pricing: A New Theory* (London: Zed Books, 1987); and Michael Shafer, "Capturing the Mineral Multinationals: Advantage or Disadvantage?" in Theodore H. Moran, ed., *Multinational Corporations* (Lexington, Mass.: Lexington Books, 1985), 33.

66. N. Iwase, "Recycling and Substitution," in S. Sideri and S. Johns, eds., *Mining for Development in the Third World* (New York: Pergamon Press, 1980), 266–274.

67. This rise and drop was aggravated by the Japanese accumulation of stocks to hedge against shortages in the boom period and the sales of these stocks during the economic recession.

68. *American Metal Market*, February 9, 1978, p. 10a. See also Theodore Panayotou, "OPEC as a Model for Copper Exporters: Potential Gains and Cartel Behavior," *The Developing Economies* (June 1979): 203–219.

69. Mikesell, *The World Copper Industry*, 199.

70. Kenji Takeuchi, John E. Strongman, Shunichi Maeda, and C. Suan Tan, *The World Copper Industry: Its Changing Structure and Future Prospects*, World Bank Staff Commodity Working Papers (Washington: World Bank, 1987).

71. For recent works on this subject, see Jack A. Finlayson and Mark W. Zacher, *Managing International Markets* (New York: Columbia University Press, 1988); Alfred Maizels, *Commodities in Crisis: The Commodity Crisis of the 1980s and the Political Economy of International Commodity Prices* (Oxford, England: Clarendon Press, 1992); and Gamani Corea, *Taming Commodity Markets: The Integrated Program and the Common Fund in UNCTAD* (New York: St. Martin's Press for Manchester University Press, 1992).

10

East-West Economic Relations during and after the Cold War

The Cold War ended definitively in August 1991 with the failure of a coup directed against Mikhail Gorbachev's political and economic reforms engineered by senior members of the Soviet Communist Party. After the attempted coup, the Soviet Union itself fell apart, Russia became a separate country, and the Communist Party was abolished—albeit temporarily—by its recently elected president, Boris Yeltsin.[1] One could say that the Cold War ended earlier. The acquiescence of the Soviet Union in the replacement of the Communist government of Poland with an elected coalition government including anti-Communist Solidarity leaders in 1989, the fall of Communist governments in Czechoslovakia, Bulgaria, and Romania, the unification of Germany, the return of Soviet troops from Afghanistan and many parts of Eastern Europe, and the holding of competitive elections in Russia might also be cited as key turning points. But the world knew that there would be no more Soviet Union after 1991, and without the Soviet Union there could be no Cold War.

The end of the Cold War was bound to bring about major changes in the economic institutions established in the Soviet bloc and between those countries and the rest of the world during the Cold War. Even before the end of World War II, economic institutions within the bloc had to be compatible with the central planning mechanisms that were mandated for all Communist countries by Josef Stalin. While a number of experiments with decentralization were conducted by various members of the bloc after the death of Stalin, central planning remained the essence of the Communist economic system. Furthermore, central planning and state ownership were part of the Marxist-Leninist economic philosophy and were also intimately connected with **nomenklatura,** a system of giving out responsible positions to loyal citizens (many of whom were Communist Party members) and designed to preserve the dominant role of the Communist Party.

Thus, wherever and whenever experiments with decentralization and liberalization threatened to disturb nomenklatura or reduce the power of the Communist Party, the experiments were soon terminated.

Understanding the strengths and weaknesses of central planning is part of the broader question of explaining why the Soviet system eventually collapsed. Central planning was replaced in most formerly Communist countries with a much greater emphasis on market mechanisms and a reduced emphasis on the promotion of state enterprises. Russia, and the other newly independent states (NIS) that formed after the breakup of the Soviet Union, along with the former communist states of central and eastern Europe tried to make the transition to capitalist economic systems, but not all of them did so rapidly or with complete success. In a number of former Soviet bloc countries, the economic transition took place at the same time that the political system was moving toward more democratic forms of government. In some cases, the early losses of the old Communist parties in the new electoral systems were reversed because of dissatisfaction with the results of economic reforms (e.g., Hungary in 1994). A key question for the industrialized countries of the West, therefore, was where and how to support the democratization process without disturbing movements toward privatization and liberalization of the economy.

Some Communist countries—most notably the People's Republic of China—remained committed to maintaining the dominant role of the Communist Party in politics. Despite the decision to remain Communist, these countries underwent major changes in their way of interacting with the world economy, especially China and, more recently, Vietnam. The most interesting question that the survival of communism in these countries raised was—and still is—how long they could maintain their communist regimes while, at the same time, transforming themselves into market economies.

One has to know something about the institutions that were in place until the end of the Cold War to understand the problems of transition. For this reason, the first part of this chapter will be devoted to describing them, starting with those that governed relations between the Communist world and the industrialized capitalist countries. The next section deals, therefore, with the construction of those institutions after World War II.

East-West Economic Relations in the Early Cold War Period

The British and American planners constructing the new international economic order between 1943 and 1947 (see Chapter 2) both desired and expected that the East would be part of the postwar system. Between the wars, the Soviet Union had been separated from the international economic system by the West's opposition to the Communist regime and by Stalin's autarkic development policy, but it was never completely isolated. From the time of the Russian Revolution until the early 1930s, when the collapse of world trade led to a collapse of trade with the West, the Soviet Union traded with the developed countries and with the United States in particular.[2] During this period, Soviet imports of Western raw materials and technology made an important contribution to Soviet growth, and a form of U.S.-Soviet economic interaction revived during the war years through U.S. lend-lease assistance.[3]

Some doubted the Soviet Union's interest in or ability to join the liberal multilateral system envisioned by the postwar planners.[4] United States officials, however, actively sought the Soviet Union's participation in the postwar economic order as a way to encourage political harmony, promote trade, and thereby encourage prosperity. Thus, the United States pressed for Soviet adherence to the Bretton Woods agreements and seriously considered giving a $10-million loan to the Soviet Union for postwar recovery.[5]

Western planners never questioned the participation of Eastern Europe in the postwar economic order. The countries of Eastern Europe had been closely integrated with the West, especially Western Europe, in the interwar period. In 1938, for example, Western Europe accounted for about 60 percent of Eastern Europe's exports and imports.[6] Czechoslovakia and Poland, which had been on the side of the Allies during the war, were invited to attend the international monetary and trade conferences. The United Nations Relief and Rehabilitation Administration was created in 1943 to help Eastern and Southern Europe recover after their liberation.[7] As late as 1947, Western European countries assumed "a substantial and ready resumption" of trade of principal goods with the East.[8]

Nevertheless, the economic relationship between the capitalist countries of the West and the Communist countries of the East became one of independence and confrontation. The Cold War led to an effort on both sides to separate the economies of East and West and to use that separation as a tool of political confrontation. The Soviet Union refused to join the Western economic order and, with the new Communist states of Eastern Europe, created a separate economic system. The Western states tried, for political and military reasons, to isolate the Communist economies and to integrate those of the developed market states.

The Creation of an Eastern Economic Bloc

The creation of a separate Eastern economic system was part of the Soviet Union's postwar policy of dominance in Eastern Europe and of its international political strategy.[9] Marxist ideology and concerns about postwar security provided the justification for Soviet control. According to Marxist theory, the formation of a separate Eastern economic bloc would deepen the crisis of world capitalism and speed its inevitable demise. Stalin stated that denying the Eastern markets to the West would decrease Western exports, create idle industrial capacity, and lead to the inevitable internal economic and political collapse of capitalism.[10] The formation of a separate socialist bloc would insulate the East from the coming economic chaos in the West and enhance socialist economic development.[11] The primary motivation, however, was political. A separate Eastern economic bloc, in the Soviet Union's view, would provide a buffer zone of friendly, that is, Communist states on its borders and would prevent Germany or other "hostile" Western powers from posing a threat of military invasion. Furthermore, the Soviet Union would obtain access on favorable terms to the resources of Eastern Europe—raw materials and capital equipment—that could be used to rebuild the Soviet Union after the war and to advance its economic development.

Through wartime diplomacy, military occupation, and coups d'état, the Soviet Union established Communist satellite regimes in all the states of Eastern Europe.[12] The Soviet Union, in cooperation with national Communist leaders, restructured the economies of Eastern Europe, introducing state ownership of the means of production, central planning, and the Soviet model of economic growth based on self-sufficiency and all-around industrialization.[13] The Soviet Union also built a socialist international economic system centered on the Soviet Union, which had a low level of interaction with the West.

The Soviet Union refused to join the new international economic institutions created by the West and prevented eligible satellites from participating in Western institutions. Although the Soviet Union participated in the Bretton Woods conference, it refused to ratify the Bretton Woods agreements and become a member of the International Monetary Fund (IMF) or the International Bank for Reconstruction and Development (IBRD, also called the World Bank).[14] Czechoslovakia and Poland, which initially joined the IMF and the World Bank, withdrew in 1950 and 1954, respectively, under strong Soviet pressure.[15]

Although invited, the Soviet Union refused to attend the preparatory meetings and international negotiations that led to the Havana Charter. Czechoslovakia and Poland participated in the Havana negotiations, although they did not ratify the charter. No Eastern states were contracting parties of the General Agreement on Tariffs and Trade (GATT).[16] The Soviet Union rejected the U.S. offer of aid under the Marshall Plan and refused to allow Poland and Czechoslovakia, the two Eastern states offered Marshall Plan aid, to accept U.S. aid and join the Organization for European Economic Cooperation (OEEC), the European organization established to coordinate European use of Marshall Plan funds.[17]

The institutional expression of the Eastern bloc was the Council for Mutual Economic Assistance (CMEA or Comecon). This economic organization, whose members included the Soviet Union and the states of Eastern Europe (except Yugoslavia), was established in 1949 as the Eastern response to the Marshall Plan. The communique issued at the time of its formation stated that the Eastern states formed Comecon in order to reinforce economic cooperation in the face of "the dictatorship of the Marshall Plan, which would have violated their sovereignty and the interests of their national economies."[18] Comecon pursued technical cooperation and joint planning, but its main function was to reorient trade eastward and to buttress the new political relationship between the Soviet Union and Eastern Europe.

Through Comecon and a series of bilateral trade agreements between the Soviet Union and the satellite countries, Eastern European trade was redirected from West to East. In 1938, 10 percent of Eastern exports went to Eastern countries including the Soviet Union, 68 percent to Western Europe, 4 percent to the United States and Canada, and 5 percent to Latin America. By 1953, 64 percent of Eastern exports went to Eastern countries, 14 percent to Western Europe, less than 1 percent to the United States, Canada, and Latin America.[19] In the first postwar decade, trade tended to benefit the Soviet Union, which was able to negotiate extremely favorable prices for its imports and exports.[20] One notorious example was the Polish-Soviet agreement under which Poland agreed to deliver large quantities of coal to the Soviet Union at a very favorable price.[21]

The Soviet Union's access to the planning process of the satellite countries also served to reorient economic flows. The Soviet Union's system of state ownership and central planning was imposed on Eastern Europe.[22] Eastern Europe's economic plans were prepared with the assistance of Soviet economic advisers by handpicked economists trained in the Soviet Union.[23] Because trade was controlled centrally, economic planners determined by administrative decisions to shift trade from West to East. Under their plans, Eastern European states produced and exported those products desired by the Soviet Union. Through long-term trade agreements, the Soviet Union obliged Czechoslovakia, for example, to emphasize production of heavy machinery, equipment, and arms instead of following the original Czech plan for more diversified production.[24]

Reparations imposed on the former Axis countries were an important element in the relationship between Eastern Europe and the Soviet Union. In East Germany, the Soviet Union unilaterally dismantled factories and claimed goods from current production for the Soviet army and the Soviet economy. The total value of these transfers has been estimated at $18 billion in 1950 dollars. In Hungary, Romania, and Bulgaria, the Soviet Union also dismantled factories and claimed goods from current production, the total value of which has been estimated at close to $2 billion.[25]

Financial ties were also redirected from West to East. Eastern European currencies were made inconvertible (on inconvertibility, see below). The nationalization of foreign investment disrupted private capital flows. The Soviet Union and most of the satellites were not eligible for IMF or IBRD assistance, and they rejected Marshall Plan aid. The principal source of external financing for Eastern Europe was credit from the Soviet Union for the purchase of raw materials and equipment from the Soviet Union.[26]

Finally, after the war, the Soviet Union acquired as reparations numerous German industrial enterprises operating in Hungary, Romania, and Bulgaria (former allies of Germany). These enterprises operated primarily as joint companies with the local national government. They enjoyed preferential taxes and access to foreign exchange and raw materials and often offered favorable prices to the Soviet Union. Because of their powerful and preferential position, these companies became a source of intrabloc conflict and were liquidated after 1954.[27]

Western economic warfare increased the East's self-imposed isolation. Following the establishment of Communist regimes in the Soviet-occupied states of Eastern Europe, Soviet pressure on Iran and Turkey, the outbreak of civil war in Greece, and political instability in Western Europe, U.S. policymakers concluded that their hopes for postwar cooperation with the Soviet Union were unrealistic. The East's rejection of Marshall Plan assistance, the coup in Czechoslovakia, and the Berlin blockade of 1948 confirmed the U.S. view that the Soviet Union was a political and military threat to the West.

In addition to building a united and prosperous Western economy and creating a powerful Western military alliance, the aim of United States and Western policy was to deny the Soviet Union and its allies economic resources that would enhance their military capability and political power. The Western strategic embargo began in full force with the passage of the U.S. Export Control Act of 1949. This act, which remained in force for twenty years, authorized the president to "prohibit or curtail" all commercial exports and to establish a licensing system to regulate exports to Communist countries. Any product that had military applicability or that would contribute to the military or economic potential of a Communist state was placed on the restricted list.[28]

The United States sought, with mixed success, to persuade other Western states to impose similar embargoes. In 1949 under U.S. pressure, the Coordinating Committee (CoCom) was set up to discuss and coordinate Western strategic embargo lists. Although it had no binding authority, CoCom succeeded in drawing up an international list of restricted items for its fifteen members.[29] However, the difference in views between the United States and its allies over the goals and content of the economic embargo became a source of tension throughout the postwar era. For the United States, the strategic embargo was intended to impair not only the East's military strength but also its political and economic power. The U.S. embargo therefore was directed at nonmilitary goods that would enhance economic performance and development as well as at military goods. The Europeans and Japanese, who had a greater economic stake in trade with the East than the United States did, felt that a broad embargo would encourage greater Eastern solidarity without hindering military and political capability. Thus, they advocated a more limited definition of strategic goods—namely, those with direct military implications.[30] As a result of allied resistance, the international list was less comprehensive than the U.S. control list.

The United States also used the Johnson Debt Default Act of 1934 to deny financial resources to the East. An effort to compel countries to repay World War I debts, the Johnson Act prohibited private persons or institutions from extending credit to a foreign government in default on obligations to the United States. Following World War II, the Johnson Act was amended to exempt members of the IMF and the World Bank—that is, virtually all states except those in the East. Yugoslavia, which was a member of the Fund and the Bank, and East Germany, Albania, and Bulgaria, which had no outstanding debts, were not affected.[31] The Johnson Act's restrictions were reinforced by a disagreement between the United

States and the Soviet Union on the settlement of the USSR's substantial World War II lend-lease debt.[32] Other NATO (North Atlantic Treaty Organization) countries did not restrict Eastern access to credit, and an effort by the United States to impose restrictions through international agreement failed.[33] Another form of economic warfare was to deny the East access to Western markets. In 1951 at the height of tensions in Korea, the U.S. Congress passed the Trade Agreements Extension Act, which withdrew all trade concessions negotiated with the Soviet Union and any Communist country (except Yugoslavia). As a result, products from Eastern countries remained subject to the onerous Smoot-Hawley tariffs. Many European states also adopted restrictions on imports from Communist countries.[34]

Thus the East and the West, mainly for political reasons, established separate international economic systems with separate institutions, rules, and patterns of interaction. At the height of economic separation during the Korean War, East-West trade was actually lower in absolute terms than it had been in 1937.[35] After the end of the Korean conflict and the death of Stalin in 1953, the political-security conflict eased somewhat. As a result, Eastern policies of regional economic isolation were modified; the West's control list was shortened; Western Europe, Canada, and Japan negotiated most-favored-nation agreements with Eastern Europe and the Soviet Union and reduced trade restrictions; and East-West trade increased.[36] From 1953 to 1958 Eastern exports to the West doubled, and from 1958 to 1963 they nearly doubled again.[37]

Nevertheless, as long as the Cold War continued, East-West trade remained unimportant as a percentage of both world trade and the total trade of East and West.[38] Although both Eastern and Western Europe favored greater commerce and took steps in that direction, the United States and the Soviet Union continued, for political reasons, to reject any major change in East-West economic relations. The large, self-sufficient economies of the superpowers enabled them to be less influenced by the potential economic advantages of interaction than their smaller and more trade-oriented partners were and more influenced by overriding political and security concerns.

Forces of Change in the East

The easing of political tensions as well as the growing problems of the Eastern economic system emerged as forces encouraging the East to end its isolation from the West. The period of U.S.-Soviet détente—the lessening of tensions—in the early 1970s set the stage for change in both East and West. By the early 1970s, the Soviet Union had achieved effective equality with the United States in strategic weapons. Nuclear parity enabled Soviet leaders to view the West with more confidence, to modify the fear of military invasion, and to entertain the idea of limiting expenditures on strategic weapons. Because of the change in nuclear capability, the Soviet Union believed the West would be more willing to discuss arms limitations and to seek political accommodation. The combination of Soviet nuclear parity and greater Soviet flexibility in foreign policy led the United States and its Western allies to look more favorably on easing conflict with the Soviet Union.[39]

While political changes were necessary, internal economic problems were the major motivation for opening economic relations with the West. Serious economic difficulties in agriculture and the industrial sector emerged in the 1960s and reached near-crisis proportions by the 1980s, particularly in the Soviet Union.

Agriculture was the first problem to affect the Soviet Union's international policy. Low agricultural productivity, a longstanding problem, had several causes: collectivization that gravely injured the peasantry; excessive interference in local farm management by the large and unwieldy Soviet agricultural bureaucracy; inadequate infrastructure in many areas ranging from roads to storage facilities; a lack of incentives given the weak links between effort and reward; and poor inputs from the industrial sector.[40] Periodic efforts to improve agricultural productivity had been undermined by the Soviet agricultural bureaucrats for whom any change in the prevailing system was a threat to their power. Despite significant capital investment in the years after 1960, productivity of the Soviet agricultural sector in the 1980s stood at 20 to 25 percent of U.S. productivity according to Soviet statistics and at 10 percent of U.S. productivity according to Western measures.[41]

In the 1960s, the Soviet Union, once a food exporter, became a net importer of food from the West (see Figure 10-1). In part, this was because of a decision to improve the diet by increasing meat consumption, which increased the need for grain for feedstock. Furthermore, before 1960, the Soviet Union had adjusted to crop shortfalls by reducing domestic consumption. After 1960, Soviet leaders could no longer impose such hardships on their people without political risk. So, when shortfalls occurred, the Soviet Union turned to the international market to purchase grain.[42] Between 1960 and 1985, Soviet imports of food increased from $613 million to $16.4 billion—an increase of 2500 percent—while food exports increased 82 percent from $702 million to $1.3 billion.[43]

The first major purchase—7 million tons—was made in 1964 following a disastrous crop in 1963. Subsequently, grain was regularly imported in large amounts—about 4 million tons per year—primarily from Canada (see again Figure 10-1). In 1972 another particularly bad harvest forced the Soviet Union to import over 19 million tons of grain from the United States and to make smaller purchases from other countries. The disruption caused by these large purchases led the United States to press the Soviet Union to sign a five-year agreement that stabilized Soviet purchases, committed the United States to make grain available up to fixed amounts, and provided for consultations on larger purchases. With the exception of the period of the grain embargo imposed after the invasion of Afghanistan in 1979 (see below), the Soviet Union made regular purchases of U.S. grain. The grain agreement was regularly renewed until it lapsed at the end of 1995. By the 1980s, Soviet grain imports averaged approximately 37 million tons per year.

Figure 10-1   Soviet Grain Harvests and Net Imports in Millions of Metric Tons, 1950–1990

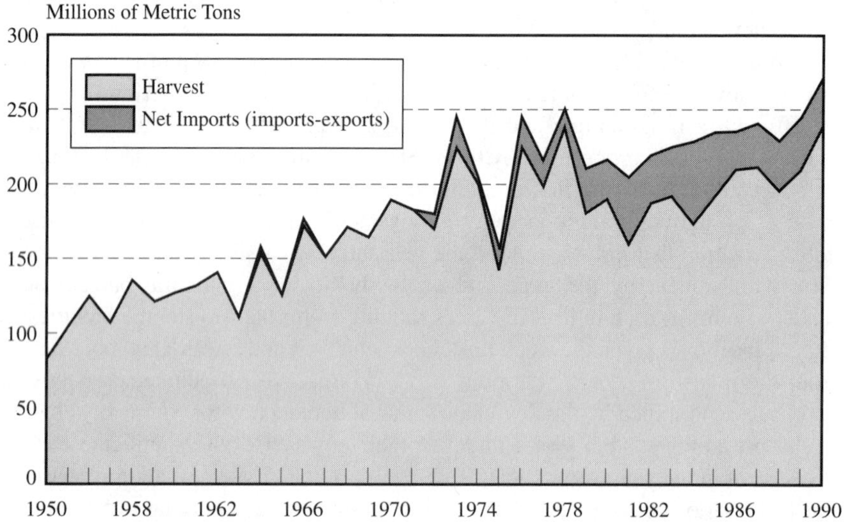

Millions of Metric Tons

SOURCE: Marshall Goldman, *Gorbachev's Challenge* (New York: Norton, 1987), 33; Marshall Goldman, *What Went Wrong with Perestroika?* (New York: Norton, 1991), 79.

Industrial growth has also been a problem for the Eastern system. In the 1950s and 1960s, the Soviet Union and Eastern Europe achieved high rates of industrial growth by a significant expansion in the labor force—the employment of women, the transfer of labor from agriculture to industry, and long working hours—and by the rapid increase in capital formation at the expense of agriculture and of improvement in the standard of living.[44] By 1960, however, this type of expansion, known as extensive growth, began to reach its limits. Comecon's growth rates declined from an average of 6 percent per year in the 1950s to about 4 percent in the early 1970s.[45] By the early 1980s, growth had fallen to 1 to 2 percent (see Figure 10-2). By the late 1980s, the Soviet economy experienced negative growth rates (see Figure 10-3).

The slowing of growth in the Soviet Union was mirrored by lower growth rates in the rest of bloc (see Figure 10-4, page 326). All of the Eastern European members of the bloc experienced a steady decline in growth rates. Like the Soviet economy, their economies began to contract at the end of the 1980s.

Growth slowed for a number of reasons. The Eastern states needed to shift to intensive growth, which is achieved by improving productivity—that is, the efficiency of production. Intensive growth relies primarily on the application of technology: advanced machinery and production processes, modern computer and communications technology, sophisticated management techniques, and

Figure 10-2   Average Annual Growth in Real GNP in the Soviet Union and Eastern Europe, 1961–1985, in Percentages

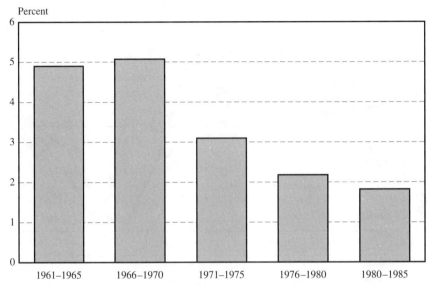

SOURCE: Central Intelligence Agency, *Handbook of Economic Statistics 1988* (Washington: Government Printing Office, 1988), 33.

Figure 10-3   Annual Real Growth in GNP at Market Prices in the Russian Federation, 1981–1994, in Percentages

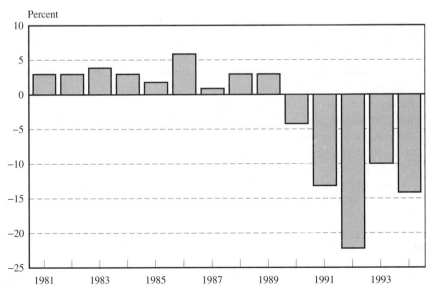

SOURCE: World Bank, *World Data '95 CD-ROM* (Washington: World Bank, 1995).

Figure 10-4   Annual Real Growth in GNP at Market Prices in Eastern Europe, 1980–1994, in Percentages

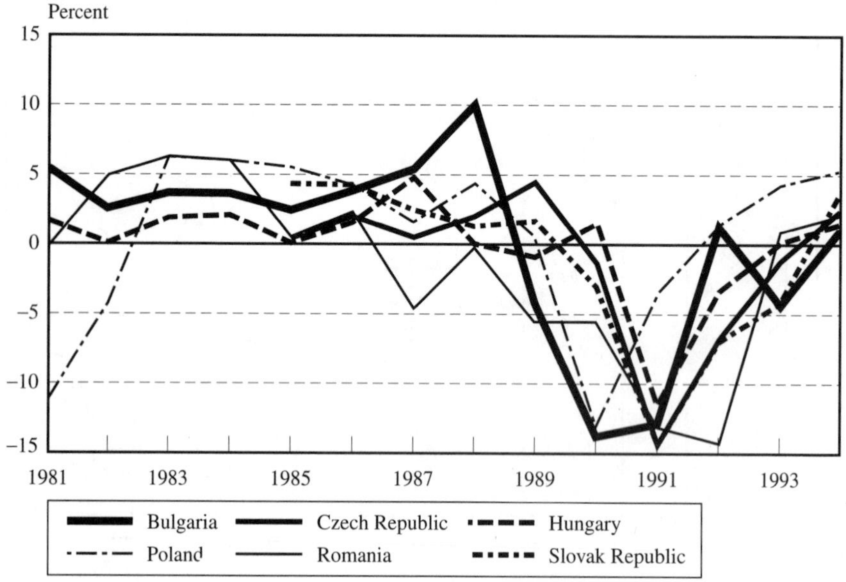

Source: World Bank, *World Data '95 CD-ROM* (Washington: World Bank, 1995).

energy. After the 1960s, Eastern plans emphasized the need to achieve growth through improved productivity and the development and application of technology, although there was little progress toward achieving this goal.

The Eastern system encountered severe difficulties in improving productivity, largely because of the central planning system. In the West, markets by and large determined the allocation of resources. Supply and demand determine price, which then determines production and consumption. In the East, planners allocated resources. They distributed resources for production and investment, determined production targets, and set prices.

Such a system discouraged innovation, productivity improvements, and quality. There was little incentive for plant managers to experiment with new technology. Rewards were based on fulfillment or overfulfillment of quantitative goals and not on improving the quality of the product or the production process. Indeed, there were disincentives to experiment with new methods because they threatened to interrupt production at least temporarily and thus to jeopardize fulfillment of the quantitative goals. Furthermore, the absence of competition and the existence of guaranteed markets eliminated incentives for managers to cut costs or improve quality. Above all, prices did not provide a guide to help managers determine what goods were needed by consumers and how to improve productivity by lowering costs.[46]

Research and development were also ineffective. Despite great emphasis on scientific research, there was little relationship between research and actual production. Unlike the West, where most research is carried out by private enterprise, research in the East was generally carried on in research institutes that had few links with production facilities. Scientists and engineers were thus not positioned to respond directly to the needs of industry or to make industry responsive to scientific development.[47] As a result of these systemic biases, the East fell far behind the West in the development of technology. For example, it was estimated that the United States had a lead over the Soviet Union in the late 1980s of eight to ten years in advanced microcircuits and nine to fifteen years in mainframe computers.[48]

In the 1960s and 1970s, the Eastern countries tried to solve the problem of technology and productivity through limited national economic reforms, intra-Comecon trade, and greater trade with the West. In the mid-1960s, managers were given greater freedom to decide what to produce and how, incentives were based on profit as well as quantitative goals, and prices were made more "rational." But the reforms did not go far enough. They were strongly opposed by party conservatives and government bureaucrats who saw their power threatened by the potential new power of the plant managers and who eventually reasserted centralized control.[49] The exception was Hungary, which for a time gave greater autonomy to individual enterprises and reformed its price system to reflect more closely supply and demand.[50] Other Eastern regimes were unwilling to risk real reform and introduced only mild changes. By 1970, many of these had been rescinded. Thus the Eastern economies continued to stagnate.[51]

The East also attempted to solve the problem of technological development and intensive growth through Comecon. An effort began in the late 1950s to revitalize Comecon and change it from a tool of Soviet dominance to a tool of development. Attempts were made to increase trade within the bloc, as it was hoped that trade would lead to economies of scale, force competitiveness, and thus encourage modernization. Trade was encouraged by an agreement on methods for establishing trade prices, a clearing institution (the International Bank for Economic Co-operation), and programs for national specialization in production. Technological cooperation was also encouraged.[52] However, Comecon trade remained hampered for economic and political reasons by internal biases against trade other than bilateral trade: lack of complementarity with the Eastern economies, the poor quality of goods, unsatisfactory currency arrangements, and political unwillingness to delegate power to a supranational body—especially one in which the Soviet Union had a powerful voice. Trade within Comecon had been characterized by bilateral arrangements between the Soviet Union and Eastern European countries rather than multilateral integration among all Comecon nations.[53] Moreover, intrabloc technological cooperation was not up to the task of overcoming systemic biases against technological innovation. In the 1980s

Comecon remained stagnant, although members agreed to establish diplomatic relations with the EC and expressed the desire to increase joint production efforts and improve the intra-Comecon trade pricing mechanisms.[54] But little was actually done to implement change.

Finally, the East sought to bridge the technology gap and achieve intensive growth by acquiring foreign technology. The Soviet Union's seven-year plan of 1959–1965 set the stage by calling for economic modernization through the development and application of technology and by allowing technological imports from the West to eliminate lags in technological development in the Soviet Union.[55] In 1959, Premier Nikita Khrushchev announced that the Soviet Union intended to make major purchases of technology—patents, licenses, entire plants—from the West.[56] One example was a 1966 agreement with Fiat, the Italian automaker, to build an automobile plant in the Soviet Union. This $1.5 billion project involved the purchase of licenses and equipment, the training of Soviet technicians in Italy, and the use of Western personnel in the Soviet Union.[57]

Industrial cooperation agreements between Western firms and Eastern European enterprises became increasingly important in the early 1970s. For the East, they were intended to provide Western technology, improve competitiveness in the West, and reduce foreign exchange needs. The West sought greater access to Eastern markets and the opportunity to reduce costs. West Germany, which was by far the most active in seeking such agreements, entered into more than 200 agreements with Comecon nations in the 1970s.[58] However, by the end of the decade both partners were disappointed with the results. The time lag for implementing projects was so long that by the time plants were built the technologies were no longer new. Some Western firms had only provided access to second-class technology, thus denying the East enhanced competitiveness in the West, and the scarcity of foreign exchange limited further agreements. The Western firms found that Third World industrializing countries with a more liberal investment climate offered the West better investment opportunities.

Western technology, however, had little impact on Soviet and Eastern European productivity and growth. As we shall see, there were financial constraints on the East's ability to purchase Western technology. Furthermore, despite the easing of CoCom controls, the West was not willing to sell sophisticated technologies that could contribute to the East's military strength. For example, Western computer and telecommunications technologies that were critical for modern production were also particularly sensitive for military reasons. Most important, foreign technology imports had little impact as long as there was no reform in the domestic economic system that would permit their effective use.

By the 1980s, the Eastern economic system was in need of drastic economic reform. Growth rates declined steadily, investment and productivity remained low. From 1981 to 1985, growth in the Soviet Union averaged only 1.8 percent and total factor productivity declined to 0.9 percent compared with 1.9 percent from 1975 to 1980.[59] Soviet agricultural problems were so great that some products were rationed and lines for goods became long in major Soviet cities.

Between 1983 and 1985 the growth rate of agricultural production per capita actually fell 2 percent.[60] Shortages of all consumer products caused public dissatisfaction, creating a potential political challenge to the regime. At the same time, the Soviet Union faced a number of political reversals. The war in Afghanistan had become a costly economic drain that was unpopular at home and damaged Soviet relations abroad. In Poland, labor unrest arising in part from economic problems challenged the legitimacy of the Communist regime in that important Soviet ally.

East-West Economic Relations: From the 1960s to the End of the Cold War

East-West economic relations between 1947 and 1989 were influenced primarily by the desire of the United States to isolate the Soviet Union and its Communist allies from the capitalist world economy, and the acceptance of this policy (with some important exceptions) by the other major industrialized nations of the West. There were important differences over how to enforce export controls and when to resume economic relations as the Cold War ground to a close, but there was an underlying consensus until the Cold War ended that the East Bloc was not to be permitted to benefit in any meaningful way from the growing economic flows that came with the recovery of Europe and the reconstruction of Japan.

Still, there was a debate within the West about whether to use economic incentives to win concessions in either foreign policy issues or in domestic reforms in the East. There were a number of experiments, particularly after 1972, with holding out promises of increased trade or investment flows in exchange for changes in the behavior of the Soviet Union and the rest of the Eastern bloc.

The Western Europeans, for both economic and political reasons, were more anxious to trade with the Soviet Union and its allies than the United States. Japan was constrained by ongoing political disputes over the Soviet occupation of several Japanese islands. United States policymakers have been caught between their desire to expand trade for economic and political reasons and their feeling that the East should not get something for nothing, that Western trade concessions should be linked to Eastern political concessions or to an easing in political and security relations. The experience of the past thirty years indicated that U.S. trade with Comecon countries was in large part a function of domestic political considerations in the United States and the state of diplomatic relations between the United States and the Soviet Union.

For example, in the mid-1960s, the Johnson administration tried to expand East-West trade in order to encourage greater pluralism in Eastern Europe and greater stability in relations between the United States and the Soviet Union. Beginning in 1966, the administration pushed for trade legislation to authorize the president to enter into commercial agreements with a Communist country and to grant most-favored-nation status to individual European countries not receiving such treatment (Yugoslavia and Poland were receiving it).[61] Despite strong administration support, Congress refused to pass such legislation and blocked the administration's policy because of concern about Soviet involvement in the war in Vietnam. After the Soviet invasion of Czechoslovakia in 1968, President Johnson abandoned the policy.

The early 1970s saw a renewal of U.S. interest in expanding East-West trade. In 1972, at the same time as the signing of the SALT I agreement, President Nixon and Chairman Brezhnev established a high-level, joint commercial commission that then negotiated a series of agreements designed to normalize U.S.-Soviet commercial relations and to open the way for increased trade and financial flows. Most important was an agreement on commerce and the settlement of the Soviet lend-lease debt. Because it was to open the way for Soviet access to private credits, this was of great economic importance to the Soviet Union. The United States agreement to grant most-favored-nation status to the Soviet Union had great political significance as a symbol of the end of the Soviet Union's exclusion from the West's international economic system. Other agreements made available U.S. Commodity Credit Corporation loans for Soviet purchase of U.S. grain exports and Export-Import Bank financing for exports to the Soviet Union.

Certain members of Congress, recognizing that these agreements gave the Soviet Union the financing it needed and a new level of political acceptance, sought to use the most-favored-nation status and Eximbank credits as a lever to force the Soviet Union to change its internal policies on emigration. Senator Henry Jackson and Representative Charles Vanik developed a proposal to link most-favored-nation treatment and Eximbank loans for the Soviet Union and Eastern Europe to freer policies of emigration in these countries. And they offered that proposal as an amendment to the U.S. trade bill which the administration needed to launch the Tokyo Round. After resisting the Jackson-Vanik amendment for two years, the Nixon administration capitulated on the assumption that the Soviet Union would change its policies in return for the inducements of credits and trade.[62] At the same time, Congress also enacted restrictions on Soviet access to Eximbank financing that would operate even if the Soviet Union satisfied emigration requirements.[63]

The Jackson-Vanik linkage plus the Eximbank restrictions proved to be more than the Soviet government was willing to accept. The Eximbank provision meant that even a major capitulation such as permitting greater emigration would lead to only small credits. Furthermore, external commercial relations, no matter how important, were not worth the price of internal political change. The Soviet Union refused to give any assurances regarding emigration and charged the United States with interfering in its internal affairs. In January 1975 the United States and the Soviet Union agreed to nullify the 1972 commercial agreement.

The Carter administration policy followed a similar pattern. The administration early on indicated a desire for higher levels of U.S.-Soviet trade and urged the Congress to repeal restrictions on most-favored-nation status and Eximbank credits. Administration officials also indicated that "attempts to use economic pressure to achieve noneconomic concessions are likely to be ineffective."[64] This position was initially tested by the administration's concern over human rights in the Soviet Union. Following the jailing of political dissidents and slander conviction of U.S. journalists, President Carter proposed embargoing the export of computers and oil-drilling equipment to the Soviet Union. More important was the Soviet Union's invasion of Afghanistan in December 1979, which ended the Carter effort to expand economic relations.

The invasion of Afghanistan terminated the 1970s era of détente and led to a shift in U.S. policy from efforts to improve East-West economic relations to a return to economic sanctions. Before the invasion, Soviet expansionism in several Third World countries and the extensive Soviet military buildup of the 1970s gave rise to the feeling that U.S. policy toward the Soviet Union had created too many opportunities for Soviet foreign policy that had been left unanswered by the United States. After the invasion, further political conflicts—over Poland's and the Soviet Union's shooting down of a Korean Airlines jet—plus a general hardening of Soviet-American relations led to a severe deterioration in U.S.-Soviet economic relations.

President Carter saw the invasion of Afghanistan as an indication of growing Soviet expansionism and particularly of Soviet designs on the nearby Persian Gulf oil fields. He withdrew the SALT II arms control treaty from consideration by the Senate and, in January 1980, announced new economic sanctions against the Soviet Union: an embargo on all sales of wheat and other grains to the Soviet Union above the amount authorized under the terms of the 1975 U.S.-Soviet grain agreement; an embargo on sales of high-technology goods to the Soviet Union; tightened restrictions on the sale of oil and gas exploration and production equipment to the Soviet Union; the suspension of service by the Soviet purchasing commission office in New York; and a more restrictive regime of access to U.S. ports for Soviet ships.[65] As a result, U.S. exports to the Soviet Union fell from $3.6 billion to $1.5 billion between 1979 and 1980.[66] Exports of U.S. grain to the Soviet Union fell from $2.8 billion in 1979 to $1.0 billion in 1980, accounting for most of the decline in U.S. exports.[67]

President Reagan adopted an even harder line with the Soviet Union, increasing military expenditures, initially downplaying arms control negotiations, and providing military support to anti-Communist forces such as the Contras in Nicaragua.[68] The Reagan administration also sought to use trade as a stick to punish the East for policies such as the invasion of Afghanistan or the imposition of martial law in Poland and generally to deny to the East the Western technology and hard currency that would enhance the Soviet bloc's economic development and military strength.

Ironically, one of the first steps taken by the Reagan administration in early 1981 was to lift the grain embargo and to announce that the administration would not use grain as a foreign policy tool. The reason for this departure from President Reagan's hard-line policy was one of domestic politics. The highly controversial grain embargo had become an issue in the 1980 campaign, with President Carter defending the embargo and candidate Reagan insisting that it was both ineffective and economically inequitable and that, if elected, he would end it. Despite the removal of the embargo, the Soviet Union, citing U.S. unreliability, refused to increase its purchases of U.S. grain and limited its imports to the amount it was committed to purchase under the terms of the grain agreement.

With this exception, the Reagan administration pursued a policy of economically isolating the Soviet Union. The administration maintained embargoes on the export of oil and gas exploration equipment and high-technology goods to the Soviet Union, tightened the enforcement of export controls generally, and favored more stringent export control legislation. The administration adopted a broad definition of the strategic goods that were to be denied to the Soviet Union, including not only defense or defense-related equipment but also many items that had either a limited or indirect impact on the East's military capability.

The Reagan administration also tried to use CoCom and NATO to impose this view of strategic exports on the West European allies. One such effort involved a U.S. attempt to stop its Western European allies from helping to build a pipeline from Siberian gas fields to customers in Western Europe. The United States viewed the plan to trade Western pipeline technology and credits for Soviet natural gas supplies as a dangerous extension of West European energy dependence on the Soviet Union and as a way of giving advanced technology to the Soviets, not only with reduced hard currency cost, but also with subsidized credits from Western governments. The Western European governments were unsympathetic to the U.S. position. From their viewpoint, energy dependence would be limited and manageable; indeed Soviet natural gas would reduce Europe's dependence on Middle Eastern oil. Furthermore, earnings and employment from the pipeline were important to the European economies, which were in the midst of a deep recession. From the European perspective, the United States was hypocritical in its efforts to block the pipeline deal when it was selling sorely needed grain to the Soviet Union.

After unsuccessfully trying to persuade the CoCom allies that they should not participate in the pipeline project, the Reagan administration imposed sanctions preventing U.S. or foreign companies using U.S.-licensed designs and technology from participating in the pipeline. Since many U.S. companies and U.S. technologies were already under contract to be used in the pipeline, this embargo brought immediate protests from Western European governments who ordered their national companies to fulfill their contracts with the Soviet Union. The United States retaliated with sanctions against those companies, forbidding them to deal with U.S. firms. After a year of heated controversy, the pipeline issue was settled: the Europeans agreed to a review of embargo policy and the U.S. agreed to lift the pipeline embargo.[69]

Gorbachev's Economic and Political Reforms

In March 1985, Mikhail Gorbachev became General Secretary of the Communist Party and began a program to address these economic, political, and foreign policy problems.[70] His first steps were tentative, especially in domestic economic matters. The earliest signs of change were in foreign policy. Gorbachev argued that the possibility of nuclear holocaust and the nature of contemporary world problems such as the environment made the world interdependent and called for a more cooperative foreign policy.[71] He adopted several key foreign policy initiatives: he called for a defensive military strategy; he signed an agreement with the United States on intermediate-range nuclear weapons and pursued negotiations on strategic and short-range nuclear weapons; he announced a unilateral reduction of conventional forces in Europe; he agreed to accept greater autonomy in Eastern Europe and to withdraw Soviet troops from Afghanistan; and he took steps to improve relations with the People's Republic of China. These foreign policy initiatives not only eased political and military confrontations but also enabled the Soviet Union to focus more attention and resources on domestic economic reform. Under his domestic political policy known as **glasnost** or openness, Gorbachev improved his government's human rights policy including greater emigration, allowed more freedom in public discussion and the arts, and took steps toward greater democratization of the political process. In 1989, for example, he implemented a reform of the political system, creating a presidency and more open elections. Political reform was also designed to facilitate economic reform, in particular, by providing a popular check on the powerful, conservative bureaucracy.[72]

In the economic arena, Gorbachev announced a policy known as perestroika, or restructuring of the Soviet economy.[73] Initially, perestroika was directed at "perfecting" the planning mechanisms and improving the planned economy through greater discipline. In 1987, it turned to systemic change. According to Gorbachev's plan for the industrial sector, decision making—with a number of exceptions—was to be decentralized from central planners to individual firms. Under the Law on State Enterprise adopted in June 1987, the central planning system was to be phased out by 1991 and replaced by annual plans drafted by individual firms. Central planners would develop voluntary guidelines for individual enterprises, establish long-term economic objectives, issue state orders for products of critical importance to the economy and national defense, and negotiate with firms to obtain those products. Instead of responding to obligatory targets set by central planners, firms would pursue revenue and profit. Individual enterprises would be responsible for production, sales, and investment. They would have more freedom to hire and fire workers and to set wages. Under the new law, they would also face the possibility of bankruptcy.

New markets responsive to these more autonomous enterprises were to be developed. Decisions on capital flows once made by state planners were to be made instead by newly liberalized financial markets. The existing system of centralized supply would be replaced by a wholesale distribution system that was to be responsive to the decisions of individual enterprises.

Reform of the agricultural system was also on the agenda. Gorbachev's "new agrarian policy" adopted in 1989 called for decentralization and a greater role for the private sector. The state bureaucracy was to be dismantled; decision making would be delegated to regional and local levels; agricultural enterprises, like industrial enterprises, were to pursue profits and to be self-financing; prices were to become more flexible; there was to be greater scope for private farming through lifetime leases of farms with the possibility of passing leases on to children.

Perestroika also had an international dimension. Part of Gorbachev's plan, albeit a minor part, was to improve trade and financial interaction with the West in order to speed the restructuring process. Many of the reforms designed to improve productivity and quality would have helped to promote exports and earn needed foreign exchange, but only if they had the desired effect. In addition, in 1986, the Soviet Union announced a plan to decentralize the trade system and end the monopoly of the Ministry of Foreign Trade over trade transactions. A number of ministries, authorities, and enterprises were authorized to conduct foreign trade directly through foreign trade organizations under their control. In 1986, the Soviet Union also requested observer status in the GATT, arguing that domestic economic reforms would remove impediments to its participation in a market-oriented organization. The Western countries, fearful that Soviet involvement would politicize the GATT, suspicious of Soviet motives, and wanting to see if reform really did move the Soviet Union toward a market-oriented economy, denied the request.[74]

The Soviet government also pursued economic cooperation with Western firms in order to promote exports and to obtain Western technology. In a major departure from previous policy, the government issued new guidelines that allowed foreign equity and management participation in joint ventures. Some Western firms responded. For example, Combustion Engineering signed the first U.S.-Soviet joint venture in 1987 to manufacture instrumentation and control systems for petroleum refining. In 1989, the Soviet government and a consortium of five major U.S. companies—RJR Nabisco, Eastman Kodak, Johnson & Johnson, Archer Daniels Midland, and Mercator—signed an agreement that enabled the companies to proceed with feasibility studies to explore joint ventures in a variety of sectors. Western Europeans were quicker to initiate joint ventures than U.S. and Japanese firms. To finance these and other ventures, the Soviet Union increased its borrowing from Western financial institutions (see below on Eastern borrowing from the West). Finally, Soviet policymakers considered various schemes for making the ruble convertible, including the possibility of introducing a convertible or "hard" ruble for international transactions that could be backed by gold, foreign exchange, or exports (see below on ruble inconvertibility).[75]

After 1985, the Reagan administration began to review its policy and to consider shifting from economic sanctions to economic inducements. The setting for this change was, as before, a thaw in East-West political-security relations. Gorbachev's foreign policy initiatives eliminated important sources of conflict such as the Soviet presence in Afghanistan and changes in some of the most aggressive aspects of Soviet military strategy. U.S.-Soviet summits were revived. Arms control talks led to the successful conclusion of the INF agreement that limited medium-range nuclear weapons in Europe and to progress on limiting conventional forces in Europe. Some administration officials came to believe that trade and finance could be used to support Gorbachev and his allies who supported the new thinking in foreign policy, glasnost and perestroika.[76] U.S. allies in Western Europe, less fearful of Gorbachev's Soviet Union and as usual interested in greater trade, urged a more moderate policy on the United States and specifically pressed for an easing of CoCom controls. Finally, the need to reduce the huge U.S. budget deficit led to pressure for reducing military expenditures, which could be justified in a more friendly East-West environment.

The Reagan administration's steps on the economic front were cautious: reestablishment of the U.S.-U.S.S.R. Joint Commercial Commission at the ministerial level to discuss improving economic relations and encouragement of "commercially viable joint ventures complying with the laws and regulations of both countries."[77] Following the Soviet withdrawal from Afghanistan, the Bush administration eased export controls somewhat. With the political revolution in Eastern Europe in the fall of 1989, U.S. policy shifted toward using trade and investment to promote change in the East. At the Malta Summit in December 1989, President Bush called for opening markets to the Soviet Union and endorsed observer status for the USSR in the GATT after the completion of the Uruguay Round.

At the same time, Western European countries moved further and faster than the United States to increase economic flows with the East. For all the economic and political reasons we have discussed, many countries of Western Europe were more interested than the United States in economic and political rapprochment with the East. Furthermore, Gorbachev deliberately courted Western Europe, publicly advocating the concept of a "common European home."[78] Finally, at the 1989 world economic summit, the European Union was given the lead Western role in opening relations with Eastern Europe.

One indication of this special focus on Europe was the official request by Comecon in 1988 for the establishment of diplomatic relations with the European Union. In addition, individual Comecon countries sought preferential trade agreements with the EU. Such a relationship proved attractive to Western Europe in general and, in particular, to West Germany. As the leading trade partner of the Soviet Union and Eastern Europe and in continuing pursuit of its *Ostpolitik*, West Germany took a strong interest in increasing economic relations with the East, especially since it wanted to keep alive the possibility of reuniting with East Germany. West Germany responded positively to the interest of the East in increased political ties with the European Union; and German firms, with the support of their government, have aggressively pursued trade and joint-venture opportunities and signed numerous trade and joint-venture agreements with the Russians, the Eastern Europeans, and the new countries created after the breakup of the Soviet Union. Germany has been a major source of aid credits and balance of payments support to the Soviet successor states since 1989 (although it cut back the level of its commitments in 1990 after it realized how much it would cost to integrate East Germany into the European Union).

The Failure of Perestroika

The policies actually implemented in 1988 by the Gorbachev government differed somewhat from the plans announced in 1987. Decision-making power was transferred from the economics ministries of the government to the managers of individual enterprises under the Law on State Enterprises after it came into force in January 1988. The ministries lost their power to appoint managers of enterprises. However, many prices were still controlled centrally, and the ministries were theoretically still in control of allocating inputs to enterprises. In addition, the ministries still controlled the research institutes, other vital sources of economic and business information, and international trade (via their power to grant export licenses). Some prices were freed selectively so that there would be room for profit-making ventures on the part of the managers, but this was done purely at the discretion of the bureaucracy.

The unanticipated result was that "What began as a Chinese-style experiment with capitalism at the margin transformed itself into a collapse of the central allocation mechanism."[79] The ministries could not guarantee the allocation of inputs because they could no longer insist upon fulfillment of production quotas. The managers therefore turned to a self-help system combining personal connections, barter, and bribery to obtain the necessary inputs to keep their enterprises going. The inevitable outcome was a major decline in production and general failure of the system. Real GNP declined by 4 percent in 1990 and 19 percent in 1991 (see again Figure 10-3). Since privatization efforts were still quite modest at this point, price increases for consumer goods led not to increased productive capacity but rather to inflationary pressures, massive shortages, supply bottlenecks, and higher monopoly rents for state enterprises. Whatever subsidy element was involved in Soviet consumer prices was quickly reduced under the new policy.

Senior economic bureaucrats in the Soviet government responded to this crisis by insisting on rapid privatization of state enterprises. Although these ministers preferred continued state ownership, under perestroika privatization was the only way to retain control over their own sources of revenues (which depended mainly on the cash flows generated by the firms). The kind of privatization they advocated involved extensive cross-holdings of shares in firms that were already linked by vertical ties—firms that were "upstream" and "downstream" from the major producers in any given industry—in order to maintain the intra-industry relationships that had existed under the pre-perestroika system. In addition, they favored transfer of ownership to the existing managers of firms rather than the sale of assets on the open market. Such an approach would enable them to preserve their own power and privileges in the new system.

In 1988, workers were given the right to strike, a right denied since the time of Stalin. As a result, there was a very rapid increase in wages. The more productive workers had to be bribed to stay on the job so as not to go to work for the "cooperatives" that sprang up everywhere in the 1988–1991 period. The cooperatives were thinly disguised private operations that lived off the supposedly "redundant" but actually quite valuable assets purchased on very favorable terms from the state enterprises. Managers of the state enterprises pursued profit-making opportunities in the cooperatives rather than in their own firms, because the cooperatives were not as heavily burdened with obsolete production equipment and unproductive workers as the state enterprises.

Workers in some state enterprises were given some control over management. This resulted in a low incidence of layoffs, even in severely overmanned firms. Of course, many workers had a stake in preserving the state enterprises because they were likely to suffer loss of their jobs and reductions in wages in genuinely private enterprises. Nevertheless, the collapse of the central government's control over its own revenues and its power to allocate resources made the future of state enterprises look bleak indeed. Thus, increasingly, the ministries, the managers, the more productive workers in state enterprises, and many local government officials supported a form of privatization called "spontaneous privatization," which amounted to the expropriation of state-owned assets for the private benefit of those individuals.

There was renewed debate about economic reforms in 1990, with a number of new proposals for speeding up the privatization process and further liberalizing the economy. However, Gorbachev, worried about opposition to quickening the pace of reform from conservative forces in the Communist Party, opposed further reforms at this time.[80] That he was right to worry became evident in August 1991 when those forces attempted a coup d'état. When the coup failed, the conservatives were neutralized politically and pro-reform elements of the new Russian government of Boris Yeltsin were able to dominate the scene. Gorbachev was forced to resign after his halfhearted attempts to salvage the leading role of the Communist Party failed and the Soviet government in Moscow was replaced by the Russian government.

Problems of Transition from Communism

The transition from Communism has both a political and economic side. The political side generally involves the creation of a multiparty electoral system, the dismantling of authoritarian institutions (like the secret police) without undermining public order, and the institutionalization of the political rights and freedoms that go along with a more liberal political system. The economic side involves the replacement of central planning with a market system. This usually involves the elimination of price controls, the privatization of state enterprises, and the creation of new economic instruments and institutions that allow the government to extract resources from and stabilize the private economy.

The timing of these measures is critical. If one allows prices to be determined by market forces without rapidly privatizing state enterprises, then the state enterprises, which are usually monopoly suppliers, can simply charge higher prices without increasing production. If one frees controlled prices and privatizes state enterprises without creating the appropriate state and market institutions to prevent irresponsible or criminal behavior by market actors, then the country may end up with a system unable to rein in corruption. If the government fails to create market stabilizing mechanisms, then the country may suffer from excessive inflation, rapid currency devaluations, low rates of private investment, and high rates of unemployment for prolonged periods of time.

The government of an economy in transition takes on a variety of new roles, many of them unfamiliar. It must police the marketplace to prevent gross malfeasance. The government must guarantee the property rights of private firms and individuals and adjudicate economic disputes among them. It has to ensure transparency of prices for both producers and consumers so that they can respond correctly to market signals. The central bank has to concern itself with monitoring and controlling the rate of growth of the money supply in order to prevent excessive inflation. Finally, the government has to adopt and promulgate new accounting procedures so that it can collect taxes from private businesses to replace the revenues previously obtained from state enterprises.

It cannot be assumed that government officials will have the knowledge or the will to do all of the above in a timely and effective manner. They are sure to meet resistance from a variety of public and private actors. Some countries will have more difficulty than others in achieving the efficiency gains that are connected with the end of central planning because of differences in their resource endowments, accumulated investments in human and physical capital, and abilities to make the required institutional changes. Therefore, the speed and consequences of economic transition will vary significantly from country to country.

Yeltsin: Crisis and Reform

Boris Yeltsin faced two major economic challenges when he came to power in 1991: stabilizing the Russian economy in the face of **hyperinflation** and restarting the process of creating a market economy that had been aborted under Gorbachev. In November 1991, Yeltsin appointed Yegor T. Gaidar as his First Deputy Prime Minister. Gaidar, an economist, was only thirty-five years old and had no political experience. He brought into office with him a commitment to continue the economic reforms that had been interrupted in the last years of

Gorbachev's rule. Gaidar's first task was to stabilize the Russian economy. The drop in government revenues, but not in government spending, led to a major budget deficit in 1991 equivalent to 21.2 percent of GDP (see Figure 10-5). In January 1992 alone, consumer prices increased by 296 percent. The annual inflation rate for 1992 was almost 2,500 percent.[81]

The Russian central bank dealt with the deficit in the worst possible manner from the standpoint of limiting inflation: it simply issued more currency. The governor of the central bank, Viktor Geraschenko, was appointed by the Parliament—not the president—in July 1992. Geraschenko immediately issued vast amounts of cheap credits to the state enterprises.[82] The money supply increased by more than 700 percent in 1992. Confidence in the ruble plummeted, and many Russian enterprises insisted on payment in **hard currencies** instead of rubles even for domestic transactions. It was not until the late spring of 1993 that the Ministry of Finance, by that time under the control of Boris Federov, agreed to limit state subsidies in order to reduce the budget deficit and the inflationary pressures it was causing. The rate of inflation remained between 15 and 20 percent per month through the end of 1994, finally dropping to less than 5 percent per month starting in mid-1995.

Yeltsin appointed Anatoly Chubais to be the head of the State Committee on the Management of State Property (GKI) in November 1991, a position Chubais

Figure 10-5   Budget Deficits/GDP and Growth in Retail Prices in the Former Soviet Union and Russia, 1985–1991, in Percentages

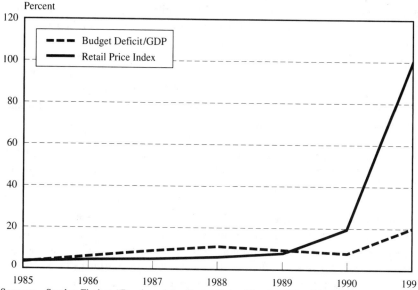

SOURCE: Stanley Fischer, "Russia and the Soviet Union Then and Now," in Olivier J. Blanchard, Kenneth A. Froot, and Jeffrey D. Sachs, eds., *The Transition in Europe: Country Studies*, vol. 1 (Chicago: University of Chicago Press, 1994), 234.

held until 1996. The GKI represented the interests of the central government in the privatization of state enterprises. Chubais and Yeltsin favored a mandatory "commercialization" of state enterprises. Under commercialization, the state enterprises would be converted into joint stock companies with shares that were to be publicly traded on stock exchanges and with boards of directors to represent the interests of shareholders. This idea, already tried in Poland, was designed to both speed up the process of privatization and reduce incentives for corruption.

Under the new privatization scheme, all the state enterprises were divided into three main categories according to their locus of control: federal, provincial (*oblast*), or municipal. The governmental responsibility for privatization was then divided according to this scheme. This approach gave the provincial and local governments—which had previously opposed it on the principle that privatization would lead to shutting down of factories in their locality—a stake in privatization. It also reduced incentives for the appropriation of central government assets by the coalitions of managers, workers, and local governments discussed above.

Russia launched its privatization program in 1992. Tens of thousands of small and medium-sized enterprises under the control of local authorities were sold through auctions and tender offers. The mass privatization program, directed at medium and large-scale enterprises, utilized employee buyouts and voucher auctions to transfer ownership. Enterprises selected one of three privatization options, all of which gave enterprise insiders—workers and management—an opportunity to hold a majority of enterprise shares. To achieve fairness, the Government distributed privatization vouchers free to every Russian to enable them to acquire shares in enterprises through voucher auctions. Remaining blocks of shares were reserved for the government. While some Russians traded their vouchers for cash or participated in the auctions, many more sold their vouchers to investment funds. During the first year of the program, however, investment funds could acquire no more that 10 percent ownership in any single enterprise.

Voucher privatization was considered a success in terms of creating a whole new class of property owners with a stake in the reform process. Between 1992 and mid-1994 when voucher privatization was completed, over 15,000 medium and large-scale enterprises employing 80 percent of Russia's industrial workforce were privatized. Over 75 percent of small enterprises were privatized by June 1994.[83] The transfer of ownership, however, did not result in enterprise restructuring. Indeed, the prevalence of insider ownership, lack of capital, and continuing responsibility to provide social services for employees obstructed enterprises reform.

In July 1994, President Yeltsin initiated a second phase of privatization based on sale of enterprise shares for cash. The objective was to complete the privatization of larger state-owned enterprises, raise funds for federal and local government budgets, and generate investment funds for privatized firms. The Government also hoped to attract investors, including foreigners, who would intensify enterprise restructuring. The program entailed sales of government-owned shares of already privatized companies as well as blocks of shares in enterprises not yet privatized. While cash privatization proceeded relatively well at the municipal and regional levels, the federal program suffered from delays due to policy struggles and the ruble crash of October 1994 which shook confidence and diverted the attention of policy makers. Ultimately only 136 firms were put up for sale under the program, and bidding was sluggish. The Government had expected to raise some $2 billion in revenues for the budget; in the end less than $1 billion was raised.[84]

In September 1995, the Government announced a new Loans-for-Shares Program in an effort to raise substantial sums from the sale of shares of more than 20 of Russia's crown jewel companies. These included the oil companies Lukoil, Yukos and Surgutneftegaz; the non-ferrous metals giant Norilsk Nickel; the Far Eastern Shipping Company; and the Bratsk Timber Complex.[85] Under the program, the Government would auction share-backed securities to Russian banks and other institutions. In return for these loans, the banks were to receive an immediate voice in management and a commitment to receive equity shares of the companies three years down the road when the value of the shares was expected to have increased dramatically. The program was widely criticized as non-transparent and dominated by insider deals, and was terminated after the initial transactions.

As privatization and efforts at macroeconomic stabilization proceeded, resistance to reform mounted, especially from the Duma or Parliament which had been elected under the prior regime and which was dominated by the Communists. The Duma's opposition to Gaidar as the leader and symbol of the reform program forced President Yeltsin to dismiss him from office in December 1992. Gaidar remained as an economic adviser to Yeltsin, but his governmental role was taken by Chernomyrdin, also an advocate of reform. In an effort to offset continued Duma opposition to his program, Yeltsin called for a referendum on economic reform on April 25, 1993. With 64 percent of the electorate voting, 59 percent expressed confidence in the leadership of Boris Yeltsin and 53 percent approved of the policies pursued by the government since 1992.[86]

In October 1993, Yeltsin faced his most serious political challenge by breaking the resistance of a group of dissident members of the Russian Parliament led by Alexandr Rutskoi and Ruslan Khasbulatov in a quickly suppressed but bloody rebellion. The Parliament had voted to impeach Yeltsin, and Yeltsin retaliated by dissolving Parliament and calling for new elections. The opposition occupied the Parliament building (the Russian "White House"). The Russian Army backed Yeltsin against the rebels in the fighting that ensued, sending a volley of cannon-fire into the White House and capturing the opposition leaders.

Parliamentary elections held in December 1993 resulted in a major defeat for Russia's Choice, the reformist political party led by Yegor Gaidar and Boris Federov. Russia's Choice was expected to win a large majority of the seats in the State Duma, the lower house of the Russian Parliament. Although it won the largest bloc of seats, the nationalistic Liberal Democratic Party led by Vladimir Zhirinovsky won almost as many seats in what was seen as a major upset for Russia's Choice. The rapid drop in industrial production in 1992 and 1993—together with continued high inflation rates—had made Gaidar and other economic reformers very unpopular, despite progress made toward reducing hyper-inflation.[87] The liberal reformers suffered further losses in the parliamentary elections of December 1995, and Yeltsin himself had to mass a major campaign in 1996 to win a second term as Russia's president.

Russian Foreign Economic Policies and the West's Response

Pursuing an aggressive foreign economic policy of integration with the Western international economy was, of necessity, part of managing the severe domestic crises that the Yeltsin government faced at the end of 1991. The rapid decline in the value of the ruble contributed to inflation by raising the prices of imports, but it also made Russian exports more competitive internationally. The various efforts to stabilize the Russian economy after 1992, especially efforts to reduce the budget deficit and to reduce inflation, eventually helped to reduce the downward pressures on the ruble. Russia also continued to face difficulties of dealing with its heavy burden of foreign debt. Faced with economic crisis and the huge challenge of a transition to a market economy, Yeltsin turned to the West and to major international economic bodies like the G-7, the World Bank, and the International Monetary Fund for help.

In a historic development, the G-7 leaders invited President Yeltsin to the London economic summit of the G-7 in the summer of 1991. At that meeting, President Yeltsin requested increased economic assistance and political support for Russian membership in the IMF and World Bank. Pleased by Yeltsin's economic policies including his efforts to privatize Russian state enterprises, the G-7 countries strongly supported Russian membership in the IMF and World Bank. However, because they remained concerned about Yeltsin's commitment to sustained reform, they held back on making major new commitments for economic aid. Most of the aid to Russia at this time came from Germany, as part of German payments to speed the removal of Russian troops from the former East Germany. The developed countries had set up a new multilateral bank in May 1990, the European Bank for Reconstruction and Development (EBRD), to channel aid into Russia, the other former Soviet Republics, and Eastern Europe.[88] Both aid and FDI flows to Russia were constrained, however, by worries about the commitment of the Russian government to economic reforms.

The G-7 took a major step toward supporting economic reform in Russia in 1993, just prior to the referendum on reform called by President Yeltsin. In April 1993, at a special meeting of G-7 foreign and finance ministers in Tokyo, a major assistance package was put together. This included approximately $34 billion in new financial flows: $13 billion in loans from the IMF, $1.5 billion in loans from the World Bank, a new G-7 Privatization Fund, an additional $10 billion in export credits from G-7 countries, and $6.5 billion in U.S. aid (which included aid to other former Soviet Republics). About $2.5 billion in loans were made available immediately. The package was finalized at the July 1993 economic summit in Tokyo.[89] The new flows, plus the IMF and World Bank conditions requiring stabilization and privatization, proved to be a major economic and political boost to Russia's reform program.

Following the 1993 program, the IMF and World Bank engaged in intensive and regular dialogue with Russia on its macroeconomic policy and its structural reform program. Support and pressure from these two institutions contributed to the stabilization and reform efforts described above. In 1996, for example, the Fund and Russia concluded a new lending arrangement of $10 billion to support stabilization which was monitored and disbursed on a monthly basis. At the same time, the developed countries supported Russian reform in other ways: ending CoCom controls on trade with Russia and the former Communist countries, beginning negotiations for Russian membership in the WTO, rescheduling Russian debt. As a symbol of growing Russian integration into the institutions of the West, Russia became a regular participant in the discussion of political, though not economic, issues at the G-7 summits.

Russia achieved many but not all of its foreign economic policy goals by the mid 1990s. It was accepted as a member in the IMF and the World Bank, although it had not yet become a member of the WTO and the OECD. Its ruble had become a convertible currency but only for current account transactions. It began to receive increased flows of foreign aid and trickles of FDI. It was included in the political part of the G-7 summits. Most importantly, it created the economic breathing space needed to carry out the major domestic reforms that might bring the Russian economy out of its doldrums.

Economic Reform in Eastern Europe

In the wake of dramatic political changes in 1989, Eastern Europe also moved toward economic reform. The pace there was sometimes quicker, sometimes slower than in Russia. Even before the political revolution of 1989, which ended the domination of the Communist Party in a number of countries, some Eastern European states had adopted economic reforms. Hungary had gone farthest by allowing more competitive pricing, reducing subsidies, introducing personal income and value-added taxes, liberalizing the financial sector and foreign trade sector, and introducing a bankruptcy law.[90] The impetus for Hungary's economic reform, which had come from some sectors within the Communist Party, was poor economic performance in the 1980s and the need to service the country's foreign debt. Political reform, aimed at allowing greater pluralism and the right of association, had gone hand in hand with economic reform and even outpaced it. Poland had gone farthest in political reform by legalizing Solidarity and other trade unions, introducing free elections, granting opposition parties seats in Parliament, and easing censorship of the press.[91]

When the coalition government with Solidarity participation took over in

Poland in September 1989, it had to deal with hyperinflation, chronic shortages of goods, a large trade deficit, and a debt crisis. Tadeusz Mazowiecki, the new prime minister, selected Leczek Balcerowicz, a young Polish economist, to implement a rapid stabilization program that, consistent with the advice of Harvard economist Jeffrey Sachs, included the freeing of prices and the liberalization of domestic and international trade. This program of rapid transition to capitalism was later to be called "the big bang." Although Solidarity was largely a movement of independent labor representatives like Lech Walesa, the new government supported a policy of reducing real wages to compensate for overly generous wage increases of the 1988–1989 period. Subsidies to state enterprises were cut back drastically, as were plans for new state investments. The government stabilized the zloty, Poland's currency, and made it fully convertible into foreign currencies. Finally, in early 1990, official creditors agreed to a generous rescheduling of Poland's official debt and in 1991 to a 50-percent reduction in that debt (see Figure 10-6).

The Polish stabilization program reduced annual inflation from 600 percent in 1990 to 71 percent in 1991 to 42 percent in 1992. The cost of stabilization, however, was quite high. In 1990, GDP decreased by 12 percent, real wages fell by 33 percent. Many government expenditures, even in basic areas like health and education, were cut to reduce the budgetary deficit.[92]

The new Polish government embarked on a privatization program in July 1990, in which state enterprises were converted into joint stock companies (this was called "commercialization") and the government was empowered to sell off its interest in the firms after a two-year transition period or to close them down. But two years after the big bang, only 11 percent of Polish state enterprises had been

Figure 10-6   Long-Term Debt Outstanding in Russia and Eastern Europe in Current Dollars, 1970–1993

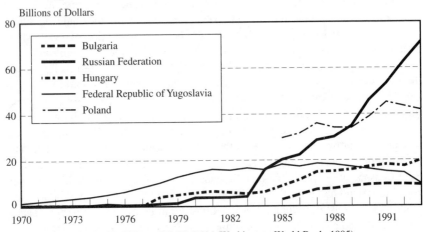

SOURCE: World Bank, *World Data '95 CD-ROM* (Washington: World Bank, 1995).

privatized. The top-down approach to privatization adopted in Poland—which had worked well in the case of East Germany because the privatization board (the Treuhandanstalt) was controlled mainly by West Germans—did not work well.[93]

Hungary proceeded more rapidly initially than Poland or Russia in pursuing privatization, but then slowed its pace markedly. Thanks to economic reforms implemented prior to 1989, liberalization of the Hungarian economy was somewhat easier than in other countries. In addition, as in Russia, a significant amount of spontaneous privatization took place in Hungary after 1989. The Hungarians were not as successful as the Russians in moving away from spontaneous privatization to a more genuine form of privatization. The electoral success of a reconstituted version of the Hungarian Communist Party in 1994 slowed the pace of reform considerably.

Czechoslovakia, now split into the Czech Republic and the Slovak Republic, like Poland, pursued privatization vigorously for small enterprises but more slowly for larger state enterprises. Part of the problem, as in Russia later, was dealing with the various stakeholders, and particularly with the managers and organized labor.[94] One could argue that the Czech and Slovak republics combined features of the Hungarian and Polish approaches to economic reform.

No formerly Communist country in Eastern Europe approached East Germany in the rapidity and depth of its transition to a market economy. East Germany had the benefit of being integrated into a larger industrialized capitalist nation in 1990, inheriting all the legal institutions (with a few notable exceptions) of West Germany, and receiving major subsidies from the German federal government, which were designed to bring its infrastructure and capital stock quickly up to the West German standards. The Communists in East Germany were completely delegitimized by the acts of the regime prior to 1989 and the West German political parties quickly established a dominant role in East German politics after 1990. The transition in former East Germany was not accomplished without dislocations, however, as high levels of unemployment accompanied a general decline in living standards, especially for those on fixed incomes. As Germany recovered from the shock of unification, however, these problems began to abate.

As in Russia, the immediate impact of economic reforms in Eastern Europe was a drop in production and increased unemployment. In some cases, hyperinflation was deeply embedded and hard to stamp out. People who were used to steady jobs and stable incomes, even if low by Western standards, began to vote against the governments who had implemented economic reforms. Some voters, especially in the former Soviet Union, wanted to return to central planning. Partly to head off this opposition, social spending increased in the mid 1990s, with much of the new spending allocated for early-retirement plans designed to increase overall labor productivity.[95] There were signs of a turnaround in the Eastern European economies by the mid 1990s (see again Figure 10-4), but genuine prosperity was still a distant prospect for most of Eastern Europe's people.

China

For most of the postwar period, China, like the Soviet Union and Eastern Europe, was isolated from the Western trading and financial system. China pursued a policy of independent economic development that was based not only on Marxist-Leninist theory but also on China's historical experience with foreign occupation and exploitation beginning with the Opium Wars and unequal treaties of the nineteenth century and ending with the Japanese occupation in the twentieth century. Following the victory of the Communists in 1949, Mao Tse-tung declared that China would "lean to one side," that is, emphasize its relationship with the Soviet Union. A treaty of friendship, alliance, and mutual assistance against aggression by Japan or "any other state" (a veiled reference to the United States) was signed in February 1950. During the 1950s, China relied exclusively on the Soviet Union for technology transfers, capital equipment, and financial support. Originally, joint-stock companies in mining and other natural resources, like those in Eastern Europe after the war, were the preferred form of aid; these were liquidated after Stalin's death. In addition, the Soviet Union lent China $60 million a year from 1950 to 1955 and another $26 million a year from 1954 to 1959.[96] Thousands of Chinese went to Moscow for technical training, while thousands of Soviet technicians worked in China on over 330 industrial projects.[97] Domestically, Mao followed the Soviet model of urban-led industrialization based on the Marxist-Leninist tenets of collectivization, state ownership of the means of production, and central planning. China's strategy of independence was reinforced by its isolation by the West. The United States refused to recognize the People's Republic of China and maintained diplomatic relations with Taiwan.

China's relations with the West were particularly strained as the Korean War developed. Following China's attack on U.S. troops in Korea in 1950, the United States imposed a complete embargo on China. The United Nations, which continued to recognize Taiwan until 1971, also imposed an embargo on the export of strategic materials to China in 1951 in response to their "aggression" in Korea.[98] As a result, trade with the West was minimal. China's total trade with all noncommunist countries amounted to only $550 million in 1952.[99]

As the fifties progressed, the Sino-Soviet alliance deteriorated. A history of border disputes and mistrust between the Soviet Union and China undergirded their differences, which were exacerbated in the 1950s by ideological disputes. When Khrushchev began his de-Stalinization campaign and his policy of peaceful coexistence with the West, Mao accused him of revisionism. A struggle ensued over doctrinal purity and whether the Chinese or the Soviet Communist Party would be the rightful leader of the international Communist movement. Eventually the Soviet Union retracted its offer to help China develop nuclear weapons, and in 1960 all of the Soviet Union's technical and economic advisors were ordered to return to Moscow.

Beginning in the late 1950s, China had adopted a policy of self-sufficiency. China turned inward, and in 1958 it embarked on the Great Leap Forward, a plan to modernize its industry and increase output by way of structural changes and greater ideological purity. Agriculture had already been collectivized, but grain production had stagnated during the 1950s. Further concentration of collectives was encouraged to produce a mass mobilization of the energies of the rural laborers. The collectives were encouraged to place a priority on small-scale local industry to provide for the needs of the farmers. Economic management was decentralized and more responsibility was given to the local Communist parties. Although Mao believed that ideological incentives could unlock the potential of the workers, productivity declined as collectivization continued. This decline in productivity, combined with the withdrawal of Soviet advisors, the decentralization of the economy, and bad weather conditions, led to disaster for the Chinese economy. China's GNP decreased by one-third in 1960. The poor harvest resulted in large-scale starvation and malnutrition. The decentralization of the economy led to the breakdown of industry and transportation, and eventually to widescale demoralization. In 1959, the crisis reached such proportions that Mao was forced to step down from the chairmanship of China (although he remained chairman of the Communist Party). The communes were broken down, some private plots were restored, and control was returned to nonparty managers.

Although China's domestic economy began to recover in the mid-1960s, it suffered another major economic setback during the Cultural Revolution, from 1966 to 1976. In his search for ideological purity, Mao incited the public to rebel against the party, which Mao felt had lost its revolutionary fervor. Major party leaders, educators, and factory managers were purged and parts of the country fell into anarchy. The economy was crippled as basic institutions fell apart and as China deepened its isolation from world contact. Eventually the army was forced to intervene to restore order. Throughout the 1960s, China decreased its trade in real terms and repaid all of its outstanding loans in order to achieve complete self-sufficiency.[100] It had no diplomatic and few economic ties with the United States and continued to be subject to export controls and other U.S. restrictions on trade.

As the 1960s drew to a close, pressures for change began to force China away from its isolationism. The Great Leap Forward and the Cultural Revolution left China technologically backward and politically isolated. Population growth continued to strain China's ability to feed its people. The most important impetus for change at the time, however, was political. Relations with the Soviet Union had continued to deteriorate, and in 1969 the two countries came close to war on the Sino-Soviet border. In 1969, China, motivated by its desire to form a tactical alliance against the Soviet Union, began sending diplomatic signals indicating its willingness to open relations with the West.

Improving relations with Beijing was an important component of Nixon and Kissinger's policy of détente. In their view, China offered a counterbalance in the U.S. relations with the Soviet Union. Accordingly, the Nixon administration responded to China's signals and indicated its interest in improving relations. Some of the U.S. unilateral trade barriers were removed, and the United States voted to support the entry of the PRC into the United Nations, although it voted against expelling Taiwan. In 1972, at the time of President Nixon's dramatic visit to China, the U.S. and Chinese governments issued the Shanghai Communique—the first of three Joint U.S.-PRC Communiques—in which the United States established its "one China" policy by acknowledging that "all Chinese on either side of the Taiwan Strait maintain there is but one China and that Taiwan is a part of China." At the same time, the United States and China signed a bilateral trade agreement and trade resumed after a twenty-six year interruption. Through the seventies, bilateral trade grew steadily to reach $4.0 billion in 1979 (see Figure 10-7). However, it remained a small fraction of the overall trade of both nations.

The second Joint Communique between the U.S. and the PRC was signed in 1979 during the Carter presidency. It formally changed U.S. diplomatic recognition from Taipei to Beijing. At the same time, the U.S. and China negotiated a third Joint Communique which resolved a number of political questions regarding U.S. unofficial relations with Taiwan, particularly U.S. arms sales.

During the 1970s Japanese-Chinese relations also improved. China's trade with Japan grew rapidly once diplomatic relations were reestablished in 1972. Total bilateral trade between Japan and China was $1 billion in 1972.[101] By 1979, bilateral trade had increased fourfold, to $4.3 billion (see Figure 10-8). This growth continued into the 1980s, growing fifteen times in value in fifteen years. China's main export to Japan was crude oil; Japan won contracts to build various chemical and steel plants in China.[102] On the political side, tension

Figure 10-7   U.S. Trade with China in Current Dollars, 1963–1994

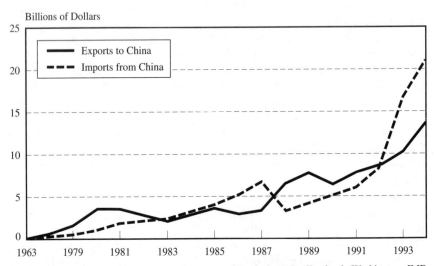

SOURCE: International Monetary Fund, *Direction of Trade Statistics Yearbook* (Washington: IMF, 1995), 924; General Agreement on Tariffs and Trade, *International Trade 1987–1988* (Geneva: GATT, 1988), table AA5.

Figure 10-8   Japanese Trade with China in Current Dollars, 1963–1994

Billions of Dollars

SOURCE: International Monetary Fund, *Direction of Trade Statistics Yearbook* (Washington: IMF, 1995), 924; General Agreement on Tariffs and Trade, *International Trade 1987–1988* (Geneva: GATT, 1988), table AA5.

remained between China and Japan due to continuing Chinese resentment over Japan's wartime occupation.

One of the most important events in recent Chinese history occurred in 1978, when Deng Xiaoping consolidated his power and initiated a profound reform of the Chinese economy. China's need to embark on economic reform can be traced to many of the same inherent weaknesses of the Communist system that the Soviet Union experienced. Under the socialist economic model, China's economy was forced to bear the burden of inefficient allocation of resources and lack of incentives for workers, resulting in poor agricultural and industrial performance. Flexibility and technological change were discouraged, resulting in an increasing technological gap between China and the West, which adversely affected its economic and military capabilities.

Deng's reforms affected both the domestic economy and China's external relations, and they focused on four areas: agriculture, industry, science and technology, and defense.[103] Beginning in the agricultural area, China implemented a "household responsibility system," which contracted work out to individuals and families and gave them more power to manage their own production decisions and more latitude to engage in economic activities outside the central state economy. Peasants were allowed to lease their own farm plots from their collectives and, after producing a certain quota for the state, to sell the rest of their production on an open market. China's 1982 constitution declared that the existence of an individual economy would complement, not threaten, the socialist economy.

Another way in which agricultural production has been encouraged is through price reform. The government has allowed prices for agricultural products to increase across the board and has also stimulated production of certain products, such as vegetables and meat, by increasing their prices even further. In 1984 farmers were allowed to contract land from the communes for fifteen-year periods and transfer the rights to their farmland to other people, although the state still owned the means of production. In 1988, farmers were actually allowed to buy and sell "land use rights," the closest a socialist economy had come to allowing private ownership of land. The household responsibility system was extended into other sectors of the rural economy, such as light industry, fishing, and restaurants. Since 1985, purchase quotas for agricultural production have been replaced by open market transactions.

Reforms in the industrial sector focused on the development of light industry, to correct for previous overemphasis on heavy industry. In 1981, for the first time, production in light industries equaled that of heavy industries. The largest growth was in small village enterprises. Firms began to be responsible for locating their own raw materials and customers. Their profits, although taxed by the state, were theirs to keep. Since 1985, 55 percent of all industrial products have been sold on the open market. The initial results of reform were strong. Agriculture improved from 4.2 percent average annual growth between 1953 and 1977 to 12.3 percent growth from 1978 to 1983. Industrial growth slowed from 10.8 percent to 6.8 percent in the respective periods, but overall national income increased from 6.1 percent average annual growth before the reforms to 8 percent growth from 1978 to 1983.[104] Between 1978 and 1993, real GNP expanded at an average annual rate of 9 percent, quadrupling in size.[105] Although China's rapid rate of economic growth was impressive, its per capita income was still quite low, between $1,000 and $2,000 by recent estimates.[106]

As Chinese economic reforms progressed and the government relinquished some of its central planning functions, it became evident that further price reform would also be necessary to allow the market to work. Goods, labor and land markets were also decontrolled, although some residual controls remained on land sales and prices. The state kept control over the financial sector through continued state ownership of banks and bureaucratic allocation of credit through the banking system. Since 1986, innovations have occurred in the development of interbank markets in some cities and the opening of money markets in Beijing, Shenyang, and Shanghai.[107] New forms of financial intermediaries, such as insurance companies and leasing operations, began to function. But the financial system was still dominated by state-owned banks.[108]

In its external affairs, China adopted a new open door policy that placed new emphasis on diplomatic relations with the West and the role of international trade, finance, and foreign investment in China's economic development. China's trade increased rapidly after 1978, after stagnating in the sixties (see Figure 10-9). Its strategy was to earn enough hard currency through its exports of textiles, petroleum,

Figure 10-9   China's Foreign Trade in Current Dollars, 1978–1993

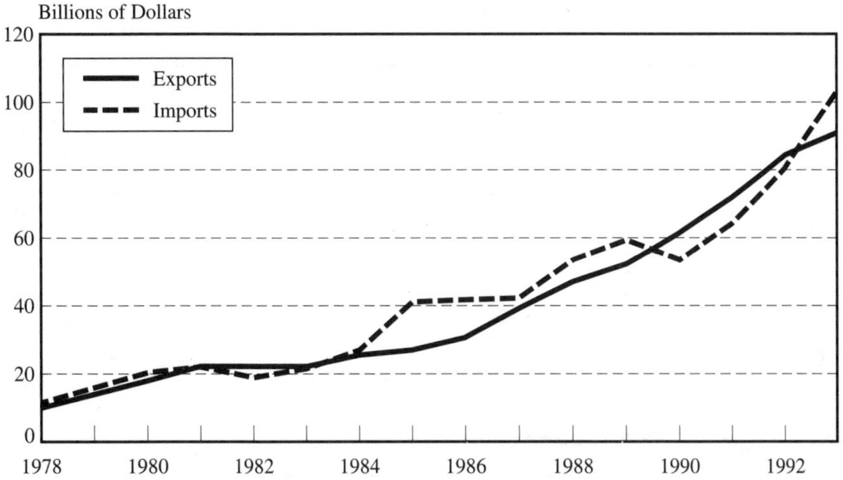

Billions of Dollars

SOURCE: Nicholas Lardy, *China in the World Economy* (Washington: Institute for International Economics, 1994), 30.

and other goods to support necessary capital and technology imports. China also depended on receipts from tourism, foreign investments, and transfers from overseas Chinese to bolster its foreign exchange reserves. The most important imports were heavy capital goods, iron and steel, oil- and gas-exploring and processing equipment, and, to a lesser extent, grain. After 1984, regulations on imports of consumer goods were relaxed, which led to occasional trade deficits.

China's largest trading partner in the 1980s and early 1990s was Japan (see above). Hong Kong was China's second largest trading partner, because of substantial indirect trade relations between China and other East Asian countries such as Taiwan and South Korea. Since no trade officially existed between these countries, the goods passed through Hong Kong. The EU as a whole was China's third largest trading partner, though the United States had more trade with China than any single member state of the EU (see Figure 10-10). Both Europe and the United States experienced deficits in their trade with China in the early 1990s, in marked contrast with Japan's growing trade surplus with that country. In 1995, the U.S. trade deficit with China approached $34 billion. Trade with the Communist bloc decreased from 70 percent of China's total trade in the 1950s to approximately 8 percent in the late 1980s, though this might increase again if the Russian and East European economies begin to grow faster.[109] China's total trade (exports and imports) increased by a factor of ten between 1978 and 1993 (see again Figure 10-9).

U.S.-Chinese trade relations were cemented on July 7, 1979, when the two countries signed a trade agreement that granted China most-favored-nation trad-

Figure 10-10   The European Union's Trade with China in Current Dollars, 1963–1993

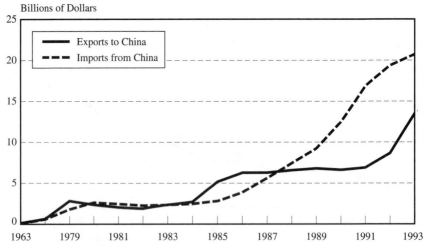

SOURCE: International Monetary Fund, *Direction of Trade Statistics Yearbook* (Washington: IMF, 1994); General Agreement on Tariffs and Trade, *International Trade 1987–1988* (Geneva: GATT, 1988), table AA5.

ing status. However, because China remained a non-market economy, MFN treatment was limited by the Jackson-Vanik amendment to the 1974 Trade Act, requiring the U.S. President to certify each year that China permitted citizens to leave the country. The agreement both reduced U.S. tariffs on Chinese imports and made China eligible for Export-Import Bank financing. The pact also provided for the establishment of commercial trade offices in the two countries. In addition, President Reagan played the China card by encouraging trade with that country. Export controls were relaxed, allowing approximately one-third of U.S. exports to China in recent years to consist of high-technology equipment.[110] Under the Reagan administration, trade with China grew, so that by 1988, U.S. exports to China amounted to $6.6 billion, compared with $1.7 billion in 1979 (see Figure 10-7).[111]

In order to pursue a more active trade policy, China has had to restructure its system of foreign trade. Beginning in 1988, the system was decentralized so that state-owned trade corporations and manufacturers could make their own export and import plans. In addition, factories were allowed to retain up to 80 percent of the export earnings that exceed their export targets. On the other hand, factories were increasingly asked to become responsible for their own losses. For foreign traders, the system was more difficult. Instead of negotiating with one central trade authority, as before, they now had to court three organizations: the central trade authority, the provincial trading firms, and the manufacturers themselves. China's desire to increase its trade also led it to apply in July 1986 to become a contracting party to the GATT.[112] However, bringing a partially reformed, non-market economy with a thriving export sector into the GATT/WTO with rules designed for market economies would prove difficult.

In the financial realm, China signaled the end of its isolationism by joining the International Monetary Fund and World Bank in 1980. Financially, it increased its borrowing from Western financial markets and international organizations, although it was wary of incurring an excessive debt burden. By the end of 1993, China's total long-term debt outstanding was approximately $70 billion (see Figure 10-11).[113] China has also become a large aid recipient (total ODA of around $4.4 billion in 1992), both through multilateral organizations and through bilateral loans from the developed countries (especially Japan) that are intended to boost trade.[114]

Another major change for China is its new interest in encouraging foreign direct investment and joint ventures with the West. Like many developing countries, China hopes to benefit from technology transfers embodied in these investments and also to take advantage of revenues generated from the exports created by these companies. China has taken many steps to encourage foreign investment. It opened five special economic zones (SEZs), which encourage foreign investment and production for export by offering favorable tax treatment, special profit repatriation agreements, and other inducements to foreign investors. Fourteen other coastal cities offer similar incentives. A joint-venture law was passed in April 1988, to provide a legal framework for foreigners doing business in China. Modifications were made in labor regulations to allow foreign compa-

Figure 10-11   Long-Term Debt Outstanding in China in Current Dollars, 1971–1993

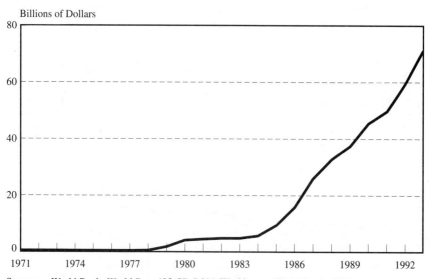

SOURCE: World Bank, *World Data '95 CD-ROM* (Washington: World Bank, 1995).

nies to hire and fire employees freely; in general, Chinese companies must have permission to hire and fire workers. Although thousands of joint and cooperative ventures have been created, many barriers remained.[115] Primary among these is the limited convertibility of the renminbi (China's currency). China has restrictive foreign exchange regulations that hinder foreign investment and profit repatriation. In addition, infrastructural problems, excessive bureaucracy, worker attitudes, and differences in management attitudes have been cited as barriers to more joint ventures.

The very rapid growth of the Chinese economy, however, served as a major inducement for the growth of inward flows of foreign direct investment in the early 1990s (see Figure 10-12). China received over $12 billion in foreign direct investment in 1992 and over $25 billion in 1993. Much of this investment came from overseas Chinese investors in Taiwan, Hong Kong, and Singapore, but many U.S., European, and Japanese multinational firms also increased their presence in China in the early 1990s. Much of this investment has gone into export-oriented production enclaves in the south and eastern coastal areas, Beijing, and the northeast and thus, has had only a limited effect on other parts of the country.

Despite China's economic successes thus far, there remain many barriers to continued change. Although the basic premise of reform is now well accepted, there has been strong conservative opposition to the speed and extent of economic reforms. High inflation rates in 1987 and 1988 resulted in fears of an overheated economy, which strengthened the position of the conservatives and

Figure 10-12   Inflows of FDI into China in Current Dollars, 1982–1994

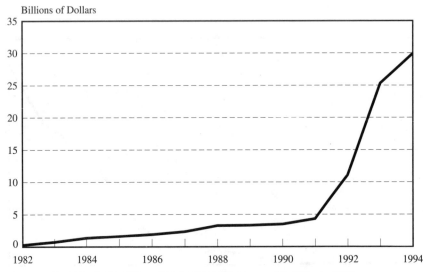

Source: World Bank, *World Data '95 CD-ROM* (Washington: World Bank, 1995).

allowed them to occasionally stop and even roll back the process of reform. Ongoing concerns about unemployment with its potential economic and political consequences have been a barrier to reform of the state enterprises.

Conservatives have also resisted pressures for greater political reform. Indeed, thus far, China's reform process has been notable by the absence of political reform. Student demonstrations for more democratic politics became common in the 1980s before erupting into widespread demonstrations for more political liberalization in 1989. The confrontation between the students and the army in Tiananmen Square in June 1989 demonstrated the strength of the desire for political participation and freedom to choose where to live and work—but it just as clearly demonstrated the government's determination not to allow it.

China's reform policy has thus proceeded unevenly. For example, in mid-1989, in the wake of the Tiananmen crisis, China took a major step backward from its market-based reforms when Prime Minister Li Peng announced a return to central planning in many sectors of its economy. The new policy was presented as a temporary austerity measure to regain control of the economy, but it is a reminder that China's road to reform will continue to be unpredictable. The main concerns of the government were the decentralization of power to the separate provinces, especially the wealthy special economic zones, and the social unrest that was symptomatic of the inequalities caused by the half-reformed economy. This step backward was accompanied by the apparent victory of the more conservative element of the Chinese government. In the 1990s, as the aging Deng Xiaoping ceded control of government policy, reform momentum was again slowed by the absence of a powerful, reformist leader.

In addition to political opposition, there are other structural and ideological problems with the reform process. The riskiest part of the reform process, price reform, has not been fully implemented. Prices of daily necessities, basic urban services and key commodities remain controlled in an effort to curb inflation. The half-adjusted system places strains on the economy. Transition problems in moving from centrally determined to market prices have resulted in severe shortages in some areas. The uneven development of different regions has also been unsettling, resulting in regional discontent and internal migration problems. Corruption has caused some dissatisfaction and is a growing problem, although most Chinese equate reforms with profits and prosperity. Finally, reform efforts may be slowed by bottlenecks in the energy and transportation sectors and general infrastructure, which have been neglected in recent years.

Despite important changes, China remains a highly centralized, socialist system. Nevertheless, China's economic reforms have produced greater aggregate economic growth than the economic reforms undertaken in Russia and Eastern Europe. This is primarily because the Chinese pre-reform economy was much less developed, more heavily dependent on agriculture and, thus, benefited greatly from agricultural reforms and the movement of rural workers to the cities.[116] Prices for state enterprises were rationalized prior to decontrol, making the transition somewhat easier for them. In addition, China was more careful than Russia to pursue its reforms in a context of macroeconomic stability. As a result, it has not suffered the sort of hyperinflation that characterized the Russian economy between 1991 and 1995.[117] Finally, some scholars argue that China benefitted greatly from a major influx of investments by overseas Chinese entrepreneurs, investments not available to Russia because of its ambivalence toward inflows of foreign direct investments and the dearth of overseas Russians. The question, however, was whether the very rapid growth of the 1980s and early 1990s was sustainable and if not whether Chinese Communism would be able to endure a future period of low growth.

During the process of reform, China has continued its policy of opening to the outside world. U.S.-Chinese trade and investment has surged. However, there have been barriers to close relations between China and the United States. From the Chinese perspective, the continued friendly, but unofficial, relations of the United States with Taiwan and its arms sales to Taiwan are major issues. The unofficial visit in June 1995 by Taiwan's President Lee Teng-hui to his *alma mater,* Cornell University, was considered a provocation by the Chinese. In 1996 at the time of Taiwan's first democratic presidential election, China began once again to threaten Taiwan with military intervention, provoking the United States to reaffirm its commitment to peaceful resolution of disputes between China and Taiwan and to send two aircraft carriers to the region.

The United States has been understandably concerned about the growth in its trade deficit with China in recent years. Trade disputes regarding textiles and intellectual property have resulted in U.S. threats of sanctions and have strained the relationship. From the perspective of the United States, barriers to improved relations include political repression such as occurred in 1989, human rights issues, China's abortion policy, China's policies toward Taiwan, and Chinese arms sales to Pakistan and Iran. These concerns have become linked politically with the annual decision of the President regarding MFN. Nonetheless, economic ties between China and the United States have become a more important part of and a stabilizing force in the overall relationship.

China has also pursued closer economic and political relations with several European countries and with Japan. China's economic opening to the West has been welcomed by Western business executives who see the enormous potential of the Chinese market. China in turn has gained much technology and trade from relations with the West. Insofar as these relationships become regularized, they can become a force for continued openness. Finally, in the late 1980s China began a new rapprochement with the Soviet Union that led to summit meetings between Gorbachev and Deng Xiaoping, and, after the breakup of the Soviet Union, between Boris Yeltsin and Jiang Zemin.

China remains a major regional power, and has been increasingly interested in becoming an international player. This interest in playing a role on the world stage has given China further incentive to liberalize its trade and financial relations, to pursue the modernization of its economy and to continue to achieve rapid rates of economic growth.

East-West Economic Relations since the End of the Cold War

The end of the Cold War presented the world economy and its system of management with an unprecedented set of challenges. The most difficult challenge was that faced by the new governments: how to manage the transition from planned to market economies and from authoritarian to democratic political systems. Such a transition was without historical precedent and, thus, there were few principles or theories let alone practical experience to guide the process. The transformation of national economies varied from country to country depending on the existing level of development and the characteristics of the local economy. Thus, eastern European countries and China benefitted from a shorter experience with communism while Russia's economy suffered from the legacy of over sixty years of state management.

Political reform, the transition from authoritarian to more democratic regimes, accompanied economic reform and also varied from country to country. China, still governed by a communist party, followed a more limited path to political liberalization while the countries of the former Soviet bloc moved more rapidly toward democracy. Scholars debated the optimum sequencing of reform—whether, for example, the Asian model of Korea and Taiwan where economic reforms preceded and let to political reforms or the eastern Europe and Russian model of simultaneous reforms was preferable. In the real world, however, each country followed its own path.

A second challenge facing the governments of the West was the need to dismantle many of the institutions constructed to prosecute the Cold War. The principle change was the regime for export controls. That regime had become increasingly unpopular even before the end of the Cold War, not just in Europe, but also with many U.S. firms and industries that wanted to sell products to the communist countries but were unable to do so because of export controls. High-technology companies, such as telecommunications, computer equipment, and software companies, in particular, pressed for changes in export controls after 1991.

The Clinton administration made a number of changes in export controls, including significant liberalization of export controls on sales of telecommunications and computing equipment to Russia, China, and other formerly communist countries in 1994. The U.S. export control regime based on containing communism was now focused more on countries—Cuba, North Korea, Iran, Iraq, Syria, and Libya—which supported terrorist activities.[118] CoCom, which had been the basis for multilateral export controls, lapsed in 1995 and was transformed into a new, looser arrangement called the New Forum. This arrangement included Russia, the Czech Republic, Hungary, Poland and the Slovak Republic as co-founders. Its main purpose was to limit exports of weapons as well as dual-use goods and technologies, i.e., those with both civilian and military applications, to countries that might engage in terrorism and military adventurism.

A third major challenge raised by the end of the Cold War was the integration of the new market economies into the systems of management developed by the West. The former communist countries sought to integrate themselves into the capitalist world economy not only to benefit from trade and investment but also as part of a larger effort to make their political and economic transitions irreversible. The rest of the world, especially the industrialized capitalist world, had to decide how and on what terms to allow the former communist countries to join their economic regimes. The new market economies, for their part, had to decide whether they could accept the discipline and play by the long-established rules of the multilateral system.

One of the goals of many of the east European countries was to join the European Union. EU members were of two minds on expanding to the east. Some, especially Germany, felt it was essential for political as well as economic reasons to bring the eastern Europeans into the union. Others felt Europe needed to be "deepened," i.e., the Maastricht agreements needed to be implemented, before it could be "widened." Thus, the EU negotiated association agreements providing for gradual movement toward free trade with the expectation of eventual membership. But the timing of that membership remained open, as the EU contemplated its future structure.

Another goal of the former non-market economies was to join the existing multilateral institutions. As we have seen, the members of the former Soviet bloc joined the International Monetary Fund and the World Bank and benefitted from financial support from those institutions. A new multilateral bank, the European Bank for Reconstruction and Development, was created to assist eastern Europe and the Newly Independent States (NIS) in their reform. Many of the new market economies of eastern Europe joined the World Trade Organization while others including Russia and the People's Republic of China applied for membership in the WTO. The applications of Russia and China to join the world trading regime raised, in turn, the fundamental challenge of the transition of these countries to market economies, the question of their ability to achieve domestic economic reform which would enable them to accept the rules and disciplines of the prevailing regime.

NOTES

1. The Communist Party was later reinstated.
2. Marshall I. Goldman, *Détente and Dollars: Doing Business with the Soviets* (New York: Basic Books, 1975), 4–20.

3. Anthony C. Sutton, *Western Technology and Soviet Economic Development, 1917 to 1930* (Stanford, Calif.: Hoover Institution on War, Revolution and Peace, 1968); and Anthony C. Sutton, *Western Technology and Soviet Economic Development, 1930 to 1945* (Stanford, Calif.: Hoover Institution on War, Revolution and Peace, 1971).

4. See, for example, Jacob Viner, "International Relations Between State-Controlled National Economics," *American Economic Review* 54 (March 1944): 315–329.

5. John Lewis Gaddis, *The United States and the Origins of the Cold War, 1941–1947* (New York: Columbia University Press, 1972): 18–23, 174–197.

6. William Diebold, Jr., "East-West Trade and the Marshall Plan," *Foreign Affairs* 26 (July 1948): 710.

7. On the United Nations Relief and Rehabilitation Administration, see E. F. Penrose, *Economic Planning for the Peace* (Princeton: Princeton University Press, 1953), 145–167.

8. Diebold, "East-West Trade and the Marshall Plan," 715.

9. For a discussion of motives and policies, see Zbigniew K. Brzezinski, *The Soviet Bloc: Unity and Conflict*, rev. ed. (Cambridge: Harvard University Press, 1967), 3–151.

10. Stalin, Joseph, *Economic Problems of Socialism in the USSR* (New York: International Publishers, 1952), 26–30. Stalin was not alone in his predictions of postwar economic problems in the West. Many Western economists and policymakers were also concerned. See Gaddis, *The United States and the Origins of the Cold War.*

11. On Marxist justification, see Zygmunt Nagorski, Jr., *The Psychology of East-West Trade* (New York: Mason and Lipscomb, 1974), 58–59.

12. See, for example, Gaddis, *The United States and the Origins of the Cold War*; and Adam B. Ulam, *Expansion and Coexistence: The History of Soviet Foreign Policy, 1917–1967* (New York: Praeger, 1968), 314–455.

13. See Nicholas Spulber, *The Economics of Communist Eastern Europe* (New York: Technology Press of MIT, John Wiley, 1957).

14. See Charles Prince, "The USSR's Role in International Finance," *Harvard Business Review* 25 (autumn 1946): 111–128.

15. See J. Keith Horsfield, ed., *The International Monetary Fund, 1945–1965*, vol. 1, *Chronicle* (Washington: International Monetary Fund, 1969), 263, 359–364.

16. Clair Wilcox, *A Charter for World Trade* (New York: Macmillan, 1949), 164–167. Czechoslovakia was a contracting party to the GATT, but the United States suspended its application of GATT provisions to that country in 1948 after a communist government came to power.

17. See Ulam, *Expansion and Coexistence*, 432–440. It is debated whether or not the U.S. offer of aid to the Soviet Union was serious. In any case the Soviet rejection was clear. For a critical analysis of U.S. policy, see Joyce Kolko and Gabriel Kolko, *The Limits of Power: The World and the United States Foreign Policy, 1945–1954* (New York: Harper and Row, 1972), 359–383. For a more recent analysis of Stalin's reaction to the Marshall Plan, see Michael J. Hogan, "American Marshall Planners and the Search for a European Neocapitalism," *American Historical Review* 90 (February 1985), 44–72.

18. Michael Kaser, *Comecon: Integration Problems of the Planned Economies* (London: Oxford University Press, 1965), 1–12; and Michael Marrese, "CMEA: Effective but Cumbersome Political Economy," in Ellen Comisso and Laura D'Andrea Tyson, eds., *Power, Purpose, and Collective Choice: Economic Strategy in Socialist States* (Ithaca, N.Y.: Cornell University Press, 1986).

19. Nicholas Spulber, "East-West Trade and the Paradoxes of the Strategic Embargo," in Alan A. Brown and Egon Neuberger, eds., *International Trade and Central Planning: An Analysis of Economic Interactions* (Berkeley and Los Angeles: University of California Press, 1968), 114.

20. Paul Marer, "The Political Economy of Soviet Relations with Eastern Europe," in Steven J. Rosen and James R. Kurth, eds., *Testing Theories of Economic Imperialism* (Lexington, Mass.: Lexington Books, 1974), 244–245.

21. Ibid., 234. After the disturbances in Poland in 1956, the Soviet Union agreed to a reimbursement for the inequitable price of coal.

22. Under market systems like those in the West, the allocation of resources—decisions about what to produce, how to produce it, and to whom to distribute it—is determined mostly by private supply and demand. Under a centrally planned system, such decisions are made by a central state planning organization.

23. See Brzezinski, *The Soviet Bloc*, 101.

24. Marer, "The Political Economy," 247–249.

25. Ibid., 233–235.

26. Spulber, *The Economics of Communist Eastern Europe.*

27. Ibid., 166–223.

28. For a discussion of earlier actions, see Gunnar Adler-Karlsson, *Western Economic Warfare, 1947–1967: A Case Study in Foreign Economic Policy* (Stockholm: Almqvist and Wiksell, 1968), 5 and, for the text of the Export Control Act, see 217–219. For an excellent discussion of the Export Control Act and its consequences, see Michael Mastanduno, *Economic Containment: CoCom and the Politics of East-West Trade* (Ithaca, N.Y.: Cornell University Press, 1992). See also John P. Hardt and George Holliday, *U.S.-Soviet Commercial Relations: The Interplay of Economics, Technology Transfer, and Diplomacy*, for the Subcommittee on National Security Policy and Scientific Developments of the Committee on Foreign Affairs (Washington: Government Printing Office, June 19, 1973), 48–49.

29. Members were the United States, Canada, Japan, Belgium, Denmark, France, Greece, Italy, Luxembourg, the Netherlands, Norway, Portugal, Turkey, the United Kingdom, and West Germany (that is, all the NATO members except Iceland, plus Japan). Spain joined in 1985 after becoming a member of NATO; Australia joined in 1989.

30. Adler-Karlsson, *Western Economic Warfare*, 1–6, 31–45; and Mastanduno, *Economic Containment*, chs. 3–4. For a summary of Western European and Japanese views on CoCom, see Angela Stent, *East-West Technology Transfer: European Perspectives*, The Washington Papers, vol. 8, no. 75 (Beverly Hills, Calif.: Sage Publications, 1980); and Stephen Sternheimer, *East-West Technology Transfer: Japan and the Communist Bloc*, The Washington Papers, vol. 8, no. 76 (Beverly Hills, Calif.: Sage Publications, 1980), 12–23.

31. Romania, Hungary, and Poland became eligible when they joined the International Monetary Fund and the World Bank in 1972, 1981, and 1986, respectively.

32. Hardt and Holliday, *U.S.-Soviet Commercial Relations*, 55–58; and Samuel Pisar, *Coexistence and Commerce Guidelines for Transactions Between East and West* (New York: McGraw-Hill, 1970), 107–109 .

33. See Goldman, *Détente and Dollars*, 52; and Pisar, *Coexistence and Commerce*, 111–114. The Berne Union, a group of governmental and private credit insurance organizations in the developed market economies, agreed to limit commercial credits to the East to five years and to require an initial cash payment of at least 20 percent of the purchase price. The agreement was nonbinding, however, and proved ineffective.

34. Pisar, *Coexistence and Commerce*, 102–107. For other U.S. restrictions on imports, see Goldman, *Détente and Dollars*, 98–102.

35. Spulber, "East-West Trade and the Paradoxes of the Strategic Embargo," 114.

36. Adler-Karlsson, *Western Economic Warfare, 1947–1967*, 83–99; and Franklyn D. Holzman, *International Trade Under Communism—Politics and Economics* (New York: Basic Books, 1976), 138–143.

37. Joseph Wilczynski, *The Economics and Politics of East-West Trade* (New York: Praeger, 1969), 56.

38. U.S. Department of State, *The Battle Act Report 1973*, Mutual Defense Assistance Control Act of 1951, Twenty-Sixth Report to Congress (Washington: Government Printing Office, 1974), 22; and Spulber, "East-West Trade and the Paradoxes of the Strategic Embargo," 114.

39. John Lewis Gaddis, *The Long Peace: Inquiries into the History of the Cold War* (New York: Oxford University Press, 1987). It has to be noted, however, that the period of rule of Leonid Brezhnev was not one of good U.S.-Soviet relations, but rather of temporary détente, ending around 1974, followed by increasing tension and escalation of hostilities, especially with the invasion of Afghanistan in 1978 and the coming to office of Ronald Reagan in 1981.

40. See Ann Goodman, Margaret Hughes, and Gertrude Schroeder, "Raising the Efficiency of Soviet Farm Labor: Problems and Prospects," in U.S. Congress, Joint Economic Committee, *Gorbachev's Economic Plans*, vol. 2, 100–125.

41. Goodman et al., 102.

42. See Goldman, *Détente and Dollars*, 27–31.

43. Central Intelligence Agency, *Handbook of Economic Statistics 1987* (Washington: CIA), 100.

44. Joseph Wilczynski, *Socialist Economic Development and Reforms: From Extensive to Intensive Growth Under Central Planning in the USSR, Eastern Europe, and Yugoslavia* (New York: Praeger, 1972), 26–33.

45. Franklyn D. Holzman and Robert Legvold, "The Economics and Politics of East-West Relations," *International Organization* 29 (winter 1975), 277–278.

46. See, for example, Alec Nove, *The Soviet Economic System*, 3rd ed. (London: Routledge, 1986).

47. See Wilczynski, S*ocialist Economic Development and Reforms*, 234–237; Bruce Parrott, *Politics and Technology in the Soviet Union* (Cambridge: MIT Press, 1983); Goldman, *Détente and Dollars*, 32–33; and Holzman and Legvold, "The Economics and Politics of East-West Relations," 278. The problems of technology did not apply to the space and military sectors; rather, advances in these fields were made possible by the close relationship of research with end users, competition among research units and with the West, and preferences on supplies.

48. U.S. Congress, Joint Economic Committee, "The Soviet Economy in 1988: Gorbachev Changes Course," Report by the Central Intelligence Agency and Defense Intelligence Agency to the Subcommittee on National Security Economics, April 14, 1989; and John P. Hardt and Richard F. Kaufman, "Gorbachev's Economic Plans: Prospects and Risks," in U.S. Congress, Joint Economic Committee, *Gorbachev's Economic Plans*, vol. 1, Study Papers submitted to the Joint Economic Committee (Washington: Government Printing Office, 1987), IX.

49. Wilczynski, *Socialist Economic Development and Reforms*; and Nagorski, *The Psychology of East-West Trade*, 104–156.

50. Marshall Goldman, "Two Roads to Economic Reform: Hungary and the German Democratic Republic" in *Gorbachev's Challenge, Economic Reform in the Age of High Technology* (New York: Norton, 1987), 148–174; and Ellen Comisso and Paul Marer, "The Economics and Politics of Reform in Hungary," *International Organization* 40 (spring 1986): 421–454. There is still some controversy about the extensiveness of Hungarian economic reforms, yet many people in the communist world focused on the Hungarian experiments with reform as a possible answer to their economic problems.

51. Holzman and Legvold, "The Economics and Politics of East-West Relations," 288.

52. See Wilczynski, *Socialist Economic Development and Reforms*, 218–220, 252.

53. Josef Van Brabant, "CMEA Institutions and Policies versus Structural Adjustment: Comments on Chapter 5," in Josef C. Brada, Ed A. Hewett, and Thomas A. Wolf, eds., *Economic Adjustment and Reform in Eastern Europe and the Soviet Union* (London: Duke University Press, 1988), 170–184.

54. For divergent views on Comecon policies in the 1980s, see chapters by Josef van Brabant and Marie Lavigne in *Economic Adjustment and Reform in Eastern Europe and the Soviet Union*, 140–184.

55. Pisar, *Coexistence and Commerce*, 35.

56. John P. Hardt, George D. Holliday, and Young C. Kim, *Western Investment in Communist Economies: A Selected Survey on Economic Interdependence*, U.S. Senate, 93rd Cong., 2nd sess., Subcommittee on Multinational Corporations of the Committee on Foreign Relations, 1974, 1–2.

57. See U.S. House, Committee on Banking and Currency, Subcommittee on International Trade, *The Fiat-Soviet Automobile Plant and Communist Economic Reforms*, 98th Cong., 2nd sess., 1967.

58. Klaus Bolz, "Industrial Cooperation," in Reinhard Rode and Hanns D. Jacobsen, eds., *Economic Warfare or Détente: An Assessment of East-West Economic Relations in the 1980s* (Boulder, Colo.: Westview Press, 1985), 63–73.

59. Joint Economic Committee Report, ix.

60. UNCTAD, *Handbook of International Trade and Development Statistics 1988* (New York: United Nations, 1988), 452.

61. U.S. Senate, 89th Cong., 2nd sess., Bill 5-3363.

62. P.L. 93-618, the Trade Act of 1974.

63. The Export-Import Bank Act Amendments of 1974, P.L. 93-646.

64. "Appendix," in U.S. Congress, Joint Economic Committee, *Issues in East-West Commercial Relations*, 292. See also similar statements by Secretary of Commerce Juanita Kreps and a State Department spokesperson, 290, 296–297.

65. See Zbigniew Brzezinski, *Power and Principle: Memoirs of the National Security Advisor, 1977–1981* (New York: Farrar, Straus, Giroux, 1983), especially ch. 12; and Fred Halliday, *The Making of the Cold War* (London: Verso, 1983), for accounts of the development of President Carter's foreign policy. See also Raymond Garthoff, *Détente and Confrontation: American-Soviet Relations from Nixon to Reagan* (Washington: The Brookings Institution, 1985).

66. International Monetary Fund, *Direction of Trade Statistics, Yearbook 1983* (Washington: International Monetary Fund, 1983), 399.

67. U.S. Department of Commerce, *Office of East European and Soviet Affairs* (Washington: Government Printing Office, 1984).

68. Strobe Talbott and Michael Mandelbaum, *Reagan and Gorbachev* (New York: Vintage Books, 1987). For a more specific discussion of changes in U.S. East-West trade with the Soviet Union, see Bruce Parrott, ed., *Trade, Technology and Soviet American Relations* (Bloomington: Indiana University Press, 1985).

69. Bruce Jentleson, *Pipeline Politics: The Complex Political Economy of East-West Energy Trade* (Ithaca, N.Y.: Cornell University Press, 1986).

70. See Mikhail Gorbachev, *Perestroika: New Thinking for Our Country and the World* (New York: Harper and Row, 1987); Zbigniew Brzezinski, *The Grand Failure: The Birth and Death of Communism in the Twentieth Century* (New York: Scribner's, 1989); Anders Åslund, *Gorbachev's Struggle for Economic Reform*, 2nd ed. (Ithaca, N.Y.: Cornell University Press, 1991); and Brendan Kiernan, *The End of Soviet Politics: Elections, Legislatures, and the Demise of the Communist Party* (Boulder, Colo.: Westview Press, 1993).

71. See David Holloway, "Gorbachev's New Thinking," *Foreign Affairs* 68 (winter 1989): 66–81; and Robert Legvold, "Soviet Foreign Policy," *Foreign Affairs* op. cit., 82–98.

72. See Seweryn Bialer, "Gorbachev's Move," *Foreign Policy* (fall 1987): 59–87; and Brendan Kiernan, *The End of Soviet Politics*.

73. Gorbachev, *Perestroika*; Padma Desai, *Perestroika in Perspective: The Design and Dilemmas of Soviet Reform* (Princeton, N.J.: Princeton University Press, 1989); Marshall I. Goldman, *What Went Wrong with Perestroika?* (New York: Norton, 1992); Ed A. Hewett, *Reforming the Soviet Economy: Equality versus Efficiency* (Washington: The Brookings Institution, 1988); and Jerry F. Hough, *Opening Up the Soviet Economy* (Washington: The Brookings Institution, 1988).

74. Joan F. McIntyre, "Soviet Efforts to Revamp the Foreign Trade Sector," in U.S. Congress, Joint Economic Committee, *Gorbachev's Economic Plans*, vol. 2 (Washington: Government Printing Office, 1987), 501–503.

75. Financial Times, April 4, 1989, p. 2.

76. See Marshall D. Shulman, "The Superpowers: Dance of the Dinosaurs," *Foreign Affairs* 66 (spring 1988), 494–550.

77. Department of State, "Joint Summit Statement," *Bulletin*, December 10, 1987, p. 16.

78. Gorbachev, *Perestroika*, 190–209.

79. Andrei Schleifer and Robert W. Vishny, "Privatization in Russia: First Steps," in Olivier J. Blanchard, Kenneth A. Froot, and Jeffrey P. Sachs, eds., *The Transition in Eastern Europe: Volume 2: Restructuring* (Chicago: University of Chicago Press, 1994), 141.

80. See Anders Åslund, *How Russia Became a Market Economy* (Washington: Brookings Institution, 1995), 36–40.

81. Richard E. Ericson, "The Russian Economy Since Independence," in Gail W. Lapidus, ed., *The New Russia: Troubled Transformation* (Boulder, Colo.: Westview Press, 1995), 46; and Brigitte Granville, *The Success of Russian Economic Reforms* (London: Royal Institute of International Affairs, 1995), 107.

82. Maxim Boycko, Andrei Shleifer, and Robert Vishny, *Privatizing Russia* (Cambridge: MIT Press, 1995), 5.

83. OECD Economic Surveys, *The Russian Federation* 1995 (Paris: Organization for Economic Cooperation and Development, 1995), 77.

84. Russian Government Statistics.

85. "Russia Sees Budget Boost in Shares-for-Loans Plan," Reuters, downloaded from the Internet newsgroup clari.world.europe.russia, Article #9066, September 25, 1995.

86. Åslund, *How Russia Became a Market Economy*, 55.

87. Yergin and Gustafson, *Russia 2010*, 89–92.

88. Enzo R. Grilli, *The European Community and the Developing Countries* (New York: Cambridge University Press, 1993), 315–316, 327–328.

89. Susan B. Garland and Owen Ullman, with Bill Javetski, "A Sticky Summit: It Won't Be the Triumph Clinton Envisioned," *Business Week*, January 10, 1994, 38.

90. On reforms in Hungary and East Germany, see Marshall Goldman, *Gorbachev's Challenge*, 148–173.

91. On reforms in Poland, see Urszula Plowiec, "Economic Reform and Foreign Trade in Poland," in Brada, Hewitt, and Wolf, *Economic Adjustment and Reform in Eastern Europe and the Soviet Union*, 340–369.

92.. Alain de Combrugghe and David Lipton, "The Government Budget and the Economic Transformation of Poland," in Blanchard et al., *The Transition in Eastern Europe*, 114; and Tadeusz Kowalik, "The Great Transformation and Privatization: Three Years of Polish Experience," in Christopher G. A. Bryant and Edmund Mokrzycki, eds., *The New Great Transformation? Change and Continuity in East-Central Europe* (New York: Routledge, 1994).

93. Andrew Berg, "The Logistics of Privatization in Poland," in Blanchard et al., *The Economic Transition in Eastern Europe*, vol. 2; and Wendy Carlin and Colin Mayer, "The Treuhandanstalt: Privatization by State and Market," also in the Blanchard volume.

94. Vick Duke and Keith Grime, "Privatization in East-Central Europe: Similarities and Contrasts in Its Application," in Bryant and Mokrzycki, *The New Great Transformation?*

95. "Eastern Europe: Paradox Explained," *The Economist*, July 22, 1995, 52.

96. John King Fairbank, *The United States and China*, 3rd ed. (Cambridge: Harvard University Press, 1971), 351–354.

97. Ibid.

98. Donald P. Whitaker and Rinn-Sup Shinn, *Area Handbook for the People's Republic of China* (Washington: Government Printing Office, 1972), 309.

99. U.S. Commerce Department statistics, cited in Congressional Quarterly, *China and U.S. Foreign Policy*, 2nd ed. (Washington: Congressional Quarterly, 1973), 60.

100. Nicholas R. Lardy, *China's Entry into the World Economy: Implications for Northeast Asia and the United States* (New York: University Press of America for the Asia Society 1987), 3.

101. Selzo Maysamuora, "Japan-China Trade in Retrospect—The 15th Anniversary of Normalizing Relations," in JETRO, *China Newsletter*, no. 72, (January-February 1988): 19.

102. Ibid.

103. For a summary of China's reforms, see A. Doak Barnett and Ralph N. Clough, eds., *Modernizing China: Post Mao Reform and Development* (Boulder, Colo.: Westview Press, 1986); Harry Harding, *China's Second Revolution: Reform after Mao* (Washington: Brookings Institution, 1987); and U.S. Congress, Joint Economic Committee, *China Under the Four Modernizations* (Washington: Government Printing Office, 1982). See also U.S. Congress, Joint Economic Committee, *China's Economy Looks Toward the Year 2000* (Washington: Government Printing Office, 1986).

104. Joint Economic Committee, *China's Economy Looks Toward the Year 2000*, 44–47.

105. Nicholas R. Lardy, *China in the World Economy* (Washington: Institute for International Economics, 1994), 3.

106. Ibid., 25.

107. See Phillip Grub and Bryan L. Sudweeks, "Securities Markets and the People's Republic of China," in JETRO, *China Newsletter*, no. 74, (May-June 1988): 11–16.

108. Lardy, *China in the World Economy*, 13–14.

109. Economist Intelligence Unit, *Country Profile: China, North Korea 1988–89*, (London: The Unit, 1989), 47.

110. Central Intelligence Agency, *China: Economic Performance in 1987 and Outlook for 1988* (Washington: CIA, May 1988), 8.

111. On U.S.-China trade in general, see Eugene K. Lawson, ed., *U.S.-China Trade: Problems and Prospects* (New York: Praeger, 1988).

112. As of this writing, China's application was still being considered. See "China Wants to Join the Club," *The Economist*, May 14, 1994, 35.

113. World Bank, *World Tables 1987* (Washington: World Bank, 1988), 99.

114. OECD, *Geographical Distribution of Financial Flows to Developing Countries 1987* (Paris: OECD, 1987); and Lardy, *China in the World Economy*, ch. 3.

115. "China Data," *The China Business Review*, 57, published by the National Council for U.S.-China Trade, May-June 1988.

116. Wing Thye Woo, "The Art of Reforming Centrally Planned Economies: Comparing China, Poland, and Russia," *Journal of Comparative Economics* 18 (June 1994): 276–308; Jingjie Li, "The Characteristics of Russian and Economic Reform," *Journal of Comparative Economics*, 18 (June 1994): 309–313; and Minxin Pei, *From Reform to Revolution: The Demise of Communism in China and the Soviet Union* (Cambridge: Harvard University Press, 1994).

117. Ronald I. McKinnon, "Financial Growth and Macroeconomic Stability in China, 1978–1992: Implications for Russia and Other Transitional Economies," *Journal of Comparative Economics* 18 (June 1994): 428–469; and Barry Naughton, "What Is Distinctive About China's Economic

Transition? State Enterprise Reform and Overall System Transformation," *Journal of Comparative Economics* 18 (June 1994): 470–490.
118. Thomas L. Friedman, "U.S. Ending Cubs on High-Tech Gear to Cold War Foes," *New York Times*, March 31, 1994, p. 1.

Conclusion: Globalization and the New World Order

This book has focused on two interrelated themes: the influence of politics on international economic relations and the political management of the world economy in the years since World War II. The examination of international economic relations in recent decades has revealed the many ways in which political factors have shaped economic outcomes. We have seen that the postwar security system significantly affected the postwar economic system. The creation of a bipolar diplomatic-security system following the outbreak of the Cold War between the United States and the Soviet Union led to the separation of the Eastern and Western economic systems and provided a base for the dominant role of the United States in the Western system and of the Soviet Union in the Eastern system. The end of the Cold War has led in turn to a deeper integration of the formerly Communist countries and China into the world economy.

We have also seen the influence of domestic policymaking on international economic relations. Political concerns often outweigh economic considerations in policy outcomes. The Marshall Plan, for example, was a security policy as well as an economic program. Similarly, aid by the West to the formerly Communist countries since the end of the Cold War was motivated strongly by security concerns, such as the desire to promote friendly and stable democratic political systems in the East.

In addition, trade and investment policy debates have been influenced by the mobilization of interest groups. For example, organized labor and environmental groups opposed the ratification of the North American Free Trade

Agreement in 1993, despite strong support from U.S. manufacturing interests and the Executive Branch of the government, because they thought the agreement would create downward pressure on wages and environmental standards in the United States.

Finally, and most important for us, international economic relations has itself become a political arena in which both governments and nonstate actors (like the multinational corporations) try to manage conflict and seek cooperative outcomes. These actors are searching for new ways to manage the interdependence and minimize the imbalances associated with the current world economic order. For example, as the world economy becomes more globalized and interdependent, foreign-owned multinational corporations are increasingly playing a role in the politics of their host countries, often acting to counter nationalist coalitions in both host and home countries. Thus, the globalization of the world economy has led to an internationalization of domestic politics. The line between domestic and foreign policy has been blurred.

A New World Order?

Our review of the political management of international economic relations in the years since World War II traced the system of political control established after World War II, the forces for change in the postwar order, and the factors affecting future international economic management. Each chapter of this book has offered some conclusion about the future of management in particular areas—money, trade, investment—and in particular subsystems—West, North-South, East-West. It seems appropriate, therefore, to look at the future of the system as a whole and to suggest some answers to the question of whether it will be possible to develop new forms of political management that will be able to deal with the problems of our time.

Any new international economic order will be based on political conditions different from the political bases of the Bretton Woods system: the concentration of power in a small number of states, the existence of a cluster of interests shared by those states, and the presence of a dominant power willing and able to assume a leadership role.

The future order will continue to rely on political management by a core of powerful, developed market states. The developed market economies and especially the "big five"—the United States, Japan, West Germany, France, and the United Kingdom—will remain the key actors in the system. The size and vitality of their economies will ensure their continuing leadership. Their growing interdependence will be a force for cooperation. Nevertheless, power relationships among the big five will change, affecting system management.

Japan, as the second-largest developed market economy after the United States, will certainly seek to play a more important role. As we have seen, Japan has already staked out a greater role in international monetary relations, foreign direct investment, and foreign aid. At the same time, the big three countries of

Western Europe—France, Germany, and the United Kingdom—are seeking to enhance their economic power through the creation of an internal market among the member states of the European Union. The ability of the EU to achieve its goal of a common economic system with a free flow of goods, services, money, and people will shape the role of its member states in the new order.

The management group, furthermore, will have to be broadened in some cases and some areas. Future management, if it is to be effective, will have to take into account new power centers. Some members of OPEC, for example, still have a major say in energy issues. In the area of trade and foreign investment, the advanced developing countries whose economies are now closer to the developed core than to the rest of the Third World will play a greater role in international management. States such as Brazil, Mexico, and South Korea, whose trade is of great importance to the industrialized countries, which have huge amounts of foreign investment, and which often have significant financial relations with the North, will be in a position to demand and receive access to management. Their voices will be heard to a greater extent in trade and investment negotiations. The new rich may develop cooperative relations with or even join the Organization for Economic Cooperation and Development.

Whereas some Third World countries will be involved to a greater extent in international economic decision making, the role of other states of the Third World in international economic management is unlikely to change. These less-developed countries constitute a Fourth World whose only hope is not access to decision making but a greater ability to force the powerful to listen to their demands and to perceive that it is in their self-interest to respond to them. The South's weakness and increasing fragmentation are major obstacles to the Fourth World's ability to place its demands for equity on the international agenda.

Finally, Eastern countries pose important management challenges to the system. In order to preserve stability and promote reform, the West has sought to promote the economic and political restructuring of Russia and Eastern Europe. It has also sought to integrate the formerly Communist countries as well as China and Vietnam into the Western economic system. The challenge for international management is to promote economic transition and integration of these countries into existing economic regimes.

Among the powerful core, there will remain a recognized cluster of common interests. Despite conflicts raised by economic change and in particular by economic interdependence, the developed market economies will continue to support a liberal, capitalist international economy. The postwar experience has reinforced their belief in the need to cooperate to achieve that stable and prosperous economic system. The persistence of the shared goal of cooperation was demonstrated by the behavior of the industrialized nations in the 1970s, 1980s, and 1990s. The restraint evidenced during the various money, oil, debt, and trade crises and their ability to achieve reform testify to the enduring consensus. So does the successful conclusion of the Uruguay Round and the formation of the World Trade Organization.

There are suggestions that the second tier of states—members of OPEC and the NICs among others—share at least some of the norms of cooperation currently held by the industrialized countries. Adoption by the Third World in the 1980s and 1990s of more pragmatic policies toward trade and foreign investment may be signs of movement toward greater global consensus. The NICs may be more receptive now to schemes for economic management at the international level than the rest of the Third World because they have a greater stake in that system.

Still, it seems quite likely that North-South tensions will persist. Despite the growing differentiation between the more-advanced and the least-developed Southern countries, the wealthier Southern states continue to support greater emphasis on international equity. Although the goal of equity is not rejected by the industrial core, it is not seen as a primary goal of international economic management or as a responsibility of the developed market economies. Even though the South has succeeded in putting equity on the agenda of international economic management and the developed market economies are willing to carry out some redistributive or development programs, the North so far has been unwilling to alter noticeably the established system's operation. Furthermore, some Northern critics have questioned whether equity, as demanded by the less-developed countries, is a legitimate goal. Some charge that redistribution as now conceived will benefit only a few or only a small stratum of the population of the less-developed countries and not the poorest in the poor countries. Without extensive internal political, social, and economic reform in the less-developed countries, international efforts at redistribution and development will be useless, according to many in both the North and the South. Conflict over equity and redistribution therefore is likely to continue to be a political dynamic in the new international economic order.

Finally, the new international economic order will be a system of multilateral management. In the past, the management of conflict and cooperation was carried out to a great extent by a single leader. In the nineteenth century, Great Britain was this leader, and in the postwar era, the United States took the part. The more even distribution of power among the core states in the future, however, will require the active participation of several states—that is, it will require multilateral management.

Multilateral management is difficult. Throughout history, agreement among sovereign powers in the absence of world government has proved to be a difficult and often an impossible task. Several factors, however, enhance the possible success of multilateral economic management. The basic consensus among the powerful will be an important factor; so, too, will be the experience in cooperation since World War II. Multilateral management will be facilitated by a variety of formal and informal methods of multilateral decision making developed over the last four decades. A relatively sophisticated and complex structure of cooperative mechanisms has unfolded in the postwar era, and experience in using these mechanisms has grown.

Even within a multilateral system, however, leadership will be important.

Existing institutions are insufficiently developed to manage the system without supplementary action on the part of leading nation-states. Most often, that leadership will have to come from the United States. Unless and until the European Union becomes politically unified, and the EU or Japan assumes a more assertive posture in world affairs, the United States, by the very size of its economy, will continue to be the most important international economic actor. Although the United States will be unable to manage the system by itself, management and reform will be impossible without U.S. approval, and U.S. initiatives and support for reforming multilateral regimes will be crucial to their success.

A New World Order, or a Reformed World Order?

Because of the political setting and the nature of the task, the process of international economic reform will be piecemeal and evolutionary. Reform will result, in part, from international negotiations such as multilateral trade negotiations. It will arise from the evolution by negotiation of international institutions such as the International Monetary Fund, the World Bank, and the World Trade Organization. Reform will also grow out of common law, the establishment of rules and procedures through trial and error and through ad hoc responses to problems. International monetary management through consultations among central bankers and finance ministers of the group of seven will most likely evolve through such a process. Reform will come not only from such international agreement and managed change but also from sporadic crises. It was the currency crises of the 1960s and 1970s, not international agreement, that led to the floating exchange rate system. The debt crises in Venezuela and Mexico led to a new approach to the debt problem; the Mexican peso crisis of 1994–1995 led to IMF reform. In the absence of agreed-upon rules, structures, and processes, such disturbances may multiply.

The outcome of these reform processes will not be a comprehensive international economic order. The political bases are too weak and the problems too complex to lead to anything approaching world economic management. In some areas, management will be effective and relatively comprehensive. Issues of interdependence will most likely be managed because they are of greatest concern to the developed market economies. But progress on international equity is much less likely. In most cases, the efforts of the less-developed countries to challenge the power and authority of the developed countries has failed. Evidence suggests that political weakness will continue to plague the South in the future. Some changes—aid for the least developed and greater market access in the North—will be offered by the developed market states. The Third World may also benefit indirectly from the management systems devised by the North for money, trade, and multinationals. No major redistribution, however, will occur. As a result, the conflict between the haves and the have-nots will persist as an element of international economic relations.

Finally, there is no assurance that multilateral cooperation among the major industrialized countries will continue or that it will be successful. The evolutionary process of reform is in many ways precarious, for it relies on mutual restraint and cooperation by the major powers until reform is achieved. Without agreed-upon rules, institutions, and procedures, a major economic shock could undermine cooperation and lead to economic warfare, as occurred in the 1930s. Without strong multilateral institutions such as the new WTO and the reformed IMF and the World Bank the world could gradually evolve into a series of economic blocs: a Western hemisphere block centered on the United States, Canada, and Mexico; a European-African block based on the EU; and a Pacific block built around Japan. If the multilateral system is weakened, regional management could become a hedge against the possibility of a breakdown in global multilateralism. Nevertheless, recent experience suggests that the will and ability to find mutual solutions persists and that cooperation among the powerful will continue.

Glossary

adjustment policies: **Macroeconomic** policies aimed at enabling a country to adapt its structure of production to prevailing world conditions by ending imbalances in its economy and changing its structure. They usually involve cutting governmental expenditures to reduce imbalances in the external accounts (balance of payments) and the domestic budget; expanding the supply of tradeables to improve the balance of trade; and privatizing companies owned by the public sector.

authoritarian: A political system in which the administration of government is centralized. The ruler's personality may play an important role in maintaining the system and advancing the notion and practice of extreme authority as a political virtue. It is characterized by the curtailment of individual freedoms; excessive reliance on actual, and the threat of, violence and punishment; virtual unaccountability of government officials; and the aversion of the decision-making process to consultation, persuasion and the necessity of forging a policy consensus.

Baker Plan: A plan introduced in September 1985 by U.S. Treasury Secretary James Baker to restore growth in the most heavily indebted countries. The proposed plan consisted of three parts: (1) the implementation of market-oriented structural changes to remove economic inefficiencies; (2) the provision of $20 billion in new loans over three years by commercial banks; and (3) an increase in the amount disbursed by multilateral development banks, particularly the International Bank for Reconstruction and Development, or World Bank. A host of factors prevented the Baker Plan from achieving a resurgence of growth. Efforts to carry out structural reforms were limited by political constraints. Inadequate tax systems and demands on the banking system for debt financing undermined the success of the proposed economic reforms. Finally, slow growth in the developed countries constrained their ability to provide the financial inflows prescribed by the plan.

balance of payments: An annual accounting of all economic transactions between one nation and the rest of the world. The balance of payments on current account includes the trade balance, which measures the movement of goods and some services; and the short-term capital account, which measures the flow of short-term investments and payments.

Brady Initiative: A strategy for dealing with LDC debt introduced in March 1989 by U.S. Treasury Secretary Nicholas Brady in the wake of the failure of the Baker Plan to achieve its objectives. The strategy called for a shift in emphasis from new lending to debt reduction by banks and called for making available the resources of multilateral development banks, such as the International Bank for Reconstruction and Development, or World Bank, and the International Monetary Fund (IMF), to debtor countries that adopt sound economic reform policies. In terms of debt reduction, the initiative proposed a menu of options that included voluntary exchanges of old debt for new bonds.

Bretton Woods Regime: The set of rules, institutions, and procedures developed to regulate international monetary interactions in the post-World War II period. It derived its name from the agreement forged in Bretton Woods, New Hampshire, in July 1944. This regime, which shaped the postwar international monetary relations until the United States suspended the convertibility of the dollar into gold in 1972, was founded on three political bases: the concentration of power in a small number of states, the existence of a cluster of important interests shared by those states, and the presence of a dominant power willing and able to assume a leading role. Bretton Woods participants set up the International Monetary Fund (IMF) and the International Bank for Reconstruction and Development (IBRD), or World Bank, to manage exchange rates and ensure international liquidity and deter balance-of-payments crises.

Calvo Doctrine: An economic policy approach named after Carlos Calvo (1824–1906), an Argentine diplomat. The doctrine asserts the right of host countries to nationalize foreign investments and make their own determination of what constitutes fair compensation. As such, the Doctrine rejects the right of foreign investors to lay claim to diplomatic protection or to appeal to their home governments for help since this could ultimately result in violating the territorial sovereignty and judicial independence of the host nations. By the turn of the twentieth century, the Calvo Doctrine became the main guiding principle for the policies of Latin American countries toward multinational investment. With the shift in Southern public attitudes against multinational corporations in the 1970s, many of Southern governments adopted this Latin American position, thus altering their open-door policies.

capital formation: The process that occurs when a nation's capital stock increases as a result of new investments in physical capital (plant and equipment). Unlike gross capital formation, net capital formation makes allowances for depreciation and repairs of the existing capital stock. See also **Human Capital Formation**.

capital goods: Manufactured products that are used to produce other goods.

capital markets: Financial institutions such as banks, insurance companies, and stock exchanges that channel long-term investment funds to commercial and industrial borrowers. Unlike the money market, on which lending is ordinarily short term, the capital market typically finances fixed investments like those in buildings and machinery.

capitalism: A socioeconomic system characterized by private initiative and the private ownership of factors of production. In such a system individuals have the right to own and use wealth to earn income and to sell and purchase labor for wages. Furthermore, capitalism is predicated on a relative absence of governmental control of the economy. The function of regulating the economy is achieved largely through the operation of market forces, whereby the price mechanism acts as a signaling system that determines the allocation of resources and their uses.

cartel: An organization of producers seeking to limit or eliminate competition among its members, most often by agreeing to restrict output to keep prices higher than would occur under competitive conditions. Cartels are inherently unstable because of the potential for producers to defect from the agreement and capture larger markets by selling at lower prices.

central bank: The bank that issues national currency, acts as banker to both government and private banks, and oversees the financial system. Central banks also administer national monetary policy, using their influence over the money supply and interest rates to implement macroeconomic policies.

central planning: The economic system adopted by Socialist countries. In this system, the processes of allocating resources, establishing production targets, and setting product prices are determined by government planners rather than the operation of market forces. Such a system discourages innovation, productivity, and quality. It provides little incentive for plant managers to experiment with new technology. The stress of fulfilling quantitative goals set by the state inhibits improving the quality of the product or the production process. The absence of competition and the existence of guaranteed markets eliminates incentives for managers to cut cost or improve quality. Above all, prices do not provide a guide to help managers determine what goods are needed by consumers and how to improve productivity by lowering costs.

comparative advantage: This doctrine, which received its first explicit formulation by the English economist David Ricardo (1772–1823), refers to the special ability of a country to produce a certain product or service relatively more cheaply than other products or services. Comparative advantage is determined by the relative abundance or lack of key factors of production (e.g., labor, land, and capital). It explains why a country that can afford to produce a wide range of products and services at a cheaper cost than any other country should concentrate on producing and trading in that product or service for which its cost advantage is greatest, leaving the production of other products and services, in which it maintains a positive but lower cost advantage, to other countries which have comparative cost advantages in them. As such, the concept of comparative advantage is intimately pertinent to international trade theory. It provides rationales for both specialization on the part of countries and freedom of trade. Under a pure free-trade system, each country would use its resources optimally by specializing only in those goods and/or services that it can produce more efficiently while importing the rest.

competitiveness: The ability of an entity to operate efficiently and productively in relation to other similar entities. Competitiveness has been used most recently to describe the overall economic performance of a nation, particularly its level of productivity, its ability to export its goods and services, and its maintenance of a high standard of living for its citizens.

convertibility: An attribute of a currency that enables its holders to freely exchange it into another currency, or into gold. Under the pressure of certain international monetary crises, nations might resort to suspending the convertibility of their currencies in order to ensure that holders of their currency will spend it in the country that issued it.

customs union: A union formed when two or more countries agree to remove all barriers to free trade with each other, while establishing a common external tariff against other nations. A free-trade area exists when nations remove trade barriers with each other while retaining individual tariffs against nonmembers.

debt crisis: The heavy borrowing of many newly industrializing countries, particularly those in Latin America that resulted in a prolonged financial crisis as evidence mounted indicating that some debtor nations might not be able to continue making payments on their loans. The crisis was triggered in the summer of 1982 when a number of highly indebted nations, including Mexico, Brazil, Argentina, and Poland, announced that they did not have the cash liquidity necessary to pay their creditors and, hence, raised the specter of defaulting on their loans. The debt crisis posed a threat not only to the development and political stability of the indebted nations but also to the international financial system itself.

debt rescheduling (debt restructuring): A process that occurs when a borrower and a lender renegotiate the original terms of a loan, altering the payment schedule or debt-service charges. This usually occurs when debtor nations cannot meet the payments due on loans from creditors.

debt service: The total amount of principal and interest due on a loan in a given period.

deficit: A national budget deficit occurs when a country's public spending exceeds government revenues. A current account deficit exists when exports and financial inflows from private and official transfers are worth less than the value of imports and transfer outflows. A trade deficit occurs when imports of goods and services exceed exports.

democracy: Literally, the term means power of the people (combining the Greek words demos, meaning "the people," and *kratien*, meaning "to rule"). It is usually used to describe a political system where the legitimacy of exercising power stems from the consent of the people. Accordingly, a democratic polity is often identified by the existence of constitutional government, where the power of the leaders is checked and restrained; representative institutions based on free elections, which provide a procedural framework for the delegation of power by the people; competitive parties, in which the ruling majority respects and guarantees the rights of minorities; and civil liberties, such as freedoms of speech, press, association, and religion.

dependency theory: A theory arguing that the exploitative nature of the relationship between advanced capitalist societies and the Third World has resulted in the development of the former and the underdevelopment of the latter. Because of its reliance on external sources of demand and investment opportunities, Western capitalism penetrated virtually all parts of the Third World and eventually laid down the foundations of dominance-dependence relationship structures between North and South, which tended to engender and perpetuate underdevelopment in the Third World. According to this theory, exchanges between the North and the South, such as trade, foreign investment, and aid, are asymmetric and tend to stifle the development of the latter and to reinforce their dependence. The theory also contends that local elites with vested interest in the structure of dominance and in monopolizing domestic power cooperate with international capitalist elites to perpetuate the international capitalist system.

depression: A prolonged and severe decline in national business activity, ordinarily occurring over several fiscal years. Depressions are characterized by sharply falling rates of production and capital investment; by the rapid contraction of credit; and by mass unemployment and high rates of business failure.

dumping: The practice of selling goods abroad below their normal market value or below the price charged for the same goods in the domestic market of the exporting country. Dumping can be a predatory trade practice whereby the international market, or a certain national market, is flooded with dumped goods in order to force competitors out of the market and establish a monopoly position. Oftentimes, government subsidies are used to help absorb temporarily the losses caused by predation, leading to friction among trade partners. Dumping and predation are considered to be unfair trade practices and, as such, are prohibited under many national trade laws. The most common antidumping measure is an added import duty calculated to offset the "dumping margin"—that is, the discrepancy between home price or cost and the export price.

economic development: The process of raising the level of prosperity and material living in a society through an increase in the productivity and efficiency of its economy. In less industrialized regions, this process is believed to be achieved by an increase in industrial production and a relative decline in the importance of agricultural production.

economic efficiency: Production that is organized to minimize the ratio of inputs to outputs and to produce goods at minimum cost in money and resources. This typically occurs where input prices are used to find the least expensive production process.

economic nationalism: The set of practices that dominated international economic interactions during the interwar years and eventually brought about the collapse of the international monetary system in the 1930s. Foremost among these practices are instituting competitive exchange rate devaluations, formation of competing monetary blocs, adoption of beggar-thy-neighbor trade policies, and aversion to the norms of international cooperation.

eurocurrencies: Currencies held outside their country of issue, such as dollars (Eurodollars) deposited in banks outside the United States, mostly in Europe. Eurocurrency markets are generally free from most national controls, so they are a flexible outlet for deposits and a source of loans for major international corporations and for national governments. This is also true of Eurobonds, or securities issued on loosely controlled international markets.

European Economic Community (EEC): An economic bloc that was established in 1957 by the signing of the Treaty of Rome agreed to by the six countries of Belgium, France, Italy, Luxemburg, the Netherlands, and West Germany. The organization is now called the European Union, its current membership having increased to fifteen. The signatories of the Treaty of Rome agreed to work for the gradual formation of a full customs union; the elimination of all barriers to the free movement of capital, labor and services; and the harmonization of agricultural, industrial, trade and transportation policies.

exchange rate: The price of a currency expressed in terms of other currencies or gold. Fixed exchange rates prevail when governments agree to maintain the value of their currencies at preestablished levels. This is also known as maintaining parity. Floating exchange rates allow the market to determine the relative value of currencies.

Exon-Florio Amendment: An amendment to the Omnibus Trade Bill of 1988 named after its sponsors Senator J. James Exon and Representative James J. Florio. It extends the scope of the International Investment and Trade in Services Act (IITSA) of 1976, which established a mechanism to monitor foreign investment in the United States, to prohibit mergers, acquisitions, or takeovers of American firms by foreign interests when such actions are deemed injurious to the national security of the United States.

export-oriented development (export-led growth): A development strategy designed to expand the overseas markets for a country's manufactured products by improving their competitiveness abroad—that is, by developing and enhancing domestic export industries. The mainstay of export-oriented development does not lie in eliminating all protection. Rather, it is based on eliminating the bias against exports: maintaining realistic exchange rates that do not discriminate against exports; reducing import barriers for inputs to the export sector; as well as removing any other export disincentives such as export taxes. In many countries, export-led growth involves government promotion of exports through favorable credit terms for exporters, tax incentives, undervalued exchange rates that decrease export prices, encouragement of foreign investment in export industries, and direct subsidies for targeted sectors.

external indebtedness: The total amount of money owed by a government to lenders outside the country.

factor endowment: The original share of the inputs needed to produce other commodities. These inputs or factors of production are broadly classified into land, labor, capital, and entrepreneurship. The availability of these factors of production helps set the price for and determine the supply of commodities produced for domestic use and for international trade.

factors of production: Economic resources or inputs that are employed in the process of production. These are usually divided into two main categories: human resources and nonhuman resources. Human resources include two main composites: labor, which includes all human physical and mental talents and efforts employed in producing goods, such as manual labor, managerial and professional skills, etc; and entrepreneurship or entrepreneurial organization, which encompasses everything that facilitates the organization of the other composite factors for productive purposes, such as innovation, risk taking, and applications analysis. Nonhuman resources include two other composites: land, which includes the entire stock of a nation's natural resources such as territory, mineral deposits, forests, airspace, territorial waters, water power, wind power, and the like; and capital, which includes all man-made aids to production, such as buildings, machinery, and transportation facilities.

fast track negotiating authority: The congressional delegation of negotiating authority to the president of the United States in the area of reducing tariffs by specific amounts without subsequent congressional approval. The practice, which was begun in 1934 to avoid the pressure of special interest groups for protection, was used during the Tokyo and Uruguay Rounds of the multilateral trade negotiations under the GATT and during the negotiations for the North American Free Trade Agreement (NAFTA).

fiscal policies: An outgrowth of Keynesian economics, fiscal policies refer to the use of government tax and spending policies to achieve desired macroeconomic goals. Accordingly, they involve discretionary efforts to adjust governmental tax and spending to induce changes in economic incentives and, hence, to stabilize fluctuations in aggregate demand. These discretionary adjustments in the government tax and spending levels are believed to effect desired changes in aggregate demand; to manipulate subsequent levels of employment, disposable income, consumption and economic activity; and to smooth fluctuations in nominal gross national product (GNP). Fiscal policies could be stimulative and expansionary, or contractionary and restrictive. As such, a budget deficit or a tax cut is considered to be stimulative (i.e., providing a fiscal stimulus) because it is believed to generate a rise in national wealth and investment. In contrast, a budget surplus achieved by raising taxes is considered to be contractionary because it is believed to reduce aggregate demand.

Foreign Direct Investment (FDI): Financial transfers by a multinational corporation from the country of the parent firm to the country of the host firm to finance a portion of its overseas operations. Foreign direct investment occurs when a corporation headquartered in one nation invests in a corporation located in another nation, either by purchasing an existing enterprise or by providing capital to start a new one. In portfolio investment, on the other hand, foreign investors purchase the stock or bonds of national corporations but do not control those corporations directly.

free trade: A situation that exists when the international exchange of goods is neither restricted nor encouraged by government-imposed trade barriers. Subsequently, the determination of the distribution and level of international trade is left to the operation of market forces.

Generalized System of Preferences (GSP): An arrangement that was introduced and negotiated under the auspices of UNCTAD. According to this agreement, a preferential tariff treatment is granted by Northern states to manufactured and semimanufactured products imported from developing countries. This system was designed to increase the export earnings and to promote the economic growth and industrialization of developing countries.

glasnost (openness): A domestic initiative of political reform introduced by Soviet president Mikhail Gorbachev in the mid-1980s to allow more freedom in public discussion and the arts, and to foster the process of the democratization of the political process.

gold standard: An international monetary system in which the value of a currency is fixed in terms of gold. A government whose currency is on the gold standard agrees to convert it to gold at a preestablished price. This creates a self-regulating mechanism for adjusting the balance of payments, since disequilibria can be remedied by inflows and outflows of gold.

Gross National Product (GNP): The monetary value of a nation's total output of goods and services, usually during a one-year period. Gross national product at factor cost is based on the total earnings of all national factors of production (wages, rent, interest, profits). Gross national product at market cost is computed by adding total national expenditures on consumption, foreign and domestic investment, and government spending on goods and services. Unlike net national product (NNP), gross national product makes no deductions for depreciation of the machinery used for production.

hard currencies: Freely convertible currencies that can be used to finance international trade, such as those held in national foreign exchange reserves. Soft currencies, on the other hand, are not freely convertible and are not held as reserve currencies.

human capital formation: Investment in education and research that results in an improvement in human skills and knowledge.

hyperinflation: A rapidly accelerating rate of inflation that is perilous to a country's economy because it undermines the ability of its currency to perform its traditional functions (i.e., standard of value, store of value, and reliable medium of exchange), and occasions a shift in the utilization of the nation's resources from productive efforts toward speculation. Hyperinflation could cause a high exponential rise in prices in as short a period as a single month.

Import-Substituting Industrialization (ISI): An inward-looking development strategy designed to reduce imports by setting up domestic industries behind protective walls to produce previously imported products. The strategy involves the adoption of protectionist trade policies (import tariffs, quantitative controls, multiple exchange rates, etc.) to allow "infant" industries to develop and grow, and encouragement of the inward flow of foreign direct investment especially in manufacturing. Once the infant stage is completed, protection can be removed and free trade resumed. Typically, ISI starts with the production of consumer goods in the hope of moving to intermediate goods and then to capital goods in the future. In most cases, the strategy fails to generate capital savings sufficient to finance the transition from producing one type of goods to another. The reason is that substitution in the area of consumer durables usually leads to the expansion of imports in the areas of intermediate and capital goods needed for the production of the consumer goods. ISI also tends to create industries that are not internationally competitive while at the same time weakening traditional exports.

infant industry: An industry in its early stages of development, unable to withstand competition from overseas competitors. It is usually argued that in order to guarantee the success and growth of such an industry, tariffs, import quotas and other barriers to international trade need to be imposed so as to provide the industry with protection from international competition and to allow it to achieve cost competitiveness by exploiting economies of scale and employing new, productivity-enhancing technologies. The industry is believed to grow out of the infantile stage when it is able to compete with foreign competitors in a system of free trade.

inflation: A persistent upward movement in the general price of goods and services that ordinarily results in a decline of the purchasing power of a nation's currency. Inflation resulting from government action to stimulate the economy is known as reflation. Disinflation is a downward movement of wages and prices that erases the effects of a previous round of price increases. Price inflation is most likely to set in under either one (or a combination) of the following conditions: (1) an increase in demand at a time when supply of labor is tight and industrial capacity is fully utilized; (2) a lack of congruence between increases in wage rates and increases in productivity; (3) a sharp decline in the sources of supply; and (4) a rise in the money supply that is faster than increases in output.

infrastructure: The communication networks, transportation systems, and public services needed to conduct business. These are often considered to be public or collective goods because individuals and firms will not supply them in adequate quantities and they are, as a result, at least partly financed with public funds and are therefore often subject to government regulation. Social infrastructure refers to human services such as education and health care that affect the quality of the workforce.

intellectual property: Property rights granted to creators of inventions or ideas embodied in products or production technologies for the purpose of promoting creativity in the arts and innovation in the economy. Legally sanctioned intellectual property rights include patents, copyrights, trademarks, and semiconductor chip designs. These property rights generally grant their holders a temporary monopoly for the sale of the right to use the item in question, allowing them to fix whatever price they deem adequate compensation for their creative efforts.

interdependence: A relationship of mutual dependence characterized by mutual sensitivity and mutual vulnerability on the part of all the parties involved. As such, managing interdependence requires the coordination of national economic policies and the observance of some international discipline in the formulation of policies that have always been the prerogative of national governments. Economic interdependence has led to the growing convergence of the economies of developed countries. The rapid accumulation of physical and human capital, the transfer of technology, and the growing similarities of wages have narrowed the differences in factor endowments, which are the basis for comparative advantage and trade.

interest rate: The cost of money that fluctuates (rises and falls) in correspondence with changes in the demand for and supply of money. Moreover, the interest rate varies over the length of a loan or deposit as well as the type of financial instrument.

intermediate inputs: Goods, like steel, that are used to produce finished products or final goods, like automobiles. The value of intermediate inputs is not counted directly in calculating gross national product (GNP). Demand for these inputs (derived demand) is related to demand for the final goods they help to produce.

internalization theory: A theory explaining why firms may prefer direct foreign investment to alternative ways of doing business, like exporting and licensing. The Ownership Location and Internalization theory (OLI) contends that firms expand abroad in order to internalize activities in the presence of transaction costs arising from market imperfections just as they expand domestically for similar reasons. Since it is generally less expensive for local firms to conduct business activities in their home markets than for foreign firms, the extra costs connected with doing business abroad must be offset by advantages that a particular foreign firm may have (such as managerial or marketing techniques or new production processes). Because knowledge is a public good, a firm's profits from developing that knowledge cannot be optimized if the firm resorts to such open market practices as exporting or licensing. Consequently, the firm internalizes the market by setting up a foreign subsidiary that can ensure maximum control over the use of that knowledge.

International Bank for Reconstruction and Development (IBRD); also known as the **World Bank:** A public international organization created by the Bretton Woods agreement to facilitate the postwar economic recovery. With capital provided by member states, the IBRD sought to achieve its objectives by extending loans at market rates to cover foreign exchange needs of borrowing countries, thus making possible a speedy postwar recovery and promoting economic development. Currently, the IBRD is the world's foremost intergovernmental organization involved in the external financing of projects aimed at fostering the economic growth of developing countries.

International Commodity Agreements (ICAs): Accords between producers and consumers aimed at stabilizing or increasing the price of particular products. ICAs may be of three types or combinations thereof: buffer-stock schemes, whereby price is managed by purchases or sales from a central fund at times of excessive fluctuation; export quotas, whereby price is managed by assigning production quotas to participating countries in order to control supply; and multilateral contracts, whereby the importing countries sign contracts commiting them to buy certain quantities at a specified low price when the world market falls below that price and the exporting countries agree to sell certain quantities at a fixed price when the world market price exceeds the maximum.

International Monetary Fund (IMF): A public international organization created by the Bretton Woods agreement in 1994 as the main instrument of international monetary management. The IMF helps countries with payments deficits by advancing credits to them. Originally, its approval was made necessary for any change in exchange rates. It advises countries on policies affecting the monetary system. The IMF is provided with a fund composed of member countries' contributions in gold and in their own currencies. The system of weighted voting allows the United States to exert a preponderant influence in this body.

intervention: An action taken on the part of one or more central banks in order to influence exchange rates. Since the move to a system of floating rates, the Group of Five (G-5) (the United States, Japan, France, Germany, and Britain) has attempted to coordinate intervention in currency markets, usually by buying and selling currency, to achieve target rates.

Invisible Hand Doctrine: Coined by Adam Smith in his pioneering book Inquiry into the Nature and Causes of the Wealth of Nations (1776), the term is used as a rationale for laissez-faire as the best economic policy. The doctrine argues that individuals, in their quest to advance their self-interests, are led, as if by an invisible hand, to achieve the best good for all. Accordingly, government intervention in the economy would distort the automatic, self-adjusting nature of economic life. Competition among individuals inspired by their selfish motives will automatically further the best interests of society as a whole.

isolationism: A foreign policy doctrine that calls for the curtailment of a nation's international relations and the avoidance of entangling alliances. Isolationism constituted a key plank in the U.S. foreign policy approach, with a few short periods of aberration, between the War of Independence and World War II. This foreign policy of nonentanglement was made possible mainly by the geopolitical detachment of the United States. The ratification of the United Nations Charter by the Congress in 1945, which inaugurated an era of internationalism in U.S. foreign policy, brought to an effective end the era of isolationism where the United States avoided incurring any binding political obligations to other nations. In fact, modern trade, communication technologies, and military weapons make isolationism a virtual impossibility for any nation in our time.

keiretsu: Japanese business confederations composed of allied financial and industrial companies. As part of their keiretsu obligations, Japanese companies usually hold each other's stocks. The keiretsu system can be an effective barrier to foreign investment by making it difficult for a foreign firm to acquire a firm that is a member of a keiretsu.

Keynesianism: A school of economics inspired by the theoretical contributions of John Maynard Keynes (1883–1946), an English economist. Keynes argued that government spending and investment function as means of disbursing purchasing power into the economy and, hence, affect the demand for consumer goods in the same way as private investment. He suggested increasing government expenditures during deflationary periods and decreasing it during inflationary periods as a means of manipulating aggregate spending and income. By prescribing governmental intervention to maintain adequate levels of employment, Keynesianism paved they way for the growth of the welfare state in the wake of the Great Depression.

liberalism: A school of economics that relies primarily on a free market with the minimum of barriers to the flow of private trade and capital. Underdevelopment in the Third World, according to this school, stems from certain domestic economic policies of the developing country, which tend to accentuate market imperfections; reduce productivity of land, labor, and capital; and intensify social and political rigidities. The adoption of market-oriented domestic policies is the optimal way to remedy these weaknesses.

locomotive theory: An economic theory calling for a coordination of national economic policies and advocating that countries with payments surpluses follow expansionary policies that would serve as engines of growth for the rest of the world. It was adopted by the Carter administration in the late-1970s as the basis of the U.S. strategy for global economic growth.

macroeconomics: The branch of economics that analyzes patterns of change in aggregate economic indicators such as national product, the money supply, and the balance of payments. Governments attempt to influence these indicators by implementing macroeconomic policies.

managed trade: Managed trade regimes arise when industrialized countries adopt industrial policies domestically—forms of government intervention designed to shift comparative advantages within countries toward high value-added and/or high technology production—and then attempt to modify existing international trade regimes to prevent the use of such industrial policies from becoming a new form of protectionism. An example of this is the U.S.-Japanese Semiconductor Trade Agreement of 1986.

market forces: The dynamic occurring when competition among firms determines the outcome in a given situation, and a supply-and-demand equilibrium is reached without government intervention.

Marshall Plan (European Recovery Program): An American program of grants and loans instituted to assist the recovery of Western Europe after World War II. The program had two main objectives: to prevent the occurrence of a collapse in the international economic system similar to the one that occurred during the interwar period and to prevent the formation of Communist systems in Western Europe. It eventually became the tool of U.S. leadership in Europe as it allowed the United States to play a key role in financing international trade, encouraging European trade competitiveness, and fostering regional trade liberalization in Europe.

Marxism (and Neo-Marxism): A school of thought inspired by the theoretical and philosophical formulations of Karl Marx. The fundamental component of the economic dimension of Marxism is predicated on the surplus value theory. Marx argued that under a capitalist system the value of commodities depends on the labor that is put into producing them. However, workers are paid only a small proportion of that value, sufficient to enable them to pay only for the goods necessary to maintain their average consumption. The difference between the actual value of the labor exerted by the workers and the wages that they receive is the surplus value, which is the source of all profits, rent, and interest income that goes to the owners of capital. The system inevitably produces poverty by underpaying workers and overpaying capitalists. It is also vulnerable to periodic economic depressions and unemployment which exacerbate poverty. Marxism (and neo-Marxism) also maintains that the imperialist drive to dominate and exploit Third World countries is intrinsic to capitalism. Accordingly, the theory argues that Third World countries are poor and exploited because of their history as subordinate elements in the world capitalist system. This condition will persist as long as they remain part of that system. As such, the only appropriate strategy for Third World development is revolutionary: the obliteration of the world capitalist system and its replacement with an international socialist system.

mercantilism: A theory originating in the seventeenth century, when certain trading states made it their goal to accumulate national economic wealth and, in turn, national power by expanding exports and limiting imports. Some analysts and policymakers have charged that countries pursuing protectionist trade policies in the twentieth century are following a similar strategy, which they termed neomercantilism.

microeconomics: The branch of economics that analyzes the market behavior of individual consumers and firms. The interaction of these individual decision makers creates patterns of supply and demand that fix the prices of goods and factors of production and determine how resources will be allocated among competing uses.

monetary policies (monetarism): Policies designed to manage the size of the nation's money supply in a manner that fosters investment and economic growth. These policies are usually inspired by the monetarist theory thatattributes economic instability to disturbances in the monetary sector. Monetary policies, therefore, attempt to influence variables like the balance of payments, currency exchange rates, inflation, and employment by increasing or decreasing interest rates and controlling the money supply.

monopoly: A market structure with only a single seller of a commodity or service dealing with a large number of buyers, which results in closing entry into the industry to potential competitors. Consequently, due to the absence of a competitive supply of goods on the market, the seller usually has complete control over the quantity of goods released into the market and the ability to set the price at which they are sold. This results in a lower level of production and a higher price than would occur under more competitive market conditions.

monopsony: A market structure with only a single buyer of a product who is able, therefore, to set the buying price. The classic examples include the demand for labor in a one-company town and the purchase of all output from certain mines by a large manufacturer.

Most-Favored Nation (MFN): The GATT principle stipulating that "any advantage, favor, privilege, or immunity granted by any contracting party to any product originating in or destined for any other country shall be accorded immediately and unconditionally to the like product originating in or destined for the territories of all other contracting parties." It is a guarantee of nondiscrimination or equal treatment in trade relations.

Multinational Corporation (MNC): A business enterprise that retains direct investments overseas and that maintains value-added holdings in more than one country. A firm is not really multinational if it just engages in overseas trade or serves as a contractor to foreign firms. A multinational firm sends abroad a package of capital, technology, managerial talent, and marketing skills to carry out production in foreign countries.

national treatment: A GATT rule designed to prevent discrimination against foreign products after they enter a country. It requires countries to give imports the same treatment as they give products made domestically in such areas as taxation, regulation, transportation, and distribution. It also requires them to treat foreign-owned enterprises no less favorably than domestically owned ones.

New International Economic Order (NIEO): The view advocated by the less-developed and developing countries mainly in the 1970s which argued that the open monetary, trade, and financial system perpetuated their underdevelopment and subordination to the developed countries. They called for the dismantling of the Western-dominated international economic order and its replacement with a new international economic regime that better serves the interests of Third World countries. They also sought a North-South dialogue on issues ranging from transfer of technology and capital, to redistribution of global economic benefits, to rapid economic development in the South.

Newly Industrializing Countries (NICs): Countries that have a high level of economic growth and export expansion, outpacing the less-developed countries but not as industrialized as the developed countries. Middle-income countries like Mexico, Brazil, and Portugal are considered NICs, as are the Four Tigers (Hong Kong, Singapore, South Korea, and Taiwan). Government policies played a central role in the initial stages of industrialization in the NICs. Targeted industries were promoted through import protection, tax incentives, and subsidies.

nomenklatura: A Communist institution which was designed to preserve the dominant role of the Communist Party by giving out responsible positions to those loyal to the regime. Started by Stalin, nomenklatura included a list of positions in all levels of government and society that the government or the Communist Party controlled. It was used as a reward system to attract people to the Communist Party and to maintain Party discipline.

nonconcessional loans: Loans offered on terms set by the market, so that interest rates and payment schedules are determined by the relative supply of investment funds; also called "hard loans." Concessional loans, or "soft loans," are offered on terms more generous than those prevailing in the market.

Nontariff Barriers (NTBs): These are measures designed to discriminate against imports, without levying taxes directly on merchandise, or to offer assistance to exports and thus have trade-distorting consequences. They include quotas, by which government determines the amount of a commodity that can be imported, procurement policies, customs procedures, agricultural policies, health and sanitary regulations, national consumer and environmental standards, voluntary restraint agreements (VRAs), and a broad range of other laws and regulations that insulate the domestic economy from international competition. The success of the GATT in removing quotas and tariffs had the unintended consequence of the emergence of "the new protectionism" through an increase in the use of nontariff barriers. Unlike the regulation and removal of quotas and tariffs, NTBs do not lend themselves easily to international control. They are usually an integral part of national economic and social policies and, as such, are considered national prerogatives beyond the scope of international regulation.

obsolescing bargain theory: A theory advanced to explain the dynamics of the activities of multinational corporations. The theory contends that the firm's initial good bargaining position, stemming from such advantages as superior technology, vis-à-vis the host country's government encourages it to invest in foreign countries. However, once the firm has made an investment, the bargaining advantage may slowly shift to the host country. The host country will then attempt to negotiate more favorable terms with the foreign investor. That is so because the technology may mature and become more easily accessible to the host country's firms, and the host country may learn how to gain better access to global capital and final product markets.

oligopoly: A market structure in which a few companies dominate an industry. This concentration often leads to collusion among manufacturers, so that prices are set by agreement rather than by the operation of the supply and demand mechanism. For an oligopoly to exist, the few companies do not need to control all the production or sale of a particular commodity or service. They only need to control a significant share of the total production or sales. As in a monopoly, an oligopoly can persist only if there are significant barriers to entry to new competitors. Obviously, the presence of relatively few firms in an industry does not negate the existence of competition. The existing few firms may still act independently even while they collude on prices. In an oligopolistic market, competition often takes the form of increased spending on marketing and advertising to win brand loyalty rather than on reducing prices or increasing the quality of products.

oligopoly theory: A theory proposed to explain the genesis of multinational investments.

The theory argues that firms are prompted to move abroad by their desire to exploit the market power they possess through control over such factors as unique products, marketing expertise, control of technology and managerial skills, or access to capital. The oligopolistic competition for global market shares makes firms match each other's moves in entering new foreign markets.

perestroika (restructuring): An economic initiative launched by Soviet president Mikhail Gorbachev in the mid-1980s in an attempt to move the Soviet economy in the market direction and to open up trade, finance, and investment relations with the West. The initiative envisioned the decentralization of industrial decision making from central planners to individual firms; the creation of financial markets to determine capital flows; scrapping the system of centralized supply and replacing it by a wholesale distribution system; and improving trade and financial interactions with the West. Because perestroika was implemented in a halting and ultimately unsuccessful manner, it had the unintended consequence of hastening the decline of the Soviet economy and ultimately helped bring about the breakup of the Soviet empire.

predatory pricing: The practice of allowing the prices of goods produced by a firm to decline to unprofitable levels in order to underprice other firms and, in turn, increase the firm's market share or drive its competitors completely out of the market. This unfair practice is usually characteristic of a large multiproduct and/or multimarket firm that can offset its losses in one product or market with profits made from other products or in other markets.

price supports: A form of government subsidy for the production of commodities. The market price of certain goods is fixed at a level that guarantees the producer an "adequate" return on investment. That price is not determined by the free interaction of supply and demand but rather by government regulators, and often the government purchases surpluses that remain unsold at an artificially high fixed price. See also Subsidies.

primary products: Unprocessed or partially processed goods, often used to produce other goods. They include agricultural commodities such as grain and vegetables, and raw materials such as iron ore and crude petroleum.

principal supplier procedure: A GATT negotiating rule that requires negotiations to take place among actual or potential "principal suppliers," where the latter are defined as nations accounting for 10 percent or more of a given product in world trade.

product cycle theory: A theory advanced to explain the tendency of multinational companies to move from exporting to undertaking foreign direct investments in overseas production to service foreign demand. The theory argues that firms invest abroad when their main products become "mature" in domestic markets. As the initial high-growth stage of domestic product commercialization ends and the domestic market becomes saturated (growth in demand slows down and new competitors arise), the firm begins to look for new sources of demand abroad in order to maintain its growth. This is achieved by establishing foreign subsidiaries with lower costs so that the firm can remain competitive in its home market while also improving its access to foreign markets.

productivity: The amount of product created by one unit of a given factor of production over a stated period of time. Productivity expresses the marginal relationship of inputs to outputs and measures the economic efficiency of production. Productivity indicators ordinarily relate output to a single factor of production, creating measures like labor productivity, capital productivity, and land productivity. Measures of multifactor productivity, in contrast, combineproductivity indicators for multiple factors of production (labor and capital, for example) to produce a single overall measure of productivity growth.

protectionism: The use of import tariffs, import licenses, quota restrictions on imports, and other nontariff barriers to protect local industry from competition with imported goods and services.

recession: A short-term decline in national business activity, usually lasting for at least three consecutive quarters of a fiscal year. Recessions are characterized by rising unemployment rates and falling rates of production, capital investment, and economic growth, but these declines are not as severe nor as persistent as those that occur during depressions.

reciprocity: The practice of offering trade concessions, such as tariff reductions, by one country in return for similar concessions by other countries. Reciprocal agreements help countries to avoid any likely balance-of-payment deficits inherent in unilateral tariff reductions. They also have the advantage of being politically feasible, since the trade concessions can be billed by the government as being more advantageous to its country's interests than to those of the other country.

rent: Earnings that can accrue to a unique factor of production in excess of the amount which that factor could earn in its next best alternative employment. An example of this is the case of a trained doctor who can earn $100,000 per year. If he could not earn his living practicing medicine, his next best alternative career, for example nursing, would earn him $24,000 per year. His economic rent, therefore, is $76,000.

Research and Development (R&D): The systematic or organized efforts aimed at the formation or advancement of knowledge and the application of that knowledge to the development of new products and production processes as well as to the improvement and refinement of existing products and production processes. R&D encompasses activities that can be divided into three groupings: basic research, applied research, and development. Basic research refers to efforts aimed at expanding knowledge in the sciences, both natural and social. Applied research aims at the formulation of engineering concepts and methods as well as the invention of machines and techniques that can be used as inputs in the process of production. Development is the process of refining and perfecting a new kind of product or activity in order to facilitate its mass production and/or commercialization. Usually both governmental and private (business as well as nonprofit) institutions share the responsibility of undertaking basic research.

reserve currency: Currencies that are held by governments and institutions outside the country of issue and are used to finance international economic transactions, including trade and the payment of debts. Stable, easily convertible currencies issued by major trading nations like the United States, Germany, and Japan are generally included in national reserves.

revaluation: A change in the official rate at which one currency is exchanged for another or for gold. Devaluation reduces the relative value of the currency and creates a mechanism for adjusting balance of payments deficits, since it lowers the price of exports abroad and raises the price of imports at home. This mechanism will not function during periods of competitive devaluation when the devaluation of one currency causes other nations to follow suit.

services: Economic activities that are intangible, such as banking, tourism, insurance, and accounting, in contrast to goods that are tangible, such as automobiles and wheat. Services account for an ever-increasing part of the trade of the industrialized countries.

socialism: An economic and political system in which private property is abolished and the means of production (i.e., capital and land) are collectively owned and operated by the community as a whole in order to advance the interests of all. In Marxist ideology, socialism is considered an intermediate stage in the inevitable transformation of capitalism into Communism. A socialist society is envisioned as being characterized by the dictatorship of the proletariat; the existence of a high degree of cooperation and equality; and the absence of discrimination, poverty, exploitation, and war. With the nonexistence of private ownership, the private profit motive is eliminated from economic life. Consequently, market forces do not play a role in organizing the process of production. Instead, large-scale government planning is employed to ensure the harmonious operation of the process of production.

sovereignty: The principle that the state exercises absolute power over its territory, system of government, and population. Accordingly, the internal authority of the state supersedes that of all other bodies, both inside and outside its territories; and the state emerges as the ultimate arbiter of its grievances vis-à-vis others. Sovereignty theoretically preserves the territorial inviolability of the state and its independence from outside authorities. In practice, the sovereignty of smaller and weaker states is limited and even the larger and stronger states confront a world in which various forms of interdependence, economic and otherwise, diminish their claims to a territorial monopoly of control. In addition, international law and international regimes (like the GATT) limit the exercise of sovereignty by those states that recognize their utility. This does not prevent governments from cherishing the idea of national sovereignty, however.

spot market: A market in which commodities sell at prices fixed by supply and demand at the time of sale. The forward market, on the other hand, exchanges promises to buy or sell commodities in the future at a preestablished "forward" price.

stabilization programs: Deflationary policy packages designed to reduce a country's trade deficit as well as imbalances in its balance of payments and domestic resource use by cutting down the levels of public and private expenditures.

stagflation: An economic downturn characterized by the simultaneous existence of stagnation and persistent and intractable inflation. In the light of conventional economic theory, the condition of stagnation is puzzling since each of the above two conditions (i.e., stagnation and inflation) is considered a correction for the other. For instance, the phenomenon of inflation, which is caused by the existence of an excess of money pursuing too few goods in the market, is usually considered a spur for slack demand. The simultaneous existence of slack demand and rising prices is usually explained by the rigidity of prices in modern economies. The downward inflexibility of prices in modern economies occasioned mainly by the attitudes of resistance on the part of workers and company management to lessened growth and to cuts in wages and prices, makes any economic slowdown less effective in curtailing price rises than is expected by conventional economic analysis.

stagnation: The utilization of an economy's resources below their potential. Stagnation might occur for two reasons: (1) the growth of the rate of output below the rate of population growth; and (2) the existence of insufficient aggregate demand that may prevent an economy from achieving its potential despite its capacity for sufficient growth.

structuralism: A school of thought that contends that the international market structure perpetuates backwardness and dependency in the Third World and fosters dominance by the developed countries. As such, unregulated international trade accentuates international inequalities, due to the declining terms of trade for the South, and creates a dual economy by giving rise to an export sector that has little effect on the rest of the economy. Foreign investment in the South leads to a net flow of capital to the developed North and tends to concentrate in export sectors, thereby aggravating the dual economy and the negative effects of trade. However, unlike Marxism and Neo-Marxism which argue that the international system is immutable, structuralism argues that the system is amenable to reform. Rather than prescribing a socialist revolution, the structuralist prescription for promoting economic development in the South focuses on four types of policy changes: (1) import-substituting industrialization; (2) increased South-South trade and investment; (3) regional integration; and (4) population control.

subsidies: Grants of money made to either the seller or a buyer of a certain product or service, thereby altering the price or cost of that particular product or service to the recipient of the subsidy in a way which affects the output. Governments usually make payments to domestic producers to offset partially their costs of producing and selling certain goods and services. Subsidies are commonly used to support infant firms just entering a new market, and to bail out older firms suffering from intensified competition. Subsidies are also used to promote the development of high technology industries, even when these are questionable candidates for "infant industry" status.

supply-side economics: A school of economics holding that decreasing impediments to the supply and efficient use of factors of production, such as reductions in the tax rates, increases incentives and shifts the aggregate supply curve. Hence, supply-side economists argue that since taxation and government regulation "crowd out" investment, taxes and government regulations ought to be reduced in an effort to stimulate savings, investment, and growth.

tariff: Taxes imposed on commodity imports based either on the value of the good or on a fixed price per unit. The tariff is usually levied by a national government when the imports cross its customs boundary. Protective tariffs attempt to shelter selected domestic industries by restricting the quantity and raising the price of competing imports, while revenue-producing tariffs are enacted mainly to increase government income. Some tariffs comprise fixed duties on a variety of imported products. However, in most cases, tariffs are ad valorem duties—that is, they are a percentage of the imported products' value.

tariff-jumping hypothesis: A hypothesis that explains foreign direct investments. Its proponents maintain that firms resort to foreign direct investments in order to jump over existing tariff or nontariff barriers in host countries.

tariffication: A pledge made by countries engaged in the use of nontariff barriers (NTBs) to replace these barriers with actual tariffs that can be reduced in future trade negotiations.

terms of trade: The relationship between the prices of a nation's imports and those of its exports. Nations face declining terms of trade when import prices rise faster than export prices, while rising terms of trade occur when relative export prices grow faster.

trade barriers: Government restrictions on the free import or export of merchandise. They include tariff and nontariff barriers, which attempt to shelter selected domestic industries from international competition.

trade preference system: The practice of offering lower tariffs on imports from a specified country or group of countries. Accordingly, a trade preference constitutes a violation of the most favored nation (MFN) principle of nondiscrimination among trading partners in the setting of tariff levels.

transfer prices: The practice of inflating the price of imports or decreasing the value of exports among the affiliated companies of a multinational corporation in order to enable a subsidiary to evade national taxation in a high-tax country.

vertical integration: The attempt to own and control activities that are both "upstream" and "downstream" from the core business of a firm. A good example is the petroleum industry, in which multinational petroleum firms tend to own oil production facilities, refineries, and retail outlets for refinery products—the entire chain of activities from production to commercialization.

Voluntary Export Restraints (VERs): See Voluntary Restraint Agreements.

Voluntary Restraint Agreements (VRAs): Bilateral, and sometimes secret, agreements stipulating that low-cost exporters "voluntarily" restrict exports to countries where their goods are threatening industry and employment, and thus forestall official protective action on the part of the importing country. They are usually used to get around the GATT restrictions on quantitative import restrictions. Because of their ostensible "voluntary" nature on the part of both the importer and the exporter, VRAs are considered consistent with the GATT norms of reciprocity. However, in actuality, VRAs result in the same outcome as that resulting from unilaterally imposed quantitative import restrictions. That is, the price of the goods subject to VRAs in the country of destination tend to rise because demand remains relatively constant while supply diminishes.

welfare state: A nation in which the government undertakes large-scale action to ensure the provision of social goods and benefits. These welfare programs are usually provided at public expense with little or no cost to the recipient of the services. Policy prescriptions advanced by proponents of the welfare-state emphasize securing a minimum standard of living for all citizens where no one is denied an essential service which might be available to others; the production of social goods and services; the control of the business cycle; and the manipulation of total output to allow for social costs and revenues. Among the instruments of the modern welfare state are progressive taxes, social security, unemployment insurance, agricultural subsidies, and government-subsidized housing programs.

Acronyms

ACP	African, Caribbean, and Pacific
AFTA	Asean Free Trade Area
AID	Agency for International Development
ANCOM	Andean Common Market
APEC	Asia Pacific Economic Corporation
ASEAN	Association of South-East Asian Nations
BIS	Bank for International Settlements
BIT	Bilateral Investment Treaty
BP	British Petroleum
CACM	Central American Common Market
CAP	Common Agriculture Policy of the European Community
CARICOM	Caribbean Common Market
CEAO	West African Economic Community
CED	Committee for Economic Development (United States)
CFIUS	Committee on Foreign Investment in the United States
CIA	Central Intelligence Agency (United States)
CIEC	Conference on International Economic Cooperation
CIPEC	Conseil Intergouvernmental des Pays Exportateurs de Cuivre
CMEA	Council for Mutual Economic Assistance (Comecon)
CoCom	Coordinating Committee
CRB	Commodity Research Bureau
CTC	Center on Transnational Corporations (United Nations)
DLF	Development Loan Fund
EBRD	European Bank for Reconstruction and Development
EC	European Community
ECCAS	Economic Community of Central African States
ECOSOC	Economic and Social Council (United Nations)
ECOWAS	Economic Community of West African States
ECU	European Currency Unit
EEC	European Economic Community
EFTA	European Free Trade Area
EMI	European Monetary Institute
EMS	European Monetary System
EMU	European Monetary Union
EPZ	Export Processing Zone
ERM	Exchange Rate Mechanism
ESCB	European System of Central Banks
EU	European Union
FDI	Foreign Direct Investment
FDIC	Federal Deposit Insurance Corporation (United States)
FIRA	Foreign Investment Review Agency (Canada)
FOGS	Functioning of the GATT System
FTA	Free Trade Association
GAB	General Arrangements to Borrow
GATT	General Agreements on Tariffs and Trade

388

GDP	Gross Domestic Product
GKI	State Committee on the Management of State Property (Russia)
GNP	Gross National Product
GSP	Generalized System of Preferences
GSTP	Global System of Trade Preferences
G-5	Group of Five
G-7	Group of Seven
G-77	Group of Seventy-Seven
H-O	Hecksher-Ohlin
HST	Hegemonial Stability Theory
IBA	International Bauxite Association
IBRD	International Bank for Reconstruction and Development (The World Bank)
ICA	International Commodity Agreement
ICSID	International Center for the Settlement of Investment Disputes
IDA	International Development Agency (United Nations)
IEA	International Energy Agency
IFAD	International Fund for Agricultural Development
IFC	International Finance Corporation
IITSA	International Investment and Trade in Services Act
ILO	International Labor Organization
IMF	International Monetary Fund
INF	Intermediate-Range Nuclear Force
ISI	Import-Substituting Industrialization
ITO	International Trade Organization
JEI	Japan Economic Institute
JETRO	Japan External Trade Organization
LAIA	Latin American Integration Association
LDC	Less Developed Country
LTA	Long Term Arrangement (for international trade in textiles)
Mercosur	Southern Cone Common Market (South America)
MFA	Multi-Fiber Arrangement
MFN	Most Favored Nation
MIGA	Multilateral Investment Guarantee Agency
MITI	Ministry of International Trade and Industry (Japan)
MNC	Multinational Corporation
MNE	Multinational Enterprise
MOSS	Market Opening Sector Specific
MTN	Multilateral Trade Negotiations
MYRA	Multi-Year Rescheduling Agreement
NAFTA	North American Free Trade Agreement
NATO	North Atlantic Treaty Organization
NIC	Newly Industrializing Country
NIEO	New International Economic Order
NIS	Newly Independent State
NNP	Net National Product
NTB	Nontariff Barrier
OAPEC	Organization of Arab Petroleum Exporting Countries
OAS	Organization of American States
OAU	Organization of African Unity
ODA	Official Development Assistance

OECD	Organization for Economic Cooperation and Development
OEEC	Organization for European Economic Cooperation
OLI	Ownership, Location, and Internalization
OMA	Orderly Marketing Agreement
OPEC	Organization of Petroleum Exporting Countries
OPIC	Overseas Private Investment Corporation
PRI	Partido Revolucionario Institucional (Mexico)
R&D	Research and Development
RTAA	Reciprocal Trade Agreements Act (United States)
SADC	Southern African Development Community
SALT	Strategic Arms Limitation Talks
SDR	Special Drawing Right
SEA	Single European Act
Sematech	Semiconductor Manufacturing Technology
SEZ	Special Economic Zone (China)
SII	Structural Impediments Initiative
TNC	Transnational Corporation
TNE	Transnational Enterprise
TPM	Trigger Price Mechanism
TRIM	Trade-Related Investment Measure
TRIP	Trade-Related Intellectual Property
UAE	United Arab Emirates
UMA	Arab Maghreb Union
UN	United Nations
UNCTAD	United Nations Conference on Trade and Development
UNCTC	United Nations Commission on Transnational Corporations
UNDP	United Nations Development Program
UNICE	European Employers' Union
UPEB	Unión de Paises Exportadores de Banana
USSR	Union of Soviet Socialist Republics
VER	Voluntary Export Restraint
VLSI	Very Large Scale Integrated (electronic circuits)
VRA	Voluntary Restraint Agreement
WHO	World Health Organization
WIPO	World Intellectual Property Organization
WTO	Warsaw Treaty Organization
WTO	World Trade Organization

Selected Bibliography

The bibliography reflects the organization of the book. The first section on general and theoretical works lists general studies and collections that encompass the broad subject of international political economy. The three bibliographical headings that follow denote the three-part division of the study: the Western system, the North-South system, and the East-West system. Each of these has a general subsection that cites works encompassing subtopics for the particular subsystem. Other subtopics correspond to the chapter subdivisions: money, trade, investment, and so on. With a few exceptions, individual articles from general works already cited under general subdivisions are not cited specifically under the various topical headings.

Publications by governmental and intergovernmental organizations are treated in three ways. Important official studies are included in the appropriate category in the first four sections. Important official serial publications are included in a separate category entitled official publications. Finally, because of space limitations some items are not listed. For example, because the U.S. Congressional hearings' bearing on the politics of international economic relations are voluminous, they are not repeated here, but are, however, cited in the notes. Those who wish to pursue research in this field should note the significance of hearings such as the Bretton Woods agreements, the Marshall Plan, the North Atlantic Treaty Organization, various trade and foreign aid hearings, and hearings on the problems of the international monetary system, the influence of multinational corporations, and East-West relations. Similar material from international organizations has also been excluded from the bibliography. Researchers should note the importance of proceedings of various United Nations bodies such as the General Assembly and UNCTAD and the voluminous material generated by international organizations such as the IMF and IBRD, the GATT, the OECD, and regional organizations.

Major newspapers and journals useful for the study of international political economy are cited in a final section.

General and Theory

Ashworth, William. *A Short History of the International Economy Since 1850.* London: Longman, 1975.

Axelrod, Robert. *The Evolution of Cooperation.* New York: Basic Books, 1984.

Baldwin, David A. *Economic Statecraft.* Princeton N.J.: Princeton University Press, 1985.

———, ed. *Neorealism and Neoliberalism: The Contemporary Debate.* New York: Columbia University Press, 1993.

Baran, Paul A. *The Political Economy of Growth.* New York: Monthly Review Press, 1968.

———, and Paul M. Sweezy. *Monopoly Capital: An Essay on the American Economic and Social Order.* New York: Monthly Review Press, 1966.

Bhagwati, Jagdish N., ed. *Economics and World Order: From the 1970s to the 1990s.* New York: Macmillan, 1972.

Camps, Miriam, and Catherine Gwin. *Collective Management: The Reform of International Economic Organizations.* New York: McGraw-Hill, 1981.

Carr, Edward Hallet. *The Twenty Years' Crisis, 1919–1939: An Introduction to the Study of International Relations*, 2nd ed. New York: St Martin's, 1962.

Cooper, Richard N. "Economic Interdependence and Foreign Policy in the Seventies." *World Politics* 24 (January 1972): 159–181.

_____. *The Economics of Interdependence: Economic Policy in the Atlantic Community.* New York: McGraw-Hill, 1968.

Cox, Robert W. *Production, Power and World Order: Social Forces in the Making of History.* New York: Columbia University Press, 1987.

Gerschenkron, Alexander. *Economic Backwardness in Historical Perspective: A Book of Essays.* Cambridge: Belknap Press of Harvard University Press, 1962.

Gilpin, Robert. *War and Change in World Politics.* Cambridge, England: Cambridge University Press, 1983.

Goldstein, Judith, and Robert O. Keohane, eds. *Ideas and Foreign Policy: Beliefs, Institutions, and Political Change.* Ithaca, N.Y.: Cornell University Press, 1993.

Gourevitch, Peter. "The Second Image Reversed: The International Sources of Domestic Politics." *International Organization* 32 (autumn 1978): 881–912.

_____. *Politics in Hard Times: Comparative Responses to International Economic Crises.* Ithaca, N.Y.: Cornell University Press, 1986.

Hamilton, Alexander. "Report on the Subject of Manufactures," in Arthur Harrison Cole, ed. *Industrial and Commercial Correspondence of Alexander Hamilton Anticipating His Report on Manufacturing.* New York: Kelley, 1968.

Hart, Jeffrey A. *Rival Capitalists: International Competitiveness in the United States, Japan, and Western Europe.* Ithaca, N.Y.: Cornell University Press, 1992.

Hawtrey, Ralph G. *Economic Aspects of Sovereignty,* 2nd ed. London: Longman, 1952.

Hecksher, Eli F. *Mercantilism,* 2 vols. Mendel Shapiro, trans. London: Allen and Unwin, 1935.

Hirsch, Fred, and John H. Goldthorpe, eds. *The Political Economy of Inflation.* Cambridge: Harvard University Press, 1978.

Hirschman, Albert O. *National Power and the Structure of Foreign Trade.* Berkeley: University of California Press, 1945.

_____. *Exit, Voice, and Loyalty: Response to Decline in Firms, Organizations, and States.* Cambridge: Harvard University Press, 1970.

Hoffmann, Stanley. "Obstinate or Obsolete? The Fate of the Nation-State and the Case of Western Europe." *Daedalus* 45 (summer 1966): 862–915.

Jacobson, Harold K. *Networks of Interdependence: International Organizations and the Global Political System.* New York: Knopf, 1979.

Kennedy, Paul. *The Rise and Fall of the Great Powers: Economic Change and Military Conflict from 1500 to 2000.* New York: Random House, 1987.

Keohane, Robert O. *After Hegemony: Co-operation and Discord in the World Political Economy.* Princeton: Princeton University Press, 1984.

_____, ed. *Neo-Realism and Its Critics.* New York: Columbia University Press, 1986.

_____, and Joseph S. Nye, Jr., eds. *Transnational Relations and World Politics.* Madison: University of Wisconsin Press, 1972.

_____, and Joseph S. Nye, Jr. Power and Interdependence: World Politics in Transition. Boston: Little, Brown, 1977.

Kindleberger, Charles P. *Power and Money: The Economics of International Politics and the Politics of International Economics.* New York: Basic Books, 1970.

_____. *The World in Depression, 1929–1939.* Berkeley: University of California Press, 1973.

_____. *The International Economic Order: Essays on Financial Crisis and International Public Goods.* Cambridge: MIT Press, 1989.

Knorr, Klaus. *Power and Wealth: The Political Economy of International Power.* New York: Basic Books, 1973.

_____. *The Power of Nations: The Political Economy of International Relations.* New York: Basic Books, 1975.

Krasner, Stephen D., ed. *International Regimes.* Ithaca, N.Y.: Cornell University Press, 1983.

Lenin, V. I. *Imperialism: The Highest Stage of Capitalism.* New York: International Publishers, 1939 [1917].

Lindblom, Charles E. *Politics and Markets: The World's Political-Economic System.* New York: Basic Books, 1977.

List, Friedrich. *The National System of Political Economy.* New York: Kelley, 1966.

Magdoff, Harry. *The Age of Imperialism: The Economics of U.S. Foreign Policy.* New York: Monthly Review Press, 1969.

Marx, Karl. *The Marx-Engels Reader.* Robert C. Tucker, ed. New York: W. W. Norton, 1972 [1848].

Morse, Edward L. Foreign Policy and Interdependence in Gaullist France. Princeton: Princeton University Press, 1973.

_____. *Modernization and the Transformation of International Relations.* New York: Free Press, 1976.

North, Douglass C. *Structure and Change in Economic History.* New York: W. W. Norton, 1981.

Olson, Mancur, Jr. *The Logic of Collective Action: Public Goods and the Theory of Groups.* Cambridge: Harvard University Press, 1971.

_____. *The Rise and Decline of Nations: Economic Growth, Stagflation, and Social Rigidities.* New Haven: Yale University Press, 1982.

Ostrom, Elinor. *Governing the Commons: The Evolution of Institutions for Collective Action.* New York: Cambridge University Press, 1990.

Oye, Kenneth, ed. *Cooperation Under Anarchy.* Princeton: Princeton University Press, 1986.

Perroux, François. *L'Economie du XXe Siècle,* 3rd ed. Paris: Presses Universitaires de France, 1969.

Polanyi, Karl. The Great Transformation. Boston: Beacon Press, 1957.

Robbins, Lionel. *The Economic Causes of War.* New York: Howard Fetig, 1968.

Rogowski, Ronald. *Commerce and Coalitions: How Trade Effects Domestic Political Alignments.* Princeton: Princeton University Press, 1989.

Rosecrance, Richard. *The Rise of the Trading State: Commerce and Conquest in the Modern World.* New York: Basic Books, 1986.

Ruggie, John G., ed. *The Antinomies of Interdependence: National Welfare and the International Division of Labor.* New York: Columbia University Press, 1983.

Schmitt, Hans O. "Mercantilism: A Modern Argument." *The Manchester School of Economic and Social Studies* 47 (June 1979): 93–111.

Schumpeter, Joseph A. *Capitalism, Socialism and Democracy.* New York: Harper and Row, 1950.

Shonfield, Andrew. *Modern Capitalism: The Changing Balance of Public and Private Power.* London: Oxford University Press, 1969.

Smith, Adam. *An Inquiry into the Nature and Causes of the Wealth of Nations.* New York: Modern Library, 1937.

Snidal, Duncan. "The Limits of Hegemonic Stability Theory." *International Organization* 39 (1985): 579–614.

Staley, Eugene. *War and the Private Investor.* Garden City, N.Y.: Doubleday, 1935.

Strange, Susan. "International Economics and International Relations: A Case of Mutual Neglect." *International Affairs* 46 (April 1970): 304–315.

_____. "What Is Economic Power and Who Has It?" *International Journal* (Canada) 30 (spring 1975): 207–224.

Tucker, Robert W. *The Inequality of Nations.* New York: Basic Books, 1976.

Viner, Jacob. "Power vs. Plenty as Objectives of Foreign Policy in the Seventeenth and Eighteenth Centuries." *World Politics* 1 (October 1948): 1–29.

Wallerstein, Immanuel. *The Modern World System: Capitalist Agriculture and the Origins of the European World-Economy in the Sixteenth Century.* New York: Academy Press, 1974.

Waltz, Kenneth N. *Theory of International Politics.* Reading, Mass.: Addison-Wesley, 1979.

Whitman, Marina V. N. *Reflections of Interdependence: Issues for Economic Theory and U.S. Policy.* Pittsburgh, Pa.: University of Pittsburgh Press, 1979.

Wu, Yuan-Li. *Economic Warfare.* Englewood Cliffs, N.J.: Prentice-Hall, 1952.

Young, Oran. *International Cooperation: Building Regimes for Natural Resources and the Environment.* Ithaca, N.Y.: Cornell University Press, 1989.

The Western System

General

Bergsten, C. Fred, and William R. Cline. *The United States-Japan Economic Problem*. Policy Analysis in International Economics, n. 13. Washington: Institute for International Economics, 1985.

Bressand, Albert. "Mastering the World Economy." *Foreign Affairs* 16 (1983): 747–772.

Calleo, David P. *Beyond American Hegemony: The Future of the Western Alliance*. New York: Basic Books, 1987.

Camps, Miriam. *"First World" Relationships: The Role of the OECD*. Paris: Atlantic Institute, 1975.

Cohen, Stephen D. *The Making of United States International Economic Policy*. New York: Praeger, 1977.

DeMenil, George, and Anthony M. Solomon. *Economic Summitry*. New York: Council on Foreign Relations, 1983.

Destler, I. M. *Making Foreign Economic Policy*. Washington: Brookings Institution, 1980.

Douglas, Gordon K., ed. *The New Interdependence: The European Community and the United States*. Lexington, Mass.: Lexington Books, 1979.

Gardner, Richard N. *Sterling-Dollar Diplomacy in Current Perspective: The Origins and Prospects of Our International Economic Order*. New York: Columbia University Press, 1980.

Katzenstein, Peter, ed. *Between Power and Plenty: Foreign Economic Policies of Advanced Industrial States*. Madison: University of Wisconsin Press, 1978.

McCracken, Paul W., et al. *Towards Full Employment and Price Stability: A Report to the OECD by a Group of Independent Experts*. Paris: OECD, 1972.

Ostry, Sylvia, and Gilbert R. Winham, eds. *The Halifax G-7 Summit: Issues on the Table*. Halifax, N.S., Canada: Center for Foreign Policy Studies, Dalhousie University, 1995.

Promoting World Recovery: A Statement on Global Economic Strategy. Washington: Institute for International Economics, 1982.

Putnam, Robert, and Nicholas Bayne. *Hanging Together: Cooperation and Conflict in the Seven-Power Summits*. Cambridge: Harvard University Press, 1987.

Japan in the World Economy

Abbeglen, J. C., and George Stalk Jr. *Kaisha: The Japanese Corporation*. New York: Basic Books, 1985.

Anchordoguy, Marie. *Computers, Inc. Japan's Challenge to IBM*. Cambridge: Harvard University Press, 1989.

Balassa, Bela, and Marcus Noland. *Japan in the World Economy*. Washington: Institute for International Economics, 1988.

Calder, Kent. *Crisis and Compensation: Public Policy and Political Stability in Japan, 1949–1986*. Princeton: Princeton University Press, 1988.

Choate, Pat. *Agents of Influence: How Japan Manipulates America's Political and Economic System*. New York: Simon and Schuster, 1990.

Dore, Ronald. *British Factory, Japanese Factory: The Origins of National Diversity in* Industrial Relations. Berkeley: University of California Press, 1973.

_____. *Flexible Rigidities: Industrial Policy and Structural Adjustment in the Japanese Economy 1970–1980*. Stanford: Stanford University Press, 1986.

_____. *Taking Japan Seriously: A Confucian Perspective on Leading Economic Issues*. Stanford: Stanford University Press, 1987.

Friedman, David. The Misunderstood Miracle: Industrial Development and Political Change in Japan. Ithaca, N.Y.: Cornell University Press, 1988.

Gerlach, Michael. *Alliance Capitalism*. Berkeley: University of California Press, 1992.

Inoguchi, Takashi, and Daniel I. Okimoto, eds. *The Political Economy of Japan*. Vol. 2, *The Changing International Context*. Stanford: Stanford University Press, 1988.

Ito, Tadashi. *The Japanese Economy*. Cambridge: MIT Press, 1992.

Johnson, Chalmers. *MITI and the Japanese Miracle: The Growth of Industrial Policy, 1925–1975.* Stanford: Stanford University Press, 1982.

Kernell, Samuel, ed. *Parellel Politics: Economic Policymaking in the United States and Japan.* Washington: Brookings Institution, 1991.

Lincoln, Edward J. Japan: Facing Economic Maturity. Washington: Brookings Institution, 1988.

_____. *Japan's Unequal Trade*. Washington: Brookings Institution, 1990.

Magaziner, Ira C., and Thomas M. Hout. *Japanese Industrial Policy: A Descriptive Account of Postwar Developments with Case Studies of Selected Industries*. London: Policy Studies Institute, January 1980.

Morris-Suzuki, Tessa. *The Technological Transformation of Japan: From the Seventeenth to the Twenty-first Century*. New York: Cambridge University Press, 1994.

Noble, Gregory. "The Japanese Industrial Policy Debate," in Stephan Haggard and Chung-In Moon, eds., *Pacific Dynamics: The International Politics of Industrial Change*. Boulder, Colo.: Westview Press, 1989.

Okimoto, Daniel I. *Between MITI and the Market*. Stanford: Stanford University Press, 1989.

_____, and Thomas P. Rohlen, eds. *Inside the Japanese System: Readings on Contemporary Society and Political Economy*. Stanford: Stanford University Press, 1988.

Ozaki, Robert S. *The Control of Imports and Foreign Capital in Japan*. New York: Praeger, 1972.

Patrick, Hugh, ed. *Japan's High Technology Industries: Lessons and Limitations of Industrial Policy*. Seattle: University of Washington Press, 1986.

_____, and Henry Rosovsky, eds. *Asia's New Giant: How the Japanese Economy Works*. Washington: Brookings Institution, 1976.

Pempel, T. J. *Policy and Politics in Japan*. Philadelphia: Temple University Press, 1982.

Prestowitz, Clyde V., Jr. *Trading Places: How We Allowed Japan to Take the Lead*. New York: Basic Books, 1988.

Sakakibara, Eisuke. *Beyond Capitalism: The Japanese Model of Market Economics*. Lanham, Md.: University Press of America for the Economic Strategy Institute, 1993.

Samuels, Richard J. *The Business of the Japanese State: Energy Markets in Comparative and Historical Perspective*. Ithaca, N.Y.: Cornell University Press, 1987.

Tsuru, Shigeto. *Japan's Capitalism: Creative Defeat and Beyond*. New York: Cambridge University Press, 1993.

Vogel, Ezra. *Japan as Number One*. Cambridge: Harvard University Press, 1979.

_____. *Comeback Case by Case: Building the Resurgence of American Business*. New York: Simon and Schuster, 1985.

Yamamura, Kozo, and Yasukichi Yasuba, eds. *The Political Economy of Japan*. Vol. 1, *The Domestic Transformation*. Stanford: Stanford University Press, 1987.

Yamazawa, Ippei. *Economic Development and International Trade: The Japanese Model*. Ippei Yamazawa, trans. and rev.. Honolulu: East-West Center, Resource Systems Institute, 1990.

Recent Works on Europe in the World Economy

Archer, Clive, and Fiona Butler. *The European Community: Structure and Process*. New York: St. Martin's Press, 1992.

Calingaert, Michael. *The 1992 Challenge from Europe: Development of the European Community's Internal Market*. Washington: National Planning Association, 1988.

Hufbauer, Gary C., ed. *Europe 1992: An American Perspective*. Washington: Brookings Institution, 1990.

Keohane, Robert O., and Stanley Hoffman, eds. *The New European Community: Decisionmaking and Institutional Change*. Boulder, Colo.: Westview Press, 1991.

Kirchner, Emil J. *Decision-making in the European Community: The Council Presidency and European Integration*. New York: Manchester University Press, 1992.

Lodge, Juliet, ed. *The European Community and the Challenge of the Future*, 2nd ed. New York: St. Martin's Press, 1993.

Sbragia, Alberta M., ed. *Euro-Politics: Institutions and Policymaking in the "New" European Community*. Washington: Brookings Institution, 1992.

Tsoukalis, Loukas. *The New European Economy: The Politics and Economics of Integration*. New York: Oxford University Press, 1992.

International Monetary System

Aliber, Robert Z. *The Political Economy of Monetary Reform*. London: Macmillan, 1977.

Aronson, Jonathan D. *Money and Power: Banks and the World Monetary System*. Beverly Hills, Calif.: Sage Library of Social Research, 1977.

Bergsten, C. Fred, and John Williamson. *The Multiple Reserve Currency System*. Cambridge: MIT Press, 1983.

_____, ed. *International Adjustment and Financing*. Washington: Institute for International Economics, 1991.

Bernstein, Edward M., et al. *Reflections on Jamaica*. Princeton: International Finance Section, Department of Economics, Princeton University, 1976.

Block, Fred L. *The Origins of International Economic Disorder: A Study of United States International Monetary Policy from World War II to the Present*. Berkeley: University of California Press, 1977.

Bordo, Michael D., and Barry J. Eichengreen, eds. *A Retrospective on the Bretton Woods System: Lessons for International Monetary Reform*. Chicago: University of Chicago Press, 1993.

Branson, William H., Jacob A. Frenkel, and Morris Goldstein, eds. *International Policy Coordination and Exchange Rate Fluctuations*. Chicago: University of Chicago Press, 1990.

Bryant, Ralph C. *International Financial Mediation*. Washington: Brookings Institution, 1987.

Cairncross, Alec, and Barry J. Eichengreen. *Sterling in Decline: The Devaluations of 1931, 1949, and 1967*. Oxford: Basil Blackwell, 1983.

Clarke, Stephen V. O. *Central Bank Co-operation, 1924–1931*. New York: Federal Reserve Bank of New York, 1967.

Cline, William R. *International Debt: Systemic Risk and Policy Response*. Cambridge: MIT Press, 1983.

Cohen, Benjamin J. *Organizing the World's Money*. New York: Basic Books, 1977.

_____. *In Whose Interest?: International Banking and American Foreign Policy*. New Haven: Yale University Press, 1986.

Cohen, Stephen D. *International Monetary Reform, 1964–69*. New York: Praeger, 1970.

Cooper, Richard N., et al. *The International Monetary System Under Flexible Exchange Rates: Global, Regional, National*. Cambridge, Mass.: Ballinger, 1982.

Dale, Richard, with Richard P. Maltione. *Managing Global Debt*. Washington: Brookings Institution, 1983.

Destler, I. M., and C. Randall Henning. *Dollar Politics: Exchange Rate Policymaking in the United States*. Washington: Institute for International Economics, 1989.

De Vries, Margaret G. *The International Monetary Fund, 1966–1971: The System Under Stress*. Washington: International Monetary Fund, 1976.

Diebold, William, Jr. *Trade and Payments in Western Europe: A Study in Economic Cooperation, 1947–1951*. New York: Harper, 1952.

Eichengreen, Barry J. *Golden Fetters: The Gold Standard and the Great Depression, 1919–1939*. New York: Oxford University Press, 1992.

_____. *Hegemonic Stability Theories of the International Monetary System*. Washington: The Brookings Institution, 1987.

_____, ed. *Monetary Regime Transformations*. Aldershot, Hants., England: Edward Elgar, 1992.

_____. "European Monetary Integration." *Journal of Economic Literature* 31 (September 1993), 1321–1357.

_____. *International Monetary Arrangements for the 21st Century*. Washington: Brookings Institution, 1994.

_____, and Jeffry A. Frieden, "The Political Economy of European Monetary Integration: An

Analytical Introduction." *Economics and Politics* 5 (July 1993): 85–104.

_____, and Jeffry A. Frieden, eds. *The Political Economy of European Integration*. Boulder, Colo.: Westview Press, 1994.

_____, A. K. Rose, and Charles Wyplosz. *Is There a Safe Passage to EMU?* Fontainebleau: INSEAD, 1994.

European Community, Committee for the Study of Economic and Monetary Union. *Report on Economic and Monetary Union in the European Community* (The Delors Report). Brussels: European Community, 1989.

Fratianni, Michele, and Jürgen von Hagen. *The European Monetary System and European Monetary Union*. Boulder, Colo.: Westview, 1992.

_____, and Theo Peters, eds. *One Money for Europe*. New York: Praeger, 1978.

_____, and Dominick Salvatore, eds. *Monetary Policy in Developed Economies*. Westport, Conn.: Greenwood, 1993.

Frieden, Jeffry A. "Invested Interests: The Politics of National Economic Policies in a World of Global Finance." *International Organization* 45 (autumn 1991), 425–452.

_____. "Exchange Rate Politics: Contemporary Lessons from American History." *Review of International Political Economy 1* (spring 1994), 81–103.

Funabashi, Yoichi. *Managing the Dollar: From the Plaza to the Louvre*. Washington: Institute for International Economics, 1988.

Garrett, Geoffrey. "The Politics of Maastricht." *Economics and Politics*, 5 (July 1993), 105–123.

Gibson, Heather D. *The Eurocurrency Markets, Domestic Financial Policy and International Instability*. New York: St. Martin's, 1989.

Goodman, John. *Monetary Sovereignty: The Politics of Central Banking in Western Europe*. Ithaca, N.Y.: Cornell University Press, 1992.

Gowa, Joanne. *Closing the Gold Window: Domestic Politics and the End of Bretton Woods*. Ithaca, N.Y.: Cornell University Press, 1983.

Group of Thirty. *The Problem of Exchange Rates: A Policy Statement*. New York: Group of Thirty, 1982.

Helleiner, Eric. *States and the Reemergence of Global Finance: From Bretton Woods to the 1990s*. Ithaca, N.Y.: Cornell University Press, 1994.

Hewlett, Sylvia Ann, Henry Kaufman, and Peter B. Kenen. *The Global Repercussions of U.S. Monetary and Fiscal Policy*. New York: Ballinger, 1984.

Horsefield, J. Keith, ed. *The International Monetary Fund, 1945–65: Twenty Years of International Monetary Cooperation*, 3 vols. Washington: International Monetary Fund, 1969.

Ilgen, Thomas L. *Autonomy and Interdependence: U.S.-Western European Monetary and Trade Relations, 1958–1984*. Totowa, N.J.: Roman and Allanheld, 1985.

Kaufmann, Hugo. *Germany's International Monetary Policy and the European Monetary System*. New York: Brooklyn College Press, 1985.

Kennedy, Ellen. *The Bundesbank: Germany's Central Bank in the International Monetary System*. London: Pinter, 1991.

King, Kenneth. *U.S. Monetary Policy and European Responses in the 1980s*, Chatham House Paper 16. London: Routledge, 1982.

Kojm, Christopher, ed. *The Problem of International Debt*. New York: H. W. Wilson, 1984.

Ludlow, Peter. *The Making of the European Monetary System*. London: Butterworth Scientific, 1982.

Machlup, Fritz. *Remaking the International Monetary System: The Rio Agreement and Beyond*. Baltimore: Johns Hopkins Press, 1968.

Marris, Stephen. *Deficits and the Dollar: The World Economy at Risk*. Washington: Institute for International Economics, 1987.

McKinnon, Ronald I., "Optimum Currency Areas." *American Economic Review* 53 (September 1963): 717–715.

_____. *The Eurocurrency Market*. Princeton: International Finance Section, Department of Economics, Princeton University, 1977.

Mundell, Robert A. "A Theory of Optimum Currency Areas." *American Economic Review* 51 (September 1961): 657–665.

_____, and Jacques J. Polak. *The New International Monetary System*. New York: Columbia University Press, 1977.

Odell, John. *U.S. International Monetary Policy: Markets, Power and Ideas as Sources of Change*. Princeton: Princeton University Press, 1982.

Padoan, Pier Carlo. *The Political Economy of International Financial Instability*. London: Croom Helm, 1986.

Pauly, Louis. Opening Financial Markes: Banking Politics on the Pacific Rim. Ithaca, N.Y.: Cornell University Press, 1988.

Princeton University International Finance Section. "International Monetary Cooperation: Essays in Honor of Henry Wallich." *Essays in International Finance*, n. 169. Princeton: Princeton University International Finance Section, 1987.

Rowland, Benjamin M., ed. *Balance of Power or Hegemony: The Interwar Monetary System*. New York: New York University Press, 1976.

Sandholtz, Wayne. "Choosing Union: Monetary Politics and Maastricht." *International Organization* 47 (winter 1993): 1–39.

_____, ed. *International Economic Relations of the Western World, 1959–1971*. Vol. 2, *International Monetary Relations*. London: Oxford University Press, 1976.

Shonfield, Andrew. *Sterling and British Policy: A Political Study of an International Currency in Decline*. New York: Oxford University Press, 1971.

Solomon, Robert. *The International Monetary System: 1945–1976: An Insider's View*. New York: Harper and Row, 1976.

Spero, Joan E. *The Failure of the Franklin National Bank: Challenge to the International Banking System*. New York: Columbia University Press, 1980.

Spindler, J. Andrew. *The Politics of International Credit*. Washington: Brookings Institution, 1984.

Stabler, Elizabeth. "The Dollar Devaluation of 1971 and 1973." *U.S. Commission of the Organization of the Government for the Conduct of Foreign Policy, Appendix*, vol. 3. Washington: Government Printing Office, 1976.

Strange, Susan. *Sterling and British Policy: A Political Study of an International Currency in Decline*. London: Oxford University Press, 1971.

_____. "The Dollar Crisis 1971." *International Affairs* 48 (April 1972): 191–215.

_____. *Casino Capitalism*. Oxford and New York: Basil Blackwell, 1986.

Triffin, Robert. *Europe and the Money Muddle: From Bilateralism to Near Convertibility, 1947–1956*. New Haven, Conn.: Yale University Press, 1957.

_____. *Gold and the Dollar Crisis: The Future of Convertibility*. New Haven, Conn.: Yale University Press, 1960.

_____. *Evolution of the International Monetary System: Historical Reappraisal and Future Perspectives*. Princeton, N.J.: International Finance Section, Department of Economics, Princeton University, 1964.

_____. "The International Role and Fate of the Dollar." *Foreign Affairs* 57 (winter 1978–79): 269–286.

Tsoukalis, Loukas. *The Politics and Economic of European Monetary Integration*. London: Allen and Unwin, 1977.

_____. *The Political Economy of International Money*. London: Royal Institute of International Affairs/Sage Publications, 1985.

Ungerer, Horst. The European Monetary System: Recent Developments. Washington: International Monetary Fund Occasional Papers No. 48, 1986.

Wachtel, Howard M. *The Money Mandarins: The Making of a Supranational Economic Order*. New York: Pantheon Books, 1986.

Wallich, Henry C. *The Failure of International Monetary Reform, 1971–74*. London: Nelson, 1977.

_____, et al. *World Money and National Policies*. New York: Group of Thirty, 1983.

Wihlborg, Clas, Michele Fratianni, and Thomas D. Willett, eds. *Financial Regulations and Monetary Arrangements after 1992*. New York: North Holland, 1991.

Williamson, John, and Marcus Miller. *Targets and Indicators: A Blueprint for International Coordination of Economic Policy*. Washington: Institute for International Economics, 1987.

Woolley, John T. *Monetary Politics: The Federal Reserve and the Politics of Monetary Policy*. Cambridge, England: Cambridge University Press, 1984.

Yeager, Leland. *International Monetary Relations*. New York: Harper and Row, 1966.

Trade among Developed Market Economies

Aggarwal, Vinod K. *Liberal Protectionism: The International Politics of Organized Textile Trade.* Berkeley: University of California Press, 1985.

Aho, C. Michael, and Jonathan David Aronson. *Trade Talks: America Better Listen!* New York: Council on Foreign Relations, 1985.

Anania, Giovanni, Colin A. Carter, and Alex F. McCalla, eds. *Agricultural Trade Conflicts and the GATT: New Dimension in U.S.-European Agricultural Trade Relations.* Boulder, Colo.: Westview, 1994.

Baldwin, Robert E. *Non-Tariff Distortions of International Trade.* Washington: Brookings Institution, 1970.

_____. *The Political Economy of U.S. Import Policy.* Cambridge: MIT Press, 1986.

Bauer, Raymond A., Ithiel de Sola Pool, and Lewis Anthony Dexter. *American Business and Public Policy: The Politics of Foreign Trade.* Chicago: Aldine-Atherton, 1972.

Bayard, Thomas O. and Kimberly Ann Elliott. *Reciprocity and Retaliation in U.S. Trade Policy.* Washington: Institute for International Economics, 1994.

Bhagwati, Jagdish N. *Protectionism.* Cambridge: MIT Press, 1988.

_____. *The World Trading System at Risk.* Princeton: Princeton University Press, 1991.

_____, and Hugh T. Patrick. *Aggressive Unilateralism: America's 301 Trade Policy and the World Trading System.* Ann Arbor: University of Michigan Press, 1990.

Blackhurst, Richard, Nicolas Marian, and Jan Tumlir. *Adjustment, Trade and Growth in Developed and Developing Countries.* GATT Studies in International Trade, no. 6. Geneva: General Agreement on Tariffs and Trade, 1978.

Boltuck, Richard, and Robert E. Litan, eds. *Down in the Dumps: Administration of Unfair Trade Laws.* Washington: Brookings Institution, 1991.

Brown, William Adams, Jr. *The United States and the Restoration of World Trade: An Analysis and Appraisal of the ITO Charter and the General Agreement on Tariffs and Trade.* Washington: Brookings Institution, 1950.

Camps, Miriam, and William Diebold, Jr. *The New Multilateralism: Can the World Trading System Be Saved?* New York: Council on Foreign Relations, 1983.

Caves, Richard E., Jeffrey A. Frankel, and Ronald W. Jones. *World Trade and Payments: An Introduction.* New York: HarperCollins, 1993.

Cline, William R. *Trade Policy in the 1980s.* Washington: Institute for International Economics, 1983.

Conybeare, John A. C. *Trade Wars: The Theory and Practice of International Commercial Rivalry.* New York: Columbia University Press, 1987.

Curran, Timothy J. "Politics of Trade Liberalization in Japan." *Journal of International Affairs* 37 (summer 1983): 105–122.

Curzon, Gerard. *Multilateral Commercial Diplomacy: The General Agreements on Tariffs and Trade and Its Impact on National Commercial Policies and Techniques.* London: Michael Joseph, 1965.

Dam, Kenneth W. *The GATT: Law and International Economic Organization.* Chicago: University of Chicago Press, 1970.

Destler, I. M. *American Trade Politics: System Under Stress.* Washington: Institute for International Economics/New York: Twentieth Century Fund, 1986.

_____, and John Odell. *Anti-Protection: Changing Forces in U.S. Trade Politics.* Washington: Institute for International Economics, 1987.

Diebold, William, Jr. *The End of the I.T.O.* Princeton: International Finance Section, Department of Economics and Social Institutions, Princeton University, 1952.

_____. "Adapting Economies to Structural Change: The International Aspect." *International Affairs* (London) 54 (October 1978): 573–588.

_____. *Bilateralism, Multilateralism and Canada in U.S. Trade Policy.* Cambridge, Mass.: Ballinger, 1988.

Dixit, Avinash, and Victor Norman. *Theory of International Trade*. New York: Cambridge University Press, 1980.

Dosi, Giovanni, Keith Pavitt, and Luc Soete. *The Economics of Technological Change and International Trade*. London: Harvester Wheatsheaf, 1990.

Drake, William J., and Kalypso Nicolaïdes. "Ideas, Interests, and Institutionalization: 'Trade in Services'." *International Organization* 46 (winter 1992): 37–100.

Feketekuty, Geza. *International Trade in Services: An Overview and Blueprint for Negotiations*. Cambridge, Mass.: Ballinger/Washington: American Enterprise Institute, 1988.

Finger, J. Michael, ed. *Antidumping: How It Works and Who Gets Hurt*. Ann Arbor: University of Michigan Press, 1993.

———, H. Keith Hall, and Douglas Nelson. "The Political Economy of Administered Protection." *American Economic Review* 72 (1982): 452–466.

Frankel, Jeffrey A., and Miles Kahler, eds. *Regionalism and Rivalry: Japan and the United States in Pacific Asia*. Chicago: University of Chicago Press, 1993.

Gadbaw, R. Michael, and Timothy J. Richards, eds. *Intellectual Property Rights: Global Consensus, Global Conflict?* Boulder, Colo.: Westview Press, 1988.

General Agreement on Tariffs and Trade. *The Tokyo Round: A Report by the Director-General of GATT*. Geneva: GATT, 1979.

Goldstein, Judith. *Ideas, Interests, and American Trade Policy*. Ithaca, N.Y.: Cornell University Press, 1993.

Grinspun, Ricardo, and Maxwell A. Cameron. *The Political Economy of North American Free Trade*. New York: St. Martin's Press, 1993.

Grossman, Gene M., ed. *Imperfect Competition and International Trade*. Cambridge: MIT Press, 1992.

Hathaway, Dale E. *Agriculture and the GATT: Rewriting the Rules*. Washington: Institute for International Economics, 1987.

Haus, Leah. *Globalizing the GATT: The Soviet Union's Successor States, Eastern Europe, and the International Trading System*. Washington: Brookings Institution, 1992.

Hill, Brian. *The Common Agricultural Policy: Past, Present and Future*. New York: Methuen, 1989.

Hindley, Brian, and Eri Nicolaides. Taking the New Protectionism Seriously, Thames Essay No. 34. London: Trade Policy Research Centre, 1983.

Hine, R. C. *The Political Economy of European Trade: An Introduction to the Trade Policies of the EEC*. New York: St. Martin's Press, 1985.

Hopkins, Nicholas. *Completing the GATT Uruguay Round: Renewed Multilateralism or a World of Regional Trading Blocs?* Wilton Park Paper 61. London: Her Majesty's Stationery Office, 1992.

Hopkins, Raymond F., and Donald J. Puchala, eds. "The Global Political Economy of Food." *International Organization* 32 (summer 1978): entire issue.

———. *Global Food Interdependence: Challenge to American Foreign Policy*. New York: Columbia University Press, 1980.

Horlick, Gary N., "How the GATT Became Protectionist: An Analysis of the Uruguay Round Draft Final Antidumping Code." *Journal of World Trade* 27 (October 1993): 5–17.

Hufbauer, Gary C., Diane T. Berliner, and Kimberly A. Elliot. *Trade Protection in the United States: Thirty-one Case Studies*. Washington: Institute for International Economics, 1986.

Institute for Contemporary Studies. *Tariffs, Quotas and Trade: The Politics of Protectionism*. San Francisco: Institute for Contemporary Studies, 1979.

Jackson, John H. *The World Trading System: Law and Policy of International Economic Relations*. Cambridge: MIT Press, 1989.

Johnson, D. Gale, Kenzo Hemmi, and Pierre Lardinois. *Agricultural Policy and Trade: Adjusting Domestic Programs in an International Framework*. New York: New York University Press, 1986.

Kock, Karin. *International Trade Policy in the GATT, 1947–67*. Stockholm: Almqvist and Wiksell, 1969.

Krasner, Stephen D. "State Power and the Structure of International Trade." *World Politics* 28 (April 1976): 317–343.

_____."The Tokyo Round: Particularistic Interests and Prospects for Stability in the Global Trading System." *International Studies Quarterly* 23 (December 1979): 491–531.

Krugman, Paul R., ed. *Strategic Trade Policy and the New International Economics.* Cambridge: MIT Press, 1986.

_____. *Rethinking International Trade.* Cambridge: MIT Press, 1990.

_____. *Peddling Prosperity: Economic Sense and Nonsense in the Age of Diminished Expectations.* New York: Norton, 1994.

Lenway, Stefanie Ann. *The Politics of U.S. International Trade: Protection, Expansion and Escape.* Marshfield, Mass.: Pitman Publishing, 1985.

Lustig, Nora, Barry P. Bosworth, and Robert Z. Lawrence, eds. *North American Free Trade: Assessing the Impact.* Washington: Brookings Institution, 1992.

Metzger, Stanley D. *Lowering Nontariff Barriers: U.S. Law, Practice and Negotiating Objectives.* Washington: Brookings Institution, 1974.

Milner, Helen V. *Resisting the Protectionist Temptation: Global Industries and the Politics of International Trade.* Princeton: Princeton University Press, 1988.

Nau, Henry, ed. *Domestic Trade Politics and the Uruguay Round.* New York: Columbia University Press, 1989.

Nivola, Pietro S. *Regulating Unfair Trade.* Washington: Brookings Institution, 1993.

Organization for Economic Cooperation and Development. *National Policies and Agricultural Trade.* Paris: OECD, 1987.

Oye, Kenneth A. *Economic Discrimination and Political Exchange: World Political Economy in the 1930s and 1980s.* Princeton: Princeton University Press, 1992.

Paarlberg, Robert L. *Fixing Farm Trade: Policy Options for the United States.* Cambridge: Ballinger, 1988.

Padoan, Pier-Carlo, and Paolo Guerrieri, eds. *The Political Economy of European Integration.* London: Harvester Wheatsheaf, 1989.

Patterson, Gardener. *Discrimination in International Trade: The Policy Issues. 1945–65.* Princeton: Princeton University Press, 1966.

Penrose, E. F. *Economic Planning for the Peace.* Princeton: Princeton University Press, 1953.

Preeg, Ernest H. *Traders and Diplomats: An Analysis of the Kennedy Round Negotiations under the General Agreement on Tariffs and Trade.* Washington: Brookings Institution, 1970.

Reich, Robert B. "Beyond Free Trade." *Foreign Affairs* 16 (spring 1983): 747–772.

Rhodes, Carolyn. *Reciprocity, U.S. Trade Policy and the GATT Regime.* Ithaca, N.Y.: Cornell University Press, 1993.

Richardson, J. David. "The Political Economy of Strategic Trade Policy." *International Organization* 44 (winter 1990): 107–135.

Ruggie, John G., ed. *Multilateralism Matters: The Theory and Praxis of an Institutional Form.* New York: Columbia University Press, 1993.

Runge, Carlisle Ford. *Freer Trade, Protected Environment: Balancing Trade Liberalization and Environmental Interests.* New York: Council on Foreign Relations Press, 1994.

Schattschneider, Elmer Eric. *Politics, Pressures and the Tariff.* Englewood Cliffs, N.J.: Prentice-Hall, 1935.

Schonfield, Andrew, ed. *International Economic Relations of the Western World, 1959–1971.* Vol. 1, *Politics and Trade.* London: Oxford University Press, 1976.

Schott, Jeffrey J. *The Uruguay Round: An Assessment.* Washington: Institute for International Economics, 1994.

_____, and Murray G. Smith. *The Canada-United States Free Trade Agreement: The Global Impact.* Washington: Institute for International Economics, 1988.

Strange, Susan. "The Management of Surplus Capacity: Or How Does Theory Stand Up to Protectionism 1970s Style?" *International Organization* 33 (summer 1979): 303–334.

Taylor, Paul. *The Limits of European Integration.* London: Croom Helm, 1983.

Tyson, Laura D'Andrea. *Who's Bashing Whom? Trade Conflict in High-Technology Industries.* Washington: Institute for International Economics, 1992.

U.S. Congress. *The Mercantilist Challenge to the Liberal International Trade Order.* A study prepared for the use of the joint Economic Committee. Congress of the United States, December 29, 1982. Washington: Government Printing Office, 1982.

Verdier, Daniel. *Democracy and International Trade: Britain, France, and the United States, 1860–1990*. Princeton, N.J.: Princeton University Press, 1994.

Walter, Ingo. *Global Competition in Financial Services: Market Structure, Protection and Liberalization*. Cambridge, Mass.: Ballinger, 1988.

Wilcox, Clair. *A Charter for World Trade*. New York: Macmillan, 1949.

Winham, Gilbert R. *International Trade and the Tokyo Round Negotiations?* Princeton: Princeton University Press, 1987.

———. *The Evolution of International Trade Agreements*. Toronto: University of Toronto Press, 1992.

Woolcock, Stephen, Jeffrey Hart, and Hans van der Ven. *Interdependence in the Postmultilateral Era*. Lanham, Md.: University Press of America, 1985.

Zysman, John, and Laura Tyson. *American Industry in International Competition: Government Policies and Corporate Strategies*. Ithaca, N.Y.: Cornell University Press, 1983.

The Multinational Corporation in Developed Market Economies

Agarwal, Jamuna P. "Determinants of Foreign Direct Investment: A Survey." *Weltwirtschaftliches Archiv* 116 (1980): 737–773.

Agmon, Tamir, and Charles P. Kindleberger. *Multinationals From Small Countries*. Cambridge: M.I.T. Press, 1977.

Aliber, Robert Z. *The Multinational Paradigm*. Cambridge: MIT Press, 1993.

Aoki, Masahiko, Bo Gustafsson, and Oliver E. Williamson, eds. *The Firm as a Nexus of Treaties*. London: Sage Publications, 1990.

Apter, David, and Louis W. Goodman, eds. *The Multinational Corporation and Social Change*. New York: Praeger, 1976.

Bailey, David, George Harte, and Roger Sugden. *Transnationals and Government: Recent Policies in Japan, France, Germany, the United States and Britain*. New York: Routledge, 1994.

Ball, George W. "Cosmocorp: The Importance of Being Stateless." *Columbia Journal of World Business* 2 (November-December 1967): 25–30.

———, ed. *Global Companies*. Englewood Cliffs, N.J.: Prentice-Hall, 1979.

Baranson, Jack. *Technology and the Multinationals: Corporate Strategies and a Changing World Environment*. Lexington, Mass.: Lexington Books, 1978.

Barnet, Richard J., and John Cavanagh. *Global Dreams: Imperial Corporations and the New World Order*. New York: Simon and Schuster, 1994.

Barnet, Richard J., and Ronald E. Müller. *The Global Reach: The Power of the Multinational Corporations*. New York: Simon and Schuster, 1974.

Bassing, Reza. *Power v. Profit: Multinational Corporation-Nation State Interaction*. New York: Arno, 1980.

Behrman, Jack N. *National Interests and the Multinational Enterprise. Tensions among the North Atlantic Countries*. Englewood, Cliffs, N.J.: Prentice-Hall, 1970.

———. *U.S. International Business and Governments*. New York: McGraw-Hill, 1971.

Bergsten, C. Fred, Thomas Horst, and Theodore H. Moran. *American Multinationals and American Interests*. Washington: Brookings Institution, 1978.

Braunerhjelm, Pontus. *Multinational Corporations, Country Characteristics, and Clustering in Foreign Direct Investment*. Stockholm: Industriens Untredningsinstitut, 1994.

Buckley, Peter J., and Mark Casson. *The Economic Theory of the Multinational Enterprise*. New York: St. Martin's Press, 1985.

———, eds. *Multinational Enterprises in the World Economy: Essays in Honor of John Dunning*. Brookfield, Vt.: Edward Elgar, 1992.

Canada. Task Force on the Structure of Canadian Industry. *Foreign Ownership and the Structure of Canadian Industry*. Ottawa: Queen's Printer, 1968.

Cantwell, John, ed. *Multinational Investment in Modern Europe: Strategic Interaction in the Integrated Community*. Brookfield, Vt.: Edward Elgar, 1992.

_____. *Transnational Corporations and Innovatory Activities*. New York: Routledge for the UNC-TAD Program on Transnational Corporations, 1994.

Caves, Richard E. *Multinational Enterprise and Economic Analysis*. Cambridge, England: Cambridge University Press, 1982.

Chandler, Alfred D. *The Visible Hand: The Managerial Revolution in American Business*. Cambridge: Belknap Press of Harvard University Press, 1977.

_____. *Scale and Scope: The Dynamics of Industrial Capitalism*. Cambridge: Belknap Press of Harvard University Press, 1990.

Cohen, Bernard J. *Multinational Firms and Asian Exports*. New Haven: Yale University Press, 1975.

Cohen, Stephen S., and John Zysman. *Manufacturing Matters: The Myth of the Post-Industrial Economy*. New York: Basic Books, for the Council on Foreign Relations, 1987.

Cowhey, Peter, and Jonathan D. Aronson. *Managing the World Economy: The Consequences of Corporate Alliances*. New York: Council on Foreign Relations Press, 1993.

Cox, Robert W. "Labor and Transnational Relations." *International Organization* 25 (summer 1971): 554–584.

Cox, Robert W. "Labor and the Multinationals." *Foreign Affairs* 54 (January 1976): 344–365.

Culem, Claudy G. "The Locational Determinants of Direct Investments among Industrialized Countries." *European Economic Review* 32 (April 1988): 885–904.

Culpan, Refik, ed. *Multinational Strategic Alliances*. New York: International Business Press, 1993.

Curzon, Gerard, and Victoria Curzon, eds. *The Multinational Enterprise in a Hostile World*. London: Macmillan, 1977.

Dassbach, Carl H. A. *Global Enterprises and the World Economy: Ford, General Motors, IBM, and the Emergence of the Transnational Enterprise*. New York: Garland, 1989.

Doz, Yves L. *Strategic Management in Multinational Companies*. New York: Pergamon Press, 1986.

Driscoll, Robert E., and Jack N. Behrman, eds. *International Industrial Integration*. Cambridge, Mass.: Oelgeschlager, Gunn, and Hain, 1983.

Dunning, John H. *International Production and the Multinational Enterprise*. London: Allen and Unwin, 1981.

_____. *Explaining International Production*. London: Unwin Hyman, 1988.

_____. *Multinational Enterprises and the Global Economy*. Reading, Mass.: Addison-Wesley, 1992.

_____. *The Globalization of Business*. New York: Routledge, 1993.

_____, ed. *The Multinational Enterprise*. London: Allen and Unwin, 1971.

_____, ed. *Multinational Enterprises, Economic Structure and International Competitiveness*. New York: Wiley, 1985.

_____, ed. The Theory of Transnational Corporations. New York: Routledge, 1993.

Emmott, Bill. *Japan's Global Reach: The Influences, Strategies and Weaknesses of Japan's Multinational Companies*. London: Century, 1991.

Encarnation, Dennis J. *Rivals Beyond Trade: America versus Japan in Global Competition*. Ithaca, N.Y.: Cornell University Press, 1992.

Ethier, Wilfred J. "The Multinational Firm." *Quarterly Journal of Economics* 101 (November 1986): 805–833.

_____, and James R. Markusen. *Multinational Firms, Technology Diffusion and Trade*. Osaka, Japan: Institute of Social and Economic Research, Osaka University, 1993.

Fayerweather, John. "International Transmission of Resources," in John Fayerweather, ed. *International Business Management: A Conceptual Framework*. New York: McGraw-Hill, 1969.

_____. "Elite Attitudes Toward Multinational Firms: A Study of Britain, Canada, and France." *International Studies Quarterly* 16 (December 1972): 472–490.

_____. *Foreign Investment in Canada: Prospects for National Policy*. White Plains, N.Y.: International Arts and Sciences Press, 1973.

Feld, Werner. *Multinational Corporations and U.N. Politics: The Quest for Codes of Conduct*. Elmsford, N.Y.: Pergamon Press, 1980.

Franko, Lawrence G. *The European Multinationals: A Renewed Challenge to American and British Big Business*. New York: Harper and Row, 1976.

Frischtak, Claudio R., and Ricnard S. Newfarmer, eds. *Market Structure and Industrial Performance*. New York: Routledge, 1994.

Froot, Kenneth A., ed. *Foreign Direct Investment*. Chicago: University of Chicago Press, 1993.

———, and Jeremy C. Stein. "Exchange Rates and Foreign Direct Investment: An Imperfect Capital Markets Approach." *Quarterly Journal of Economics* 106 (November 1991): 1191–1217.

Gervais, Jacques. *La France face aux investissements étrangers: Analysé par secteurs*. Paris: Éditions de l'Enterprise Moderne, 1963.

Ghoshal, Sumantra, and D. Eleanor Westney, eds. *Organization Theory and the Multinational Corporation*. New York: St. Martin's Press, 1993.

Gilpin, Robert. *U.S. Power and the Multinational Corporation: The Political Economy of Foreign Direct Investment*. New York: Basic Books, 1975.

Gilroy, Bernard M. *Networking in Multinational Enterprises: the Importance of Strategic Alliances*. Columbia: University of South Carolina Press, 1993.

Goldberg, Paul M., and Charles P. Kindleberger. "Toward a GATT for Investment: A Proposal for Supervision of the International Corporation." *Law and Policy in International Business* 2 (summer 1970): 295–323.

Gourevitch, Peter, and Paolo Guerrieri, eds. *New Challenges to International Cooperation: Adjustment of Firms, Policies and Organizations to Global Competition*. La Jolla: University of California, San Diego, International Relations and Pacific Studies, 1993.

Graham, Edward M., and Michael E. Ebert. "Foreign Direct Investment and National Security: Fixing the Exon-Florio Process." *The World Economy* 14 (September 1991): 245–268.

Graham, Edward M. and Paul R. Krugman. *Foreign Direct Investment in the United States*, 3rd ed. Washington: Institute for International Economics, 1995.

Hedlund, Gunnar, and Lars Otterbeck. *The Multinational Corporation, the Nation State and the Trade Unions: A European Perspective*. Kent, Ohio: Comparative Administration Research Institute, Kent State University, 1977.

Hood, Neil, and Stephen Young. *The Economics of Multinational Enterprise*. London: Longman, 1979.

Huntington, Samuel P. "Transnational Organizations in World Politics." *World Politics* 25 (April 1973): 333–368.

Hymer, Stephen. "The Efficiency (Contradictions) of Multinational Corporations." *American Economic Review* 60 (May 1970): 441–448.

———. *The International Operations of National Firms: A Study of Direct Foreign Investment*. Cambridge: MIT Press, 1976.

———. *The Multinational Corporation: A Radical Approach*. Robert Cohen et al., eds. Cambridge, England: Cambridge University Press, 1979.

Johanson, Jan, et al. *Internationalization, Relationships and Networks*. Uppsala, Sweden: Acta Universitatis Upsaliensis, 1994.

Johnstone, Allan W. *U.S. Direct Investment in France: An Investigation of French Charges*. Cambridge: M.I.T. Press, 1965.

Julius, DeAnne. *Global Companies and Public Policy: The Growing Challenge of Foreign Direct Investment*. London: Pinter, 1990.

Kindleberger, Charles P., ed. *The International Corporation: A Symposium*. Cambridge: MIT Press, 1970.

———, and David B. Audretsch, eds. *The Multinational Corporation in the 1980s*. Cambridge: MIT Press, 1983.

Kobrin, Stephen J. *Managing Political Risk Assessment*. Berkeley: University of California Press, 1982.

Kogut, Bruce, and Sea J. Chang. "Technological Capabilities and Japanese Foreign Direct Investment in the United States." *Review of Economics and Statistics* 73 (August 1991): 401–413.

Kojima, Kiyoshi. *Direct Foreign Investment: A Japanese Model of Multinational Business Operations*. London: Croom Helm, 1978.

Levitt, Kari. *Silent Surrender: The Multinational Corporation in Canada*. New York: St. Martin's, 1970.

Lipson, Charles. *Standing Guard: Protecting Foreign Capital in the Nineteenth and Twentieth Centuries.* Berkeley: University of California Press, 1985.

Litvak, Isaiah A., and Christopher J. Maule, eds. *Foreign Investment: The Experience of Host Countries.* New York: Praeger, 1970.

Lunn, John. "Determinants of United States Direct Investment in the EEC: Further Evidence." *European Economic Review* 13 (January 1980): 93–101.

Magaziner, Ira, and Mark Patinkin. *The Silent War: Inside the Global Business Battles Shaping America's Future.* New York: Vintage, 1989.

Mandel, Ernest. *Europe vs. America: Contradictions of Imperialism.* New York: Monthly Review Press, 1970.

Mason, Mark. *American Multinationals and Japan: The Political Economy of Japanese Capital Controls, 1899–1980.* Cambridge: Harvard University Press, 1992.

_____, and Dennis Encarnation, eds. *Does Ownership Matter? Japanese Multinationals in Europe.* New York: Oxford University Press, 1994.

Moran, Theodore H. *American Economic Policy and National Security.* New York: Council on Foreign Relations, 1993.

_____, ed. *Multinational Corporations: The Political Economy of Foreign Direct Investment.* Lexington, Mass.: Lexington Books, 1985.

_____, ed. *Governments and Transnational Corporations.* New York: Routledge, 1993.

Mowery, David C. *Alliance Politics and Economics: Multinational Joint Ventures in Commercial Aircraft.* Cambridge: Ballinger, 1987.

_____, ed. *Collaborative Ventures in U.S. Manufacturing.* Cambridge, Mass.: Ballinger, 1988.

Mytelka, Lynn K., ed. *Strategic Partnerships: States, Firms, and International Competition.* Rutherford, N.J.: Fairleigh Dickinson University Press, 1991.

Ohmae, Kenichi. *Triad Power.* New York: Free Press, 1985.

_____. *The Borderless World.* New York: Free Press, 1989.

Organization for Economic Cooperation and Development. *National Treatment for Foreign-Controlled Enterprises.* Paris: OECD, 1993.

_____. *The OECD Guidelines for Multinational Enterprises.* Paris: OECD, 1994.

Parkhe, Arvind. "Interfirm Diversity, Organizational Learning, and Longevity in Global Strategic Alliances." *Journal of International Business Studies*, 22 (Fourth Quarter 1991): 579–601.

Patrick, Hugh, and Larry Meissner, eds. *Japan's High Technology Industries: Lessons and Limitations of Industrial Policy.* Seattle: University of Washington Press, 1987.

Pearce, Robert D. *The Growth and Evolution of Multinational Enterprise: Patterns of Geographical and Industrial Diversification.* Brookfield, Vt.: Edward Elgar, 1993.

Prahalad, C. K. and Yves Doz. *The Multinational Mission.* New York: Free Press, 1987.

Reardon, John J. *American and the Multinational Corporation: The History of a Troubled Partnership.* Westport, Conn.: Praeger, 1992.

Reich, Robert B., "Who Is Us?" *Harvard Business Review* 68 (January-February 1990): 53–64.

_____. *The Work of Nations.* New York: Knopf, 1991.

Reich, Simon. "Roads to Follow: Regulating Direct Foreign Investment." *International Organization*, 43 (autumn 1989): 543–584.

Robinson, John. *Multinationals and Political Control.* New York: St. Martin's, 1983.

Rubin, Seymour J. "Developments in the Law and Institutions of International Economic Relations: The Multinational Enterprise at Bay." *The American Journal of International Law* 68 (July 1974): 475–488.

Rugman, Alan M., and Lorraine Eden, eds. *Multinationals and Transfer Pricing.* London: Croom Helm, 1985.

Safarian, Albert E. *Governments and Multinationals: Policies in the Developed Countries.* Washington: British North American Commission, 1983.

_____. *Multinational Enterprise and Public Policy: A Study of the Industrial Countries.* Brookfield, Vt.: Edward Elgar, 1993.

Savary, Julien. *French Multinationals.* New York: St. Martin's Press, 1984.

Servan-Schreiber, Jean-Jacques. *The American Challenge*, Ronald Steel, trans. New York: Atheneum, 1968.

Spencer, Linda M. *American Assets: An Examination of Foreign Investment in the United States.* Arlington, Va.: Congressional Economic Leadership Institute, 1988.

Stopford, John M., and Louis T. Wells. *Managing the Multinational Enterprise.* New York: Basic Books, 1972.

Stopford, John M. and John H. Dunning. *Multinationals: Company Performance and Global Trends.* London: Macmillan, 1983.

Tang, Roger Y. W. *Transfer Pricing in the 1990s: Tax and Management Perspectives.* Westport, Conn.: Quorum, 1993.

Teece, David. *The Multinational Corporation and the Resource Cost of International Technology Transfer.* Cambridge, Mass.: Ballinger, 1986.

Thomsen, Stephen, and Phedon Nicolaides. *The Evolution of Japanese Direct Investment in Europe: Death of a Transistor Salesman.* New York: Harvester Wheatsheaf, 1991.

Thomsen, Stephen, and Stephen Woolcook. *Direct Investment and European Integration.* London: Royal Institute for International Affairs, 1993.

Tolchin, Susan, and Martin Tolchin. *Buying into America: How Foreign Money Is Changing the Face of Our Nation.* New York: Times Books, 1988.

Twomey, Michael J. *Multinational Corporations and the North American Free Trade Agreement.* Westport, Conn.: Praeger, 1993.

United Nations. *Report of the Group of Eminent Persons to Study the Impact of Multinational Corporations on Development and on International Relations.* New York: United Nations, 1974.

U.S. Senate Committee on Foreign Relations. *Multinational Corporations and United States Foreign Policy.* Hearings before the Subcommittee on Multinational Corporations of the Committee on Foreign Relations, 93rd and 94th Congresses, 1973-1976. Washington: Government Printing Office, 1973–1976.

van Tulder, Rob and Gerd Junne. *European Multinationals in Core Technologies.* New York: Wiley, 1988.

Vernon, Raymond. "International Investment and International Trade in the Product Cycle." *Quarterly Journal of Economics* 80 (May 1966): 190–207.

_____. *Sovereignty at Bay: The Multinational Spread of U.S. Enterprises.* New York: Basic,1971.

_____, ed. *Big Business and the State: Changing Relations in Western Europe.* Cambridge: Harvard University Press, 1974.

_____. *Storm Over the Multinationals: The Real Issues.* Cambridge: Harvard University Press, 1977.

_____. "Multinationals: No Strings Attached." *Foreign Policy*, 35 (winter 1978–79): 121–134.

Vogel, Ezra. *Comeback Case by Case: Building the Resurgence of American Business.* New York: Simon and Schuster, 1985.

Wakasugi, Ryuhei. "Is Japanese Foreign Direct Investment a Substitute for International Trade?" *Japan and the World Economy* 6 (May 1994): 45–52.

Wallace, Cynthia Day. *Legal Control of the Multinational Enterprise: National Regulatory Techniques and the Prospects for International Controls.* The Hague, Netherlands: Martinus Nijhoff, 1982.

Weinberg, Paul J. *European Labor and Multinationals.* New York: Praeger, 1978.

Wilkins, Mira. *The Maturing of the Multinational Enterprise: American Business Abroad from 1914 to 1970.* Cambridge: Harvard University Press, 1975.

_____. *The Emergence of Multinational Enterprise: American Business Abroad from the Colonial Era to 1914.* Cambridge: Harvard University Press, 1970.

Williamson, Oliver E. *Markets and Hierarchies.* New York: Free Press, 1975.

_____. *The Economic Institutions of Capitalism: Firms, Markets, and Relational Contracting.* New York: Free Press, 1985.

Womack, James P., Daniel T. Jones, and Daniel Roos. *The Machine That Changed the World.* New York: Rawson Associates, 1990.

Yoshino, Michael. *Japan's Multinational Enterprises.* Cambridge: Harvard University Press, 1976.

Yoon, Young-Kwan. "The Political Economy of Transition: Japanese Foreign Direct Investments in the 1980s." *World Politics* 43 (October 1990): 1–27.

Young, Stephen, Neil Hood, and James Hamill. *Foreign Multinationals and the British Economy.* London: Croom Helm, 1988.

The North-South System

General and Theory

Adelman, Irma and Cynthia Morris. *Economic Growth and Social Equity in Developing Countries.* Stanford: Stanford University Press, 1973.

Amin, Samir. *Accumulation on a World Scale.* New York: Monthly Review Press, 1974.

_____. *Unequal Development: An Essay on the Social Formations of Peripheral Capitalism.* New York: Monthly Review Press, 1976.

_____. *Delinking: Towards a Polycentric World.* London: Zed Books, 1990.

_____. *Intinéraire Intellectuel.* Paris: Éditions L'Harmattan, 1993.

Amsden, Alice H. *Asia's Next Giant: South Korea and Late Industrialization.* New York: Oxford University Press, 1989.

Apter, David E. *Rethinking Development: Modernization, Dependency, and Postmodern Politics.* Newbury Park, Calif.: Sage Publications, 1987.

Arndt, Heinz W. *Economic Development: The History of an Idea.* Chicago: University of Chicago Press, 1987.

Bairoch, Paul. *Révolution industrielle et sous-développement.* Paris: Sedes, 1963.

Balassa, Bela. *Comparative Advantage, Trade Policy and Economic Development.* New York: New York University Press, 1989.

_____. *New Directions in the World Economy.* London: Macmillan, 1989.

Baran, Paul A. *The Political Economy of Growth.* New York: Monthly Review Press, 1957.

_____, and Paul M. Sweezy. *Monopoly Capital: An Essay on the American Economic and Social Order.* New York: Monthly Review Press, 1966.

Barratt-Brown, Michael. *After Imperialism*, rev. ed. New York: Humanities Press, 1970.

_____. *The Economics of Imperialism.* Harmondsworth, England: Penguin, 1974.

Bauer, Peter T. *Dissent on Development: Studies and Debates on Development Economics.* Cambridge: Harvard University Press, 1972.

_____. *Equality, the Third World and Economic Delusion.* Cambridge: Harvard University Press, 1981.

Bernard, Mitchell, and John Ravenhill. "Beyond Product Cycles and Flying Geese: Regionalization, Hierarchy, and the Industrialization of East Asia." *World Politics* 47 (January 1995): 171–209.

Bhagwati, Jagdish N. "Immiserizing Growth: A Geometrical Note." *Review of Economic Studies* 25 (June 1958): 201–205.

_____. *The Economics of Underdeveloped Countries.* New York: McGraw-Hill, 1966.

_____, ed. *The New International Economic Order: The North-South Debate.* Cambridge: M.I.T. Press, 1977.

_____. "Development Economics: What Have We Learned?" *Asian Development Review* 2 (1984): 23–38.

_____. *Essays in Development Economics*, 2 vols. Cambridge: MIT Press, 1985.

_____, and John G. Ruggie, eds. *Power, Passions and Purpose: Prospects for North South Negotiations.* Cambridge: MIT Press, 1984.

Boulding, Kenneth, and Tapan Mukerjee, eds. *Economic Imperialism: A Book of Readings.* Ann Arbor: University of Michigan Press, 1972.

Caporaso, James, ed. "Dependence and Dependency in the Global System." *International Organization* 32 (winter 1978): entire issue.

_____. *A Changing International Division of Labor.* Boulder, Colo.: Lynne Rienner, 1987.

Cardoso, Fernando H., and Enzo Faletto. *Dependency and Development in Latin America.* Marjory Mattingly Urquidi, trans. Berkeley: University of California Press, 1979.

Chenery, Hollis, Montek S. Ahluwalia, C. L. G. Bell, John J. Duloy, and Richard Jolly. *Redistribution with Growth: Policies to Improve Income Distribution in Developing Countries in the Context of Economic Growth.* New York: Oxford University Press for the World Bank, 1974.

_____, Sherman Robinson, and Moshe Syrquin. *Industrialization and Growth.* New York: Oxford University Press for the World Bank, 1986.

_____, and T.N. Srinivasan, eds. *Handbook of Development Economics.* New York: North Holland, 1989.

Chichilnisky, Graciela, and Geoffrey M. Heal. *The Evolving International Economy*. New York: Cambridge University Press, 1987.

Cockcroft, James D., André Gunder Frank, and Dale L. Johnson. *Dependence and Underdevelopment: Latin America's Political Economy*. Garden City, N.Y.: Anchor, 1972.

Cohen, Benjamin J. *The Question of Imperialism: The Political Economy of Dominance and Dependence*. New York: Basic Books, 1973.

Commins, Stephen, ed. *Africa's Development Challenge and the World Bank*. Boulder, Colo.: Lynne Rienner, 1988.

Cox, Robert W. "Ideologies and the New International Economic Order: Reflections on Some Recent Literature." *International Organization* 33 (spring 1979): 257–302.

_____. *Production, Power and World Order: Social Forces in the Making of History*. New York: Columbia University Press, 1987.

Dos Santos, Theotonio. "The Structure of Dependence," in K. T. Fann and D. C. Hodges, eds., *Readings in U.S. Imperialism*. Boston: Sargent, 1971.

Edwards, Sebastián. *From Despair to Hope: Crisis and Economic Reform in Latin America*. New York: Oxford University Press for the World Bank, 1995.

Elsenhans, Hartmut. *Development and Underdevelopment: The History, Economics and Politics of North-South Relations*. 2nd ed. London: Sage, 1991.

Emmanuel, Arghiri. *Unequal Exchange: A Study of the Imperialism of Trade*. New York: Monthly Review Press, 1972.

Erb, Guy F., and Valeriana Kallab, eds. *Beyond Dependence: The Developing World Speaks Out*. New York: Praeger, 1975.

Evans, Henry David. Comparative Advantage and Growth: Trade and Development in Theory and Practice. London: Harvester Wheatsheaf, 1989.

Evans, Peter. *Dependent Development: The Alliance of Multinationals, State and Local Capital in Brazil*. Princeton: Princeton University Press, 1979.

Fajnzylber, Fernando. *Unavoidable Industrial Restructuring in Latin America*. Durham, N.C.: Duke University Press, 1990.

Fann, K. T., and Donald C. Hodges, eds. *Readings in U.S. Imperialism*. Boston: Porter Sargent, 1971.

Feinberg, Richard E., and Valeriana Kallab, eds. *Adjustment Crisis in the Third World*. Washington: Overseas Development Council, 1984.

Findlay, Ronald. "The Terms of Trade and Equilibrium Growth in the World Economy." *American Economic Review*, 70 (June 1980): 291–299.

Fishlow, Albert, Carlos F. Diaz-Alejandro, Richard R. Fagen, and Roger D. Hansen. *Rich and Poor Nations in the World Economy*. New York: McGraw-Hill, 1978.

Frank, Andre Gunder. "The Development of Underdevelopment." *Monthly Review*, 18 (September 1966): 17–31.

_____. *Capitalism and Underdevelopment in Latin America: Historical Studies of Chile and Brazil*, rev. ed. New York: Monthly Review Press, 1969.

_____. *Latin America: Underdevelopment or Revolution*. New York: Monthly Review Press, 1969.

_____. *Crisis in the Third World*. New York: Holmes and Meier, 1981.

Furtado, Celso. *Economic Development of Latin America*. London: Cambridge University Press, 1970.

_____. *The Obstacles to Development in Latin America*. Charles Ekker, trans. Garden City, N.Y.: Anchor, 1970.

Galtung, Johan. "A Structural Theory of Imperialism." *Journal of Peace Research* 8 (1971): 81–117.

Gereffi, Gary, and Donald Wyman, eds. *Manufacturing Miracles: Patterns of Industrialization in Latin America and East Asia*. Princeton, N.J.: Princeton University Press, 1990.

Gosovic, Branislav, and John G. Ruggie. "On the Creation of a New International Economic Order." *International Organization*, 30 (spring 1976): 309–345.

Haberler, Gottfried. *International Trade and Economic Development*. Cairo, Egypt: Bank of Egypt, 1959.

Hadjor, Kofi Buenor, ed. *New Perspectives in North-South Dialogue: Essays in Honour of Olof Palme*. London: I. B. Tauris, 1988.

Haggard, Stephan. *Pathways from the Periphery: The Politics of Growth in Newly Industrializing Countries*. Ithaca, N.Y.: Cornell University Press, 1990.

_____. _Developing Nations and the Politics of Global Integration_. Washington: Brookings Institution, 1995.

_____, Chung H. Lee, and Sylvia Maxfield, eds. _The Politics of Finance in Developing Countries_. Ithaca, N.Y.: Cornell University Press, 1993.

Hansen, Roger D. _Beyond the North-South Stalemate_. New York: McGraw-Hill, 1979.

_____. "North-South Policy—What is the Problem?" _Foreign Affairs_ 58 (summer 1980): 1104–1128.

Haq, Khadija, and Carlos Massad, eds. _Adjustment with Growth: A Search for an Equitable Solution_. Islamabad, Pakistan: North South Roundtable, 1984.

Haq, Mahbub ul. _The Poverty Curtain: Choices for the Third World_. New York: Columbia University Press, 1976.

Hart, Jeffrey A. _The New International Economic Order: Conflict and Co-operation in North-South Economic Relations 1974–77_. New York: St. Martin's, 1983.

Helleiner, Gerald K., ed. _A World Divided: The Less Developed Countries in the International Economy_. New York: Cambridge University Press, 1976.

_____. _The New Global Economy and the Developing Countries: Essays in International Economics and Development_. Brookfield, Vt.: Edward Elgar, 1990.

_____, ed. _Trade Policy, Industrialization, and Development: New Perspectives_. Oxford: Clarendon Press, 1992.

_____, ed. _Trade Policy and Industrialization in Turbulent Times_. New York: Routledge, 1994.

_____, and Carlos F. Díaz-Alejandro. _Handmaiden in Distress: World Trade in the 1980s_. Washington: Overseas Development Council, 1982.

Hirschman, Albert O. _The Strategy of Economic Development_. New Haven: Yale University Press, 1958.

_____. _Development Projects Observed_. Washington: Brookings Institution, 1967.

_____. "The Political Economy of Import-Substituting Industrialization in Latin America." _Quarterly Journal of Economics_ 82 (February 1968): 1–32.

_____. _Journeys Toward Progress: Studies of Economic Policy Making in Latin America_. New York: Norton, 1973.

_____. "Beyond Asymmetry: Critical Notes on Myself as a Young Man and on Some Other Old Friends," _International Organization_ 32 (winter 1978): 45–50.

_____. "The Rise and Decline of Development Economics," in Albert O. Hirschman, _Essays in Trespassing: Economic to Politics and Beyond_. New York: Cambridge University Press, 1981.

Independent Commission on International Development Issues. _North-South: A Programme for Survival_. [Brandt Commission Report.] Cambridge: MIT. Press, 1980.

_____. _Common Crisis North-South: Cooperation for World Recovery_. [Second Brandt Commission Report] Cambridge: MIT Press, 1983.

Ito, Takatoshi, and Anne O. Krueger, eds. _Growth Theories in Light of the East Asian Experience_. Chicago: University of Chicago Press, 1995.

Jalée, Pierre. _The Pillage of the Third World_. Mary Klopper, trans. New York: Monthly Review Press, 1968.

_____. _The Third World in the World Economy_. Mary Klopper, trans. New York: Monthly Review Press, 1969.

_____. _Imperialism in the Seventies_. Raymond and Margaret Sokolov, trans. New York: Third World, 1972.

Jepma, Catrinus J., ed. _North-South Co-operation in Retrospect and Prospect_. New York: Routledge, 1988.

Johnson, Harry G. _Economic Policies Toward Less-Developed Countries_. New York: Praeger, 1967.

Kahler, Miles, ed. _The Politics of International Debt_. Ithaca, N.Y.: Cornell University Press, 1986.

Krasner, Stephen D. _Structural Conflict: The Third World Against Global Liberalism_. Berkeley: University of California Press, 1985.

Krueger, Anne O. _Trade and Employment in Developing Countries_. Chicago: University of Chicago Press, 1981.

_____. _Perspectives on Trade and Development_. Exeter, England: Harvester Wheatsheaf, 1990.

_____. _Economic Policy Reform in Developing Countries: The Kuznets Memorial Lectures at the Economic Growth Center, Yale University_. Cambridge, Mass.: Basil Blackwell, 1992.

Kuznets, Simon. *Economic Growth and Structure*. New York: Norton, 1965.

_____. *Modern Economic Growth: Rate Structure and Spread*. New Haven: Yale University Press, 1966.

_____. *Economic Growth of Nations: Total Output and Production Structure*. Cambridge: Belknap Press of Harvard University Press, 1971.

_____. *Population, Capital, and Growth*. New York: Norton, 1973.

Lal, Deepak. *The Poverty of Development Economics*. Cambridge: Harvard University Press, 1985.

Leamer, Edward E. *Sources of International Comparative Advantage: Theory and Evidence*. Cambridge: MIT Press, 1984.

Lewis, John, and Valeriana Kallab, eds. *Development Strategies Reconsidered*. New Brunswick, N.J.: Transaction Books for the Overseas Development Council, 1986.

Lewis, W. Arthur, "Economic Development with Unlimited Supplies of Labor." *The Manchester School of Economic and Social Studies* 22 (May 1954): 139–191.

_____. *The Theory of Economic Growth*. London: Unwin, 1955.

_____. *The Evolution of the International Economic Order*. Princeton, N.J.: Princeton University Press, 1978.

_____. "The Dual Economy Revisited." *The Manchester School of Economic and Social Studies* 47 (September 1979): 211–229.

Livingston, Steven G. "The Politics of International Agenda-Setting: Reagan and North-South Relations." *International Studies Quarterly* 36 (September 1992): 313–330.

MacEwan, Arthur. "Capitalist Expansion, Ideology and Intervention." *Review of Radical Political Economics* 4 (spring 1972): 36–58.

Magdoff, Harry. *Imperialism: From the Colonial Age to the Present*. New York: Monthly Review Press, 1978.

Markusen, James R., and Randall M. Wigle. "Explaining the Volume of North-South Trade." *Economic Journal* 100 (December 1990): 1206–1215.

Marquez, Jaime, and Peter Pauly. "International Policy Coordination and Growth Prospects of Developing Countries." *Journal of Development Economics* 25 (February 1987): 89–104.

Mehmet, Ozay. *Westernizing the Third World: The Eurocentricity of Economic Development Theories*. New York: Routledge, 1995.

Meier, Gerald M. *International Trade and Development*. New York: Harper and Row, 1963.

_____, and Dudley Seers, eds. *Pioneers in Development*. New York: Oxford University Press, 1984.

Miller, S. M., Roy Bennett, and Cyril Alapatt. "Does the U.S. Economy Require Imperialism?" *Social Policy*, 1 (September-October, 1970): 12–19.

Molana, Hamid, and David Vines. "North-South Growth and the Terms of Trade: A Model on Kaldorian Lines." *Economic Journal* 99 (June 1989): 443–453.

Mortimer, Robert A. *The Third World Coalition in International Politics*, 2nd ed. Boulder, Colo.: Westview, 1984.

Murphy, Craig. *The Emergence of the NIEO Ideology*. Boulder, Colo.: Westview, 1984.

Myint, Hla. *Economic Theory and the Underdeveloped Countries*. New York: Oxford University Press, 1971.

Myrdal, Gunnar. *Rich Lands and Poor: The Road to World Prosperity*. New York: Harper and Row, 1957.

_____. *An International Economy: Problems and Prospects*. New York: Harper and Row, 1956.

_____. *Economic Theory and Underdeveloped Regions*. London: Duckworth, 1957.

_____. *The Challenge of World Poverty*. London: Pelican, 1970.

Nabudere, Dan M. The Political Economy of Imperialism. London: Zed Press, 1977.

Nurkse, Ragnar. *Equilibrium and Growth in the World Economy: Economic Essays*. Cambridge: Harvard University Press, 1961.

_____. *Problems of Capital Formation for Underdeveloped Countries*. New York: Oxford University Press, 1953.

O'Donnell, Guillermo. *Modernization and Bureaucratic-Authoritarianism: Studies in South American Politics*. Berkeley: Institute of International Studies, 1973.

Pearson, Lester B. *Partners in Development: Report of the Commission on International Development*. New York: Praeger, 1969.

Prebisch, Raúl. *The Economic Development of Latin America and Its Principal Problems*. New York: United Nations, 1950.

Review of Radical Political Economy. "Dependence and Foreign Domination," 4 (winter 1972): entire volume.

Review of Radical Political Economy. "Facing the 1980s: New Directions in the Theory of Imperialism," 11 (winter 1979): entire volume.

Ranis, Gustav, and T. Paul Schultz, eds. *The State of Development Economics*. Oxford: Basil Blackwell, 1988.

Rosen, Steven J., and James R. Kurth, eds. *Testing Theories of Economic Imperialism*. Lexington, Mass.: Lexington Books, 1974.

Rostow, Walt W. *The Stages of Economic Growth: A Non-Communist Manifesto*. Cambridge, England: Cambridge University Press, 1962.

———. *Politics and the Stages of Growth*. Cambridge, England: Cambridge University Press, 1971.

———. *Theorists of Economic Growth from David Hume to the Present*. New York: Oxford University Press, 1990.

Rothstein, Robert L. *The Weak in the World of the Strong: The Developing Countries in the International System*. New York: Columbia University Press, 1977.

———. *Global Bargaining: UNCTAD and the Quest for a New International Economic Order*. Princeton: Princeton University Press, 1979.

———. "Regime-Creation by a Coalition of the Weak: Lessons from the NIEO and the Integrated Program for Commodities." *International Studies Quarterly* 28 (September 1984): 307–328.

———. "Epitaph for a Monument to a Failed Protest? A North-South Retrospective." *International Organization* 42 (autumn 1988): 725–750.

Ruggie, John G., ed. *Antinomies of Interdependence: National Welfare and the International Division of Labor*. New York: Columbia University Press, 1983.

Sapsford, David, Prabirjit Sarkar, and Hans W. Singer. "The Prebisch-Singer Terms of Trade Controversy Revisited." *Journal of International Development* 4 (May-June 1992): 315–332.

Sarkar, Prabirjit. "The Singer-Prebisch Hypothesis: A Statistical Evaluation." *Cambridge Journal of Economics* 10 (December 1986): 355–371.

———. "North-South Terms of Trade and Growth: A Macroeconomic Framework on Kaldorian Lines." *World Development* 22 (November 1994): 1711–1715.

Singer, Hans W. *International Development: Growth and Change*. New York: McGraw-Hill, 1964.

Sklair, Leslie, ed. *Capitalism and Development*. New York: Routledge, 1994.

The South Commission. *The Challenge to the South: The Report of the South Commission*. New York: Oxford University Press, 1990.

Stewart, Frances. *North-South and South-South: Essays on International Economics*. New York: St. Martin's Press, 1992.

Sunkel, Osvaldo. "National Development Policy and External Dependence in Latin America." *Journal of Development Studies* 6 (October 1969): 23–48.

———. "Big Business and Dependence: A Latin American View." *Foreign Affairs* 50 (April 1972): 517–532.

Swatuk, Larry A., and Timothy M. Shaw, eds. *The South at the End of the Twentieth Century: Rethinking the Political Economy of Foreign Policy in Africa, Asia, the Caribbean and Latin America*. New York: St. Martin's Press, 1994.

Sweezy, Paul M. *Modern Capitalism and Other Essays*. New York: Monthly Review Press, 1972.

Szymanski, Al. "Capital Accumulation on a World Scale and the Necessity of Imperialism." *The Insurgent Sociologist* 7 (spring 1977): 35–53.

Taylor, Lance. *Structural Macroeconomics: Applicable Models for the Third World*. New York: Basic Books, 1983.

Thirlwall, Anthony P. "A General Model of Growth and Development Along Kaldorian Lines." *Oxford Economic Papers* 38 (July 1986): 199–219.

Uri, Pierre. *Development Without Dependence*. New York: Praeger, 1976.

Viaggi, Gianni, ed. *From the Debt Crisis to Sustainable Development: Changing Perspectives on North-South Relations*. New York: St. Martin's Press, 1993.

Wade, Robert. *Governing the Market: Economic Theory and the Role of Government in East Asian*

Industrialization. Princeton: Princeton University Press, 1990.

Wallerstein, Immanuel. "Dependence in an Interdependent World." *African Studies Review* 17 (April 1974): 1–26.

_____. *The Capitalist World Economy*. Cambridge, England: Cambridge University Press, 1979.

Weiss, Thomas G. *Multilateral Development Diplomacy in UNCTAD: The Lessons of Group Negotiations, 1964–84*. New York: St. Martin's Press, 1986.

Weisskopf, Thomas E. "Theories of American Imperialism: A Critical Evaluation." *Review of Radical Political Economics* 6 (fall 1974): 41–60.

Williams, Marc. *Third World Cooperation: The Group of 77 in UNCTAD*. New York: St. Martin's Press, 1991.

Wood, Adrian. *North-South Trade, Employment and Inequality; Changing Fortunes in a Skill-Driven World*. Oxford: Clarendon Press, 1994.

North-South Aid/International Financial Flows

Altvater, Elmar, Kurt Hübner, Jochen Lorentzen, and Raúl Rojas, eds. *The Poverty of Nations: A Guide to the Debt Crisis from Argentina to Zaire*. Terry Bond, trans. London: Zed Books, 1991.

Arnau, J. Sanchez, ed. *Debt and Development in Latin America*. New York: Praeger, 1982.

Ayres, Robert L. *Banking on the Poor*. Cambridge: MIT Press, 1984.

Bacha, Edmar Lisboa, and Carlos F. Díaz-Alejandro. *International Financial Intermediation: A Long and Tropical View*, Essays in International Finance, n. 47. Princeton: Princeton University, International Finance Section; May 1982.

Baldwin, David A. *Economic Development in American Foreign Policy, 1943–1962*. Chicago: University of Chicago Press, 1966.

Bandow, Doug, and Ian Vásquez, eds. *Perpetuating Poverty: The World Bank, the IMF, and the Developing World*. Washington: Cato Institute, 1994.

Bhagwati, Jagdish N., and Richard E. Eckans, eds. *Foreign Aid*. Harmondsworth, England: Penguin, 1970.

Bird, Graham. *The International Monetary System and the Less Developed Countries*. London: Macmillan, 1978.

_____. *IMF Lending to Developing Countries: Issues and Evidence*. New York: Routledge, 1995.

Bitterman, Henry J. "Negotiation of the Bank for Reconstruction and Development." *The International Lawyer* 5 (January 1971): 59–88.

Bogdanowicz-Bindert, Christine A., ed. *Solving the Global Debt Crisis: Strategies and Controversies by Key Stakeholders*. New York: Harper and Row, 1989.

Browne, Stephen. *Foreign Aid in Practice*. New York: New York University Press, 1990.

Calvo, Guillermo, Ronald Findley, Pentti Kouri, and Jorge Barga de Macedo, eds. *Debt, Stabilization, and Development*. Cambridge, Mass.: Basil Blackwell, 1989.

Campbell, Bonnie K., ed. *Political Dimensions of the International Debt Crisis*. New York: St. Martin's Press, 1989.

Cassen, Robert, et al. *Does Aid Work? Report to an Intergovernmental Task Force*. Oxford: Clarendon Press, 1986.

Cline, William R. "Mexico's Crisis, the World's Peril." *Foreign Policy* 49 (winter 1982–83): 107–120.

_____. *International Debt Reexamined*. Washington: Institute for International Economics, 1995.

Conteh-Morgan, Earl. *American Foreign Aid and Global Power Projection: The Geopolitics of Resource Allocation*. Brookfield, Vt.: Dartmouth, 1990.

Devlin, Robert. *Debt and Crisis in Latin America: The Supply Side of the Story*. Princeton: Princeton University Press, 1989.

Dinwiddy, Bruce, ed. *European Development Policies: The United Kingdom, Sweden, France, EEC, and Multilateral Organizations*. London: Praeger for the Overseas Development Institute, 1973.

Dooley, Michael P., Eduardo Fernandez-Arias, and Kenneth Kletzer. *Is the Debt Crisis History?: Recent Private Capital Inflows to Developing Countries*. Washington: World Bank, International Economics Department, Debt and International Finance Division, July 1994.

Dornbusch, Rudiger. *Stabilization, Debt, and Reform: Policy Analysis for Developing Countries*. Englewood Cliffs, N.J.: Prentice-Hall, 1993.

_____, and Sebastián Edwards, eds. *The Macroeconomics of Populism in Latin America*. Chicago: University of Chicago Press, 1991.

Eaton, Jonathan, and Mark Gersovitz. "Debt with Potential Repudiation: Theoretical and Empirical Analysis." *Review of Economic Studies* 48 (April 1981): 481–513.

_____, Mark Gersovitz, and Joseph E. Stiglitz. "The Pure Theory of Country Risk." *European Economic Review* 30 (June 1986): 481–513.

Eberstadt, Nick. *U.S. Foreign Aid Policy: A Critique*. New York: Foreign Policy Association, 1990.

Edwards, Sebastián. "LDC Foreign Borrowing and Default Risk: An Empirical Investigation, 1976–1980." *American Economic Review*, 74 (September 1984), 726–734.

_____. *The Debt Crisis and Economic Adjustment in Latin America*. *Latin American Research Review* 24 (1989): 172–186.

_____. *The Latin American Debt Crisis*. Washington: World Bank, 1994.

_____, and Felipe Larraín, eds. Debt, Adjustment, and Recovery: Latin America's Prospects for Growth and Development. Oxford: Basil Blackwell, 1989.

Eichengreen, Barry J., and Peter H. Lindert, eds. *The International Debt Crisis in Historical Perspective*. Cambridge: MIT Press, 1989.

Ensign, Margee M. *Doing Good or Doing Well?: Japan's Foreign Aid Program*. New York: Columbia University Press, 1992.

Feinberg, Richard E., and Valeriana Kallab, eds. *Between Two Worlds: The World Bank's Next Decade*. New Brunswick, N.J.: Transaction Books, 1986.

Felix, David, ed. *Debt and Transfiguration? Prospects for Latin America's Economic Revival*. New York: M. E. Sharpe, 1990.

Fletcher, Lehman B., ed. *World Food in the 1990s: Production, Trade, and Aid*. Boulder, Colo.: Westview, 1992.

Frieden, Jeffry A. *Debt, Development, and Democracy: Modern Political Economy and Latin America, 1965–1985*. Princeton: Princeton University Press, 1991.

_____. "International Investment and Colonial Control: A New Interpretation." *International Organization* 48 (Autumn 1994): 559–594.

Gates, Marilyn. *In Default: Peasants, the Debt Crisis, and the Agricultural Challenge in Mexico*. Boulder, Colo.: Westview, 1993.

George, Susan. *The Debt Boomerang: How Third World Debt Harms Us All*. Boulder, Colo.: Westview, 1992.

Grilli, Enzo R. *The European Community and the Developing Countries*. New York: Cambridge University Press, 1993.

Gwin, Catherine. *U.S. Relations with the World Bank 1945–92*. Washington: Brookings Institution, 1994.

Haggard, Stephan, and Robert R. Kaufman, eds. *The Politics of Economic Adjustment: International Constraints, Distributive Conflicts, and the State*. Princeton: Princeton University Press, 1992.

_____, and Steven B. Webb, eds. *Voting for Reform: Democracy, Political Liberalization and Economic Adjustment*. New York: Oxford University Press, 1994.

Hayter, Teresa. *Aid as Imperialism*. Harmondsworth, England: Penguin, 1971.

_____. *Aid: Rhetoric and Reality*. London: Pluto, 1985.

Hurni, Bettina S. *The Lending Policy of the World Bank in the 1970s*. Boulder, Colo.: Westview, 1980.

Hyden, Goran. *From Bargaining to Marketing: How to Reform Foreign Aid in the 1990s*. East Lansing, Mich.: Department of Political Science, Michigan State University, 1993.

Islam, Shafiqul, ed. *Yen for Development: Japanese Foreign Aid and the Politics of Burden-Sharing*. New York: Council on Foreign Relations Press, 1991.

Kahler, Miles, ed. *The Politics of International Debt*. Ithaca, N.Y.: Cornell University Press, 1986.

Kaminsky, Graciela L. *The Debt Crisis: Lessons of the 1980's for the 1990s*. Washington: Board of Governors of the Federal Reserve System, 1994.

Kelleo, Peter M., with Nessanke E. Weerasinghe. *Multilateral Official Debt Rescheduling: Recent Experiences*. Washington: International Monetary Fund, 1988.

Killick, Tony. *The IMF and Stabilization: Developing Country Experiences*. New York: St. Martin's, 1984.

Krueger, Anne O. *Economic Policies at Cross Purposes: The United States and Developing Countries*. Washington: Brookings Institution, 1993.

Krugman, Paul. "Financing vs. Forgiving a Debt Overhang: Some Analytical Notes." *Journal of Development Economics*, 29 (November 1988), 253-268.

_____. "LDC Debt Policy," in Martin Feldstein, ed., *American Economic Policy in the 1980s*. Chicago: University of Chicago Press, 1994.

Kuczynski, Pedro-Pablo. *Latin American Debt*. Baltimore: Johns Hopkins University Press, 1988.

Lancaster, Carol, and John Williamson, eds. *African Debt and Financing*. Washington: Institute for International Economics, 1986.

Lehman, Howard P. *Indebted Development: Strategic Bargaining and Economic Adjustment in the Third World*. New York: St. Martin's Press, 1993.

Lehman, Howard P., and Jennifer L. McCoy. "The Dynamics of the Two-Level Bargaining Game: The 1988 Brazilian Debt Negotiations." *World Politics* 44 (July 1992): 600–644.

Lessard, Donald R., and John Williamson. *Capital Flight and Third World Debt*. Washington: Institute for International Economics, 1987.

Levinson, Jerome, and Juan de Onis. *The Alliance that Lost its Way: A Critical Report on the Alliance for Progress*. New York: Quadrangle, 1970.

Lewis, John P. *Pro-Poor Aid Conditionality*. Washington: Overseas Development Council, 1992.

_____, *U.S. Foreign Policy and the Third World: Agenda 1983*. New York: Praeger for the Overseas Development Council, 1983.

_____, *Development Strategies Reconsidered*. New Brunswick, N.J.: Transaction Books, 1986.

Lissakers, Karen. *Banks, Borrowers, and the Establishment: A Revisionist Account of the International Debt Crisis*. New York: Basic Books, 1991.

Little, Ian M. D., and Juliet M. Clifford. *International Aid: A Discussion of the Flow of Public Resources from Rich to Poor Countries, with Particular Reference to British Policy*. London: Allen and Unwin, 1965.

Lumsdaine, David H. *Moral Vision in International Politics: The Foreign Aid Regime 1949–1989*. Princeton: Princeton University Press, 1993.

Madrid, Raúl L. *Overexposed: U.S. Banks Confront the Third World Debt Crisis*. Boulder, Colo.: Westview, 1992.

Makin, John H. *The Global Debt Crisis: America's Growing Involvement*. New York: Basic Books, 1984.

Marichal, Carlos. *A Century of Debt Crises in Latin America*. Princeton: Princeton University Press, 1989.

Mason, Edward S., and Robert E. Asher. *The World Bank Since Bretton Woods*. Washington: Brookings Institution, 1973.

Maxfield, Sylvia. *Governing Capital: International Finance and Mexican Politics*. Ithaca, N.Y.: Cornell University Press, 1990.

McNeill, Desmond. *The Contradictions of Foreign Aid*. London: Croom Helm, 1981.

Meller, Patricio, ed. *Latin American Development Debate: Neostructuralism, Neomonetarism, and Adjustment Proceses*. Boulder, Colo.: Westview, 1991.

Milivoljevic, Marko. *The Debt Rescheduling Process*. New York: St. Martin's Press, 1985.

Miller, Norman C. *International Reserves, Exchange Rates, and Developing Country Finance*. Lexington, Mass.: Lexington Books, 1982.

Millikan, Max F., and Walt W. Rostow. *A Proposal: Key to an Effective Foreign Policy*. New York: Harper and Row, 1957.

Mosley, Paul. "The Political Economy of Foreign Aid: A Model of the Market for a Public Good." *Economic Development and Cultural Change* 33 (January 1985): 373–393.

_____. *Overseas Aid: Its Defense and Reform*. Brighton: Harvester Wheatsheaf, 1987.

Muscatelli, Vito Antonio, and David Vines. "Third World Debt and Macroeconomic Interactions Between the North and the South." *Journal of Development Studies* 27 (April 1991): 146–166.

Nafziger, E. Wayne. *The Debt Crisis in Africa*. Baltimore: Johns Hopkins University Press, 1993.

Nelson, Joan M. *Aid, Influence and Foreign Policy*. New York: Macmillan, 1968.

_____. *Fragile Coalitions: The Politics of Economic Adjustment*. New Brunswick, N.J.: Transaction Books for the Overseas Development Council, 1989.

_____. *Global Goals, Contentious Means: Issues of Multiple Aid Conditionality*. Washington: Overseas Development Council, 1993.

_____, and Stephanie J. Eglinton. *Encouraging Democracy: What Role for Conditional Aid?* Washington: Overseas Development Council, 1992.

Ohlin, Goran. *Foreign Aid Policies Reconsidered.* Paris: OECD, 1966.

O'Hanlon, Michael E. *Enhancing U.S. Security Through Foreign Aid.* Washington: U.S. Congress, Congressional Budget Office, 1994.

Organization for Economic Cooperation and Development. *Twenty-five Years of Development Cooperation.* Paris: OECD, 1985.

Orr, Robert M., Jr. *The Emergence of Japan's Foreign Aid Power.* New York: Columbia University Press, 1990.

Paarlberg, Robert L., "U.S. Agriculture and the Developing World." *Growth, Exports and Jobs in a Changing World Economy: Agenda 1988.* New Brunswick, N.J.: Transaction Books, 1988.

Packenham, R. A. *Liberal America and the Third World: Political Development Ideas in Foreign Aid and Social Science,* Princeton: Princeton University Press, 1973.

Pant, Girish P. *Foreign Aid, Economic Growth, and Cost-Benefit Analysis: Some Experiences from Nepal.* Brookfield, Vt.: Avebury, 1991.

Payer, Cheryl. *The Debt Trap: The International Monetary Fund and the Third World.* New York: Monthly Review Press, 1974.

_____. *Lent and Lost: Foreign Credit and Third World Development.* London: Zed Books, 1991.

Porter, David. *U.S. Economic Foreign Aid: A Case Study of the United States Agency for International Development.* New York: Garland, 1990.

Pratt, Cranford, ed. *Internationalism under Strain: The North-South Policies of Canada, the Netherlands, Norway, and Sweden.* (Toronto: University of Toronto Press, 1989.

_____, ed. *Middle Power Internationalism: The North-South Dimension.* Kingston, Ontario: McGill-Queen's University Press, 1990.

Ray, Edward J. *U.S. Protectionism and the World Debt Crisis.* New York: Quorum Books, 1989.

Remmer, Karen L. "The Politics of Economic Stabilization: IMF Standby Programs in Latin America, 1954–1984." *Comparative Politics* 19 (October 1986): 1–25.

Riddell, Roger C. *Foreign Aid Reconsidered.* Baltimore: Johns Hopkins University Press, 1987.

Riley, Stephen P., ed. *The Politics of Global Debt.* Houndsmills, Basingstoke, England: Macmillan, 1993.

Rix, Alan. *Japan's Foreign Aid Challenge: Policy Reform and Aid Leadership.* New York: Routledge, 1993.

Rostow, Walt W. *Eisenhower, Kennedy, and Foreign Aid.* Austin: University of Texas Press, 1985.

Sachs, Jeffrey D., ed. *Developing Country Debt and the World Economy.* Chicago: University of Chicago Press, 1989.

_____, and Susan M. Collins, eds. *Developing Country Debt and Economic Performance.* Chicago: University of Chicago Press, 1989.

_____, and Harry Huizinga. "U.S. Commercial Banks and the Developing Country Debt Crisis," *Brookings Papers on Economic Activity,* vol. 2. Washington: Brookings Institution, 1987.

Sampson, Anthony. *The Money Lenders: The People and Politics of The World Banking Crisis.* Harmondsworth, England: Penguin, 1983 (originally published by Viking Books in 1981).

Sewell, John W., Richard E. Feinberg, and Valeriana Kallab, eds. *U.S. Foreign Policy and the Third World: Agenda 1985–6.* New York: Praeger for the Overseas Development Council, 1986.

Singer, Hans W., John Wood, and Tony Jennings. *Food Aid: The Challenge and the Opportunity.* New York: Oxford University Press, 1987.

Smith, Brian. *More than Altruism: The Politics of Private Foreign Aid.* Princeton: Princeton University Press, 1990.

Spindler, J. Andrew. *The Politics of International Credit: Private Finance and Foreign Policy in Germany and Japan.* Washington: Brookings Institution, 1984.

Stallings, Barbara. *Banker to the Third World: U.S. Portfolio Investment in Latin America, 1900–1986.* Berkeley, Calif.: University of California Press, 1987.

_____, and Robert R. Kaufmann, eds. *Debt and Democracy in Latin America.* Boulder, Colo.: Westview Press, 1989.

Tisch, Sarah J., and Michael B. Wallace. *Dilemmas of Development Assistance: The What, Why and Who of Foreign Aid.* Boulder, Colo.: Westview, 1994.

Uvin, Peter. "Regime, Surplus, and Self-Interest: The International Politics of Food Aid." *International Studies Quarterly* 36 (September 1992): 293–312.

U.S. Senate. *Foreign Aid Program*, 1957. 85th Congress, 1st sess. Washington: Government Printing Office, 1957.

Vos, Rob. *The World Economy, Debt and Adjustment: Structural Asymmetries in North-South Interactions*. London: Macmillan, 1993.

_____. "Aid Flows and the International Transfer Problem in a Structuralist North-South Model." *Economic Journal* 103 (March 1993): 494–508.

Wall, David. *The Charity of Nations: The Political Economy of Foreign Aid*. New York: Basic Books, 1973.

Walters, Robert S. *American and Soviet Aid: A Comparative Analysis*. Pittsburgh: University of Pittsburgh Press, 1970.

Weeks, John F., ed. *Debt Disaster?: Banks, Governments and Multilaterals Confront the Crisis*. New York: New York University Press, 1989.

Wellons, Philip A. *Passing the Buck: Banks, Governments and Third World Debt*. Boston: Harvard Business School Press, 1986.

Williamson, John. *The Lending Policies of the International Monetary Fund*. Washington: Institute for International Economics, 1982.

_____. *IMF Conditionality*. Cambridge: MIT Press, 1983.

_____. "Debt Crisis: Lessons of the 1980s." *Asian Development Review* 9 (1991): 1–13. and Donald Lessard, eds. *Capital Flight and Third World Debt*. Washington: Institute for International Economics, 1987.

Wright-Neville, David. *The Evolution of Japanese Foreign Aid 1955–1990*. Clayton, Australia: Monash Development Studies Center, Monash University, 1991.

North-South and South-South Trade

Alting von Geusau, Frans A. M., ed. *The Lomé Convention and a New International Economic Order*. Leiden, the Netherlands: A.W. Sijthoff, 1977.

Araim, Amer Salih. *Intergovernmental Commodity Organizations and the New International Economic Order*. New York: Praeger, 1991.

Behrman, Jere R. *Foreign Trade Regimes and Economic Development: Chile*. New York: Columbia University Press, 1976.

_____. *International Commodity Agreements*. Washington: Overseas Development Council, 1977.

Belassa, Bela. "Trade Policies in Developing Countries." *American Economic Review* 61 (May 1971): 178–210.

_____. "The Developing Countries and the Tokyo Round." *Journal of World Trade Law*, 14 (March-April 1980): 93–118.

Blandford, David, Colin A. Carter, and Roley Piggott, eds. *North-South Grain Markets and Trade Policies*. Boulder, Colo.: Westview, 1993.

Campos, Roberto de Oliveiro, et al. *Trends in International Trade: A Report by a Panel of Experts*. [Haberler Report]. Geneva: The Contracting Parties to the General Agreement on Tariffs and Trade, October 1958.

Chimni, B. S. *International Commodity Agreements: A Legal Study*. New York: Croom Helm, 1987.

Cordovez, Diego. "The Making of UNCTAD: Institutional Background and Legislative History." *Journal of World Trade Law* 1 (May-June 1967): 243–328.

_____. *UNCTAD and Development Diplomacy: From Confrontation to Strategy*. Twickenham, England: Journal of World Trade Law, 1970.

Corea, Gamani. *Taming Commodity Markets: The Integrated Program and the Common Fund in UNCTAD*. New York: St. Martin's Press for Manchester University Press, 1992.

Finlayson, Jock A., and Mark W. Zacher. *Managing International Markets: Developing Countries and the International Trading Regimes*. New York: Columbia University Press, 1988.

Folke, Steen, Niels Fold and Thyge Enevoldsen. *South-South Trade and Development: Manufactures in the New International Division of Labor*. New York: St. Martin's Press, 1993.

Frank, Isaiah. "The 'Graduation' Issue for the Less Developed Countries." *Journal of World Trade Law* 13 (July-August 1979): 289–302.

Friedeberg, Alfred S. *The United Nations Conference on Trade and Development of 1964: The Theory of the Peripheral Economy.* Rotterdam, the Netherlands: Rotterdam University Press, 1969.

Gereffi, Gary. "The 'Old' and 'New' Maquiladora Industries In Mexico: What Is Their Contribution to National Development and North American Integration?" *Nuestra economía* 3 (May-August 1991): 39–63.

———, and Miguel Korzeniewicz, eds. *Commodity Chains and Global Capitalism.* Westport, Conn.: Greenwood Press, 1994.

Goodwin, Geoffrey, and James Mayall, eds. *A New International Commodity Regime.* New York: St. Martin's, 1980.

Gosovic, Branislav. *UNCTAD, Conflict and Compromise: The Third World's Quest for an Equitable World Economic Order Through the United Nations.* Leiden, the Netherlands: A.W. Sijthoff, 1972.

Gruhn, Isebill V. "The Lomé Convention: Inching Towards Interdependence." *International Organization* 30 (spring 1976): 240–262.

Haberler, Gottfried. *International Trade and Economic Development.* Cairo, Egypt: National Bank of Egypt, 1959.

Henderson, Jeffrey. *The Globalization of High Technology Production: Society, Space and Semiconductors in the Restructuring of the Modern World.* New York: Routledge, 1989.

Hudec, Robert. *Developing Countries in the GATT Legal System.* London: Trade Policy Research Center, 1987.

Krueger, Anne O. *Trade Policies and Developing Nations.* Washington: Brookings Institution, 1995.

Langhammer, Rolf J., and André Sapir. *Economic Impact of Generalized Tariff Preferences.* London: Trade Policy Research Center, 1987.

Law, Alton D. *International Commodity Agreements.* Lexington, Mass.: Lexington Books, 1975.

Levin, Jonathan V. *The Export Economies: Their Pattern of Development in Historical Perspective.* Cambridge: Harvard University Press, 1964.

Linden, Steffan B. "The Significance of GATT for Underdeveloped Countries." *Proceedings of the United Nations Conference on Trade and Development* 5 (1964): 502–532.

Linnemann, Hans, ed. *South-South Preferences: The GSTP and Trade in Manufactures.* New Delhi, India: Sage, 1992.

Lister, Marjorie. *The European Community and the Developing World: The Role of the Lomé Convention.* Brookfield, Vt.: Avebury, 1988.

Lord, Montague J. *Imperfect Competition and International Commodity Trade: Theory, Dynamics, and Policy Modelling.* Oxford: Clarendon Press, 1991.

Madeley, John. *Trade and the Poor: The Impact of International Trade on Developing Countries.* New York: St. Martin's Press, 1993.

Maizels, Alfred. *Exports and Economic Growth of Developing Countries: A Theoretical and Empirical Study of the Relationship Between Exports and Economic Growth.* London: Cambridge University Press, 1968.

———. *Commodities in Crisis: The Commodity Crisis of the 1980s and the Political Economy of International Commodity Prices.* Oxford: Clarendon Press, 1992.

McMullen, Neil, and Louis Turner with Colin L. Bradford. *The Newly Industrializing Countries: Trade and Adjustment.* London: Allen and Unwin, 1982.

McNicol, David L. *Commodity Agreements and Price Stabilization.* Lexington, Mass.: Lexington Books, 1978.

Meadows, Donella H., Dennis L. Meadows, Jorgen Randers, and William W. Behrens, III. *The Limits to Growth: A Report for the Club of Rome's Project on the Predicament of Mankind,* 2nd ed. New York: Universe Books, 1972.

Michaely, Michael, Demetris Papageorgiou, and Armeane M. Choksi. *Liberalizing Foreign Trade: Lessons of Experience from Developing Countries.* Oxford: Basil Blackwell for the World Bank, 1991.

Milner, Chris, ed. *Export Promotion Strategies: Theory and Evidence from Developing Countries.* New York: New York University Press, 1990.

Murray, Tracy. *Trade Preferences for Developing Countries.* New York: Wiley, 1977.

Nappi, Carmine. *Commodity Market Controls.* Lexington, Mass.: Lexington Books, 1979.

Nurkse, Ragnar. *Patterns of Trade and Development.* New York: Oxford University Press, 1961.

O'Donnell, Christopher. *Commodity Price Stabilization: An Empirical Analysis*. Brookfield, Vt.: Avebury, 1993.

Oman, Charles. *Globalization and Regionalization: The Challenge for Developing Countries*. Paris: Development Center, OECD, 1994.

Organization for Economic Cooperation and Development. *The Newly Industrializing Countries: Challenge and Opportunity for OECD Countries*. Paris: OECD, 1988.

Page, Sheila. *How Developing Countries Trade: The Institutional Constraints*. New York: Routledge, 1994.

Payer, Cheryl. *Commodity Trade of the Third World*. London: Macmillan, 1975.

Prebisch, Raul. "The Role of Commercial Policies in Underdeveloped Countries." *American Economic Review, Papers and Proceedings* 49 (May 1959): 251–273.

Preeg, Ernest H., ed. *Hard Bargaining Ahead; U.S. Trade Policy and Developing Countries*. New Brunswick, N.J.: Transaction Books, 1985.

Raghavan, Charkravarthi. *Recolonization: GATT, the Uruguay Round and the Third World*. Atlantic Highlands, N.J.: Zed Books, 1990.

Ravenhill, John. *Collective Clientelism: The Lomé Conventions and North-South Relations*. New York: Columbia University Press, 1985.

Reynolds, Paul D. *International Commodity Agreements and the Common Fund*. Lexington, Mass.: Lexington Books, 1978.

Sell, Susan K. "Intellectual Property Protection and Antitrust in the Developing World: Crisis, Coercion, and Choice." *International Organization* 49 (spring 1995): 315–350.

Sengupta, Arjun, ed. *Commodities, Finance and Trade: Issues in North-South Negotiations*. Westport, Conn.: Greenwood, 1980.

Sewell, John, Stuart K. Tucker, and contributors. *Growth, Exports and Jobs in a Changing World Economy: Agenda 1988*. New Brunswick, N.J.: Transaction Books, 1988.

Streeten, Paul, ed. *Toward a New Trade Policy for Development*. New York: United Nations, 1964.

_____. *Trade Strategies for Development: Papers of the Ninth Cambridge Conference on Development Problems, September 1972*. New York: Wiley, 1973.

Tussie, Diana. *The Less Developed Countries and the World Trading System: A Challenge to the GATT*. London: Frances Pinter, 1987.

Vastine, J. Robert, Jr. "United States International Commodity Policy." *Law and Policy in International Business* 9 (1977): 401–477.

Ventura-Dias, Vivianne, ed. *South-South Trade: Trends, Issues, and Obstacles to Its Growth*. New York: Praeger, 1989.

Whalley, John, ed. *Developing Countries and the Global Trading System*, 2 vols. Ann Arbor: University of Michigan Press, 1989.

Yamazawa, Ippei. *International Trade and Economic Development: A Japanese Model*. Honolulu: University of Hawaii Press, 1990.

Yoffie, David. *Power and Protectionism: Strategies of the Newly Industrializing Countries*. New York: Columbia University Press, 1983.

Foreign Investment in Less-Developed Countries

Adler, Emanuel. *The Power of Ideology: The Quest for Technological Autonomy in Argentina and Brazil*. Berkeley: University of California Press, 1987.

Alschuler, Lawrence R. *Multinationals and Maldevelopment*. New York: St. Martin's Press, 1988.

Andersson, Thomas. *Multinational Investment in Developing Countries: A Study of Taxation and Nationalization*. New York: Routledge, 1991.

Becker, David. *The New Bourgeoisie and the Limits of Dependency: Mining, Class, and Power in Revolutionary Peru*. Princeton: Princeton University Press, 1983.

Bennett, Douglas, and Kenneth Sharpe. *Transnational Corporations versus the State: The Political Economy of the Mexican Auto Industry*. Princeton: Princeton University Press, 1985.

Biersteker, Thomas. *Distortion or Development? Contending Perspectives on the Multinational Corporation*. Cambridge: MIT Press, 1978.

_____. *Multinationals, the State and Control of the Nigerian Economy*. Princeton: Princeton University Press, 1987.

Bornschier, Volker, and Christopher Chase-Dunn. *Transnational Corporations and Underdevelopment*. New York: Praeger, 1985.

Chan, Steve, ed. *Foreign Direct Investment in a Changing Global Political Economy*. London: Macmillan, 1995.

Chen, Edward K. Y., ed. *Technology Transfer to Developing Countries*. New York: Routledge for the UNCTAD Program on Transnational Corporations, 1994.

Doner, Richard F. *Driving a Bargain: Automobile Industrialization and Japanese Firms in Southeast Asia*. Berkeley: University of California Press, 1991.

Encarnation, Dennis J. *Dislodging Multinationals: India's Strategy in Comparative Perspective*. Ithaca, N.Y.: Cornell University Press, 1989.

———, and Louis T. Wells, Jr. "Sovereignty en Garde: Negotiating with Foreign Investors." *International Organization* 39 (winter 1985): 47–78.

Evans, Peter. *Dependent Development: The Alliance of Multinational, State, and Local Capital in Brazil*. Princeton: Princeton University Press, 1979.

———. *Embedded Autonomy: States and Industrial Transformation*. Princeton: Princeton University Press, 1995.

Fajnzylber, Fernando, and Trinidad Martínez Tarragí. *Las Empresas Transnacionales: Expansión a Nivel Mundial y Proyección en la Industria Mexicana*. Mexico: Fondo de Cultura Económica, 1976.

Fatemi, Khosrow, ed. *The Maquiladora Industry: Economic Solution or Problem?* New York: Praeger, 1990.

Faundey, Julio, and Sol Picciotto, eds. *The Nationalization of Multinationals in Peripheral Economies*. London: Macmillan, 1978.

Frank, Isaiah. *Foreign Enterprise in Developing Countries*. Baltimore: Johns Hopkins Press, 1980.

Frieden, Jeffry A. "Third World Indebted Industrialization: International Finance and State Capitalism in Mexico, Brazil, Algeria, and South Korea." *International Organization* 35, no. 3 (summer 1981): 407–431.

Furnish, Dale B. "The Andean Common Market's Common Regime for Foreign Investments." *Vanderbilt Journal of Transnational Law* 5 (spring 1972): 313–339.

Gereffi, Gary. *The Pharmaceutical Industry and Dependency in the Third World*. Princeton: Princeton University Press, 1983.

———, and Miguel Korzeniewicz, eds. *Commodity Chains and Global Capitalism*. Westport, Conn.: Praeger, 1994.

Goodsell, Charles T. *American Corporations and Peruvian Politics*. Cambridge: Harvard University Press, 1974.

Grieco, Joseph M. *Between Dependency and Autonomy: India's Experience with the International Computer Industry*. Berkeley: University of California Press, 1984.

Hirschman, A. O. "How to Divest in Latin America and Why." Essays in International Finance, 74. Princeton: International Finance Section, Department of Economics, Princeton University, 1969.

Hymer, Stephen. "The Multinational Corporation and the Law of Uneven Development," in Jagdish N. Bhagwati, ed., *Economics and World Order: From the 1970s to the 1990s*. New York: Macmillan, 1972.

International Labor Organization. *Multinational Enterprises and Social Policy*. Geneva: International Labor Organization, 1973.

Fröbel, Folker, Jürgen Heinrichs, and Otto Kreye. *The New International Division of Labor: Structural Employment in Industrialized Countries and Industrialization in Developing Countries*. Cambridge, England: Cambridge University Press, 1980.

Jansson, Hans. *Transnational Corporations in Southeast Asia: An Institutional Approach to Industrial Organization*. Brookfield, Vt.: Edward Elgar, 1994.

Kobrin, Stephen J. *Foreign Direct Investment, Industrialization and Social Change*. Greenwich, Conn.: Jai Press, 1977.

———. "Foreign Enterprise and Forced Divestment in LDCs." *International Organization* 34 (winter 1980): 65–88.

———. "Testing the Bargaining Hypothesis in the Manufacturing Sector in Developing Countries." *International Organization* 41 (autumn 1987): 609–638.

Lall, Sanjaya, ed. *New Multinationals: The Spread of Third World Enterprises*. London: Wiley, 1983.

LaPalombara, Joseph, and Stephen Blank. *Multinational Corporations and Developing Countries*. New York: The Conference Board, 1979.

Lim, Linda Y. C. and Pang Eng Fong. *Foreign Direct Investment and Industrialization in Malaysia, Singapore, Taiwan and Thailand*. Paris: OECD Development Center, 1991.

Marton, Katherin. *Multinationals, Technology and Industrialization: Implications and Impact in the Third World Countries*. Lexington, Mass.: Lexington Books, 1986.

Meyer-Stamer, Jorg. "The End of Brazil's Informatics Policy." *Science and Public Policy* 19 (April 1992): 99–110.

Mikesell, Raymond F., William H. Bartsch, et al. *Foreign Investment in the Petroleum and Mineral Industries: Case Studies of Investor-Host Country Relations*. Baltimore: Johns Hopkins Press, 1971.

Moran, Theodore H. *Multinational Corporations and the Politics of Dependence: Copper in Chile*. Princeton: Princeton University Press, 1974.

_____, ed. *Multinational Corporations: The Political Economy of Foreign Direct Investment*. Lexington, Mass.: Lexington Books, 1985.

_____, ed. *Governments and Multinational Corporations*. New York: Routledge, 1993.

Newfarmer, Richard S., ed. *Profits, Progress and Poverty: Case Studies of International Industries in Latin America*. Notre Dame, Ind.: University of Notre Dame Press, 1985.

Novak, Michael, and Michael P. Jackson. *Latin America: Dependency or Independence?* Washington: American Enterprise Institute, 1985.

Oman, Charles. *New Forms of International Investment in Developing Countries*. Paris: OECD, 1982.

Oseghale, Braimoh D. *Political Instability, Interstate Conflict, Adverse Changes in Host Government Policies and Foreign Direct Investment: A Sensitivity Analysis*. New York: Garland, 1993.

Penrose, Edith. "The State and the Multinational Enterprise in Less-Developed Countries," in John H. Dunning, ed., *The Multinational Enterprise*, London: Allen and Unwin, 1971.

Piñelo, Adalberto J. *The Multinational Corporation as a Force in Latin American Politics: A Case Study of the International Petroleum Company in Peru*. New York: Praeger, 1973.

Rothgeb, John. *The Modern Leviathan in the Third World: The Myths and Realities of Foreign Investment in the Third World*. New York: Praeger, 1989.

Sampson, Anthony. *The Sovereign State of ITT*. New York: Stein and Day, 1973.

Sauvant, Karl, and Farid Lavipour, eds. *Controlling Multinational Enterprises: Problems, Strategies, Counter-Strategies*. Boulder, Colo.: Westview, 1976.

Shapiro, Helen. *Engines of Growth: The State and Transnational Auto Companies in Brazil*. New York: Cambridge University Press, 1994.

Sigmund, Paul E. *Multinationals in Latin America: The Politics of Nationalization*. Madison: University of Wisconsin Press, 1980.

Singer, Hans W. "U.S. Foreign Investment in Underdeveloped Areas: The Distribution of Gains between Investing and Borrowing Countries." *American Economic Review* 40 (May 1950): 473–485.

Sklar, Richard L. *Corporate Power in an African State: The Political Impact of Multinational Mining Companies in Zambia*. Berkeley: University of California Press, 1975.

Stopford, John, and Susan Strange, with John S. Henley. *Rival States, Rival Firms: Competition for World Market Shares*. New York: Cambridge University Press, 1991.

Tugwell, Franklin. *The Politics of Oil in Venezuela*. Stanford: Stanford University Press, 1975.

Turner, Louis. *Multinational Companies and the Third World*. New York: Hill and Wang, 1973.

Ulgado, Francis M., Chwo-Ming Yu, and Anant Negandhi. *Multinational Enterprises from Asian Developing Countries: Management and Organizational Characteristics*. Atlanta: Georgia Tech Center for International Business Education and Research, 1994.

U.S. Senate. Committee on Foreign Relations, Subcommittee on Multinational Corporations. *Multinational Corporations in Brazil and Mexico: Structural Sources of Economic and Noneconomic Power*. Washington: Government Printing Office, 1975.

Vaitsos, Constantine. *Intercountry Income Distribution and Transnational Enterprises*. Oxford: Clarendon Press, 1974.

Vernon, Raymond. "Conflict and Resolution Between Foreign Direct Investors and Less Developed Countries." *Public Policy* 17 (1968): 333–351.

Wells, Louis T. *Third World Multinationals*. Cambridge: MIT Press. 1983.

Whiting, Jr., Van R. *The Political Economy of Foreign Investment in Mexico: Nationalism, Liberalism, and Constraints on Choice*. Baltimore: Johns Hopkins University Press, 1992.

Widstrand, Carl, ed. *Multinational Firms in Africa*. Uppsala, Sweden: Scandinavian Institute of African Studies, 1975.

Yang, Xiaohua. *Globalization and the Automobile Industry: The United States, Japan, and the People's Republic of China*. Westport, Conn.: Praeger, 1995.

Oil and Commodity Cartels

Aburish, Said K. *The Rise, Corruption and Coming Fall of the House of Saud*. New York: St. Martin's Press, 1994.

Adelman, Morris A. *The World Petroleum Market*. Baltimore: Johns Hopkins University Press, 1972.

Ahrari, Mohammed E. *OPEC: The Failing Giant*. Lexington: University Press of Kentucky, 1986.

Allen, Loring. *OPEC Oil*. Cambridge, Mass.: Oelgeschlager, Gunn and Hain, 1979.

Alnasrawi, Abbas. "Collective Bargaining Power in OPEC." *Journal of World Trade Law* 7 (March–April 1973): 188–207.

———. *The Economy of Iraq: Oil, Wars, Destruction of Development and Prospects, 1950–2010*. Westport, Conn.: Greenwood Press, 1994.

Araim, Amer Salih. *Intergovernmental Commodity Organizations and the New International Economic Order*. New York: Praeger, 1991.

Bergsten, C. Fred. "The Threat from the Third World." *Foreign Policy* no. 11 (summer 1973): 102–124.

Blair, John M. *The Control of Oil*. New York: Pantheon, 1976.

Boué, Juan Carlos. *Venezuela: The Political Economy of Oil*. New York: Oxford University Press for the Oxford Institute of Energy Studies, 1993.

Bromley, Simon. *American Hegemony and World Oil: The Industry, the State System, and the World Economy*. University Park: Pennsylvania State University Press, 1991.

Brown, Christopher. *The Political and Social Economy of Commodity Control*. London: Macmillan, 1980.

Chenery, Hollis B. "Restructuring the World Economy: Round II." *Foreign Affairs* 59 (1981): 1102–1121.

Cowhey, Peter F. *The Problems of Plenty: Energy Policy and International Politics*. Berkeley: University of California Press, 1985.

Crystal, Jill. *Oil and Politics in the Gulf: Rules and Merchants in Kuwait and Qatar*. New York: Cambridge University Press, 1990.

Danielsen, Albert L. *The Evolution of OPEC*. New York: Harcourt Brace Jonanovich, 1982.

Deagle, Edwin A., Jr. *The Future of the International Oil Market*. New York: Group of Thirty, 1983.

Eckbo, Paul Leo. *The Future of World Oil*. Cambridge, Mass.: Ballinger, 1976.

Eckes, Alfred E., Jr. *The United States and the Global Struggle for Minerals*. Austin: University of Texas Press, 1979.

Elm, Mostafa. *Oil, Power, and Principle: Iran's Oil Nationalization and Its Aftermath*. Syracuse, N.Y.: Syracuse University Press, 1992.

Engler, Robert. *The Politics of Oil: Private Power and Democratic Directions*. Chicago: University of Chicago Press, 1961.

———. *The Brotherhood of Oil: Energy Policy and the Public Interest*. Chicago: University of Chicago Press, 1977.

Finlayson, Jack A., and Mark W. Zacher. *Managing International Markets: Developing Countries and the Commodity Trade Regime*. New York: Columbia University Press, 1988.

Freedman, Lawrence, and Efraim Karsh. *The Gulf Conflict 1990–1991: Diplomacy and War in the New World Order*. Princeton: Princeton University Press, 1993.

Fried, Edward R. and Philip H. Trezise. *Oil Security: Retrospect and Prospect*. Washington: Brookings Institution, 1993.

Fursenko, A. A. *The Battle for Oil: The Economics and Politics of International Corporate Conflict over Petroleum, 1860–1930*. Greenwich, Conn.: Jai Press, 1990.

Gause, F. Gregory, III. *Oil Monarchies: Domestic and Security Challenges in the Arab Gulf States*. New York: Council on Foreign Relations Press, 1993.

Ghadar, Fariborz. *The Evolution of OPEC Strategy*. Lexington, Mass.: Lexington Books, 1977.

Goodwin, Geoffrey, and James Mayall, eds. *A New International Commodity Regime*. London: Croom Helm, 1982.

Gordon-Ashworth, Fiona. *International Commodity Control: A Contemporary History and Appraisal*. London: Croom Helm, 1984.

Griffin, James M., and David J. Teece. *OPEC Behavior and World Oil Prices*. London: George Allen and Unwin, 1982.

Hallwood, C. Paul. *Transaction Costs and Trade Between Multinational Corporations: A Study of Offshore Oil Production*. Boston: Unwin Hyman, 1990.

Hartshorn, J. E. *Oil Companies and Governments: An Account of the International Oil Industry in Its Political Environment*, 2nd rev. ed. London: Faber, 1967.

_____. *Oil Trade: Politics and Prospects*. New York: Cambridge University Press, 1993.

Heal, Geoffrey M., and Graciela Chichilnisky. *Oil and the International Economy*. Oxford: Clarendon Press, 1991.

Hillman, John. "Bolivia and the International Tin Cartel, 1893–1941." *Journal of Latin American Studies* 20 (1987): 83–110.

_____. "Malaya and the International Tin Cartel." *Modern Asian Studies* 22 (May 1988): 237–261.

Hiro, D. *The Longest War: The Iran-Iraq Military Conflict*. New York: Routledge, 1991.

_____, *Desert Shield to Desert Storm: The Second Gulf War*. New York: Routledge, 1992.

Holloway, Steven K. *The Aluminum Multinationals and the Bauxite Cartel*. New York: St. Martin's Press, 1988.

Hveem, Helge. *The Political Economy of Third World Producer Associations*. New York: Columbia University Press, 1978.

Ikenberry, G. John. *Reasons of State: Oil Politics and the Capacities of American Government*. Ithaca, N.Y.: Cornell University Press, 1988.

Jentleson, Bruce W. *Pipeline Politics: The Complex Political Economy of East-West Energy Trade*. Ithaca, N.Y.: Cornell University Press, 1986.

_____. *With Friends Like These: Reagan, Bush, and Saddam 1982–1990*. New York: Norton, 1994.

Kelly, J. B. *Arabia, the Gulf, and the West: A Critical View of the Arabs and Their Oil Policy*. New York: Basic Books, 1980.

Klapp, Merrie Gilbert. *The Sovereign Entrepreneur: Oil Policies in Advanced and Less Developed Capitalist Countries*. Ithaca, N.Y.: Cornell University Press, 1987.

Krasner, Stephen D. *Defending the National Interest: Raw Materials Investments and U.S. Foreign Policy*. Princeton: Princeton University Press, 1978.

_____. "Oil Is the Exception." *Foreign Policy* 14 (spring 1974): 68–90.

Litvak, Alan, and Christopher J. Maule. "The International Bauxite Agreement: A Commodity Cartel in Action." *International Affairs* 56 (spring 1980).

Maizels, Alfred. *Commodities in Crisis: The Commodity Crisis of the 1980s and the Political Economy of International Commodity Prices*. Oxford: Clarendon Press, 1992.

Mattione, Richard. *OPEC's Investments and the International Financial System*. Washington: Brookings Institution, 1985.

Mikdashi, Zuhayr. *A Financial Analysis of Middle Eastern Oil Concessions: 1901–1965*. New York: Praeger, 1966.

_____. *The Community of Oil Exporting Countries: A Study in Governmental Cooperation*. Ithaca, N.Y.: Cornell University Press, 1972.

Mikesell, Raymond F. *The World Copper Industry: Structure in Economic Analysis*. Baltimore: Johns Hopkins Press, 1979.

Mofid, K. *The Economic Consequences of the Gulf War*. London: Routledge, 1990.

Nappi, Carmine. *Commodity Market Controls: A Historical Review*. Lexington, Mass.: Lexington Books, 1979.

Noreng, Oystein. *Oil Politics in the 1980s: Patterns of International Cooperation*. New York: McGraw-Hill, 1978.

_____. *The Pressures of Oil: A Strategy for Economic Revival*. New York: Harper and Row, 1978.

Nwoke, Chibuzo. *Third World Minerals and Global Pricing: A New Theory*. London: Zed Books, 1987.

Odell, Peter R. *An Economic Geography of Oil*. New York; Praeger, 1963.
_____. *Oil and World Power: Background to the Oil Crisis*. Harmondsworth, England: Penguin, 1974.
_____, and Luis Vallenilla. *The Pressures of Oil*. London: Harper and Row, 1978.
Pearce, Joan, ed. *The Third Oil Shock: The Effects of Lower Oil Prices*. London: Royal Institute of International Affairs, 1983.
Penrose, Edith T. *The Large International Firm in Developing Countries: The International Petroleum Industry*. Cambridge: MIT Press, 1969.
Philip, George D. E. *The Political Economy of International Oil*. Edinburgh, Scotland: Edinburgh Univerity Press, 1994.
Rangarajan, L. N. *Commodity Conflict: The Political Economy of International Commodity Agreements*. London: Croom Helm, 1978.
Rauscher, Michael. *OPEC and the Price of Petroleum: Theoretical Considerations and Empirical Evidence*. New York: Springer, 1989.
Robinson, Jeffrey. *Yamani: The Inside Story*. New York: Atlantic Monthly Press, 1989.
Rouhani, Fuad. *A History of OPEC*. New York: Praeger, 1971.
Rustow, Dankwart A., and John F. Mungo. *OPEC, Success and Prospects*. New York: New York University Press, 1976.
Sampson, Anthony. *The Seven Sisters: The Great Oil Companies and the World They Made*. New York: Viking, 1975.
Schneider, Steven A. *The Oil Price Revolution*. Baltimore: Johns Hopkins University Press, 1983.
Shwadran, Benjamin. *The Middle East, Oil and the Great Powers*. New York: Praeger, 1955.
Skeet, Ian. *OPEC: Twenty-Five Years of Prices and Politics*. New York: Cambridge University Press, 1988.
Spar, Debora L. *The Cooperative Edge: The International Politics of International Cartels*. Ithaca, N.Y.: Cornell University Press, 1994.
Stobaugh, Robert, and Daniel Yergin. *Energy Future: Report of the Harvard Business School Energy Project*. New York: Random House, 1979.
Szyliowicz, Joseph S., and Bard E. O'Neill, eds. *The Energy Crisis and U.S. Foreign Policy*. New York: Praeger, 1975.
Takerichi, Kenji, John E. Strongman, Shunichi Maeda, and C. Suan Tan. *The World Copper Industry: Its Changing Structure and Future Prospects*. World Bank Staff Working Papers, no. 15. Washington: World Bank, 1987.
Tanzer, Michael. *The Political Economy of International Oil and the Underdeveloped Countries*. Boston: Beacon Press, 1969.
Tilton, John E. "Cartels in Metal Industries." *Earth and Mineral Sciences* 44 (March 1975): 41–44.
Tugwell, Franklin. *The Politics of Oil in Venezuela*. Stanford: Stanford University Press, 1975.
Turner, Louis. *Oil Companies and the International System*. London: Allen and Unwin, 1978.
U.S. Federal Trade Commission. *International Petroleum Cartel*. Staff Report to the Federal Trade Commission, 82nd Congress, 2nd sess. Washington: Government Printing Office, 1952.
Vernon, Raymond. *Two Hungry Giants: The US and Japan in the Quest for Oil and Ores*. Cambridge: Harvard University Press, 1983.
Vo, Xuan Han. *Oil, the Persian Gulf States, and the United States*. Westport, Conn.: Praeger, 1994.
Woods, Douglas W., and James C. Burrows. *The World Aluminum-Bauxite Market: Policy Implications for the United States*. New York: Praeger, 1980.
Yager, Joseph A., and Eleanor B. Steinbert, et al. *Energy and U.S. Foreign Policy: A Report to the Energy Policy Project of the Ford Foundation*. Cambridge, Mass.: Ballinger, 1974.
Yergin, Daniel. *Energy Future*. New York: Ballantine, 1981.
_____. *The Prize: The Epic Quest for Oil, Money and Power*. New York: Simon and Schuster, 1991.

East-West Economic Relations and Economic Sanctions

Adler-Karlsson, Gunnar. *Western Economic Warfare, 1947–1967: A Case Study in Foreign Economic Policy*. Stockholm, Sweden: Almqvist and Wiksell, 1968.

Aganbegyan, Abel G. *The Economic Challenge of Perestroika*. Bloomington: Indiana University Press, 1988.

Alerassool, Mahvash. *Freezing Assets: The USA and the Most Effective Economic Sanction*. New York: St. Martin's, 1993.

Altman, Oscar. "Russians Gold and the Ruble." *International Monetary Fund Staff Papers* 8 (April 1960): 415–438.

Åslund, Anders. *Gorbachev's Struggle for Economic Reform*, 2nd ed. Ithaca: Cornell University Press, 1991.

_____, ed. *The Post-Soviet Economy: Soviet and Western Perspectives*. New York: St. Martin's Press, 1992.

_____, ed. *Economic Transformation in Russia*. New York: St. Martin's Press, 1994.

_____. *How Russia Became a Market Economy*. Washington: Brookings Institution, 1995.

_____, and R. Layard, eds. *Changing the Economic System in Russia*. New York: St. Martin's Press, 1993.

Barner-Barry, Carol, and Cynthia Hody. *The Politics of Change: The Transformation of the Former Soviet Union*. New York: St. Martin's Press, 1995.

Bertsch, Gary, ed. *Controlling East-West Trade and Technology Transfer: Power, Politics and Policies*. Durham, N.C.: Duke University Press, 1988.

Blackwell, William L. *The Industrialization of Russia: A Historical Perspective*, 3rd ed. Arlington Heights, Ill.: H. Davidson, 1994.

Blanchard, Olivier J., Kenneth A. Froot, and Jeffrey D. Sachs, eds. *The Transition in Eastern Europe*, 2 vols. Chicago: University of Chicago Press, 1994.

Blinken, Anthony. *Ally Versus Ally: America, Europe and the Siberian Pipeline Crisis*. New York: Praeger, 1987.

Brada, Josef C., and Michael P. Claudon, eds. *Reforming the Ruble: Monetary Aspects of Perestroika*. New York: New York University Press, 1990.

_____. *The Emerging Russian Bear: Integrating the Soviet Union in the World Economy*. New York: New York University Press, 1991.

Brown, Alan A., and Egon Neuberger, eds. *International Trade and Central Planning: An Analysis of Economic Interactions*. Berkeley: University of Calif. Press, 1968.

Bryant, Christopher, and Edmund Mokrzycki, eds. *The New Great Transformation?: Change and Continuity in East-Central Europe*. New York: Routledge, 1994.

Burawoy, Michael, and János Lukács, *The Radiant Past: Ideology and Reality in Hungary's Road to Capitalism*. Chicago: University of Chicago Press, 1992.

Carter, Barry E. *International Economic Sanctions: Improving the Haphazard U.S. Legal Regime*. Cambridge, England: Cambridge University Press, 1988.

Clabaugh, Samuel F., and Richard V. Allen. *Trading with the Communists*. Washington: Georgetown University Center for Strategic Studies, 1968.

_____. *East-West Trade: Its Strategic Implications*. Washington: Georgetown University, Center for Strategic Studies, 1964.

Claudon, Michael P., and Tamal L. Gunter, eds. *Putting Food on What Was the Soviet Table*. New York: New York University Press, 1992.

Commisso, Ellen, and Laura D'Andrea Tyson, eds. *Power, Purpose, and Collective Choice: Economic Strategy in Socialist States*. Ithaca, N.Y.: Cornell University Press, 1986.

Crawford, Beverly, ed. *Markets, States, and Democracy: The Political Economy of Post-Communist Transformation*. Boulder, Colo.: Westview Press, 1995.

Dallin, Alexander, and Gail W. Lapidus, eds. *The Soviet System: From Crisis to Collapse*. Boulder, Colo.: Westview Press, 1995.

Dunn, John F. *All Change in Russia: The Pressure For and Against Reform*. London: Her Majesty's Stationery Office, 1992.

Ernst, Maurice, Michael Alexeev, and Paul Marer. *Transforming the Core: State Industrial Enterprises in Russia and Central Europe*. Boulder, Colo.: Westview Press, 1995.

Fallenbuchl, Zbigniew M. "Comecon Integration." *Problems of Communism* 22 (March-April 1973): 25–39.

Fan, Qimio and Peter Nolan, eds. *China's Economic Reforms: The Costs and Benefits of Incrementalism*. New York: St. Martin's Press, 1994.

Fewsmith, Joseph. *Dilemmas of Reform in China: Political Conflict and Economic Debate*. Armonk, N.Y.: M. E. Sharpe, 1994.

Fries, Steven, ed. *Transition: Private Sector Development and the Role of Financial Institutions*. London: European Bank for Reconstruction and Development, 1994.

Fukasaki, Kiichiro, and David Wall, with Mingyuan Wu. *China's Long March to an Open Economy*. Paris: OECD, 1994.

Gaidar, Egor T., and Karl Otto Pöhl. *Russian Reform/International Money*. Cambridge: MIT Press, 1995.

Garland, John S. *Financing Foreign Trade in Eastern Europe: Problems of Bilateralism and Currency Inconvertibility*. New York: Praeger, 1977.

Giffen, James H. *The Legal and Practical Aspects of Trade with the Soviet Union*. New York: Praeger, 1969.

Goldman, Marshall I. *Détente and Dollars: Doing Business with the Soviets*. New York: Basic Books, 1975.

_____. *What Went Wrong with Perestroika?* New York: Norton, 1991.

Gorbachev, Mikhail S. *Perestroika: New Thinking for Our Country and the World*. New York: Harper and Row, 1987.

_____. *The August Coup: The Truth and the Lessons*. London: HarperCollins, 1991.

Granville, Brigitte. *The Success of Russian Economic Reforms*. London: Royal Institute for International Affairs, 1995.

Grub, Phillip D., and Karel Holbik, eds. *American-East European Trade: Controversy, Progress, Prospects*. Washington: National Press, 1969.

Harding, Harry. *China's Second Revolution: Reform After Mao*. Washington: Brookings Institution, 1987.

Hewett, Ed. A. *Reforming the Soviet Economy: Equality versus Efficiency*. Washington: Brookings Institution, 1988.

_____, and Thomas A. Wolf, eds. *Economic Adjustment and Reform in Eastern Europe and the Soviet Union*. Durham, N.C.: Duke University Press, 1988.

Hillman, Arye L., and Branko Milanovic, eds. *The Transition from Socialism in Eastern Europe: Domestic Restructuring and Foreign Trade*. Washington: World Bank, 1992.

Holm, Hans Henrik, and Georg Sorenson. *Whose World Order?: Uneven Globalization and the End of the Cold War*. Boulder: Westview Press, 1995.

Holzman, Franklyn D. *International Trade Under Communism—Politics and Economics*. New York: Basic Books, 1976.

Hough, Jerry F. *Opening Up the Soviet Economy*. Washington: Brookings Institution, 1988.

Hoyt, Ronald E. *Winners and Losers in East-West Trade: A Behavioral Analysis of U.S.-Soviet Détente (1970–1980)*. New York: Praeger, 1983.

Hufbauer, Gary Clyde, Jeffrey J. Schott, and Kimberly Ann Elliott. *Economic Sanctions Reconsidered: History and Current Policy*, 2nd ed. Washington: Institute for International Economics, 1990.

Jentleson, Bruce W. *Pipeline Politics: The Complex Political Economy of East-West Energy Trade*. Ithaca, N.Y.: Cornell University Press, 1986.

Jowitt, Kenneth. *New World Disorder: The Leninist Extinction*. Berkeley: University of California Press, 1992.

Kaldor, Mary. *The Disintegrating West*. New York: Hill and Wang, 1978.

Kaser, Michael. *Comecon: Integration Problems of the Planned Economies*. London: Oxford University Press, 1965.

Kemme, David M., ed. *Technology Markets and Export Controls in the 1990s*. New York: New York University Press, 1991.

Khasbulatov, Ruslan I. *The Economic Reform in the Russian Federation (1992–1993)*. Moscow: INMARCON, 1993.

Kornai, Janos. *The Socialist System: The Political Economy of Communism*. Princeton: Princeton University Press, 1992.

Kostecki, M. M. *East-West Trade and the GATT System.* New York: St. Martin's, 1978.

Kraus, Michael, and Ronald D. Leibowitz, eds. *Perestroika and East-West Economic Relations: Prospects for the 1990's.* New York: New York University Press, 1990.

Kristof, Nicholas D. *China Wakes: The Struggle for the Soul of a Rising Power.* New York: Times Books, 1994.

Kuznetsov, Andrei P. *Foreign Investment in Contemporary Russia: Managing Capital Entry.* New York: St. Martin's Press, 1994.

Lapidus, Gail W., ed. *The New Russia: Troubled Transformation.* Boulder, Colo.: Westview, 1995.

Lardy, Nicholas R. *China's Entry into the World Economy: Implications for Northeast Asia and the United States.* New York: University Press of America for the Asia Society, 1987.

_____. *China in the World Economy.* Washington: Institute for International Economics, 1994.

Lavigne, Marie, ed. *East-South Relations in the World Economy.* Boulder: Westview Press, 1988.

Lawson, Eugene K., ed. *U.S.-China Trade: Problems and Prospects.* New York: Praeger Press, 1988.

Lazear, Edward P., ed. *Economic Transition in Eastern Europe and Russia: Realities of Reform.* Stanford: Hoover Institution Press, 1995.

Leitzel, Jim. *Russian Economic Reform.* New York: Routledge, 1995.

Leyton-Brown, David, ed. *The Utility of Economic Sanctions.* New York: St. Martin's Press, 1987.

Losman, Donald L. *International Economic Sanctions: The Cases of Cuba, Israel, and Rhodesia.* Albuquerque, N.M.: University of New Mexico Press, 1979.

Malish, Anton F., Jr. "United States-East European Trade." *Staff Research Studies*, no. 4. Washington: U.S. Tariff Commission, 1972.

Marer, Paul. "The Political Economy of Soviet Relations with Eastern Europe," in Steven J. Rosen and James R. Kurth, eds., *Testing Theories of Economic Imperialism.* Lexington, Mass.: Lexington Books, 1974.

Mastanduno, Michael. *Economic Containment: CoCom and the Politics of East-West Trade.* Ithaca, N.Y.: Cornell University Press, 1992.

McFaul, Michael. "State Power, Institutional Change, and the Politics of Privatization in Russia." *World Politics* 47 (January 1995): 210–243.

McKinnon, Ronald I. *Gradual versus Rapid Liberalization in Socialist Economies: Financial Policies in China and Russia Compared.* San Francisco: ICS Press, 1994.

Mikesell, Raymond F., and Jack N. Behrman. *Financing Free World Trade with the Sino-Soviet Bloc.* Princeton: International Finance Section, Department of Economics, Princeton University, 1958.

Nagorski, Jr., Zygmunt. *The Psychology of East-West Trade.* New York: Mason and Lipscomb, 1974.

National Academy of Science. *Balancing the National Interest: U.S. National Security Export Controls and Global Economic Competition.* Washington: National Academy Press, 1987.

Nelson, Lynn D., and Irina Y. Kuzes. *Property to the People: The Struggle for Radical Economic Reform in Russia.* Armonk, N.Y.: M. E. Sharpe, 1994.

_____. *Radical Reform in Yeltsin's Russia: Political, Economic, and Social Dimensions.* Armonk, N.Y.: M. E. Sharpe, 1995.

Nincic, Miroslav, and Peter Wallensteen, eds. *Dilemmas of Economic Coercion.* New York: Praeger, 1983.

Nove, Alec. *East-West Trade: Problems, Prospects, Issues.* The Washington Papers, 6, no. 53. Beverly Hills: Sage Publications, 1978.

_____. *The Soviet Economic System*, 3rd ed. London: Routledge, 1986.

_____. *An Economic History of the USSR.* 2nd ed. New York: Penguin, 1989.

Paarlberg, Robert. "Lessons of the Grain Embargo." *Foreign Affairs* 59 (fall 1980): 144–162.

Parrott, Bruce. *Politics and Technology in the Soviet Union.* Cambridge: MIT Press, 1983.

Perry, Charles, and Robert Pfaltzcraft Jr., eds. *Selling the Rope to Hang Capitalism? The Debate on East-West Trade and Technology Transfer.* Washington: Pergamon-Brassey, 1987.

Peterson, Peter G. *U.S.-Soviet Commercial Relationships in a New Era.* Washington: Department of Commerce, August 1972.

Pisar, Samuel. *Coexistence and Commerce: Guidelines for Transactions Between East and West.* New York: McGraw-Hill, 1970.

Poznanski, Kazimierz Z. *The Evolutionary Transition to Capitalism.* Boulder, Colo.: Westview Press, 1995.

Prince, Charles. "The U.S.S.R.'s Role in International Finance." *Harvard Business Review* 25 (autumn 1946): 111–128.

Pryor, Frederic. *The Communist Foreign Trade System.* Cambridge: MIT Press, 1963.

Przeworski, Adam. *Democracy and the Market: Political and Economic Reforms in Eastern Europe and Latin America.* New York: Cambridge University Press, 1991.

Przeworski, Adam, et al. with Pranab Bardhan, Luiz Carlos Bresser Pereira. *Sustainable Democracy.* New York: Cambridge University Press, 1995.

Rode, Reinhard, and Hanns-Dieter Jacobsen, eds. *Economic Warfare or Detente; An Assessment of East-West Relations in the 1980s.* Boulder, Colo.: Westview Press, 1985.

Roosa, Robert V., Armin Gutowski, and Michiya Matsukawa. *East/West Trade at the Crossroads: Economic Relations with the Soviet Union and Eastern Europe*, a task force report to the Trilateral Commission. New York: New York University Press, 1982.

Rowen, Henry S., Charles Wolf, and Jeanne Zlotnik, eds. *Defense Conversion, Economic Reform, and the Outlook for the Russian and Ukrainian Economies.* New York: St. Martin's Press, 1994.

Rutland, Peter. *Russia, Eurasia, and the Global Economy.* Washington: Brookings Institution, July 1995.

Sachs, Jeffrey. *Poland's Jump to the Market Economy.* Cambridge: MIT Press, 1993.

Sachs, Jeffrey, and Galen L. Stone. *Accelerating Privatization in Eastern Europe: The Case of Poland.* Helsinki: World Institute for Development Economics Research, 1991.

Saunders, Christopher T., ed. *East-West-South: Economic Interactions Between Three Worlds.* London: Macmillan, 1981.

Schmitter, Philippe C., and Terry L. Karl. "The Conceptual Traveis of Transitologists and Consolidologists: How Far to the East Should They Attempt to Go?" *Slavic Review* 53 (spring 1994): 173–185.

Schmitthoff, Clive M., ed. *The Sources of the Law of International Trade, with Special Reference to East-West Trade.* New York: Praeger, 1964.

Schnitzer, Martin. *U.S. Business Involvement in Eastern Europe: Case Studies of Hungary, Poland, and Rumania.* New York: Praeger, 1980.

Shelton, Judy. *The Coming Soviet Crash: Gorbachev's Desperate Pursuit of Credit in Western Financial Markets.* New York: Free Press, 1989.

Siebert, Horst, ed. *Overcoming the Transformation Crisis: Lessons for the Succcessor States of the Soviet Union.* Tübingen: Mohr, 1993.

Spulber, Nicholas. *The Economics of Communist Eastern Europe.* New York: Wiley, 1957.

Sternheimer, Stephen. *East-West Technology Transfer: Japan and the Communist Bloc.* The Washington Papers, no. 76. Beverly Hills: Sage Publications, 1980.

Stokes, Gail. *The Walls Came Tumbling Down: The Collapse of Communism in Eastern Europe.* New York: Oxford University Press, 1993.

Sutton, Anthony C. *Western Technology and Soviet Economic Development, 1945–1965.* Stanford: Hoover Institution on War, Revolution and Peace, 1973.

_____. *Western Technology and Soviet Economic Development, 1930 to 1945.* Stanford: Hoover Institution on War, Revolution and Peace, 1971.

_____. *Western Technology and Soviet Economic Development, 1917 to 1930.* Stanford: Hoover Institution on War, Revolution and Peace, 1968.

U.S. Congress, Joint Economic Committee. *Issues in East-West Commercial Relations.* Washington: Government Printing Office, 1979.

_____. *East European Economics Post-Helsinki.* Washington: Government Printing Office, 1977.

U.S. House of Representatives, Committee on Banking and Currency. *The FIAT-Soviet Automobile Plant and Communist Economic Reforms.* 88th Congress, 2nd sess. Washington: Government Printing Office, 1967.

Van Winkle, Jeannette. *Captial Accumulation, Financial Reform, and Investment Planning in Russia: What Is to Be Done about the Banks?* Santa Monica: RAND, 1995.

Vernon, Raymond. "The Fragile Foundations of East-West Trade." *Foreign Affairs* 57 (summer 1979): 1035–1051.

Viner, Jacob. "International Relations Between State-Controlled National Economies." *American Economic Review* 34 (March 1944): 315–329.

Wädekin, Karl-Eugen. "Soviet Agriculture's Dependence on the West." *Foreign Affairs* 60 (spring 1982): 882–903.

Watts, Nita G. M., ed. *Economic Relations Between East and West*. London: Macmillan, 1978.

Wilczynski, Joseph. *Socialist Economic Development and Reforms: From Extensive to Intensive Growth Under Central Planning in the U.S.S.R., Eastern Europe and Yugoslavia*. New York: Praeger, 1972.

———. *The Multinationals and East-West Relations*. Boulder, Colo.: Westview, 1976.

Wiles, Peter J. F. *Communist International Economics*. New York: Praeger, 1968.

World Bank. *Russian Economic Reform: Crossing the Threshold of Structural Change*. Washington: World Bank, 1992.

Wu, Yu-Shan. *Comparative Economic Transformations: Mainland China, Hungary, the Soviet Union, and Taiwan*. Stanford: Stanford University Press, 1994.

Yergin, Angela Stent. *East-West Technology Transfer: European Perspectives*. The Washington Papers, no. 75. Beverly Hills, Calif.: Sage Publications, 1980.

Yergin, Daniel, and Thane Gustafson. *Russia 2010 and What It Means for the World*. New York: Vintage, 1995.

Yevstigneyev, Ruben N., and Arkady M. Voinov. *Economic Reform and Its Interpretations in Russia*. Helsinki: World Institute for Development Economics Research, 1994.

Zaslavskaya, Tatiana. *The Second Socialist Revolution*. Bloomington: Indiana University Press, 1990.

Other Textbooks on International Political Economy

Blake, David H., and Robert S. Walters. *The Politics of Global Economic Relations*. 4th ed. Englewood Cliffs, N.J.: Prentice-Hall, 1992.

Frey, Bruno S. *International Political Economics*. New York: Basil Blackwell, 1984.

Gill, Stephen, and David Law. *The Global Political Economy: Perspectives, Problems and Policies*. Baltimore: Johns Hopkins University Press, 1988.

Gilpin, Robert. *The Political Economy of International Relations*. Princeton: Princeton University Press, 1987.

Schwartz, Herman. *States versus Markets: History, Geography and the Development of the International Political Economy*. New York: St. Martin's, 1994.

Strange, Susan. *States and Markets: An Introduction to International Political Economy*. New York: Basil Blackwell, 1988.

Newspapers and Journals

American Economic Review
American Journal of International Law
American Political Science Review
Amex Bank Review
The Banker (London)
Columbia Journal of World Business
The Economist
Euromoney
The Financial Times (London)
Foreign Affairs
Foreign Policy
Fortune
Harvard Business Review
International Affairs (London)
International Organization
International Studies Quarterly
Journal of Commerce

Journal of Common Market Studies
Journal of Development Studies
Journal of International Affairs
Journal of World Trade Law
Law and Policy in International Business
Monthly Review
The New York Times
Princeton Essays in International Finance
Princeton Studies in International Finance
Review of Radical Political Economics
The Wall Street Journal
World Business Weekly
World Development
The World Economy
World Financial Markets (Morgan Guaranty Trust Co.)
World Politics

Publications by Official Sources

Bank for International Settlements, *Annual Reports*
International Bank for Reconstruction and Development, *World Bank Atlas*
_____, *World Debt Tables*
_____, *World Development Report*
_____, *World Social and Economic Indicators*
International Bank for Reconstruction and Development and International Development Agency, *Annual Reports*
International Monetary Fund, *Annual Reports*
_____, *Direction of Trade*
_____, *Finance and Development*
_____, *IMF Survey*
_____, *International Financial Statistics*
_____, *Selected Decisions of the Executive Directors and Selected Documents*
_____, *Staff Papers*
_____, *World Economic Report*
Organization for Economic Cooperation and Development, *Flow of Financial Resources to Less-Developed Countries*
_____, *OECD Economic Outlook*
_____, *OECD Observer*
_____, Development Assistance Committee, *Development Cooperation. Review of Efforts and Policies of the Members of the Development Assistance Committee*
_____, *Statistics of Foreign Trade*
_____, *Stock of Private Direct Investments by DAC Countries in Developing Countries*
_____, *Trade by Commodities*
United Nations. *Transnational Corporations in World Development: A Reexamination*
United Nations, Center on Transnational Corporations. *Transnational Corporations in World Development, Third Survey*
United Nations, Center on Transnational Corporations. *Transnational Corporations in World Development: Trends and Prospects*
United Nations Conference on Trade and Development, *Handbook of International Trade and Development Statistics*
_____, *Review of Trade and Development*
United Nations Economic Commission for Europe, *Economic Survey of Europe*
United Nations Economic Commission for Latin America, *Economic Survey of Latin America*
U.S. Central Intelligence Agency, *Handbook of Economic Statistics*
U.S. Department of Agriculture, *Foreign Agricultural Trade of the United States*
U.S. Department of Commerce, Bureau of the Census, *Statistical Abstract of the United States*
U.S. Department of Commerce, *Survey of Current Business*
U.S. Department of State, *Bulletin*
U.S. President's Council of Economic Advisors, *Economic Report of the President*
U.S. Trade Representative, *Annual Report of the President of the United States on the Trade Agreements Program*

Acknowledgments (continued from copyright page)

Figure 2–6: Monthly Percent Change in Real Exchange Rates, 1960–1990. Source: Barry Eichengreen, *International Monetary Arrangements for the 21st Century* (Washington, D.C.: Brookings Institution Press, 1994), p. 12.

Table 4–1: Countries and Corporations: A Ranking by GNP and Sales, 1992–1993. Source: World Bank, *World Development Report 1994: Infrastructure for Development* (Washington: D.C. World Bank, 1994); and "The World's Largest Industrial Corporations," *Fortune* (July 25, 1994).

Figure 4–6: Product Cycle Theory. Source: Raymond Vernon, "International Investment and International Trade in the Product Cycle." *Quarterly Journal of Economics*, 80 (May 1996), pp. 190–207.

Figure 4–7: Exports versus Local Production of Automobiles in the United States by Japanese Firms, 1980–1990. Source: Japanese Automobile Manufacturers Association, Inc.

Figure 6–1: Bilateral Official Development Assistance by the Five Largest Industrialized Countries, Selected Periods between 1950 and 1988, in Constant 1987 Prices. Source: Stephen Browne, *Foreign Aid in Practice* (New York: New York University Press, 1990), pp. 40–41.

Figure 7–4: Imports by Industrialized Countries and Regions from the Developing Countries Facing Nontariff Barriers, 1985. Source: UNCTAD Database on Trade Control Measures as cited in Sheila Page, *How Developing Countries Trade* (New York (New York: Routledge, 1994), p. 57. Copyright ©1994 by Sheila Page. Reprinted by permission.

Figure 8–1: Inflows of FDI by LDC Region, 1975–1992, in Current Dollars. Source: Sheila Page, *How Developing Countries Trade* (New York: Routledge, 1994) p. 104. Copyright ©1994 by Sheila Page. Reprinted by permission.

Table 8–1: Export Processing Zones (EPZs) by 1990. Source: John Madeley, *Trade and the Poor: The Impact of International Trade on Developing Countries* (New York: St. Martin's Press, 1993), p. 68. Copyright © John Madeley. Reprinted with permission of St. Martin's Press, Incorporated.

Figure 10–1: Soviet Grain Harvests and Net Imports in Millions of Metric Tons, 1950–1990. Source: Marshall Goldman, *Gorbachev's Challenge* (New York: Norton, 1987), p. 33; Marshall Goldman, *What Went Wrong with Perestroika?* (New York: Norton, 1991), p. 79. Reprinted by permission of W. W. Norton & Company, Inc.

Figure 10–5: Budget Deficits/GDP and Growth in Retail Prices in the Former Soviet Union and Russia, 1985–1991, in Percentages. Source: Stanley Fischer, "Russia and the Soviet Union Then and Now," in Oliver J. Blanchard, Kenneth A. Froot, and Jeffrey D. Sachs, eds., *The Transition in Europe:Country Studies*, vol. 1 (Chicago: University of Chicago Press, 1994), p. 234.

Figure 10–9: China's Foreign Trade in Current Dollars, 1978–1993. Source: Nicholas Lardy, *China in the World Economy* (Washington, D.C.: Institute for International Economics, 1994), p. 30. Copyright © 1994 by the Institute for International Economics. Reprinted by permission. All rights reserved.

Index

Glossary terms and the pages on which they appear are set in boldface type.

LTA (Long-Term Arrangement), 232–33

Maastricht Treaty, 34, 64, 137, 358, 359
MacEwan, Arthur, 159–60
macroeconomic imbalance, 66
MacSharry, Ray (MacSharry proposals), 85
Malaysia
　and FDI, 250
　foreign investment and, 266
　and free trade, 79
　oil production in, 290, 291
Malta Summit, 335
managed trade, 6
Mandela, Nelson, 124
manufacturing, 251
Mao Tse-tung, 346, 347
market forces, 8
Marketing Opening Sector Specific (MOSS),
　70
Marshall Plan, 12–13, 54, 63, 319, 320, 321
Marxism, North-South relations and, 153–54,
　155–61
Mauritania as member of CIPEC, 310
Mazowiecki, Tadeusz, 344
Mercosur, 79, 241
Merger Regulation of 1989, 136–37
Mexico, 164
　as an emerging market, 203, 204
　capital flight and, 186
　capital outflow of, 27–28
　debt crisis and, 38, 186
　1982 debt crisis of, 188
　debt-equity swaps and, 197
　domestic austerity program of, 205
　effects of oil price war on, 294
　and FDI, 250–51, 264, 268
　financial crisis of, 43
　as first test case for debt relief, 202–3
　foreign investment and, 268
　foreign loans to, 188
　and free trade area, 78, 79
　GATT and, 203–4
　growth of, 184
　and IMF credits, 189
　inability to service foreign debt and, 187
　informatics policy of, 268
　and intellectual property, 78
　manufacturing shift to, 60
　as a model for debt management, 189
　and multi-year rescheduling agreement
　　(MYRA), 191
　NAFTA and, 130, 204
　as a new source of oil, 284
　oil production in, 290, 291
　peso crisis of, 207
　regulatory behavior of, 264–65
　role of, in oil price management, 300
　and services, 78

U.S. acquisition of national firms and, 256
U.S. emergency support to, 185
and VERs with U.S., 73
See also peso
MFN (most-favored-nation), 52, 81, 82, 87,
　229, 237, 322, 351–52
military expenditures in NATO countries, 13
Ministry of International Trade and Industry
　(MITI), 129
Model Tax Convention, 139–40
monetary management, 8–48
　and Bretton Woods agreement, 10–12,
　　16–24
　Committee on Reform of, 21
　dilemmas of, in post-Bretton Woods era,
　　24–30
　multilateral, under U.S. leadership, 13–16
　and regional monetary systems, 30–35
　in the 1990s, 44
　unilateral role of U.S. in, 12–13
　U.S. policy of, 35–43
monetary policies, 8
monopoly, 111
Morocco
　debt crisis and, 186
　and export of phosphates, 303, 304
most-favored-nation (MFN), 52, 81, 82, 87,
　229, 237, 322, 351–52
Mozambique, foreign direct investment and,
　268
MTN (multilateral trade negotiations), 54, 80,
　81, 82
Multi-Fiber Arrangement (MFA), 72, 86, 233,
　238–39, 240
multilateral contracts, 228
Multilateral Investment Guarantee Agency
　(MIGA), 181, 267, 269
multilateralism, 69
multilateral trade negotiations (MTN), 54, 80,
　81, 82
multinational corporation(s) (MNC), 96
　in Canada and Europe, 115-18
　characteristics of, 98–103, 258
　consequences of activity of, 113–15
　and FDI, 103–8, 126–27, 260–65 (*see also*
　　foreign direct investment)
　and home country
　　importance of, 113, 254–58
　　interference by, 121–24
　and internalization theory, 109–10
　jurisdictional problems involving, 103
　local control and, 249–52, 252–54
　and management of, 127–34, 134–37,
　　137–41
　and monopoly control of technology,
　　256–57
　national
　　and economic control, 118–21

and economic crisis of 1947, 11–12
effects of oil price war on, 294
Eximbank financing and, 330–31
industrial growth and, 324
and Jackson-Vanik amendment, 330
Marxist ideology and, 318–19
Ministry of Foreign Trade and, 334
and most-favored-nation status, 322, 330
as a new source of oil, 300–301
and nuclear parity, 322–23
and *perestroika,* 7
as political and military threat to West, 321
rejection of aid by U.S. and, 319
research and development and, 326
and western economies, 3
See also East-West economic relations;
Russia
Spain, exchange rate mechanism and, 32
special drawing rights (SDRs), 16, 23, 24, 36,
172, 206
special economic zones (SEZs), 353
spot market, 287, 292, 296
stabilization program, 43
stagflation, 60
Stalin, Josef, 316, 317, 318, 337
steel and VRAs, 73
strategic alliance, 102
structural change, 57–62
structuralism and North-South system,
154–61
subsidies, 51, 53, 71, 75, 83, 84–85, 86
supply-side economics, 36
Surinam, as a member of IBA, 306
Sutherland, Peter, 85–86
Sweden, European Currency Unit and, 32
Syria
role of CoCom and, 359
and Soviet Union, 169
and U.S. export controls, 357

Taiwan, 224
as an Asian "tiger," 184, 231
change in trade structure and, 231
emergence of, as industrialized country,
207–8
and FDI, 251
and foreign investment, 266
impact of aid on, 184
manufacturing shift to, 60
U.S. support of, 346, 348, 356
tariff(s), 83, 85, 86, 219, 322, 352.
See also General Agreement on Tariffs
and Trade
tariffication, 86
tariff-jumping hypothesis, 112
tax preferences, 71
technology policy, 118
terms of trade, 153

tesobonos, 204, 205
Thailand
and foreign investment, 266
and free trade, 79
growth of, 184
Thatcher government, 180
Third World, 140, 162, 301
competition over, 171
debt crisis of, 29, 206–7
and emergence of Fourth World classifica-
tion, 208
future of aid/financial flows to, 207–8
multinational corporations in, 125, 249–70
neglect of agriculture in, 174
and trade management, 220–21
Tokyo Round, 65, 80–82, 84, 86, 87, 229–30,
330
Toronto Summit, 200
total factor productivity, 69
trade
agricultural, 53
barriers to, 6, 78, 79, 81, 108
encouragement of, in Eastern Europe, 327
and the environment, 77
Havana Charter and, 50–52, 53
and intellectual property, 76–77, 240
international
H-O theory and, 160
management of, 57–62
See also General Agreement on Tariffs
and Trade
as a mechanism of capital outflow, 257
North-South system and
commodity power and, 225–30
post-war trading order of, 215–25
in the 1980s, 230–40
Uruguay Round negotiations and, 240–43
and principle of nondiscrimination, 52–53
and regionalism, 78–80
and services, 240
surge in, after World War II, 58
U.S., with Comecon countries, 329
Trade Agreement Extension Act, 322
Trade and Development Committee, 223
trade balance, 292
trade deficit, 21, 28–29, 69
trade negotiations, multilateral, 54
trade preference systems, 51
trade-related intellectual property (TRIP),
87
trade-related investment measures (TRIMs),
77, 87, 270
Trading with the Enemy Act of 1917, 121–22
transaction costs, 109
transfer prices, 120
Treaty of Rome, 31, 136, 137
trigger price mechanism, 73
Trudeau, Pierre, 125